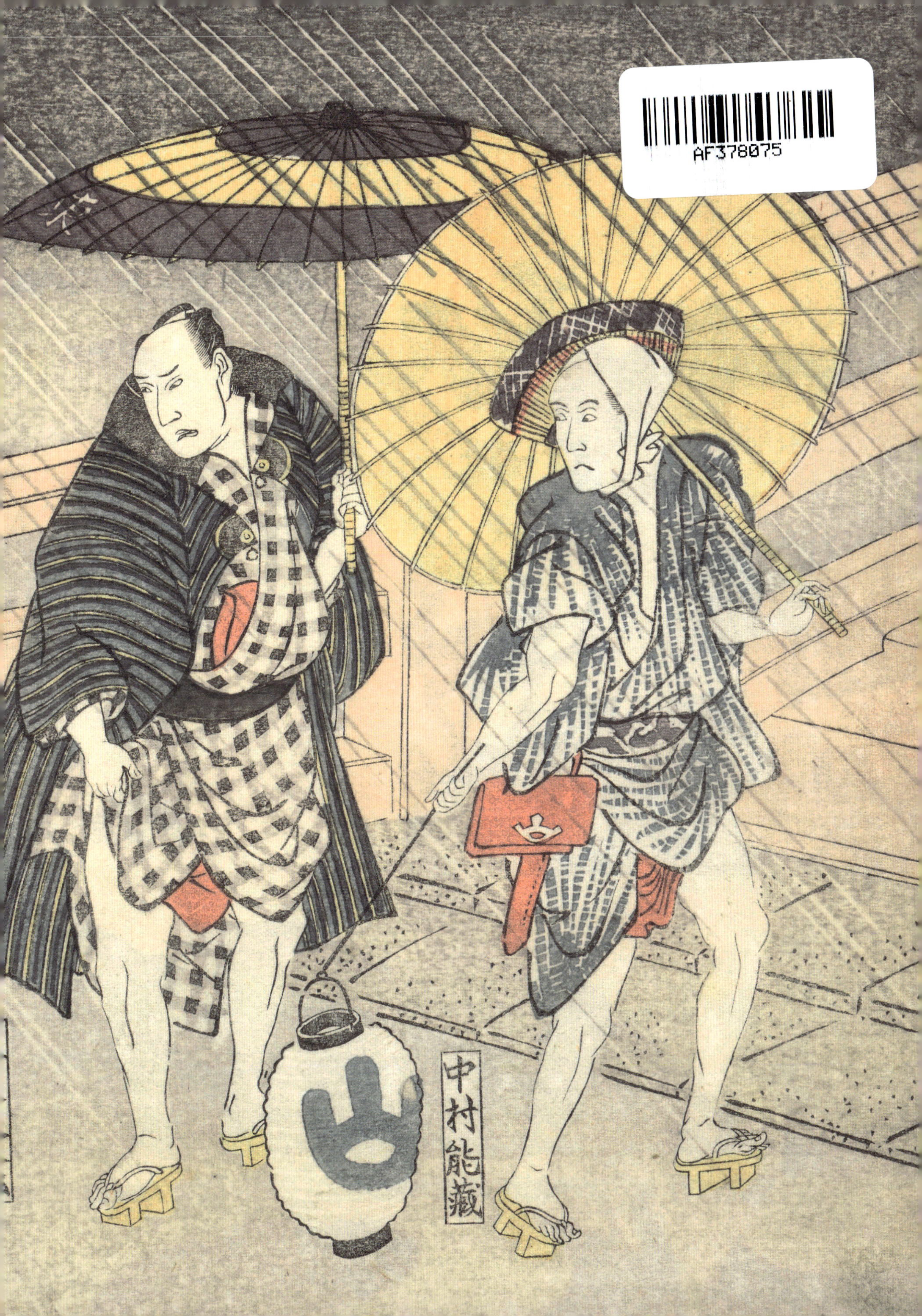
中村熊藏

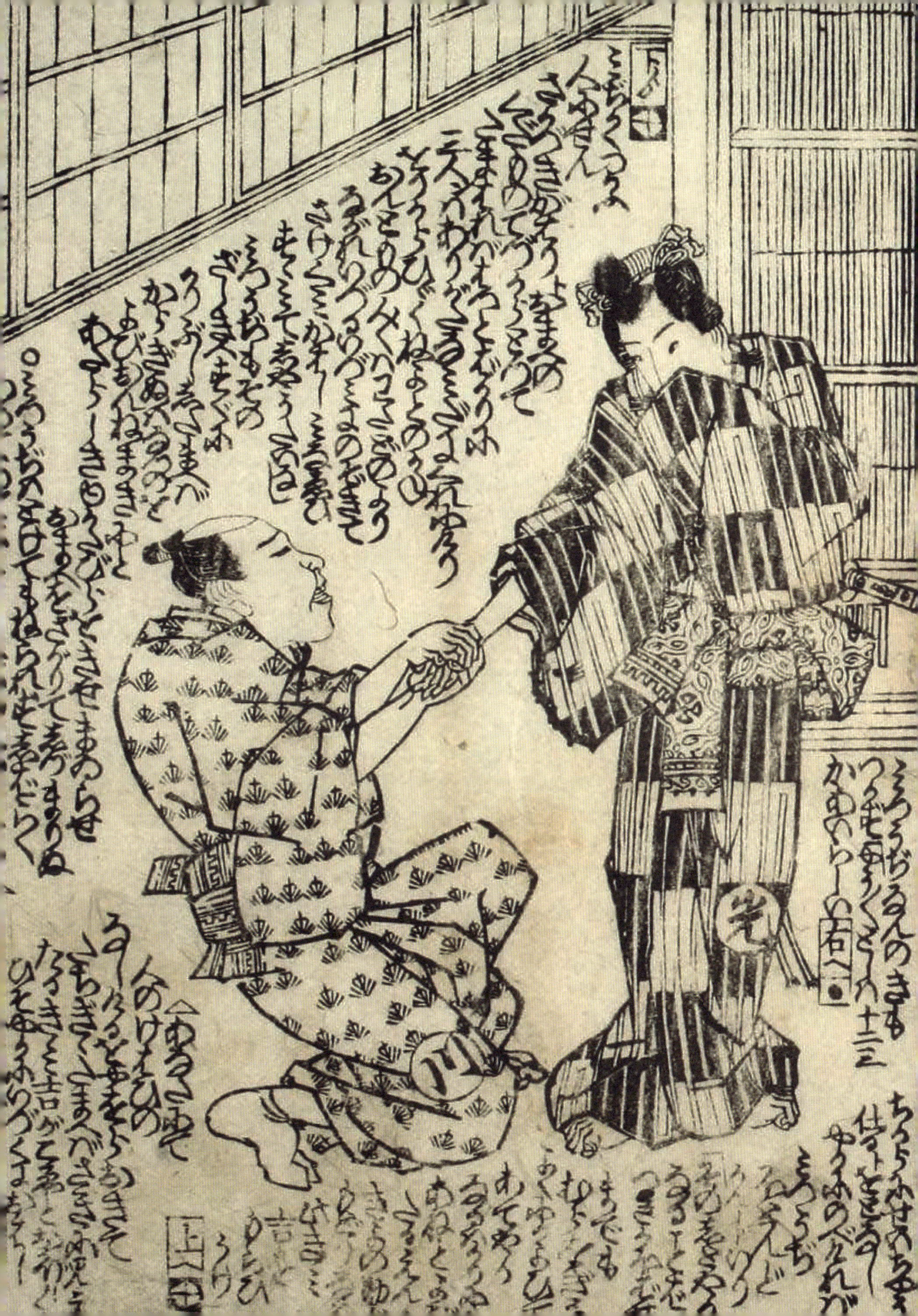

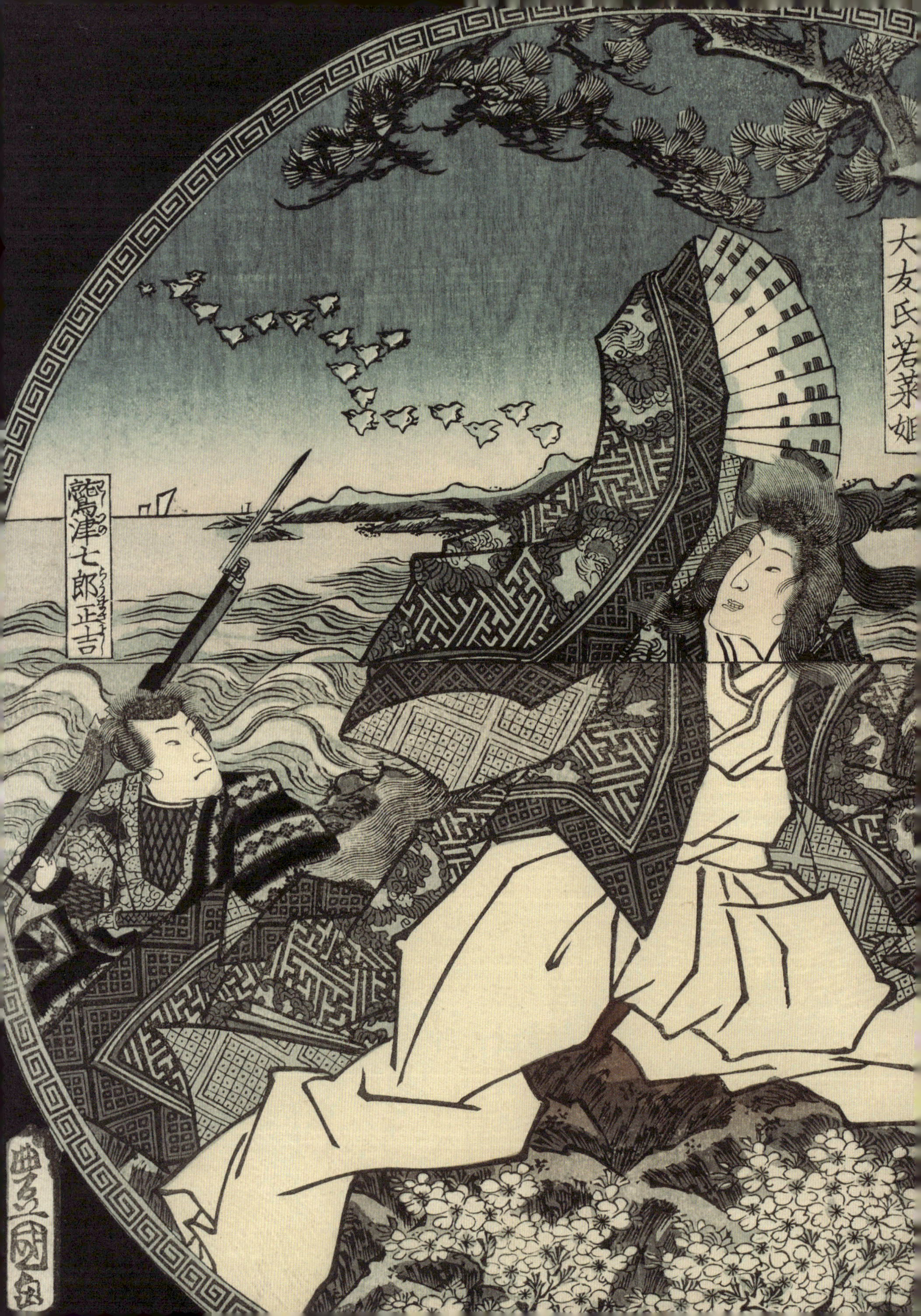
大友氏若菜姫
鷲津七郎正吉

# JAPAN'S MANGA REVOLUTION

## FROM PAINTED SCROLLS
## TO COMIC BOOKS
### 1680–1920

ANDREAS MARKS

**TUTTLE** Publishing
Tokyo | Rutland, Vermont | Singapore

# CONTENTS

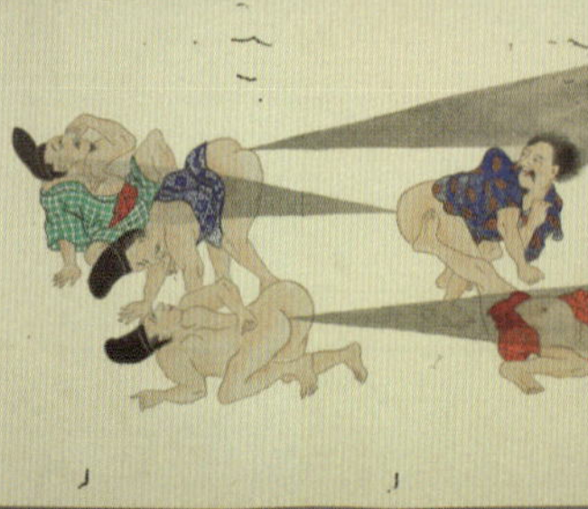



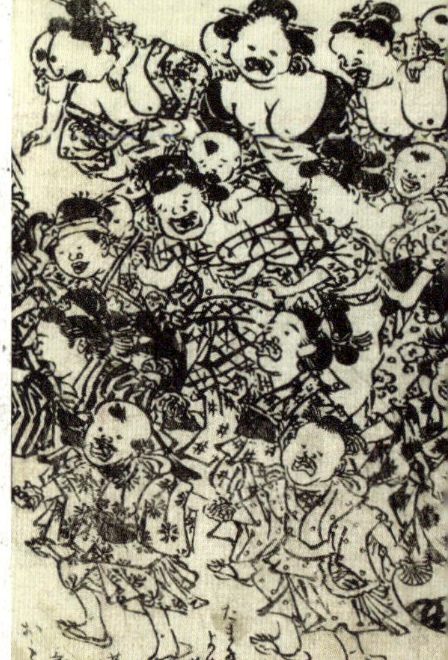

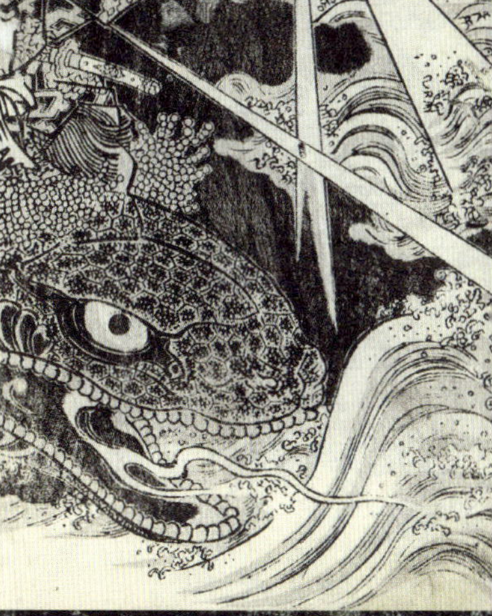

## Chapter 5  SUPERNATURAL ADVENTURE NOVELS



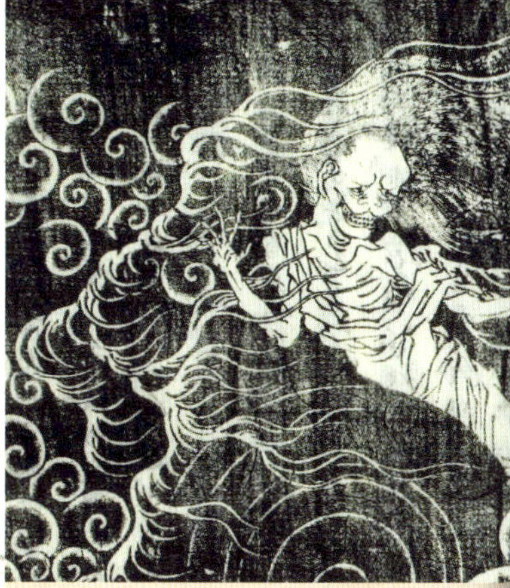

## Chapter 6  HOKUSAI'S FANTASTICAL SERIAL NOVELS



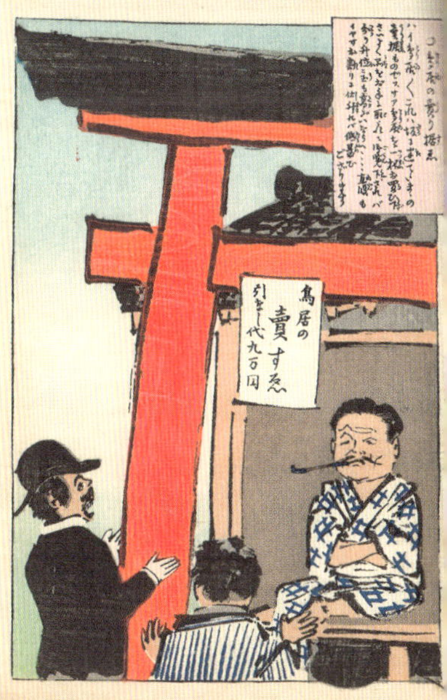

## Chapter 7  THE INFLUX OF WESTERN IDEAS



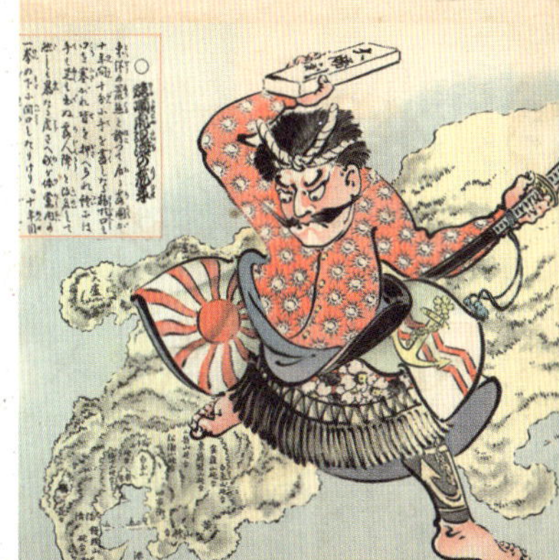

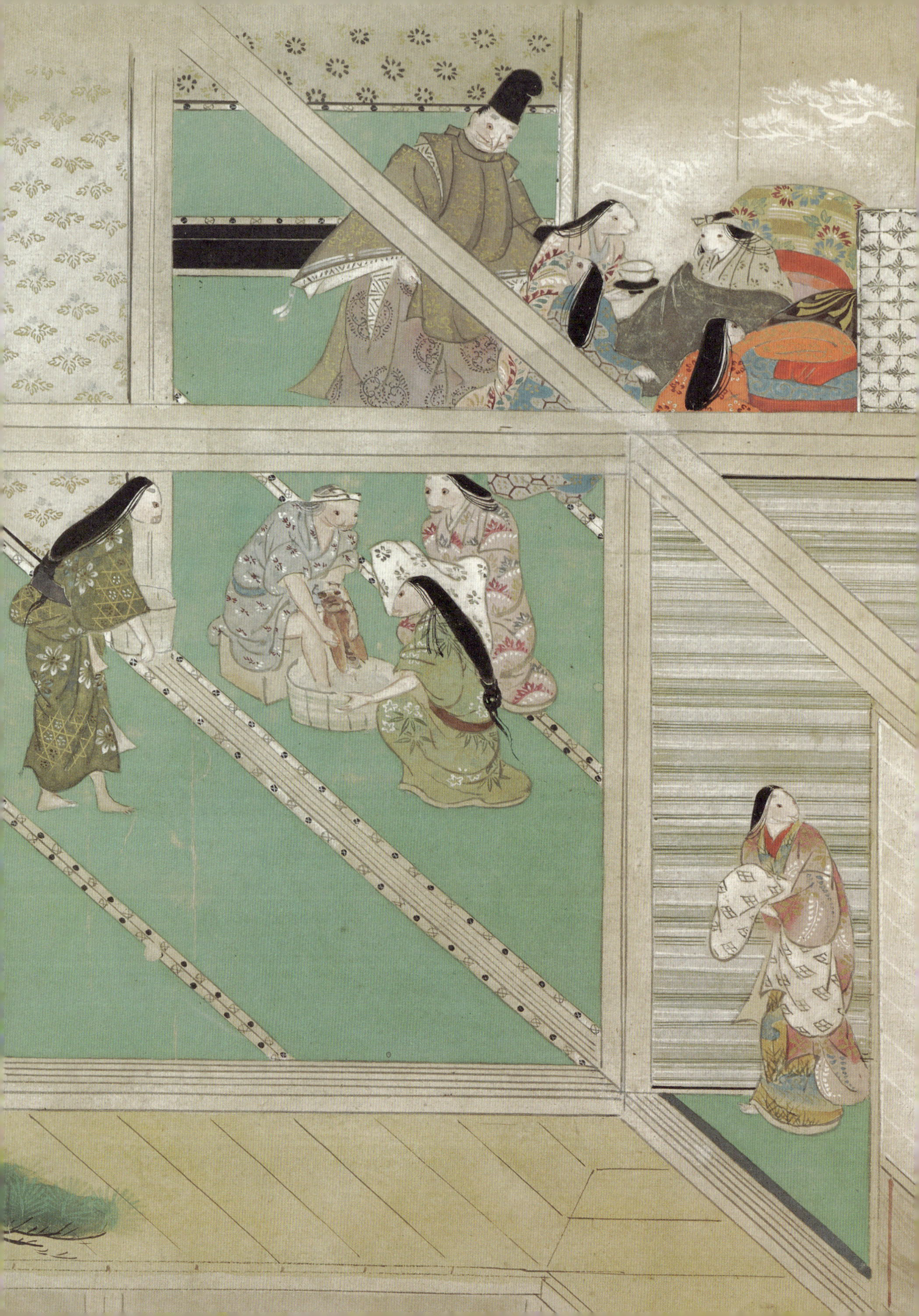

# EARLY STORYTELLING THROUGH PAINTED HANDSCROLLS

As in many other cultures, storytelling has played an important role in Japanese visual arts where a tradition of interplay between text and image developed well over a thousand years ago and it remains active today in modern "manga" storytelling cartoons and comics. Paintings on walls and ceilings in graves, and later also in temples, existed from the Kofun period (250–538), but the paintings were static and restricted to specific locations that were not accessible to everyone. Narration with the help of pictures became mobile and more widely available through the invention of picture scrolls (*emaki*). While the handscroll format originally developed in China, the combination of Japanese narrative subjects with their own decorative painting style (*yamato-e*), originated in the eighth century in a new, distinctly Japanese art form. The earliest manifestations of Japanese handscrolls that have been preserved date from the twelfth and thirteenth centuries.

Handscrolls depicting Buddhist legends, literary and historical narratives, biographies, and fables were all rendered in vibrant compositions and complemented by graceful text written in elegant calligraphy. To better show the action within an architectural structure, a painting style known as *fukinuki-yatai*, or "torn away roof," developed. At first, the predominant composition style was to separate illustrations and texts and to arrange them as alternating elements. In general, a handscroll would begin with a text segment to which the subsequent illustration was related. Next was more text followed by an illustration, and so forth. The size of the illustrations and the length of the texts could vary within a single scroll. Later, small text elements were sometimes added directly to the illustrations in order to assist the reader in identifying the locations and protagonists. Since the fourteenth century, handscrolls have existed where the text wrapped around the pictures and the separation between the text and picture elements disappeared.

Handscrolls are typically around 30 cm (1 ft) tall and can reach 10 meters (33 ft) in length. The story is read from right to left, with the right hand holding the scroll while the left unrolls it. After viewing an opening of around 60 cm (2 ft), the right hand rolls the part already seen and the left unrolls a new segment. The viewer thus controls the space that is visualized as well as the time spent examining it. Some stories are so long that they are divided into several scrolls. If a handscroll was damaged, it is possible that surviving parts were mounted as hanging scrolls. The authorship of many handscrolls remains anonymous today as the name of the painters were unlisted. Since these scrolls were hand painted, they were costly luxury items. This only changed in the seventeenth century when printing techniques became more widely used in Japan, and illustrated narratives in the form of books began to flourish.

**Opposite** Detail from *A Story of Crickets*.

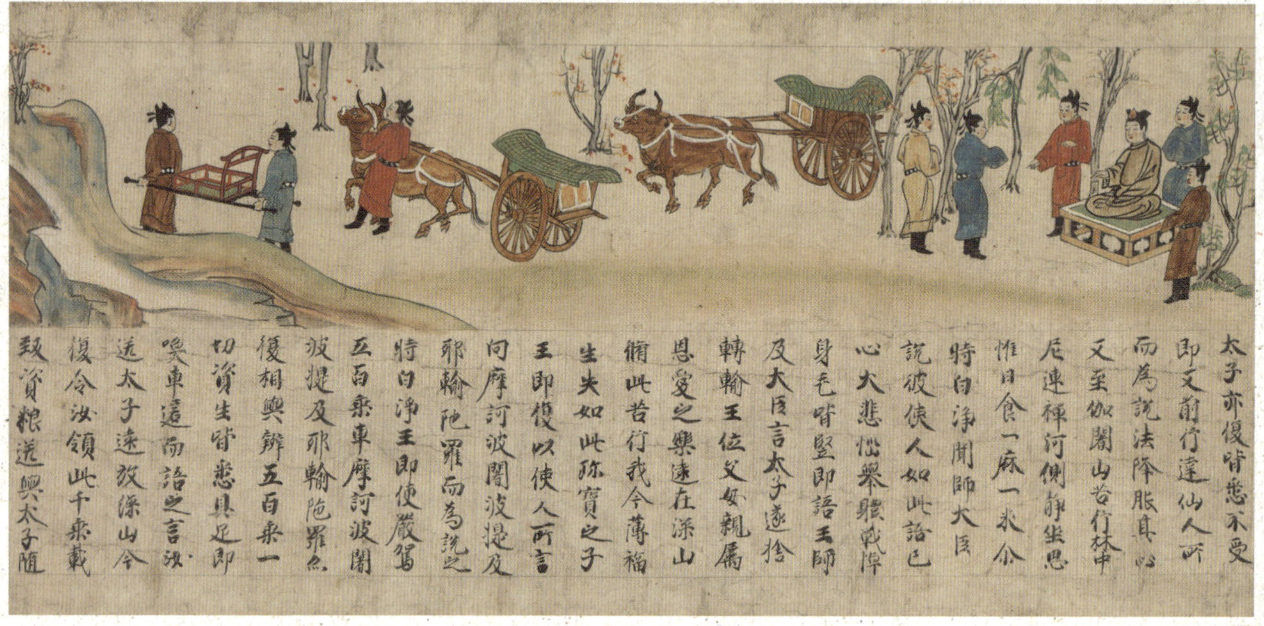

# The Illustrated Sutra of Past and Present Karma

*Kako genzai inga kyō emaki*
過去現在因果経絵巻

Late 13th century

Handscroll fragment, mounted as hanging scroll; ink and color on paper

27.6 × 56.8 cm

The Metropolitan Museum of Art, Purchase, several members of The Chairman's Council Gifts, Miriam and Ira D. Wallach Foundation and Mary and James G. Wallach Foundation Gifts, 2012 (2012.249)

This work is a segment from one version of *The Illustrated Sutra of Past and Present Karma* (*Kako genzai inga kyō emaki*), often colloquially referred to as *The Illustrated Sutra of Cause and Effect* (*E-inga kyō*). Historically of extraordinary importance as the earliest known narrative painting in Japan, it vividly portrays the lives, both past and present, of Prince Siddhartha, the historical Buddha. The earliest surviving examples of this work in Japan, dating back to the eighth century, are believed to be copies of now-lost Chinese originals from the Sui (581–618) or Tang dynasties (618–907). This version is a copy dating from the late thirteenth century.

In this artwork, Chinese-looking figures symbolizing Prince Siddhartha's father and his entourage inhabit a serene landscape featuring gentle rolling hills and trees, rendered in a limited color palette. Below the illustration, the 27-line meticulously inscribed calligraphy in standard script narrates the journey of Prince Siddhartha after leaving the palace. He travels to Mount Gaya, where his uncle resides, and dedicates six years to ascetic practices. The king dispatches ministers to monitor his son's activities and to ensure he receives one thousand cartsful of daily necessities while being closely watched.

# Illustrated Legends of the Kitano Tenjin Shrine

## Kitano Tenjin engi emaki

北野天神縁起絵巻

Late 13th century
Set of five handscrolls; ink, color, and cut gold leaf (*kirikane*) on paper
Totals: 28.8 × 689.4 cm, 28.8 × 763 cm, 28.8 × 696.3 cm, 28.8 × 571.4 cm, 28.8 × 894.5 cm
The Metropolitan Museum of Art, Fletcher Fund, 1925 (25.224a–e)

Over thirty illustrated handscrolls have survived that recount the life and afterlife of the well-known scholar, poet, and statesman Sugawara Michizane (845–903). Slandered by enemies at the imperial court in Kyoto, Michizane died in exile. The large number of extant scrolls reflects how popular he had become in the centuries to follow when the Shinto belief of the so-called Tenjin cult flourished, which mainly sought to appease tormented human spirits (*onryō*) that brought to life the random, disastrous forces of nature.

After Michizane's death, the capital was struck by a series of exceptional natural catastrophes which caused the untimely deaths of his attackers. To appease his vengeful spirit, Michizane was posthumously pardoned and promoted to high office. However, the disasters continued. In the 940s, Michizane's spirit appeared several times and made it known that he wished to be honored in a newly built shrine in the northwestern part of Kyoto, the Kitano Tenmangū, which was founded in 947. Michizane was deified as Tenjin, a god of agriculture, god of sincerity, patron of the falsely accused, and later also as god of literature and music.

Illustrations and text segments are interspersed in this important set of five scrolls. One part focuses on the life of the itinerant monk Nichizō, who reaches the palace of Enma, the King of Hell. There he learns how to pacify Michizane's spirit.

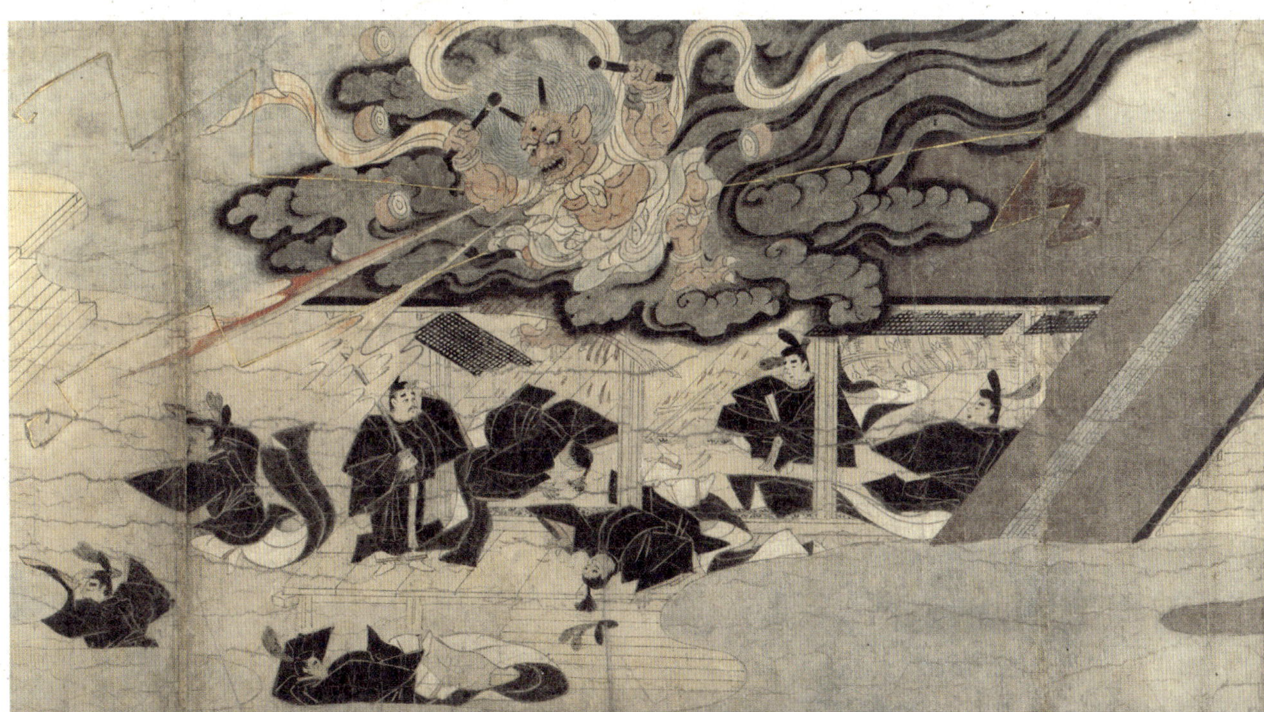

**Above** Michizane's angry spirit.

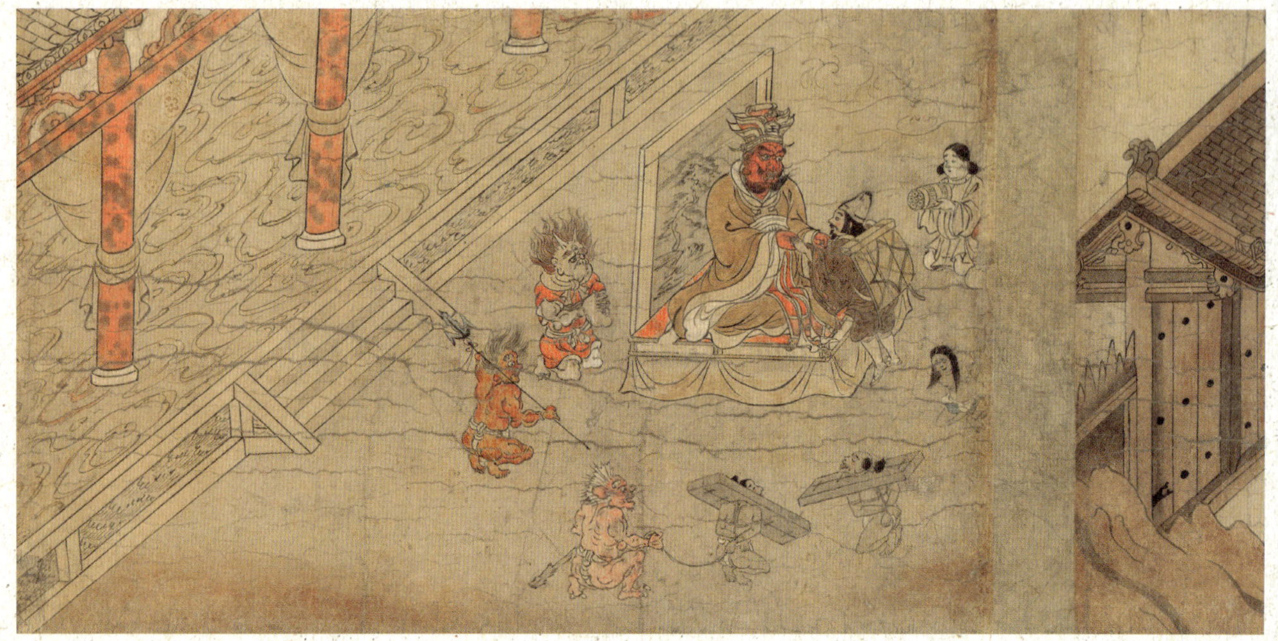

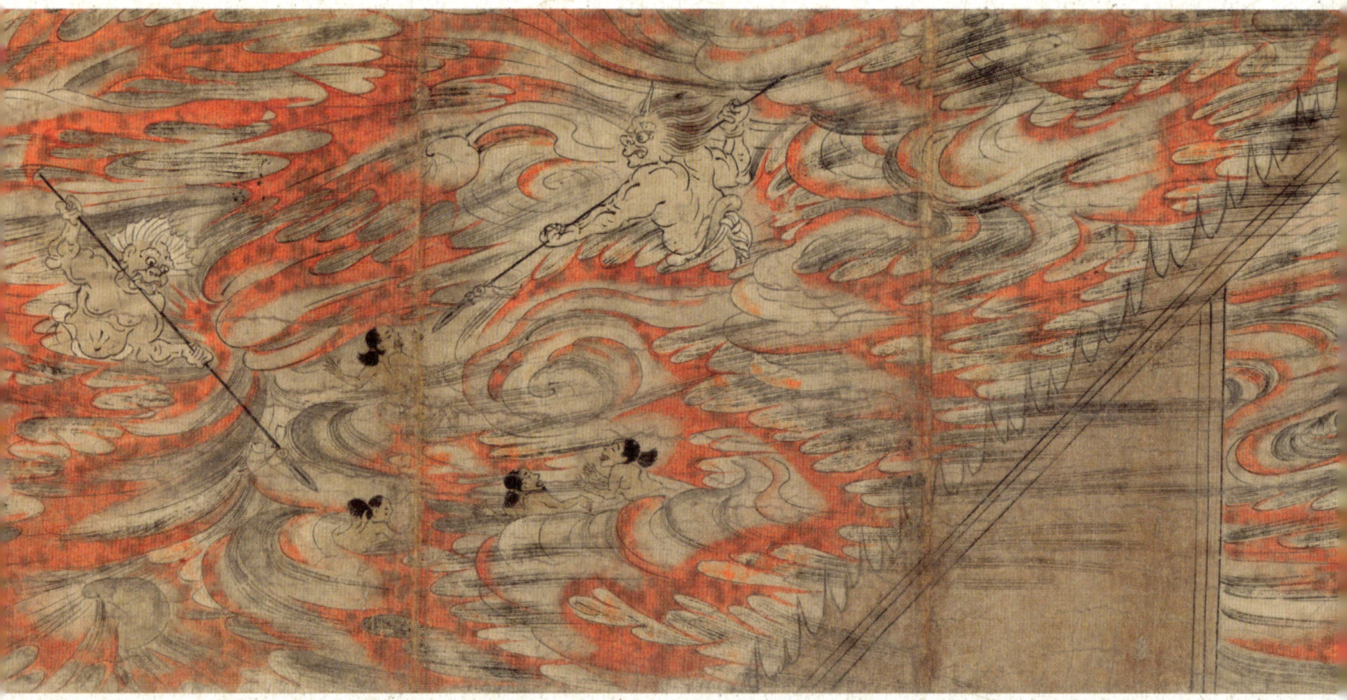

Above An eight-headed beast guards the entrance to hell.

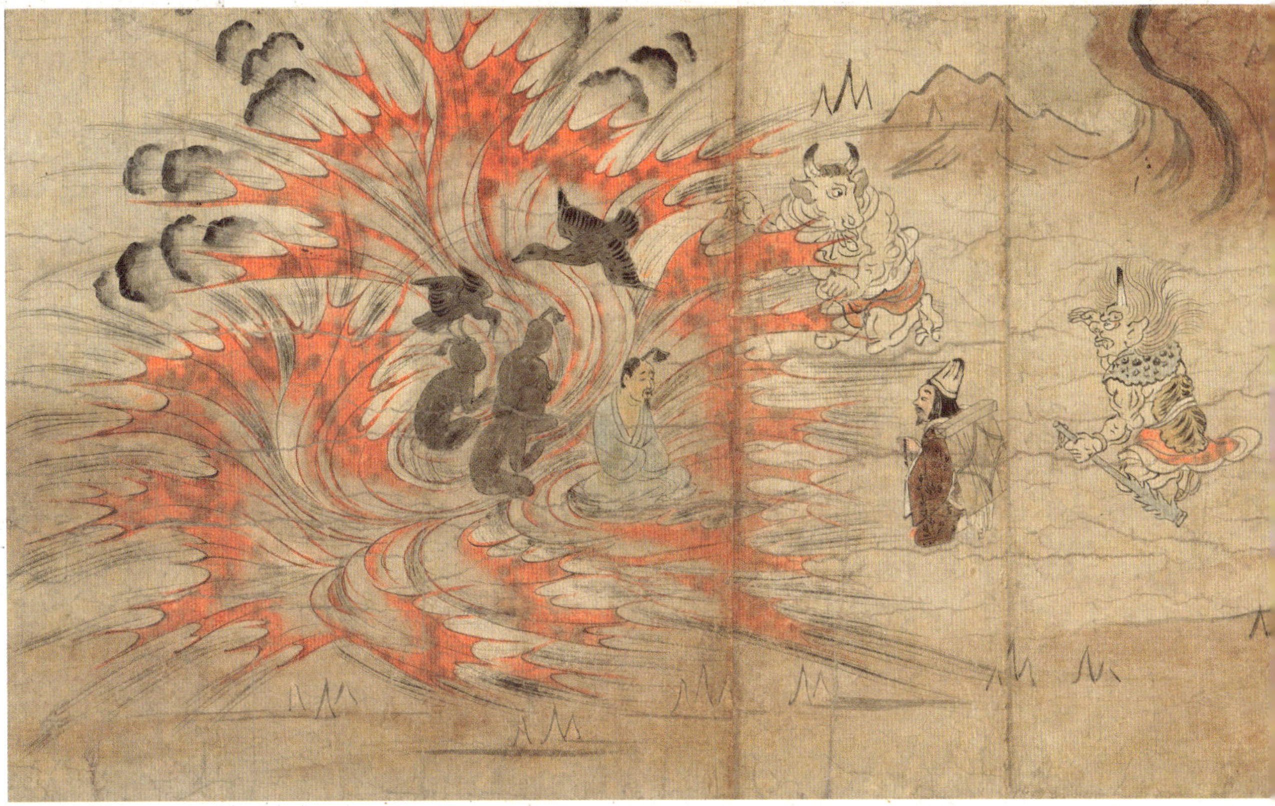

**Above** The Emperor Daigo and his servants are tormented by flames and blackbirds.

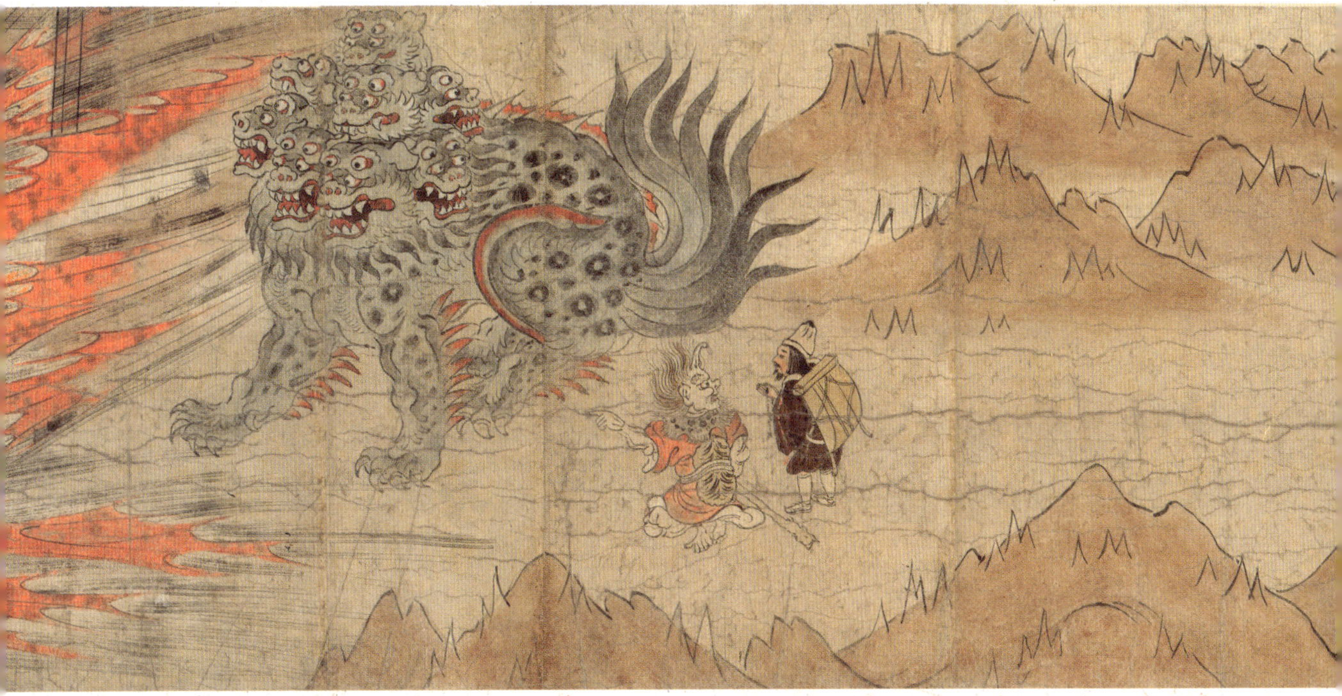

# A Scene from "Spring Shoots II" in The Tale of Genji

## *'Wakana ge' Genji monogatari emaki dankan*
「若菜下」『源氏物語』絵巻断簡

16th century
Handscroll fragment, mounted as hanging scroll; ink on paper
11.1 × 50.5 cm
Minneapolis Institute of Art, Mary Griggs Burke Collection,
Gift of the Mary and Jackson Burke Foundation (2015.79.36)

Although currently mounted as a hanging scroll, this painting constitutes a small segment from a set of handscrolls illustrating *The Tale of Genji* (*Genji monogatari*), Japan's best-known literary masterpiece that has charmed audiences for more than a thousand years. Sometimes called the world's first novel, the tale, written by the court lady Murasaki Shikibu (970/78?–1014/31?), is about romance and scandal and plays out over fifty-four chapters. Here the artist skillfully captures a scene from chapter 35, titled "Spring Shoots II" (*Wakana ge*), where Prince Genji accompanies several women on a pilgrimage. Within interior spaces defined by diagonal walls and screens, the women engage in various activities. Meanwhile, on the far right, two men sit on a veranda. Notably, the three principal female characters on the left are each identified by name.

These monochrome drawings exemplify a style known as "white drawing" (*hakubyō*). Popular during the Muromachi period (1392–1573), the delicate depictions were crafted by amateur women painters in private, aristocratic settings, and only a few of them have survived. The simple execution stands in stark contrast to the vibrant, colorful, and large folding screens typically commissioned by feudal lords and executed by professional artists.

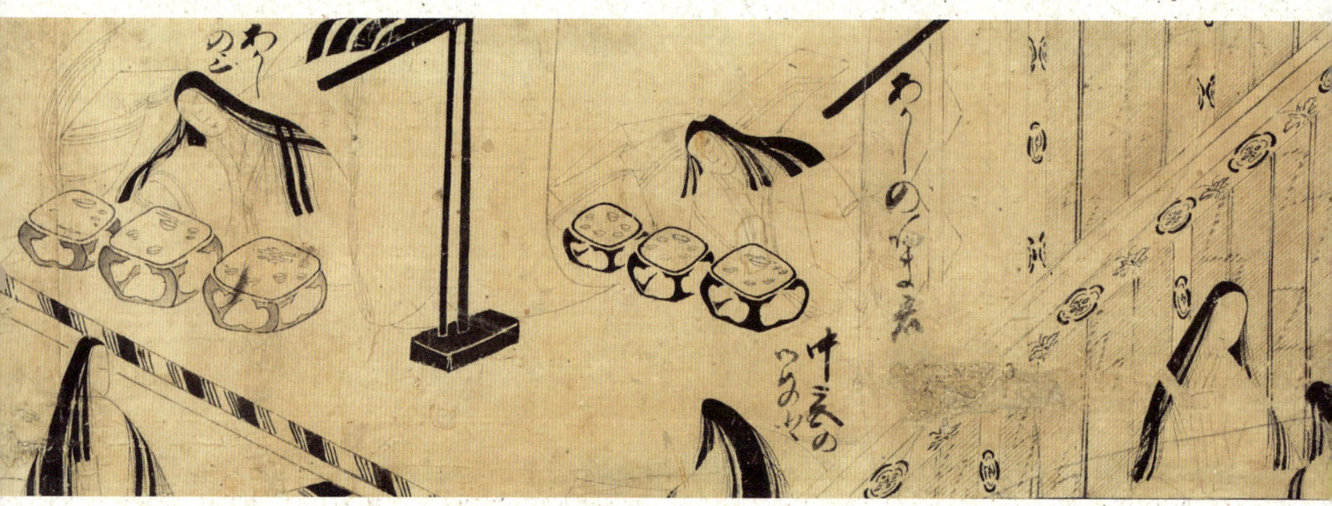

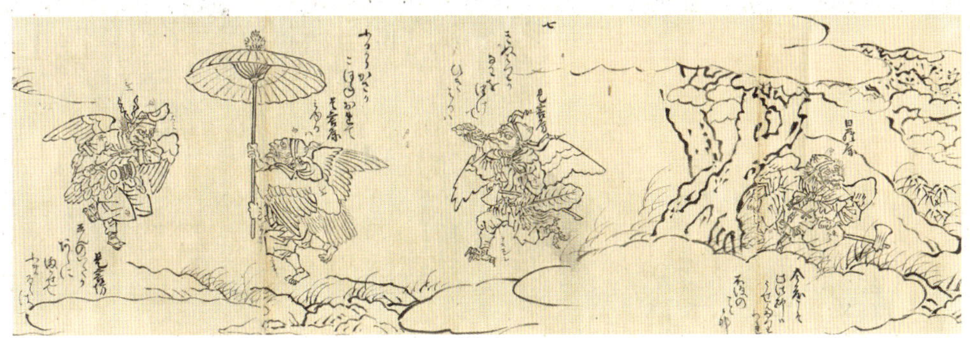

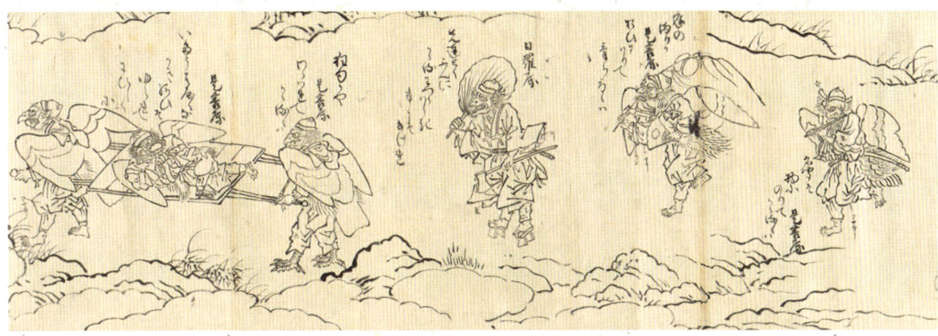

# The Story of the Monk Zegaibō

## *Zegaibō emaki*

是害坊絵巻

1587
Handscroll; ink on paper
Height: 26.7 cm
New York Public Library, Spencer Collection, Sorimachi 40

The *tengu* (lit. "celestial dog") is a type of demon which lives in the mountains and is very popular in Japanese culture. The *Chronicles of Japan* (*Nihon shoki*) from 637 includes the earliest mention of *tengu*. The thirteenth-century *Tale of the Heike* (*Heike monogatari*) contains a detailed description of them as "human, but not human; bird, but not bird; dog, but not dog; they possess feet and hands of a human, the head of a dog, wings on both sides, and can fly as well as walk."

This handscroll illustrates the story of the legendary Buddhist monk Zegaibō, a *tengu* from China who came to Japan around 966 to challenge the efficacy of prayer of the Japanese *tengu*. Unimpressed by his first encounter, he sought stronger opponents and thus visited the monastery on Mount Hiei. There Zegaibō stood no chance and was defeated three times, resulting in a broken nose and serious illness. To heal him, the *tengu* from Mount Hiei took him to the Kamo River where he eventually recovered. After a farewell party, Zegaibō returned to China, repenting his errors.

In this particular handscroll, inscriptions are presented as dialogues, much like in manga today.

# The Story of Shuten-dōji on Mount Ōe

*Ōeyama Shuten-dōji*

大江山酒呑童子

Second half 17th century
Artist: Kaihō Yūchiku (1654–1728)
Set of three handscrolls; ink, color, and gold on paper
Totals: 32.4 × 1552.2 cm, 32.4 × 2024.4 cm, 32.4 × 1747.2 cm
New York Public Library, Spencer Collection, Sorimachi 96

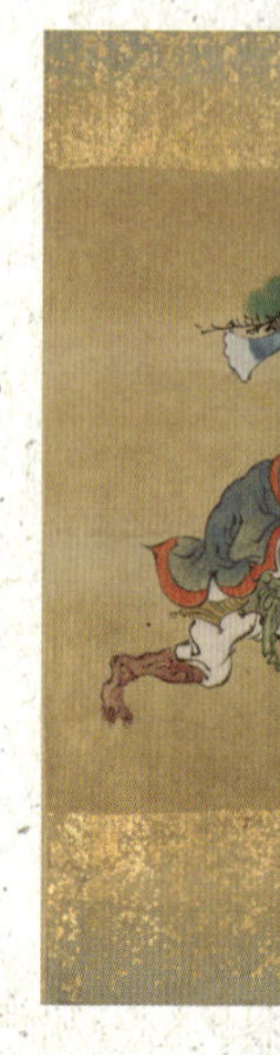

The fourteenth-century picture handscroll titled *Mount Ōe in Pictures and Words* (*Ōeyama ekotoba*), housed in the collection of the Itsuō Art Museum in Ikeda, Osaka, stands as the oldest surviving record of the legend of the ogre leader Shuten-dōji. This is another version dating from the second half of the seventeenth century.

Born with hair and teeth after an unusually long sixteen-month pregnancy, Shuten-dōji possessed the strength of a sixteen-year-old and was considered an ogre-child due to his rough temperament. Abandoned by his mother, he transformed into an ogre and resided on Mount Ōe, northwest of Kyoto, alongside his horde of ogres. Shuten-dōji and his ogre horde abducted young women and terrorized Kyoto. To end this menace, the valiant warrior Minamoto Yorimitsu (also known as Raikō; 948–1021) and his trusted allies, the Four Heavenly Kings (*Shitennō*)—Watanabe Tsuna (953–1025), Urabe Suetake (950?–1022?), Sakata Kintoki (956–1012), and Usui Sadamitsu (954–1021?)—disguised themselves as Buddhist monks. They embarked on a perilous journey to Shuten-dōji's mountain stronghold. Once admitted, they witnessed the ogres feasting on a banquet of human flesh. Seizing an opportune moment when the ogres succumbed to slumber from their indulgence, the heroes slew the entire horde, including Shuten-dōji himself. Yorimitsu beheaded the demon leader, but remarkably the severed head still attempted to bite him. In the struggle, one of the helmet's ornaments broke off, and the demon's teeth became deeply embedded in Yorimitsu's helmet, with the head stuck to it.

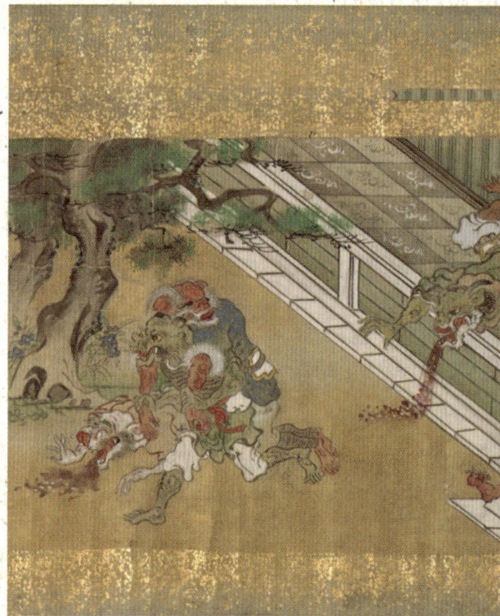

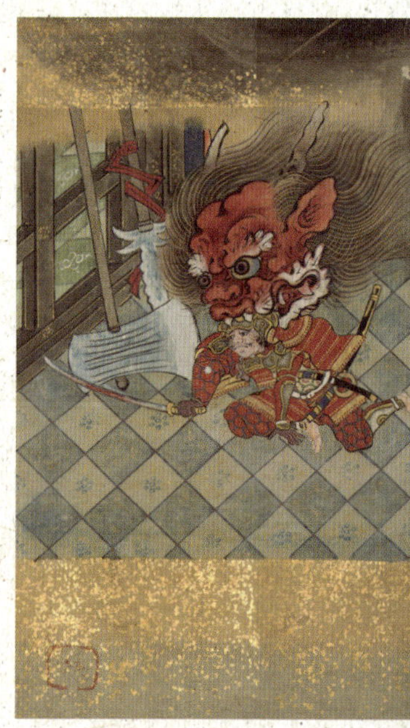

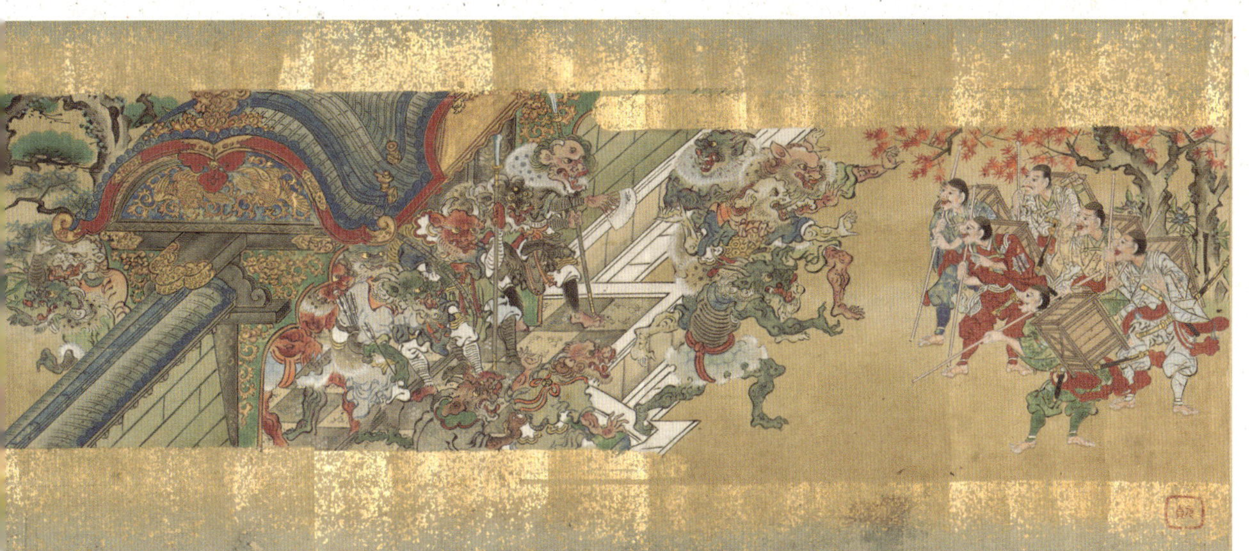

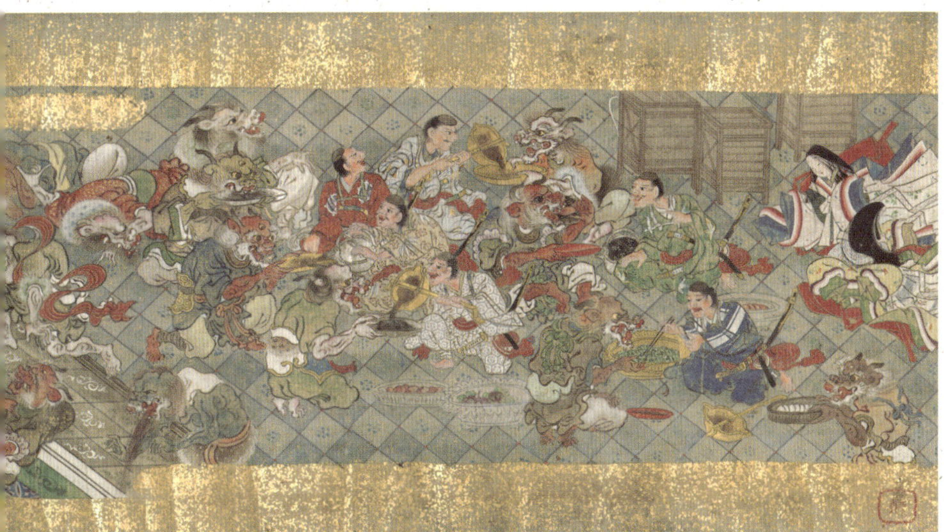

Above Minamoto Yorimitsu and his retainers arrive at Shuten-dōji's palace disguised as monks.

Left The ogres feasting on a banquet.

Below The killing of Shuten-dōji.

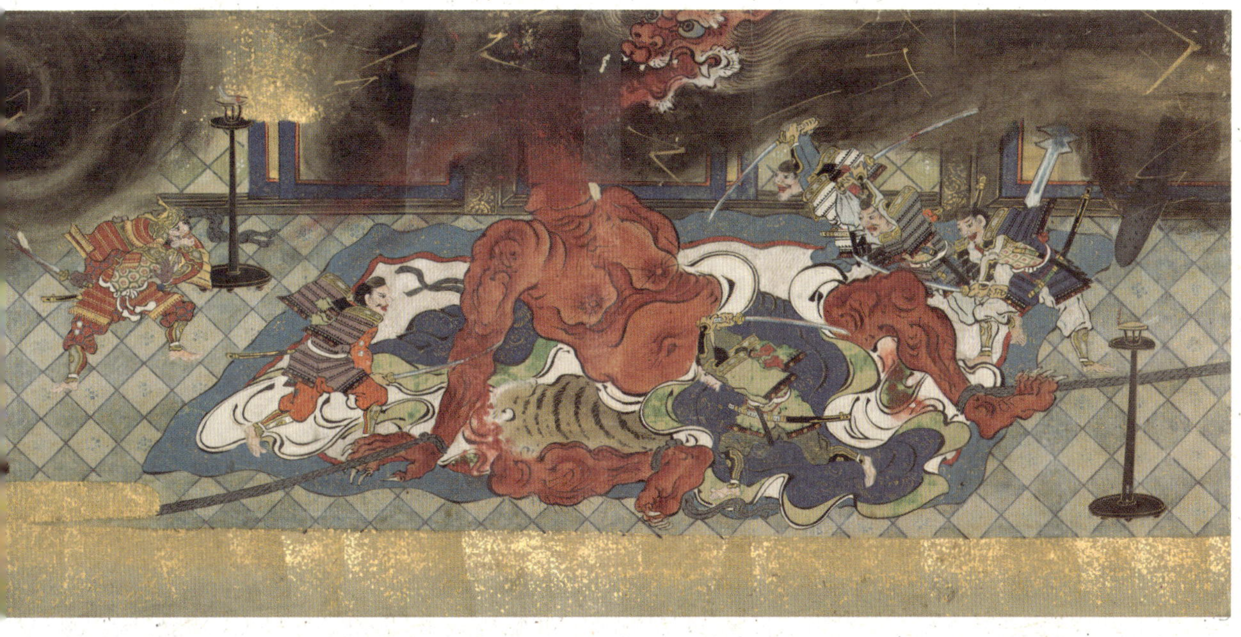

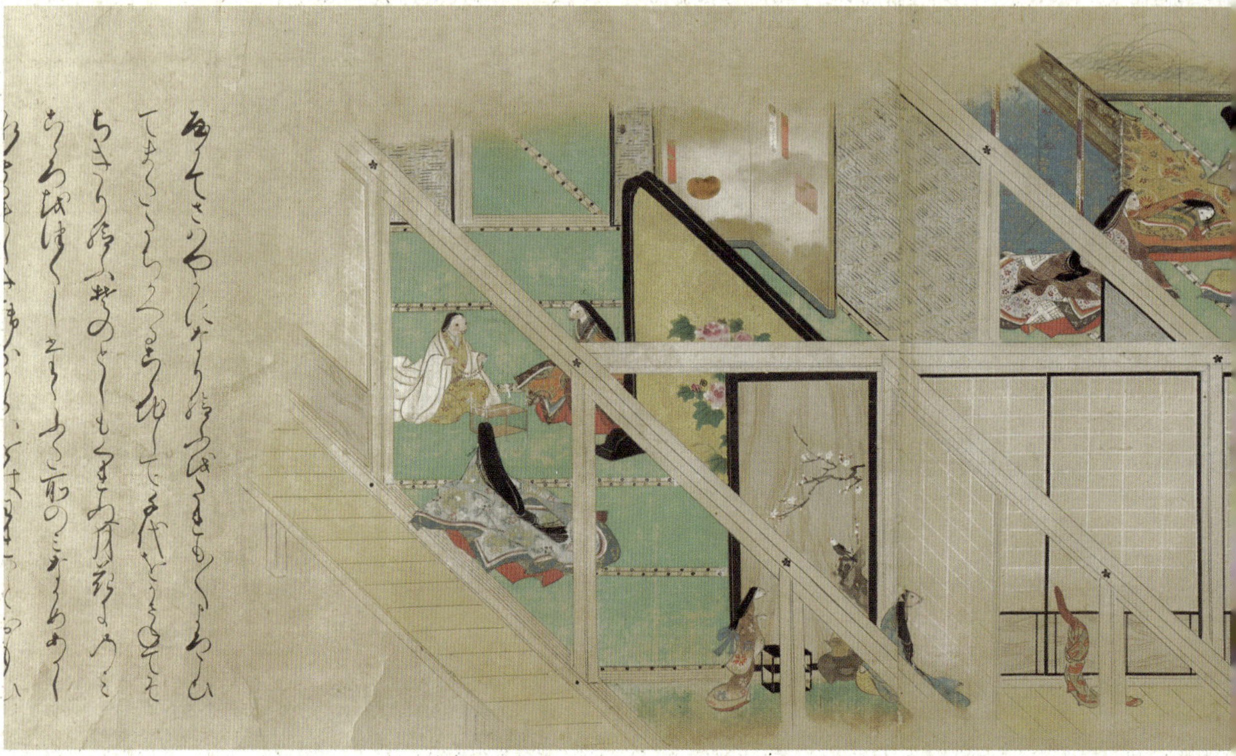

# A Story of Crickets

*Kirigirisu emaki*
きりぎりす絵巻

Second half 17th century
Artist: attributed to Sumiyoshi Jokei (1599–1670)
Handscroll; ink and color on paper
31.1 × 429.3 cm
Minneapolis Institute of Art, Anonymous Gift of Funds (84.1)

Many handscrolls recount the same cannon of stories, but this particular one features a love story in which humans are substituted by insects. The core of the story is about three contenders: a cicada, a cricket, and an evening cicada (*higurashi*) competing for the love of a beautiful jewel beetle-princess. At the end of the story, the cicada and the jewel beetle-princess are married, and the princess gives birth to a beautiful cicada boy. Typical of fairy tales,

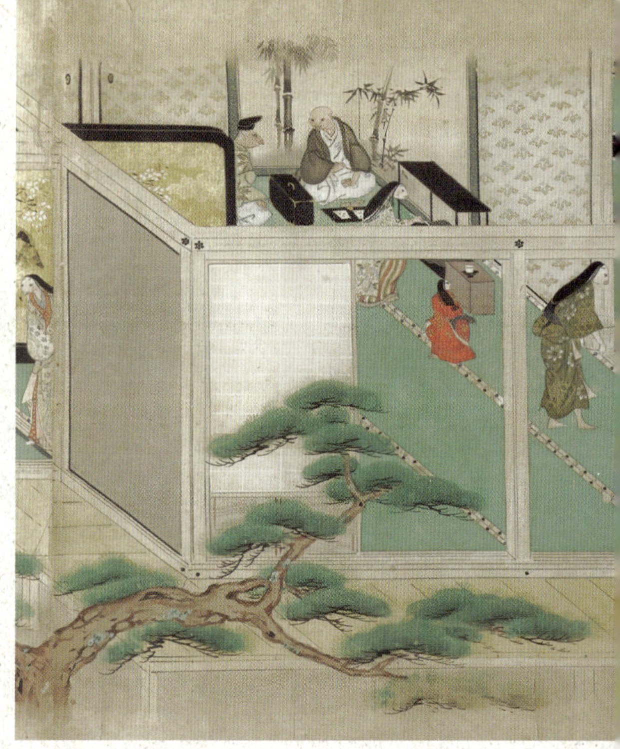

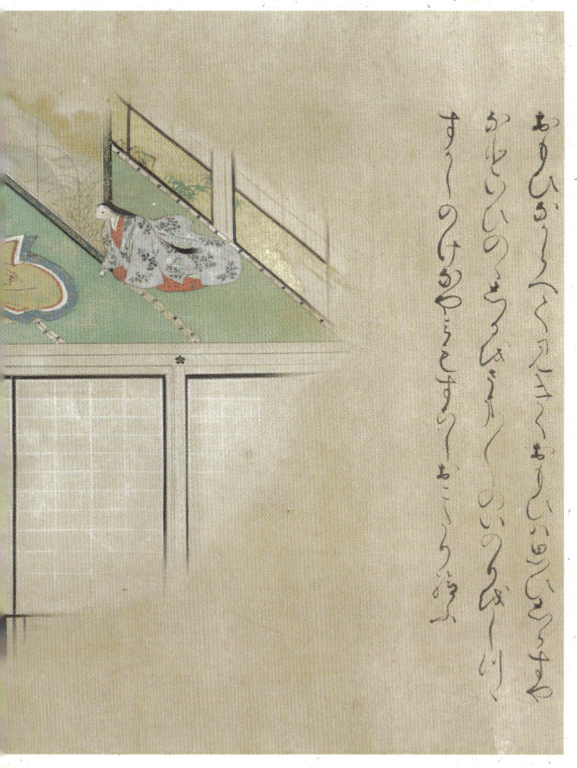

the family continues to live happily ever after. Notably, the anthropomorphic fairy tale technique employs human bodies with animal heads to vividly portray the diverse and delightful expressions of these insects, adorned in splendid attire, within their opulent houses furnished with folding screens, scrolls, dividers, and meticulously crafted details. The lavish costumes are typical for aristocrats during Japan's earlier Heian period (794–1185).

Stylistically, the painting and calligraphy are reminiscent of a handscroll of the same subject that is now in the collection of the Hosomi Museum in Kyoto. It is believed that this scroll was created as a sequel to that in the Hosomi Museum, which also has no obvious signatures or seals, but hidden in a picture of a cedar door is the seal of the painter Sumiyoshi Jokei (1599–1670).

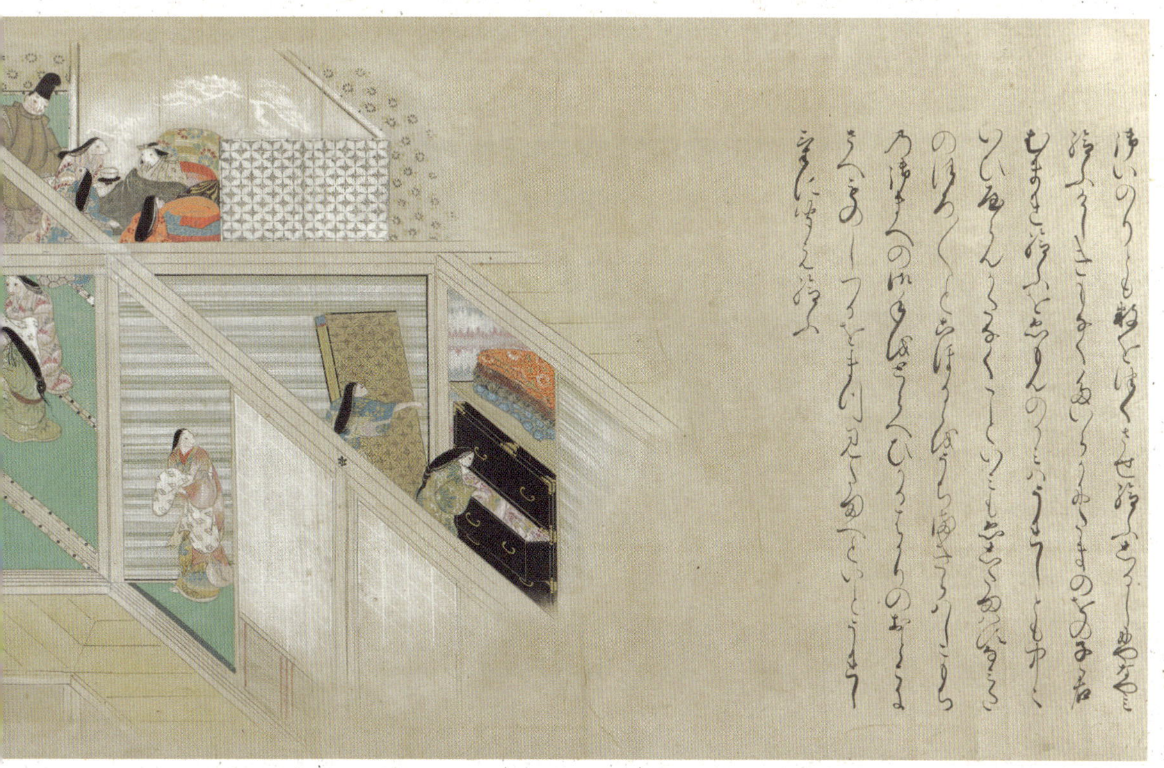

# The Fart Battles Scroll

*He-gassen emaki*

屁合戦絵巻

1846
Artist: Airan (born 1778)
Handscroll; ink and color on paper
29.6 × 1003.1 cm
Waseda University Library

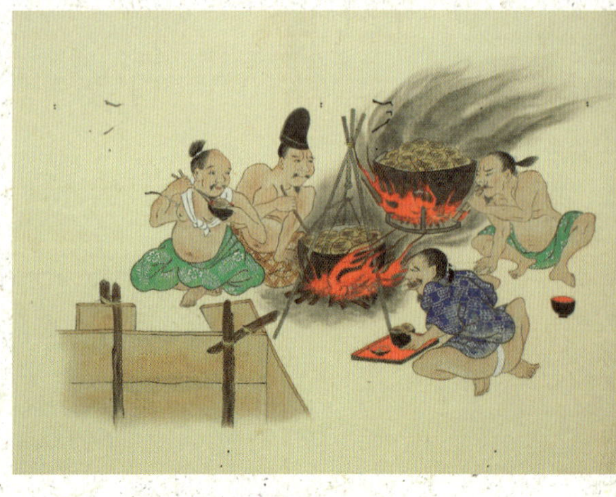

Humor is an important subject in Japanese arts, and handscrolls illustrating the effects of flatulence reach back to the Heian period (794–1185). Originally created by one or more unidentified painters, the scrolls, known as "fart battles" (*he-gassen*), depict animated scenes of men or women using farts to achieve their cause. The earliest extant copies of Fart Battles date from the fifteenth century. This copy of a handscroll from 1680 originally painted by Hishikawa Moronobu (1618–94), one of the seminal pioneers of the *ukiyo-e* genre, was painted by a certain Airan who lived in the Fukuyama domain in present-day Hiroshima.

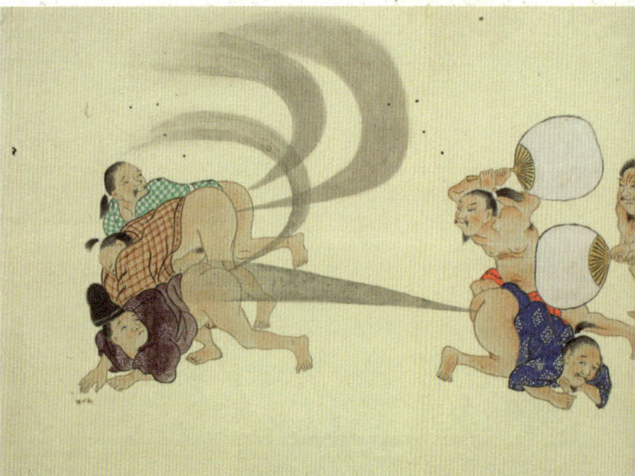

The scroll starts with a group of men, including courtiers (indicated by their lacquered black caps) as well as commoners, discussing holding a farting competition. Food that causes gas is prepared over fire and eaten by the men. Eventually, they battle with each other, bowling one another over. As the competition continues, one man farts so strongly that he blows a hole in a wooden board. Eventually, women, who can make a man hover in the air, join in. As a group they succeed in blowing over a picnic party who had enjoyed cherry blossoms, along with the six-panel folding screen that had provided the party with some privacy.

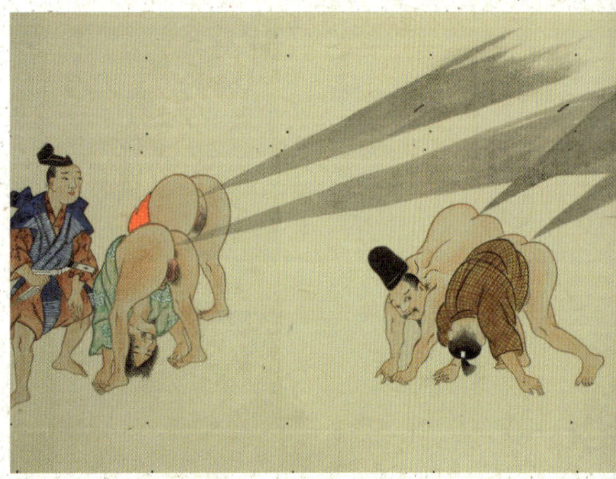

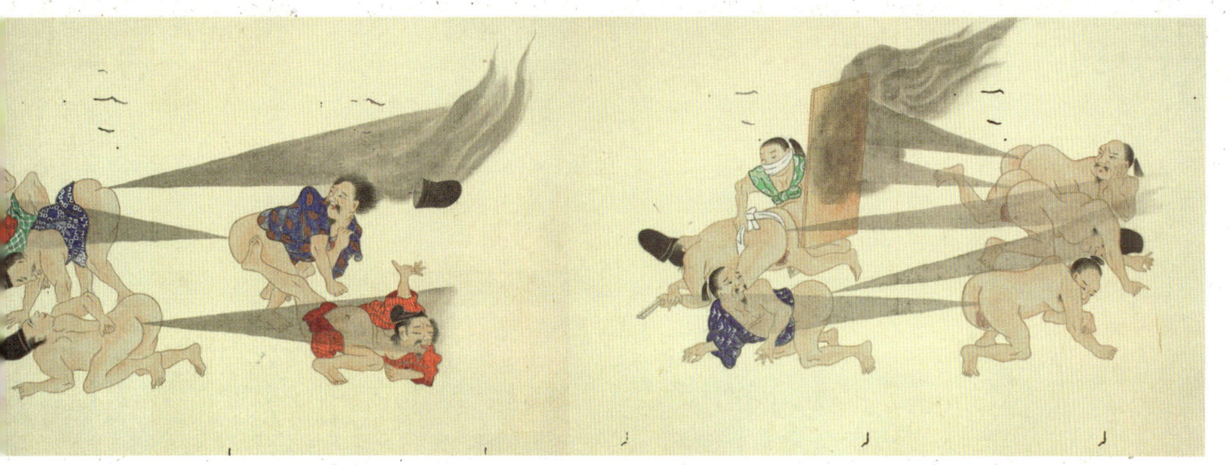

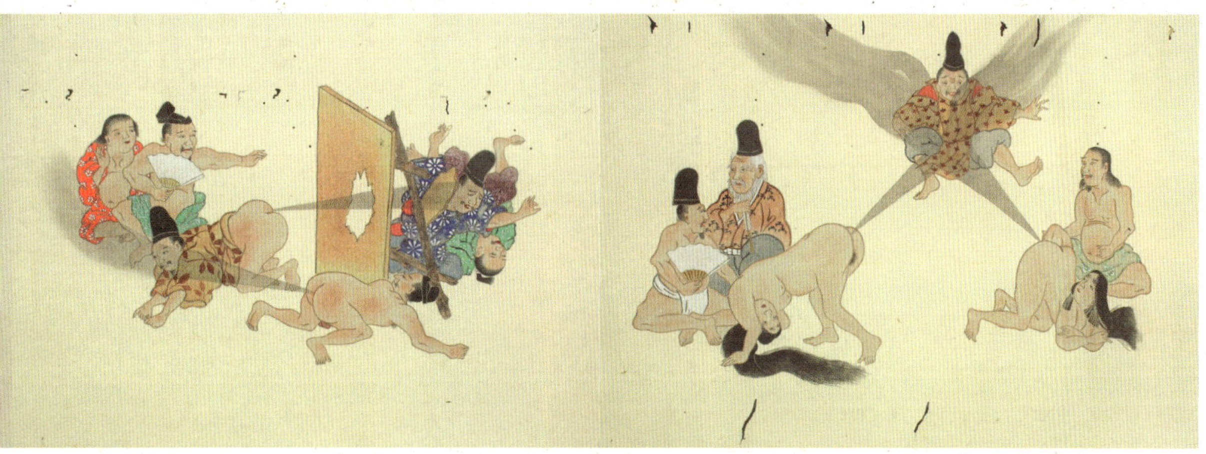

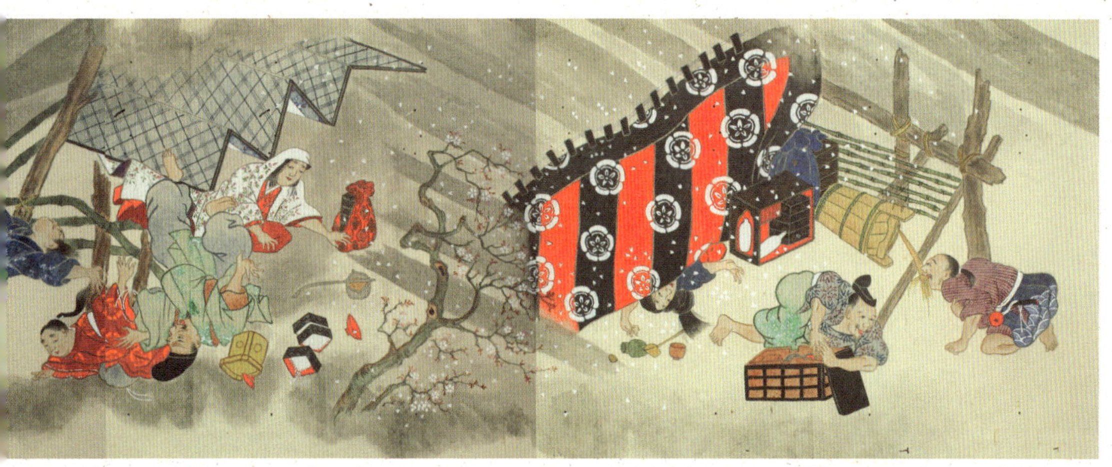

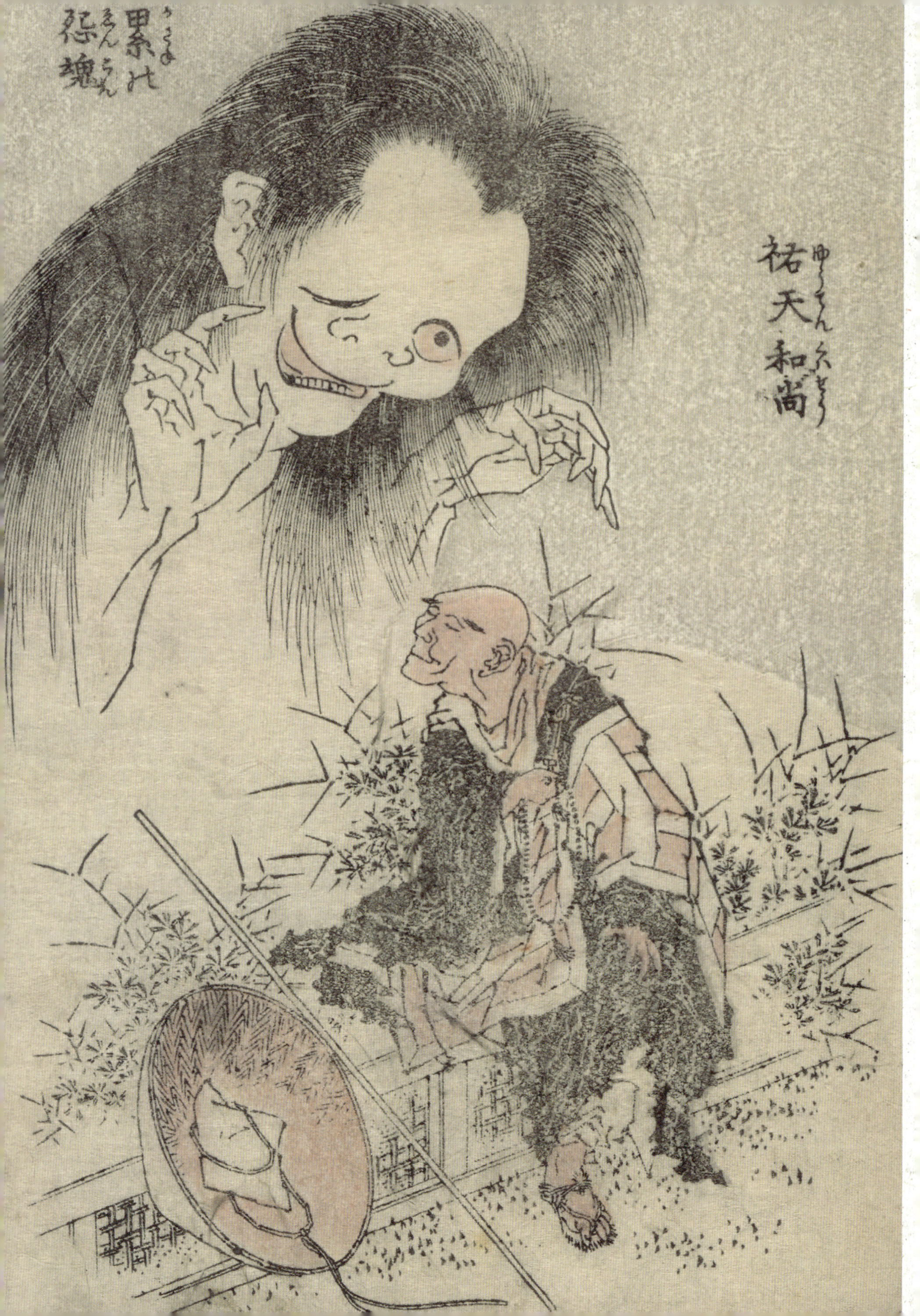
累れ怨塊
祐天和尚

# CHAPTER ONE

# EARLY USES OF THE TERM "MANGA"

The word "manga" 漫画 is a compound of two Chinese characters. "Man" literally refers to water that overflows, and in a broader sense comprises the meanings unrestrained, random, and casual. "Ga" means painting or drawing. Manga today specifically denotes storytelling cartoons or comics, but originally it only referred to simple, insular drawings that did not contain a narrative.

The earliest unquestionable appearance of the Chinese characters for manga in a Japanese publication is in the title of Suzuki Senshū's (1715–76) book *Miscellany of Casual Drawings* (*Mankaku zuihitsu*) from 1771. However, while the same characters were used, they were pronounced "mankaku" instead of "manga." The book contains no illustrations, only text. Another occurrence of the term manga is connected to the book *Hanabusa's Drawings like a Swarm of Butterflies* (*Gunchō gaei*) compiled by Suzuki Rinshō (1732–1803) in 1778. The book comprises typical drawings in the style of the influential painter Hanabusa Itchō (1652–1724). Some copies of this book carry a title slip with the subtitle *Pictorial Records of Sketches* (*Manga zukō*), but it is questionable that this subtitle predates the first volume of *Hokusai's Manga* from 1814, as a copy with this slip in the collection of the British Museum dates from 1833.

The first time the word manga appears in a text is in the 1798 book *Comings and Goings in the Four Seasons* (*Shiji no yukikai*). Manga is used to reference examples of simple drawings, and this meaning was maintained throughout the nineteenth century. The earliest confirmed appearance of manga in a book title is in 1814. That year, two books were published independently of each other: the first volume of Katsushika Hokusai's (1760–1849) famous *Hokusai's Manga* and the single-volume *Manga of One Hundred Women* (*Manga hyakujo*) by Aikawa Minwa (active 1806–21). It is unknown which of the two books was released first and if the choice of manga in their titles was coincidental or deliberate. In the 1860s and 1880s, other artists like Tsukioka Yoshitoshi (1839–92) and Kawanabe Kyōsai (1831–89) followed Hokusai's example and issued compilations of their drawing styles as manga.

Today's use of the word manga traces back to 1902 when the cartoonist Kitazawa Rakuten (1876–1955) was given a comic strip in the newspaper *Jiji Shinpō*, which he named *Jiji Manga*. Nevertheless, in the following year, Ogino Issui (dates unknown) still employed the old meaning of the word manga when he chose it for the title of his *Practical Manga* (*Ōyō manga*).

**Opposite** Detail from *Hokusai's Manga*.

# Comings and Goings in the Four Seasons

## *Shiji no yukikai*
四時交加

1798
Author: Santō Kyōden (Kitao Masanobu; 1761–1816)
Artist: Kitao Shigemasa (1739–1820)
Publisher: Tsuruya Kiemon
Woodblock printed book (*hanshibon*); ink on paper
National Diet Library

Santō Kyōden initially studied painting under Kitao Shigemasa and became a successful painter using the name Kitao Masanobu. However, Kyōden developed into an even more prolific writer who authored more than four hundred books from 1778 until his death in 1816. In 1789 and 1791, Kyōden was punished by the government for violations against censorship rules. The first one was for his illustrations of the book *Black and White Watery Mirror* (*Kokubyaku mizukagami*), written by Ishibe

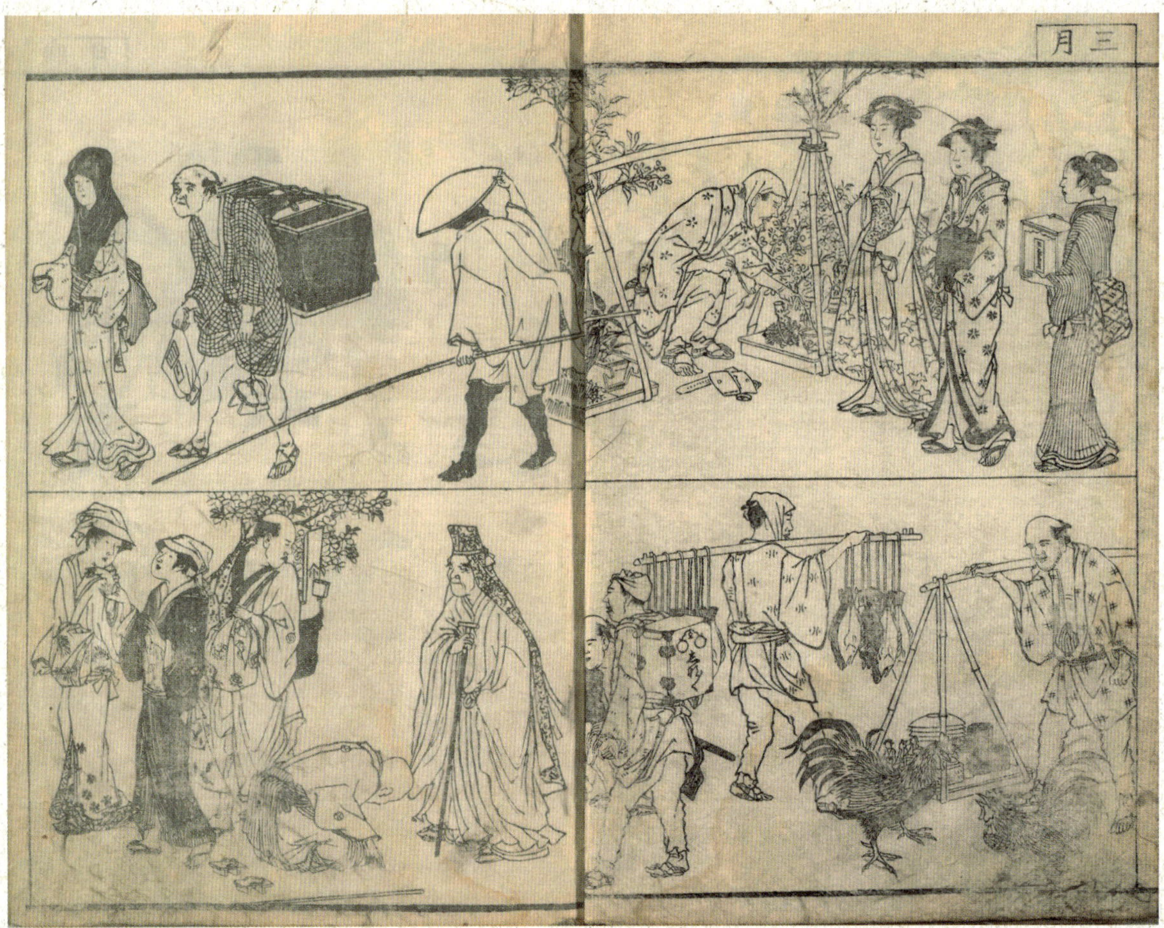

**Above** Third lunar month.

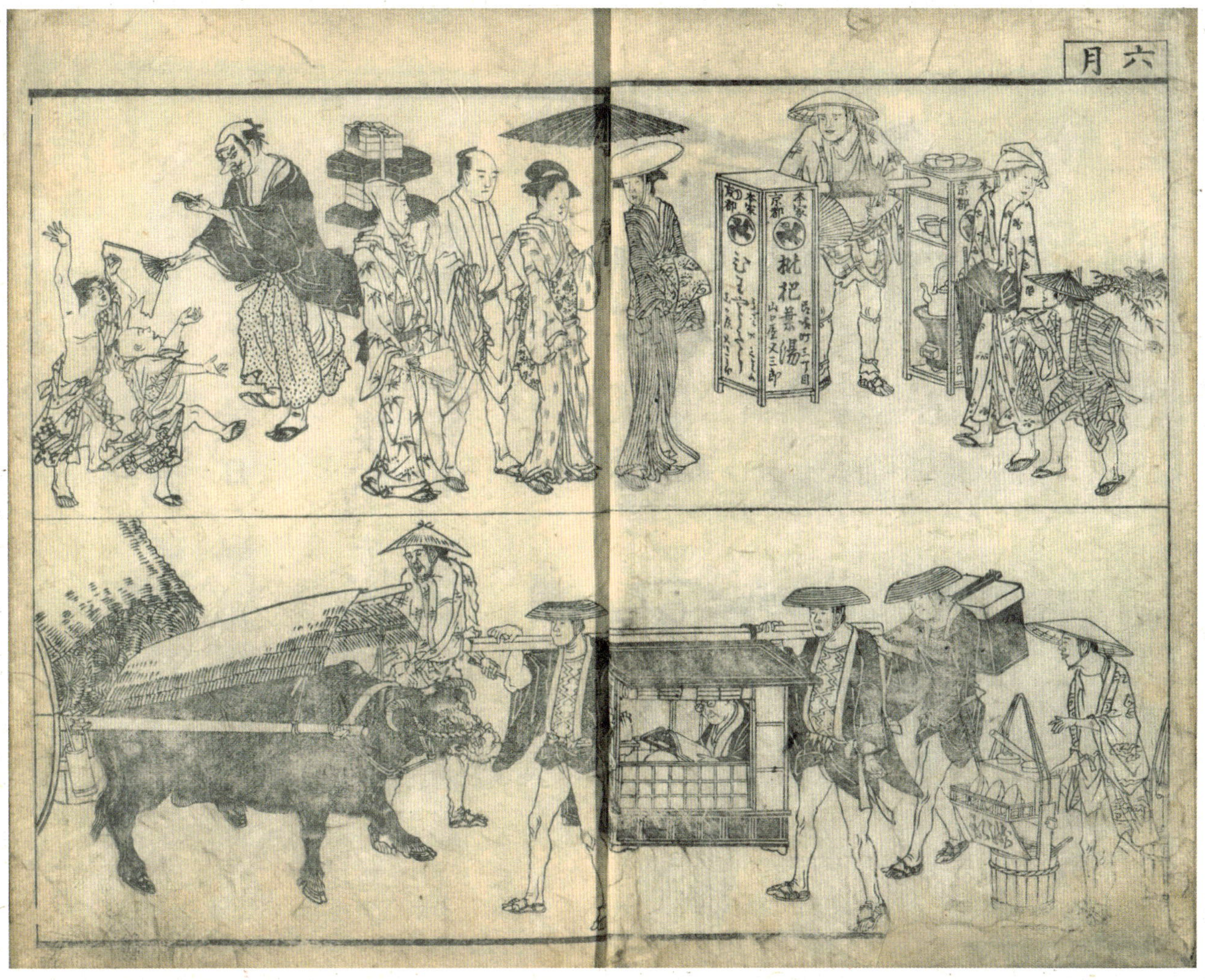



**Above** Sixth lunar month.

Kinkō (dates unknown). The second was for writing the humorous books *The Other Side of the Brocade* (*Nishiki no ura*), *A Library of Contrivances* (*Shikake bunko*), and *Courtesans' Silken Sleeves* (*Shōgi kinu burui*) without the required permissions.

*Comings and Goings in the Four Seasons* (*Shiji no yukikai*) is a compilation of drawing examples by Kyōden's teacher Shigemasa, followed by prose text by Kyōden. Shigemasa matches his drawings to a specific month of the lunar year, with each month presented in an opening separated into an upper and lower section. The drawings show women and men of all classes, from samurai to peasant, as well as various kinds of craftsmen and vendors who could be found in the Edo metropolis. This book is important because it is the earliest record of the word "manga" in a publication filled with drawing examples. Kyōden uses manga (and this intended pronunciation) in the preface, and thus is the first to publicly raise awareness of the term. Shigemasa's casual drawings of random subjects rarely interact but are lined up like people walking independently along a busy road. Contrary to what Hokusai will do a few years later in his *Manga*, Shigemasa does not repeat specific characters and neither does he offer variations on how to draw them.

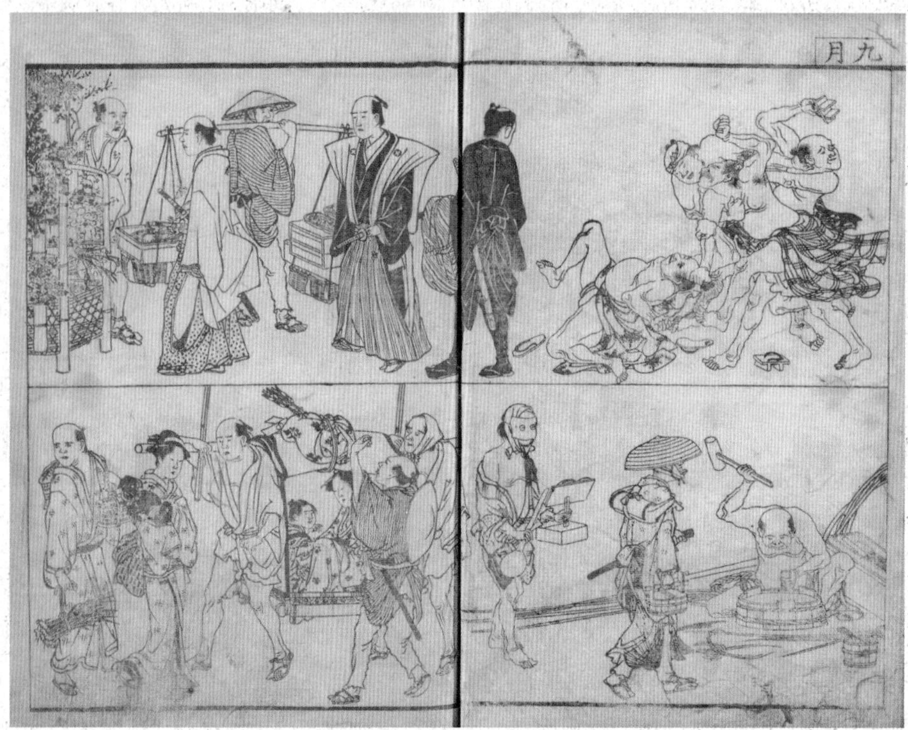

Left Ninth lunar month.

Below Twelfth lunar month.

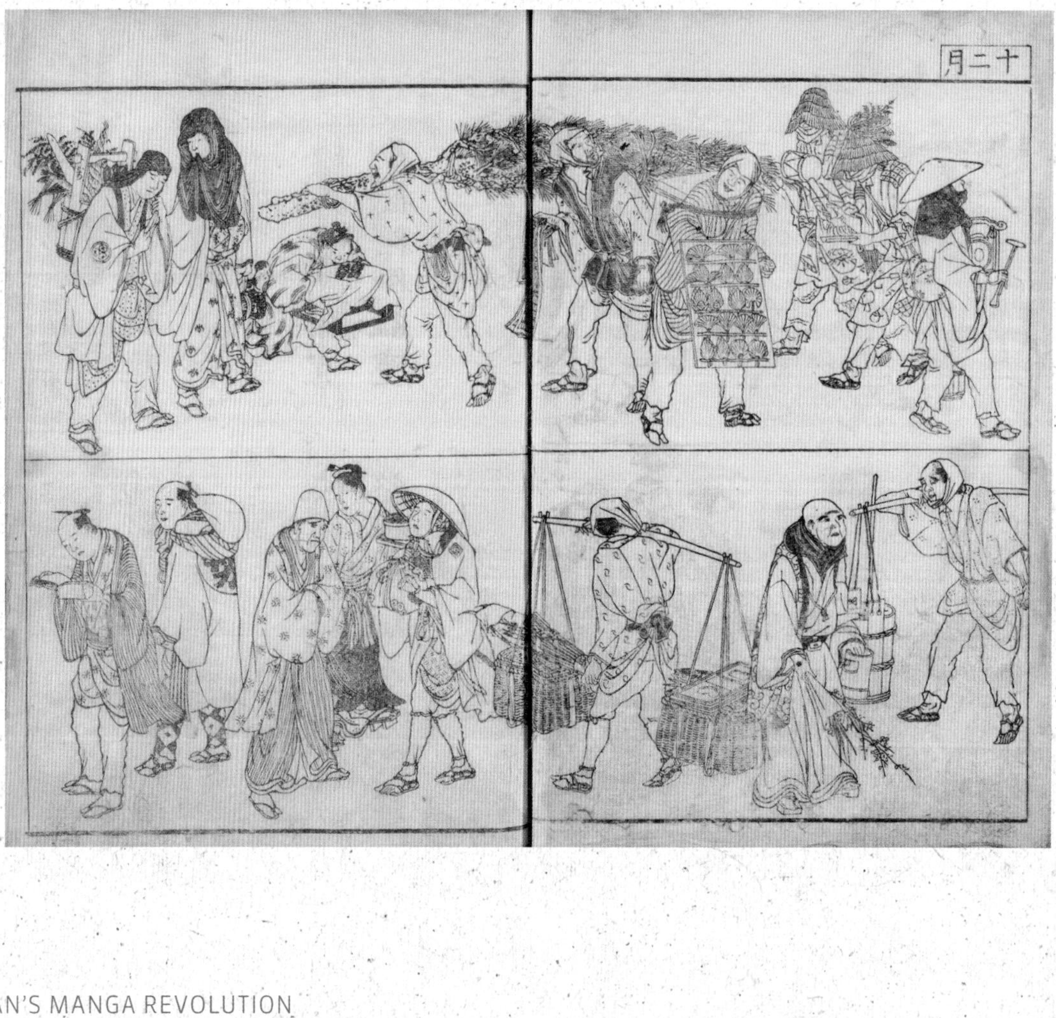

# Hokusai's Manga: Transmitting the Spirit and Revealing the Forms of Things

*(Denshin kaishu) Hokusai manga*

傳神開手　北齋漫画

1814 (vol. 1), 1815 (vols. 2–3), 1816 (vols. 4–5), 1817 (vols. 6–7), 1819 (vols. 8–10), 1833? (vol. 11), 1834 (vol. 12), 1849 (vol. 13), 1875 (vol. 14), 1878 (vol. 15)
Artist: Katsushika Hokusai (1760–1849)
Publisher: Eirakuya Tōshirō, et al.
Woodblock printed book (*hanshibon*); ink and color on paper
Smithsonian Libraries

**Below** Vol. 1, scenes of humans and animals.

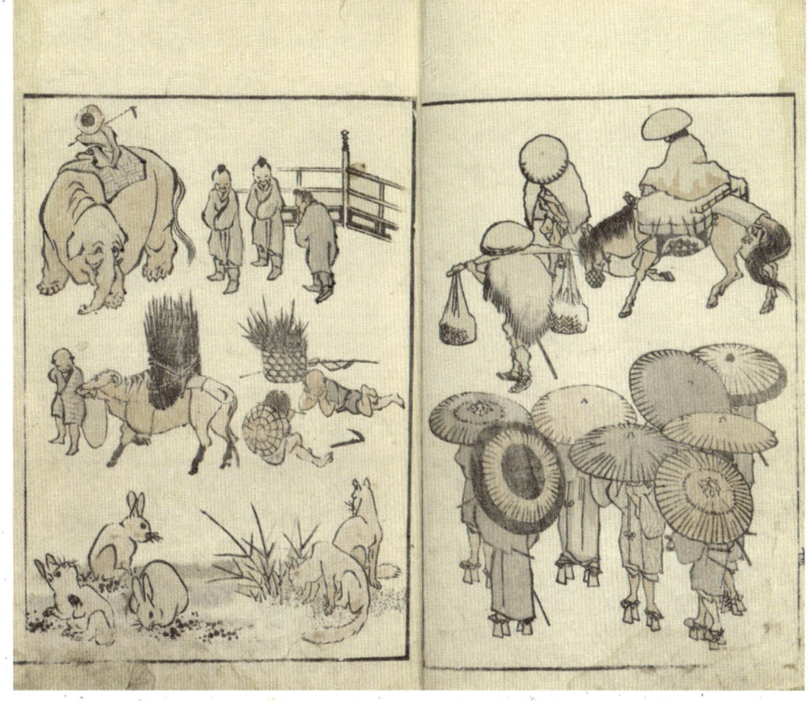

The term "manga" became widely known through *Hokusai's Manga*, Katsushika Hokusai's most famous multi-volume work, which showcases the immense breadth of the artist's talent. Provided with the subtitle *Transmitting the Spirit and Revealing the Forms of Things (Denshin kaishu)*, *Hokusai's Manga* served as a source of inspiration to many European artists in the second half of the nineteenth century and remains popular today for its vast array of drawing ideas and design possibilities. The preface of the first volume traces the inception of the books back to Hokusai's autumn visit to his student Maki Bokusen (1775–1824) in Nagoya in 1812, during which he sketched hundreds of drawings. His visit also elucidates why the production of *Hokusai's Manga* was overseen by Nagoya-based publisher Eirakuya Tōshirō, with the first volume published in 1814 and the last, volume 10, in 1819. Subsequent volumes, totaling five in all, were released over a decade later, with the final two volumes emerging in the 1870s, long after Hokusai's death. The initial ten volumes contain nearly three hundred images, reflecting the number of drawings purportedly created during Hokusai's Nagoya visit. It is plausible that Hokusai created a fresh set of drawings for the succeeding volumes during the more than decade-long hiatus until the release of volume 11 around 1833.

The compositions of Hokusai's illustrations include individual scenes, such as travelers fighting

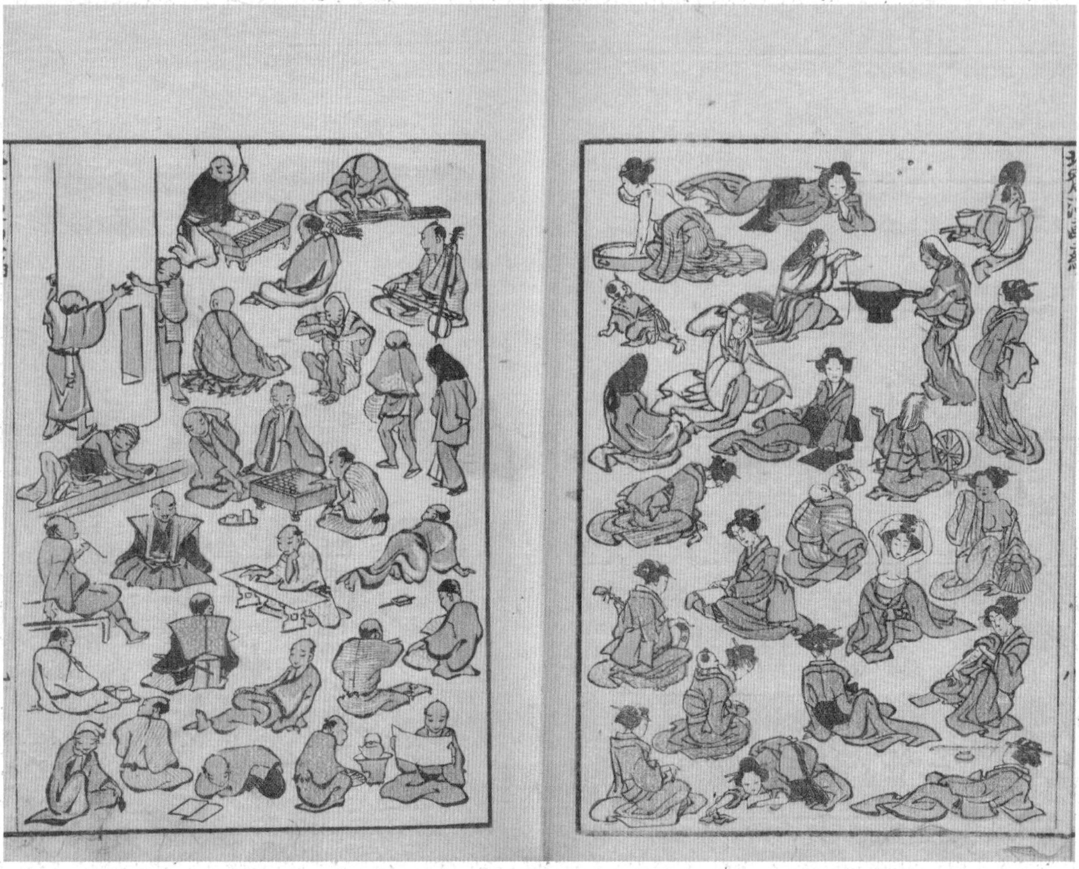

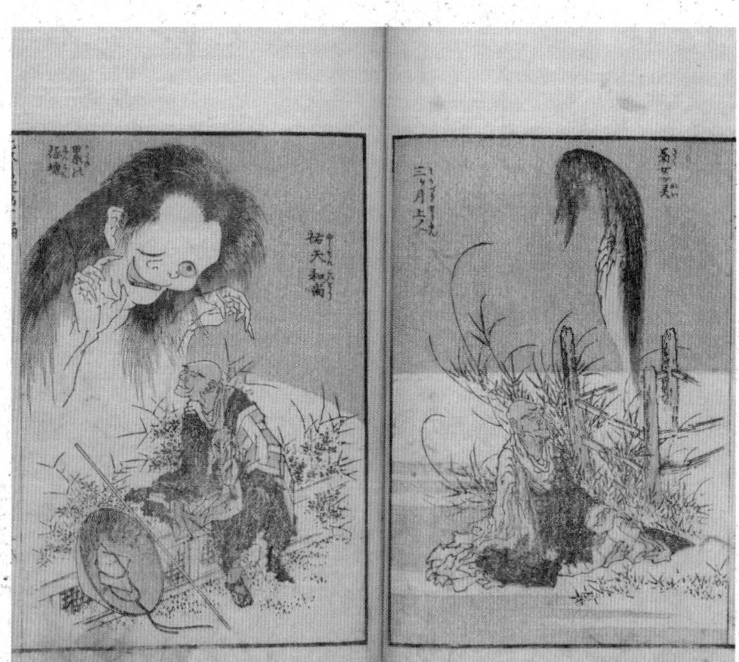

**Above** Vol. 2, men and women in various poses.

**Below** Vol. 10, Kasane and the monk Yūten; the ghost of Kiku and the monk Mikazuki.

the wind spread over an opening, which sometimes needs to be rotated by 90 degrees to be viewed properly. But the majority offer variations on the same subject, such as sumo wrestlers, trees, insects, and pistols. Hokusai later created several other drawing manuals, including *Hokusai's Album from Life* (*Hokusai shashin gafu*), *Teach Yourself the Dance* (*Odori hitori geiko*), and *The Quick Pictorial Dictionary* (*Ehon hayabiki*), but none of them reached the fame of his *Manga*, which was reprinted countless times.

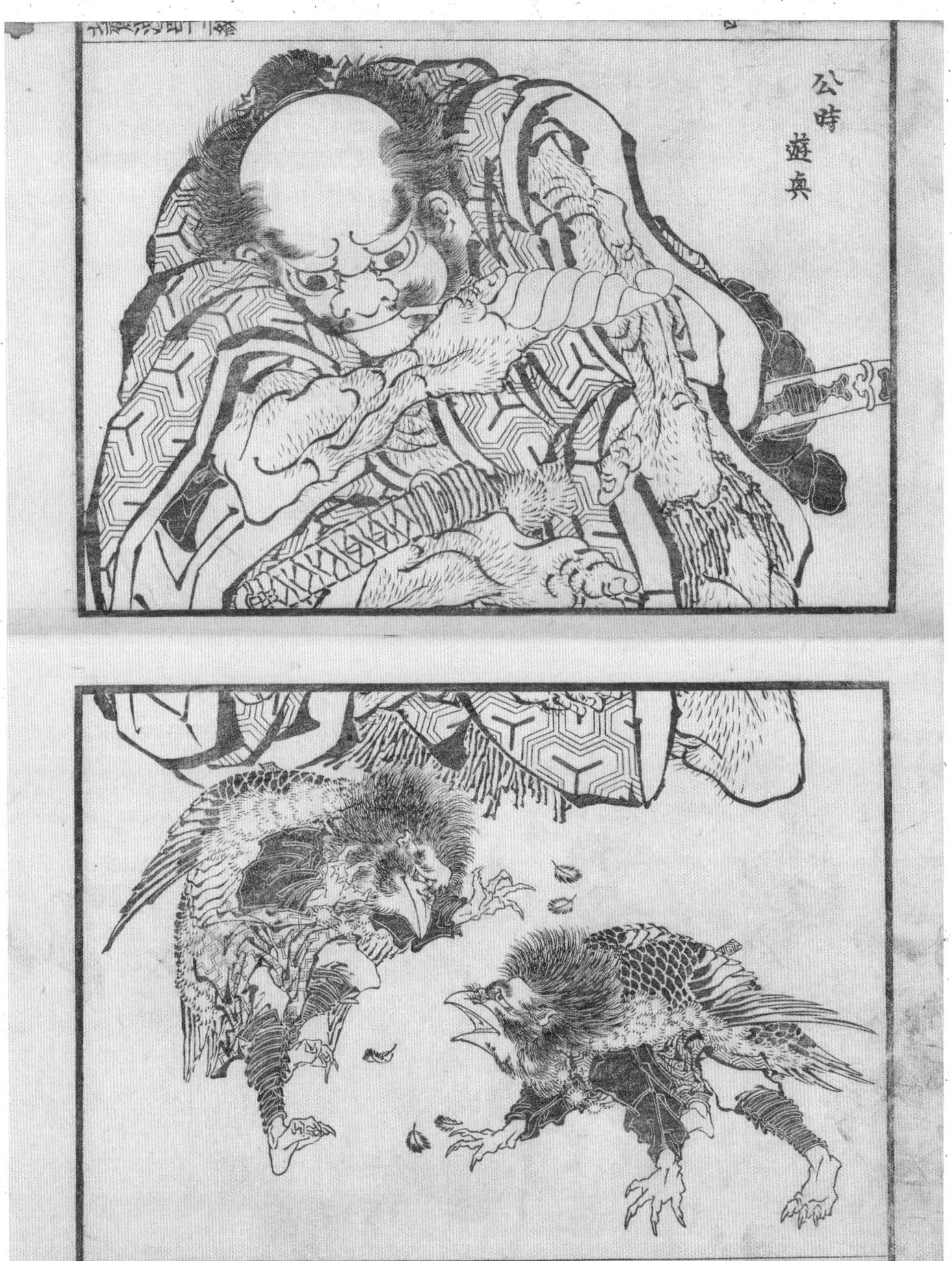


公時
遊興

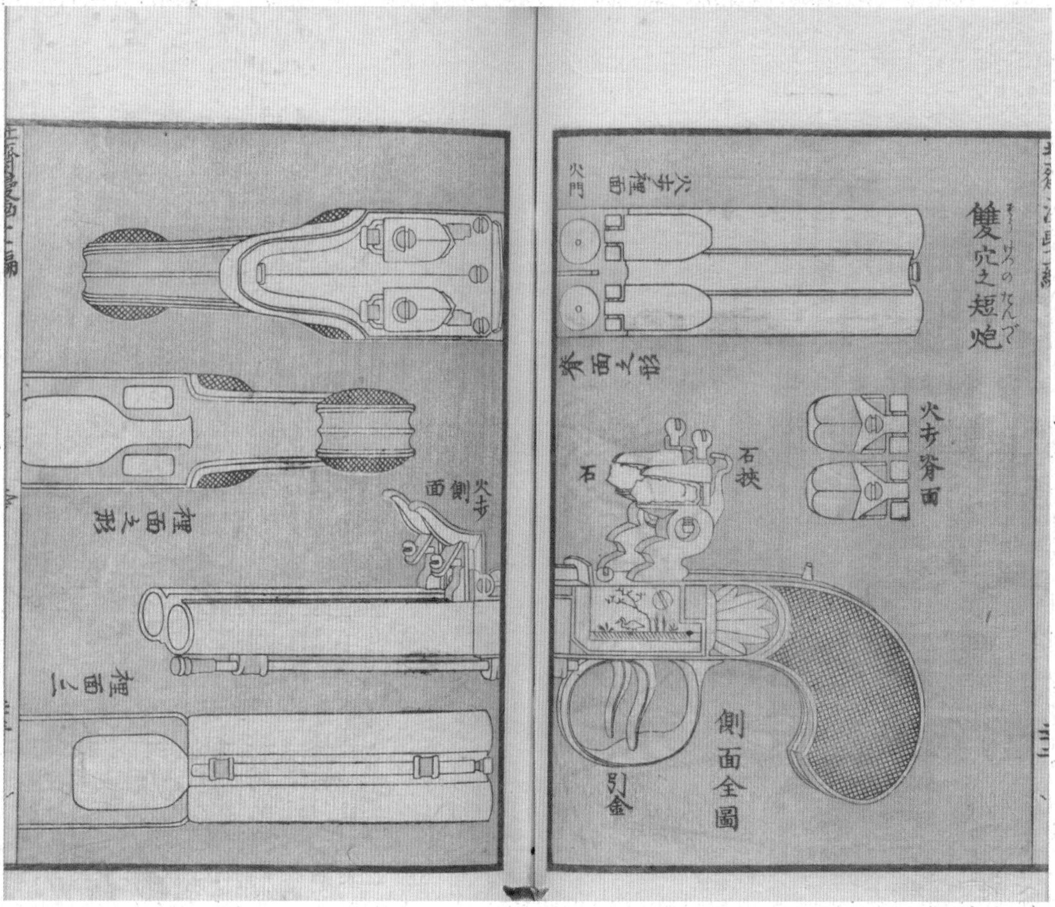

**Above** Vol. 11, flintlock pistols.

**Below left** Vol. 6, spear drills.

**Below right** Vol. 7, evening shower at Sekiya.

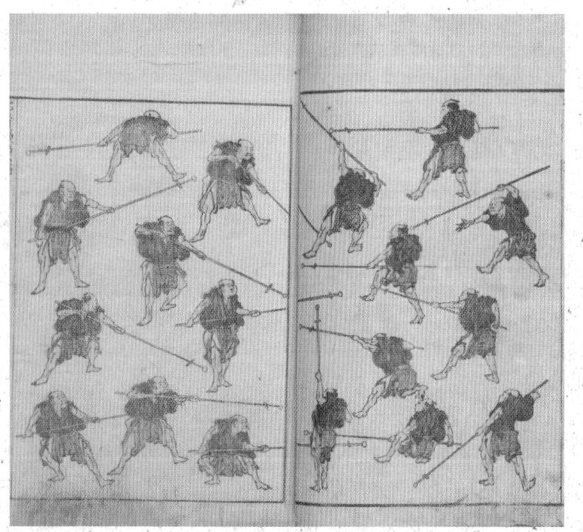

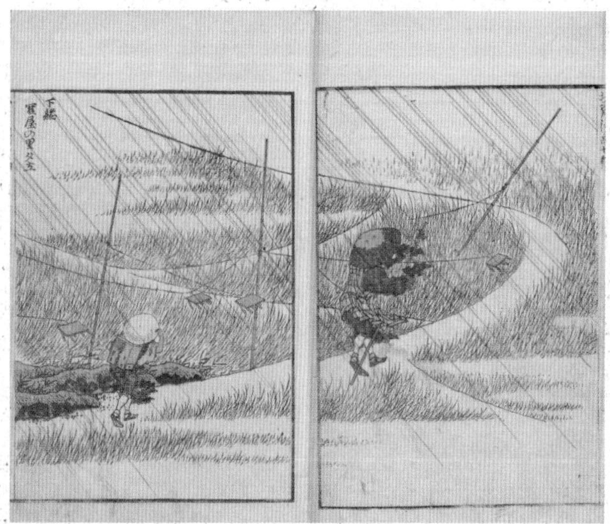

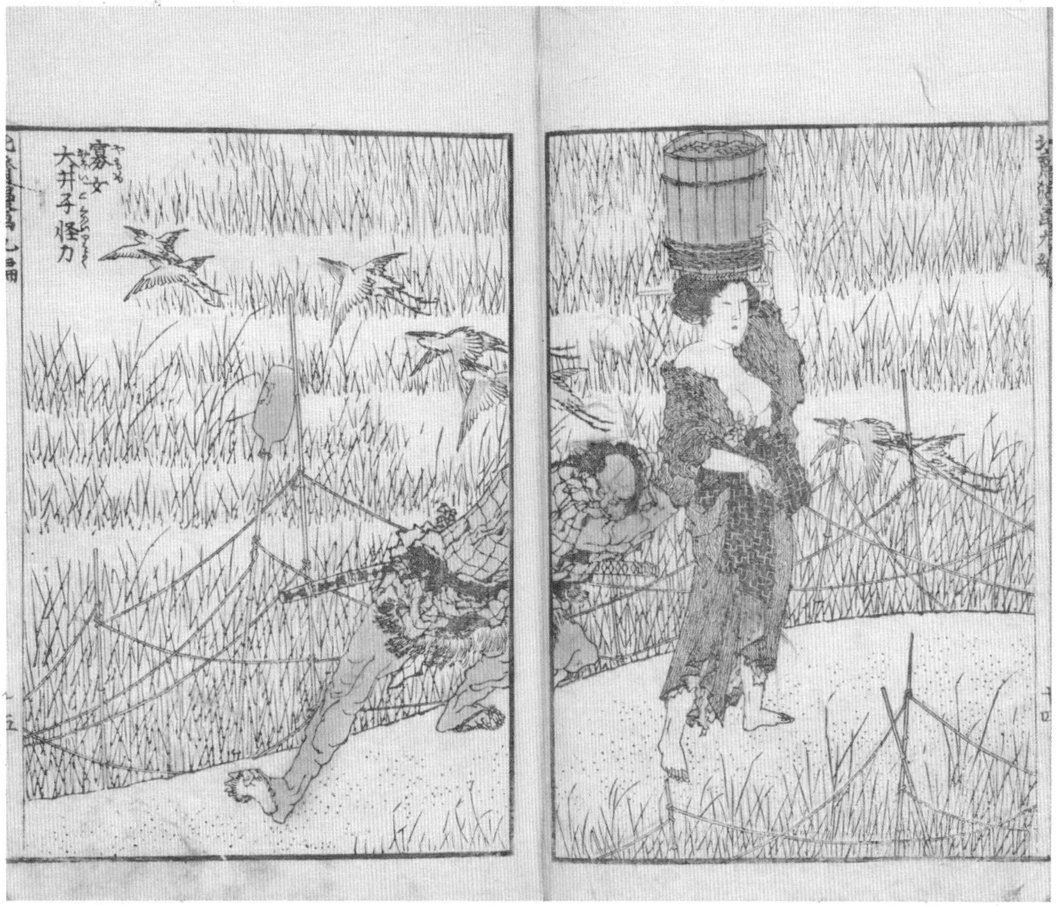

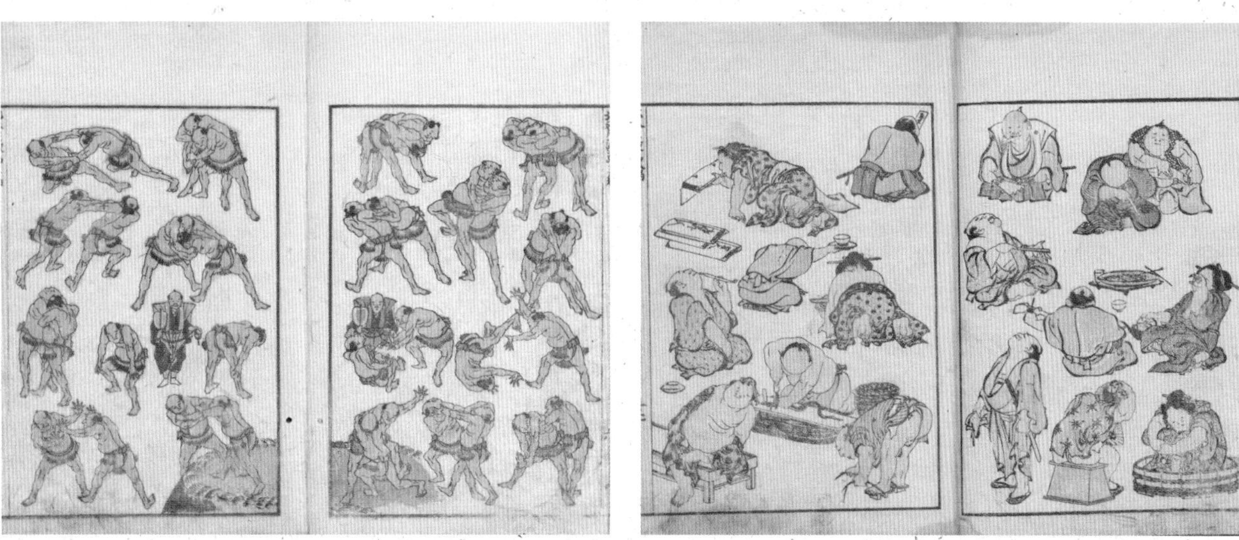

**Above** Vol. 9, the extraordinary prowess of the widow Oiko.

**Below left** Vol. 3, sumo wrestlers.

**Below right** Vol. 8, scenes of daily life.

# Manga of One Hundred Women

*Manga hyakujo*

漫画百女

1814
Artist: Aikawa Minwa (active 1806–21)
Preface: Yoshida Shinbei (dates unknown)
Publishers: Maekawa Rokuzaemon, Yanagihara Kihei, Yoshidaya Shinbei
Woodblock printed book (*ōhon*); ink and color on paper
The Metropolitan Museum of Art, Purchase, Mary and James G. Wallach Foundation Gift, 2013 (2013.782)

Not much is known about the artist Aikawa Minwa who is said to have been a student of the painter Ganku (1749/56?–1839). Minwa illustrated fewer than twenty books between 1806 and 1821, the most famous being *Kōrin's Painting Style* (*Kōrin gashiki*) from 1818, a compilation of drawings in the style of Ogata Kōrin (1658–1716), one of Japan's most beloved artists. Four years earlier, in the ninth lunar month of 1814, Minwa's *Manga of One Hundred Women* (*Manga hyakujo*) was issued by

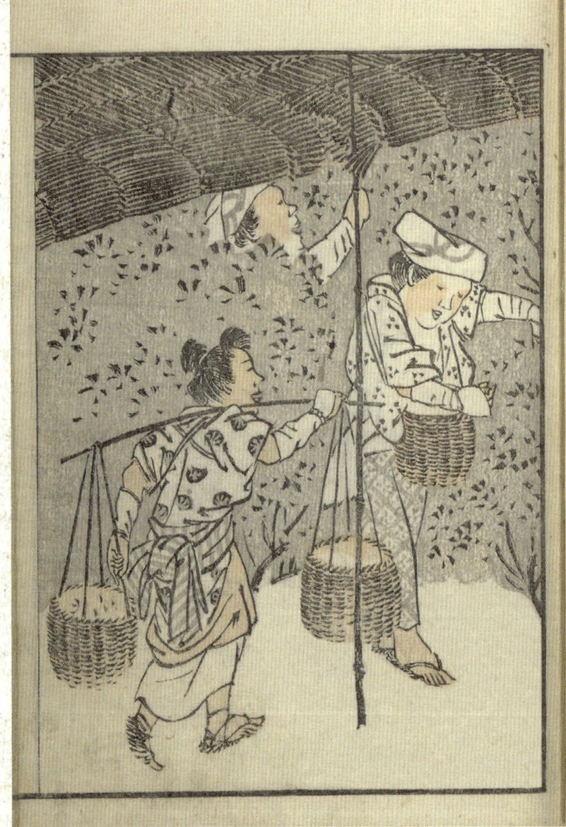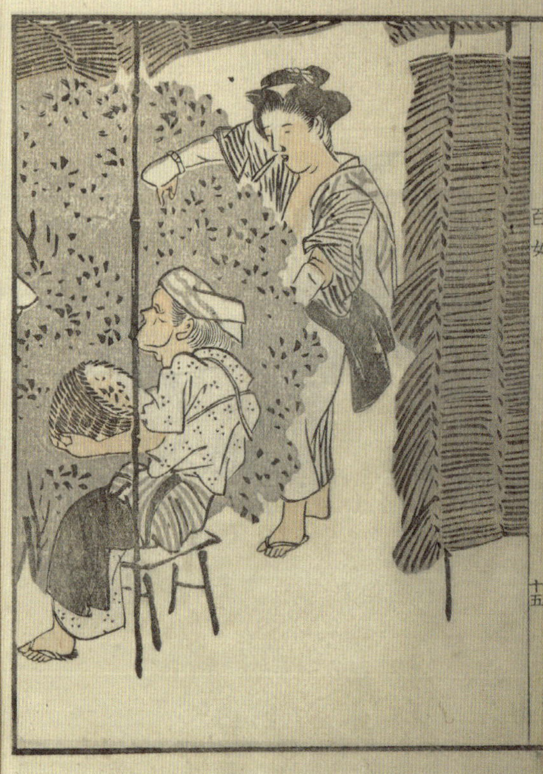

**Above** Picking tea leaves.

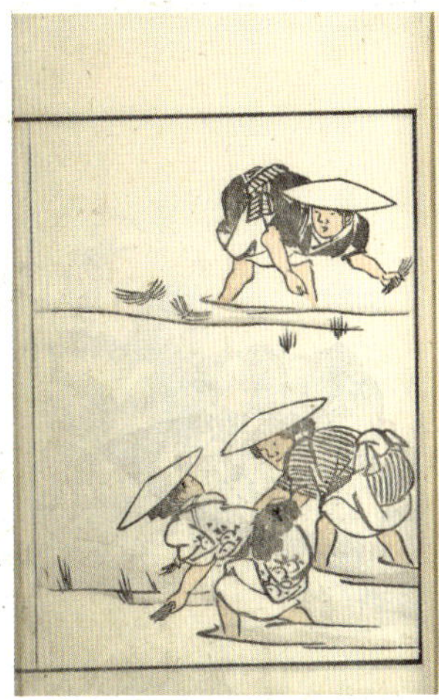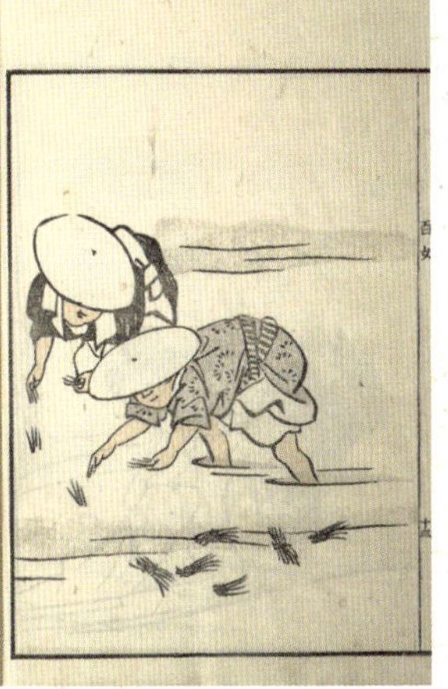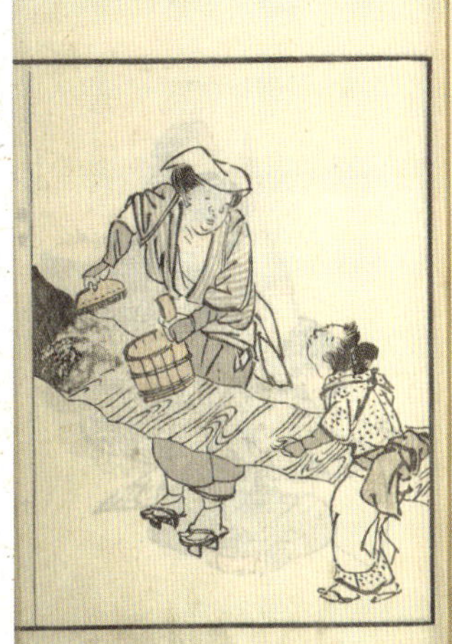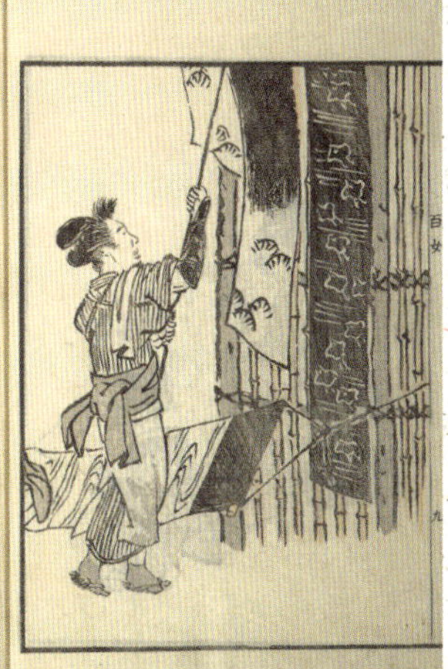

a consortium of three publishers: Maekawa Roku-zaemon in Edo (today's Tokyo), Yanagihara Kihei in Osaka, and Yoshidaya Shinbei in Kyoto.

The *Manga of One Hundred Women* contains thirty-one double-page illustrations. The drawings depict women of all classes in varying situations, such as drying bolts of cloth, planting rice in a field, and picking tea leaves, or a group of three courtesans taking a break and smoking. Minwa's illustrations are casual, as the term manga in the title suggests, and each scene is a whimsical, cohesive situation, not specifically meant as drawing models for teaching.

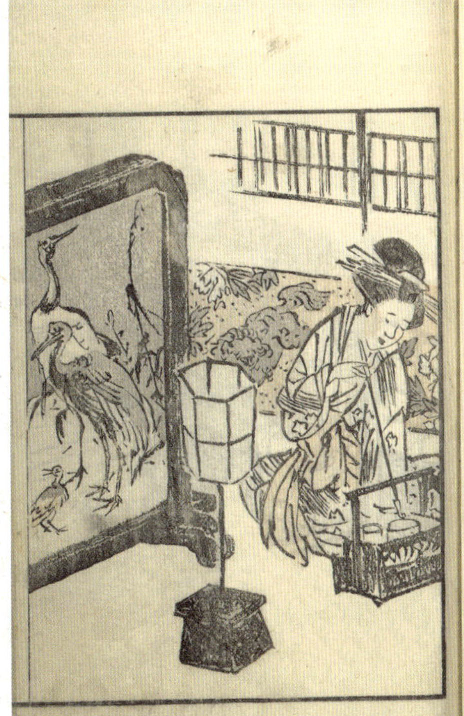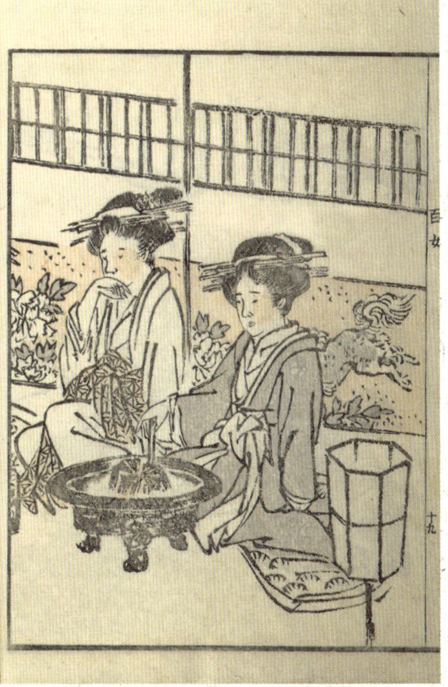

**Above left** Planting rice.

**Above right** Drying bolts of cloth.

**Left** Courtesans taking a break.

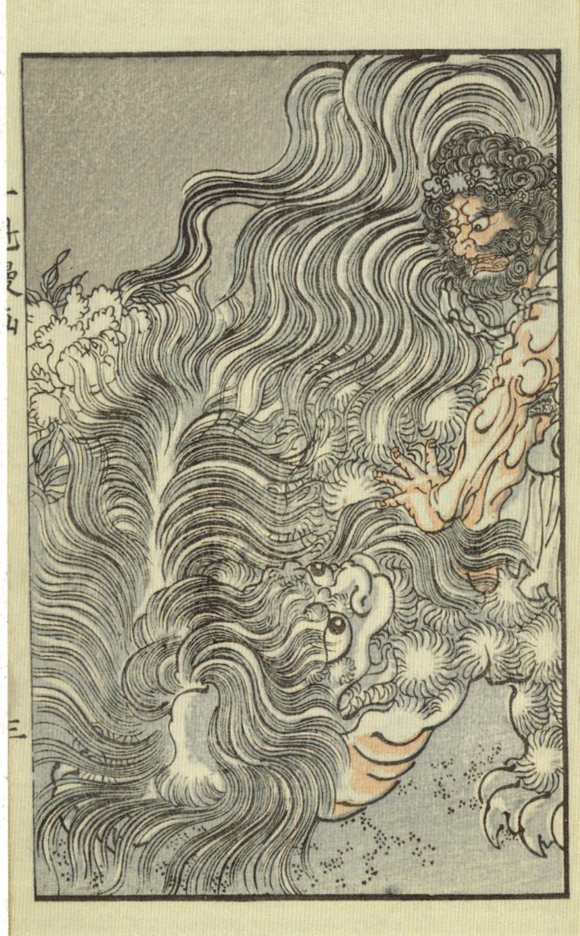
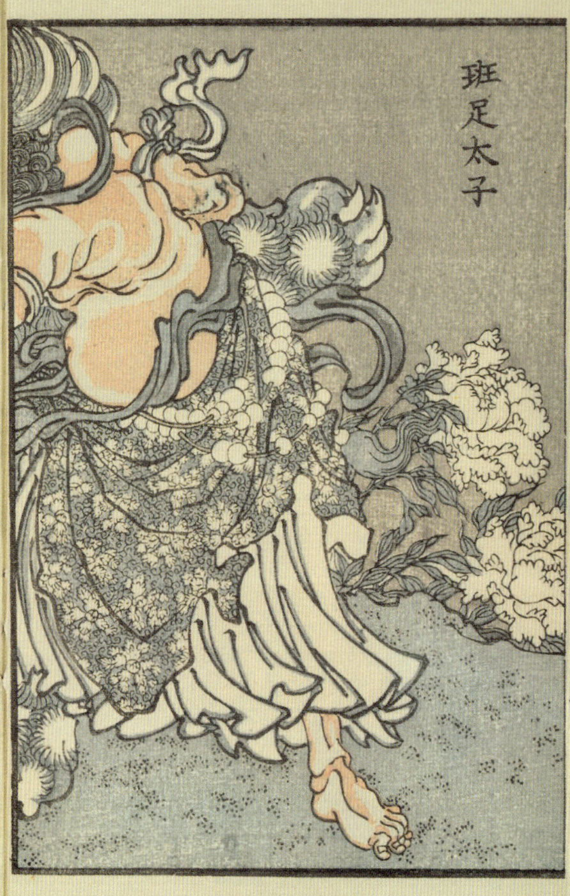


# Ikkai's Manga

*Ikkai manga*

一魁漫画

1866
Artist: Tsukioka Yoshitoshi (1839–92)
Preface: Kanagaki Robun (1829–94)
Publisher: Nakaya Tokusaburō, et al.
Woodblock printed book (*chūbon*); ink and color on paper
Minneapolis Institute of Art, The Mary Griggs Burke Endowment Fund established by the Mary Livingston Griggs and Mary Griggs Burke Foundation, gifts of various donors, by exchange, and gift of Edmond Freis in memory of his parents, Rose and Leon Freis (2017.106.251)

Tsukioka Yoshitoshi was predominantly a designer of woodblock prints but was also active as a painter and book illustrator. A student of Utagawa Kuniyoshi (1798–1861), one of the leading print artists in the mid-nineteenth century who dominated the market of warrior portraits, Yoshitoshi followed his teacher's example, and his earliest published print is a warrior scene dating from 1853. He continued to design beautiful women and actors in the Utagawa school style. In 1858, Yoshitoshi became an independent artist and focused on historical subjects. Eventually, he shifted towards realism and Western drawing styles.

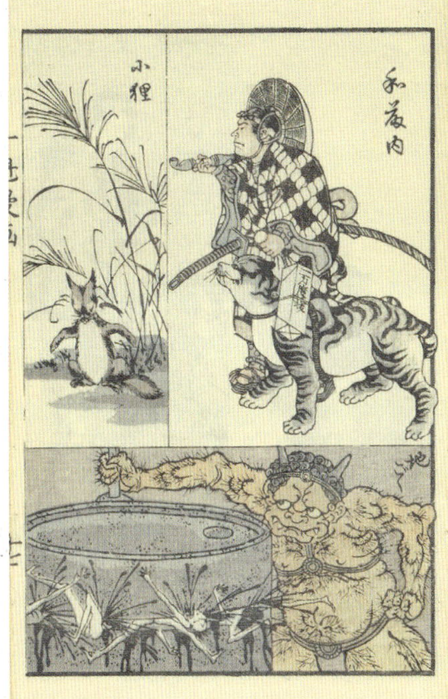
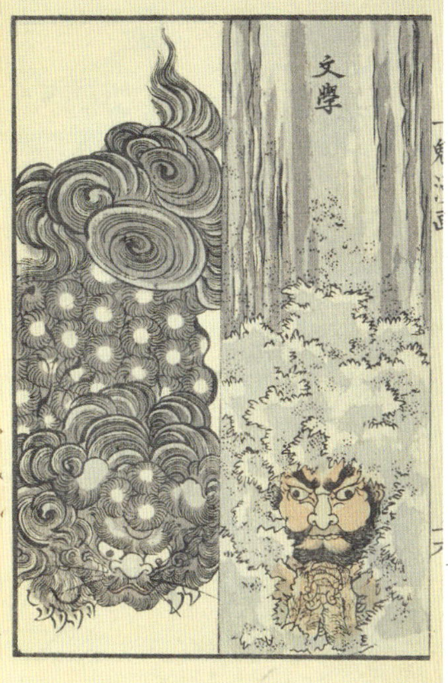



**Opposite** Prince Hansoku fights with a lion.

**Below** Konjin Chōgorō struggles with a demon.

Hokusai was fifty-four years old when the first volume of his *Manga* was published, and by 1866 thirteen volumes had been released. Yoshitoshi was exactly half as old as Hokusai when his *Ikkai's Manga* was produced. It was a rather bold move by the twenty-seven-year-old to think that his drawing style was already of such quality that it could serve as teaching material. Be that as it may, only one volume with thirty-nine pages of illustrations was produced. The publisher and owner of the blocks was Nakaya Tokusaburō, who enrolled a staggering nineteen other publishers in Edo and three in Osaka for the distribution.

The eight double-page illustrations are all of famous warriors set against a gray background, for example, the Indian Prince Hansoku fighting with a lion, and Konjin Chōgorō struggling with a demon. The other pages are separated into frames of varying sizes and feature a combination of subjects, including fish and other animals, trees, toys, townspeople, supernatural figures, and characters from folklore and history.

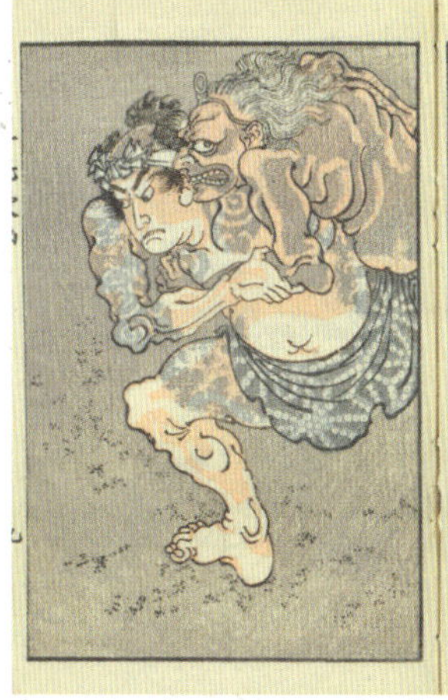
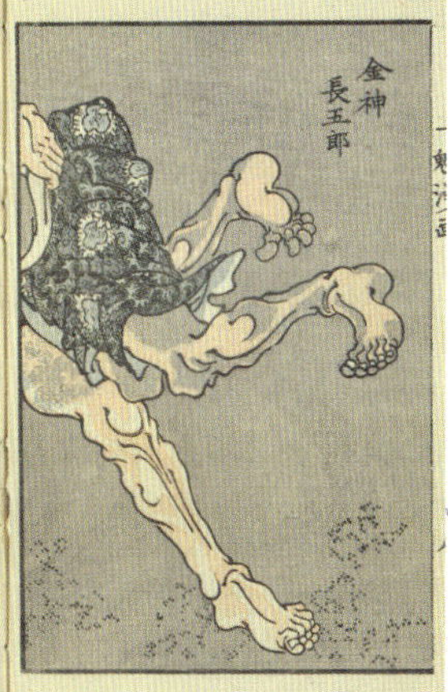



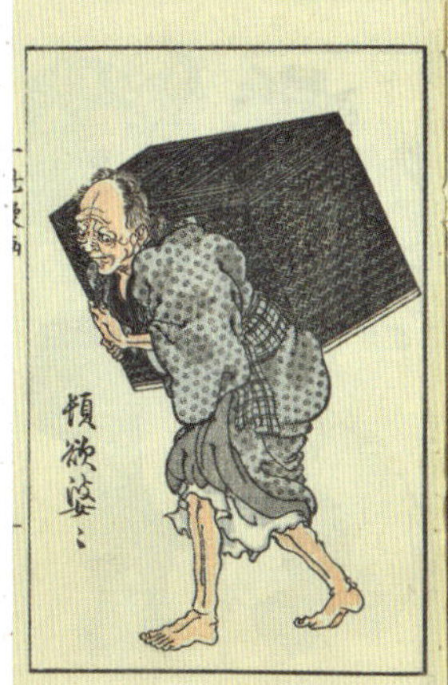
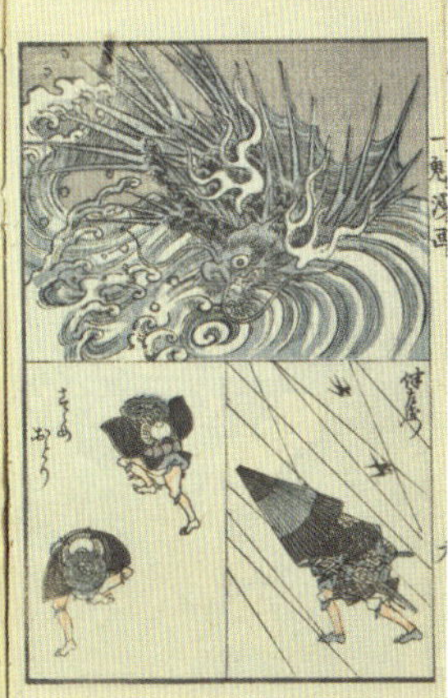

# Kyōsai's Manga

*Kyōsai manga*

暁斎漫画

1881
Artist: Kawanabe Kyōsai (1831–89)
Preface: Matsuura Hiroshi (1818–88)
Publisher: Izumiya Kichibei
Woodblock printed book (*hanshibon*); ink and color on paper
The Metropolitan Museum of Art, Purchase, Mary and James G. Wallach Foundation Gift, 2013 (2013.765)

Like Tsukioka Yoshitoshi, Kawanabe Kyōsai was a student of Utagawa Kuniyoshi (1798–1861), the foremost designer of warrior prints in the mid-nineteenth century. Before Kyōsai began designing prints in 1855, he studied painting and continued to do so throughout his career. In 1860, *Kyōsai's Album* (*Kyōsai gafu*), the artist's first illustrated book was issued, filled with people interacting and behaving in certain ways which would become frequent subjects in his future work. It took twenty-one years until

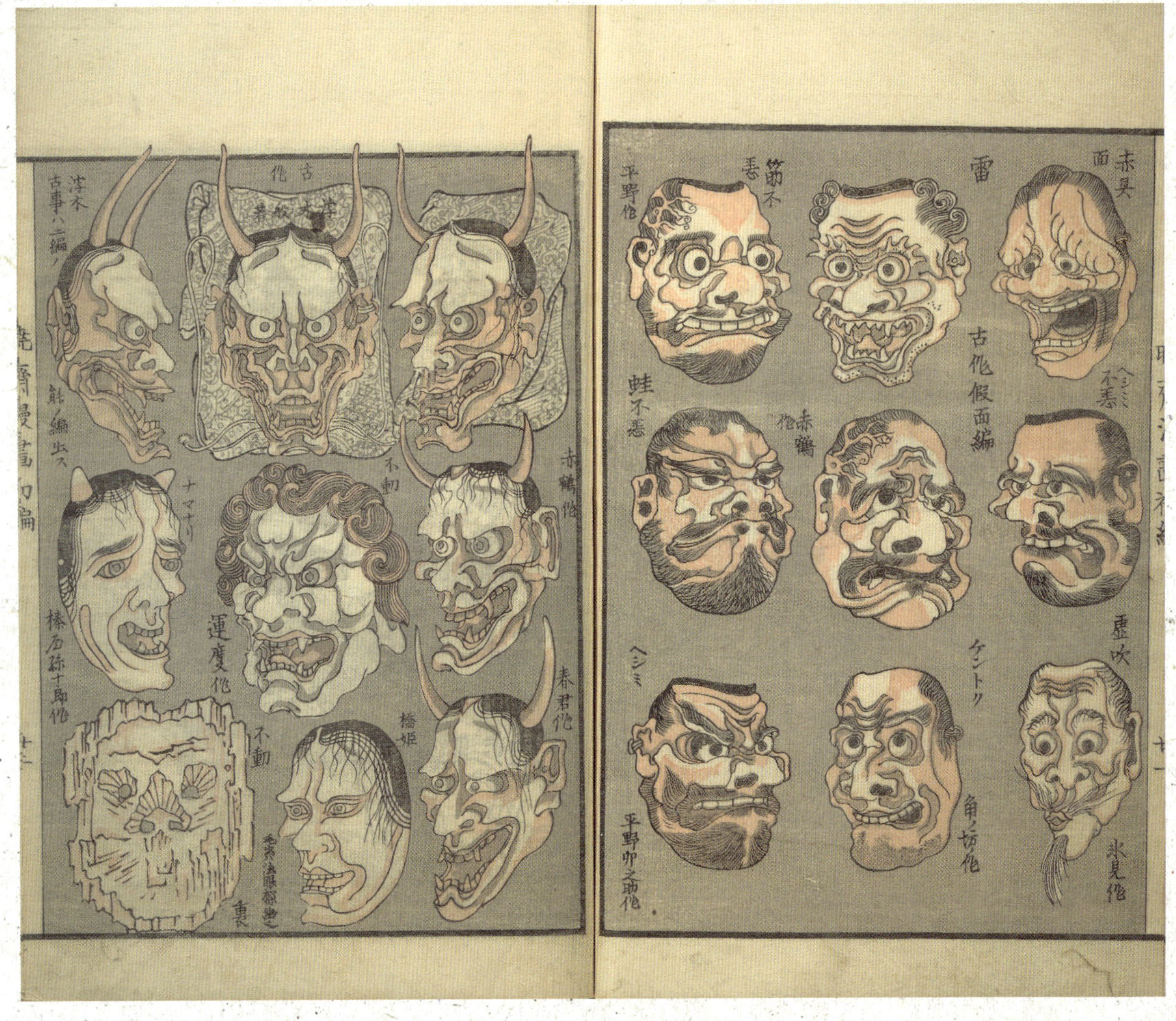

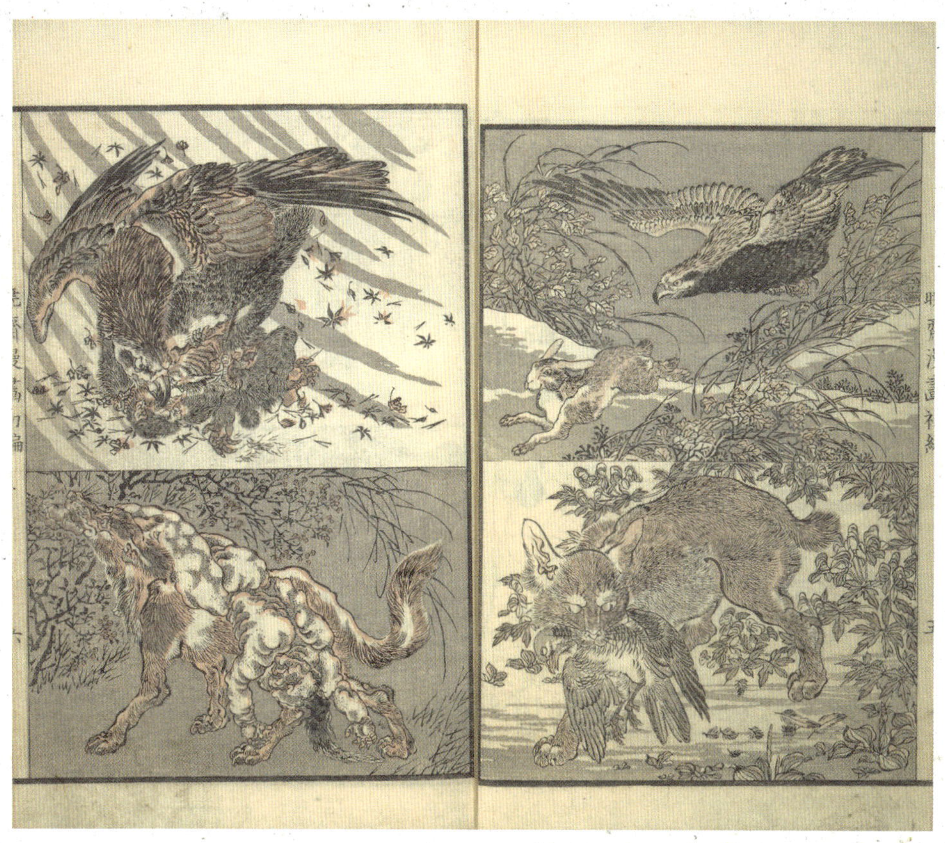

**Opposite** Masks.

**Left** Wild animals.

**Below** A cat riding a catfish.

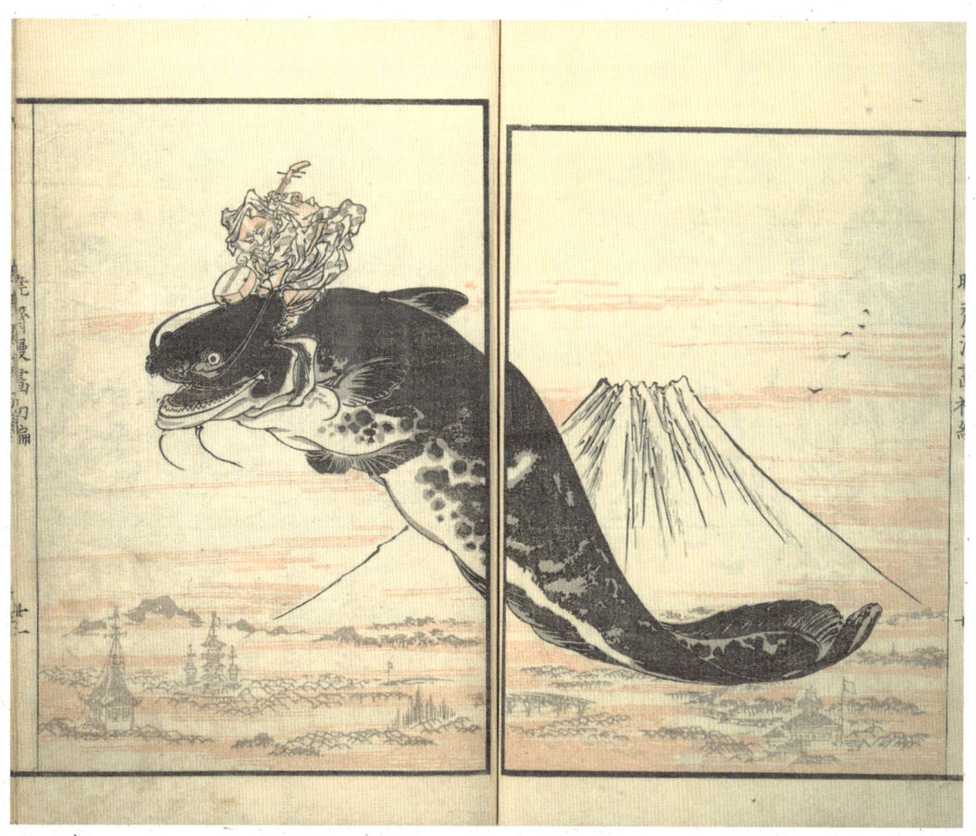

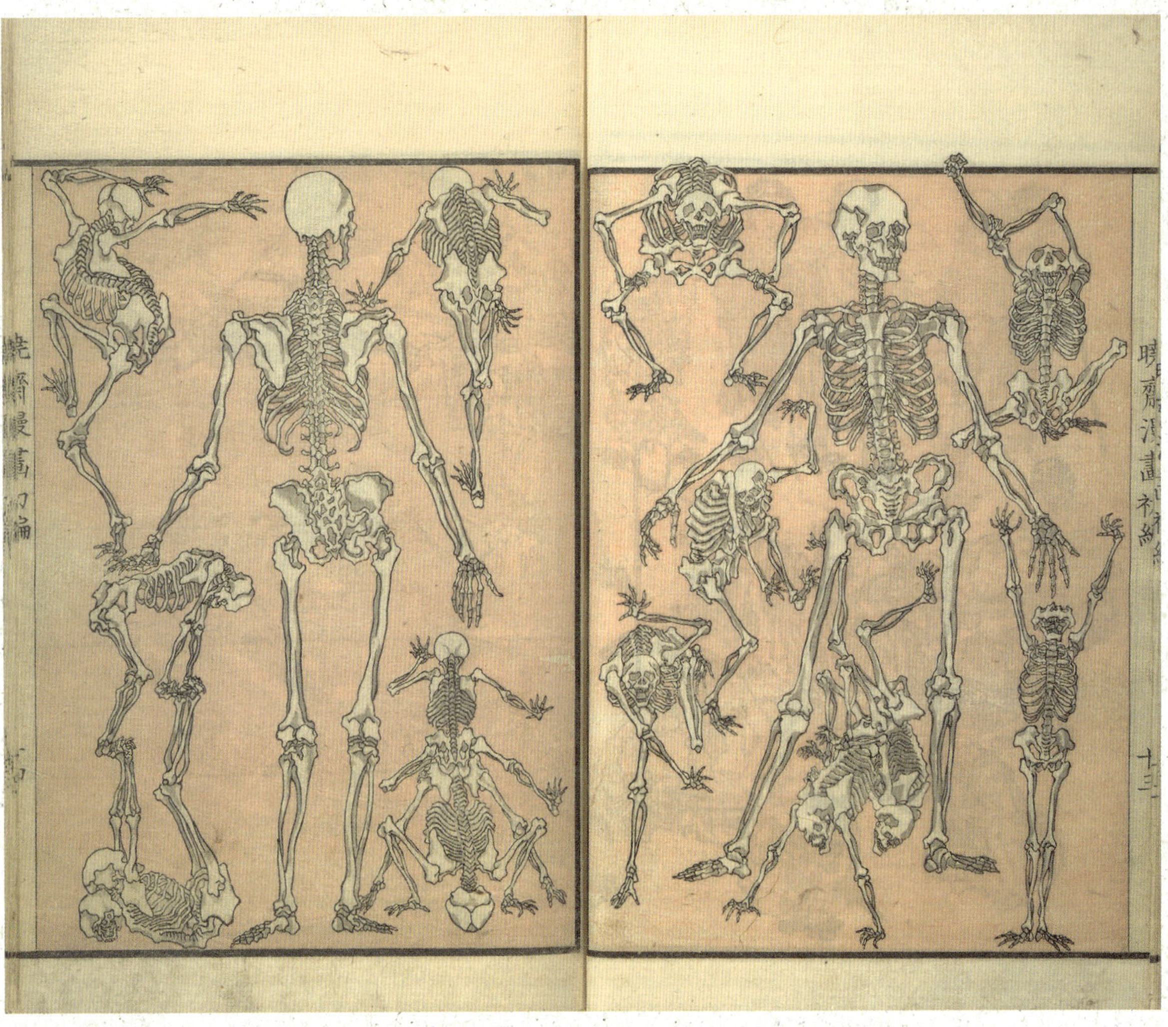

**Above** Skeletons.

more of his drawing models were published as books, and this time in three distinct publications, each produced by a different publisher: *Kyōsai's Idle Drawings* (*Kyōsai donga*) was issued by Chōjiya Heibei, et al., *Kyōsai's Drawings for Pleasure* (*Kyōsai rakuga*) by Morita Tetsugorō, et al., and *Kyōsai's Manga* by Izumiya Kichibei. The first volume of *Drawings by an Inebriated Kyōsai* (*Kyōsai suiga*) followed in 1882, and that of *Kyōsai's Treatise Through Pictures* (*Kyōsai gadan*) in 1887.

*Kyōsai's Manga* contains twenty-four double-page spreads and two single-page illustrations of comic parodies rendered in light colors. The preface by Matsuura Hiroshi explains that Kyōsai is the victim of an unconditional love of sake and at the same time is an exceptional artist. Some illustrations are titled and most are executed in great detail. By this time, Kyōsai had made a name for himself as

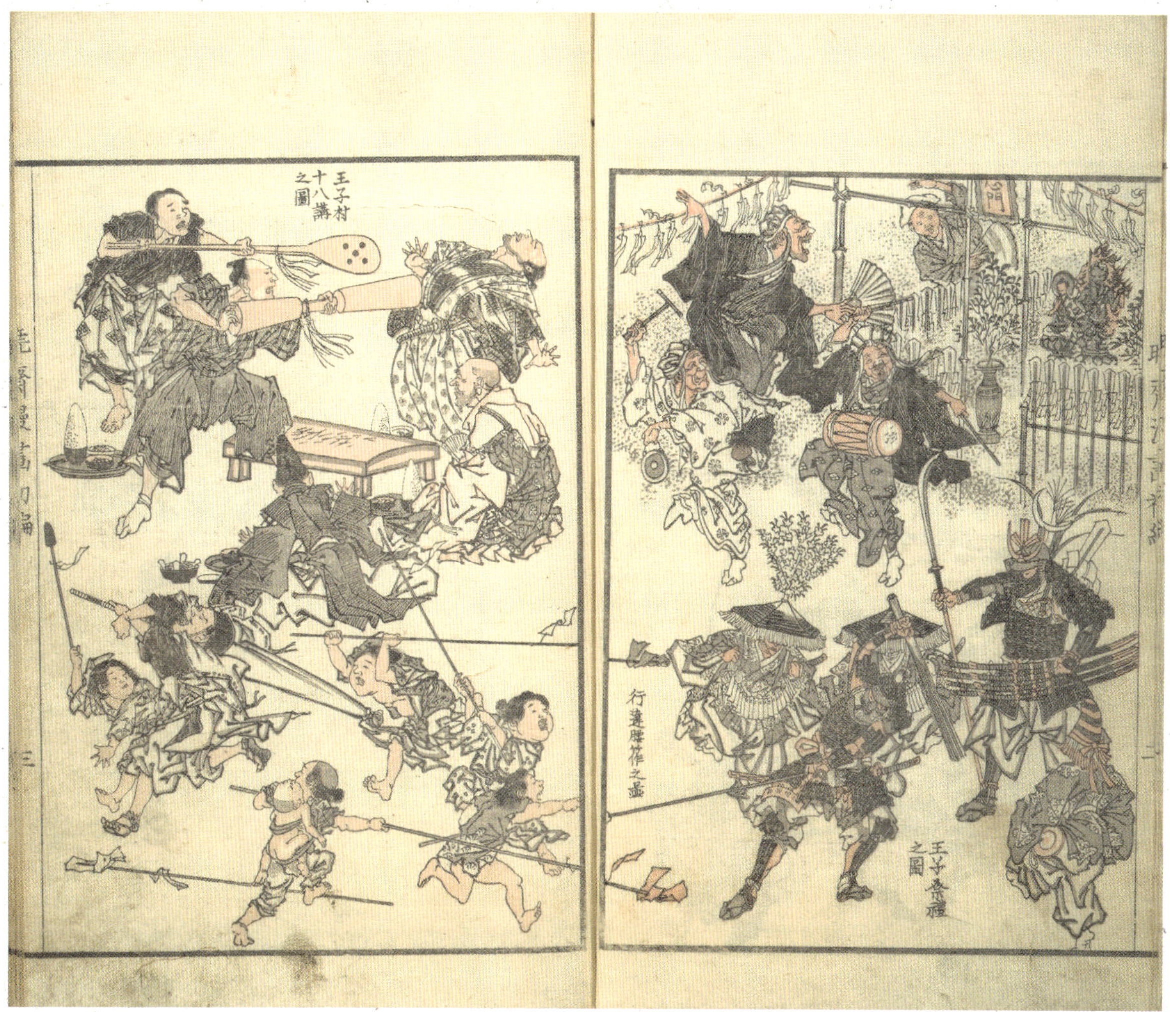

**Above** Playing games.

an unconventional artist with an extraordinary
sense of humor, albeit sometimes of a dark nature.
One opening, for example, shows four scenes of wild
animals, including a raptor in pursuit of a rabbit,
a cat that has killed a bird, an eagle picking out a
monkey's eyes, and a wolf dragging a human corpse.
Amongst the most memorable openings is that of
cavorting skeletons, and of a cat riding a flying
catfish in front of Mount Fuji.

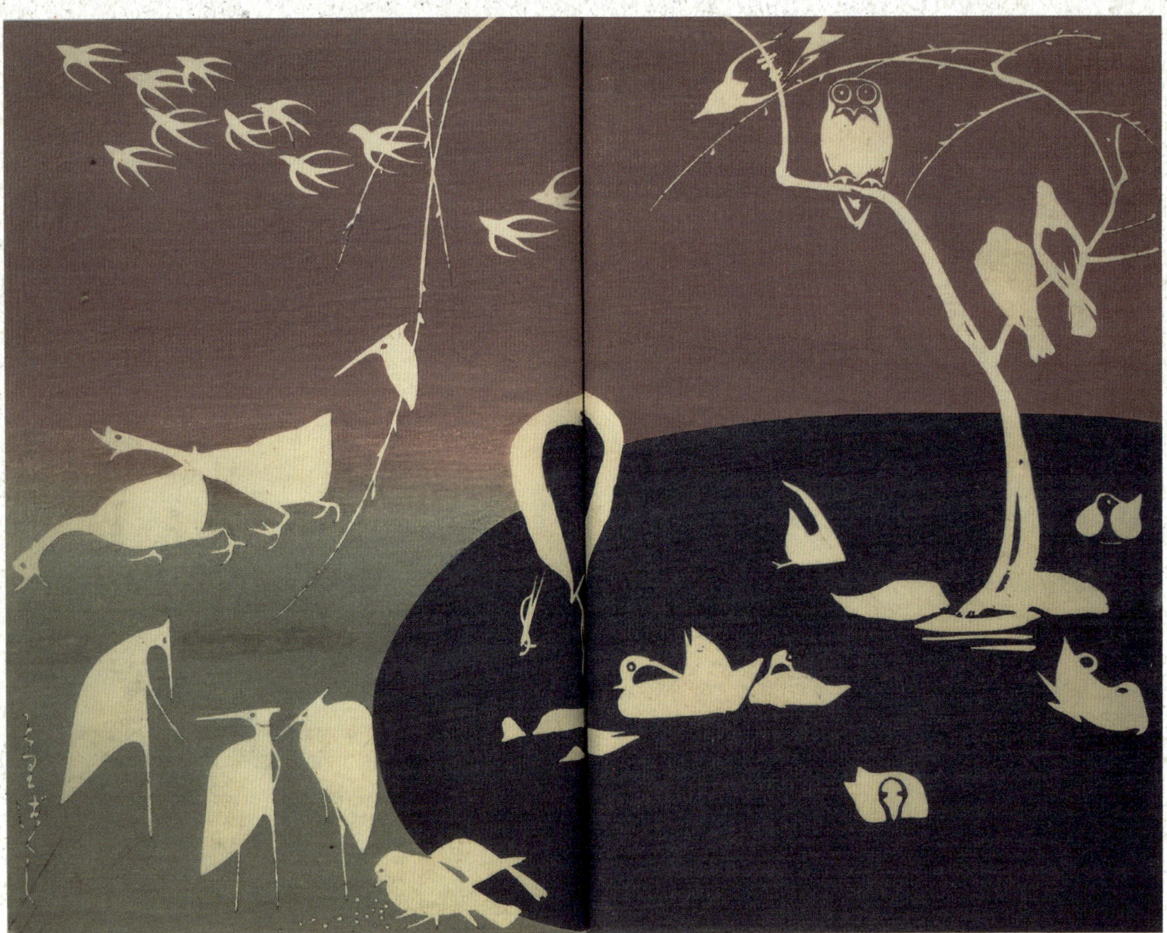

## Practical Manga

### *Ōyō manga*
応用漫画

1903 (2 vols.)
Artist: Ogino Issui (dates unknown)
Publisher: Unsōdō
Woodblock printed book (*ōhon*); ink on paper
The Metropolitan Museum of Art, Purchase, Mary and
James G. Wallach Foundation Gift, 2013 (2013.789a,b)

In 1891, Yamada Naosaburō founded the publishing
firm Unsōdō in Kyoto with the intention of special-
izing in the publication of high-quality art books.
Yamada's endeavors were successful and soon he
established a quasi-monopoly, working with leading
book artists at that time, especially Kamisaka Sekka
(1866–1942). Unsōdō released new parts of Sekka's
*All Kinds of Things* (*Chigusa*) between February
1899 and April 1903. In August 1902, Unsōdō
issued his *Textile Designs: The Sea Route* (*Senshoku
zuan: Kairo*). In April 1903 came *Humorous
Designs* (*Kokkei zuan*), and in April 1904 began
the release of *All Kinds of Butterflies* (*Chō senshu*).

In the same period came *Practical Manga*
(*Ōyō manga*), a collection of designs issued in
two volumes. Ogino Issui is mentioned as the
mastermind behind these, but there is a possibility
that he was merely the compiler whereas the
designs themselves were created by the young
Sugiura Hisui (1876–1965) who was going to
become the pioneer of modern graphic design in
Japan. Instead of presenting character studies as
in the manga books by Hokusai, Yoshitoshi, and
Kyōsai, this set features abstract designs mostly
of animal and plant motifs. While they are of
varying sizes, each one is labeled in the margin
and mentioned in the content sheets.

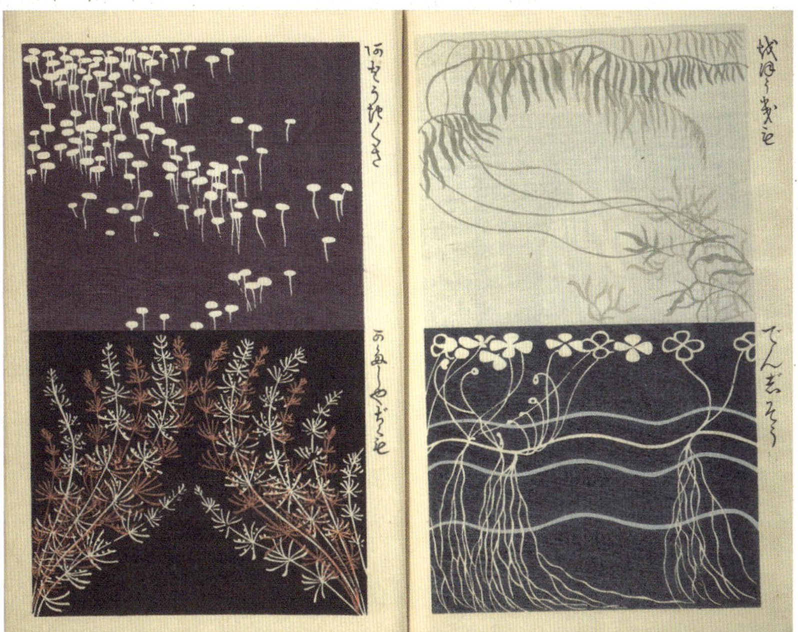

**Opposite** A collection of birds.

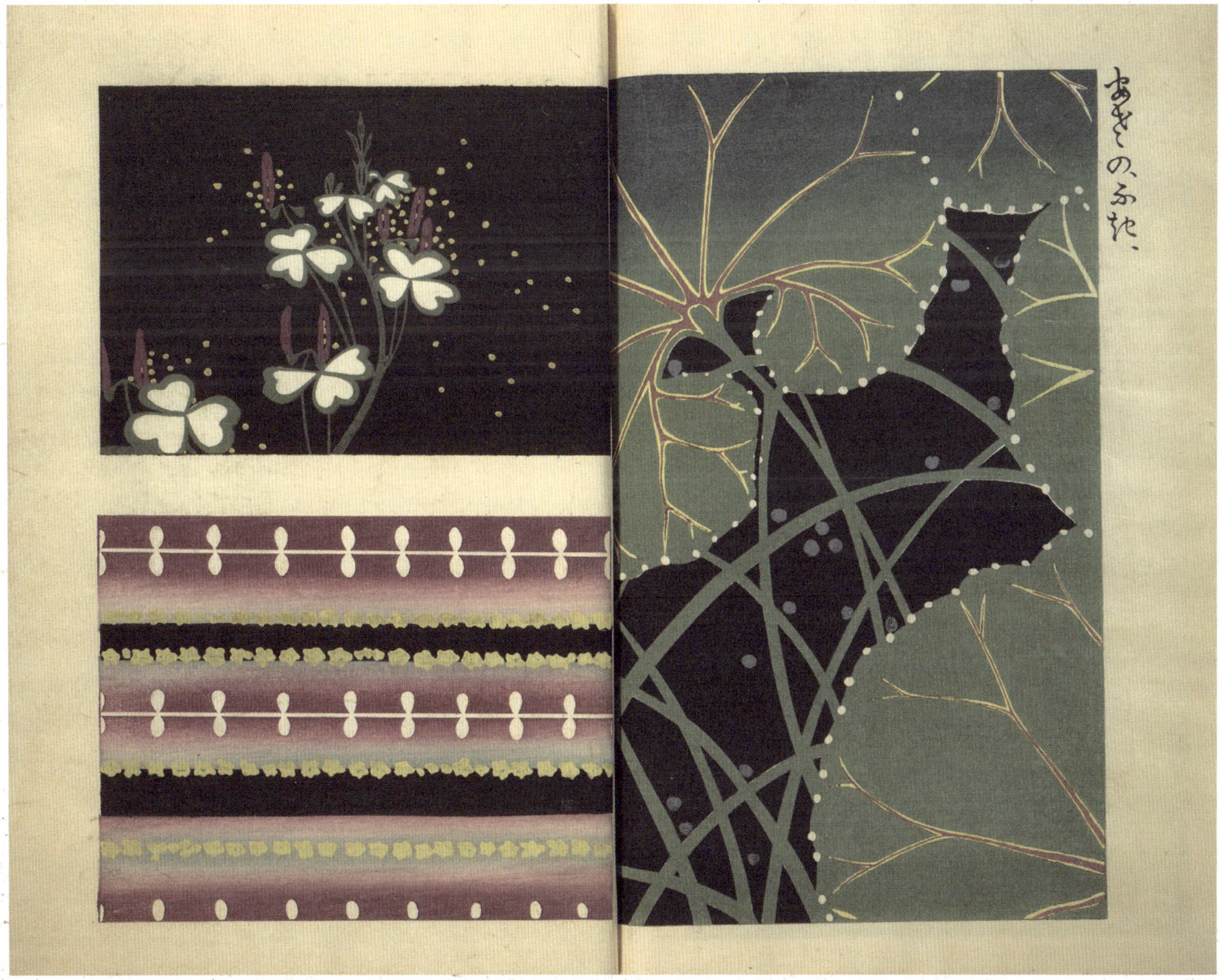

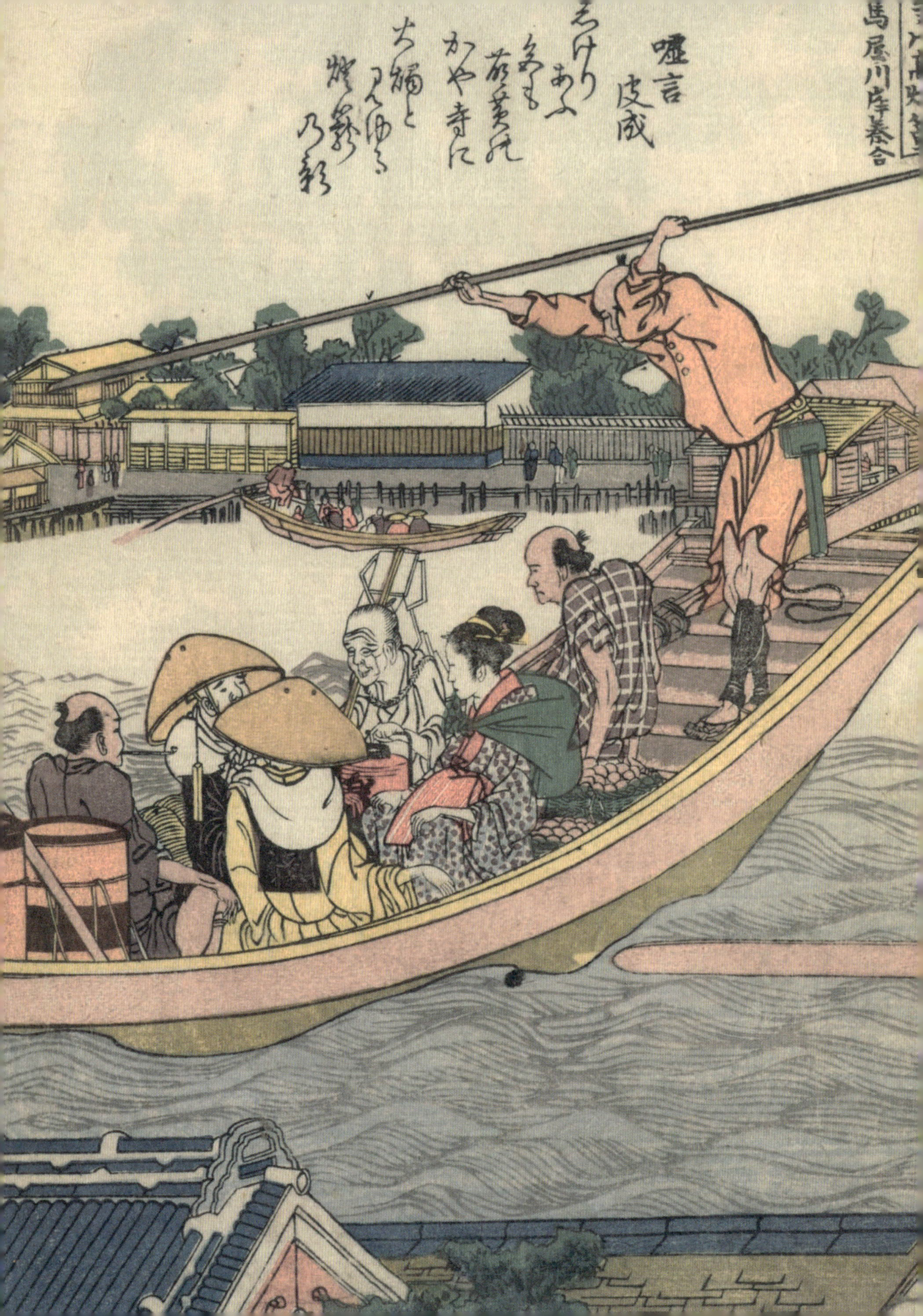

嘘言　皮成
馬屋川岸養合
そけり
ありあふ
旅美死
かや寺に
古帽と
人ゆる
遊彩
乃彩

# CHAPTER TWO

# ILLUSTRATED POETRY BOOKS

In the 1780s, the first poetry books were issued using the highest possible production methods. These deluxe picture books were printed with the utmost care, featured exceptional coloration, were enhanced by employing techniques like embossing or blind printing (*karazuri*), and further embellished with mica and gold lacquer. Such luxury books were produced for and sponsored by private clubs of amateur poets who met to compose *kyōka*—light, parodic and satirical verses filled with puns and wordplay. At the forefront of this genre was the publisher Tsutaya Jūzaburō who collaborated with the print artist Kitagawa Utamaro (ca. 1754–1806). Together they produced the outstandingly beautiful *Illustrated Book of Selected Creatures* (*Ehon mushi erami*) and *Gifts of the Ebb Tide* (*Shiohi no tsuto*).

The government became wary about the production of luxury books and in the 1790s, under the Kansei reforms, a series of conservative social and economic changes in Tokugawa Japan, prohibited them. Although the genre of poetry books continued, the new publications were no longer printed with deluxe features. In 1799, Tsutaya began working with Katsushika Hokusai (1760–1849) and released *Amusements in the Eastern Capital with Kyōka* (*Kyōka azuma asobi*), which was printed in monochrome to avert any luxury restrictions by the censors. In the following year came *Famous Places in the Eastern Capital at a Glance* (*Tōto meisho ichiran*), now in multi-color. Two years later, *Amusements in the Eastern Capital with Kyōka* was reissued in color under the title *Illustrated Book of Amusements in the Eastern Capital* (*Ehon azuma asobi*). In 1804 followed *Mountains upon Mountains: An Illustrated Book of Kyōka Poems* (*Ehon kyōka: Yama mata yama*).

Probably also in 1804, Hokusai's *Both Banks of the Sumida River at a Glance* (*Sumidagawa ryōgan ichiran*) was published, but this time not by Tsutaya. The book is remarkable for its composition as Hokusai drew a continuous panorama by connecting the pictures over all the pages, thus creating the impression for the reader of viewing a handscroll.

**Opposite** Detail from *Both Banks of the Sumida River at a Glance*.

# The Illustrated Book of Selected Creatures

## *Ehon mushi erami*
## 画本虫撰

1788 (2 vols.)
Artist: Kitagawa Utamaro (ca. 1754–1806)
Poetry: Yomo group
Publisher: Tsutaya Jūzaburō
Woodblock printed book (*ōhon*); ink on paper
Chester Beatty

*The Illustrated Book of Selected Creatures* (*Ehon mushi erami*), popularly known as the "Insect Book," is one of the most celebrated deluxe picture books of the Edo period (1603–1868). It was produced with great care by extremely skilled carvers and printers, and employs special features such as blind printing (*karazuri*) and mica (*kirazuri*). Such costly publications became prohibited with the conservative Kansei reforms of the early 1790s.

The publisher Tsutaya Jūzaburō began his business in 1774 and quickly became successful, especially in covering the popular Yoshiwara pleasure quarter in his publications. The artist Kitagawa Utamaro became a close friend of Tsutaya, who operated almost solely as his publisher. The two

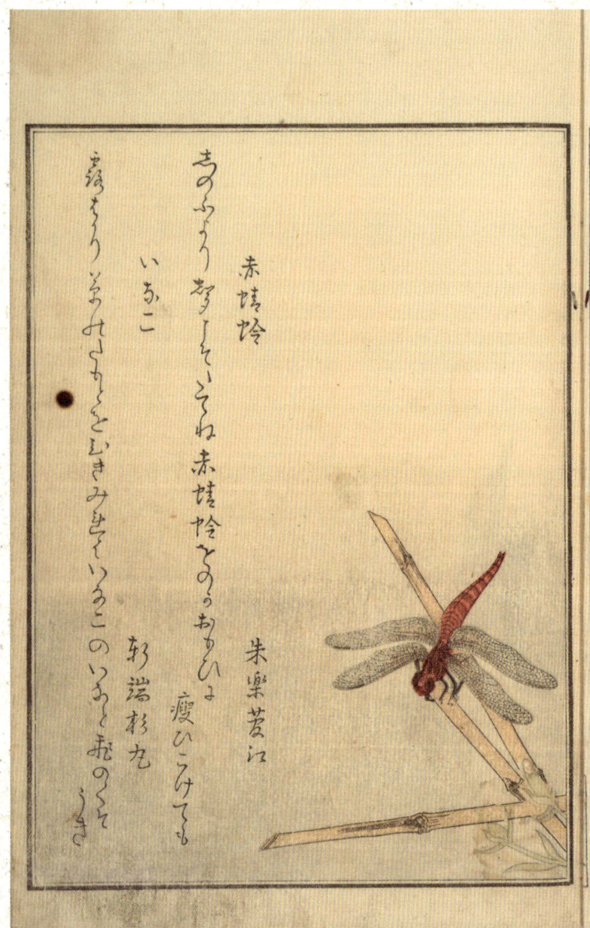
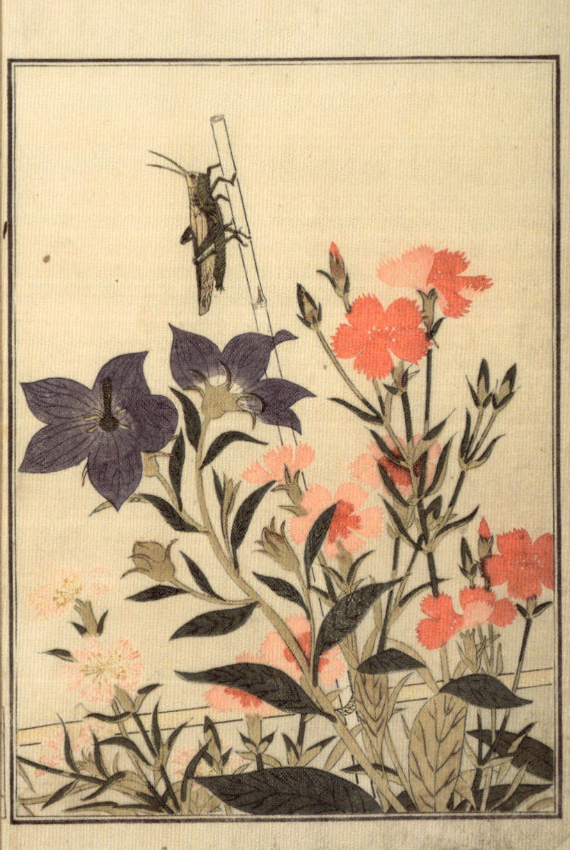

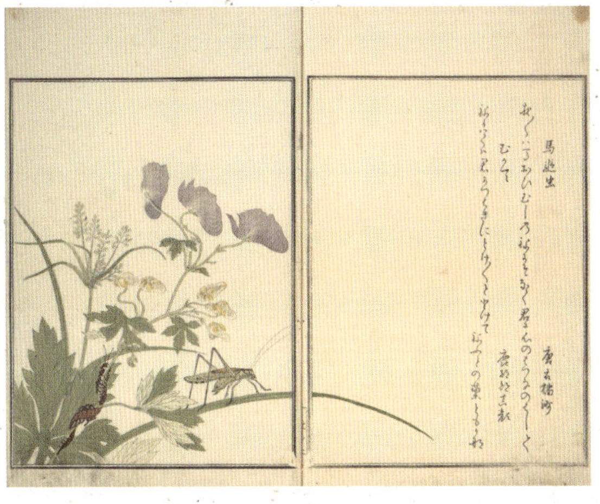

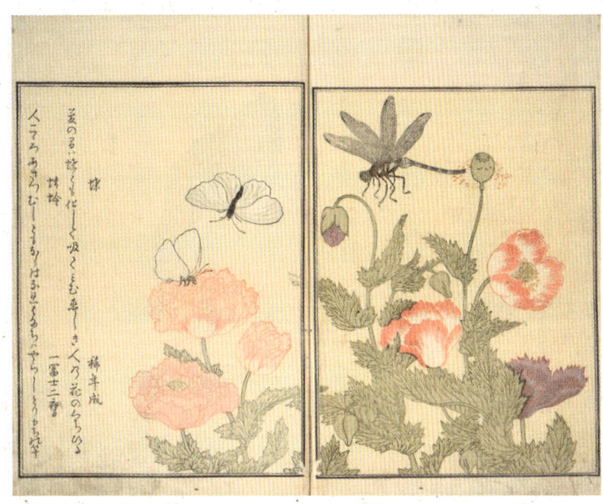

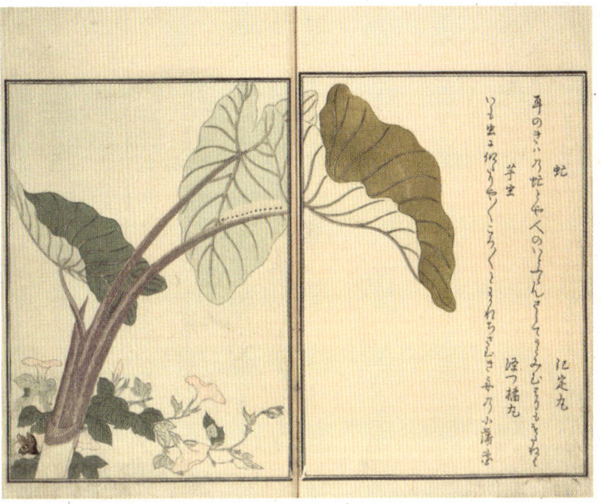

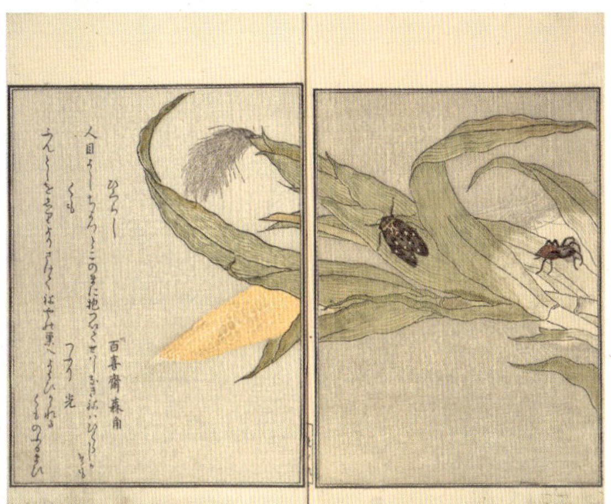

volumes of the Insect Book contain fifteen double-page illustrations of insects or small reptiles on plants. Each illustration is matched with one or more poems composed by a member of the Yomo poetry group whose leader was Ōta Nanpo (1749–1823). For every illustration, Utamaro cleverly combined different plants and creatures, drawing them in so much detail as to allow for close-up views of veins in insect wings or leaves. The poems wittily allude to the animals, and are filled with puns and double entendres of love and eroticism.

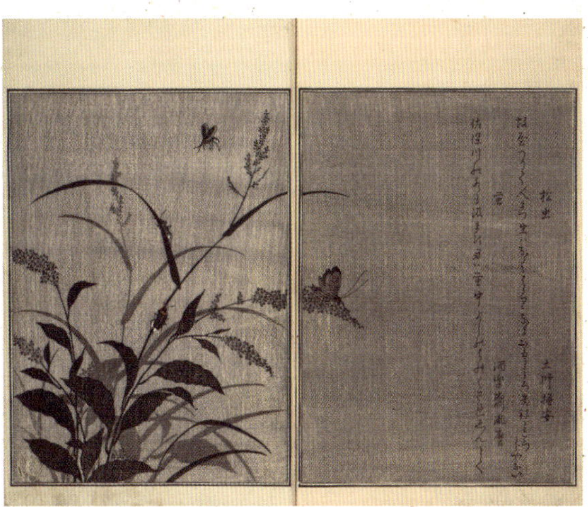

**Opposite** Red dragonfly (*akatonbo*) and locust (*inago*).

**Top** Katydid (*umaoi-mushi*) and centipede (*mukade*).

**Above** Horsefly (*abu*) and green caterpillar (*imomushi*).

**Top** Butterfly (*chō*) and dragonfly (*tonbo*).

**Center** Evening cicada (*higurashi*) and spider (*kumo*).

**Above** Tree cricket (*matsumushi*) and fireflies (*hotaru*).

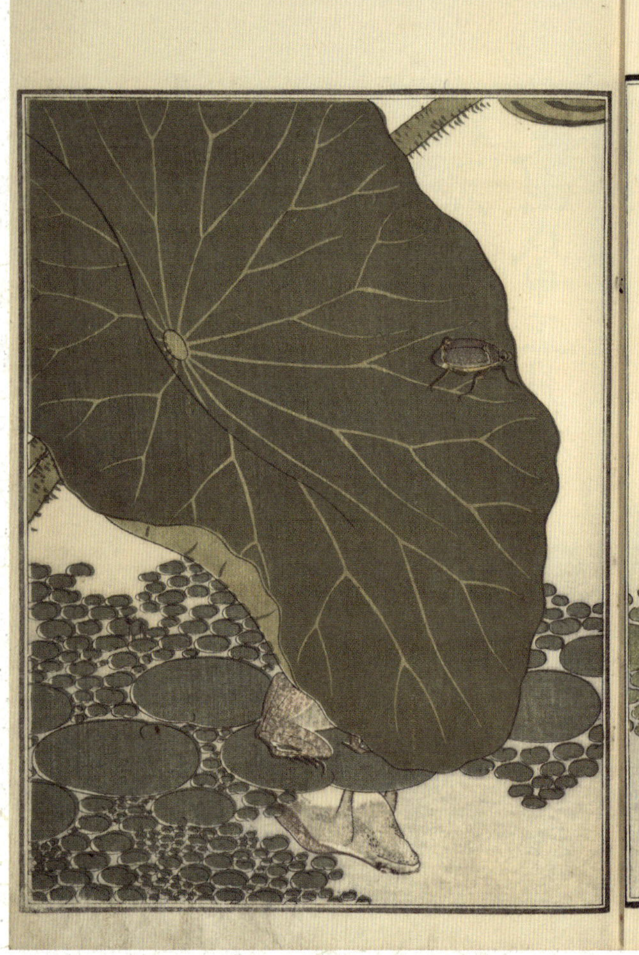

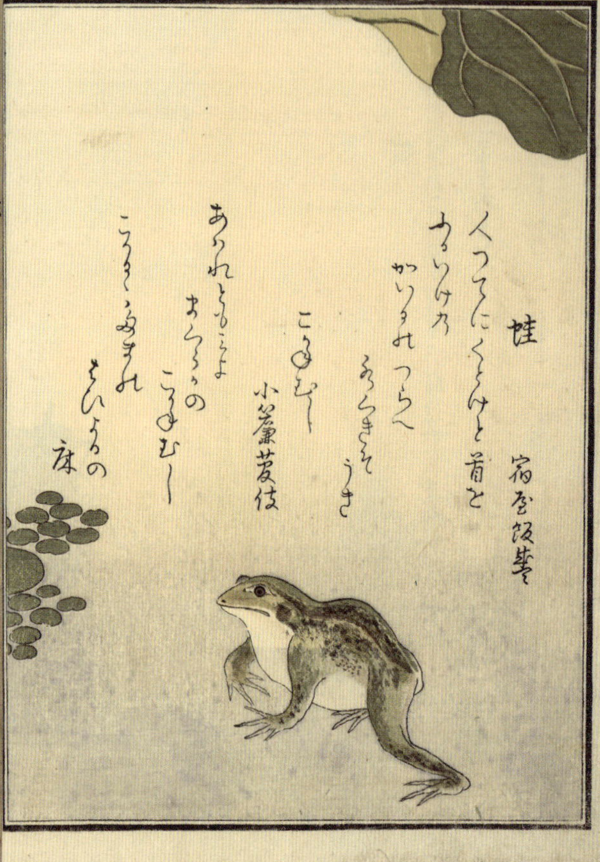

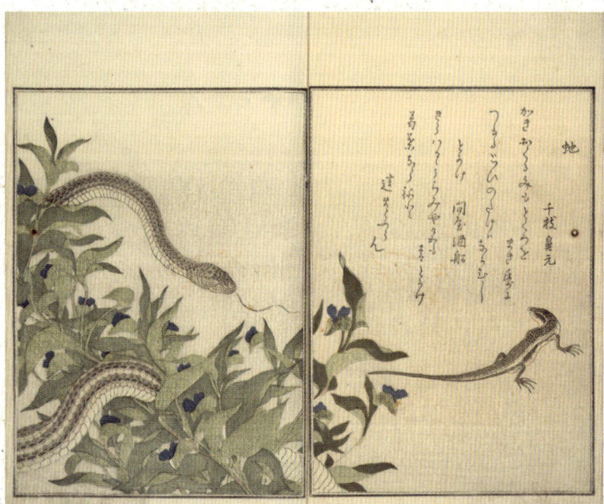

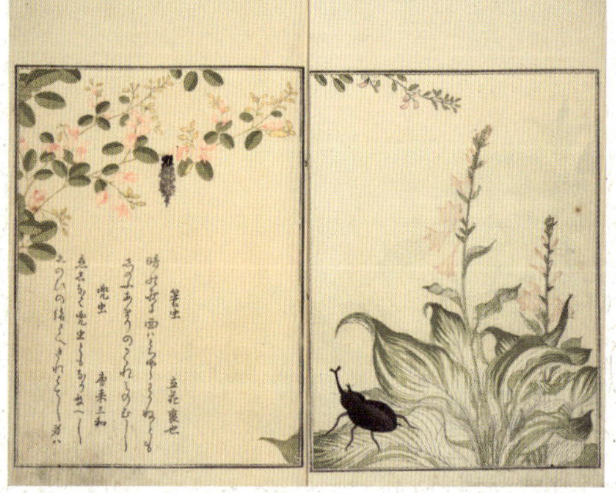

**Above** Two frogs (*kaeru*) and gold beetle (*kogane-mushi*).

**Left** Rat snake (*hebi*) and skink (*tokage*).

**Below** Bagworm (*minomushi*) and horned scarab beetle (*kabutomushi*).

# Gifts of the Ebb Tide

## *Shiohi no tsuto*
潮干のつと

1789
Artist: Kitagawa Utamaro (ca. 1754–1806)
Poetry: Yaegaki group
Preface: Akera Kankō (1740–99)
Publisher: Tsutaya Jūzaburō

Woodblock printed book (*ōhon*); ink and color on paper

The Metropolitan Museum of Art, Purchase, Mary and James G. Wallach Family Foundation Gift, in honor of John T. Carpenter, 2013 (2013.897)

After publishing *The Illustrated Book of Selected Creatures* (*Ehon mushi erami*) for the Yomo poetry group, Tsutaya Jūzaburō produced *Gifts of the Ebb Tide* (*Shiohi no tsuto*) for the Yaegaki poetry group. To meet friends in a group and then to travel and compose light parodic and satirical *kyōka* poems was a popular leisure activity in pre-modern Japan. Many such groups existed in Edo (today's Tokyo). Members sometimes used a special poetry name

**Below** Shell gathering at the beach of Shinagawa.

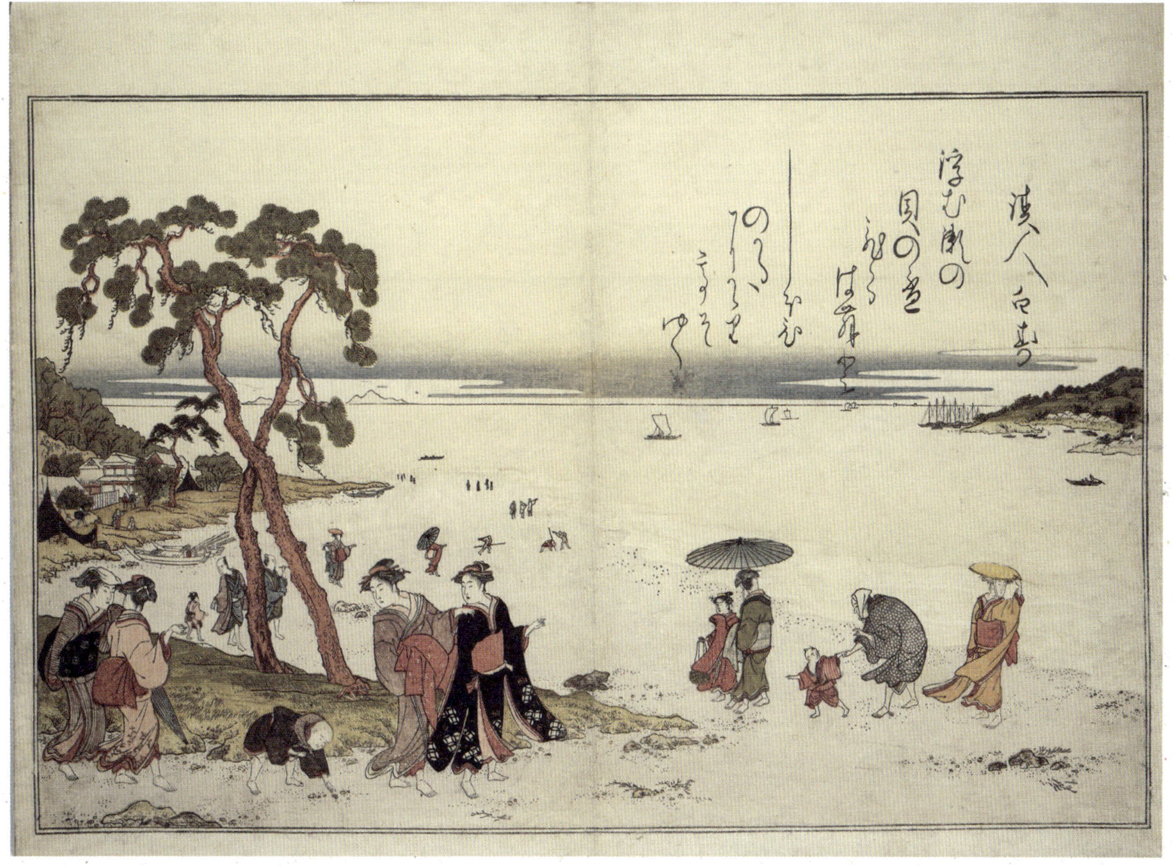

to sign their compositions and many names remain unidentified today. Tsutaya collaborated again with the print artist Kitagawa Utamaro to create another exceptional book, occasionally using mica, cut gold, and gauffrage (blind printing or embossing), and printing all the pages with immense care for exactness and detail.

The book was the result of a boat trip that the playwright Akera Kankō, leader of the Yaegaki group, and six of his friends took in the third lunar month 1788. The outing was to Sodegaura on the opposite side of Edo Bay, today located in Chiba Prefecture. The group went to gather seashells and seaweed at ebb tide, as well as to enjoy some wine on the coast. But instead of depicting the poetry group, *Gifts of the Ebb Tide* begins with an opening that captures beautiful women—Utamaro's specialty—gathering shells. It is followed by six openings that show the kinds of shells and sea creatures that the women might have encountered. Each of the openings is inscribed with six poems, signed by the authors, that relate to the images. The final opening portrays a group of women playing a game of matching shells. The scene takes place in an elegant room furnished with a folding screen decorated with a painting of peonies by a stream.

**Below** Upper-class women playing a game of matching shells.

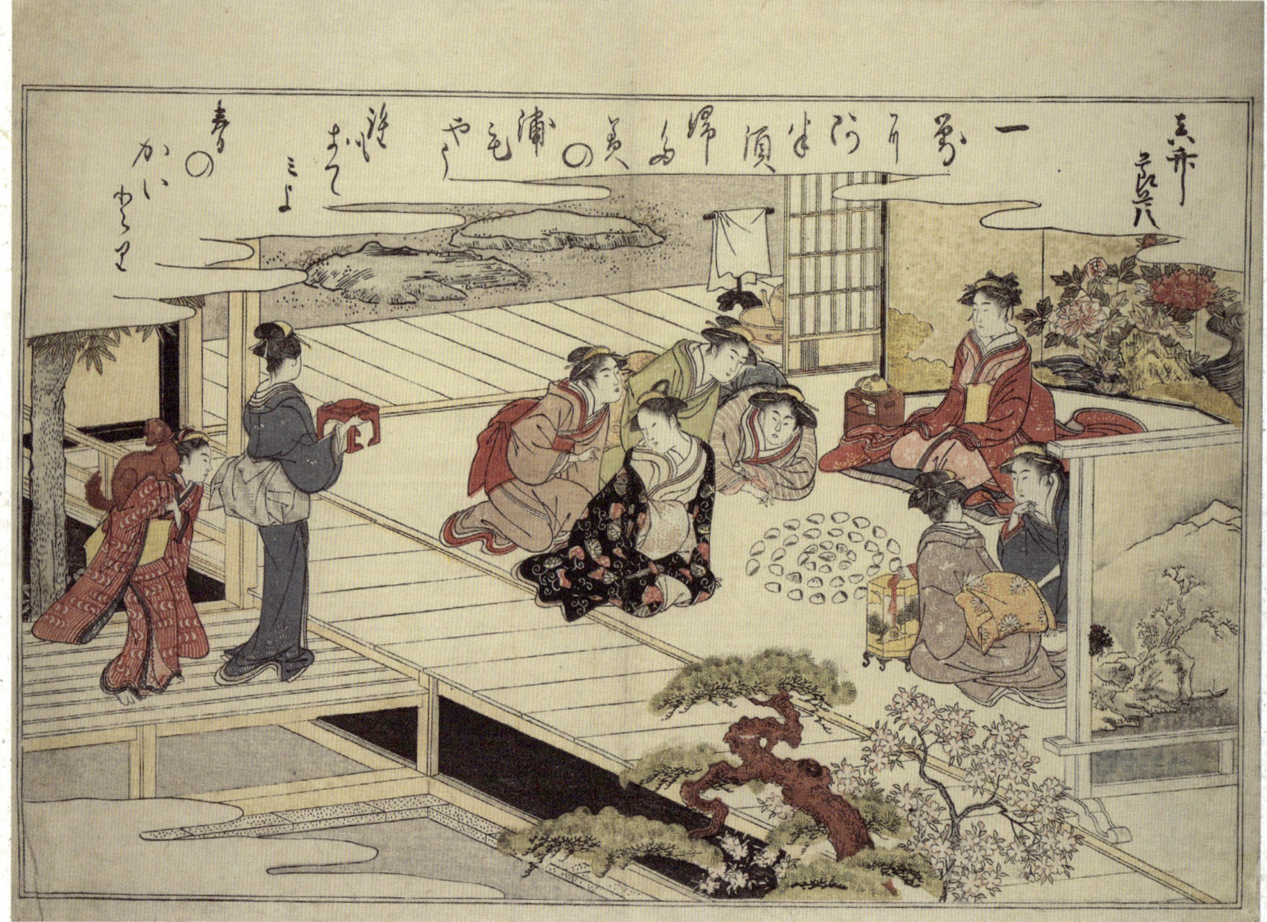

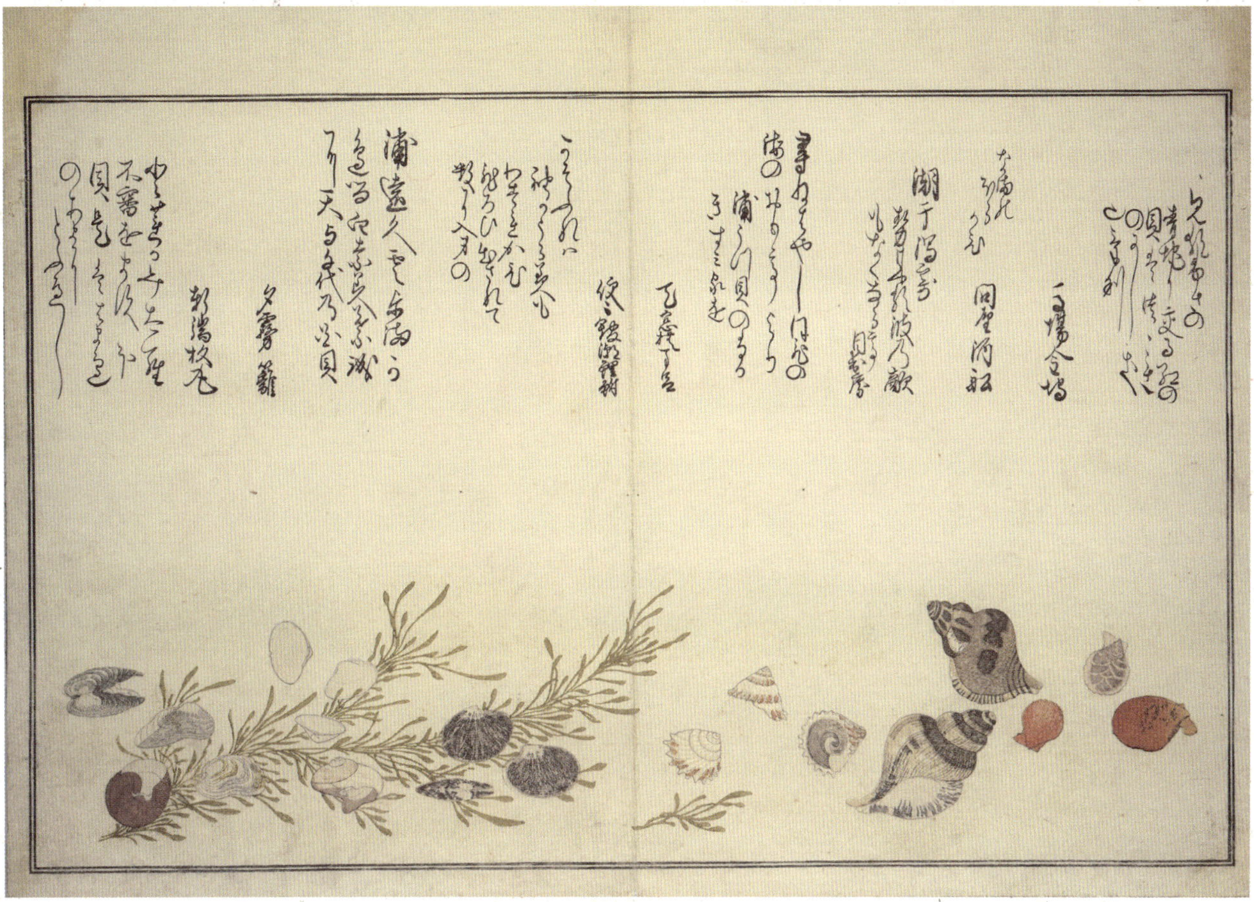

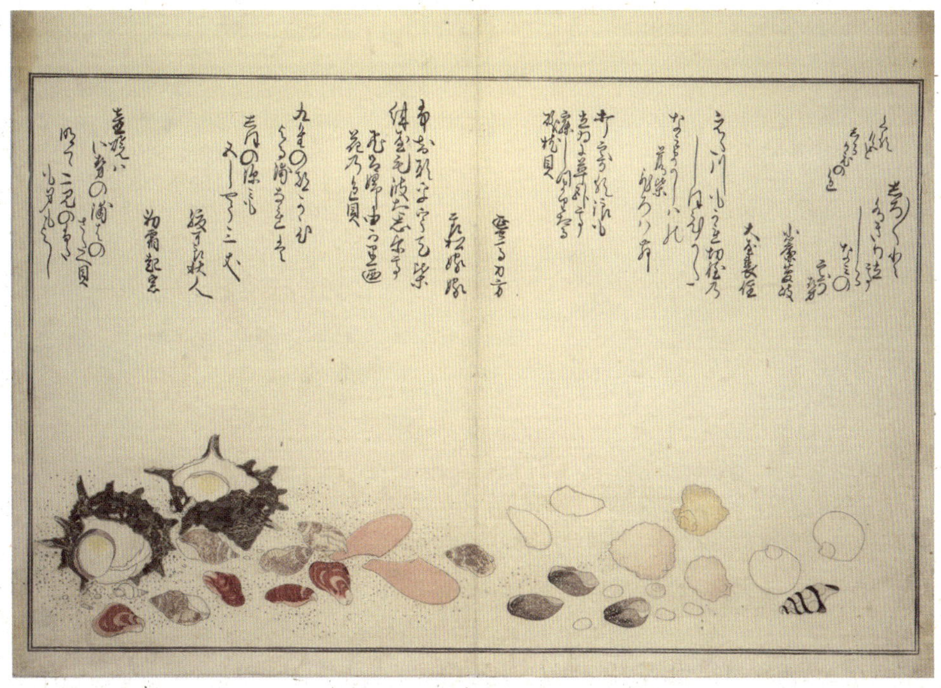

**Above and below** Assortments of shells.

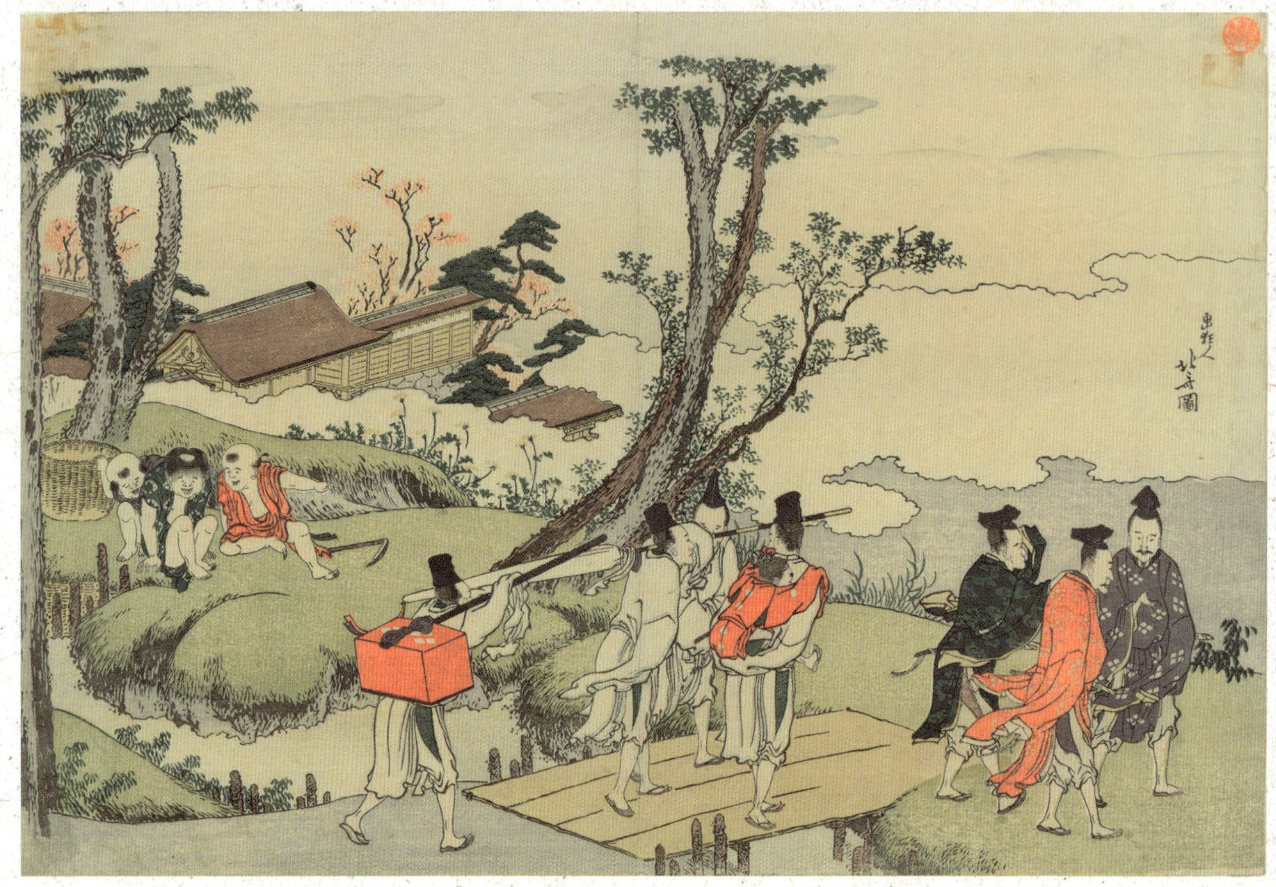

# Thirty-six Immortal Women Poets in Brocade Prints

*Nishikizuri onna sanjūrokkasen*

錦摺女三十六歌仙

1801
Artist: Chōbunsai Eishi (1756–1829); frontispiece: Katsushika Hokusai (1760–1849)
Publisher: Nishimuraya Yohachi
Woodblock printed book (*ōhon*); ink and color on paper
Chester Beatty (frontispiece); National Diet Library

Nishimuraya Yohachi's publishing house, Eijudō, began operating from as early as 1751. In the 1770s, he entered the market of single-sheet woodblock prints, at that time called *nishiki-e*, or brocade prints, but today commonly known as *ukiyo-e* (lit. "pictures of the floating world"). He quickly became one of Japan's most important publishers, staying in business until 1860. In

the mid-1780s, he began collaborations with both Chōbunsai Eishi, who specialized in portraits of beautiful women, and Katsushika Hokusai, who designed landscapes and interiors of buildings using Western perspective techniques. Prints as well as books were pre-financed by the publishers, thus enlisting popular artists for a project was more likely to achieve success than hiring lesser-known artists.

In 1801, Nishimuraya worked with both Eishi and Hokusai to publish a color book about thirty-six noblewomen in Japanese history renowned for their poetry. Grouping thirty-six poets together in an anthology was a tradition established several hundred years earlier by Fujiwara Kintō (966–1041).

*Thirty-six Immortal Women Poets in Brocade Prints* (*Nishikizuri onna sanjūrokkasen*) contains

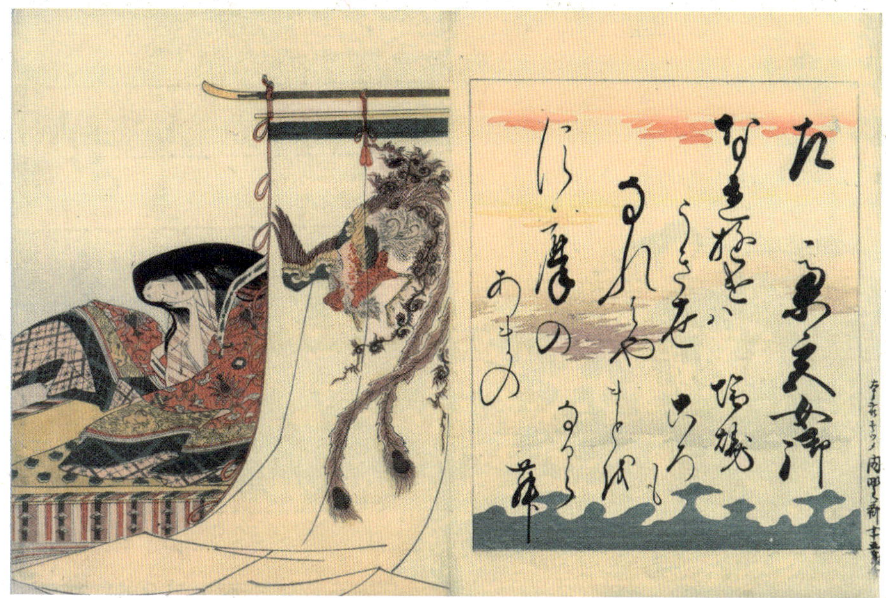



**Right** The Poetess Saigū no Nyōgo.

**Below** The Poetess Princess Shikishi.

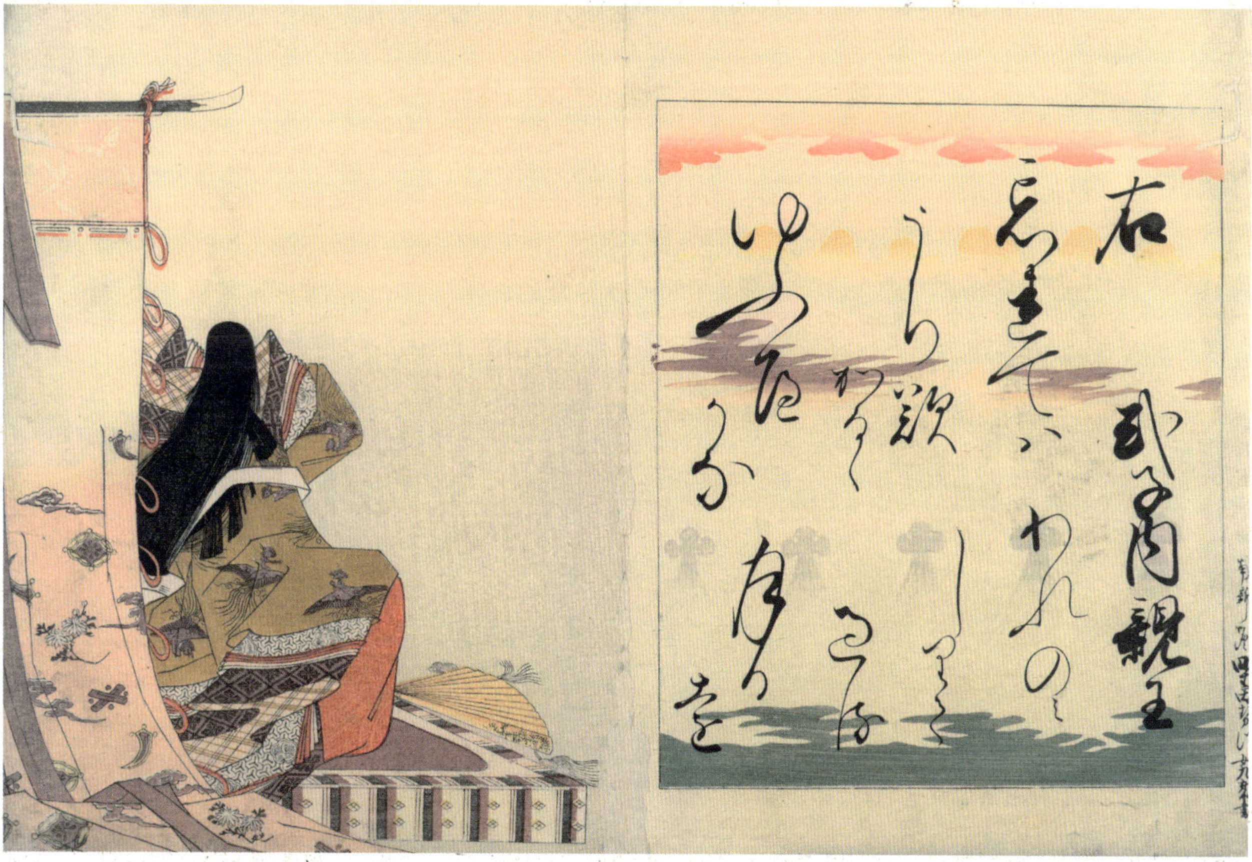

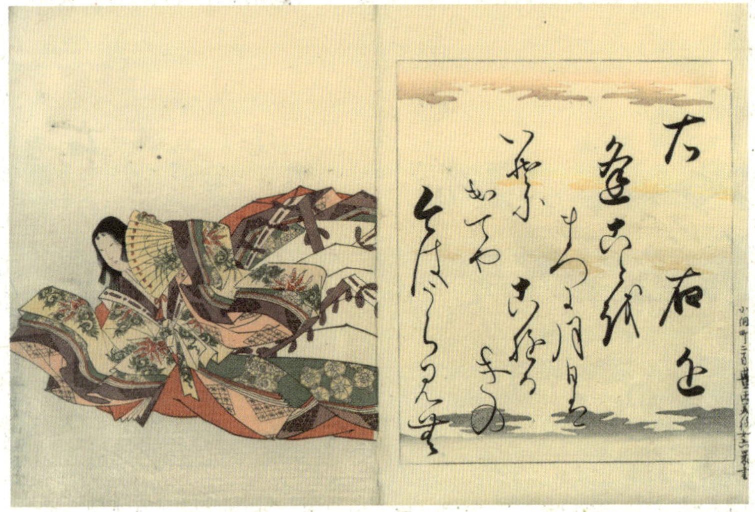



pairs of portraits of women by Eishi on the left matched with their poems on the right. The calligraphy is by thirty-six female students of the Hanagata calligraphy school, supervised by Hanagata Giyū (dates unknown). The notes in the right margin provide the ages of the girls, ranging from 5 to 14 (6 to 15 in Japanese traditional counting). Giyū's explanations at the end of the book date from 1797, indicating that Nishimuraya waited a few years until he was ready to release this venture, which he intended to be lavish, hence the use of *nishikizuri* (lit. "brocade printed") in the title. Eishi portrays the poets in luxurious dresses of the Heian period (794–1185). Hokusai was hired to design a double-page frontispiece (see p. 48) which depicts an outdoor scene of men and children.

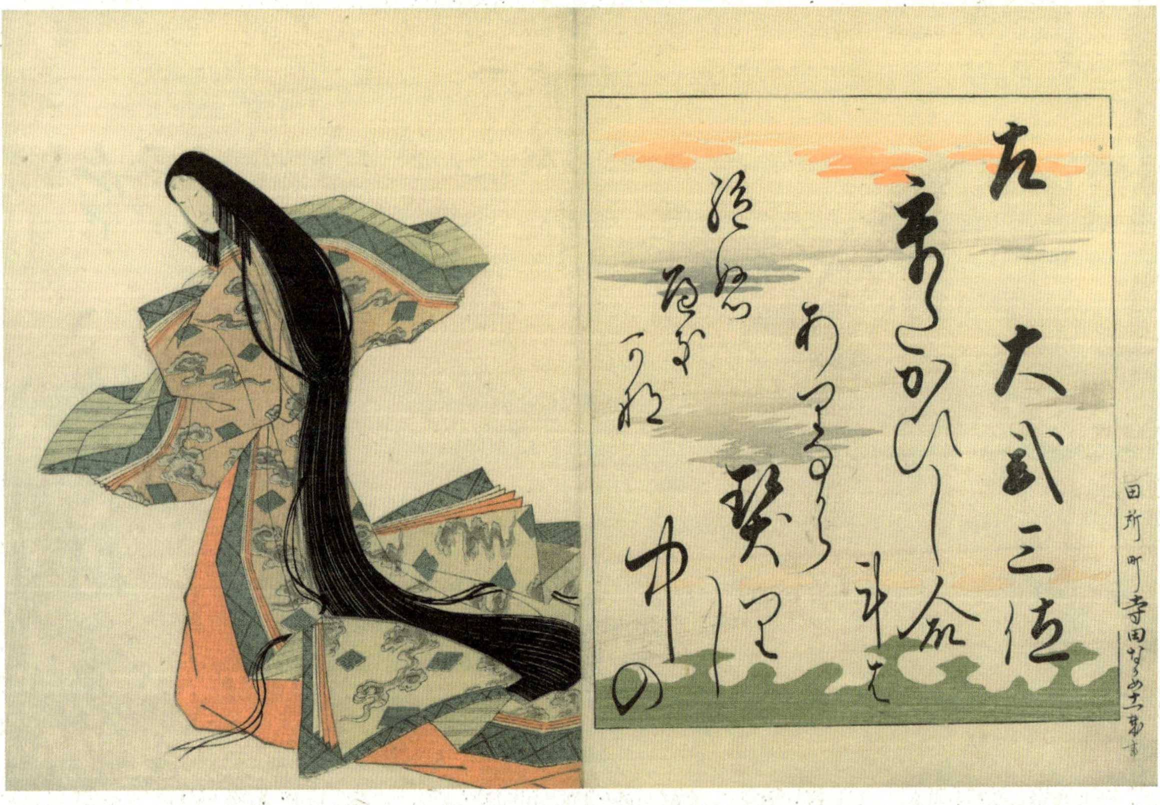

# Both Banks of the Sumida River at a Glance

*Sumidagawa ryōgan ichiran*

隅田川両岸一覧

Ca. 1804 (3 vols.)
Artist: Katsushika Hokusai (1760–1849)
Preface: Kojūrō Nariyasu (dates unknown)
Publishers: Tsuruya Kiemon, Maekawa Zenbei
Woodblock printed book (*hanshibon*); ink and color on paper
National Diet Library

The book *Both Banks of the Sumida River at a Glance* (*Sumidagawa ryōgan ichiran*) is not just another anthology of parodic *kyōka* poems but is astonishing because its illustrator, Katsushika Hokusai, connected the pictures in a continuous panorama of the two banks of the river over forty-six pages. Moreover, instead of depicting the scenery in one season and with the same weather conditions, Hokusai varies between winter scenes of snow, spring scenes with flowers, and even incorporates some rain. *Both Banks of the Sumida River at a Glance* is therefore further proof of Hokusai's unlimited imagination and, as such, cannot be understood as a simple documentary.

No copy of this book is known that provides a publication date, and scholars' opinions are divided between 1801, 1804, and 1806. The copies in the collections of The Metropolitan Museum of Art, New York, and the Rikkyo University Library, Tokyo, contain a colophon that notes the Osaka-based Maekawa Zenbei as the publisher and Hokusai's name as "Hokusai Tokimasa," which he only used between 1798 and 1813. Andō Enshi, who also worked on other Hokusai books in 1799 and 1800, is listed as the carver of the woodblocks. The preface makes mention of Senkakudō, which is the company name of the Edo-based publisher Tsuruya Kiemon. However, no colophon exists that lists

**Below** Matsuchiyama; Mukojima and Hanakawado; Sensōji Temple.

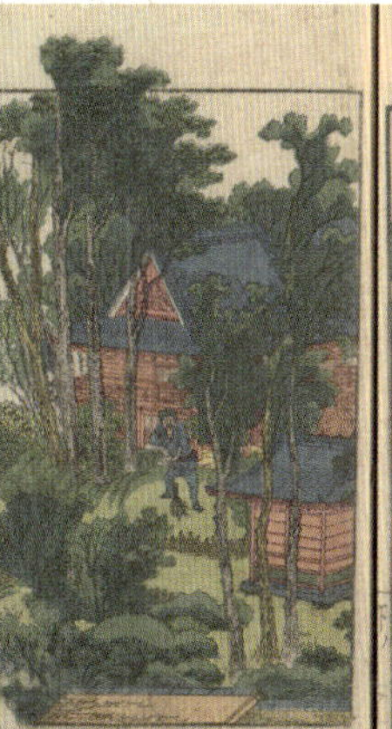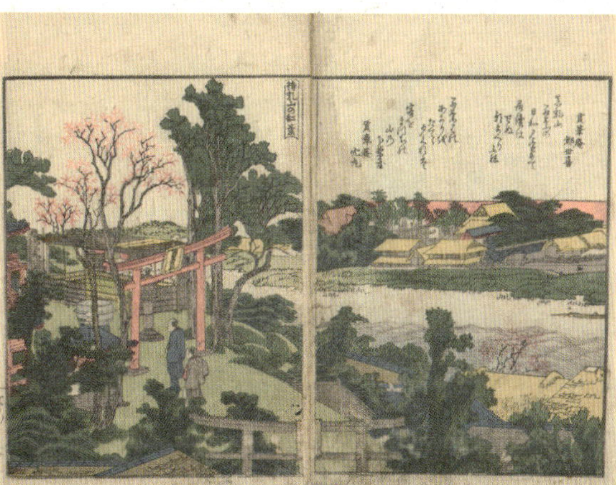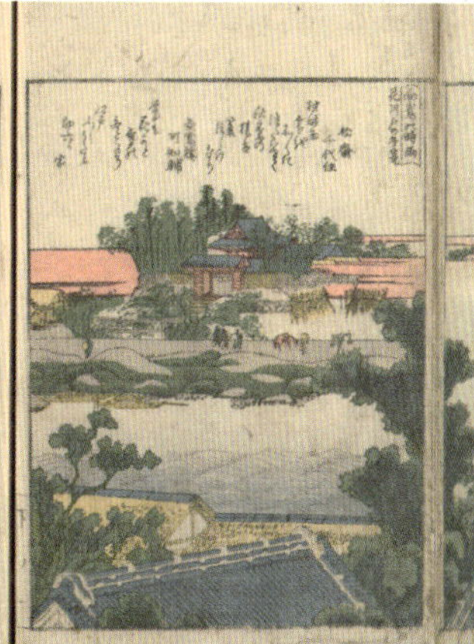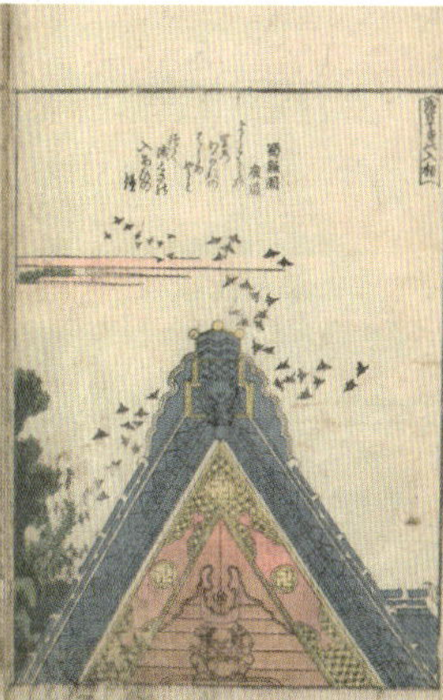

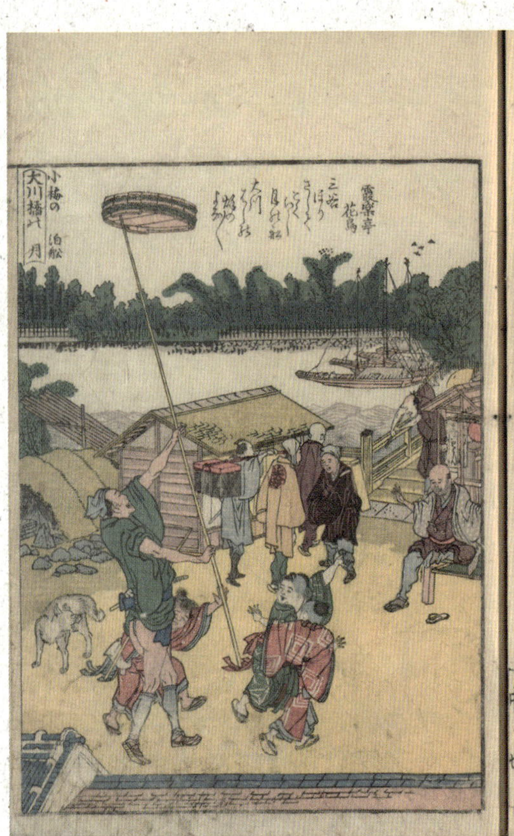

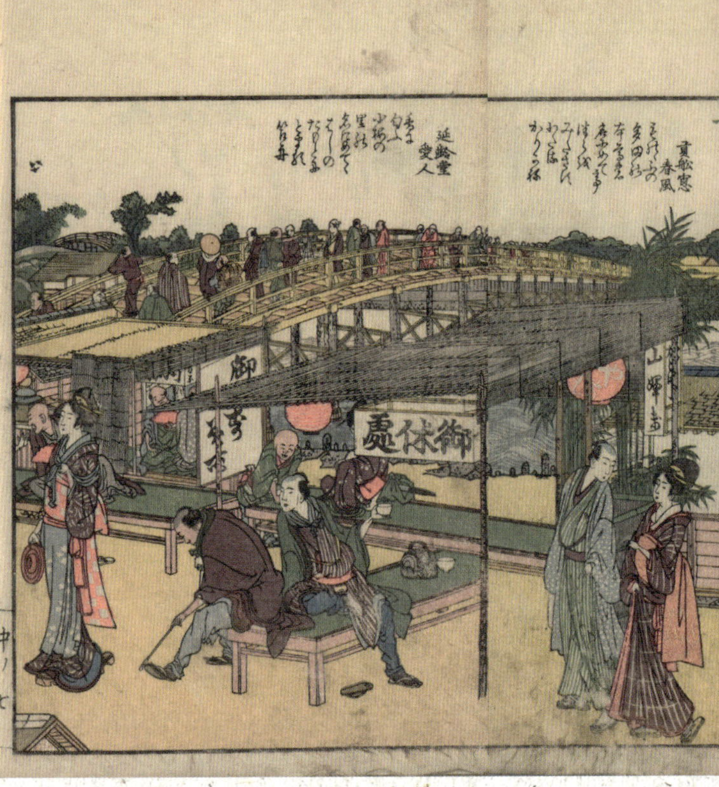

Tsuruya as the publisher of this book. The Museum of Fine Arts, Boston, has in its collection a wrapper for this book produced by Tsuruya, but Hokusai's name is given as "Saki no Hokusai Taito hitsu," which means that the wrapper was printed between 1814 and 1819 and produced for a later edition of the book. However, given Tsuruya's name in the preface and the later wrapper, it is plausible that there was also a wrapper for the first edition and that Tsuruya and Maekawa co-published the book since they operated in different cities.

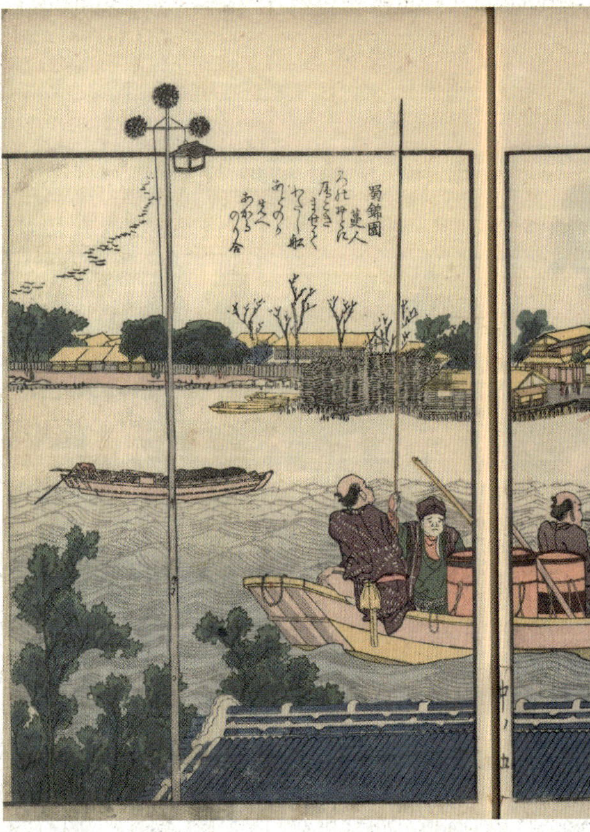

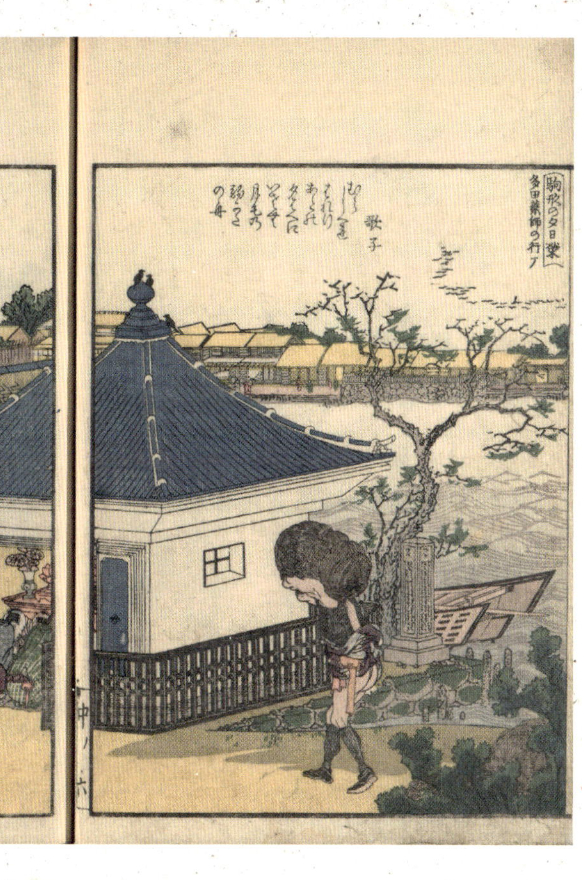

**Left** Koume; Komagata.

**Below** Onmaya Riverbank; Pine of Success.

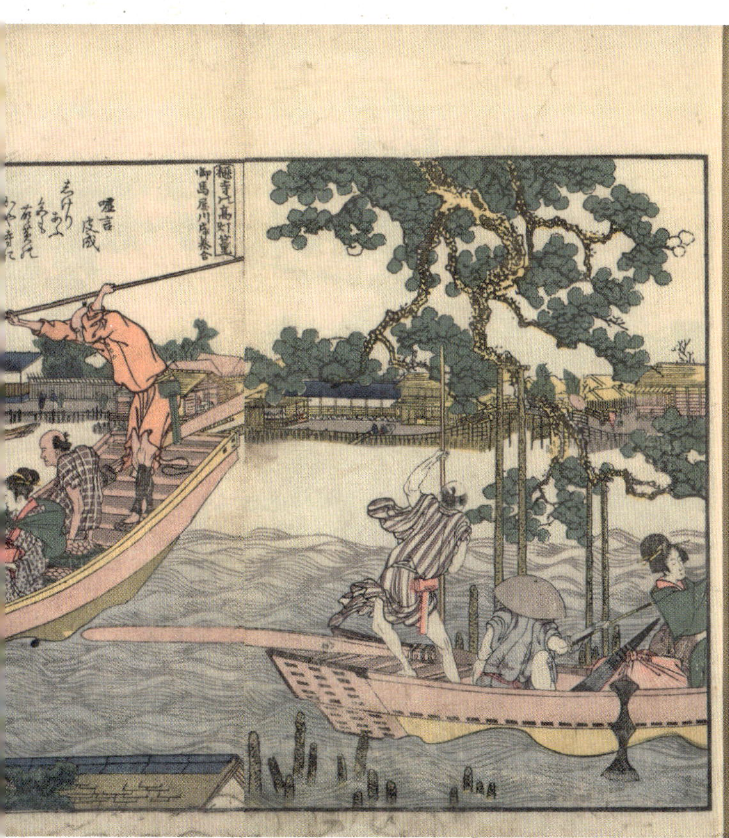

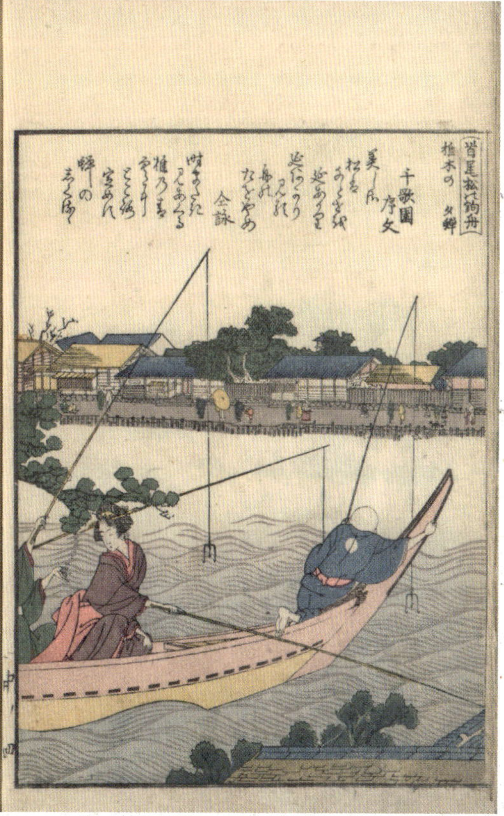

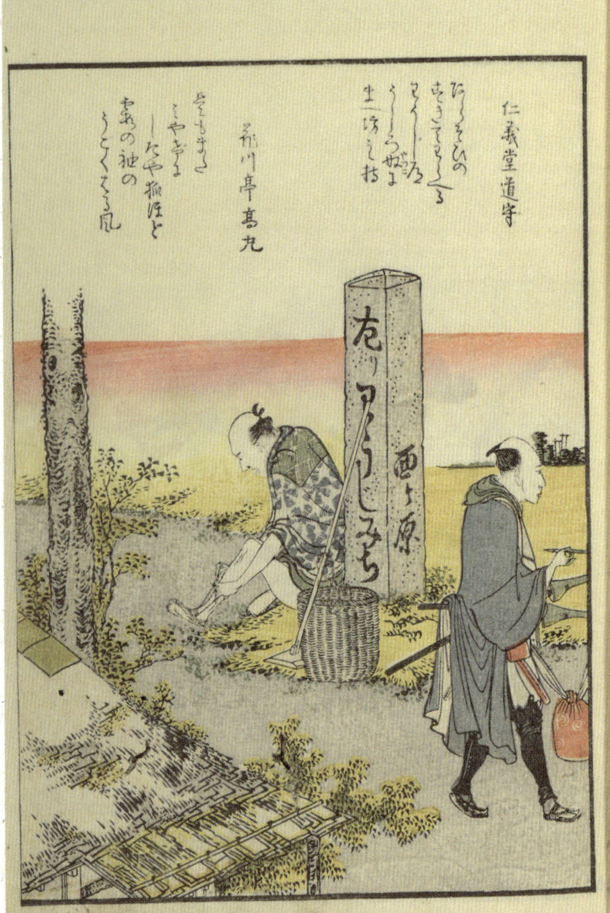

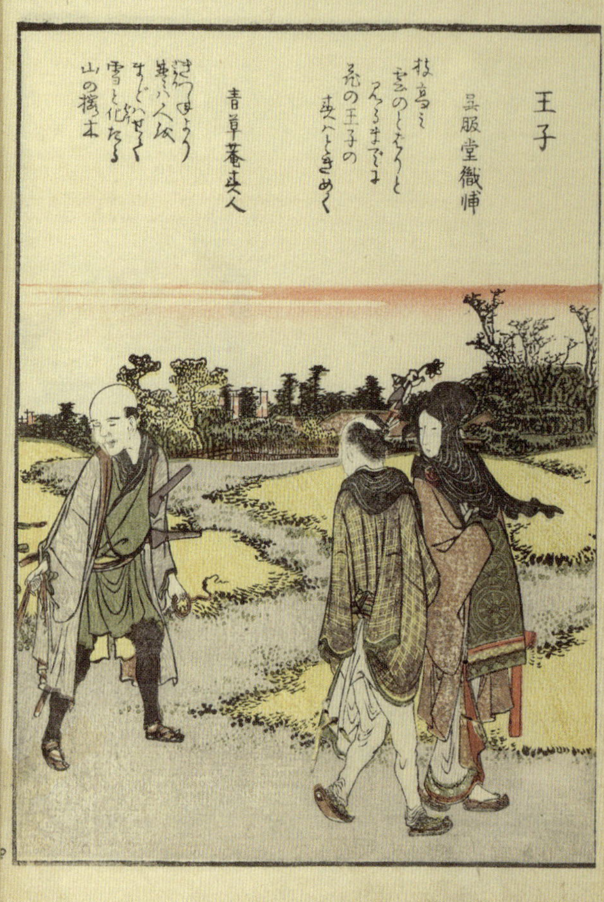

**Above** Ōji.

# Famous Places in the Eastern Capital at a Glance

## *Tōto meisho ichiran*
## 東都名所一覧

1800 (2 vols.)
Artist: Katsushika Hokusai (1760–1849)
Publisher: Tsutaya Jūzaburō
Woodblock printed book (*ōhon*); ink and color on paper
The Metropolitan Museum of Art, Purchase, Mary and James G. Wallach Family Foundation Gift, in honor of John T. Carpenter, 2013 (2013.712a, b)

*Famous Places in the Eastern Capital at a Glance* (*Tōto meisho ichiran*) is also a book of *kyōka* poetry, but contrary to *The Illustrated Book of Selected Creatures* and *Gifts of the Ebb Tide*, it was neither printed as a luxury item nor commissioned by a specific poetry group. Also published by Tsutaya Jūzaburō, he worked at this time with Katsushika Hokusai as illustrator and not with Kitagawa Utamaro. Each one of the two single pages and nineteen double pages features a specific site in Edo (today's Tokyo), at that time also referred to as the Eastern Capital (*tōto*). The single pages are inscribed with two poems by different poets, the double pages with four, except the last one which only has three, resulting in seventy-nine poems. The book begins with spring in Shinagawa and finishes with the year-end festival in Asakusa. Most of the views are outdoors, depicting the locations during the time of year they were most popular or notable, for example, Shinobazu Pond while the lotus flowers

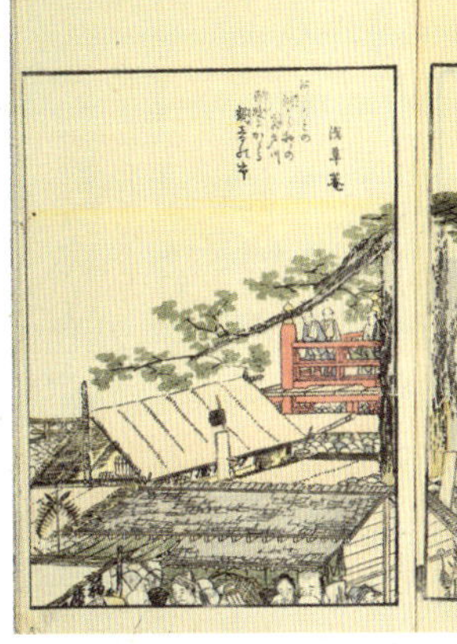
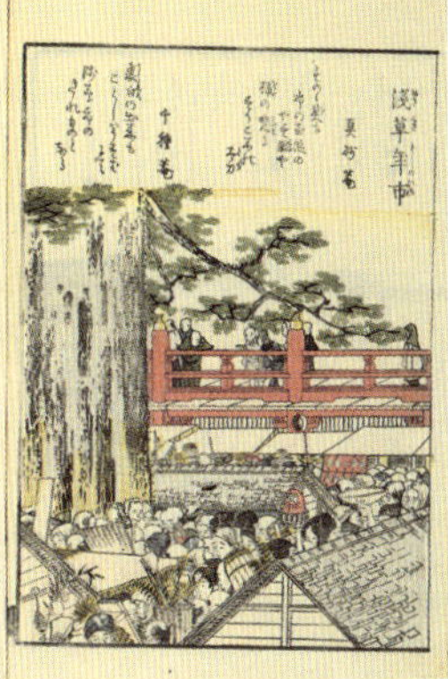

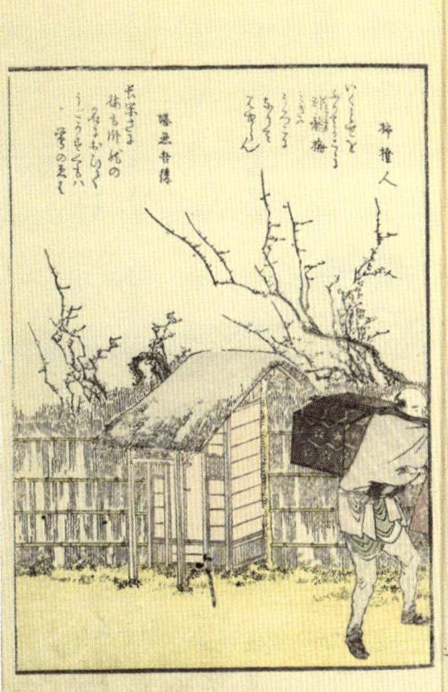
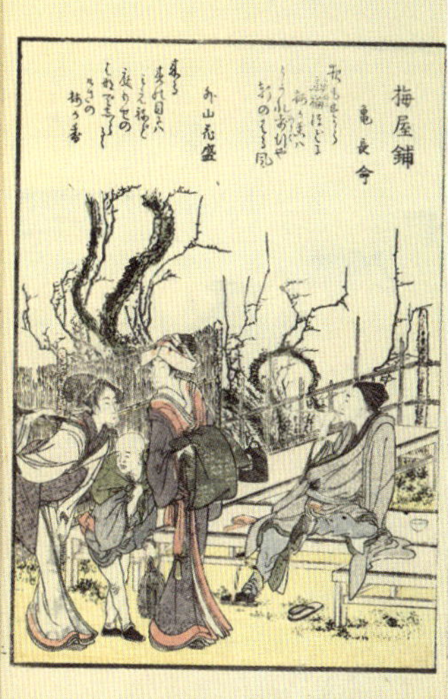

**Above** Year-end Festival in Asakusa.

**Right** Umeyashiki.

**Below** Sumida River.

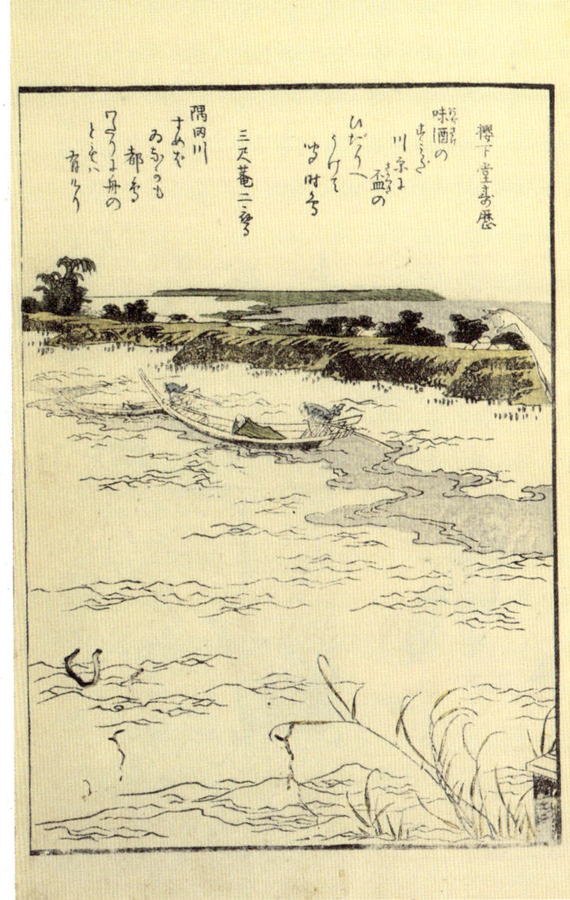
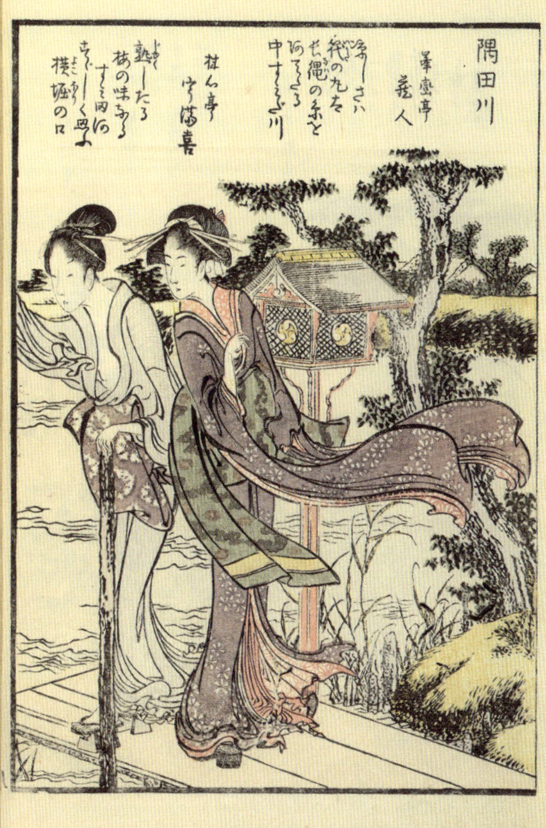

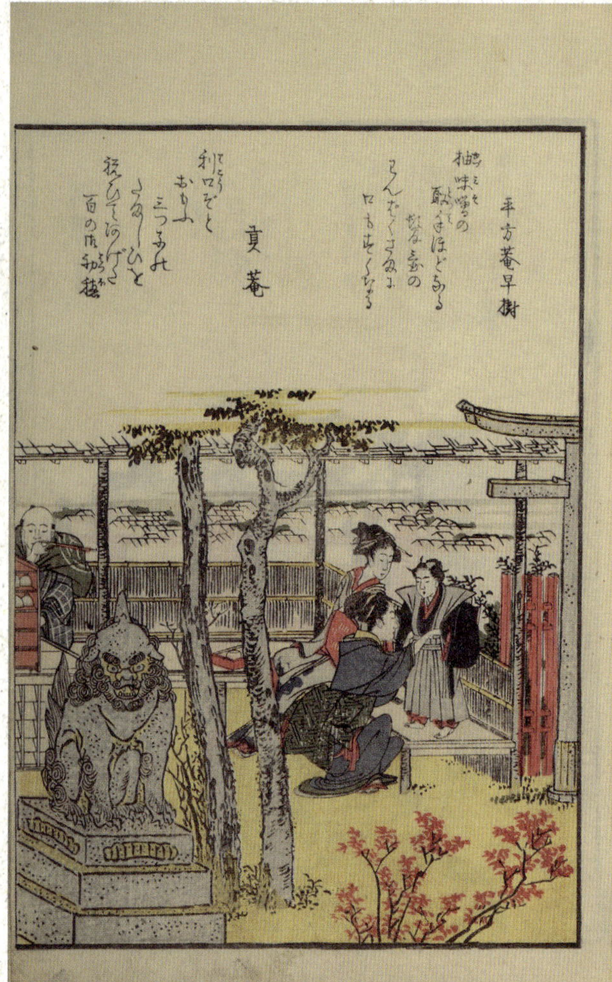
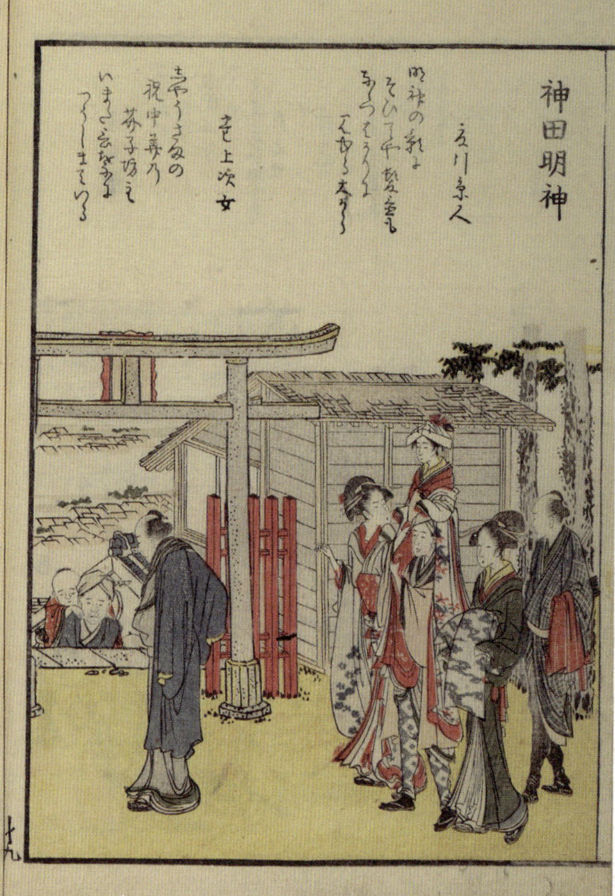

**Above** Kanda Shrine.

**Below** Shinobazu Pond.

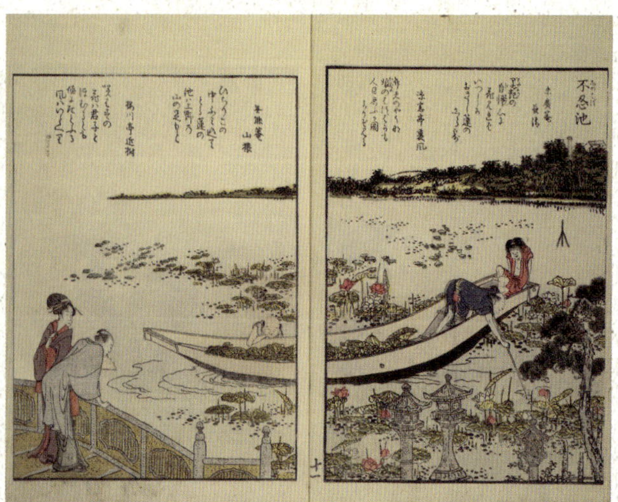

are in bloom. For Ryōgoku, Hokusai did not depict how the famous bridge spans the Sumida River or how people view the fireworks in summer, but a close-up of boats between the bridge's pylons. Remarkable also is the unconventional picture of the *kabuki* theater at Sakaichō because Hokusai does not portray famous actors on stage but instead shows the view from behind the stage, capturing the back of the actors and the front of the audience.

There is some confusion amongst scholars about the title of this book because there are two editions with two different titles. *Tōto meisho ichiran* is the original title and *Tōto shōkei ichiran* (*Scenic Views in the Eastern Capital at a Glance*) is the title of the reissue that was produced in the ninth lunar month 1815 by three publishers: Tsutaya (the original publisher), Suharaya Mohei, and Suharaya Ihachi.

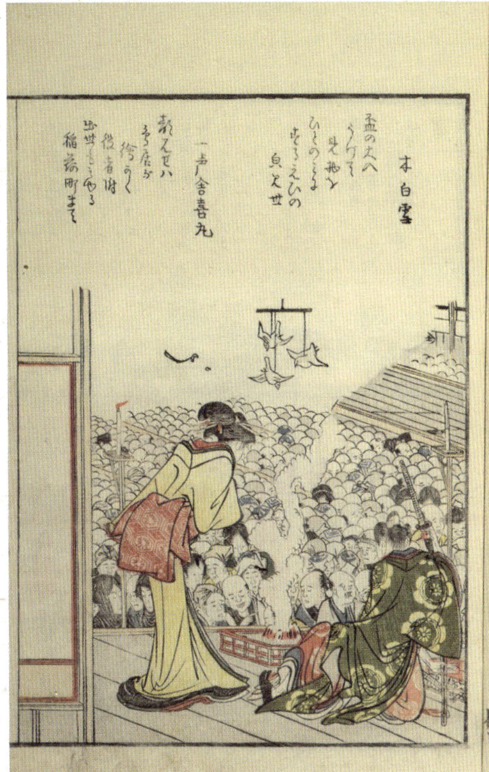
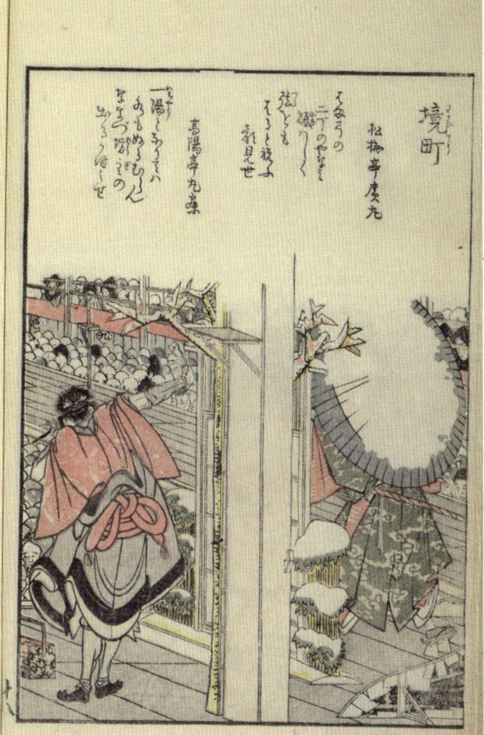

**Right** Sakaichō.
**Below** Ryōgoku.

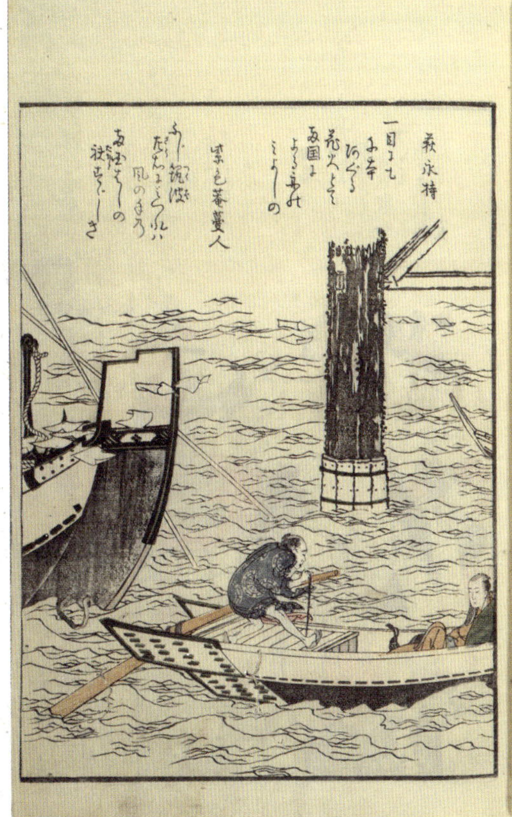
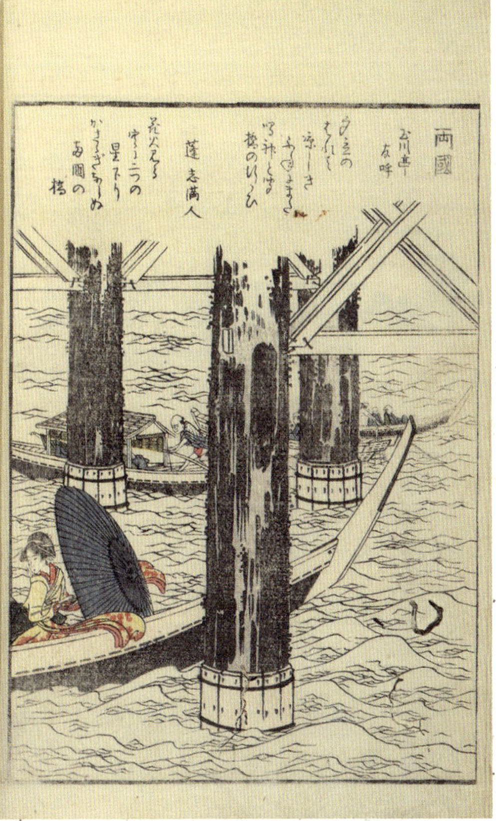

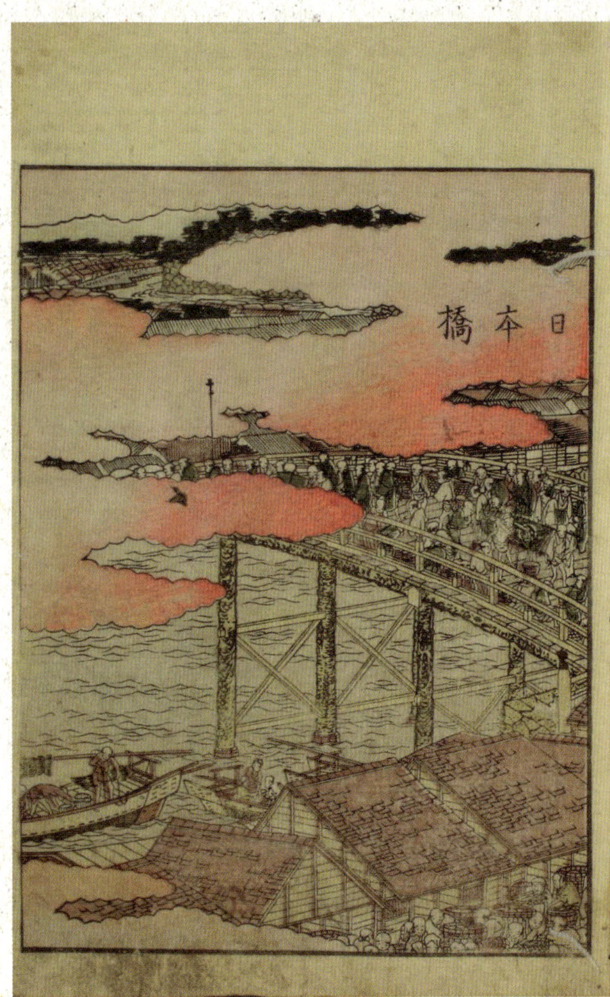
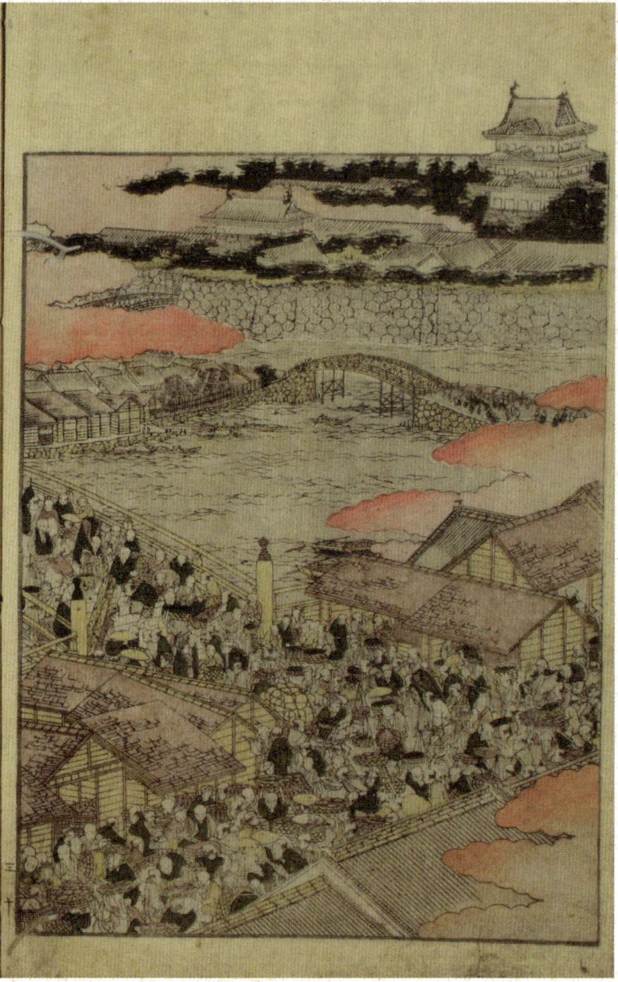


**Above** Nihonbashi Bridge.

# The Illustrated Book of Amusements in the Eastern Capital

## *Ehon azuma asobi*

畫本東都遊

1802 (3 vols.)
Artist: Katsushika Hokusai (1760–1849)
Preface: Asakusaan Ichindo (1755–1820)
Publisher: Tsutaya Jūzaburō, et al.
Woodblock printed book (*ōhon*); ink and color on paper
Waseda University Library

*The Illustrated Book of Amusements in the Eastern Capital* (*Ehon azuma asobi*) from 1802 was originally published in monochrome ink in 1799 under the title *Amusements in the Eastern Capital with Kyōka* (*Kyōka azuma asobi*). Both versions comprise the same number of illustrations by Katsushika Hokusai but are arranged differently. The original version contains nine single pages and twenty double pages of illustrations, whereas the reprint has five single pages and twenty-two double pages of illustrations. The original version is a much thicker book because it also contains seventy-eight pages of parodic *kyōka* poems that were completely omitted from the reprint, hence the change of title. The agenda for the reprint was to make the illustrations available as a picture book of famous sights in Edo (today's Tokyo). Each scene is titled with the location's name. Almost all the exterior views include cloud elements that are either straight,

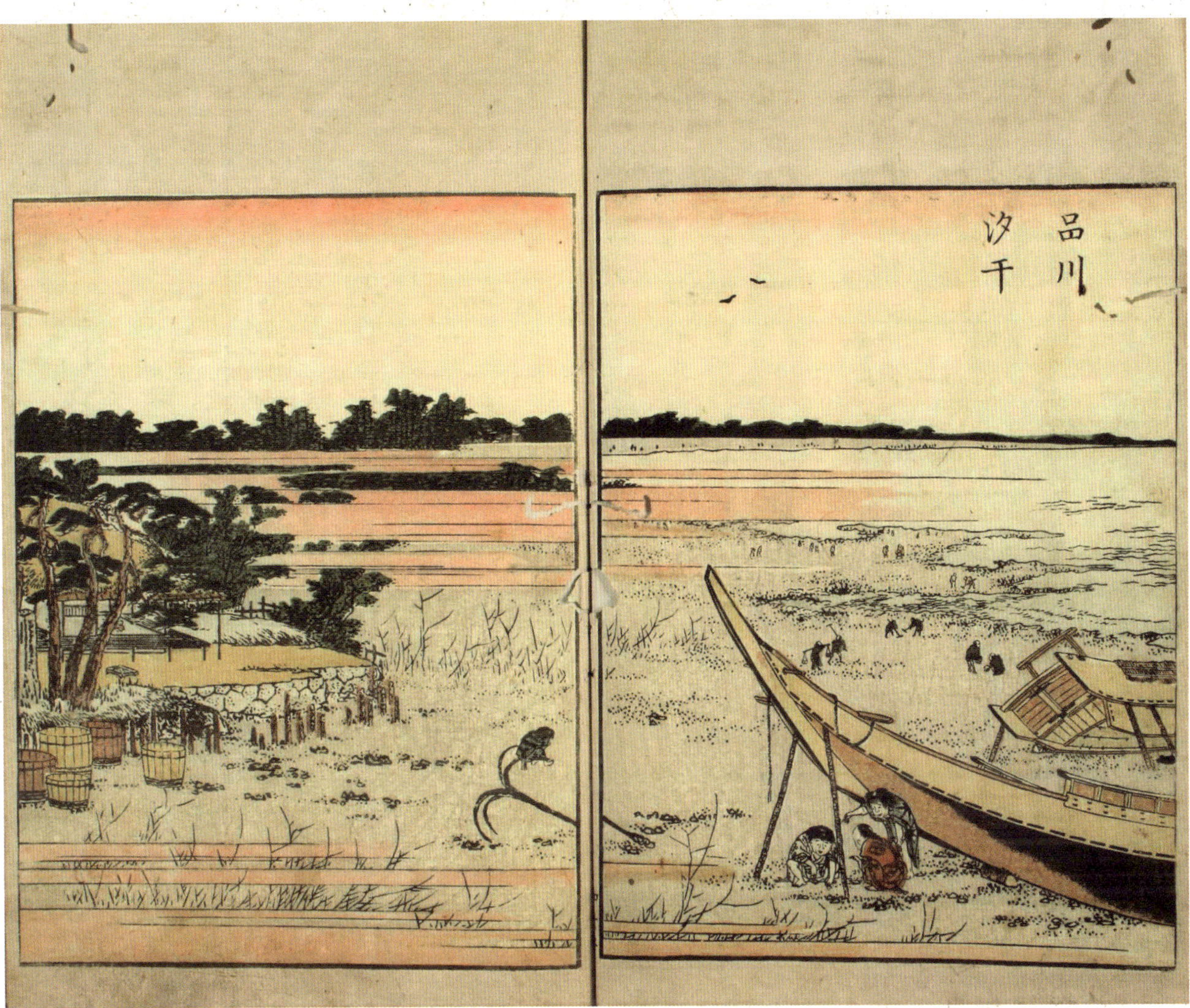



**Above** Clam digging in Shinagawa.

in horizontal bands, or as accumulations with curly edges. Most of the clouds were colored pink in the reprint.

The first illustration is an aerial view of the Shiba Shinmei Shrine during spring. The shrine grounds are sparsely populated compared with the following view of hectic traffic over the Nihonbashi Bridge, which was then considered the center of Japan and the starting point for all the major highways. The interior views include a busy doll shop in Jikkendana that has piles of boxes ready for customers to pick up. The shop of Tsutaya Jūzaburō, the publisher of this book, is also illustrated, showing how sales items were advertised at that time by announcing them on long boards that were hung outside the shop, and how single-sheet prints were sold by stacking them in piles. Shinagawa captures children playing near a boat, while in the background people are collecting clams at low tide. Another image shows the Asakusa Festival, better known today as the Sanja Festival, and how it was traditionally celebrated on the river with floats rather than with portable shrines in the streets as it is today.

**Right** Print and book store.

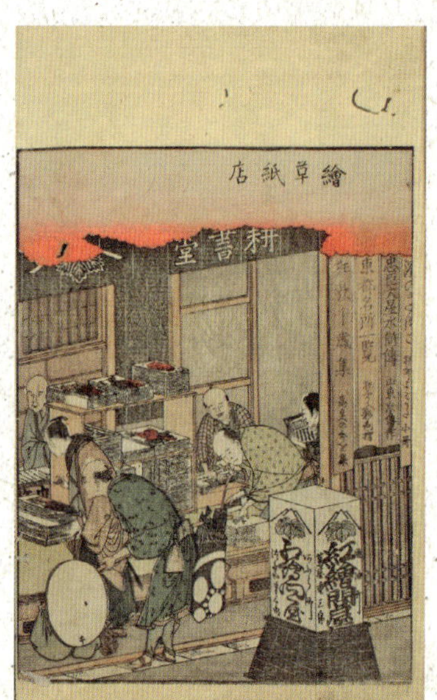

**Below** Doll shop in Jikkendana.

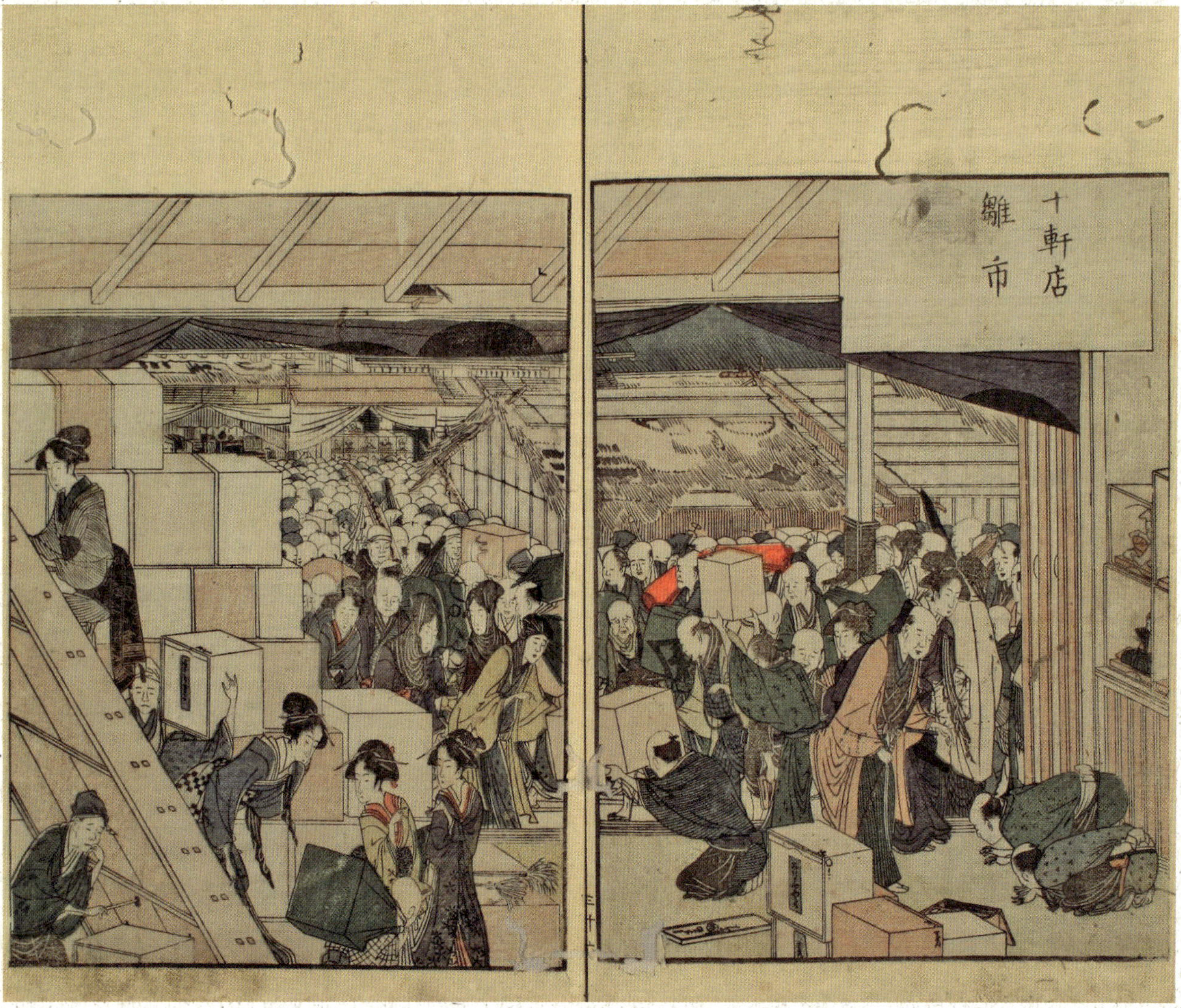

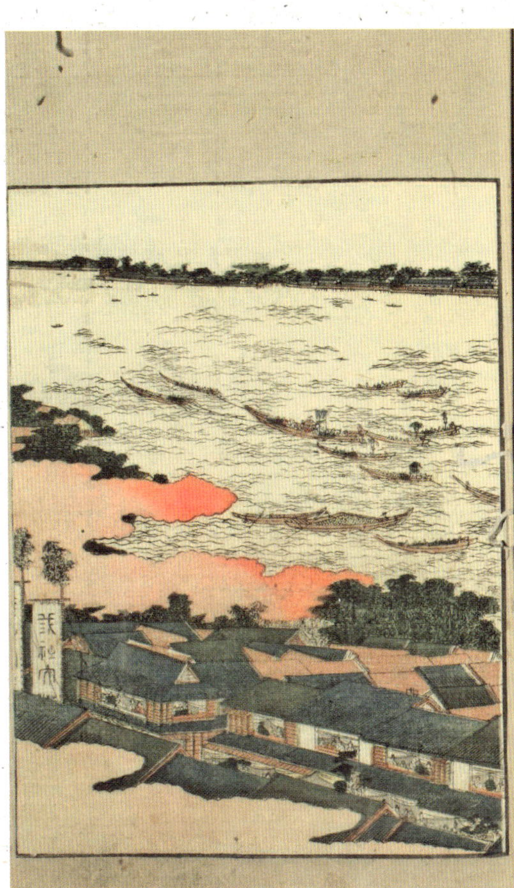
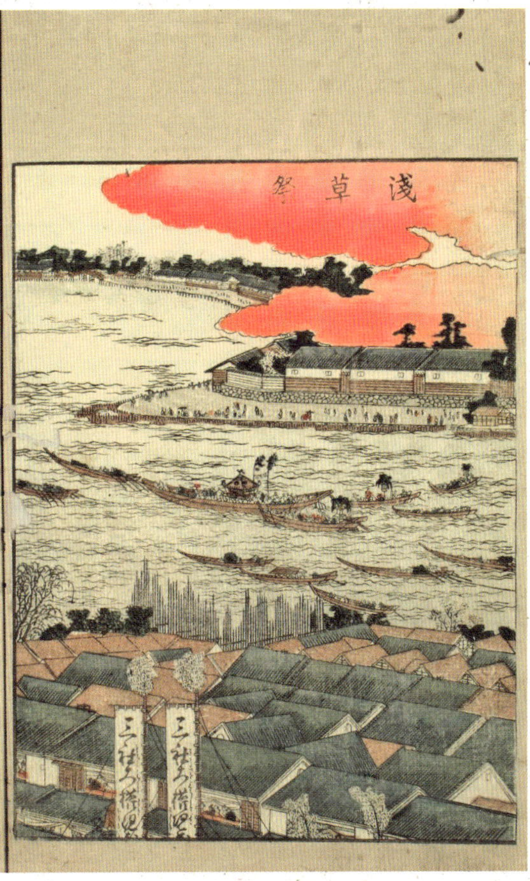

**Above** Asakusa Festival.

**Right** Armorer.

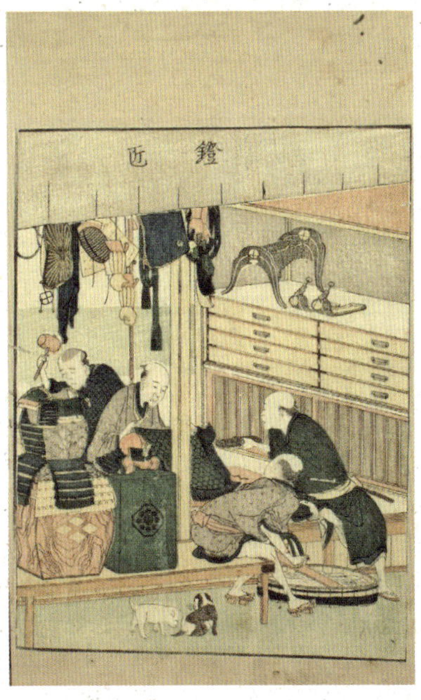

# Mountains upon Mountains: An Illustrated Book of Kyōka Poems

*Ehon kyōka: Yama mata yama*

絵本狂歌　山満多山

1804 (3 vols.)

Artist: Katsushika Hokusai (1760–1849)

Preface: Benbenkan Koryū (1756–1816)

Compiler: Ōharatei Sumikata (dates unknown)

Publisher: Tsutaya Jūzaburō

Woodblock printed book (*ōhon*); ink and color on paper

The Metropolitan Museum of Art, Purchase, Mary and James G. Wallach Family Foundation Gift, in honor of John T. Carpenter, 2013 (2013.714)

The hilly grounds on the north and northwest sides of Edo (today's Tokyo) are the subject of the illustrations by Katsushika Hokusai in the book *Mountains upon Mountains: An Illustrated Book of Kyōka Poems* (*Ehon kyōka: Yama mata yama*). Each one of Hokusai's thirty double-page illustrations is inscribed with between two and five parodic *kyōka* poems that were compiled by Ōharatei Sumikata. The illustrations themselves are untitled, leaving it to the reader to figure out the exact locations that are drawn from the districts Ichigaya, Ushigome, and Yotsuya, which are in today's Shinjuku Ward, Koishikawa (today in the Bunkyō Ward), and Aoyama (today in the Minato Ward).

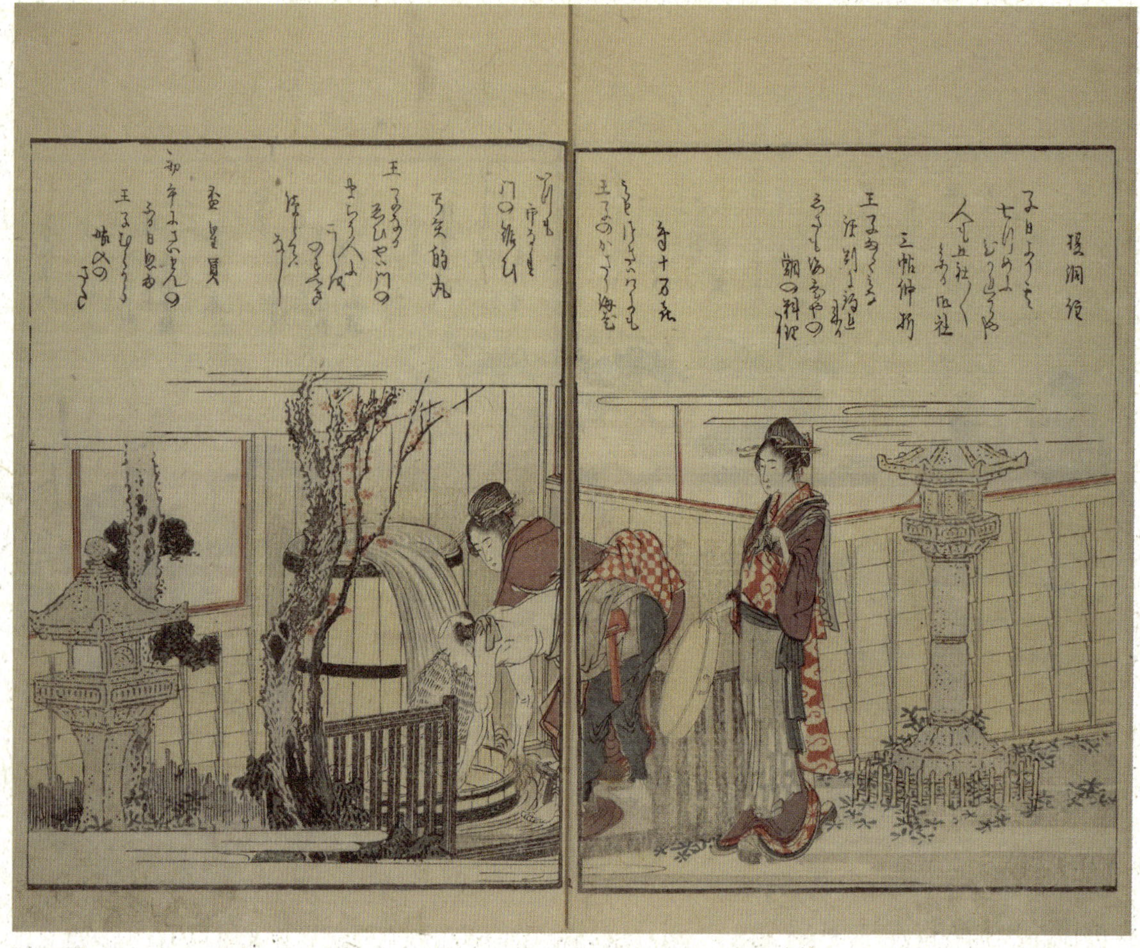

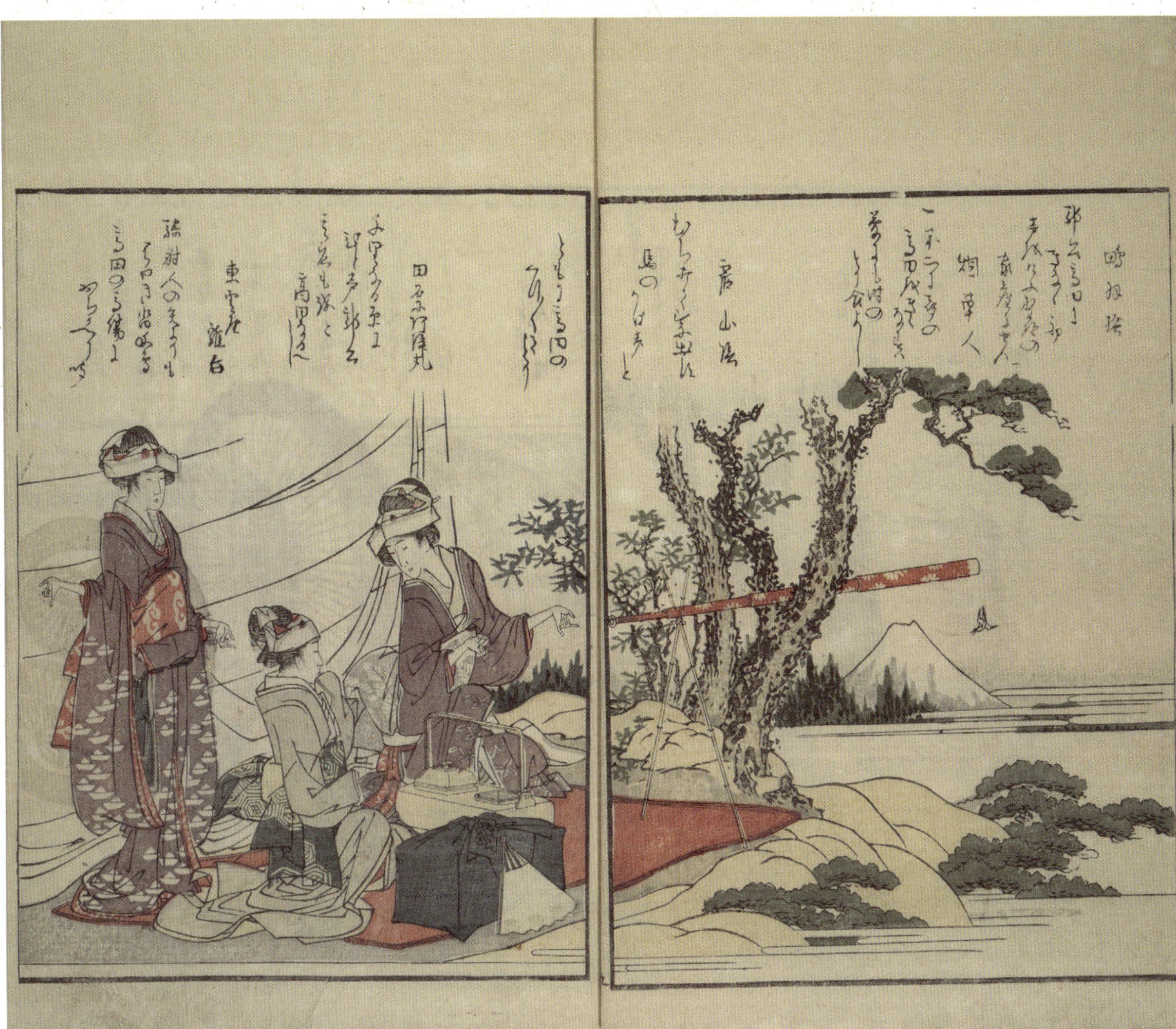

In front of a teahouse in Ōji, a man and two women are washing trays in the fountain. Three elegantly dressed women are picnicking at Takatanobaba (today Takadanobaba) next to a tree which they use to support a telescope that is pointed towards Mount Fuji. In another picture, men are fishing in the waterfall at Sekiguchi Aqueduct. Yet another illustration depicts people along the Edo River interacting with fireflies. Men and women are caught by surprise in a rainstorm near a fortified stone wall. Two women and a child are looking at the sails of distant fishing boats in Edo Bay from

**Above** Picnic at Takatanobaba.

**Opposite** Washing trays at a teahouse in Ōji.

a terrace on Atago Hill. The festivities at the shrine in Akasaka is another motif which Hokusai drew from an elevated viewpoint that is higher than the red *torii* gate at its entrance. Suwa Pond is a winter scene that shows the water covered with ice, while three women in a small boat are enjoying watching the ice break as their boat knocks into it.

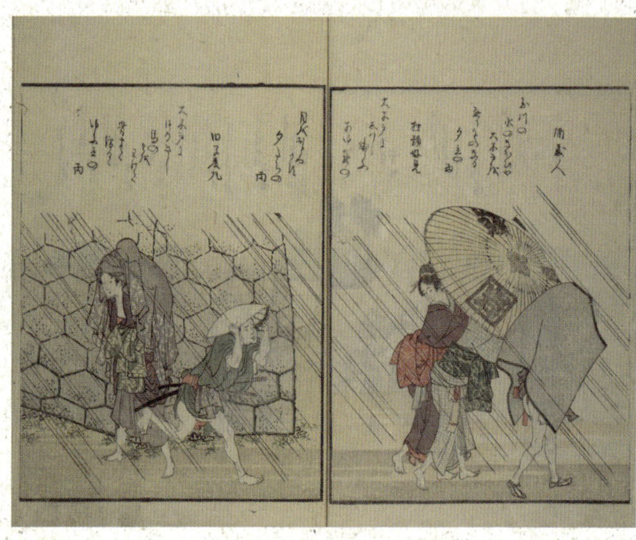

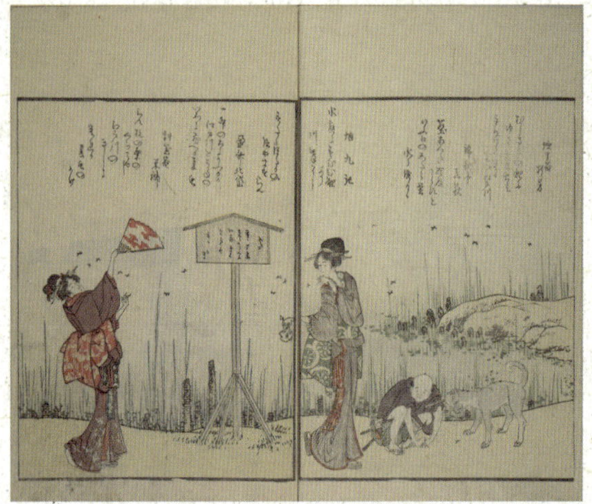

**Above** Sudden rainstorm.

**Left** Catching fireflies along the Edo River.

**Below** Fishing at Sekiguchi Aqueduct.

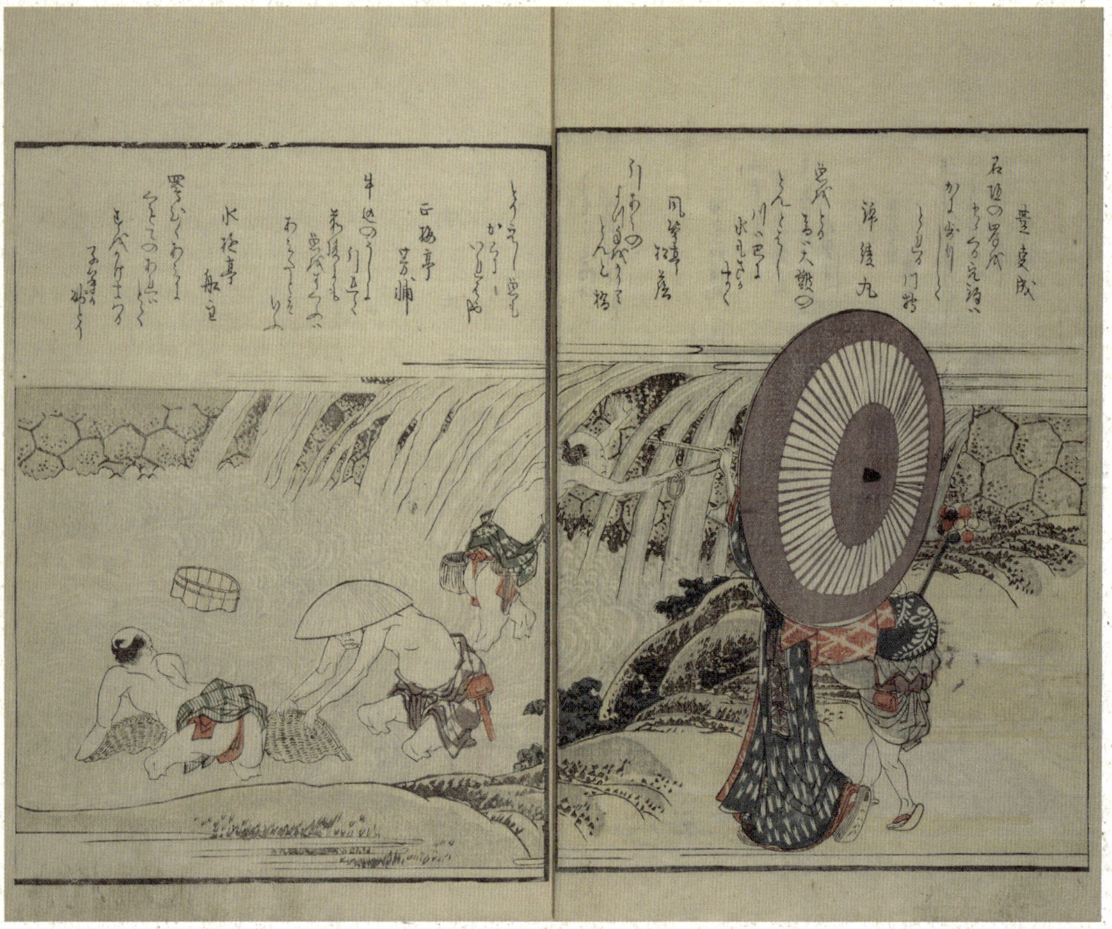

**Right** Breaking the ice on Suwa Pond.

**Below** Festival at Akasaka.

**Bottom** Distant fishing boats from Atago Hill.

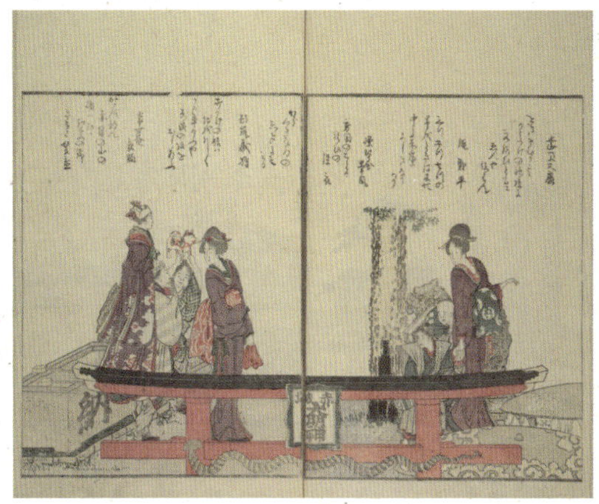

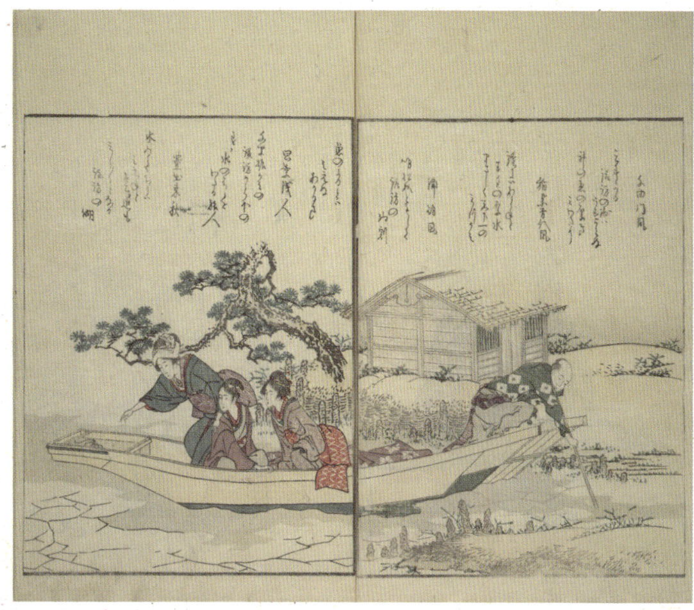

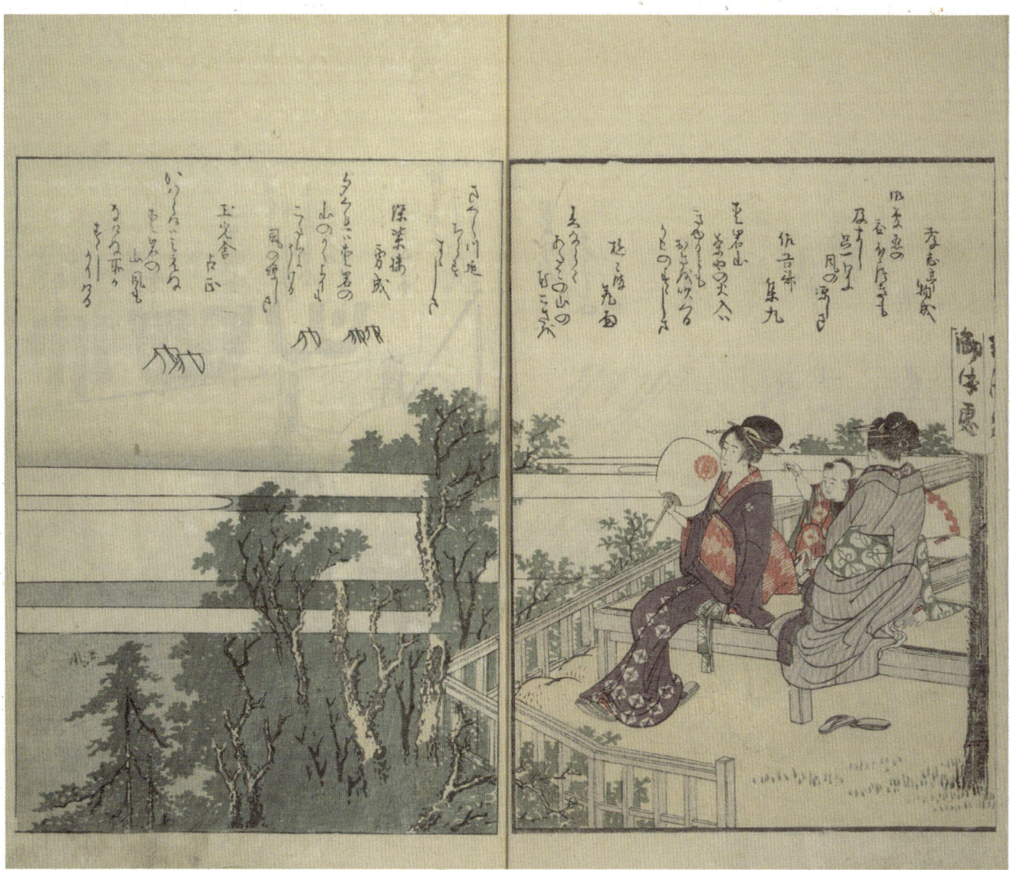

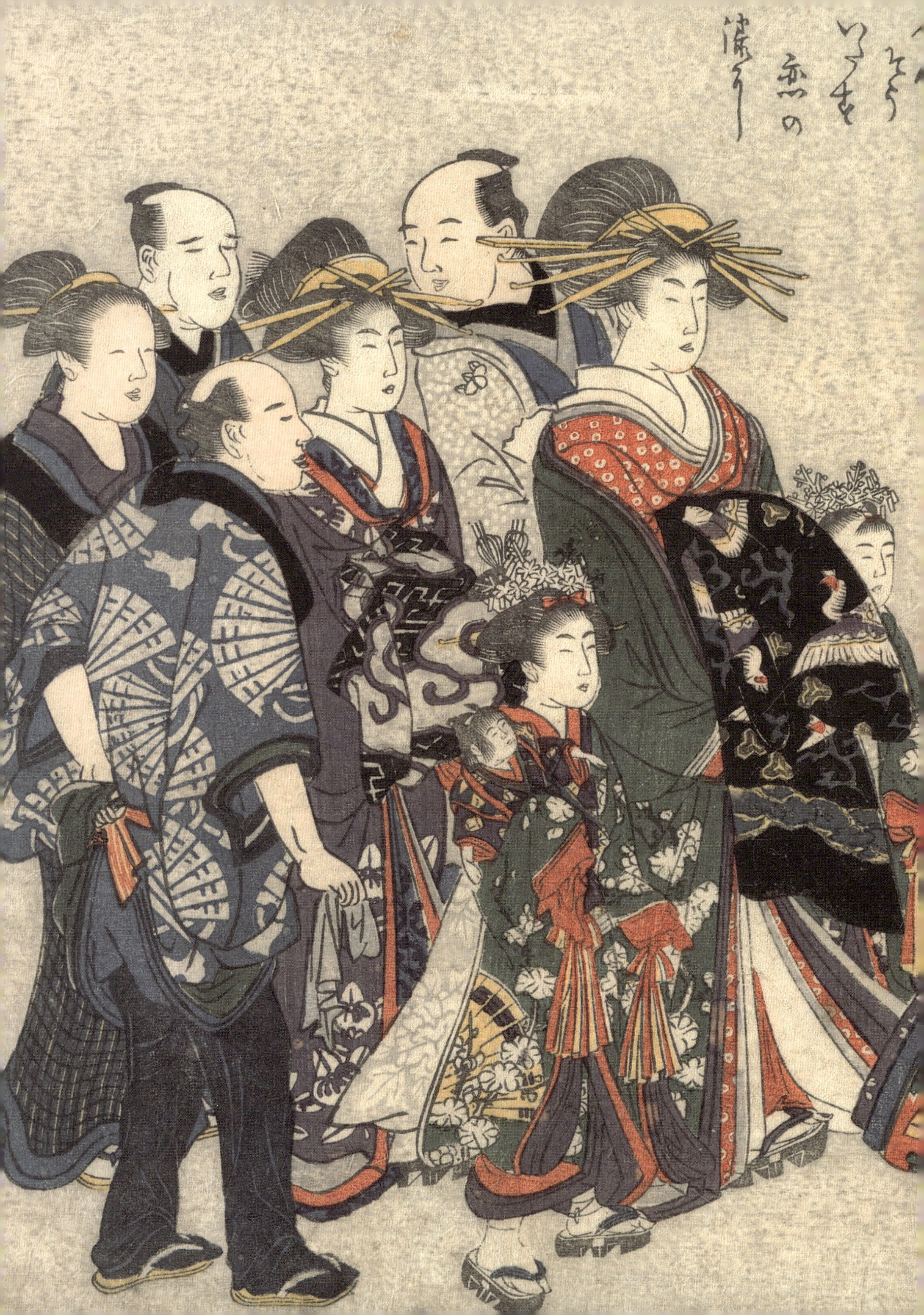

いつきを恋の流行

# CHAPTER THREE

# ACTORS, WOMEN, AND LEISURE ACTIVITIES

During the Edo period (1603–1868), almost all authors of literary works came from the samurai class. One exception was Ihara Saikaku (1642–93), the son of a wealthy merchant in Osaka. Initially Saikaku became a master of *haikai* poetry and only later began writing fictional books about the life of townspeople (*chōnin*) like himself. Some of his stories were erotic, but not of an explicit nature like *shunga*, which also existed in Japan. Saikaku's debut, *The Life of an Amorous Man* (*Kōshoku ichidai otoko*), was published in 1682 with his own illustrations. Four years later followed *The Life of an Amorous Woman* (*Kōshoku ichidai onna*), the title suggesting it was a counterpart to his earlier book, although the storyline is, in fact, very different.

In the 1660s, Hishikawa Moronobu (1618–94) moved to Edo (present-day Tokyo) and eventually became the most important book illustrator of the seventeenth century. Moronobu claimed to be the inventor of the new art form of single-sheet woodblock prints, calling himself *ukiyo eshi*, literally "floating-world picture master." In 1683, he authored and illustrated *Illustrations of Beautiful Women* (*Bijin e-zukushi*), a compilation of episodes in book form of the lives of attractive women. In *Monthly Amusements* (*Tsukinami no asobi*) from 1691, Moronobu presented annual customs and events in Edo, allowing a glimpse of daily life at that time in Japan's largest metropolis.

One of the characteristics of the Edo period was the increase in entertainment options. The *kabuki* theater developed and became enormously popular, with several theaters offering performances every month. Actors became stars, and dedicated fans avidly followed their idols not only onstage but also offstage. The latter is offered in the book *Amusements of Actors on the Third Floor* (*Yakusha sangaikyō*) from 1801, which depicts some of the popular actors at that time indulging in leisure activities. The illustrations are by Utagawa Toyokuni (1769–1825), who was a household name for portraits of actors on stage.

Famous beyond the city limits of Edo was its pleasure district, the Yoshiwara, and the high-ranking courtesans who were considered starlets. Their services were so costly that they were unattainable by most. Kitagawa Utamaro's (ca. 1754–1806) *Illustrated Book of Annual Events in the Pleasure Quarters* (*Seirō ehon nenjū gyōji*) captured the glamorous side of life in the brothels.

**Opposite** Detail from *Illustrated Book of Annual Events in the Pleasure Quarters*.

# The Life of an Amorous Man

## *Kōshoku ichidai otoko*
好色一代男

1682
Author/Artist: Ihara Saikaku (1642–93)
Publisher: Aratoya Magobei
Woodblock printed book (*ōhon*); ink on paper
National Institute of Japanese Literature

Ihara Saikaku was born into a wealthy merchant family in Osaka where he established a successful career as a poet. It was not until he was forty years old that he turned to writing fiction directed at the new bourgeoisie. During the rule of the Tokugawa shogunate (1603–1868), the country was at peace, the merchant class thrived, and cities like Osaka and Edo (today's Tokyo) developed into large metropolises with new dynamics. Townspeople were eager for new entertainment, and Saikaku's poetic and allusive style was a great success from the start. His debut novel, *The Life of an Amorous Man* (*Kōshoku ichidai otoko*), is centered around Yonosuke, a man deeply infatuated with passionate romantic interests. The descriptions and illustrations of Yonosuke's amorous affairs, while erotic are not pornographic in nature.

The book was initially published in Osaka and illustrated by Saikaku himself in a straightforward and rather simple style. By scripting the novel into fifty-four chapters, one for each year of Yonosuke's life, Saikaku alludes to the eleventh-century novel, *The Tale of Genji* (*Genji monogatari*), the most important narrative in Japan's history. Yonosuke has adventures in the brothels of the licensed pleasure quarters and is completely obsessed and consumed by his lust. At age nineteen he becomes a priest, but only for a few days

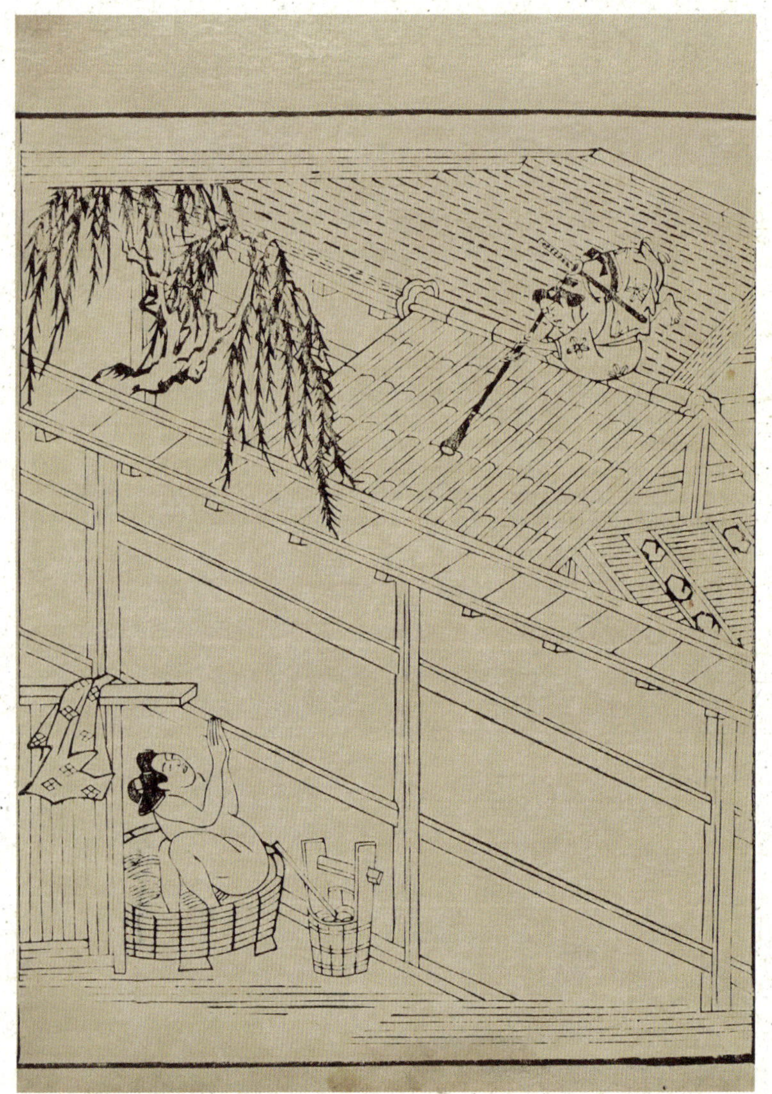

**Left** Yonosuke spies on a woman taking a bath.

as he soon realizes that this is not the life he wishes to lead. He sells his rosary and amuses himself with three young boys, which was not uncommon in Japan at that time. Once Yonosuke's father dies, he is free to seek all the pleasures he wants because of his enormous inheritance. Ultimately, the number of women in his life exceeds 3,700, and that of young men 700. At the end of his life, he sails to the Island of Women and vanishes.

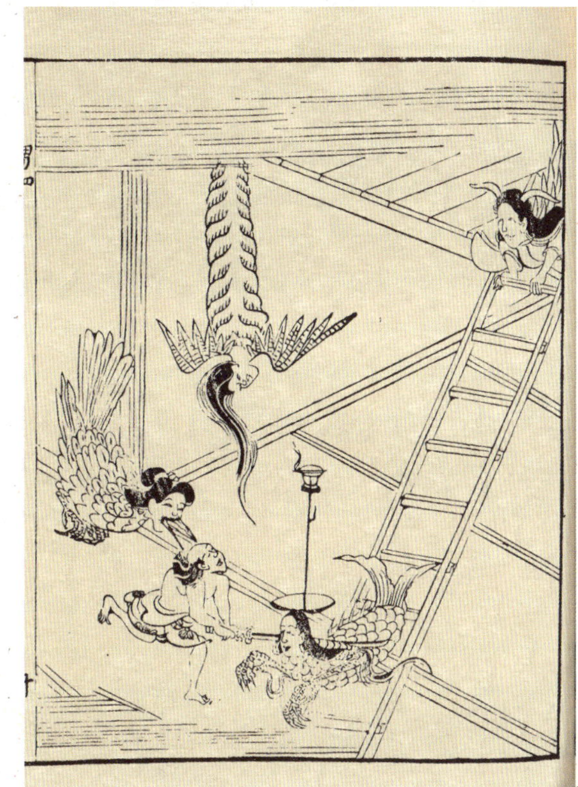

**Right** Yonosuke is tormented by the resentment of a former lover.

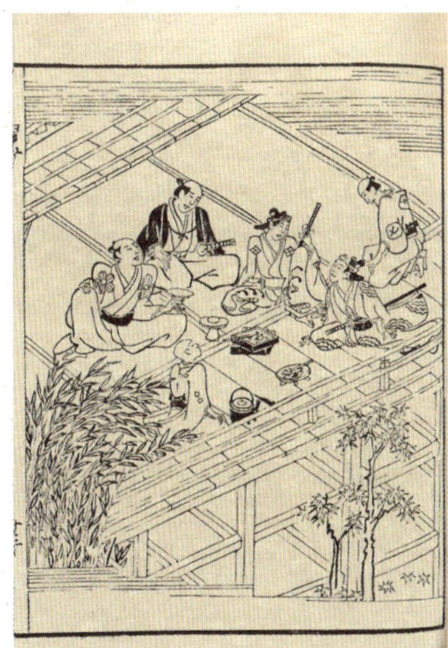

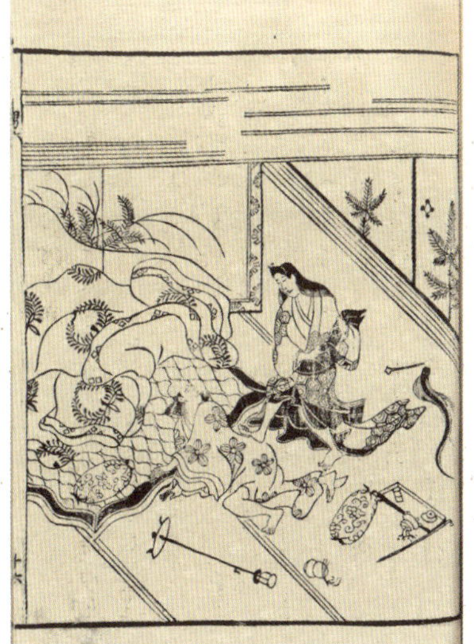

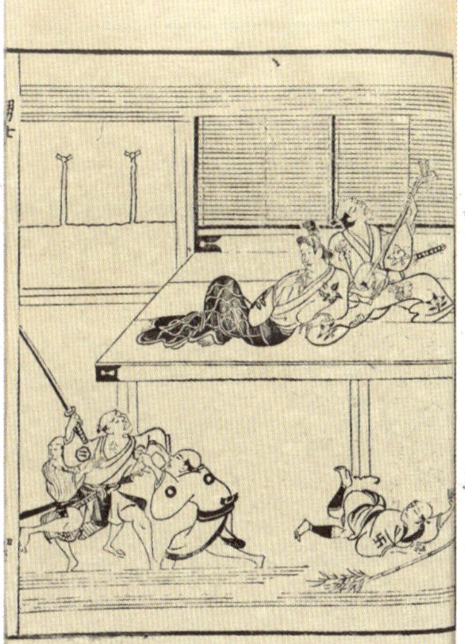

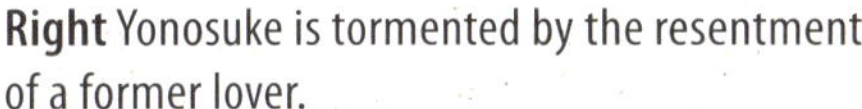

**Above left** Yonosuke arranged an amorous meeting between Sanzaburō and a monk.

# The Life of an Amorous Woman

## *Kōshoku ichidai onna*

好色一代女

1686
Author/Artist: Ihara Saikaku (1642–93)
Publisher: Okada Saburōemon
Woodblock printed book (*ōhon*); ink on paper
National Institute of Japanese Literature

Following the great success off his first novel, *The Life of an Amorous Man* (*Kōshoku ichidai otoko*), Ihara Saikaku wrote *Five Women Who Loved Love* (*Kōshoku gonin onna*), which was partially inspired by contemporary events. Four months later, *The Life of an Amorous Woman* (*Kōshoku ichidai onna*) was published, again illustrated by Saikaku himself. The story is purely fictional and intended as a counterpart to *The Life of an Amorous Man*. In the latter, Saikaku called the protagonist Yonosuke, but in *The Life of an Amorous Woman* he does not name the woman whose life he retells.

The story begins in the woods at the lonely "Hut of Fleshly Pleasures" where an old woman lives who has not renounced her way of life but is still passionate and has carnal desires. Asked about her life by two young men, the woman's recollections fill the remainder of the book. Born into a good family, she learned what was expected of her as a lady and was educated in calligraphy and needlework, which later helped her make a living. Her beauty, however, greatly ruled the first part of her life that was dominated by her nymphomania. In a vision later

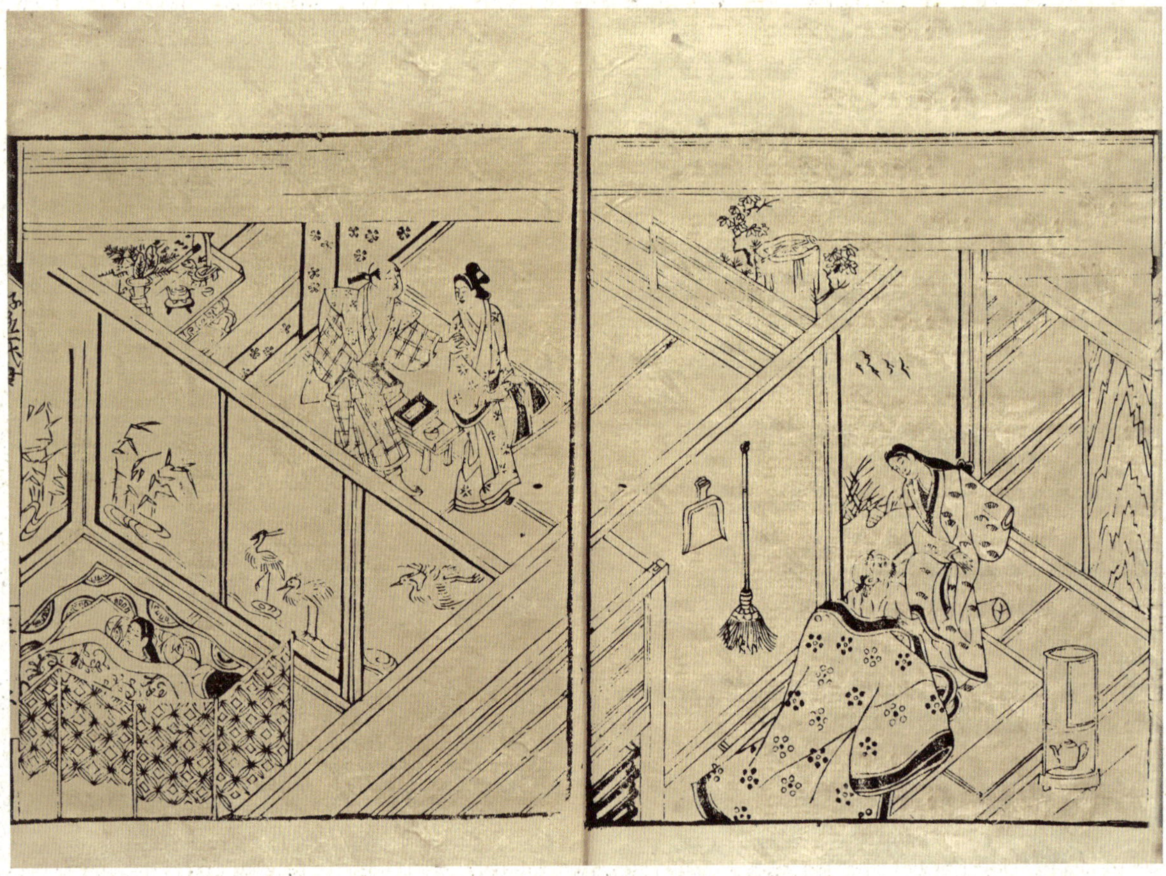

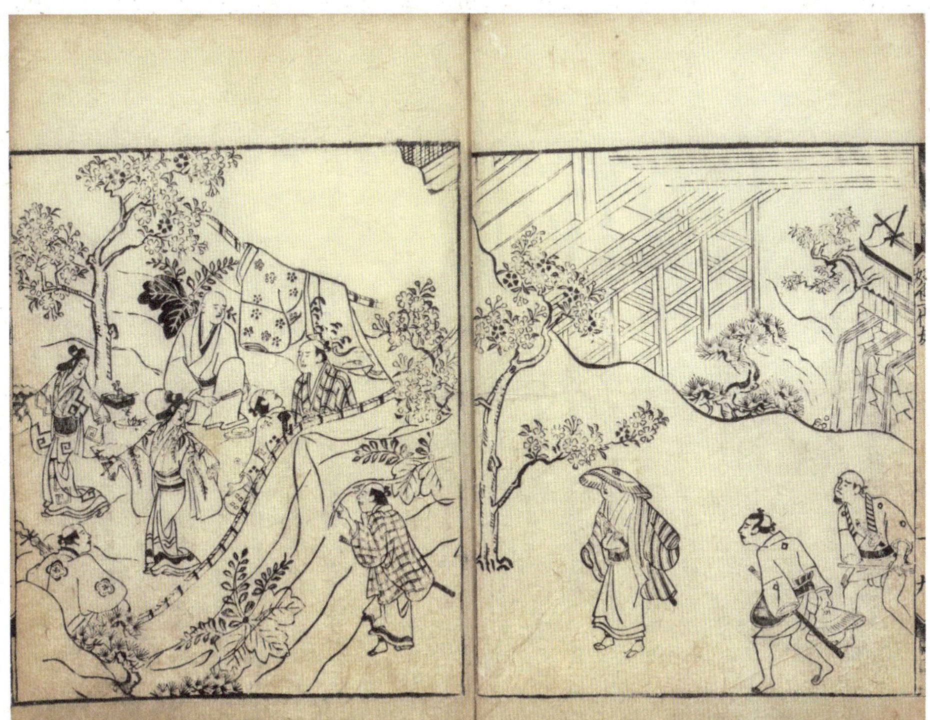



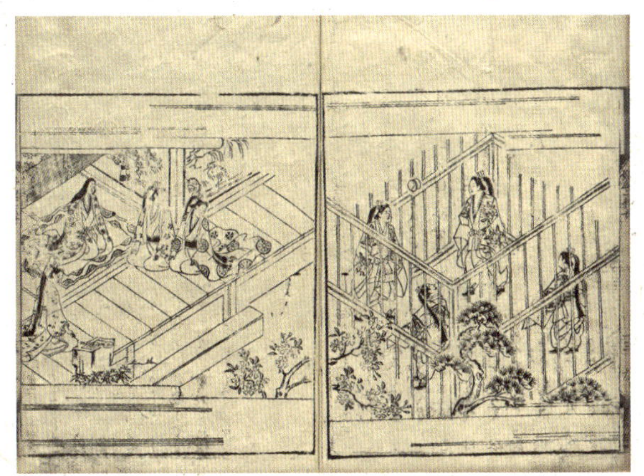

in life, she encounters ninety-five childlike figures who remind her of the children she aborted. While having multiple chances to abandon her insatiable lustful life and accept the offer of one of the men she meets to become his wife, she could never entertain the idea of being a housewife. Rather, she works as a prostitute and is so degraded from society that she becomes a common (illegal) streetwalker at night. As it was for Yonosuke, money was central, but while he enjoyed plenty of it at the end of his life, she becomes impoverished.

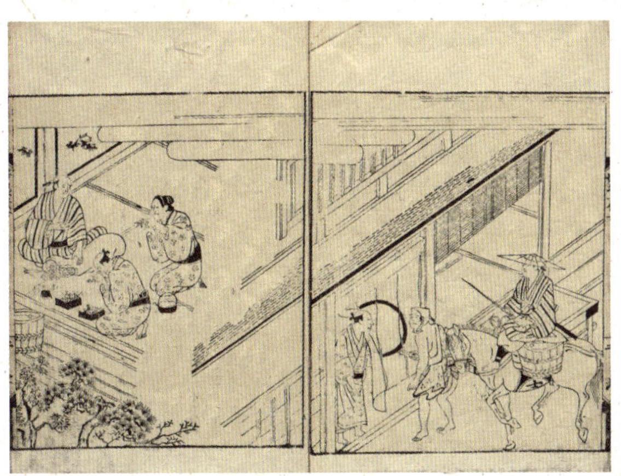

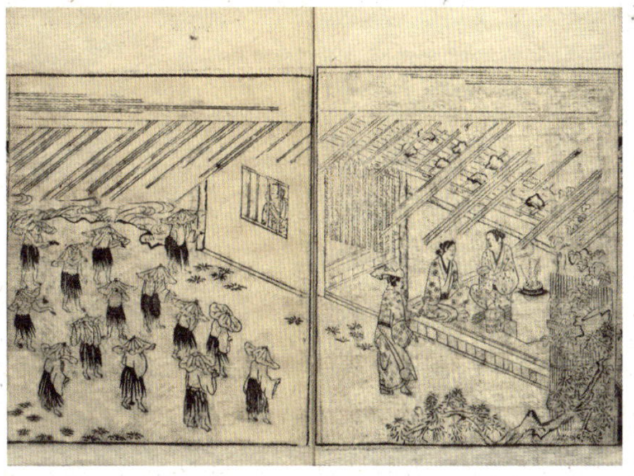

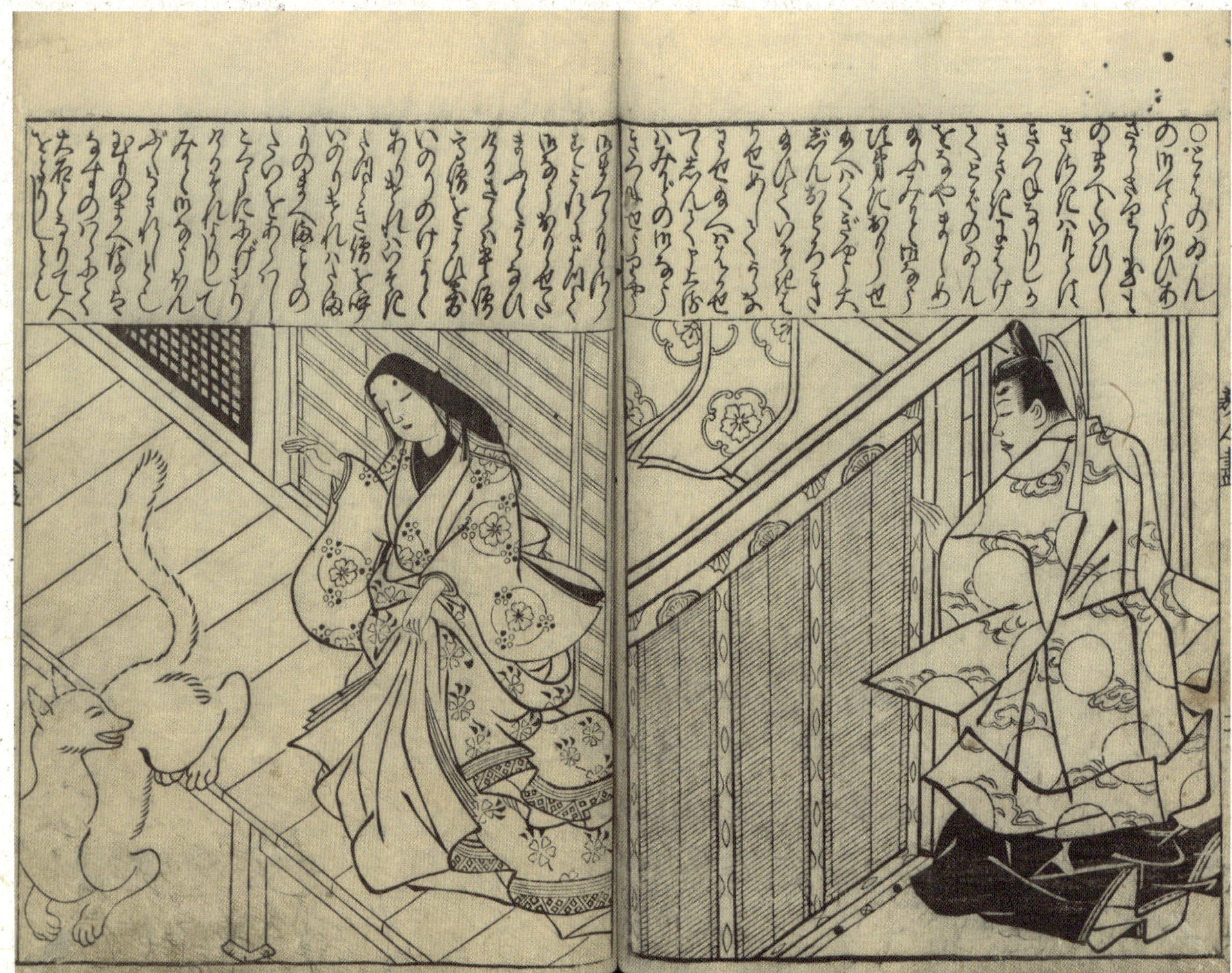

# Illustrations of Beautiful Women

*Bijin e-zukushi*

美人絵尽

1683
Author/Artist: Hishikawa Moronobu (1618–94)
Publisher: Urokogataya Sanzaemon
Woodblock printed book (*ōhon*); ink on paper
The Metropolitan Museum of Art, Rogers Fund, 1918 (JIB67a–c)

Hishikawa Moronobu was a painter who moved to Edo in the 1660s with the aim of making a name for himself as an illustrator of books. His earliest dated works are a book and a painting from 1672. By 1680, Moronobu was considered *ukiyo eshi*, literally "floating-world picture master," and he claimed to be the inventor of the new art form of single-sheet woodblock prints. A substantial number of his works are of an explicitly erotic nature. His book *Illustrations of Beautiful Women* (*Bijin e-zukushi*) is a collection of episodes in the lives of attractive women who are desired by men. Each situation is presented in an opening by a combination of illustration below and text above.

Moronobu took his subjects chiefly from Japan's rich history and literature, such as the famous *Tale of Genji* (*Genji monogatari*) from which he picked a scene from chapter 35, "Spring Shoots II" (*Wakana, ge*). Kashiwagi, the son of Prince Genji's best friend, catches a glimpse of Genji's young wife, the Third Princess. Her cat, kept on a leash since it was such a precious animal, had tried to run away and made the window blinds move so that the normally hidden

Third Princess could be seen. Fortuitously, Kashiwagi was playing a form of kickball with his friends on the court grounds and instantly fell in love with her. Despite her being married, they pursued an affair and she becomes pregnant with his child.

*Illustrations of Beautiful Women* starts in China with Yang Guifei (719–56), the consort of Emperor Xuanzong (685–762) of the Tang Dynasty, who is considered one of the four beauties of ancient China and famous for her influence on the emperor. Another scene features the fictious Tamamo-no-mae, who became a consort of Emperor Toba (1103–56) but was, in reality, a fox that caused the emperor to fall gravely ill.

**Opposite** Tamamo-no-mae, consort of Emperor Toba.

**Below left** Yang Guifei, consort of Emperor Xuanzong.

**Below right** The Third Princess and Kashiwagi.

**Bottom left** Orihime and celestial beings.

**Bottom right** The salt merchant's daughter and the prince.

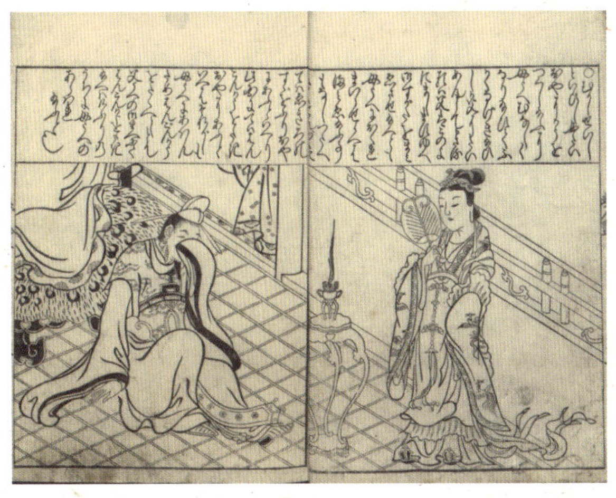

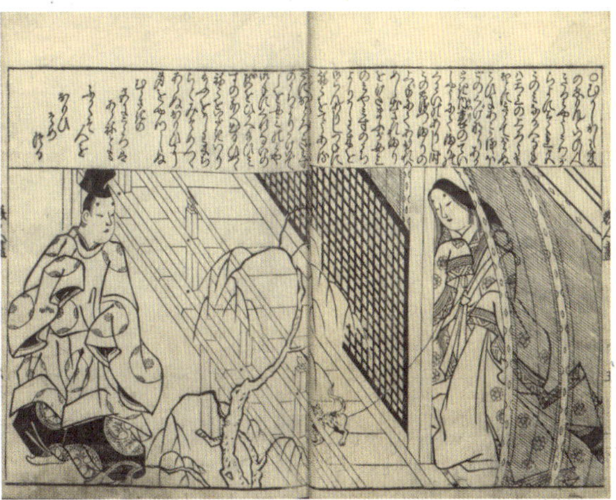

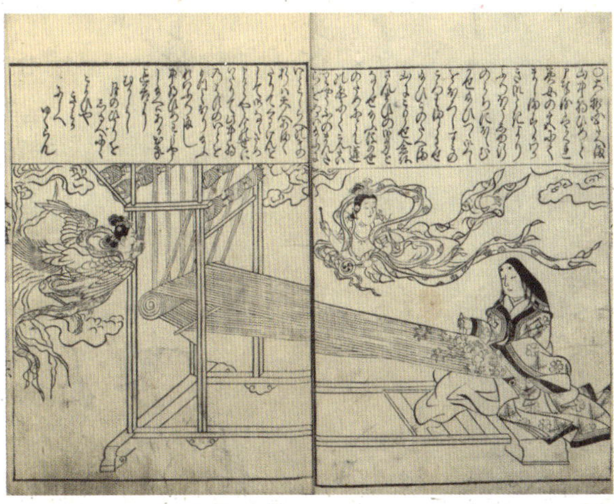

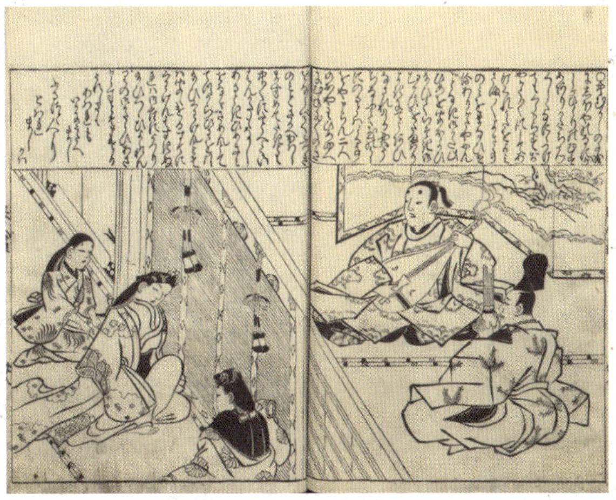

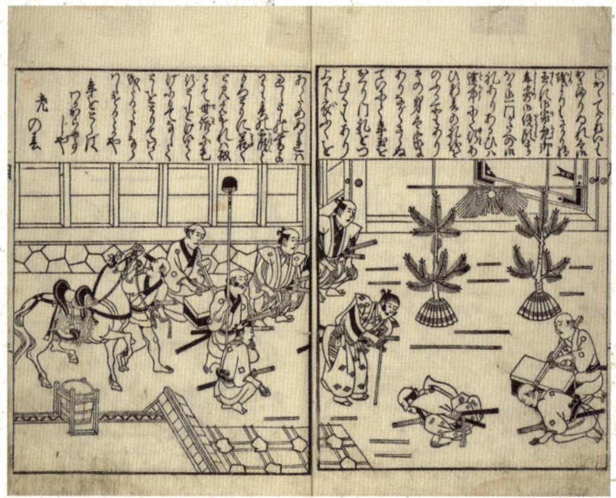

# Monthly Amusements

## *Tsukinami no asobi*
月次のあそび

1691
Author/Artist: Hishikawa Moronobu (1618–94)
Publisher: Urokogataya Magobei
Woodblock printed book (*ōhon*); ink on paper
Chester Beatty

Hishikawa Moronobu, who claimed to be the inventor of the Japanese woodblock print genre, today better known as *ukiyo-e* (lit. "pictures of the floating world"), was probably not only the illustrator of the book *Monthly Amusements* (*Tsukinami no asobi*) but also the author of its text. Each of the nineteen double-page illustrations that have an accompanying text above them, highlights a popular custom and event of the twelve months, likely in the city of Edo (today's Tokyo). Amongst the scenes is a picture of pleasure boats on the Sumida River that includes two men entertaining their friends and families with personal fireworks. Another scene captures the liveliness of the fish market, with fishers unloading their catch off their boats, vendors offering a wide variety from octopus to shellfish, and wild scenes of men haggling for the best price. One scene includes religious performers called *gannin bōzu* (lit. "petitioning monks") in black robes walking around town with small displays to celebrate the nativity of the Buddha Sakyamuni; the representation of the Buddha as

**Left** Meeting of samurai.

**Below** *Gannin bōzu* celebrate the birth of the Buddha.

**Bottom** Fish market.

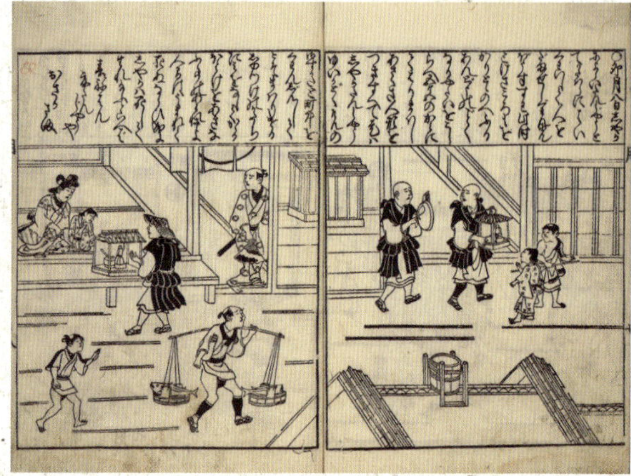

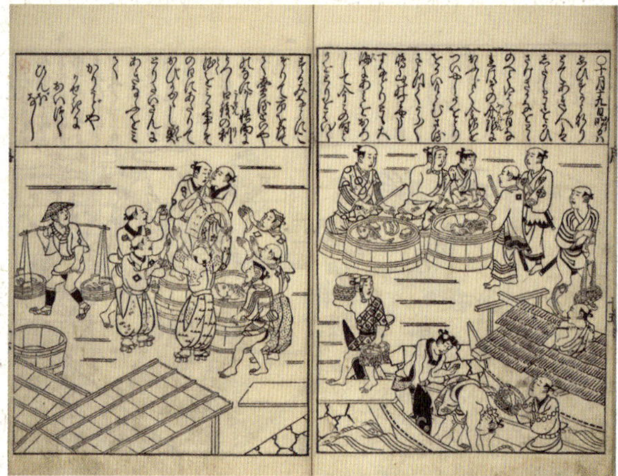

a child was probably a simple clay or wood figure. Yet another scene shows a group of samurai sitting by the water of an evening enjoying a picnic while watching the moon rise above distant mountains.

The last page of the copy in the collection of Chester Beatty contains a handwritten note that claims the book is a reissue of one by Moronobu that the publisher Kashiwaya Yoichi released in 1680. However, the alleged original publication has not been found and it is possible that the author of this note was confused and meant *Designs for Virtuous Landscape Gardens* (*Yokei tsukuri niwa no zu*), which was indeed originally released by Kashiwaya in 1680 and then reprinted in 1691.

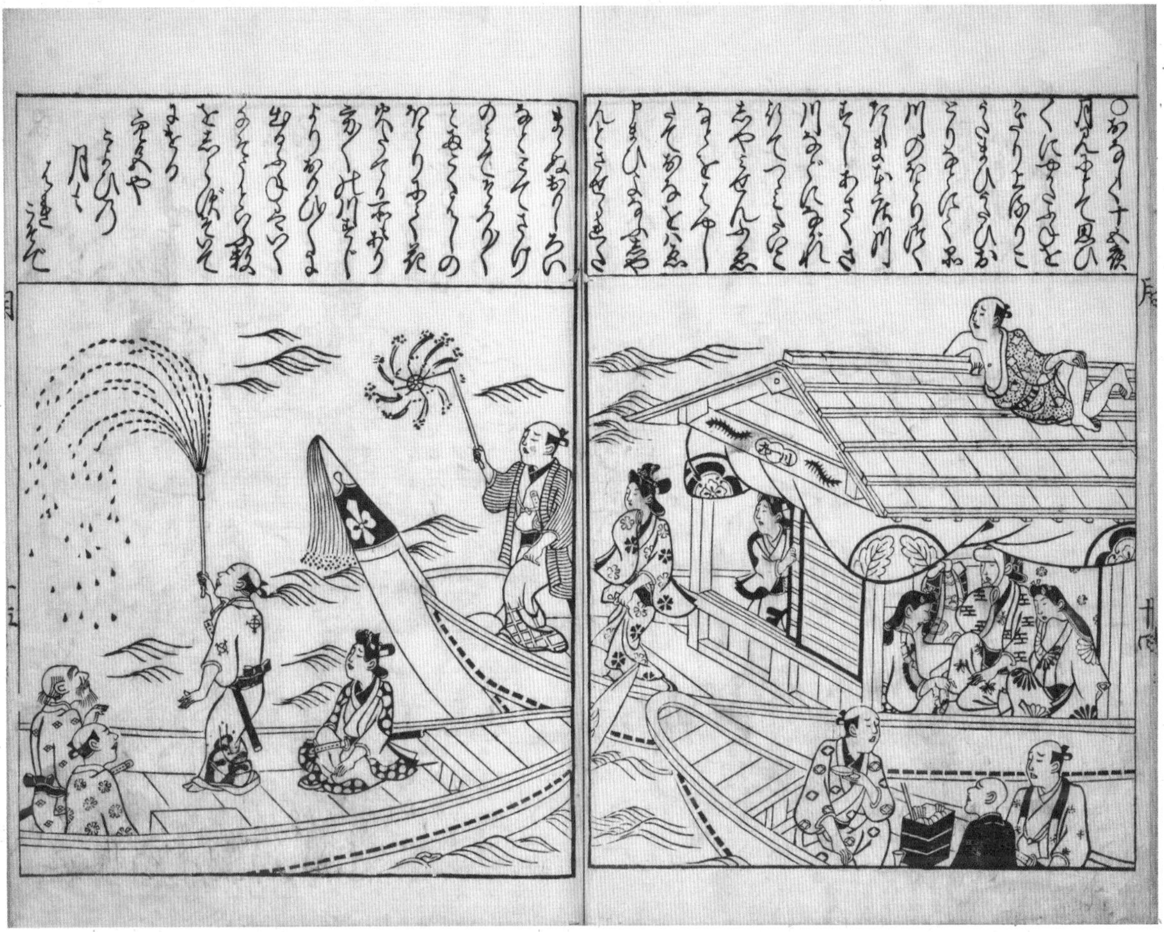

**Above** Pleasure boats on the Sumida River.

**Below left** Picnic of samurai.

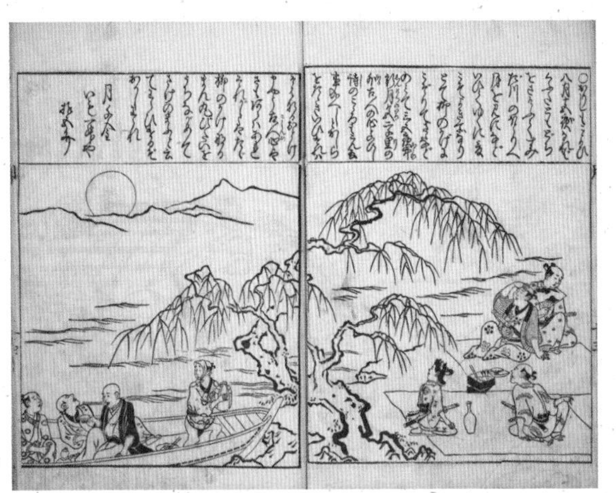 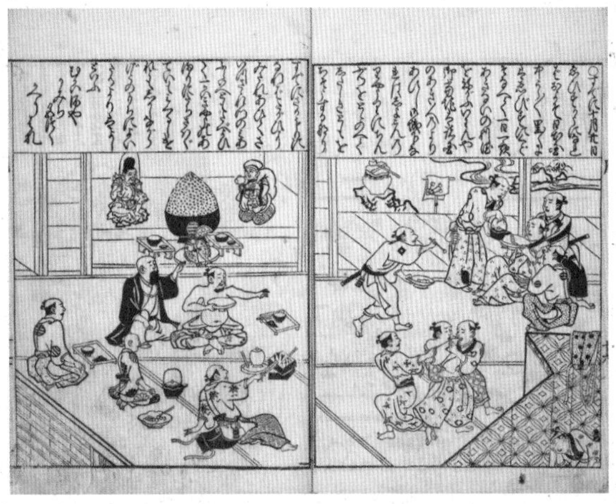

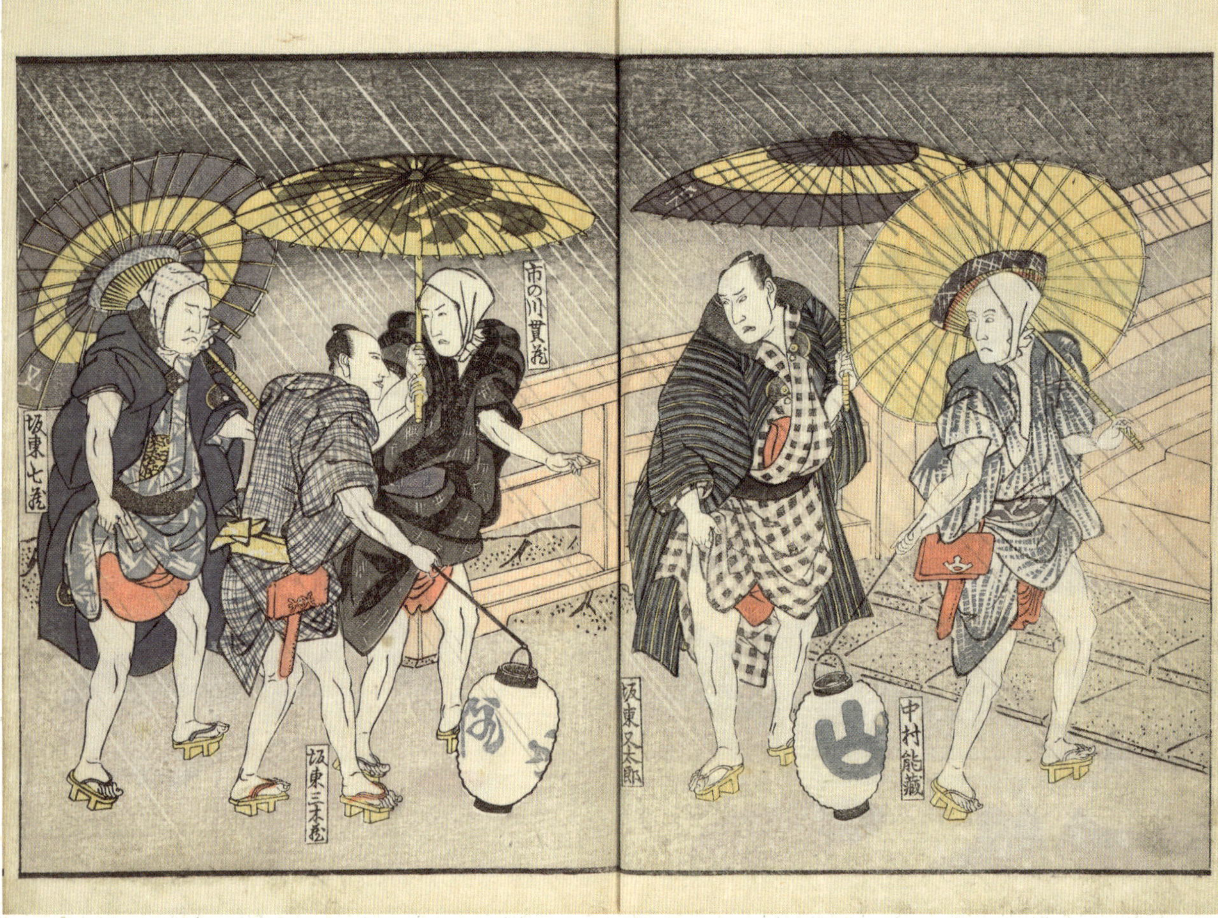

# Amusements of Actors on the Third Floor

*Yakusha sangaikyō*

俳優三階興

1801
Author: Shikitei Sanba (1776–1822)
Artist: Utagawa Toyokuni (1769–1825)
Publishers: Nishinomiya Shinroku, Yorozuya Tajiemon
Woodblock printed book (*hanshibon*); ink and color on paper
Chester Beatty

The book *Amusements of Actors on the Third Floor* (*Yakusha sangaikyō*) is the product of two leading players in the art and literature world at that time, the immensely popular designer of actor prints, Utagawa Toyokuni, and a mainstream writer of comical novels, Shikitei Sanba. Issued in two volumes, each volume contains ten full-color double-page pictures that depict popular *kabuki* actors participating in different activities offstage. The book's title alludes to the three-storied backstage dressing rooms in *kabuki* theaters. Toyokuni's personal experience and knowledge of the *kabuki* theater and its stars ensured that the reader could expect a view behind the scenes of what otherwise was off-limits. Instead of portraying actors in fictional or historical roles, they are captured in private and public situations and presented as approachable. This formula was not applied here for the first time but used twenty years earlier in the book *Actors Like Fuji in Summer* (*Yakusha natsu no Fuji*).

One of the scenes features the actors Ichikawa Dansaku (dates unknown) and Ichikawa Danzō IV (1745–1808) and his son Ichikawa Danzaburō IV

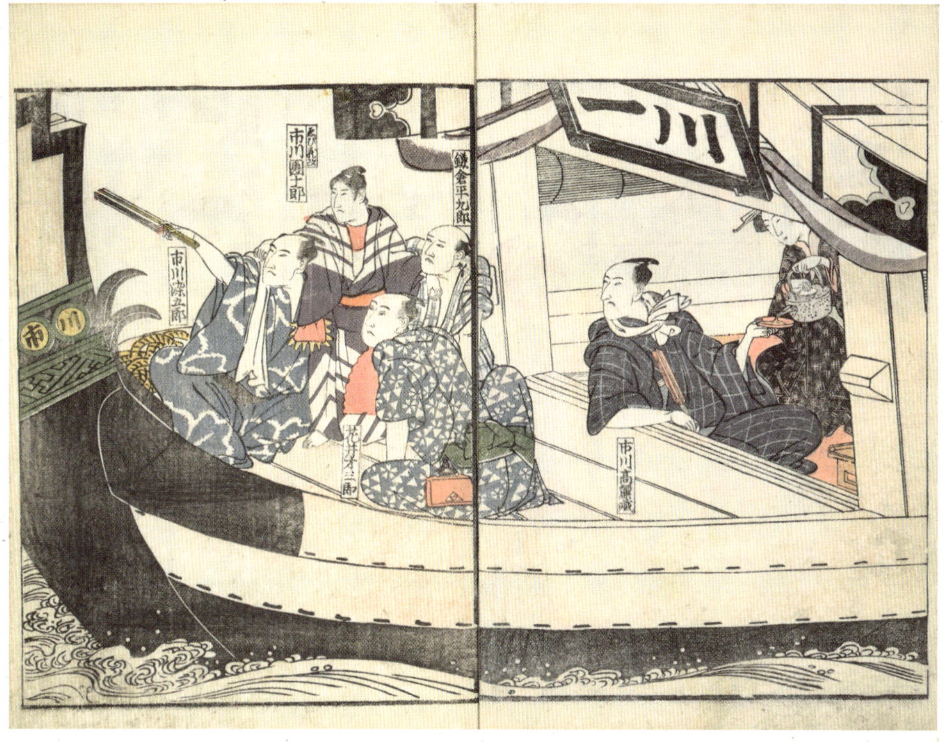



**Left** Ichikawa Somegorō, Ichikawa Danjūrō VII, Ichikawa Komazō III, and others on a pleasure boat.

**Below** Ichikawa Hakuen inscribing a paper lantern.

**Bottom** Ichikawa Dansaku, Ichikawa Danzō IV, and Ichikawa Danzaburō IV picnicking on the shore.

**Opposite** Five actors leisurely crossing a bridge on a rainy night.

(1788–1854) picnicking on the shore while watching fishers pulling in their nets. Ichikawa Somegorō (1737–1802), Ichikawa Danjūrō VII (1791–1859), Ichikawa Komazō III (1764–1838), and others are depicted enjoying a ride on a sizeable pleasure boat. Another scene shows Ichikawa Hakuen (1741–1806) inscribing a paper lantern with the stable name "Naritaya."

An interesting detail, and one that sheds light on the economics of the book publishing world at that time, is noted in the colophon of this book. While two publishers are listed to have jointly produced it, only one of them, Nishimiya Shinroku, is mentioned as the owner of the wood blocks, which means that he would have had control over any future printings.

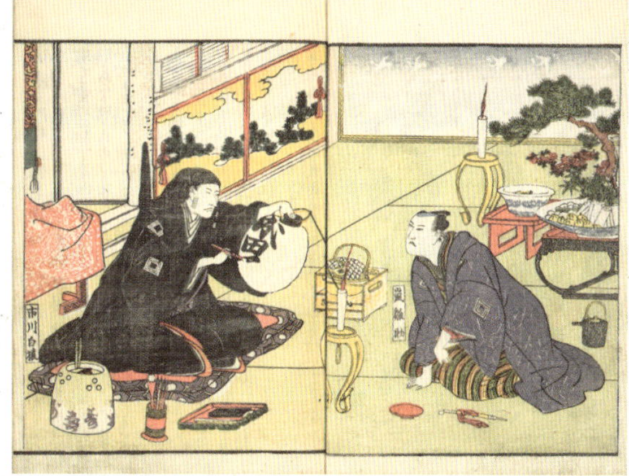

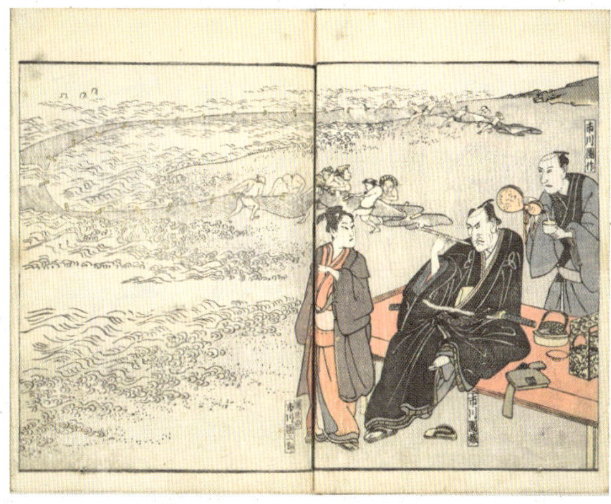

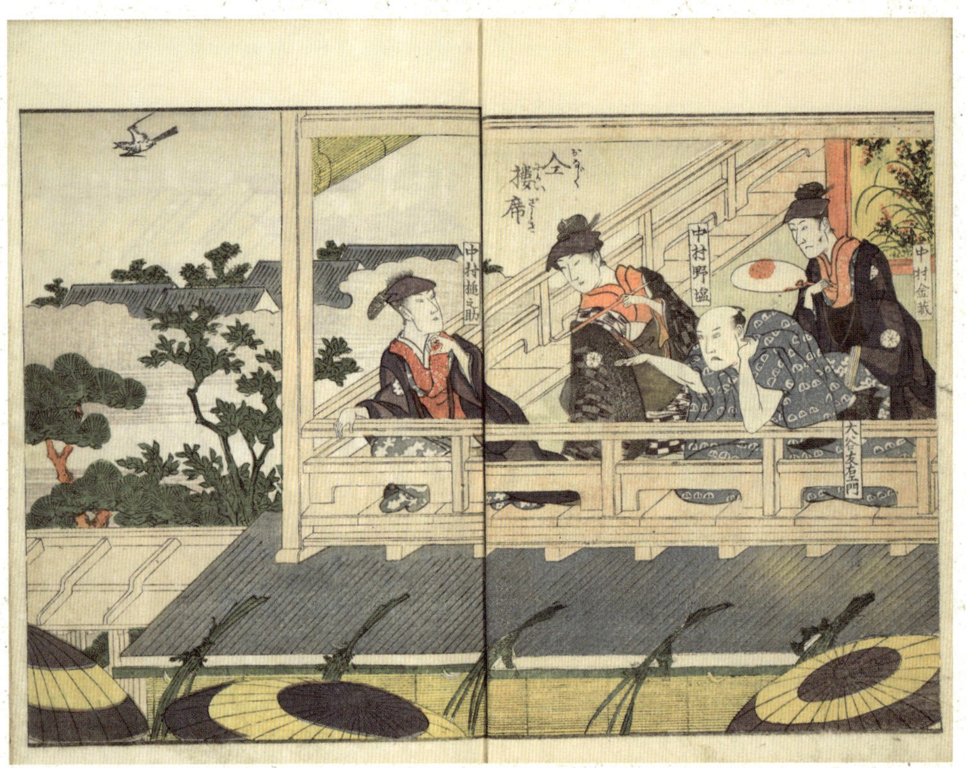

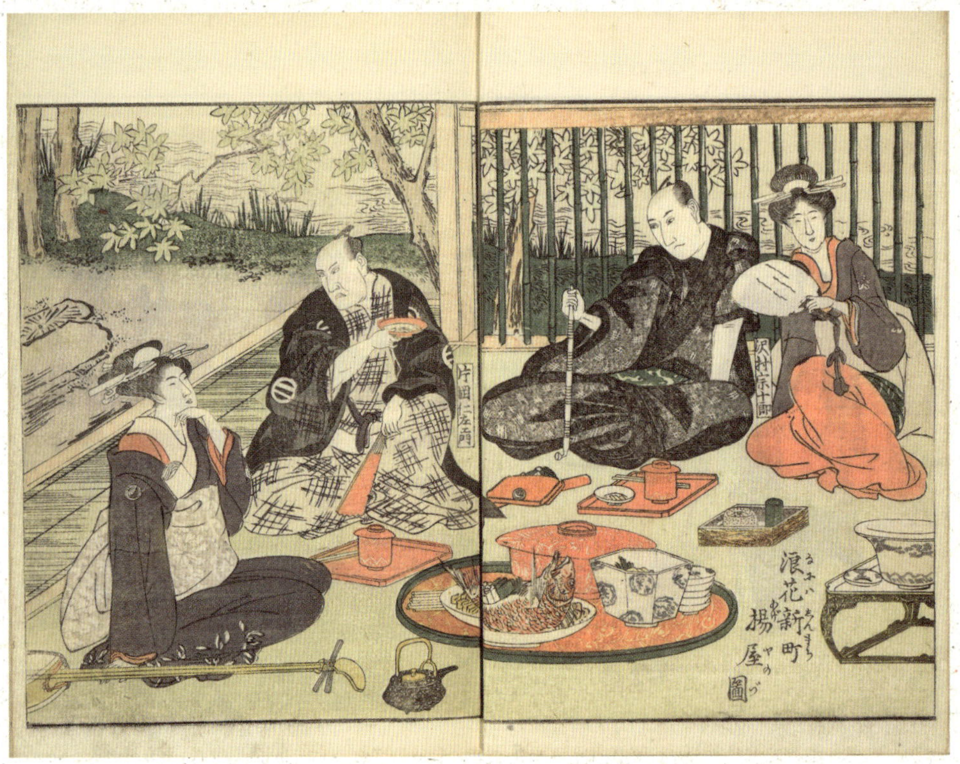

**Above left** Second floor of a pleasure house on Children's Day.

**Left** Pleasure house in Osaka's Shinmachi district.

# The Illustrated Book of Children of the East

*Ehon azuma warawa*

絵本東童郎

1804 (2 vols.)
Author: Nansenshō Somahito (1749–1807)
Artist: Utagawa Toyohiro (1773–1828)
Publisher: Izumiya Ichibei
Woodblock printed book (*hanshibon*); ink and color on paper
Ritsumeikan University Library

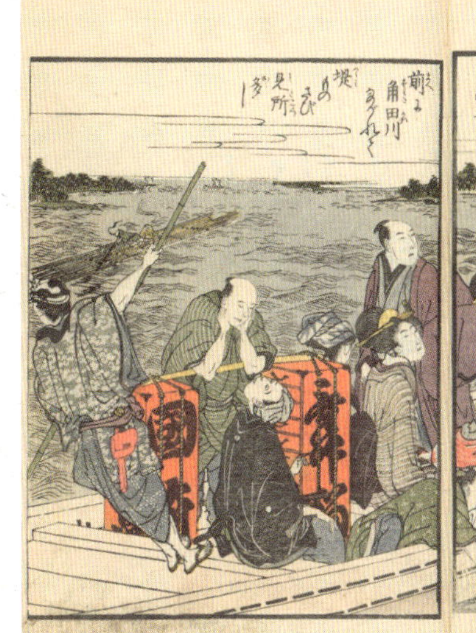

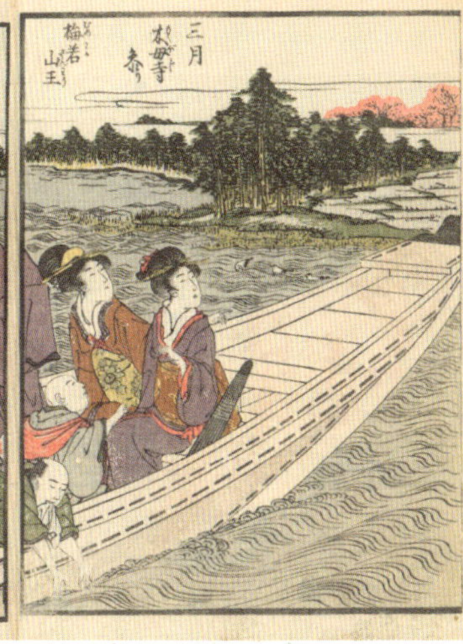

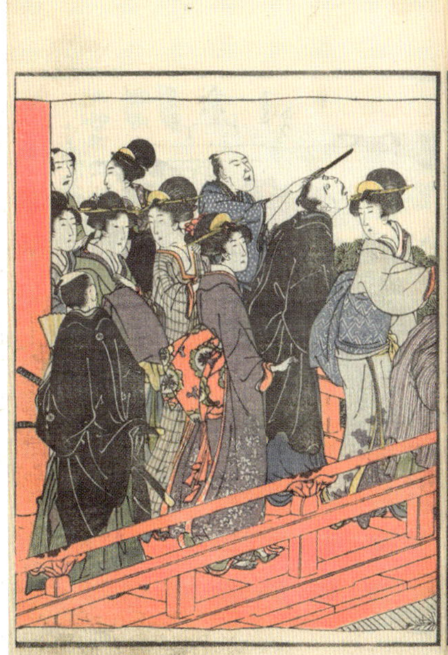

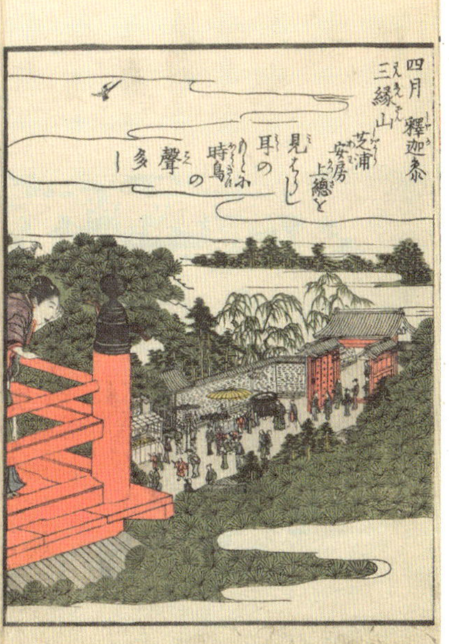

**Above** Third month, the Mokuboji Temple Festival.

**Left** Fourth month, the Shaka Festival at San'enzan Temple.

Utagawa Toyoharu (1735–1814) was the founder of the Utagawa school that dominated the print market for most of the nineteenth century. Toyoharu's leading students were Toyokuni (1769–1825), who specialized in portraits of *kabuki* actors, and Toyohiro, who concentrated more on landscapes and beautiful women. Toyohiro also illustrated dozens of novels. In the short period from 1801 to 1808, Toyohiro completed over forty book projects in collaboration with the playwright Nansenshō Somahito. *The Illustrated Book of Children of the East* (*Ehon azuma warawa*) stands out amongst them because it is not a novel but a compilation of twelve celebrations in the city of Edo (today's Tokyo), one for each lunar month. Published by Izumiya Ichibei in 1804 and printed in color, the concept is the same as for the lavish triptych series by Toyohiro and Toyokuni from 1801 that was published by Yamadaya Sanshirō. However, only triptychs related to months one to seven are known.

Each scene in *Children of the East* has a cloud band at top containing a descriptive sentence by Somahito. For the first lunar month, the choice fell on the Ehō Festival at Sannō Gongen Shrine. For the second lunar month, the Horse Day Festival (*hatsuuma-matsuri*), celebrated at the Ōji Inari Shrine, is chosen. The third features the festival at Mokuboji Temple; the fourth the Shaka Festival at San'enzan Temple; the

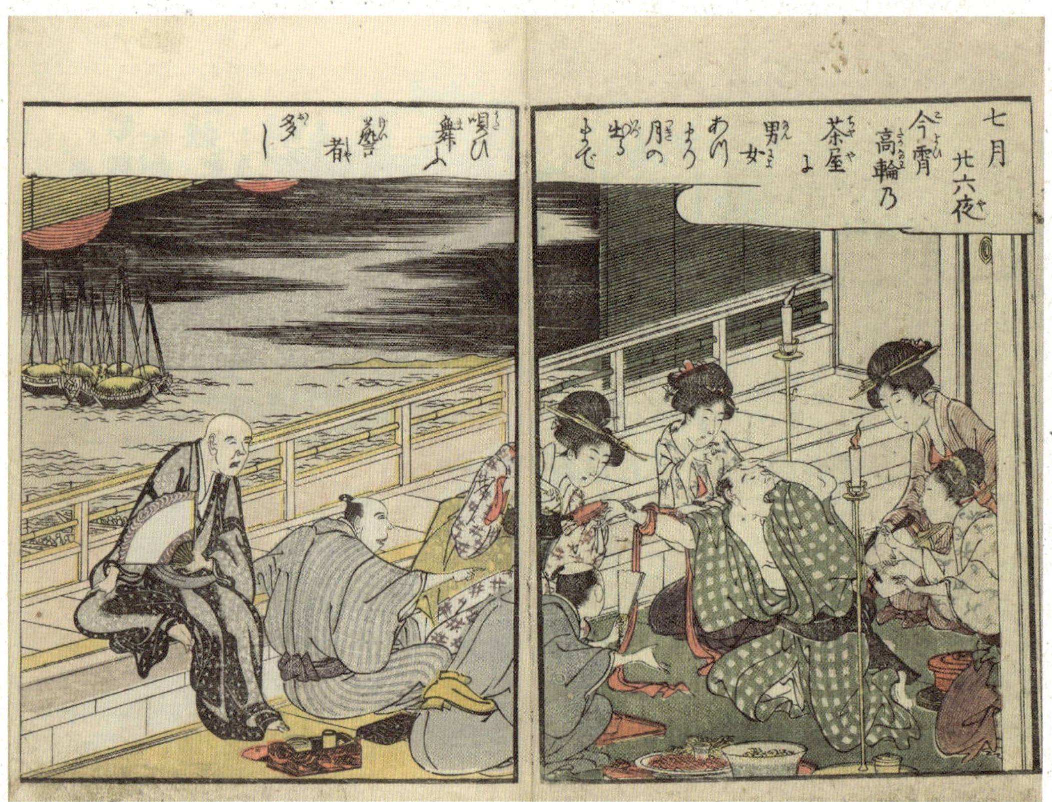

**Above** Seventh month, a teahouse party in Takanawa.    **Below** Tenth month, the Taishi Festival in Ueno.

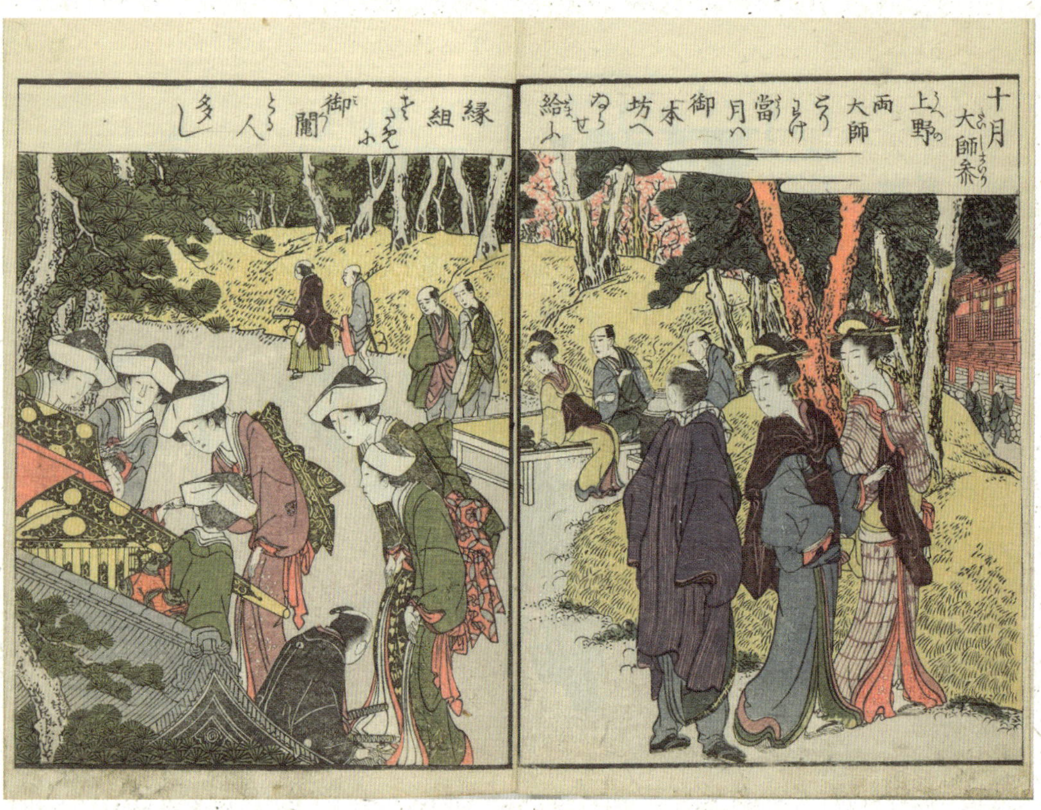

fifth is at Meguro's Fudō Myōō
Temple; the sixth is the Ten'nō
Festival in Ōdenmachō; the
seventh illustration depicts a
teahouse party in Takanawa
enjoying the moon viewing,
traditionally considered to be best
on the night of the twenty-sixth
day. The Hachiman Festival at
Tomigaoka Shrine is the motif
of the eighth; the ninth depicts
Shōgaichi (lit. "ginger fair") at
Shiba Shinmei Shrine; the tenth
shows the Taishi Festival in Ueno;
the eleventh the Okō Festival at
Honganji Temple, and the last
the Year-end Fair (*toshi no ichi*)
at Asakusa's Kinryūzan Temple.

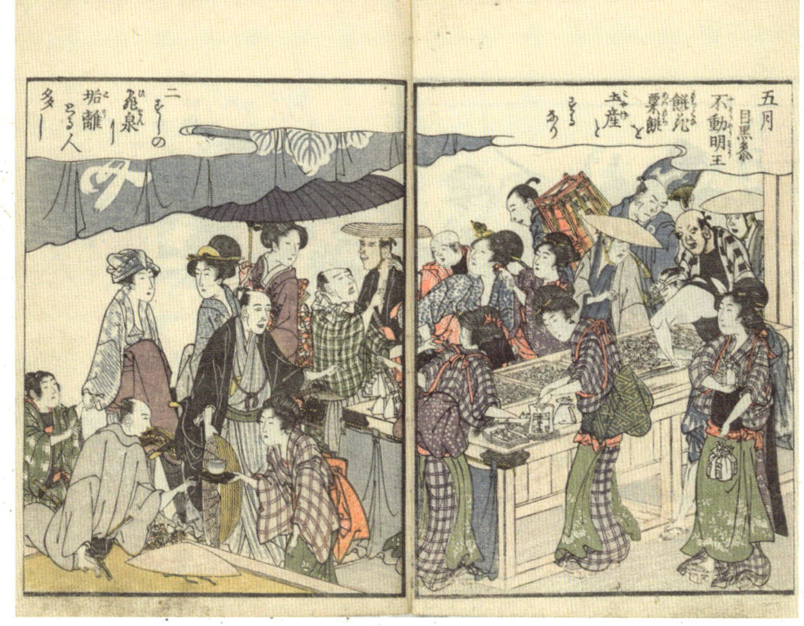

**Above** Fifth month, at Meguro's Fūdō Myōō Temple.

**Below** Eleventh month, the Okō Festival at Honganji Temple.

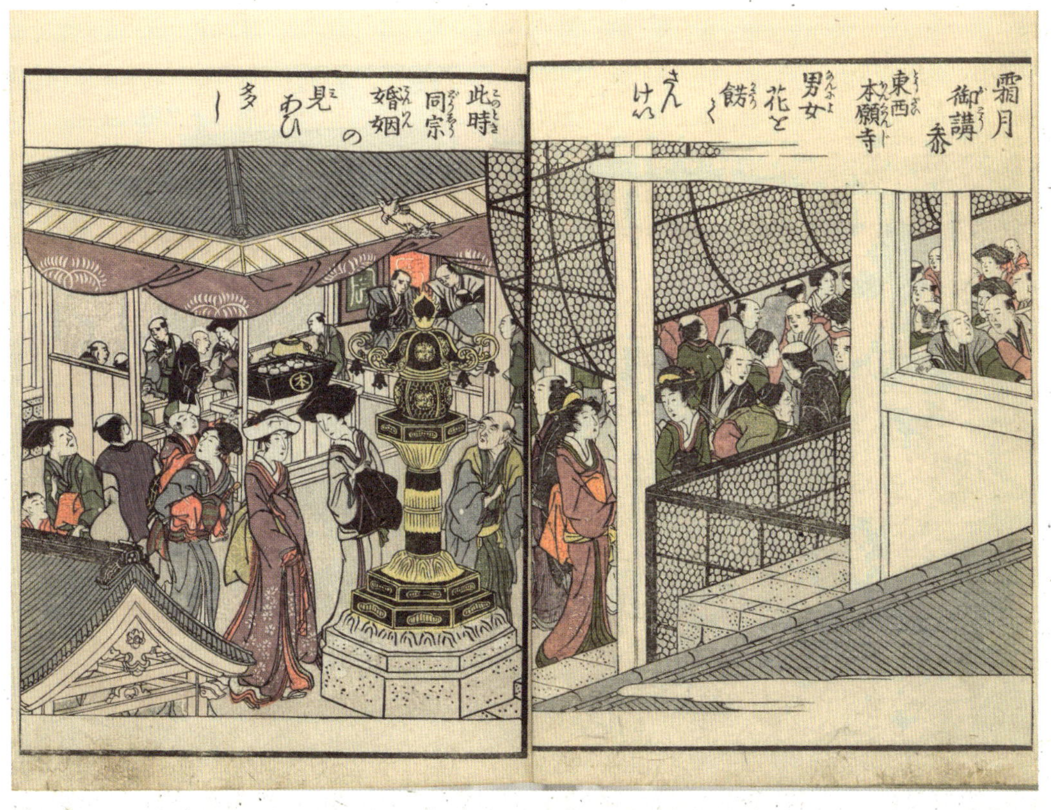

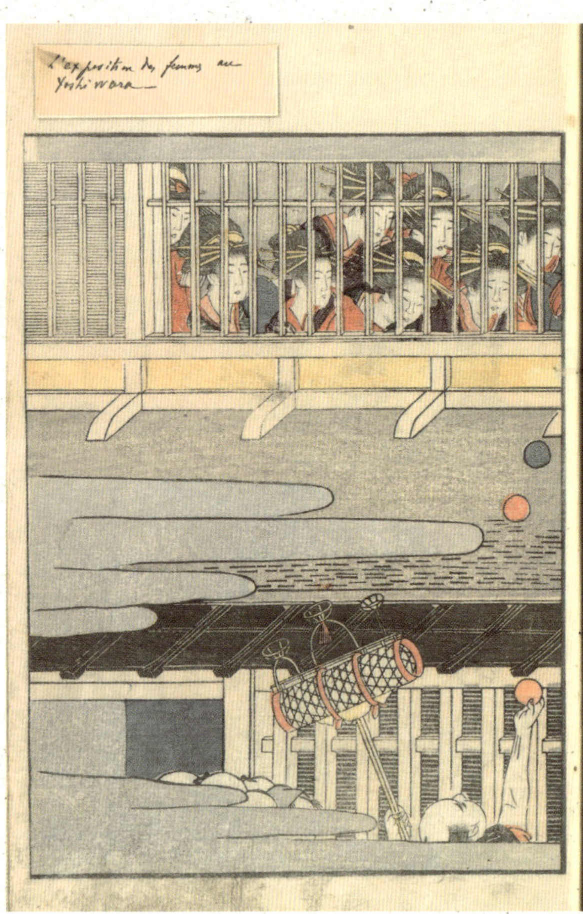


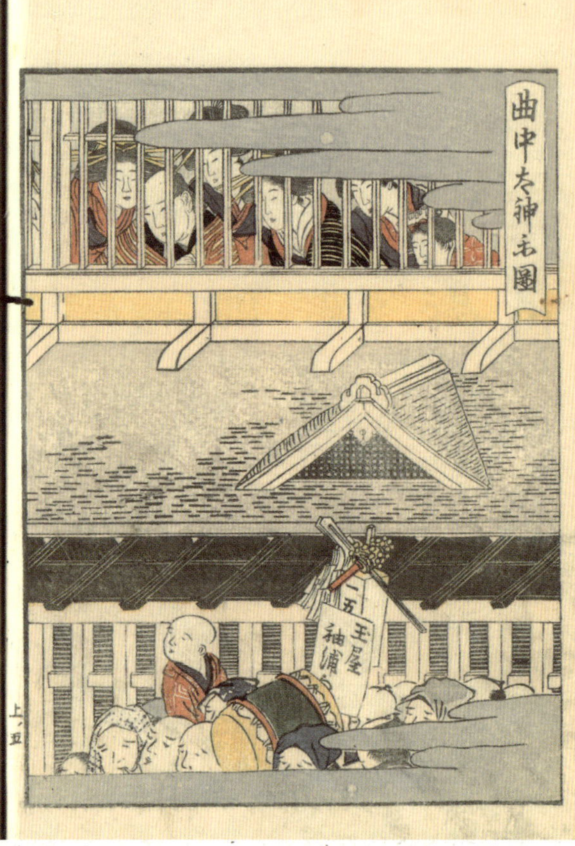


# The Illustrated Book of Annual Events in the Pleasure Quarters

## *Seirō ehon nenjū gyōji*

青楼絵本年中行事

1804 (2 vols.)

Author: Jippensha Ikku (1765–1831)

Artists: Kitagawa Utamaro (ca. 1754–1806), assisted by Kikumaro, Hidemaro, and Takemaro

Publisher: Kazusaya Chūsuke

Woodblock printed book (*hanshibon*); ink on paper

The Metropolitan Museum of Art, Purchase, Mary and James G. Wallach Family Foundation Gift, in honor of John T. Carpenter, 2013 (2013.856a,b)

The *Illustrated Book of Annual Events in the Pleasure Quarters* (*Seirō ehon nenjū gyōji*) is the result of the collaboration of the writer Jippensha Ikku and the artist Kitagawa Utamaro, who, around 1800 were amongst the most popular figures in the "floating world" of enjoying life and being entertained. Utamaro's prominence was based on his portraits of beautiful women, most of them courtesans working in the licensed brothels of Edo's pleasure quarter, the Yoshiwara. Fittingly, this book reflects on life in the Yoshiwara throughout the year, but of course depicting only the glamorous sides of beauty, fashion, and the arts. While the title suggests the focus is on annual festivities, some openings capture situations that happened more regularly, for example, "Picture of the Establishments at Night (*Yomise no zu*)" showng courtesans of different ranks behind lattice windows gawked at by men outside. The artist painting a phoenix (*hōō*) on a wall is believed to be Utamaro himself.

This book reveals an interesting fact concerning the design of the illustrations. Usually, a colophon only lists one artist as illustrator, suggesting that it is the work of a single person. This is, however, doubtful since senior artists were involved in many projects and operated a studio with students who would be available to assist. Here, the involvement of students is openly mentioned as three students are listed in the colophon: Kikumaro, Hidemaro, and Takemaro. We do not know anything about any of them other than that they were active around 1804. Unfortunately, the colophon does not provide any other details, and it remains unclear what exactly their contributions were.

The book was so popular that it was reprinted in the Meiji era (1868–1912) using new wood blocks. The copy illustrated here carries descriptive titles in French, glued on the pages by a previous owner.

**Opposite** Street performers.

**Right** Debut of a *shinzō* courtesan.

**Below left** Lantern festival.

**Below right** Adding colors to an interior painting.

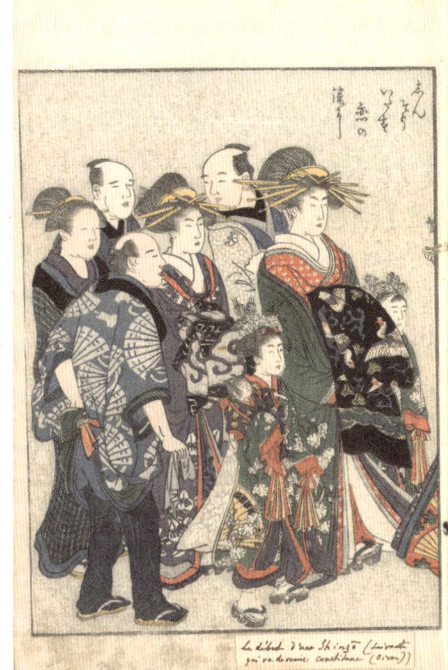
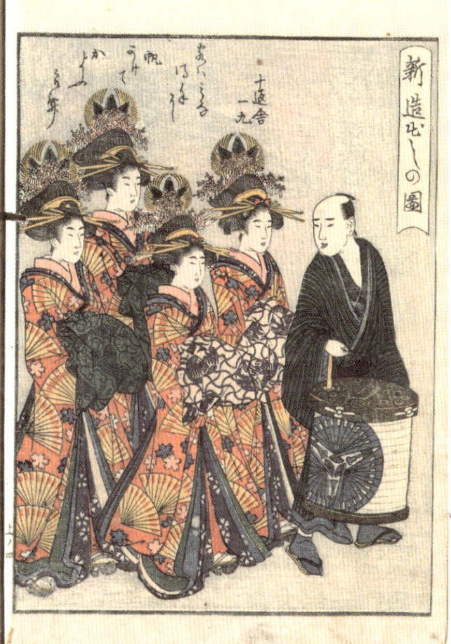

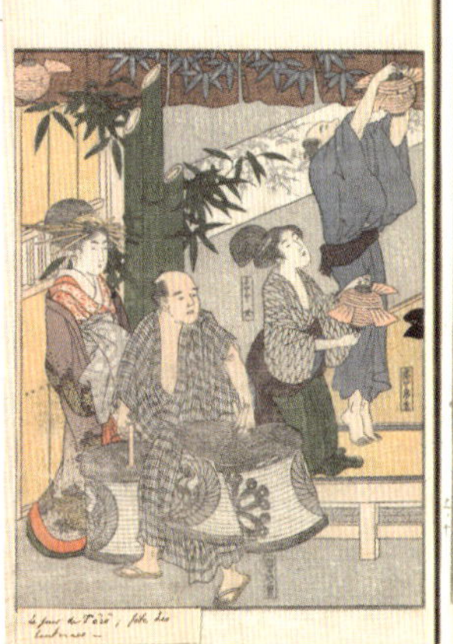
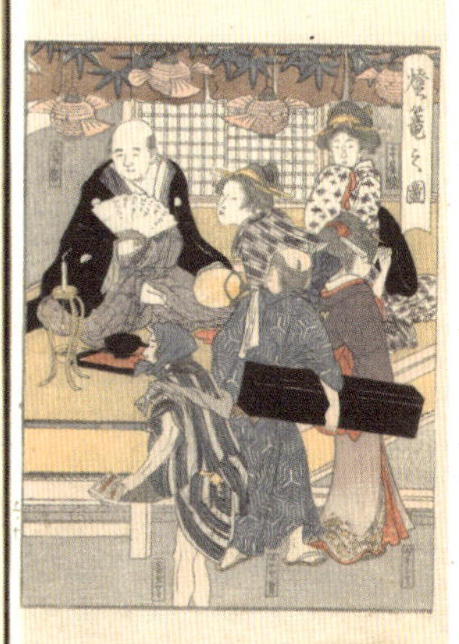

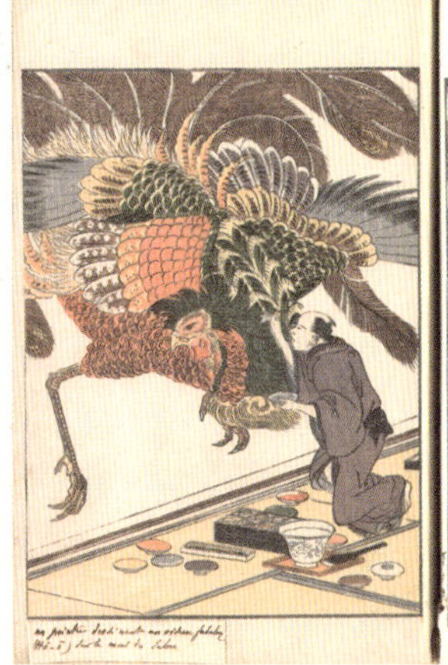
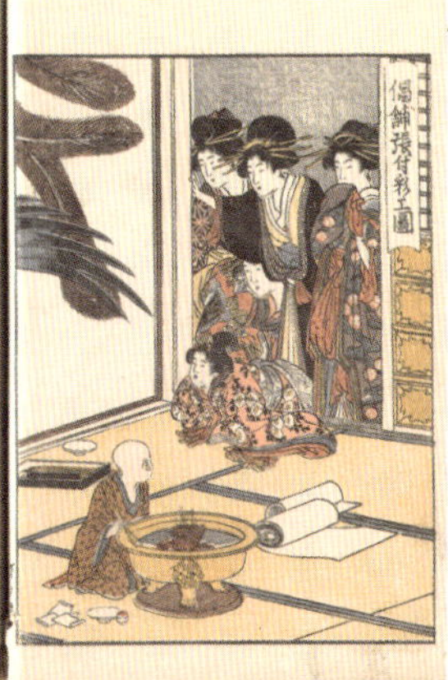

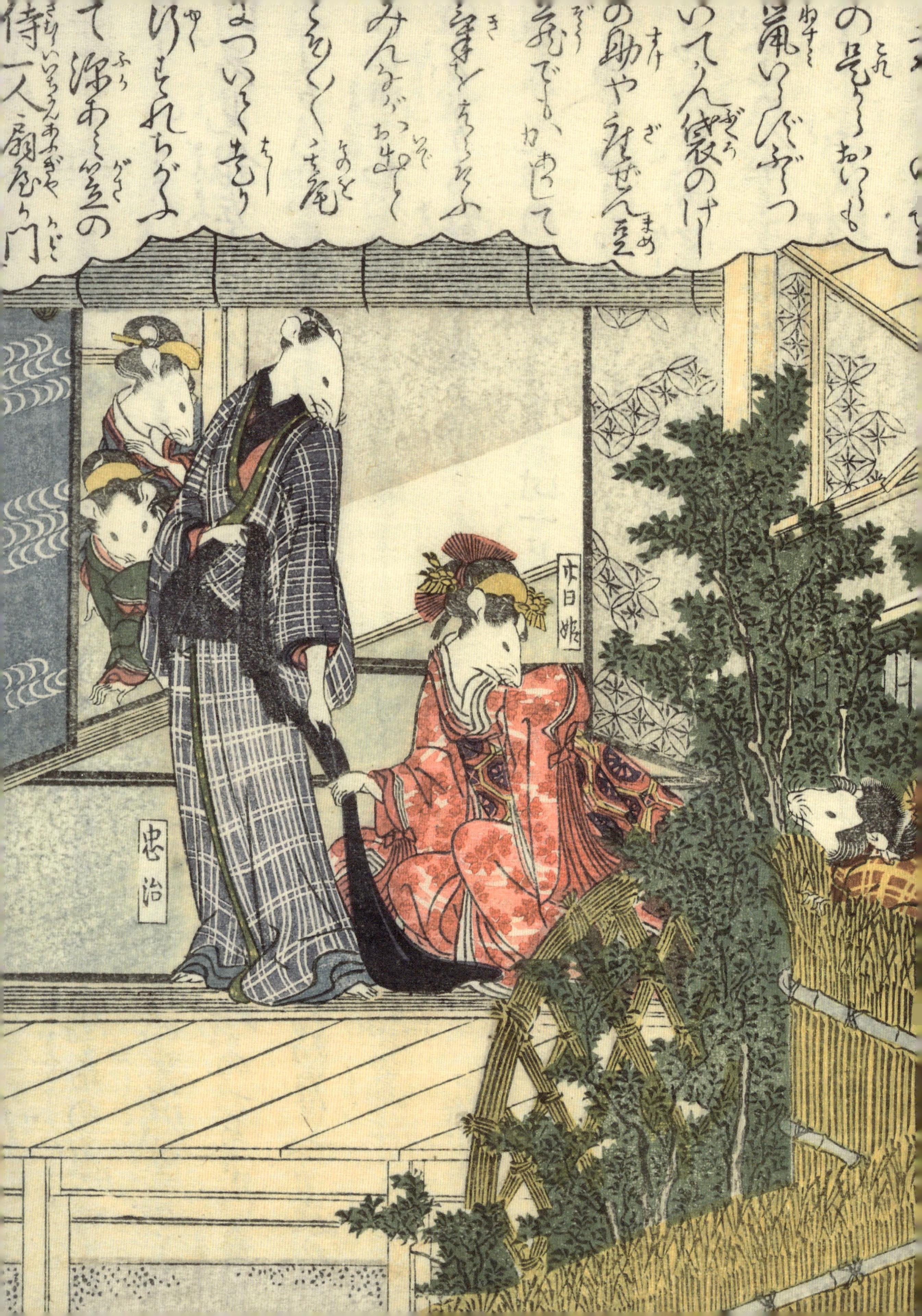

忠治
片日姫

# CHAPTER FOUR

# HUMOROUS STORIES AND FABLES

Humor plays an important role in Japanese visual arts, arguably more so than in any other Asian culture. Some of the earliest surviving paintings, such as the twelfth-century *Scroll of Frolicking Animals and People* (*Chōjū jinbutsu giga*), are of a humorous nature and indicate that interest in this subject has existed for hundreds of years. The *Scroll of Frolicking Animals and People* features linear drawings of comical anthropomorphic animals. From around 1700, similar drawings became popular and were called *toba-e* (lit. "Toba pictures") because the priest Toba Sōjō (Kakuyū, 1053–1140) has traditionally been considered to be the painter of the *Scroll of Frolicking Animals and People*. *Toba-e* were the subject of books as well as single-sheet prints, the latter chiefly by Katsushika Hokusai (1760–1849) who designed well over one hundred of them in the first half of the 1810s.

Humorous subjects were frequented in *kibyōshi* (lit. "yellow covers"), a type of illustrated story book with yellow-colored covers. The books were targeted at adults and were easy to read because they were in vernacular language, written in the widely understood syllables-based *kana* alphabet instead of Chinese characters. The texts wrapped around simple illustrations, which made these novels look like modern comic books. Since they were printed in ink only, the production effort and costs were relatively small, and thus thousands were published. Some authors, like Santō Kyōden (Kitao Masanobu; 1761–1816), specialized in writing *kibyōshi*, and continuously provided readers with an appetite for such stories with new ones.

The most successful humorous story in the Edo period (1603–1868) was *Travels on the Tōkaidō* (*Tōkai dōchū hizakurige*) written by Jippensha Ikku (1765–1831). The comic travelogue follows the adventures of Yaji and Kita (short for Yajirōbei and Kitahachi), two lazybones who embark from Edo (present-day Tokyo) on a journey on foot to the Grand Shrine in Ise. The first volume of Ikku's bestseller was released in 1802, and once he finished the narrative in 1809 he was asked to continue with a sequel that concluded in 1822. Over the following decades, the two books were reprinted many times, and in the 1870s, after Japan was opened to the West, a new fictional story written by Kanagaki Robun (1829–94) took the two protagonists overseas.

**Opposite** Detail from *Fat Tails of Lucky Mice*.

# Comic Pictures to Stop You from Yawning

## *Toba-e akubidome*
鳥羽画あくびとめ

1720
Artist: Unknown
Publisher: Terada Yoemon
Woodblock printed book (*ōhon*); ink on paper
Staatsbibliothek zu Berlin—Preußischer Kulturbesitz, Germany

The priest Toba Sōjō (Kakuyū, 1053–1140) has long been credited as the painter of the *Scroll of Frolicking Animals and People* (*Chōjū jinbutsu giga*), an important set of four handscrolls of comical anthropomorphic animals rendered with linear drawings. Similar drawings became popular from around 1700 and have been called *toba-e* ever since. Two collections of *toba-e*—*Comic Pictures on the Point* (*Toba-e ōgi no mato*) and *Comic Pictures to Stop You from Yawning* (*Toba-e akubidome*)—were compiled into books and issued in Osaka in 1720. The artist of either book is not known with certainty, but it has been speculated that *Comic Pictures on the Point* was drawn by Ōoka Shunboku (1680–1763) and *Comic Pictures to Stop You from Yawning* was created by Takehara Shunchōsai (died 1801). Unquestionably, however, the earliest work by Shunchōsai dates from 1767, and since we know that he died in 1801 it would mean he died at around age 100 in order to be the creater of this book. The confusion over his authorship may have arisen because two reprints were issued during his lifetime, in 1788 and 1793.

The book begins with a preface by Yokomizo Chinjin about whom nothing is known, followed by twenty-nine mostly double-page illustrations presenting a wide array of mishaps. The figures are drawn in caricature style with skinny limbs and gaping

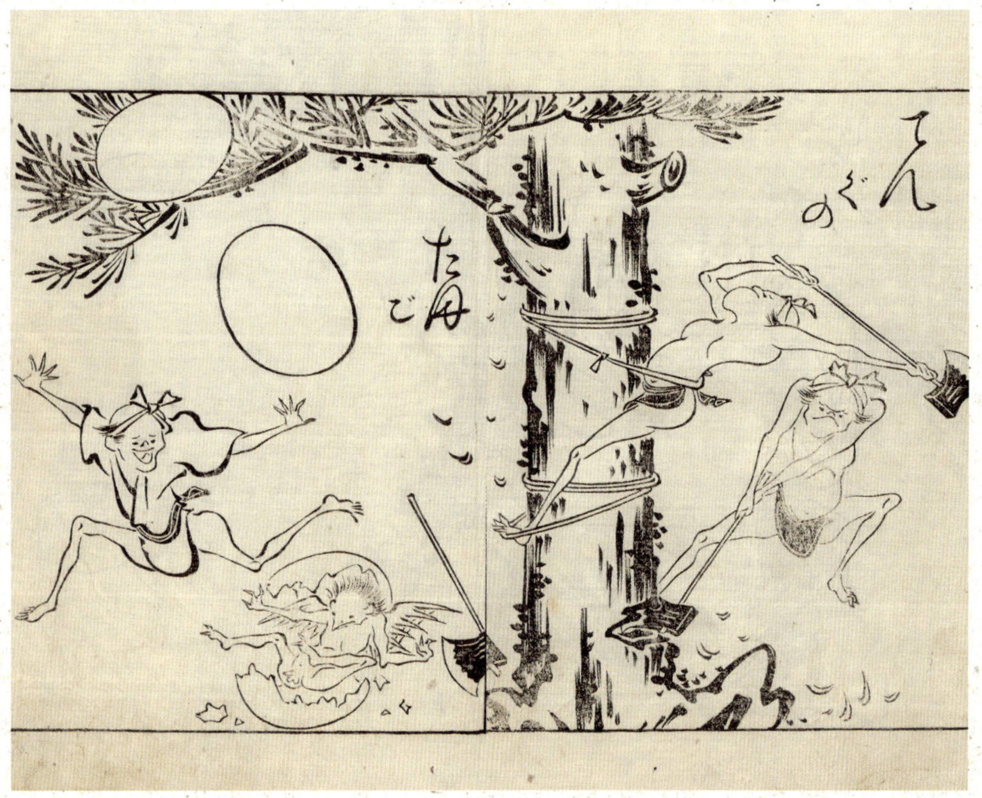

grimaces. The scene "Tengu Eggs (*Tengu no tamago*)" shows eggs with unhatched *tengu* demons falling from a tree that two men are trying to chop down. In "Coastal Fishing (*Hamatsuri*)," the hook of a fisher catches the hair of another. The scene "First Fish of the New Year (*Hatsu no uo*)" depicts one of the porters collapsing under the weight of a gigantic half-fish, while the other porter is fanned fresh air from an old man nearby. In "Mushroom Shelter (*Matsutake-kari*)," people are captured taking cover from torrential rain under a humongous mushroom.

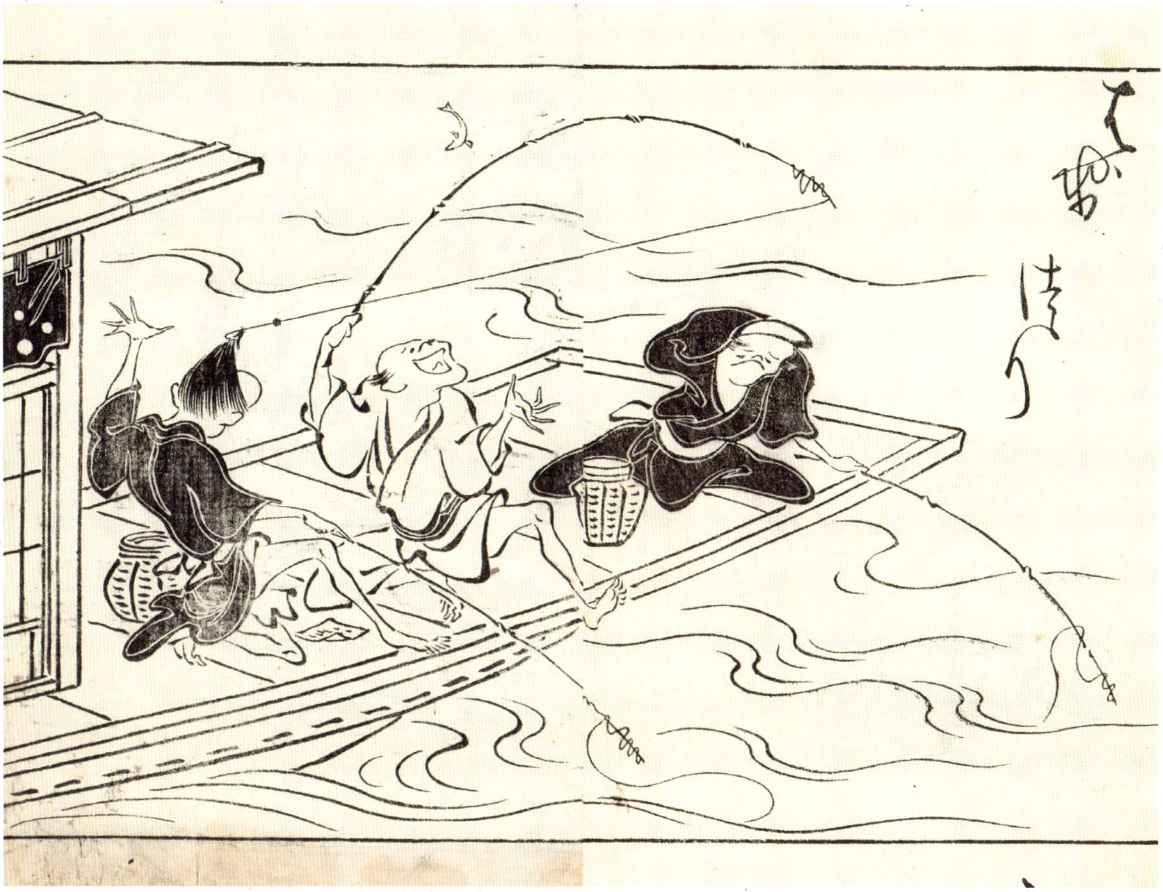

**Opposite** Tengu eggs.

**Above** Coastal fishing.

**Below left** First fish of the New Year.

**Below center** An eagle carries a man away.

**Below right** Mushroom shelter.

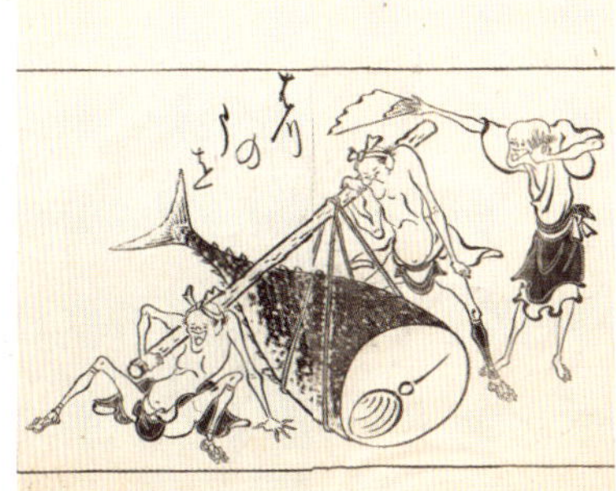

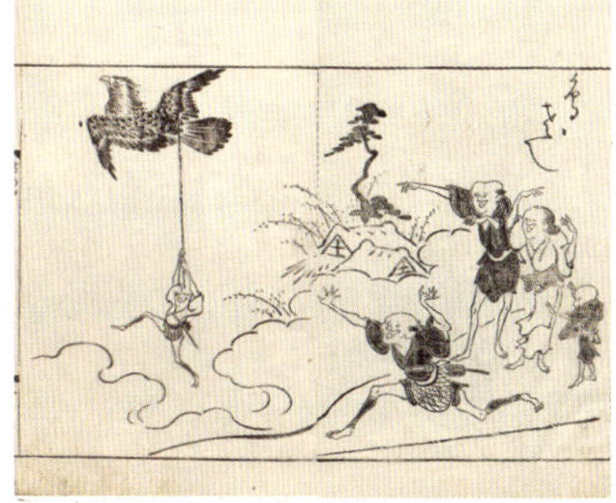

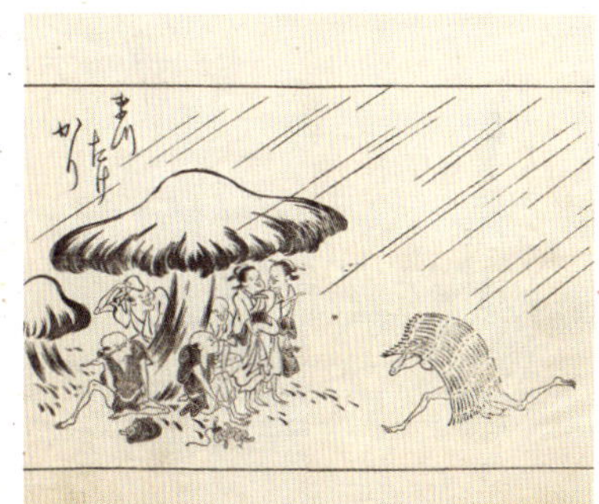

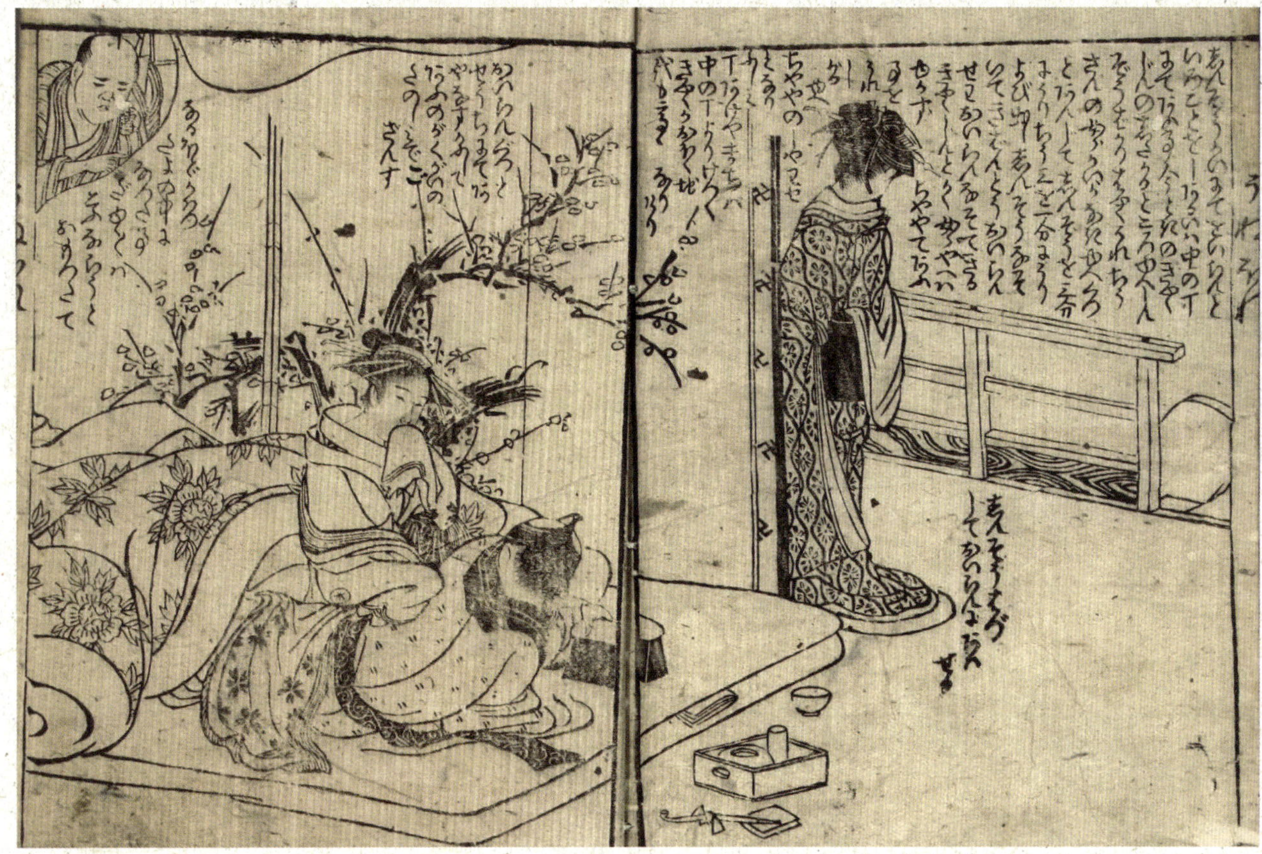

## The Mirror of Self-conceit

### *Kaitsū unubore kagami*

会通己恍惚照子

1788
Author/Artist: Santō Kyōden (Kitao Masanobu; 1761–1816)
Publisher: Nishinomiya Shinroku
Woodblock printed book (*kobon*); ink on paper
Waseda University Library

*Kibyōshi* (lit. "yellow covers") is a type of illustrated storybook that received its name from the yellow-colored covers the books were bound with. This genre was popular in the last decades of the eighteenth century when thousands of them were produced. The stories were straightforward and accessible, typically containing some sort of criticism of contemporary society with a focus on the urban culture of large metropolises like Edo (today's Tokyo) and Osaka. The illustrations of these first comic books in the world were kept simple and the texts were inserted amongst them, interspersed as necessary to fit both on the same page.

Santō Kyōden was one of the most prolific writers of *kibyōshi*, and since he was also a talented painter he provided many of them with his own illustrations. One example is *The Mirror of Self-conceit* (*Kaitsū unubore kagami*), which comprises a one-page preface followed by nine double pages and one single page of picture-text combinations.

Denjirō, the protagonist of the story, dreams of becomng a stylish visitor to the pleasure quarters but, unfortunately, his economic means leave him far from achieving that. Luck strikes when a god gives him a magical mirror with which he can see how people really are and what they think. He visits the Yoshiwara and sees through his mirror, learning that the happiness he witnesses is just an act and all behavior is superficial. He is also shocked to realize that the Yoshiwara is controlled by money. Disappointed and disgusted, Denjirō turns away and begins a life of virtue.

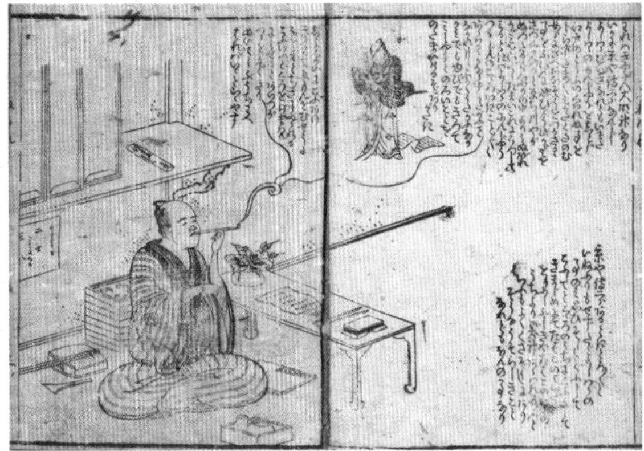

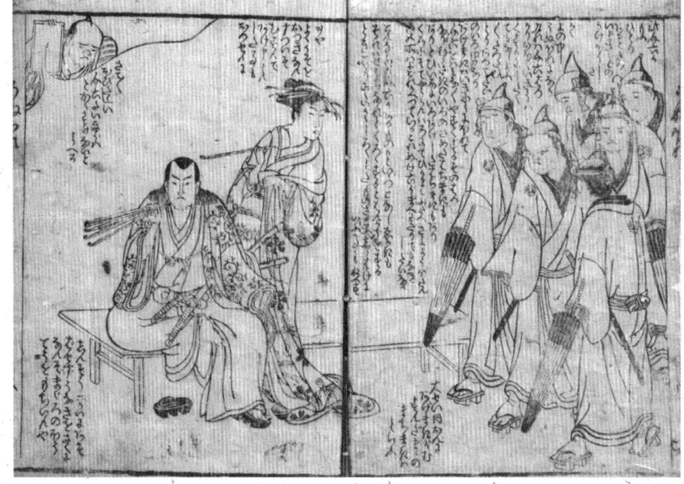

**Opposite** Denjirō dreaming of being with a courtesan.

**Left** Denjirō starts dreaming.

**Below and bottom** Denjirō's dreams.

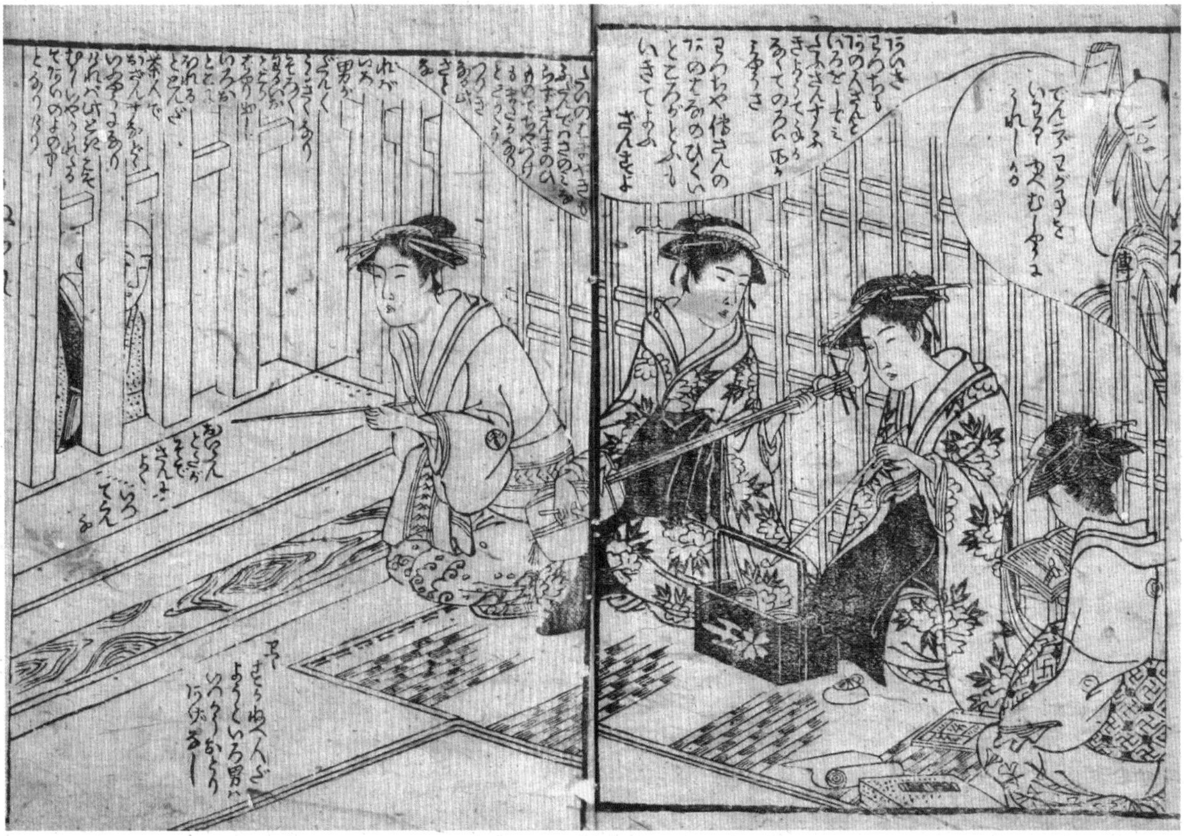

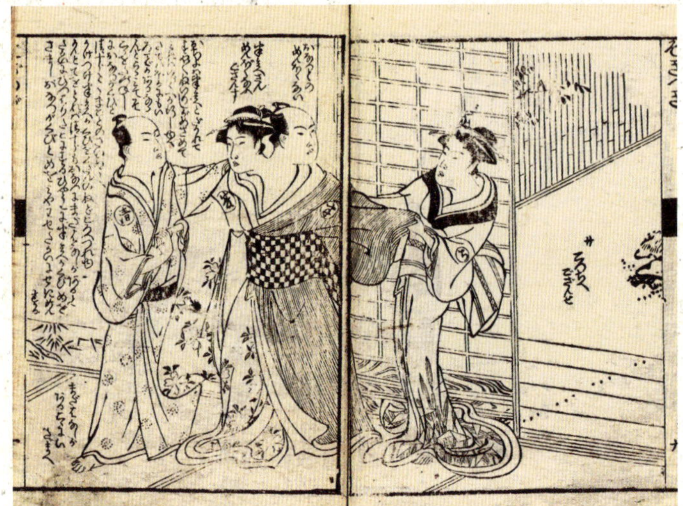







# The Unseamly Silverpiped Swingers

## *Sogitsugi gingiseru*

扮接銀烟管

1788
Author/Artist: Santō Kyōden (Kitao Masanobu; 1761–1816)
Publisher: Nishinomiya Shinroku
Woodblock printed book (*chūbon*); ink on paper
National Diet Library

Santō Kyōden is both the author and illustrator of *The Unseamly Silverpiped Swingers* (*Sogitsugi gingiseru*), which belongs to a specific genre of Japanese literature called *kibyōshi* (lit. "yellow covers") that was popular in the last decades of the eighteenth century. During their heyday, close to a hundred new books were published each year, and the writers and illustrators were under great pressure to conceive new, entertaining stories that contained social satire. *The Unseamly Silverpiped Swingers* is about a pair of conjoined bicephalous twins. Albeit a medical impossibility, they have one torso but two heads, one of which is male, named Hanbei, and the other female, Onatsu. Kyōden's tragic story shows influences of historic events, such as the unsuccessful love-suicide attempt of Onatsu and Seijūrō in 1660 and the successful double suicide of Hanbei and Ochiyo in 1722.

The story of *The Unseamly Silverpiped Swingers* is set in the sixteenth century in the countryside of Yamashiro Province, where a poor huntsman and his wife have two-headed conjoined twins which they name Oinosuke. Unable to provide for them, they sell the twins to a Kyoto sideshow. The twins assume the names Hanbei and Onatsu and are modestly successful as performers in spectacles (*misemono*). The situation becomes complex when each takes a lover, Ochiyo, the daughter of a greengrocer, and Seijūrō, a playboy. Kyōden never reveals the precise nature of the twins' genitalia but merely the enormous logistical problems of the pair having lovers. The result is profound frustration to all involved and the mutual decision that the only solution is a double, double suicide. Before that happens, the twins meet a doctor who is trained in Western medicine and promises to resolve their misery. But before we learn how exactly the impossible can be achieved, the story ends.

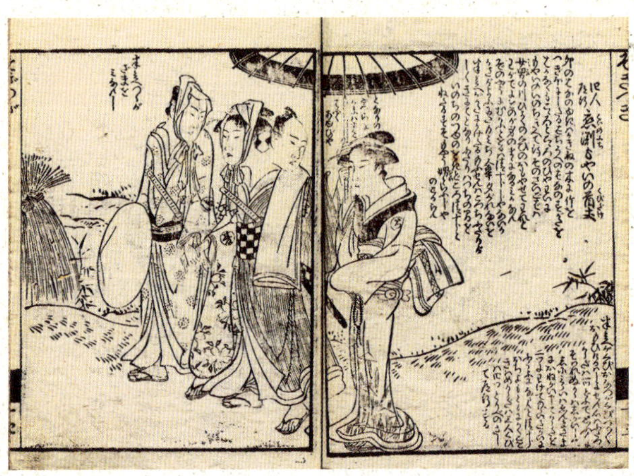

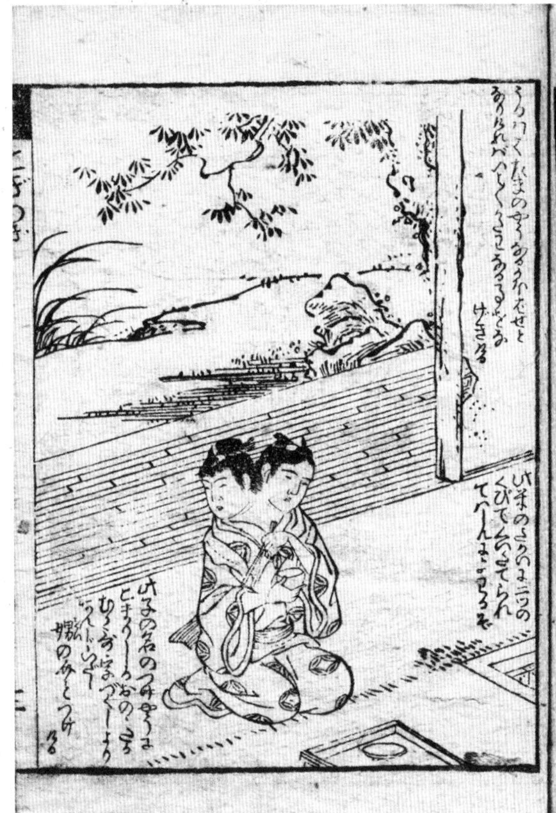
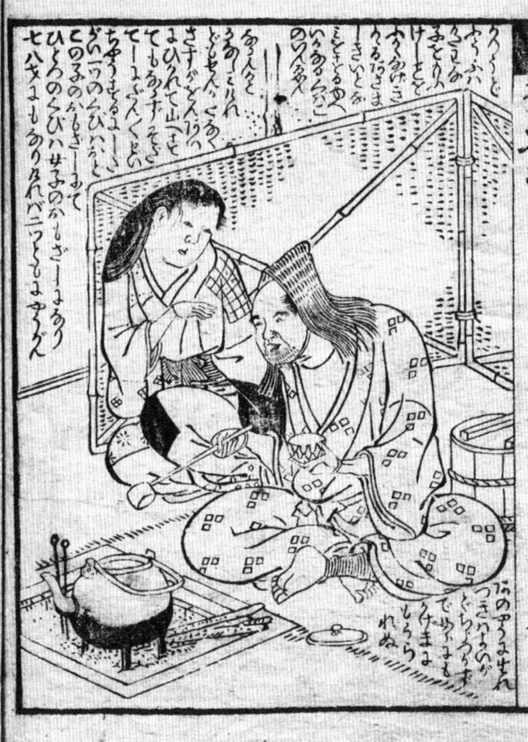
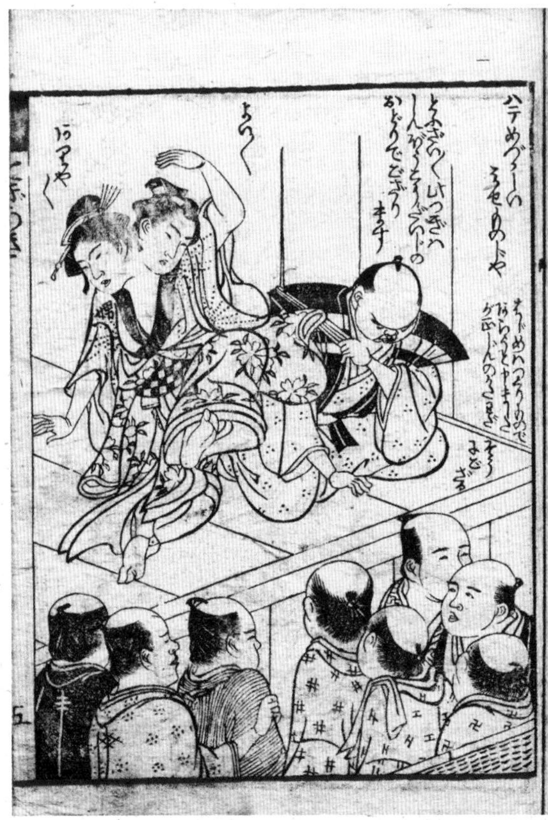
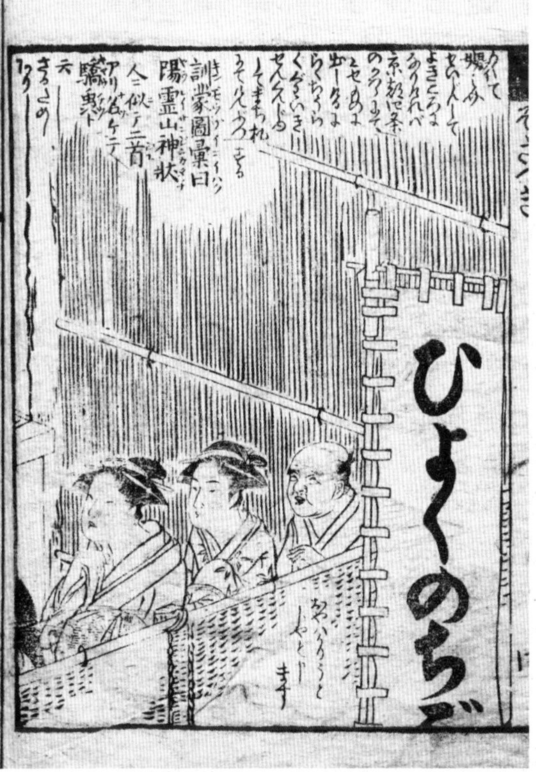

# Ancient Origins of the Tale of Momotarō

## *Mukashi-mukashi Momotarō hottan banashi*

昔々桃太郎發端話説

1793 (3 vols.)
Author: Santō Kyōden (Kitao Masanobu; 1761–1816)
Artist: Katsushika Hokusai (1760–1849)
Publisher: Tsutaya Jūzaburō
Woodblock printed book (*chūbon*); ink on paper
Waseda University Library

**Below** The nasty woman cut out the tongue of the sparrow.

**Opposite above** The sparrow family.

**Opposite below** The nasty woman receives a massive box of monsters.

For the book *Ancient Origins of the Tale of Momotarō* (*Mukashi-mukashi Momotarō hottan banashi*), the author Santō Kyōden combined two folk stories, the legend of Momotarō (lit. "peach boy") and the fable of *The Tongue-cut Sparrow* (*Shitakiri suzume*). A nasty old woman catches a young sparrow eating the paste she has prepared to weigh down her laundry. As punishment, she cuts out his tongue and the battered sparrow hastily flees. A benevolent couple who live next door to the evil woman witness the assault and begin searching for the wounded sparrow. They finally find it in his house where his mother is caring for it. The sparrow family, impressed by these good folk, dance for them, and when the couple is about to leave, they receive a mysterious box. Once they are home, they open the box and find a magical hammer that leaves a piece of gold with every strike. The evil neighbor

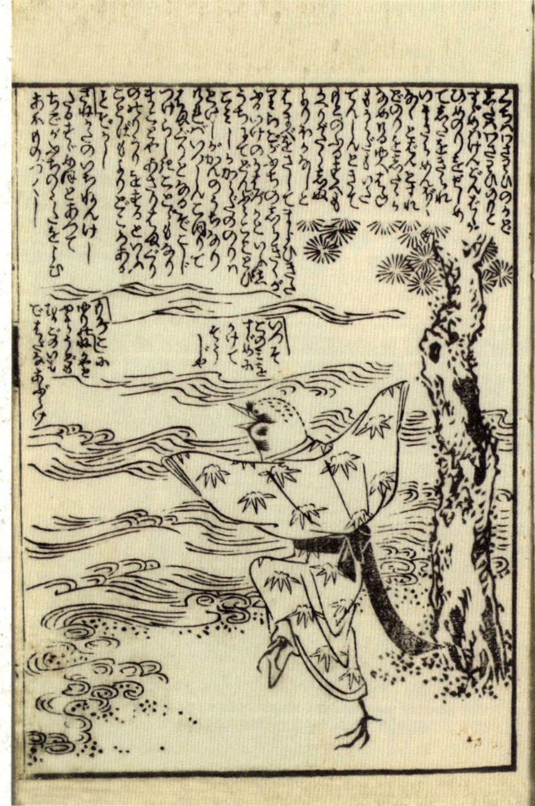

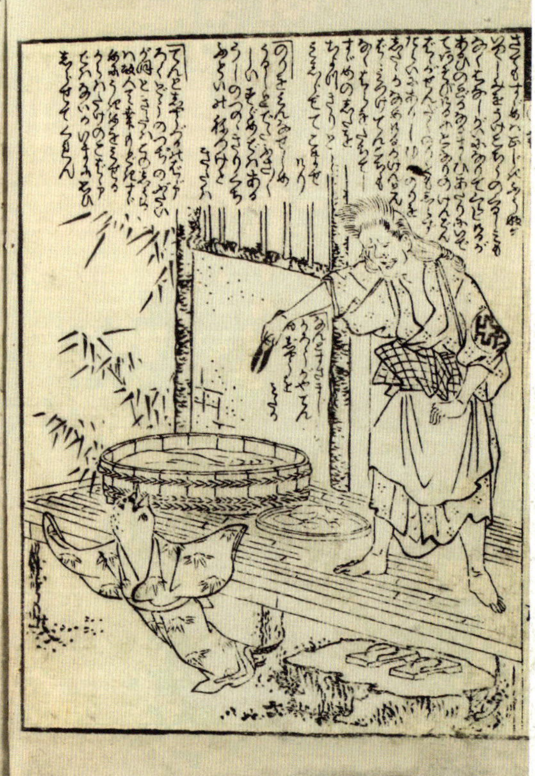

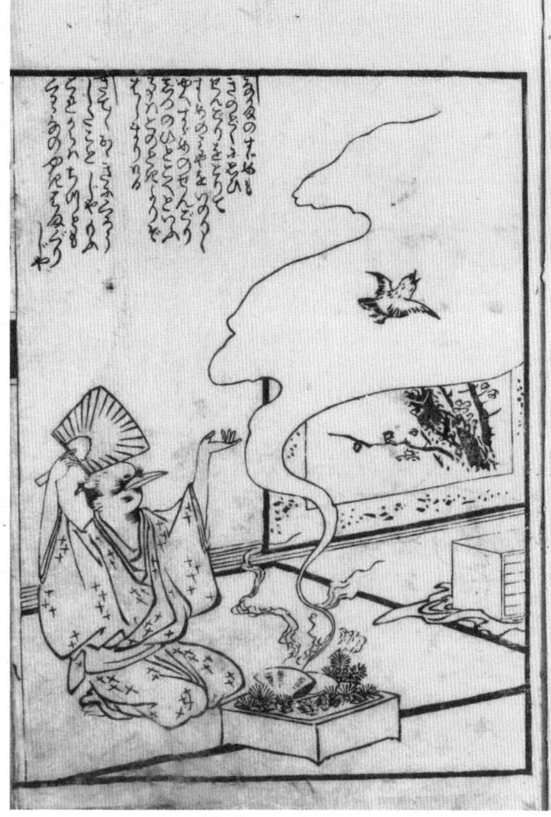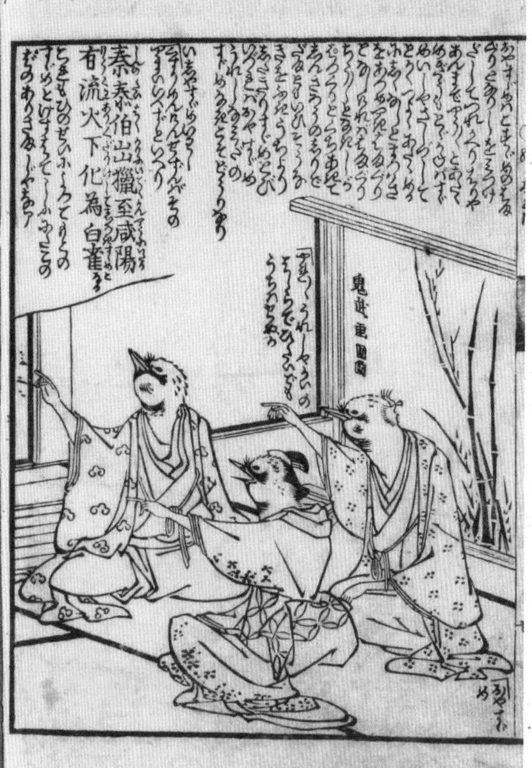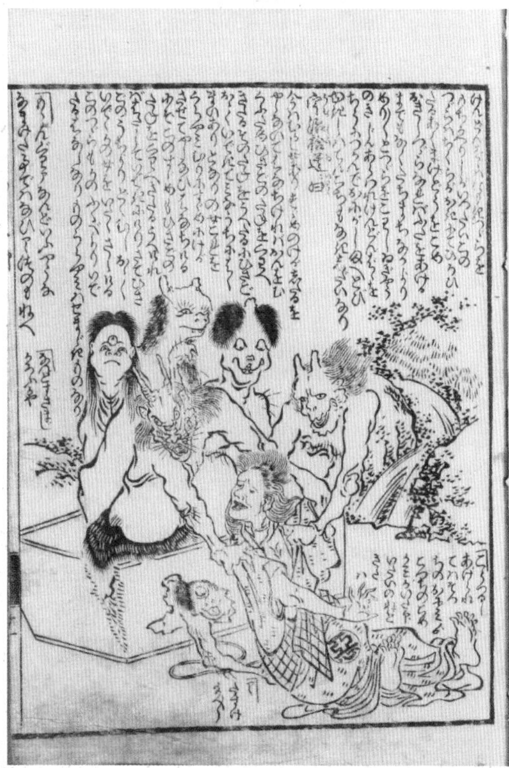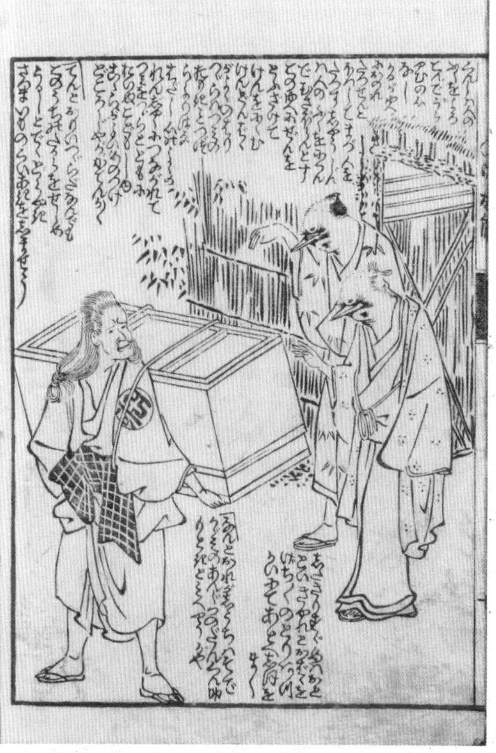

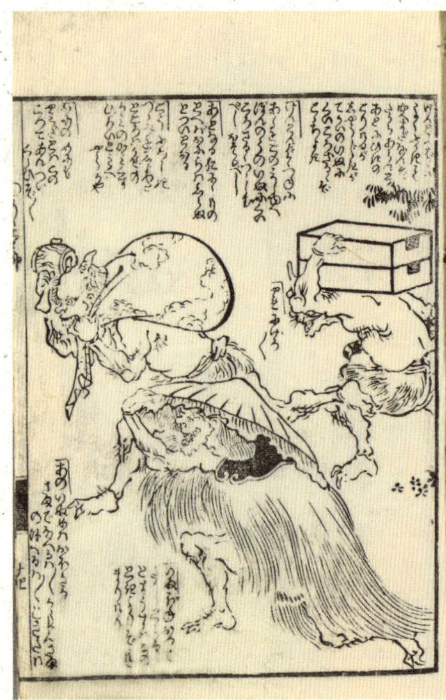

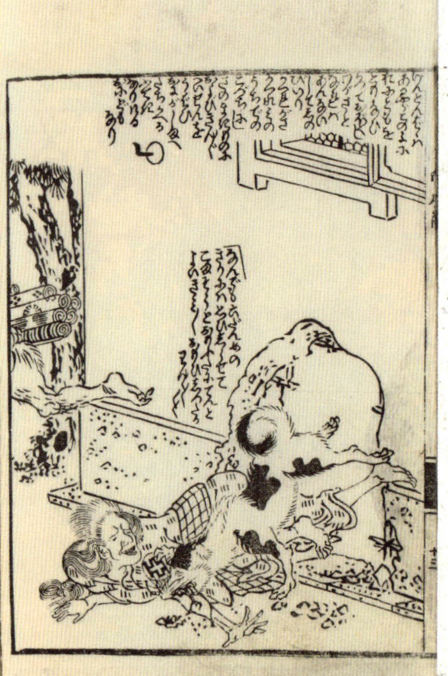



**Left** The monsters steal the belongings of the nasty woman.

**Below** The good woman finds a large peach.

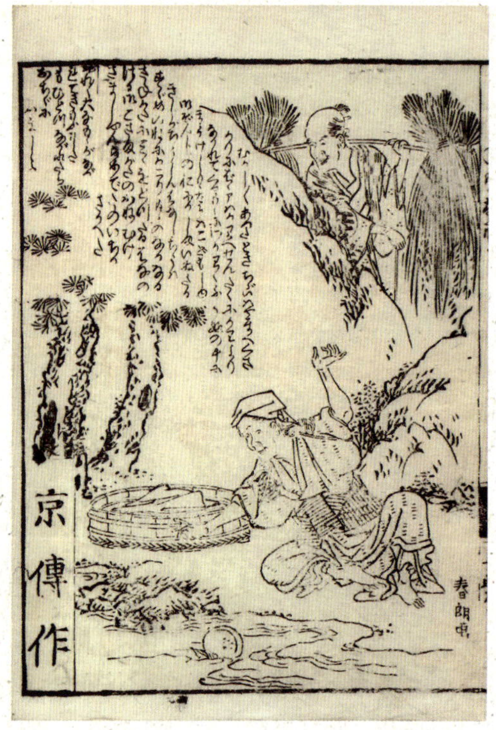


spies this from her window and does everything she can to receive an invitation to the sparrows' home. Eventually, she goes there and receives a massive box. Excited about what treasures might be inside, she opens it when she gets home and out comes a band of horned monsters that tear her to pieces and steal all her belongings. One day, the good woman is washing her clothes at a stream when she finds a large peach which will bear the superhuman Momotarō, who has the power to speak with animals and vanquish monsters.

At the time when the young Katsushika Hokusai was hired for this project, he had already made a name for himself as a designer of actor prints but was also working as a book illustrator. In this book, Hokusai skillfully renders the sparrows anthropomorphic nature by depicting them wearing kimonos and acting like humans.

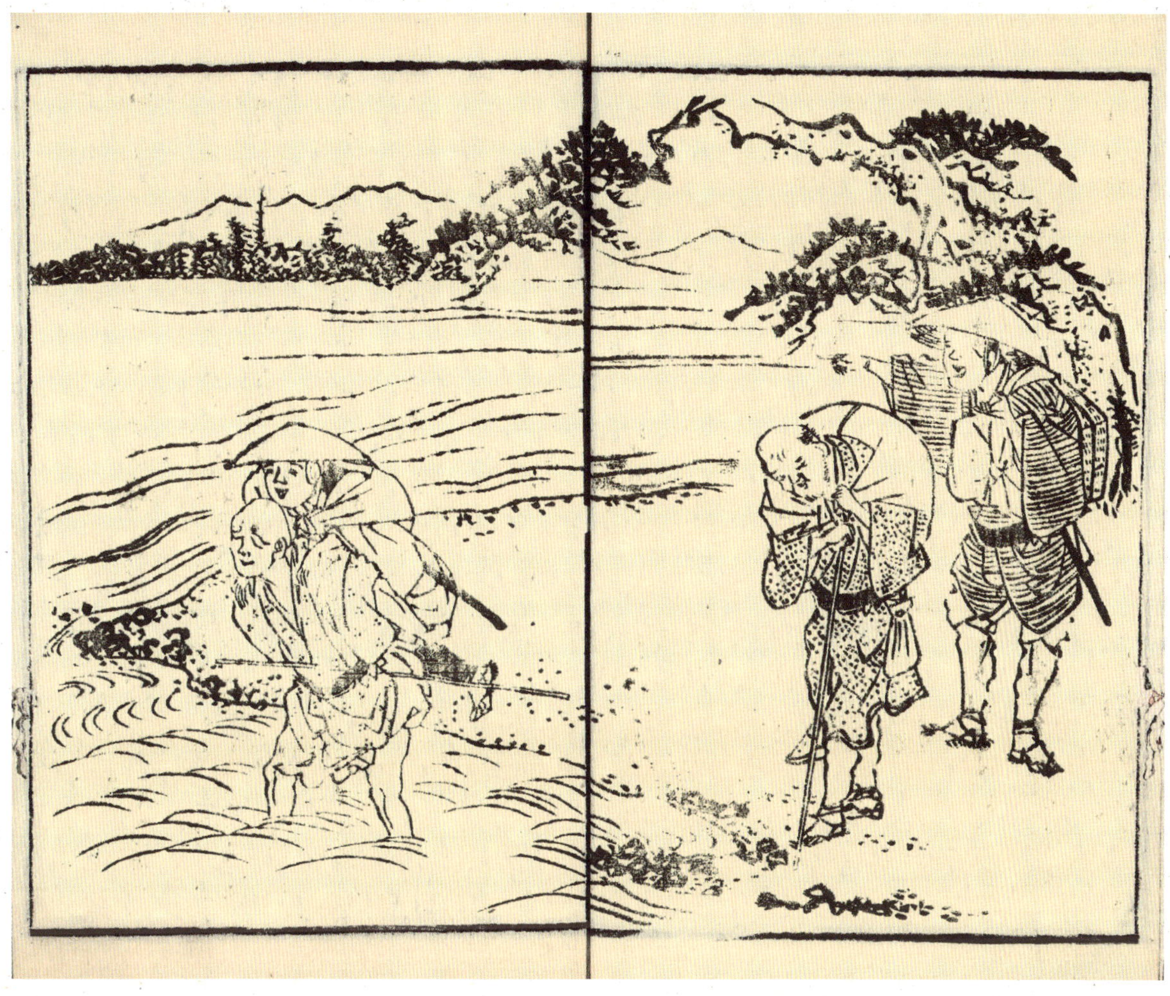



# Travels on the Tōkaidō

## *Tōkai dōchū hizakurige*
東海道中膝栗毛

1802 (vol. 1), 1803 (vol. 2), 1804 (vol. 3), 1805 (vol. 4); 1806 (vol. 5), 1807 (vol. 6), 1808 (vol. 7), 1809 (vol. 8)
Author/Artist: Jippensha Ikku (1765–1831)
Publisher: Murataya Jirōbei
Woodblock printed book (*chūbon*); ink on paper
Waseda University Library

*Tōkai dōchū hizakurige*, in English *Travels on the Tōkaidō* but commonly known as *Shank's Mare* through the 1960 translation by Thomas Satchell, is a comical novel by the popular fiction writer Jippensha Ikku. It is Ikku's most successful novel and masterpiece for which he became best known. The story follows the adventures of Yajirōbei and Kitahachi (Yaji and Kita for short), two ne'er-do-wells who

embark from Edo (today's Tokyo) on a pilgrimage. The objective is to reach the Grand Shrine in Ise along the Tōkaidō, Japan's most popular highway that connected Edo with Kyoto along the coast. During that time, travel was popular but costly, and permission was also needed. Ikku himself was an avid traveler, and his experiences are reflected in his texts. The name of the artist is not noted for the few single- and double-page illustrations interspersed within the text and it can be assumed that Ikku provided them himself. They are rather simply rendered but fit in with the comical characters and their mishaps. Publication began in 1802 and was completed in 1809. Due to its tremendous success, Ikku was hired to create a sequel (*Zoku hizakurige*),

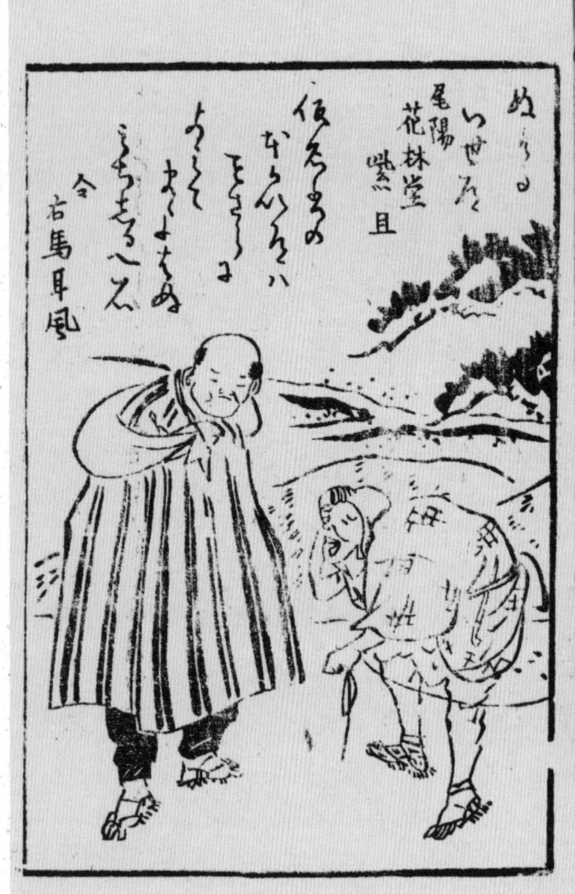
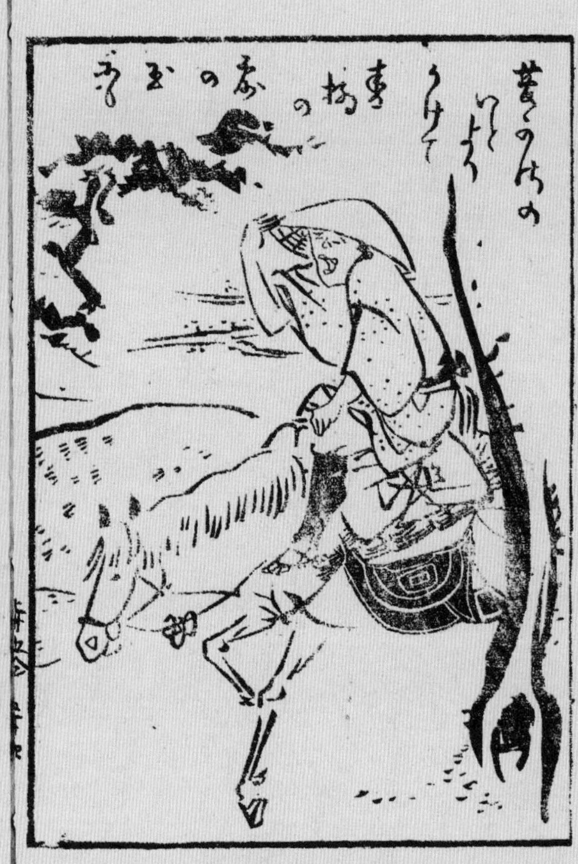

**Above** Vol. 5, traveling on horseback.

**Below** Vol. 3, a blind monk enjoying a meal.

with publication beginning in 1810 and continuing for another twelve years. For the sequel, amongst others some of Kitagawa Utamaro's (ca. 1754–1806) students, such as Tsukimaro (active ca. 1794–1836) and Shikimaro (active ca. 1810s) were hired.

In their journeys, Yaji and Kita demonstrate a rather low level of intelligence and repeatedly fail. Their focus is on finding good food and women, both common entertainments offered in the inns along the road. While they make embarrassing mistakes, such as not knowing how to use a bathtub, they are never seriously injured and are thus able to continue their journey to Kyoto and Osaka.

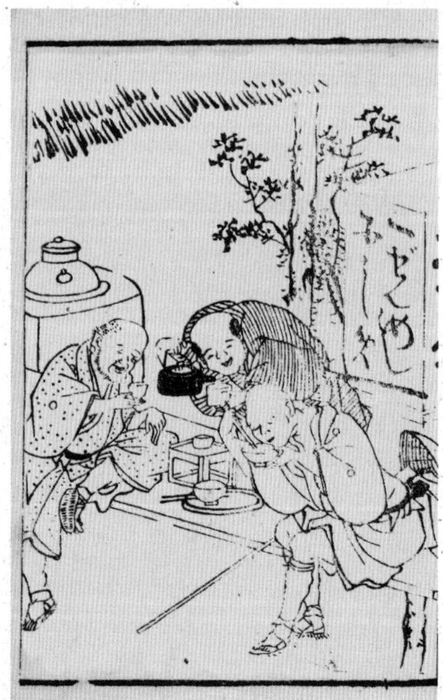

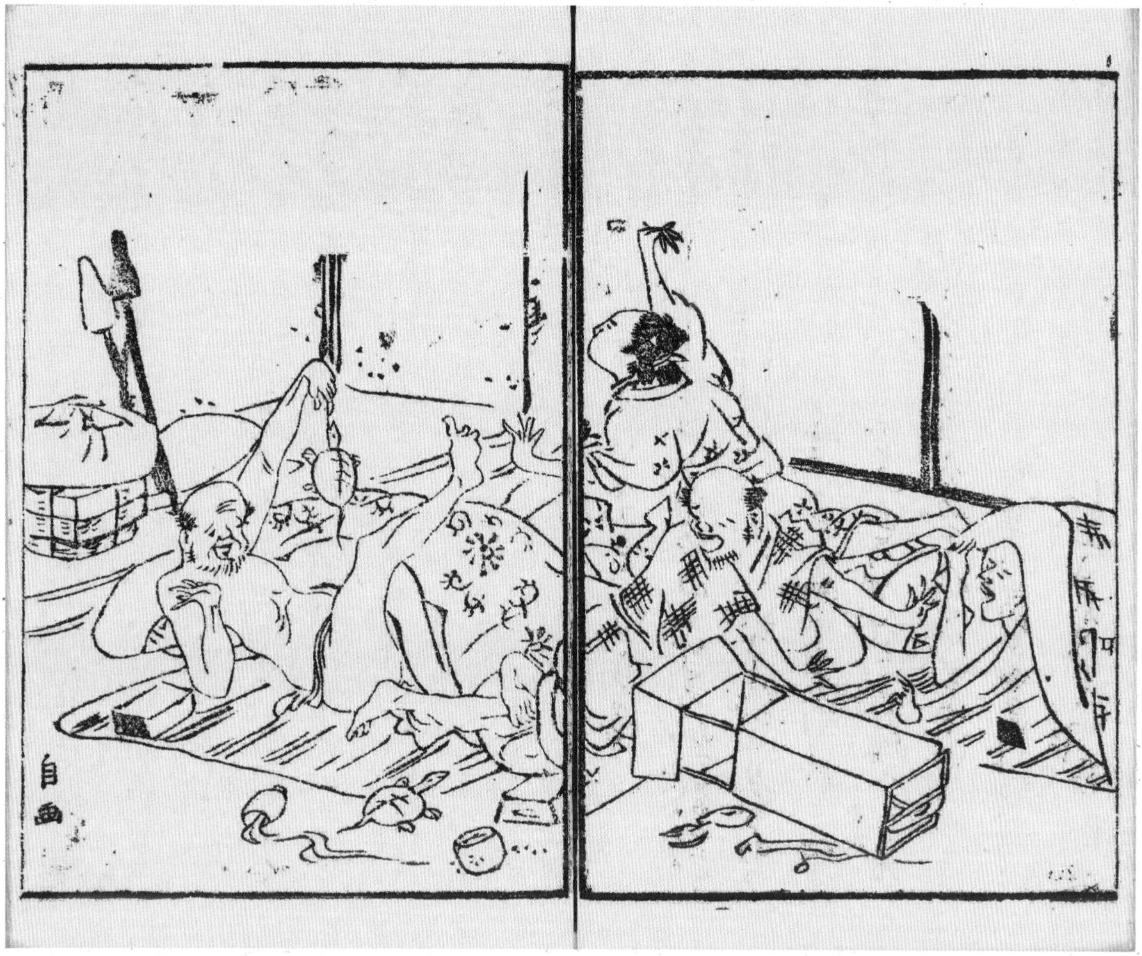

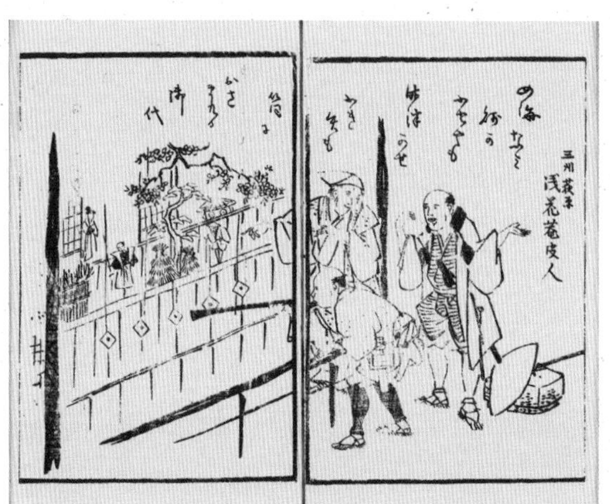

**Above** Vol. 2, woken up by snapping turtles.

**Below** Vol. 5, a blowgun contest.

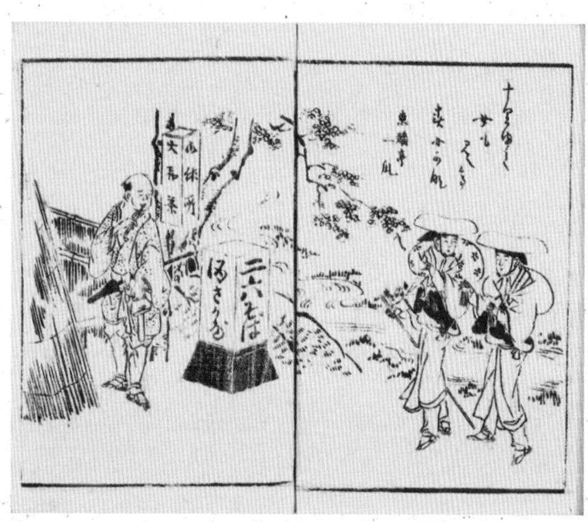

**Below** Vol. 4, two women approaching an inn.

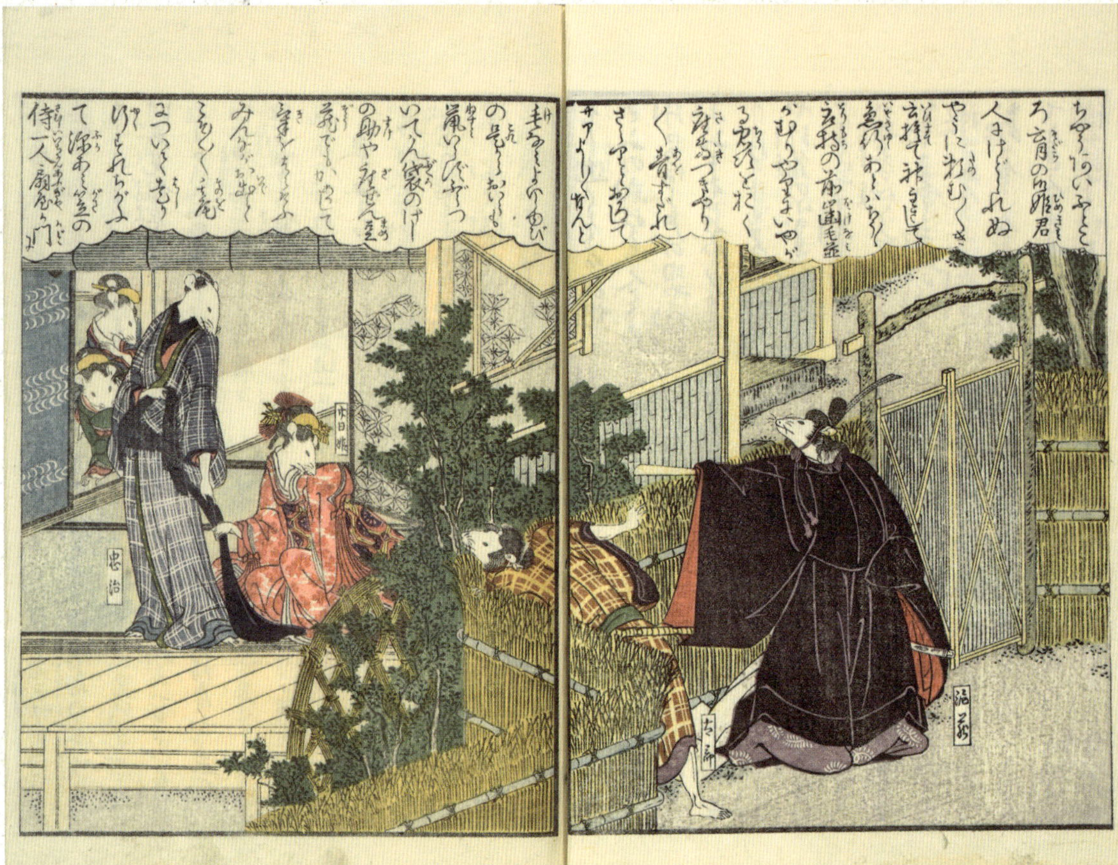

# Fat Tails of Lucky Mice

## *Fukunezumi shirio no futozao*

福鼠尻尾太棹

1804
Author: Sakuragawa Jihinari (1762–1833)
Artist: Utagawa Toyohiro (1773–1828)
Publishers: Yamadaya Sanshirō, Ōmiya Yohei
Woodblock printed book (*hanshibon*); ink and color on paper
Chester Beatty

Sakuragawa Jihinari was a playwright and professional *rakugo*, or storyteller. Outstanding amongst his publications is the book *Fat Tails of Lucky Mice* (*Fukunezumi shirio no futozao*), which was luxuriously printed in color in 1804. It seems, however, that this was done without proper permission, as five months later the magistrates in Edo confiscated the color blocks and ordered the book to be printed henceforth only in black.

*Fukunezumi*, white mice that bring luck, are the protagonists of this story. For the project, Utagawa Toyohiro, a print artist popular for his landscape designs and portraits of beautiful women, was engaged to draw the anthropomorphic mice. Toyohiro renders the mice as tall, small-headed, but elegant figures. The entertaining story is about the love between the Princess Hatsuka and the townsman Chūji that causes a commotion in the imperial family; the message: true love is hard to achieve, even amongst mice.

The first volume contains five double pages and one single-page illustration, separated by text pages. The second volume follows the same format but contains six double-page illustrations. The first and last illustrations of the combined volumes have no text, but all other double-page illustrations are furnished with a cloud band at the top containing text. On the side of each mouse character is a small cartouche inscribed with its name.

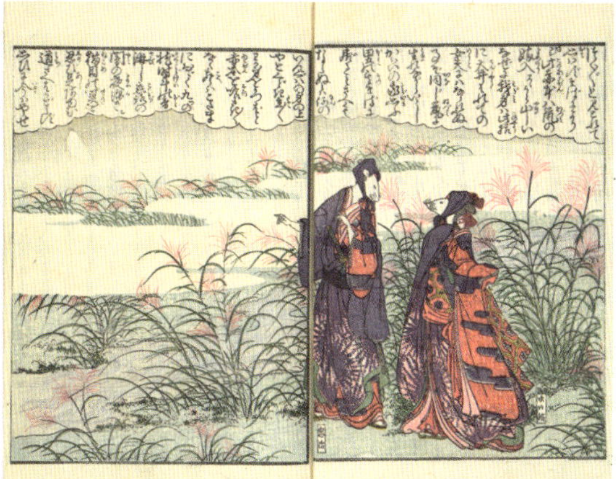

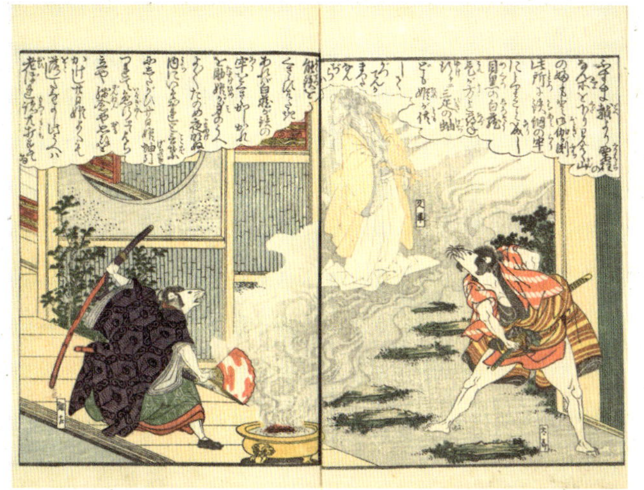

**Opposite** The love between Chūji and Hatsuka is revealed.

**Left** The apparition of Kyūso.

**Above** Chūji and Hatsuka on an outing.

**Below** Hatsuka and her entourage enjoy cherry blossoms.

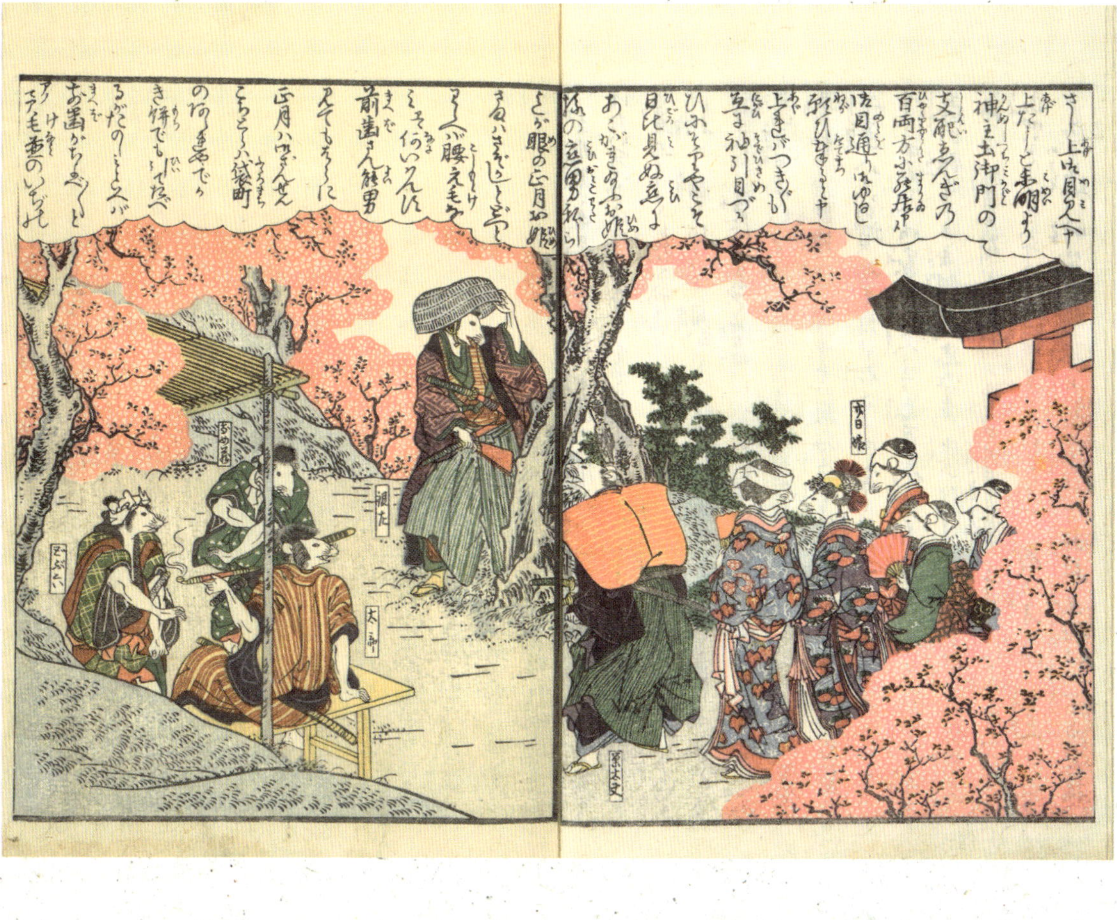

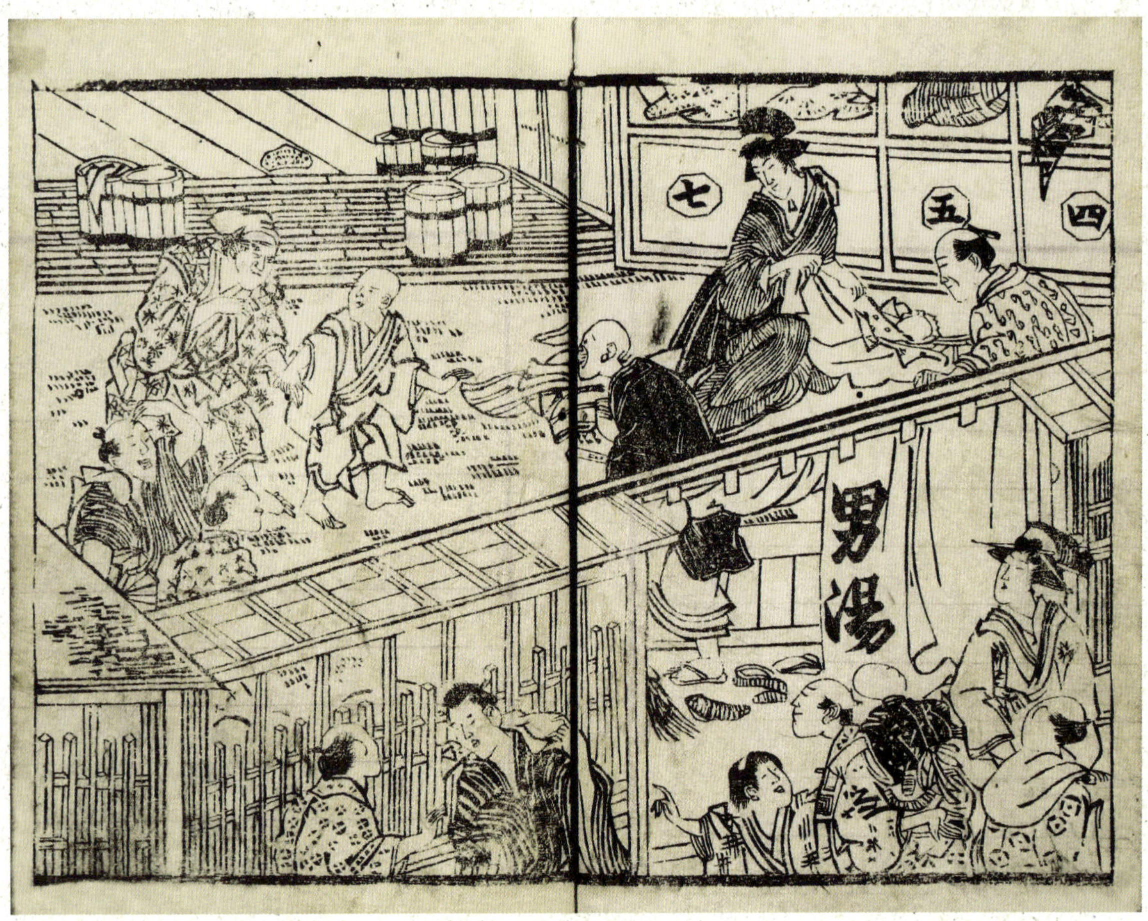

# Bathhouse to the
# Floating World

*Ukiyo buro*
浮世風呂

1809 (vol. 1), 1810 (vol. 2), 1812 (vol. 3), 1813 (vol. 4)
Author: Shikitei Sanba (1776–1822)
Artists: vol. 1: Kitao Shigemasa II (active ca. 1809–45); vols. 2–4:
Utagawa Kuninao (1793–1854)
Publishers: Ishiwatari Risuke, Nishimuraya Genroku
Woodblock printed book (*chūbon*); ink on paper
Waseda University Library

Shikitei Sanba, the son of a Shinto priest, first gained
recognition in 1799 with a comical retelling of a
dispute between two rival groups of firefighters in
Edo (today's Tokyo). One group, feeling insulted by
Sanba, attacked him and his publisher. The government punished everyone involved and Sanba was
forced to wear handcuffs for fifty days. *Bathhouse*

to the Floating World (*Ukiyo buro*) is the earlier of
two comic masterpieces that confirmed his reputa-
tion. Seven volumes were originally advertised but
only four were produced. Each volume takes place
at a specific location. The first and fourth volumes
contain stories from a men's bathhouse, the second
and third from a women's. Typically, bathhouses,
where people soaked in hot water, were a popular
place of social exchange for the common people.
Sanba retells mostly trivial chats between friends
or with strangers and captures the varying manners
of speech of the different townspeople, such as
merchants inserting advertising for their products
into their stories, or scholars frantically trying to
educate others.

The amusing text is interspersed with only a few
(mostly two-page) illustrations, thus, the text-image

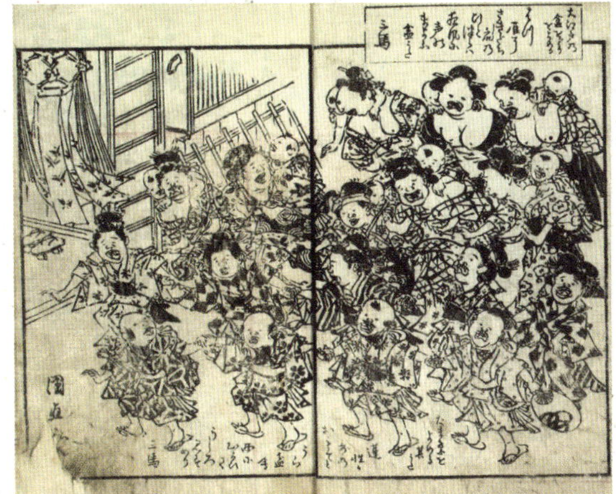

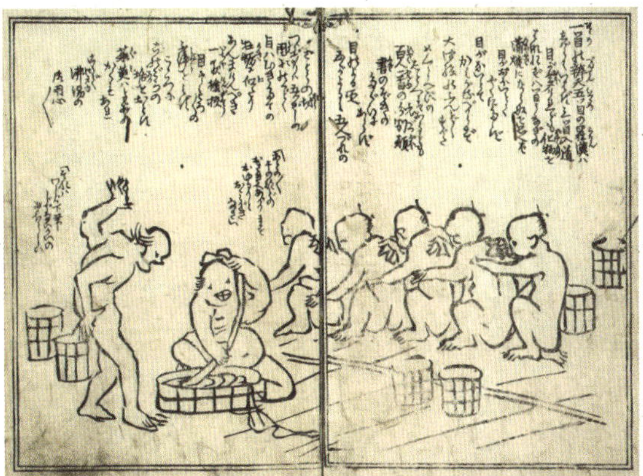



ratio is eight to one. The two artists who provided the images for the different volumes were not famous. The first volume contains eight pictures signed by Kitagawa Yoshimaru (later named Kitao Shigemasa II), which appear to be his earliest published work. The second volume also seems to be a debut work, this time for Utagawa Kuninao, a seventeen-year-old student of the popular designer of actor prints Utagawa Toyokuni (1769–1825). Hiring young and unknown artists suggests that the budget for this production was rather small, and it is likely that the publishers were reluctant to invest a lot of money in the book since they were wary about its commercial success.

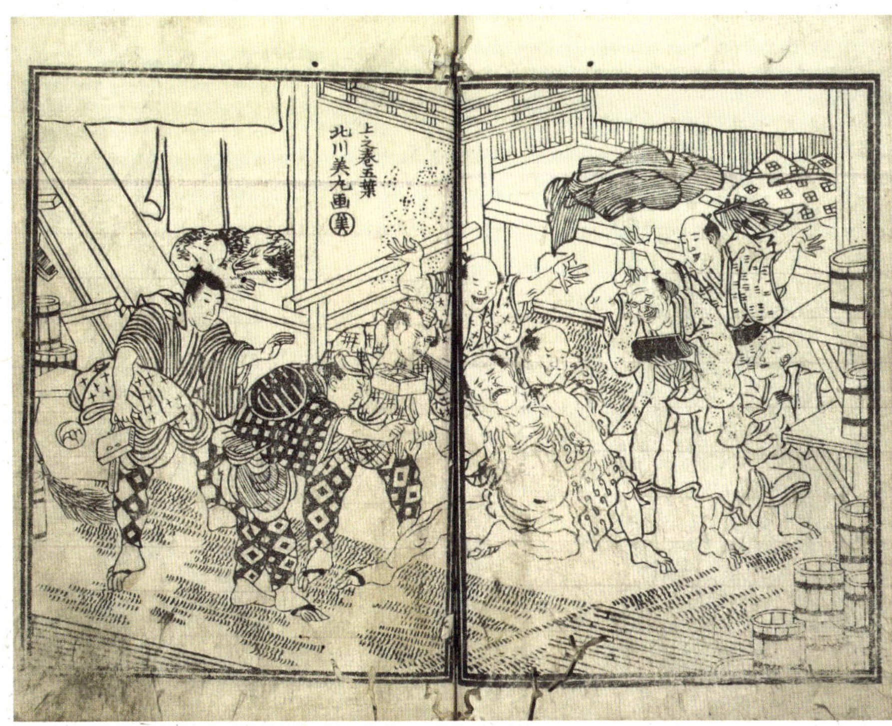

**Right** Vol. 1, Yoiyoi accidentally fell in the water.

# What Fun!

## *Otsuriki*
於都里伎

1810
Author: Jippensha Ikku (1765–1831)
Artist: Kitagawa Tsukimaro (act. ca. 1794–1836)
Publisher: Murataya Jirobei
Woodblock printed book (*chūbon*); ink on paper
Waseda University Library

Creating shadow plays was an entertaining activity, and in the book *What Fun!* (*Otsuriki*), the author Jippensha Ikku and artist Kitagawa Tsukimaro present nineteen pictures showing how to do this. Ikku was one of the most prolific writers of comical light fiction, composing over twenty novels each year between 1795 and 1801. Tsukimaro was the principal student of one of the most influential designers of woodblock prints, Kitagawa Utamaro (ca. 1754–1806), but little is known about him.

The pictures are Dutch (*Oranda*), which means they are of Western origin and therefore strange and exotic. The event where the pictures were presented is stated as a drinking party of Dutch traders in Nagasaki; the Dutch were the only Westerners allowed to do business in Japan during the Edo period (1603–1868) and only in enclaves like Nagasaki.

The book is a parody, thus Ikku's texts underline the humorous character of the book with sentences like "I feel sorry for your wife and children who rely on your excuses." It provides both the shadow image as well as how this was achieved. First, the shadow image is displayed, then after flipping the page, the reader is presented with the extraordinary effort required to achieve it. The book is conceived like a quiz game. Nothing is straightforward, and when the solution is finally

**Below** View of Maruyama Street in Nagasaki.

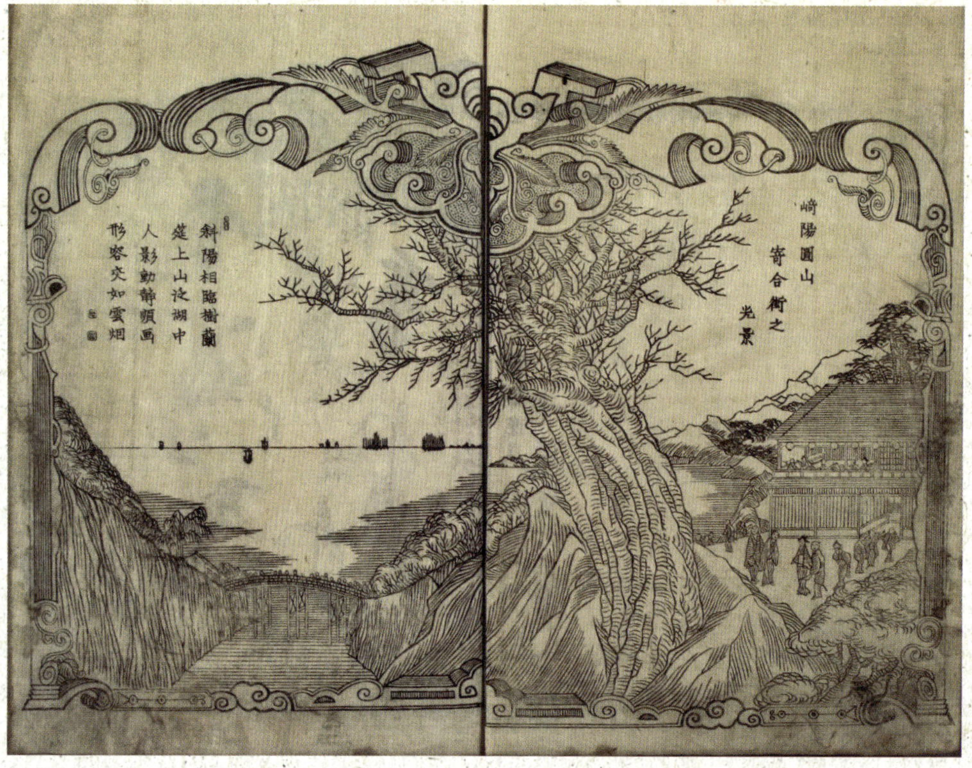

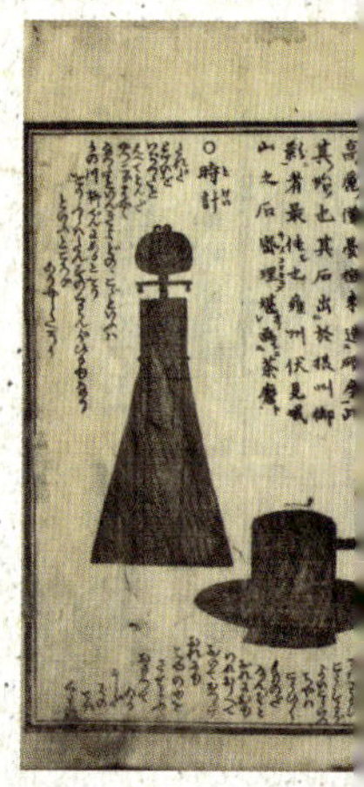

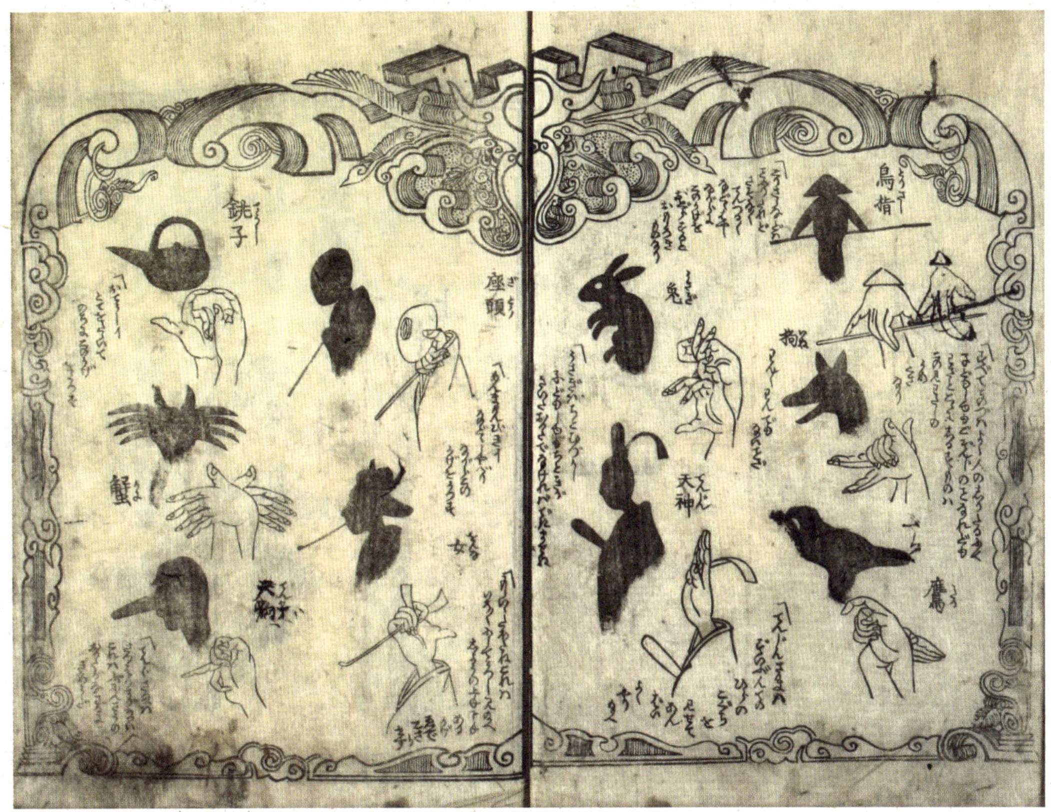

revealed, it is hilarious. A *torii* gate, for example, is achieved by three men, with two serving as beams and a third lying horizontally, balancing on the others' heads. Other shadows were achieved through acrobatics with items such as lanterns, hairpins, bridges, braziers, frogs, a duo of long arms and long legs. One spread introduces the more ordinary hand shadows that include a bird on a twig, a dog, a hawk, a rabbit, the Shinto god Tenjin, a blind monk, a woman, a kettle, a crab, and a *tengu* demon.

**Above** Hand shadows.

**Below** Figure shadows.

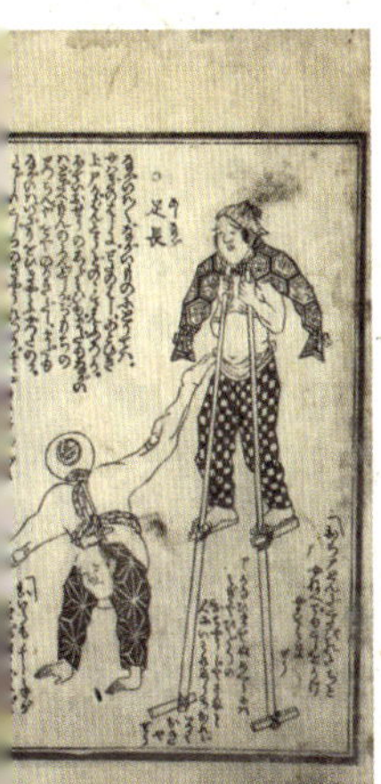

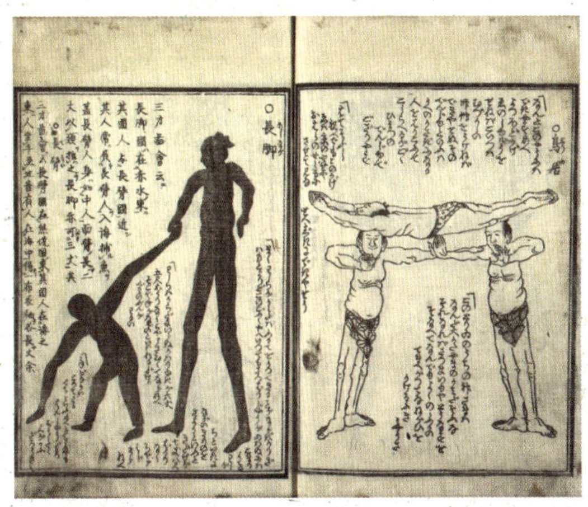

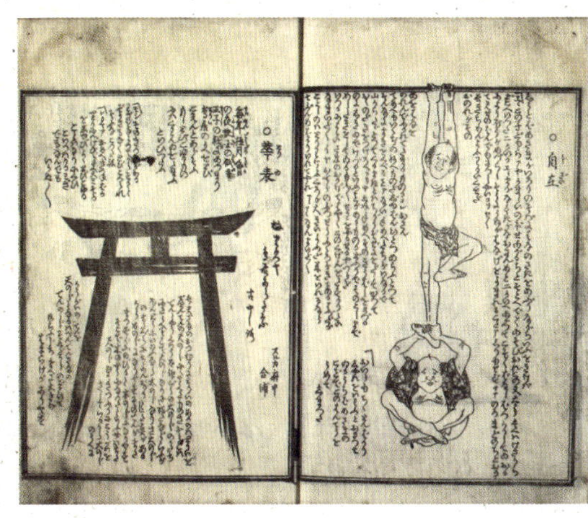

# Travels round the West

## *Seiyō dōchū hizakurige*

西洋道中膝栗毛

1870 (vols. 1–2), 1871 (vols. 3–9), 1872 (vols. 10–11), 1873 (vol. 12), ca. 1873–76 (vols. 13–14)

Author: Kanagaki Robun (1829–94)

Artists: vols. 1–4, 6–11: Utagawa Yoshiiku (1833–1904); vol. 5: Utagawa Hiroshige III (1842–94); vols. 12–14: Kawanabe Kyōsai (1831–89)

Publisher: Wan'ya Kihei

Woodblock printed book (*chūbon*); ink on paper

Waseda University Library

Jippensha Ikku scored a remarkable hit with his comic travelogue *Travels on the Tōkaidō* (*Tōkai dōchū hizakurige*) and its sequels (see p. 95), which were published between 1802 and 1822. The success continued in the decades to follow as the books were reprinted many times to meet steady demand. Japan had been secluded until the mid-nineteenth century when Western forces pried it open, causing an influx of information about faraway countries and their

**Below** A battle in Europe.

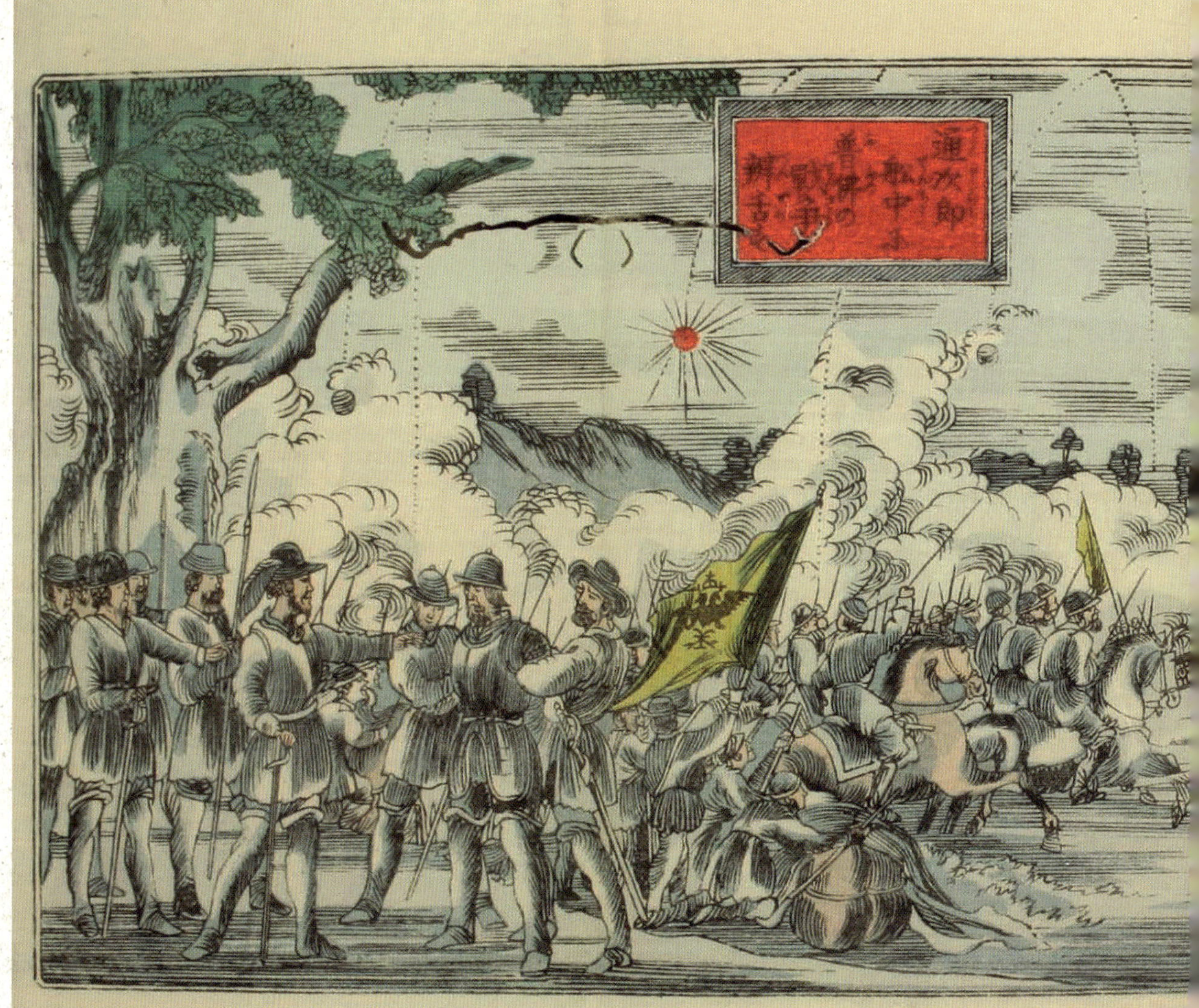

cultures. The modernization and Westernization of Japan was launched even more vigorously when Emperor Meiji (1852–1912) took the throne in 1868.

In 1870, publication began of *Travels round the West* (*Seiyō dōchū hizakurige*), written by the novelist Kanagaki Robun. This sequel to Ikku's book was an imitation composed in a style familiar to readers. Ikku's two clumsy protagonists, Yajirōbei and Kitahachi (Yaji and Kita for short), are this time not traveling in Japan but overseas, from Edo (today's Tokyo) to London. As usual, they stumble into situations where they end up embarrassing themselves.

Utagawa Yoshiiku was charged with the illustrations, and these show the same simple drawing style as those in the original novel. However, there are some exceptions, with some illustrations drawn in much greater detail and colorized. Especially remarkable is an illustration in volume 6 that folds out to a four-page spread and captures a land battle in Europe where the air is filled with cannon smoke.

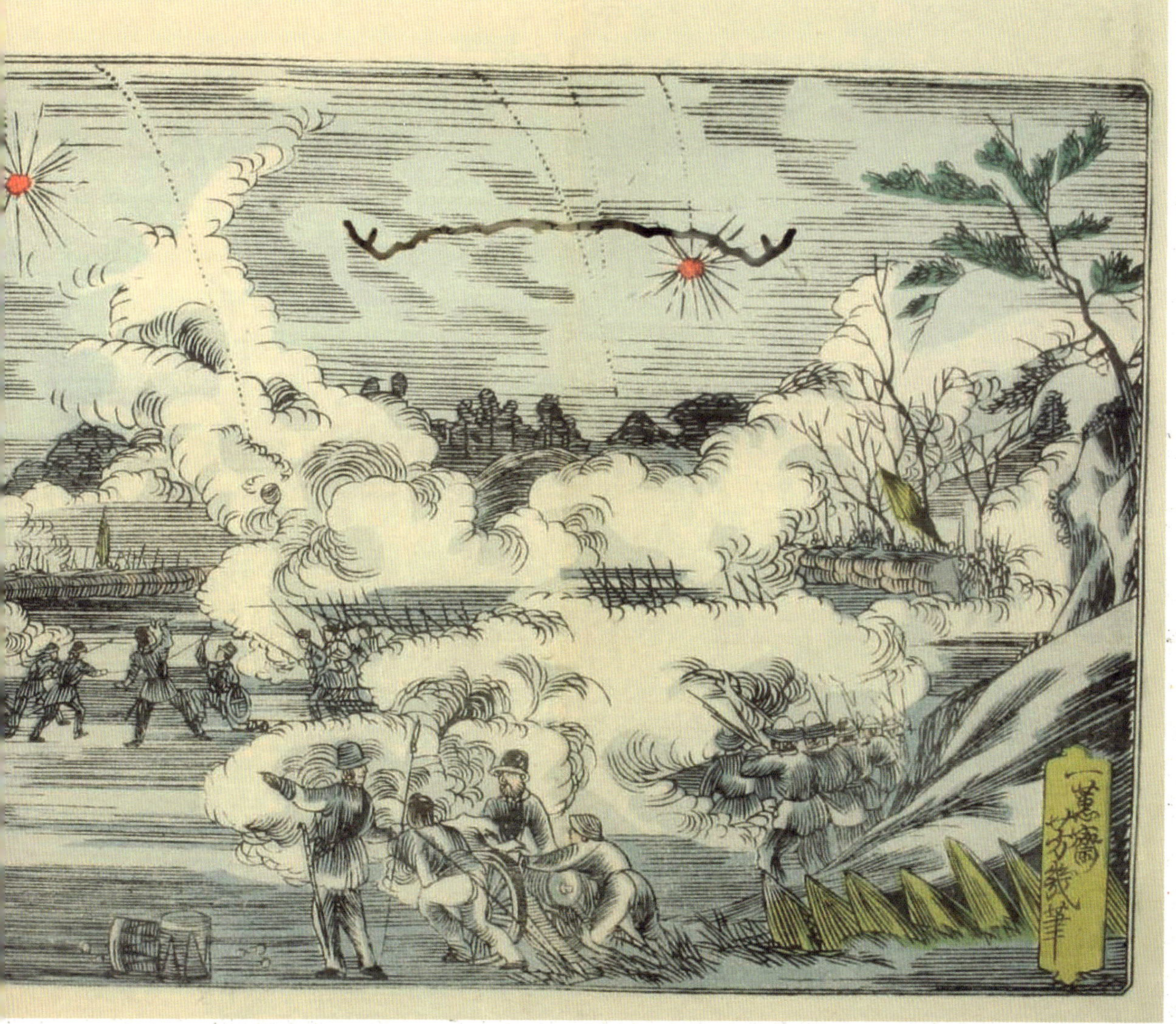

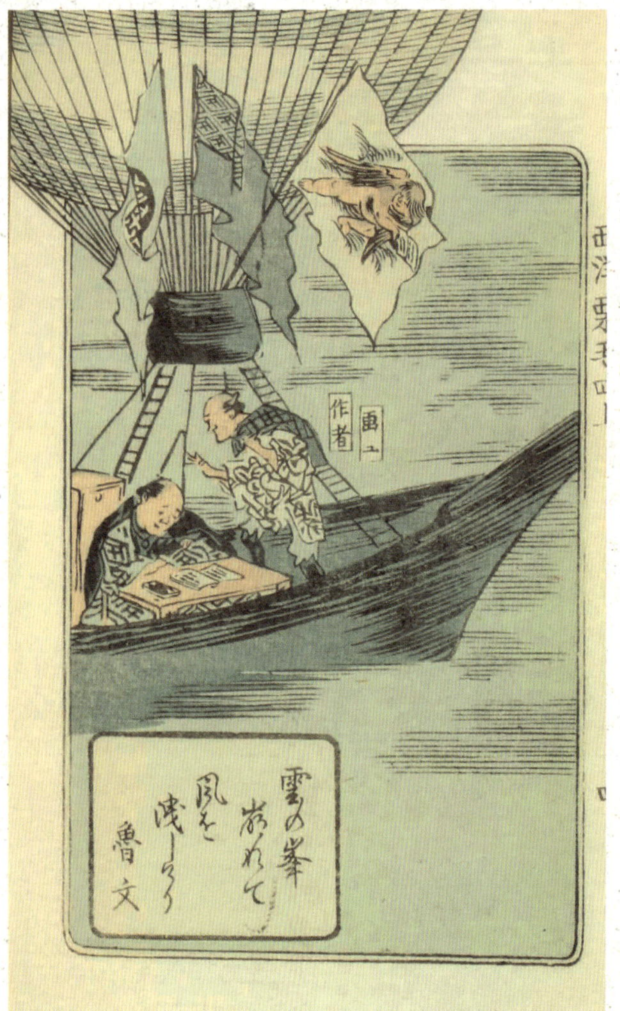

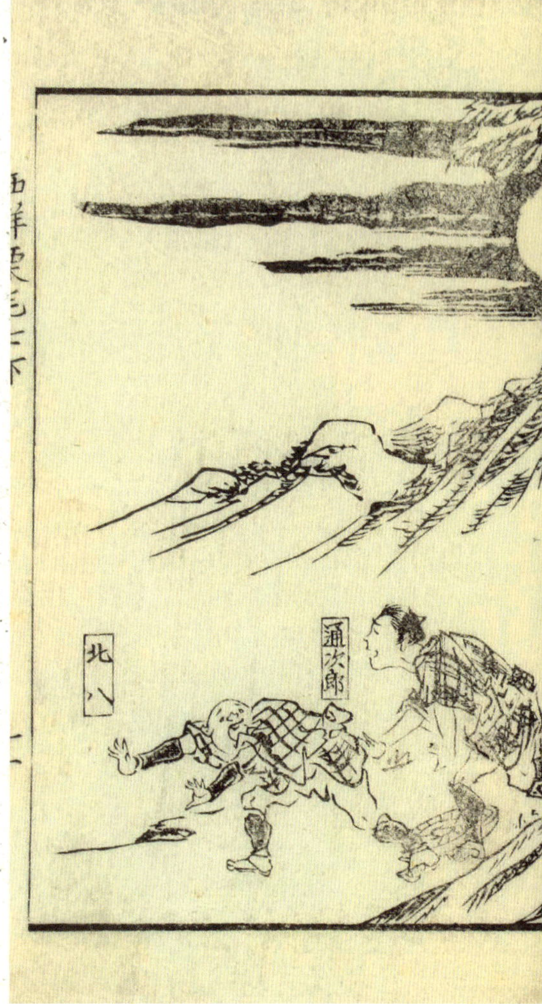

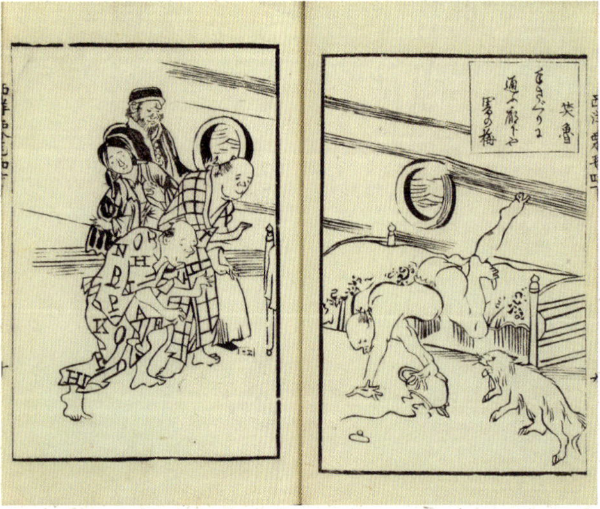

New volumes of *Travels round the West* were published until 1876, but for some reason Yoshiiku did not illustrate all of them, only up to volume 11, although volume 5 was already illustrated by Utagawa Hiroshige III. From volume 12, Kawanabe Kyōsai, who like Yoshiiku was a student of Utagawa Kuniyoshi (1798–1861), took over. Kyōsai is today much better known than Yoshiiku, especially for his mockery of contemporary society as well as his imagination of the supernatural as seen not only in his printed works but also in his large-scale paintings.

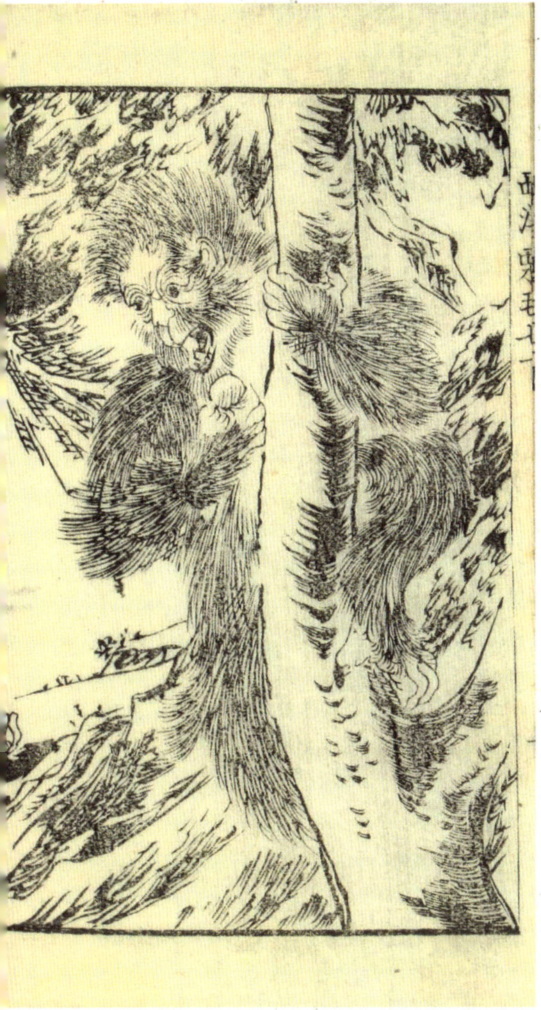

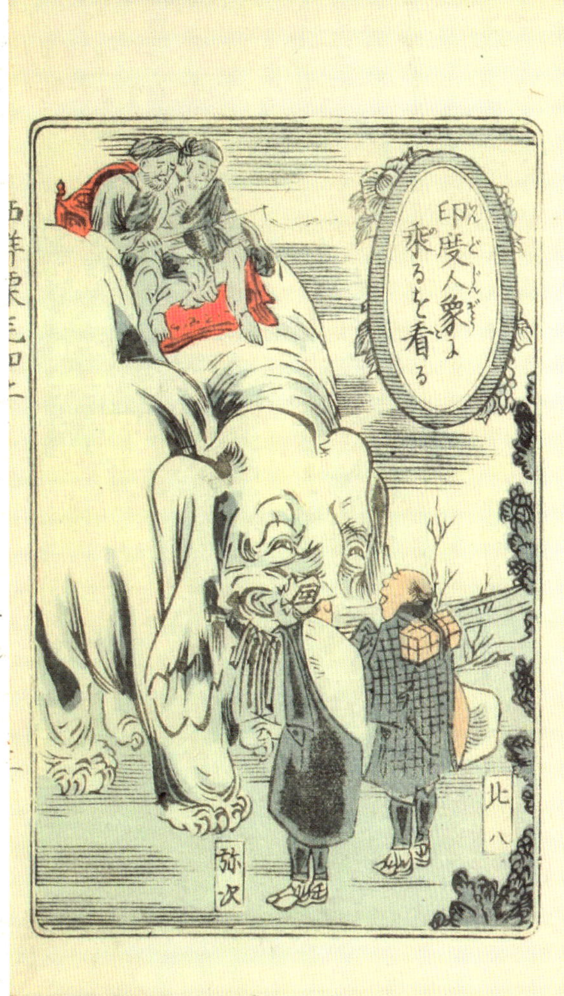


**Opposite above** Traveling by hot air balloon.

**Opposite below** On a ship.

**Above center** Night scare.

**Above right** Riding an elephant in India.

**Right** Octopus attack.

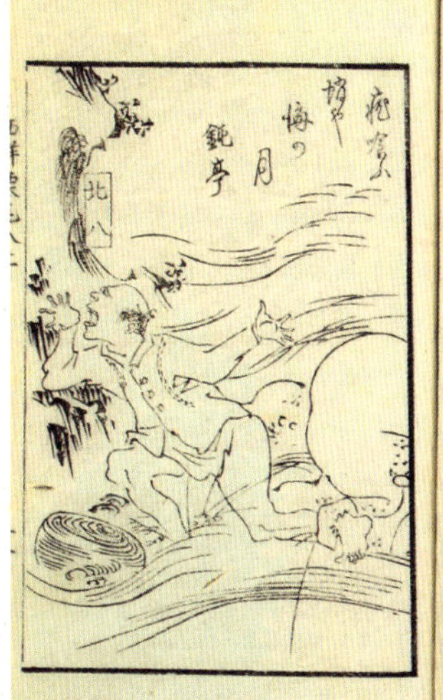

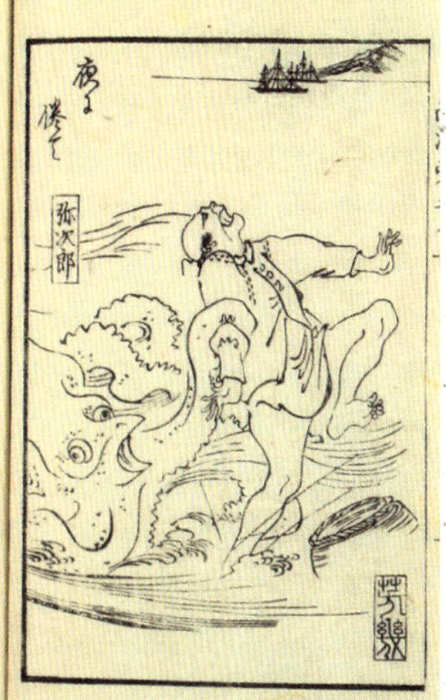

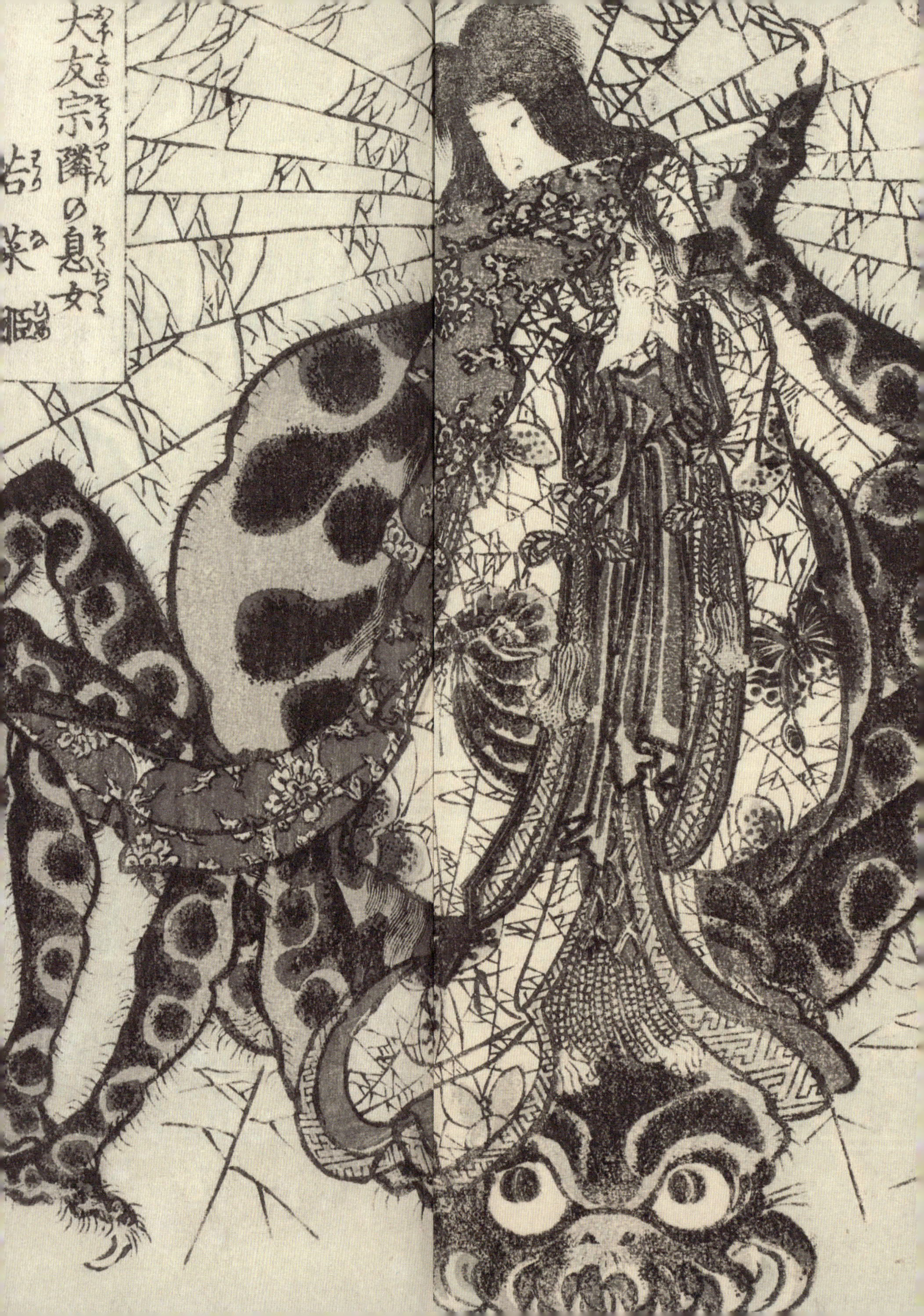
大友宗隣の息女
若菜腦

# CHAPTER FIVE

# SUPERNATURAL ADVENTURE NOVELS

As early as the eighth century, supernatural beings have been mentioned in Japanese literature, and there is probably no other culture in the world with such a rich variety of demons and ghosts. Like the humorous subjects mentioned in chapter 4, supernatural subjects were also popular in *kibyōshi* (lit. "yellow covers") storybooks, although *kibyōshi* were short stories limited to a few booklets. In the nineteenth century, adventure stories became the prime subject for serial novels as they could be published over many decades. The books were designed like handscrolls, with text elements separate from illustrations, and if a writer or artist was no longer available, someone else could take over. Readers were left in suspense at the end of each volume and were invariably eager to learn what happens next and were thus keen to purchase subsequent volumes.

The new adventure stories could be based on well-known fairy tales or historical novels from Japan or China. The famous legend about an Earth Spider (*tsuchigumo*), a demon in the form of a giant spider who was killed by the courageous warrior Minamoto Yorimitsu (also known as Raikō; 948–1021), was the inspiration for Kyokutei Bakin's (1767–1848) novel *The Spider-Woman* (*Kojorōgumo*) in 1809. Bakin was the author of another epic novel, *The Lives of the Eight Dog Warriors of the Satomi Clan* (*Nansō Satomi hakkenden*), which began publication in 1814 and was completed twenty-eight years later after an astonishing 106 booklets. Even longer was *The Tale of Shiranui* (*Shiranui monogatari*), started in 1849 by the writer Ryūkatei Tanekazu (1807–58) and finished sixty years later.

Very little information survives about the economics of the book and print market despite it being so active. In 1829, the publisher Tsuruya Kiemon released the first volume of *A Rustic Genji by a False Murasaki* (*Nise Murasaki inaka Genji*), written by Ryūtei Tanehiko (1783–1842) who used *The Tale of Genji* from the eleventh century (ca. 1000) as his source of inspiration. The combination of romance and adventure proved to be highly popular, and *A Rustic Genji* is believed to have been the bestselling book of the Edo period (1603–1868) with sales of about 15,000 copies per volume.

**Opposite** Detail from *The Tale of Shiranui*.

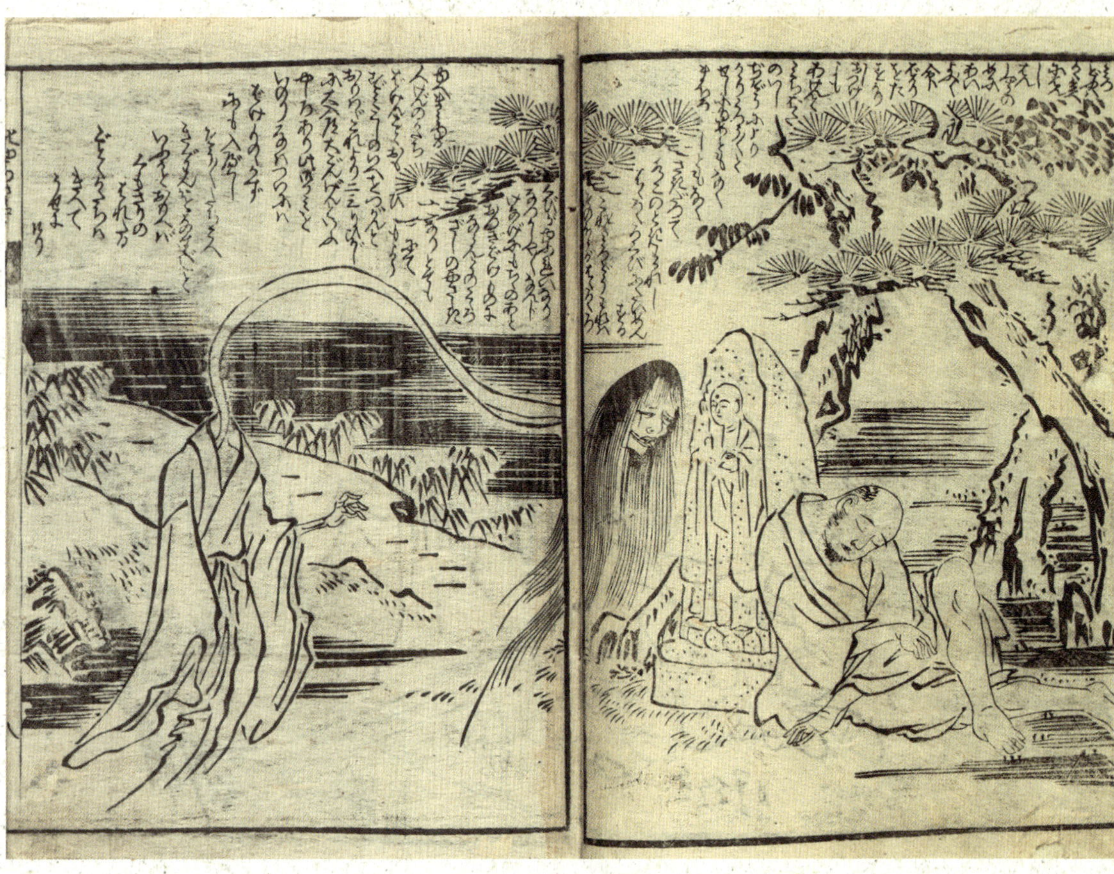

# Bonsai Trees and the Demon's Inheritance

## *Bakemono yotsugi no hachinoki*

化物世櫃鉢木

1781 (2 vols.)
Author: Iba Kashō (1747–83)
Artist: Torii Kiyonaga (1752–1815)
Publisher: Iwatoya Genpachi
Woodblock printed book (*chūbon*); ink on paper
New York Public Library, Spencer Collection, Sorimachi 497

*Bonsai Trees and the Demon's Inheritance* (*Bake-mono yotsugi no hachinoki*) is a demon story of the type that was very popular in Japan. It belongs to the literary genre known as *kibyōshi* (lit. "yellow covers"). Written with the Japanese *hiragana* alphabet instead of the more complicated *kanji* characters, *kibyōshi* were originally created for children, but adults also eventually became absorbed in these easy-to-read stories. The writer would produce the text first and then an artist was hired to illustrate it, in this case no other than Torii Kiyonaga who was well known for his prints of beautiful women.

Some demons are in distress because their chief left them to go on a pilgrimage and his son and heir, Mitsudō, transformed himself into a human to philander with women. One day, Mitsudō realizes that the woman he finds pleasure with is, in reality, a cat demon and he reveals to her that he is also a demon. Surprised by this news, she asks him why he is wasting his time in brothels instead of pursuing his own path. After his father left and his mother died, Mitsudō had no mentor and struggles to find

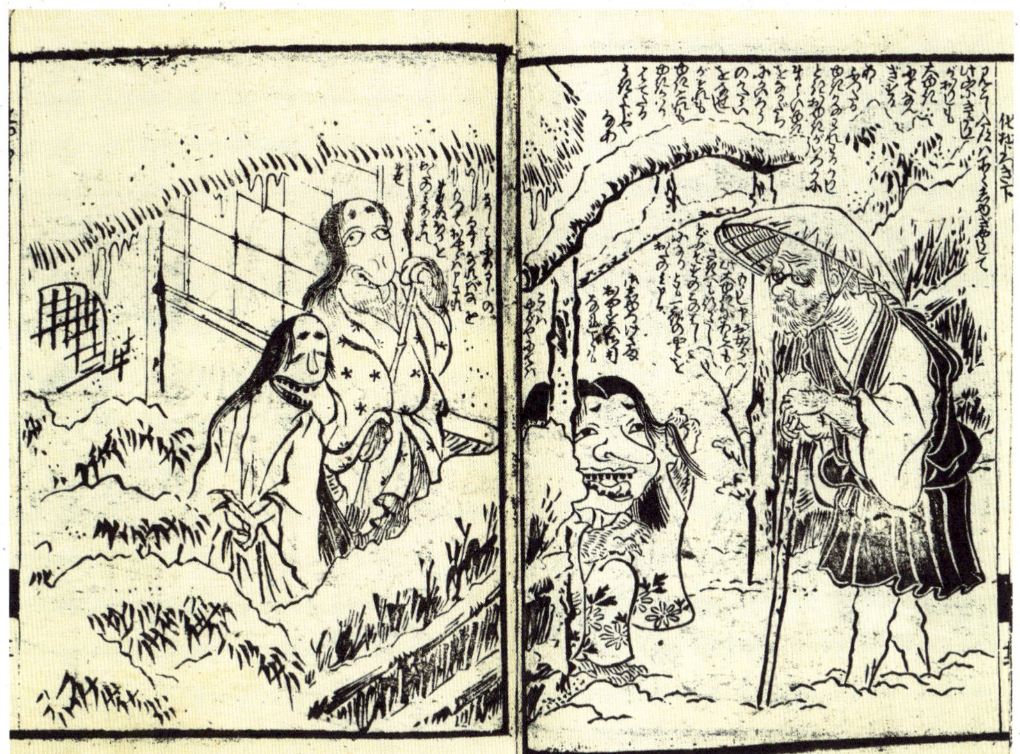

**Opposite** The ghost of Mitsudō's mother appears while he is asleep.

**Above** Mitsudō's father seeks shelter.

**Below** Three monsters chatting.

meaning in life. As a demon, he is meant to excel in scaring people. However, he fails miserably in that. After another unsuccessful experience, he has fallen asleep in a cemetery when his mother appears as a ghost. She encourages him not to give up but to visit an abandoned shrine to pray. Mitsudō follows her advice and prays for an entire week, after which the shrine's god appears and bestows on him a third eye. Now Mitsudō is scary-looking and more confident in his role as a demon.

Some time passes, and when winter arrived his father sought shelter. Horse Head gives him shelter and burns three ancient bonsai trees to warm him. After he leaves, he runs into Mitsudō and approves of his transformation. He crowns him as the new demon chief and rewards Horse Head for his generosity.

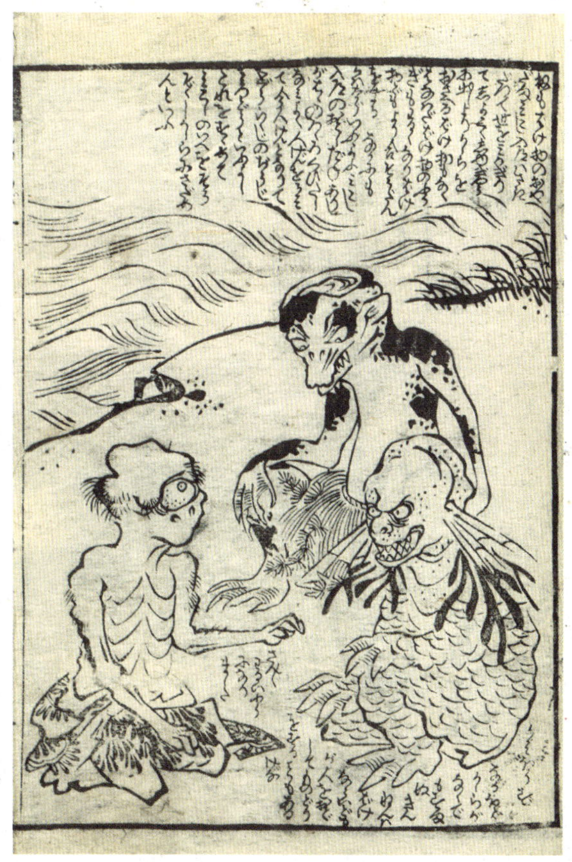

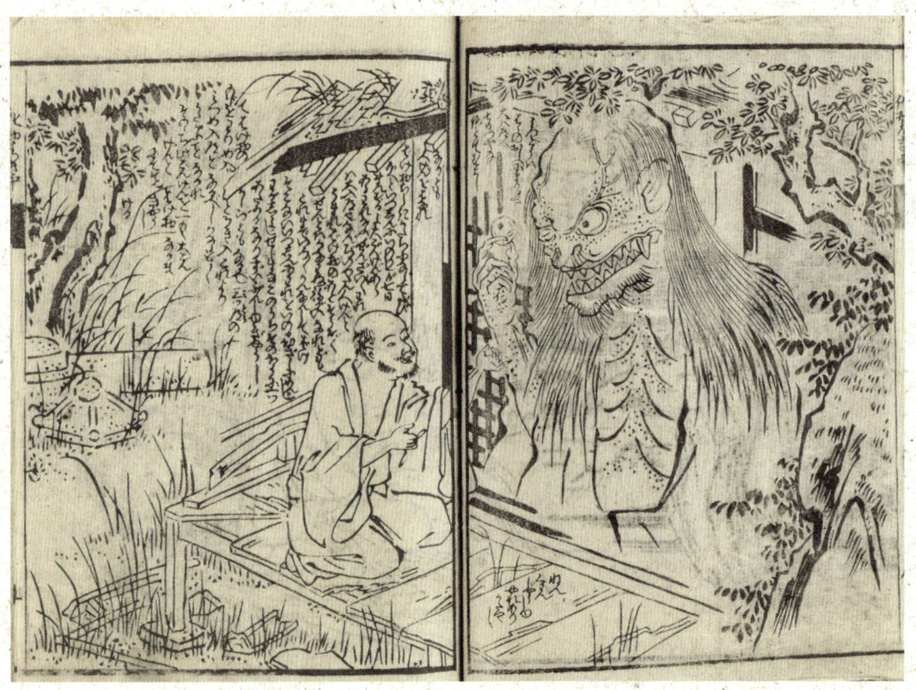

**Above** The shrine's god gives Mitsudō a third eye.

**Below** Mitsudō's father meets Horse Head.

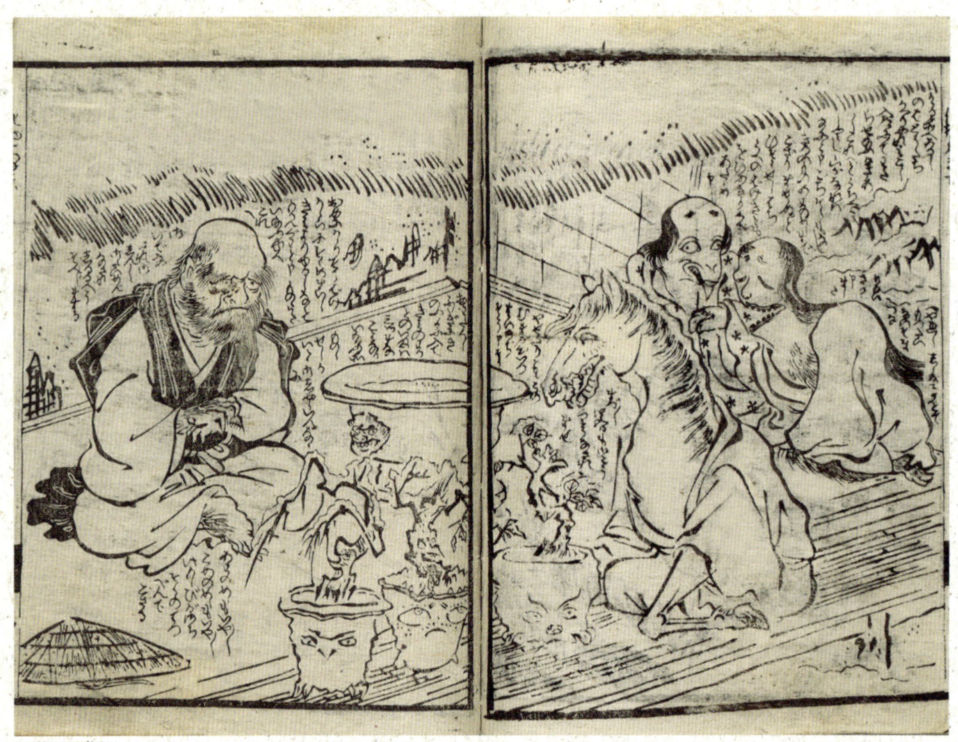

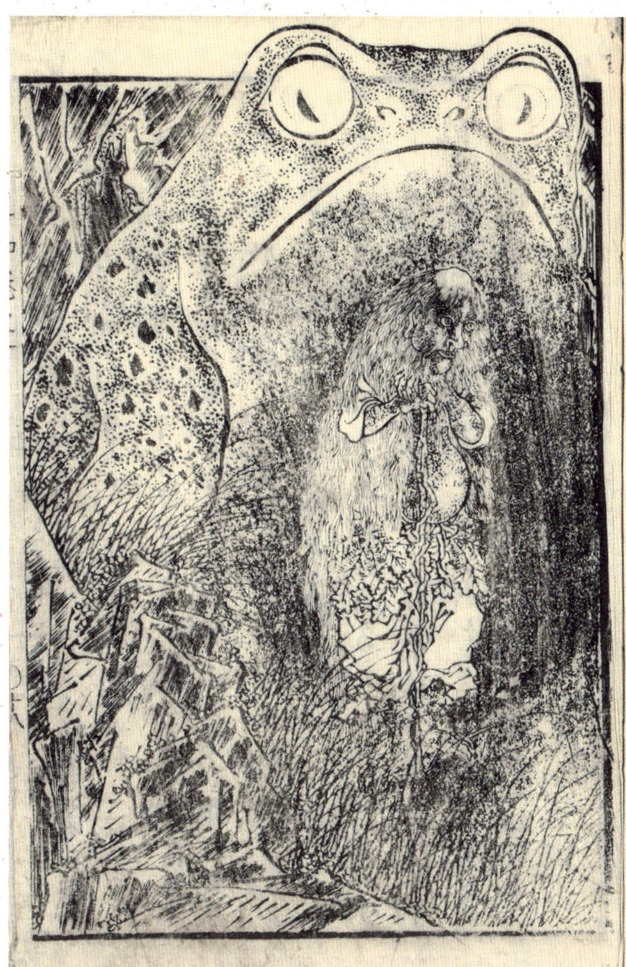

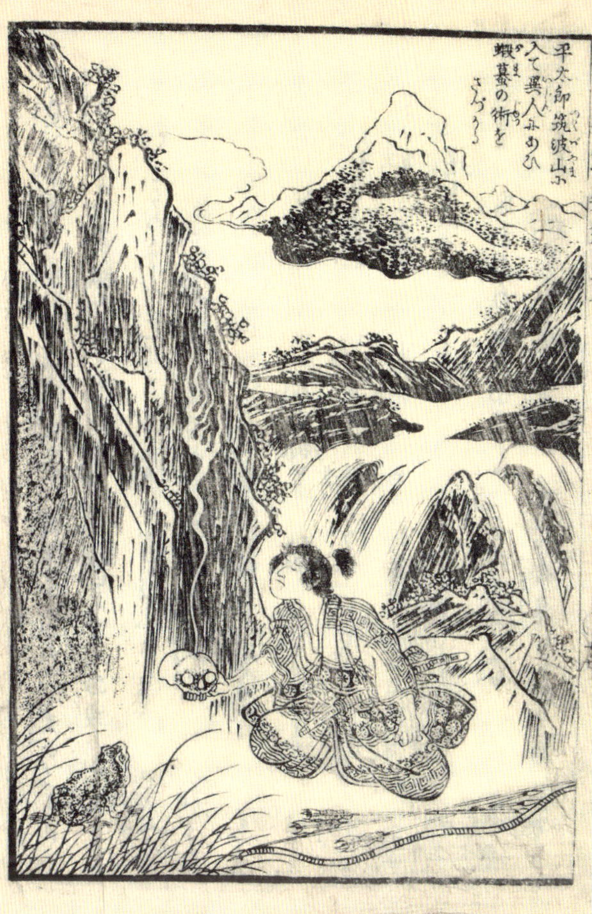


**Above** The Toad Immortal at Mount Tsukuba.

# Biography of the Loyal Utō Yasukata

*Utō Yasukata chūgi den*

善知安方忠義傳

1806 (vol. 1), 1849 (vol. 2), 1860 (vol. 3)

Authors: vol. 1: Santō Kyōden (1761–1816); vols. 2–3: Shōtei Kinsui (1795–1862)

Artists: vol. 1: Utagawa Toyokuni (1769–1825); vol. 2: Katsushika Isai (1821–80); vol. 3: Yanagawa Shigenobu II (active ca. 1823–60)

Publishers: vol. 1: Tsuruya Kiemon; vols. 2–3: Kawachiya Mohei

Woodblock printed book (*hanshibon*); ink on paper

Waseda University Library

In the novel *Biography of the Loyal Utō Yasukata* (*Utō Yasukata chūgi den*), the author Santō Kyōden (1761–1816) recounts the legend of the historical figure Utō Yasukata (dates unknown), a commander of Taira Masakado (died 940) who led an unsuccessful rebellion against the emperor. He combines it with the story of Masakado's son, Taira Yoshikado, and his sister, Princess Takiyasha (also called Satsuki). Yoshikado and Takiyasha are made the protagonists of Kyōden's story. Satsuki and her much younger half-brother, Yoshikado, narrowly manage to escape the fighting. At the foot of Mount Tsukuba, Satsuki becomes a nun and secretly raises Yoshikado. Yoshikado grows into a strong warrior and meets the hermit Nikushisen in the mountains. In reality, he is the Toad Immortal, Gama Sennin, and he reveals to Yoshikado who his father is. The siblings begin to study toad magic with Nikushisen. Yoshikado changes his name to Sōma Tarō Yoshikado because his father was born in Sōma, and Satsuki now calls herself Takiyasha.

Yoshikado ultimately leaves Mount Tsukuba and travels through the country to find supporters of his father who are willing to help him avenge his father's death. Yasukata appears as a ghost to Yoshikado, trying to discourage Yoshikado from rebelling, but Yoshikado and Takiyasha continue on their way and reach Sōma Palace. However, their evil intentions are discovered by Ōya Tarō Mitsukuni, a retainer of the powerful warlord Minamoto Yorinobu, who defeats them at the palace.

For the first volume, published by Tsuruya Kiemon in 1806, Kyōden collaborated with Utagawa Toyokuni, the leading designer of actor prints at the time. The success of the volume must have been rather limited because Tsuruya did not pursue a serial novel. In fact, it took forty-three years until the second volume was issued, long after the deaths of the initial author and illustrator. Shōtei Kinsui became the author of the second and third volumes, although the latter was not published for another eleven years.

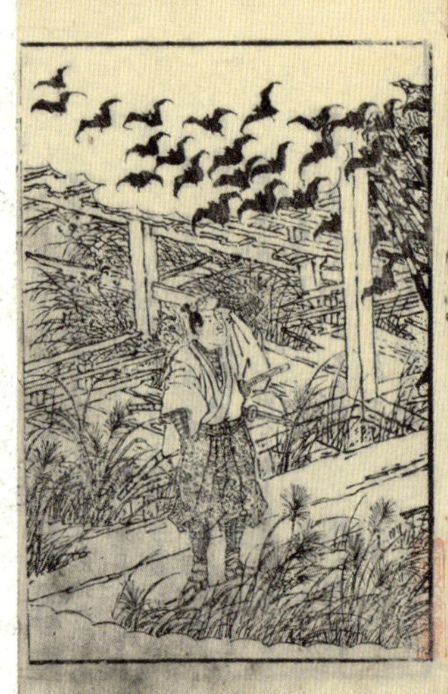
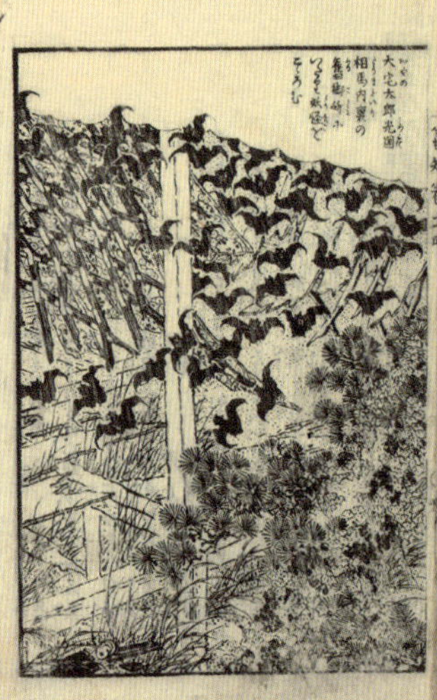
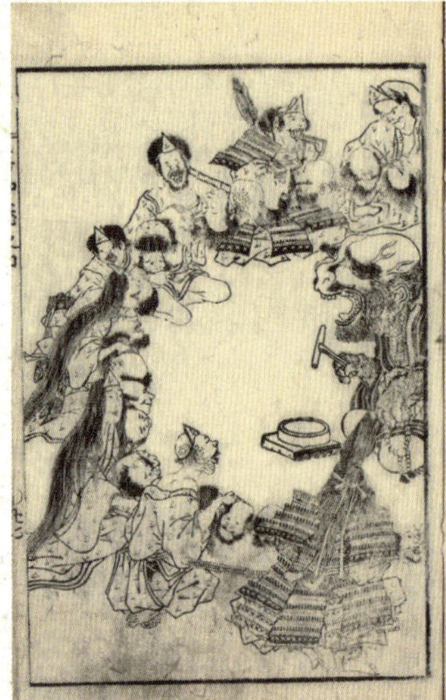
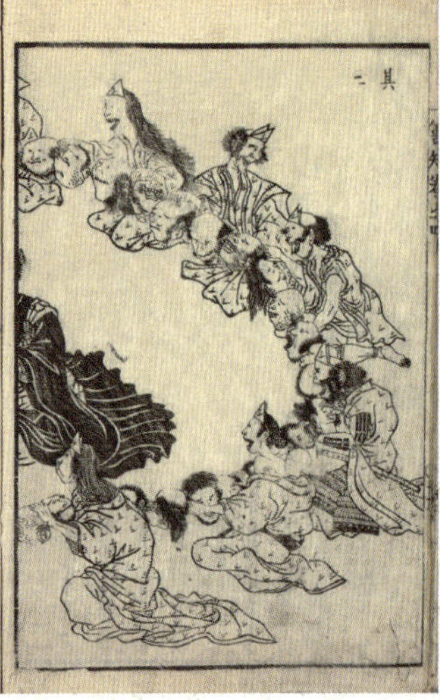
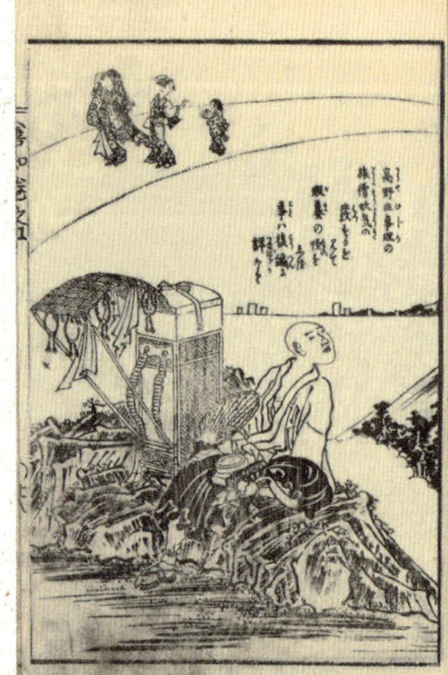
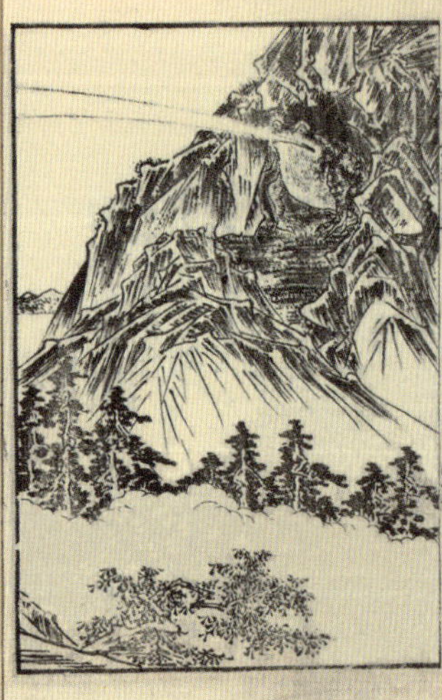

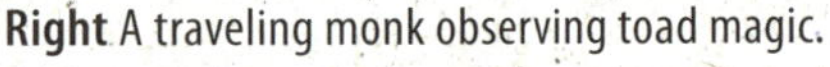
**Right** A traveling monk observing toad magic.

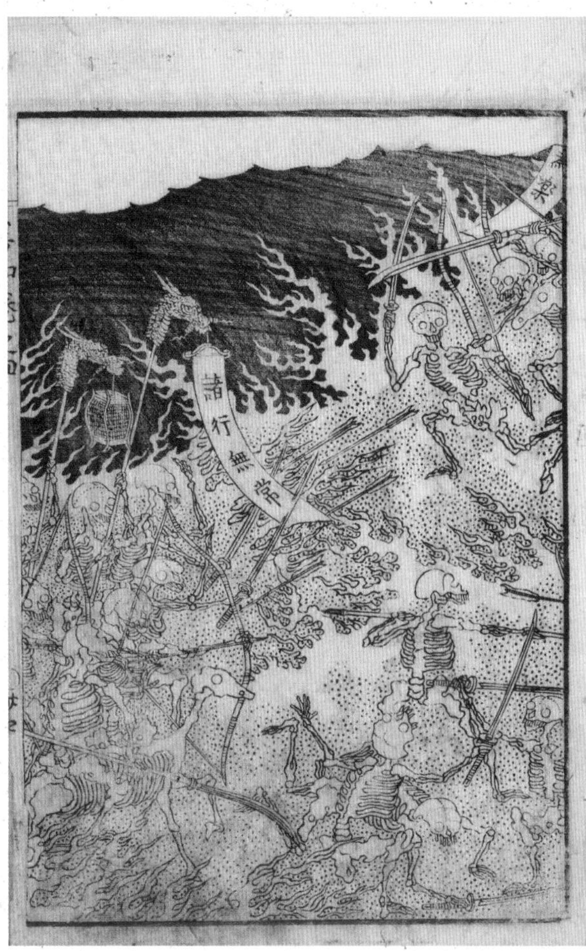
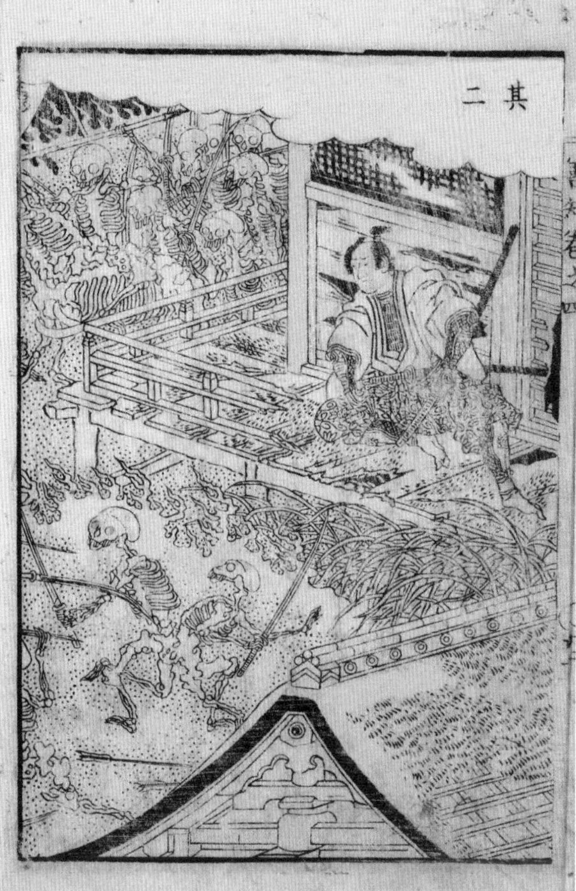


**Opposite above and center, above and right** Ōya Tarō Mitsukuni encounters monsters at Sōma Palace.

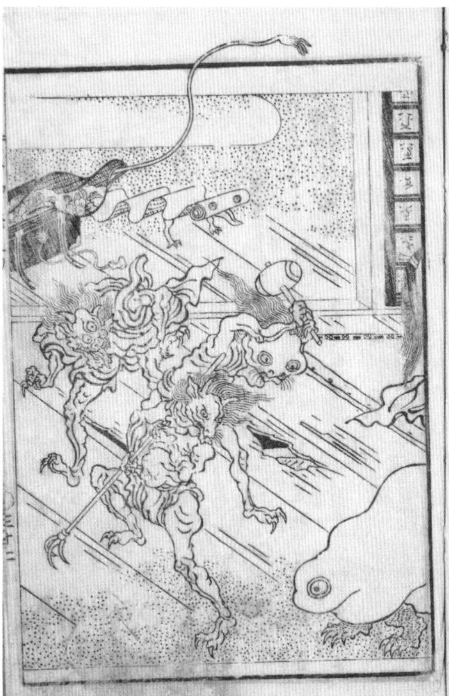
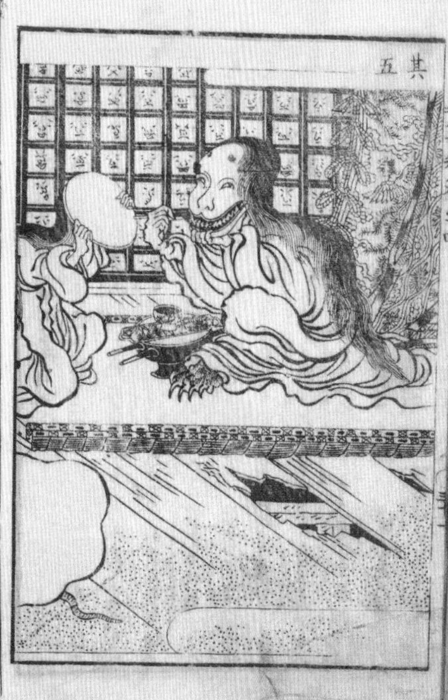

# The Spider Woman

## *Kojorōgumo*

小女郎蜘蛛

1809 (3 vols.)
Author: Kyokutei Bakin (1767–1848)
Artist: Katsukawa Shuntei (1770–1824)
Publisher: Tsuruya Kiemon
Woodblock printed book (*chūbon*); ink on paper
Tokyo Metropolitan Library, National Diet Library

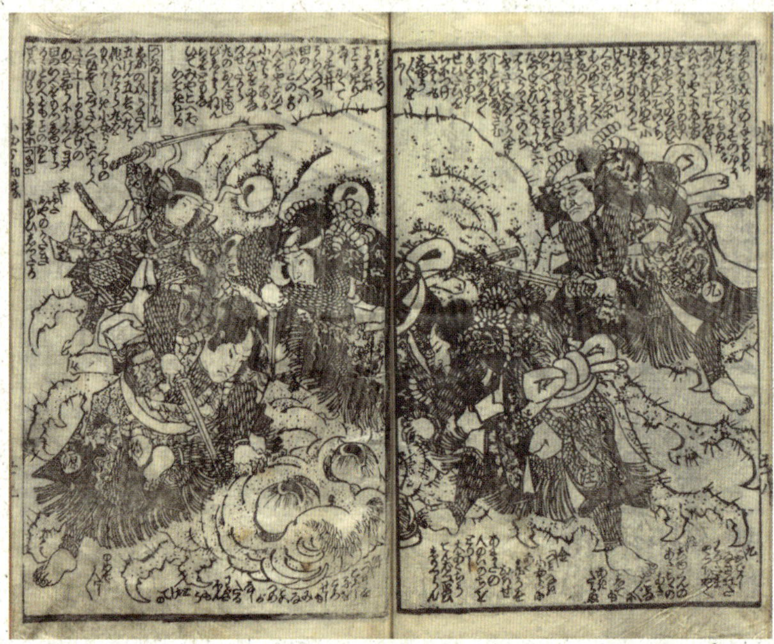

**Above** Killing the monster spider (1841/42 edition).

**Left** Killing the monster spider (1809 edition).

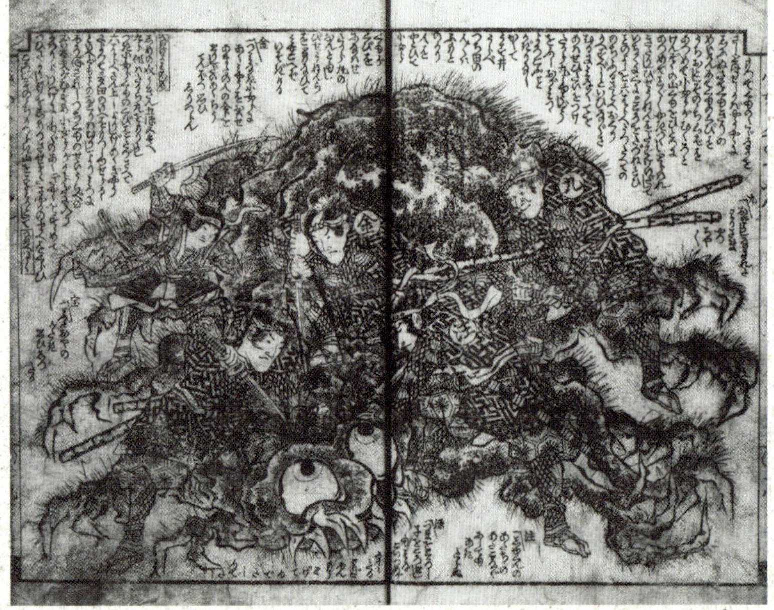

Following Kyokutei Bakin's great success with *The New Illustrated Water Margin* (*Shinpen suiko gaden*), illustrated by Katsushika Hokusai, the collaboration of the two men continued with *The New Story of Kasane's Salvation* (*Shin Kasane gedatsu monogatari*), *Snow in the Garden* (*Sono no yuki*), and *Strange Tales of the Crescent Moon* (*Chinsetsu yumiharizuki*).

In 1809, the publisher Tsuruya Kiemon produced yet another new story by Bakin, *The Spider Woman* (*Kojorōgumo*), but this time it was not Hokusai who was charged with the illustrations but the slightly younger Katsukawa Shuntei. Inspired by the legend about the Earth Spider (*tsuchigumo*), Bakin envisioned for his story a beautiful woman who was in reality a giant, murderous spider. Shuntei captured masterfully how this spider kills people until it is itself killed by a group of brave men.

Instead of reprinting the old wood blocks or having new blocks carved from the original book, the publisher Izumiya Ichibei decided to release a new edition of Bakin's story with brand-new illustrations. He hired Utagawa Kunisada (1786–1865) for the covers and Utagawa Kuniyoshi (1798–1861) for the interior—a rare collaboration of these two senior print artists. Under the new title *The Spider-Woman and a Thread Ball of Grudge* (*Kojorōgumo urami no odamaki*), the first volume was issued in 1841 and the second one followed a year later.

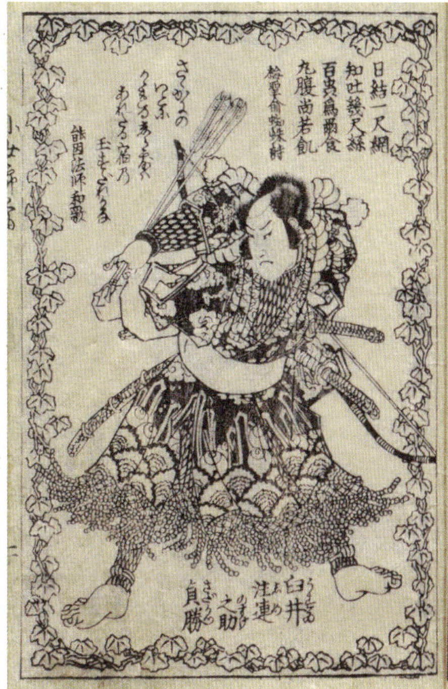

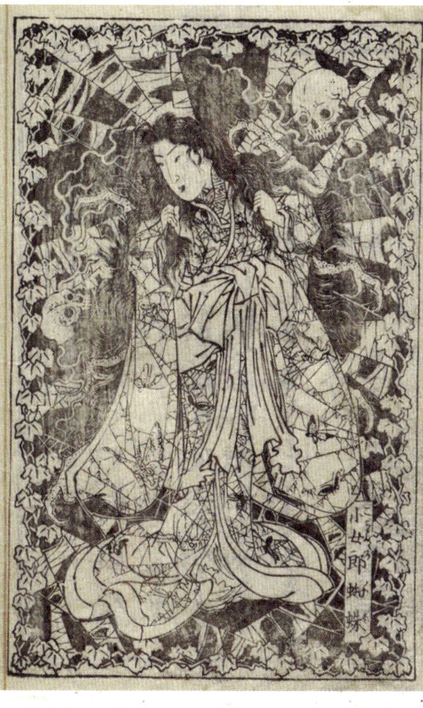

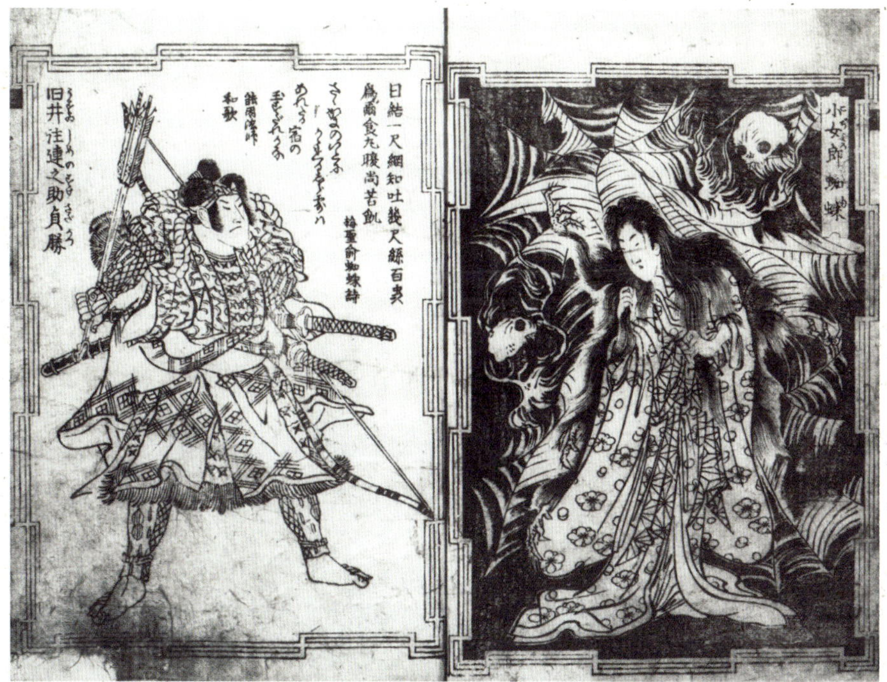

**Above left** Usui Shimenosuke Sadakatsu.

**Above right** Spider Woman (1841/42 edition).

**Far left** Usui Shimenosuke Sadakatsu.

**Left** Spider Woman (1809 edition).

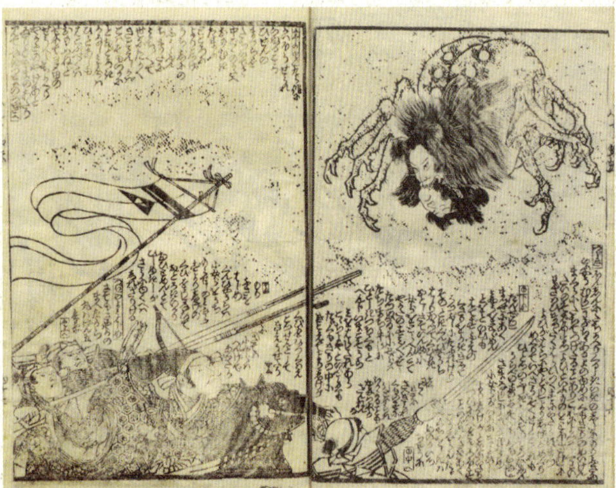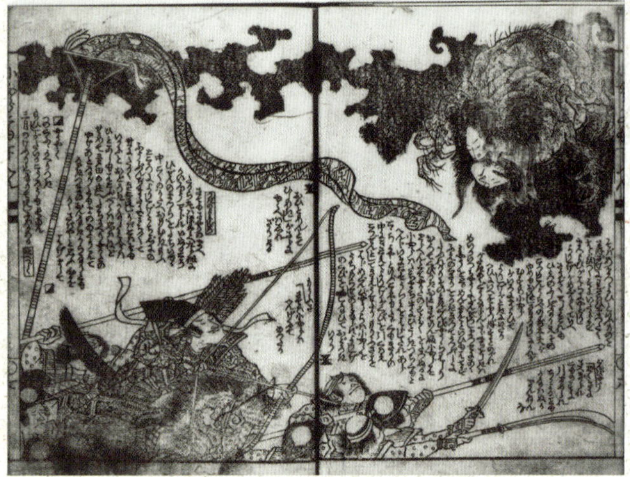

**Above** The spider monster killed a woman (1841/42 edition).

**Below** The spider monster caught a woman as prey (1809 edition).

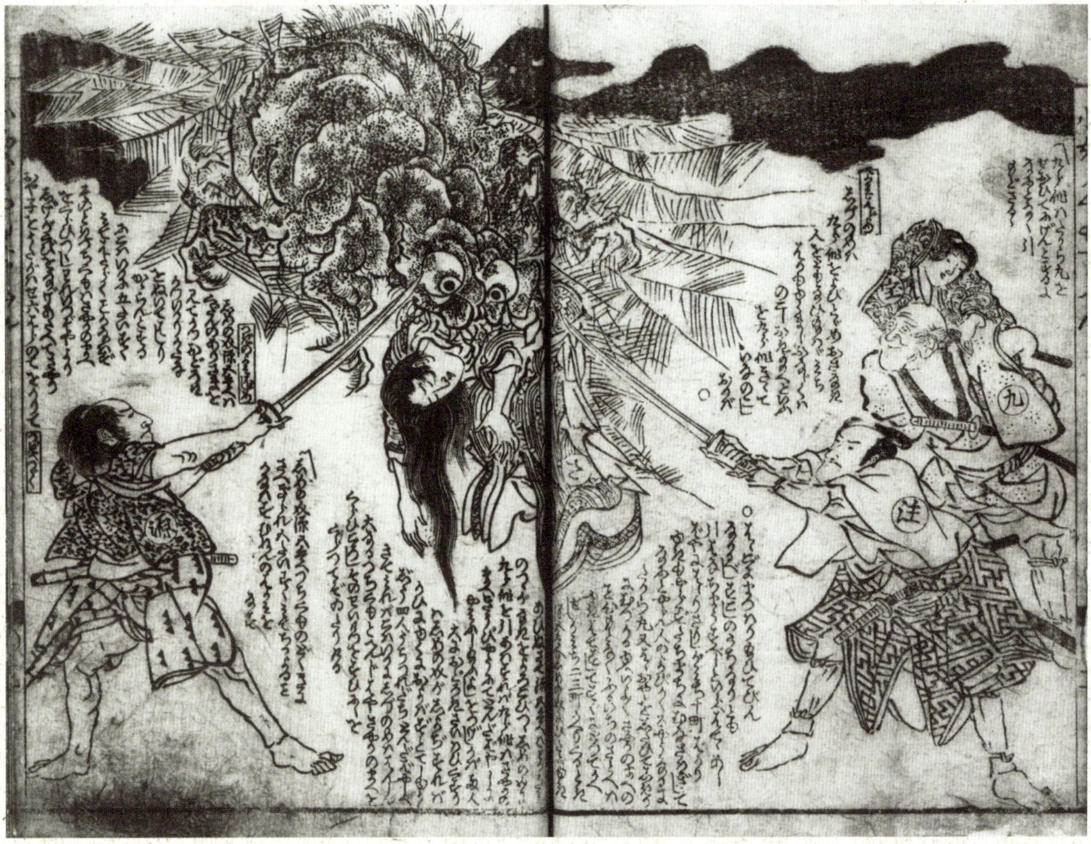

**Above** The spider monster killed a woman (1809 edition).

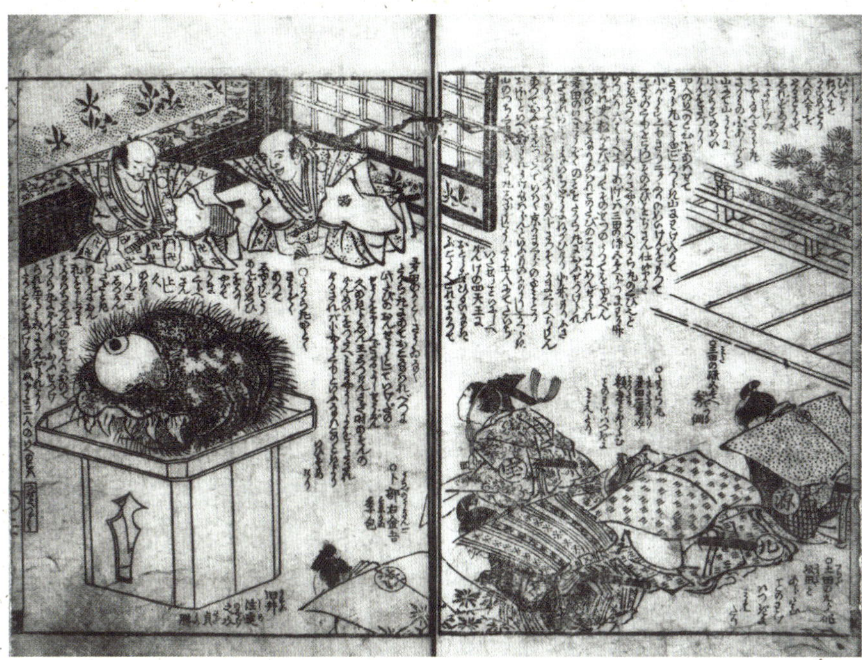

**Left** Presentation of the spider monster's head (1809 edition).

**Below** Presentation of the spider monster's head (1841/42 edition).

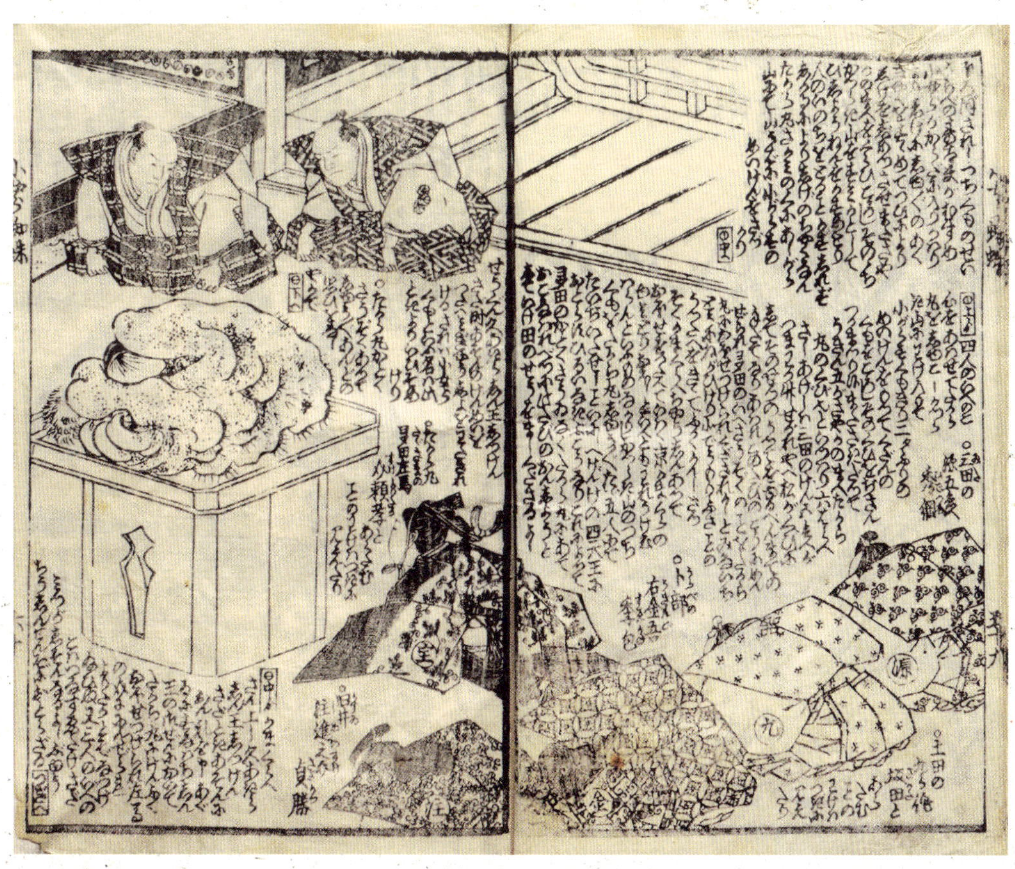

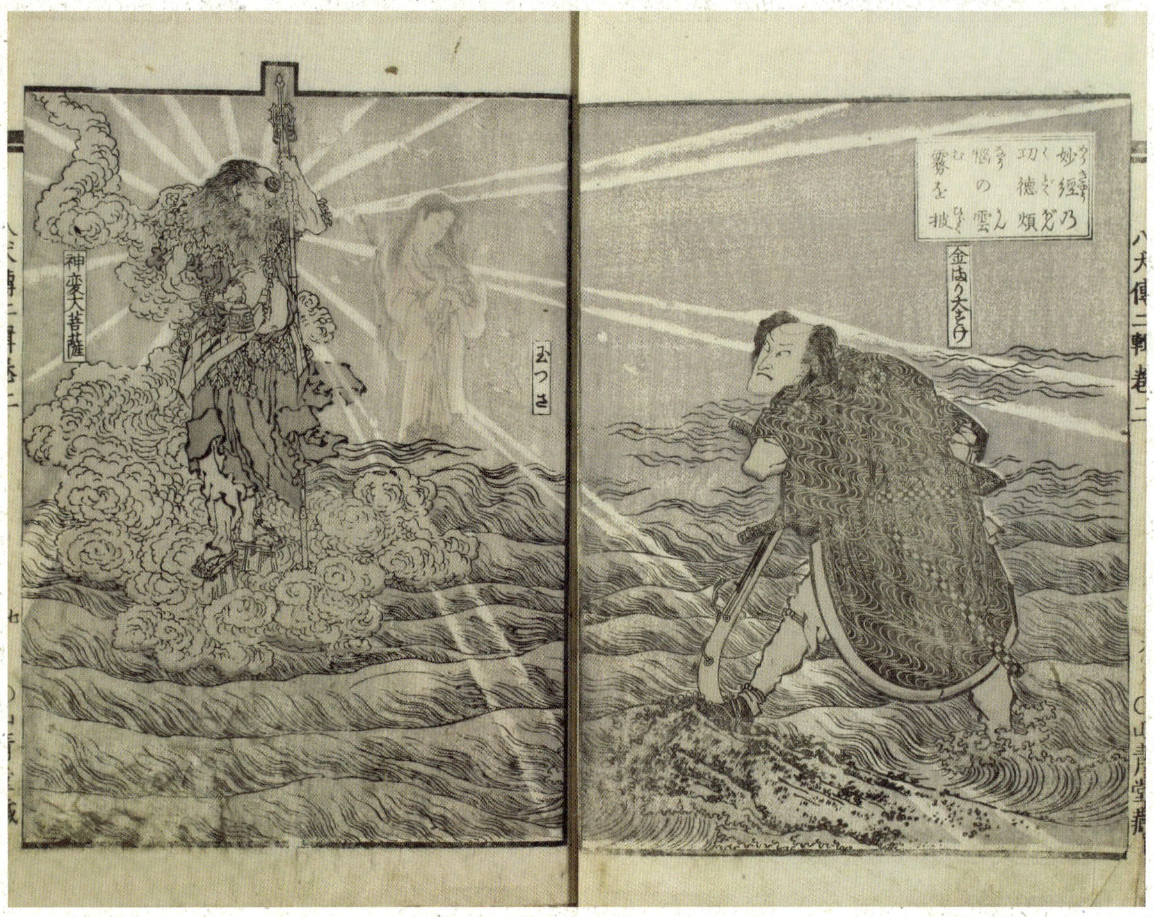

# Lives of the Eight Dog Warriors of the Satomi Clan

## *Nansō Satomi hakkenden*
南総里見八犬傳

1814 (vol. 1), 1816 (vol. 2), 1819 (vol. 3), 1820 (vol. 4), 1823 (vol. 5), 1827 (vol. 6), 1828 (vol. 7), 1832 (vol. 8 part 1), 1833 (vol. 8 part 2), 1835 (vol. 9 part 1), 1836 (vol. 9 part 2), 1837 (vol. 9 part 3), 1838 (vol. 9 part 4), 1839 (vol. 9 part 5), 1840 (vol. 9 parts 6–7), 1841 (vol. 9 parts 8–9), 1842 (vol. 9 parts 10–11)

Author: Kyokutei Bakin (1767–1848)

Artists: vols. 1–4: Yanagawa Shigenobu (1787?–1833); vols. 5–6: Yanagawa Shigenobu and Keisai Eisen (1790–1848); vols. 7–8: Yanagawa Shigenobu; vol. 9 parts 1–3: Yanagawa Shigenobu II (active ca. 1823–60); vol. 9 parts 4–5: Keisai Eisen; vol. 9 parts 6–7: Utagawa Sadahide (1807–ca. 1878); vol. 9 parts 8–9: Keisai Eisen and Yanagawa Shigenobu II; vol. 9 part 10: Keisai Eisen; vol. 9 part 11: Yanagawa Shigenobu II

Publishers: Yamazakiya Heihachi (vols. 1–6); Chōjiya Heibei (vols. 7–9)

Woodblock printed book (*hanshibon*); ink on paper

Waseda University Library

Kyokutei Bakin had been an author of popular fiction (*gesaku*) since 1790 and had written dozens of books before he embarked on his most famous project, *Lives of the Eight Dog Warriors of the Satomi Clan* (*Nansō Satomi hakkenden*). Publication of this epic novel began in 1814 and was only completed twenty-eight years later after nine volumes comprising 106 booklets. The entire story spans the period from 1441 until 1500 and is a single-epic narrative rather than consisting of independent episodes. The focus lies on the mishaps of eight warriors who discover that they share the same origin as "spirit-children" of Princess Fuse from the Satomi clan and the family dog Yatsufusa. The eight, born into different families but each carrying a surname that includes the character *inu*, or dog, eventually unite in Kazusa Province (otherwise known as Nansō) and loyally defend her clan.

The record length of the novel made it necessary to employ several different artists over the period for the illustrations, starting with Yanagawa Shigenobu, the son-in-law of Hokusai who died in 1833. Besides Shigenobu, Keisai Eisen, Yanagawa Shigenobu II, and Utagawa Sadahide provided illustrations which are single or double pages. Separated from Bakin's text pages, the illustrations identify the protagonists with brief explanatory remarks. In general, the text-image ratio is around six to one.

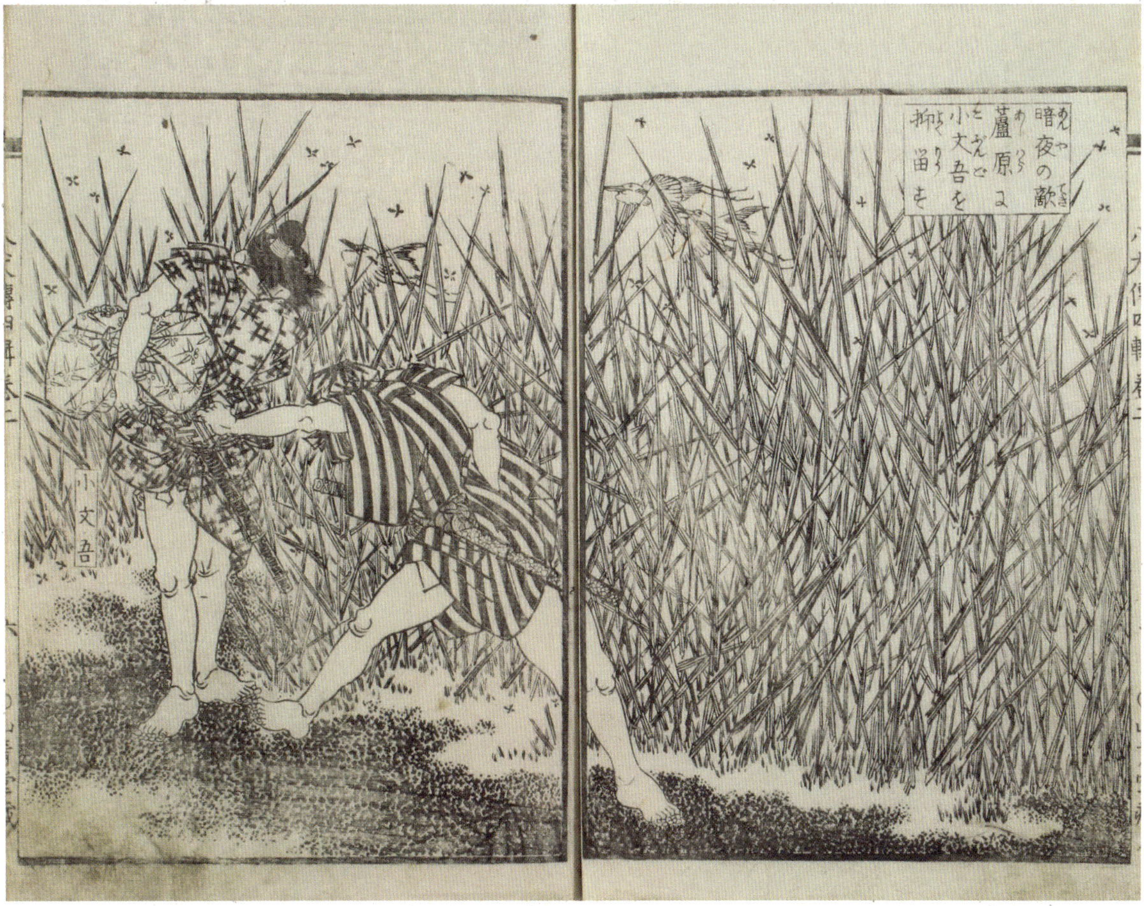

Most images are action-laden as they focus on dramatic moments within the story. The last image in volume 1 captures the newly married sixteen-year-old Fuse with her husband, the dog Yatsufusa, who won her hand by bringing Fuse's father the head of his enemy. Inuzuka Bansaku, who will be the father of the first dog warrior, is introduced in volume 2. He is portrayed retrieving the heads of two princes as well as the head of his own father, who had failed to prevent their execution.

**Opposite** Vol. 2, En no Gyōja, Tamazusa, and Kanamari Daisuke.

**Above** Vol. 4, Ashihara grabs Inuta Kobungo on a dark night.

**Below** Vol. 1, Shirazuya Kokuroku and Kanamari Hachirō.

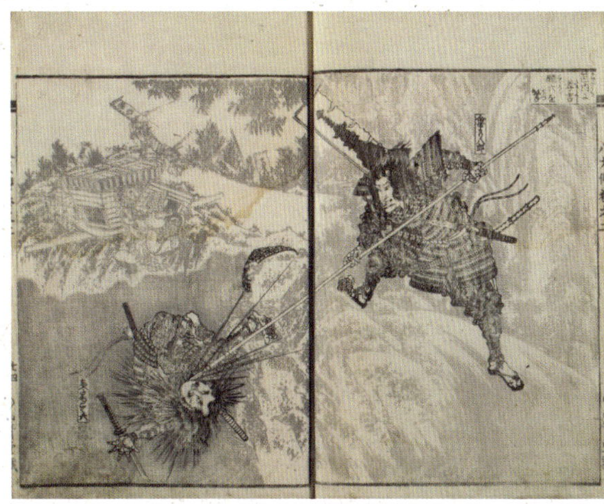

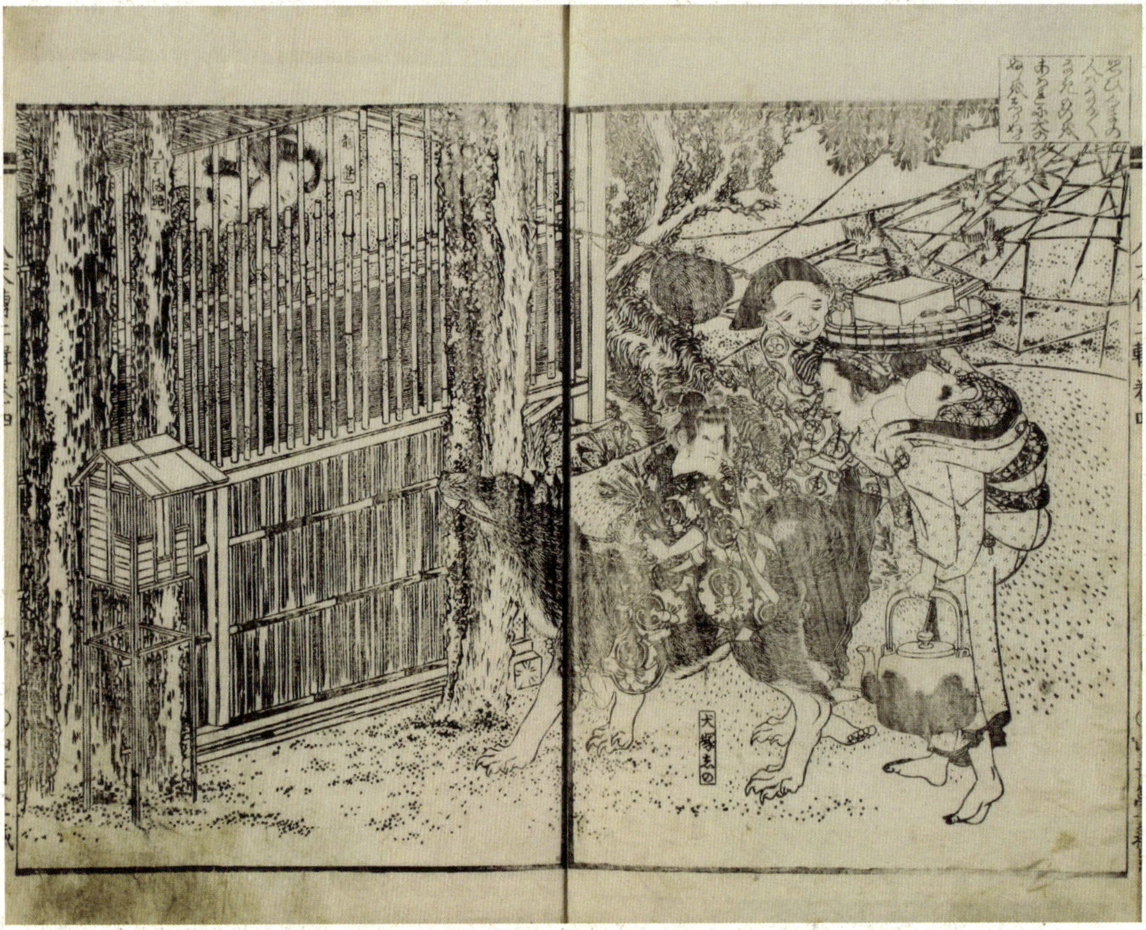

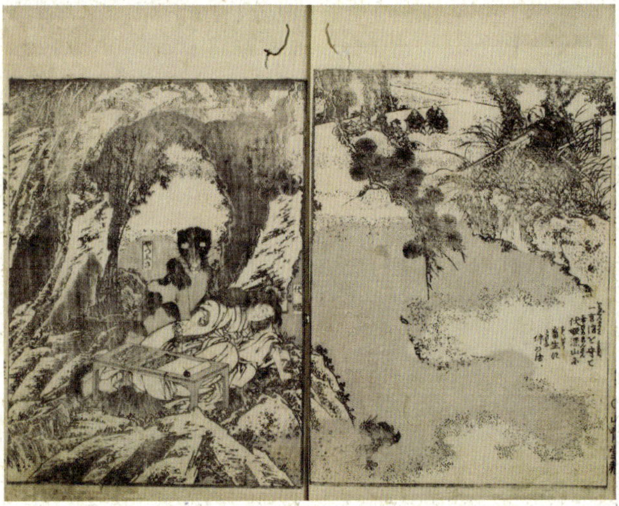

**Above** Vol. 2, Inuzuka Shino riding a dog.

**Left** Vol. 1, Princess Fuse and the dog Yatsufusa.

**Below** Vol. 3, Inuzuka Bansaku retrieving the heads of two princes and of his father.

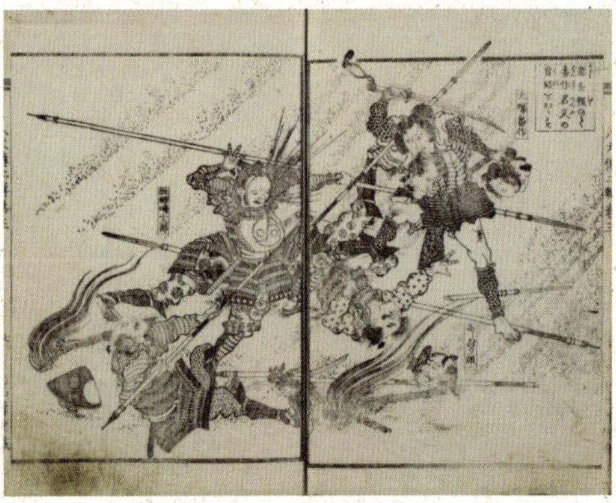

# A Rustic Genji by a False Murasaki

## *Nise Murasaki inaka Genji*

### 偐紫田舎源氏

1829 (vol. 1), 1830 (vols. 2–3), 1831 (vols. 4–5), 1832 (vols. 6–7), 1833 (vols. 8–10), 1834 (vols. 11–13), 1835 (vols. 14–17), 1836 (vols. 18–21), 1837 (vols. 22–24), 1838 (vols. 25–27), 1839 (vols. 28–31), 1840 (vols. 32–34), 1841 (vols. 35–37), 1842 (vol. 38)

Author: Ryūtei Tanehiko (1783–1842)

Artist: Utagawa Kunisada (1786–1865)

Publisher: Tsuruya Kiemon

Woodblock printed book (*chūbon*); ink on paper

Waseda University Library

*The Tale of Genji* (*Genji monogatari*), believed to be the first novel in world history, was written by the court lady Murasaki Shikibu (970/78?–1014/31?). The story about the amorous adventures of Prince Genji became enormously popular through many later versions and commentaries and was a frequent motif in the arts. Undoubtedly the most famous parody of *The Tale of Genji*, with the most overwhelming response, was *A Rustic Genji by a False Murasaki* (*Nise Murasaki inaka Genji*), set during the Muromachi period (1392–1573), which began publication in 1829. Tsuruya Kiemon the publisher, hired the popular writer Ryūtei Tanehiko to conceive a story based on *Genji* and recast with modern elements, such as the fighting scenes observed in *kabuki* plays. Tanehiko thus transposed his light and entertaining new story into fifteenth-century Japan.

**Below** Vol. 1, the assumed author of this work.

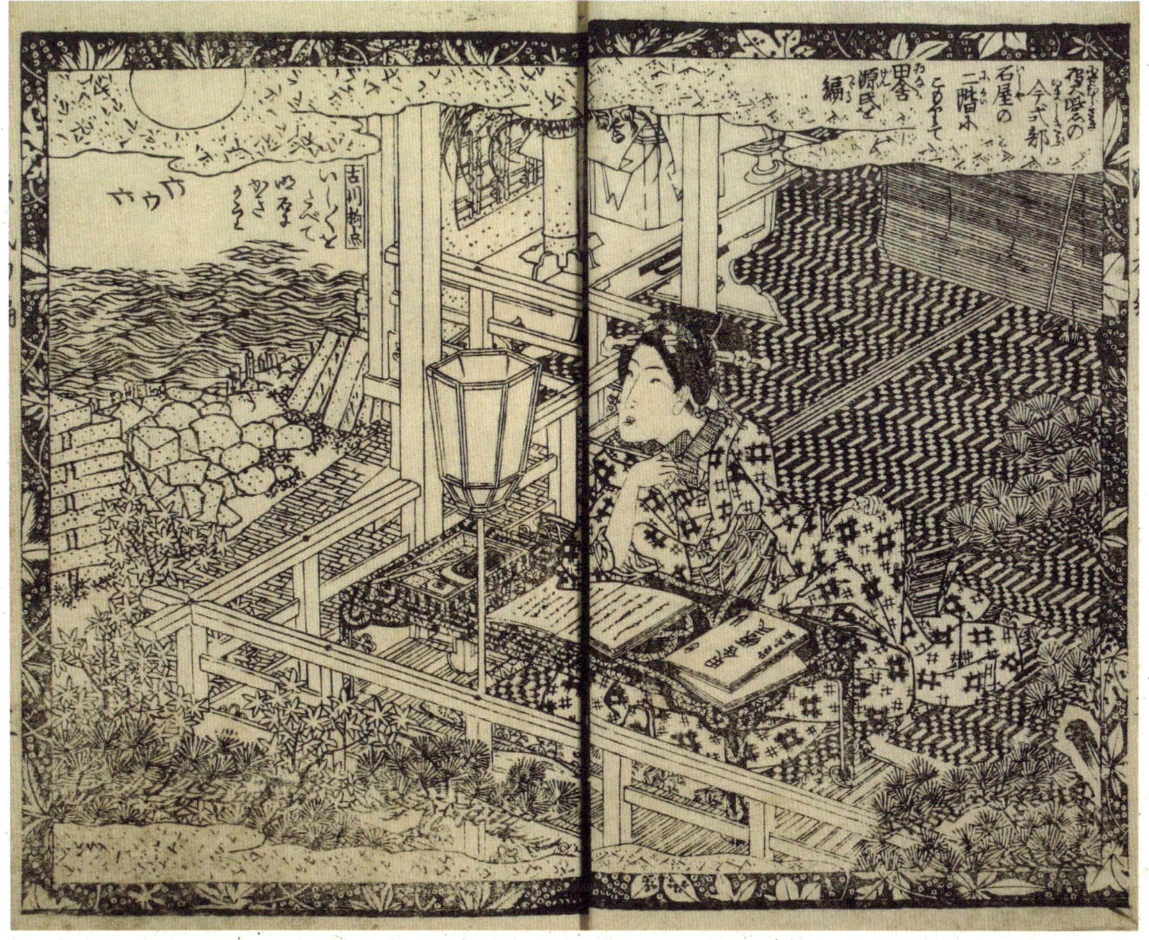

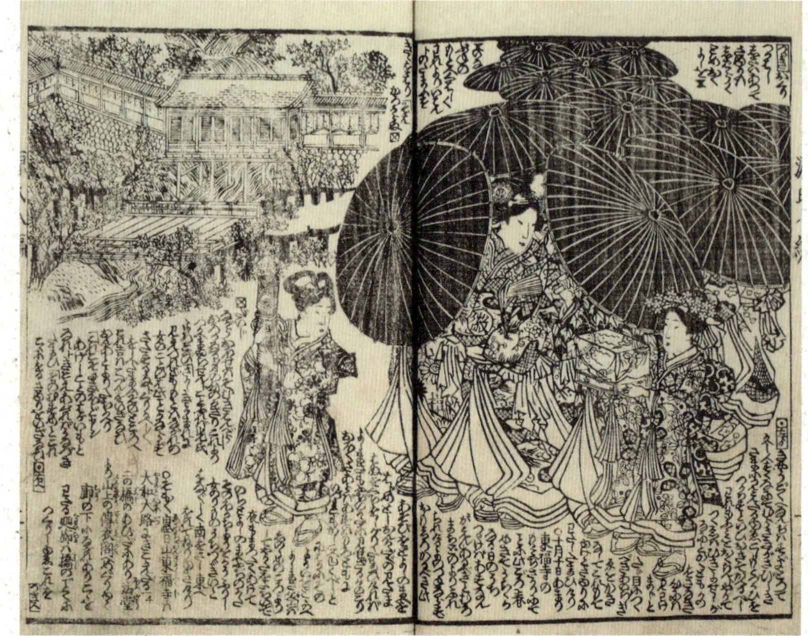

**Right** Vol. 8, a group is heading to enjoy autumn leaves at Tōfukuji Temple.

**Below** Vol. 3, Mitsuuji on the way to Karaginu's bedroom.

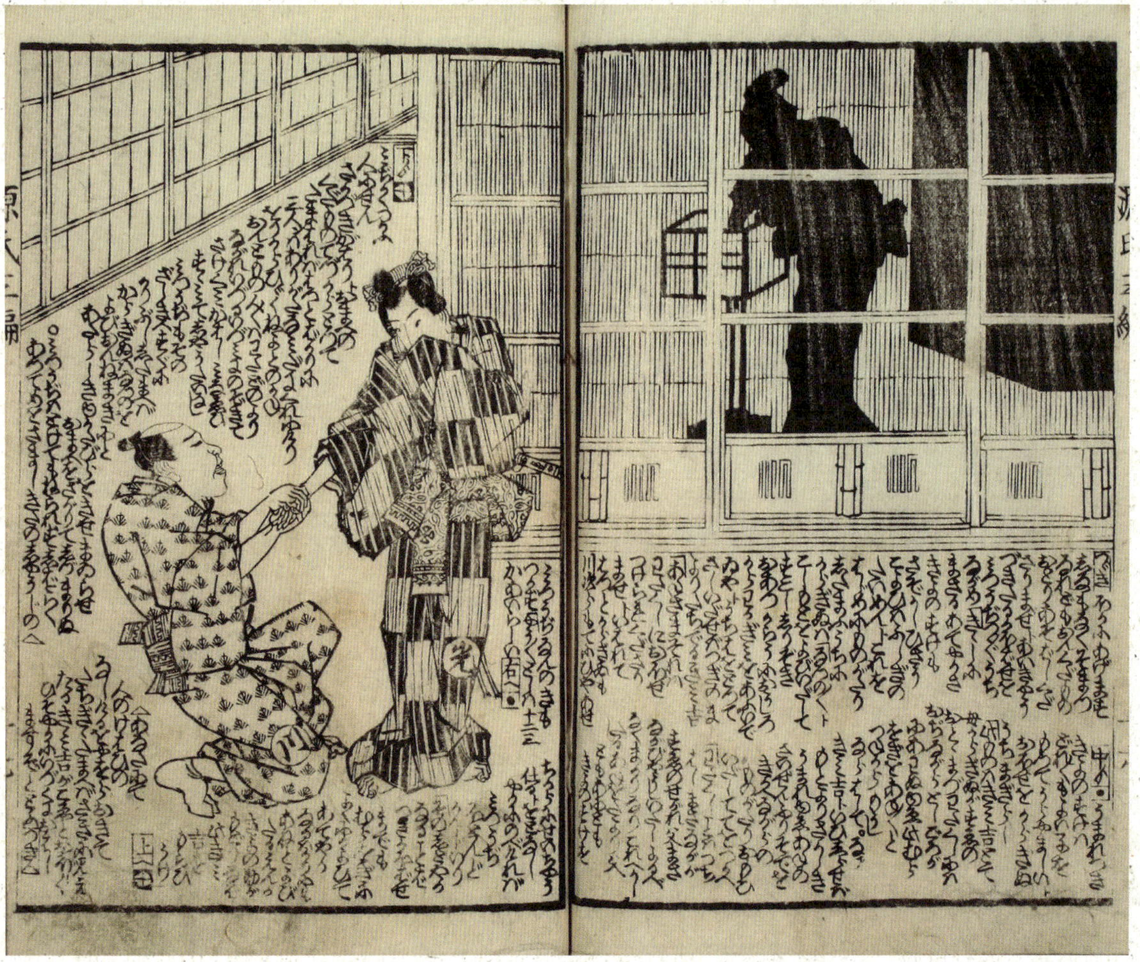

The storyline centers on Mitsuuji, who is on a quest to track down his missing family treasures but runs into amorous as well as dangerous situations. The serial novel was so successful that thirty-eight volumes were issued until 1842. However, the story was never finished because it was banned during the Tenpō Reforms, an array of economic policies introduced between 1841 and 1843, and Tanehiko died shortly after being imprisoned. Sequels began to be issued a few years later after the oppressive control by the censors weakened.

Tanehiko's text was not the only reason for the success of *A Rustic Genji*. The illustrations provided by Utagawa Kunisada, one of the most prominent print artists at the time, also played a large role. Tanehiko's closely written text encircles Kunisada's pictures. Together the two men created an enticing literary partnership that broke all sales records. At a time when 7,000 copies were under-stood to make a book a bestseller, *A Rustic Genji* is thought to have sold as many as 15,000 copies. It was the number one seller in fiction during the entire Edo period (1603–1868).

The craze for this novel was so enormous that in 1838 Kunisada began to design single-sheet prints that offered some of his illustrations enlarged and in color. A new print genre was thus born, and within the next sixty years


**Below** Vol. 5, Mitsuuji protects Tasogare from Shinonome.

**Bottom** Vol. 4, Karaginu and Muraoki play a game of Gō.

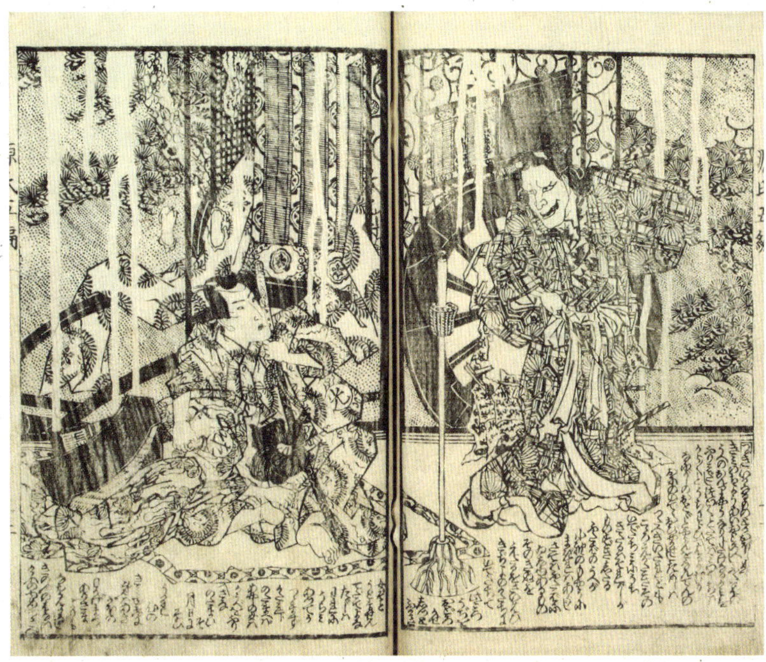

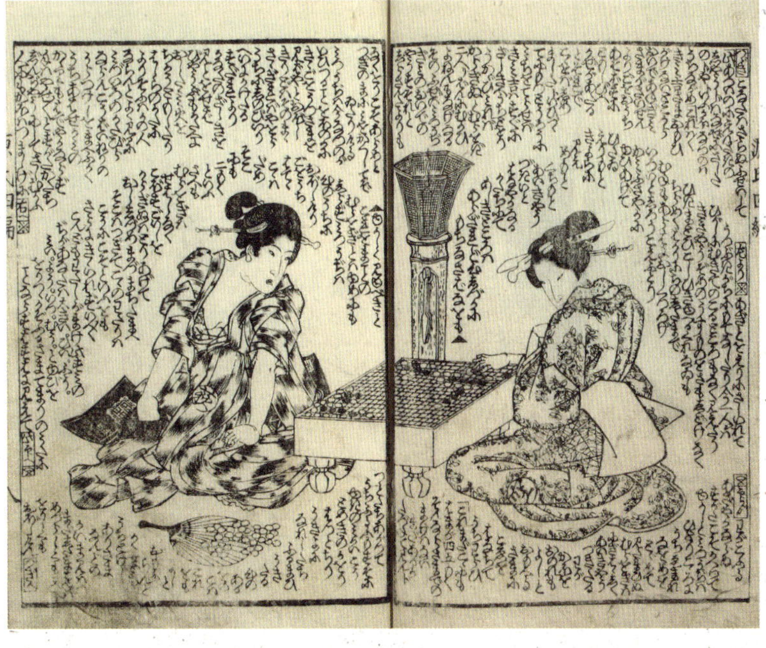

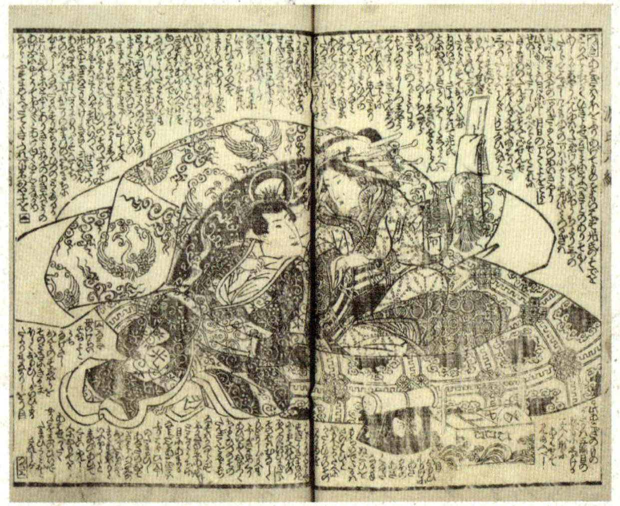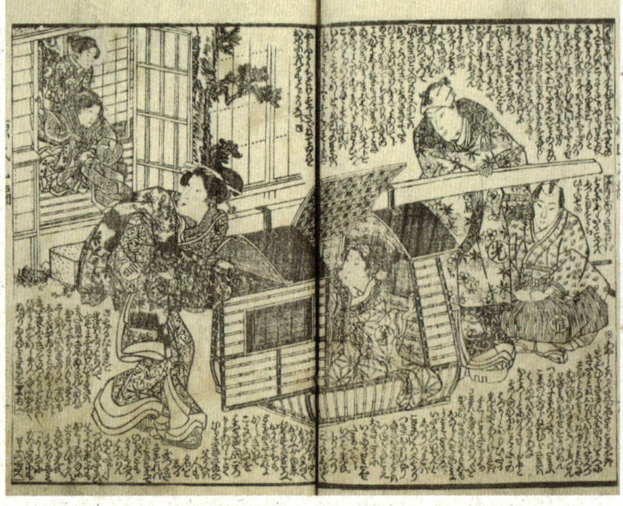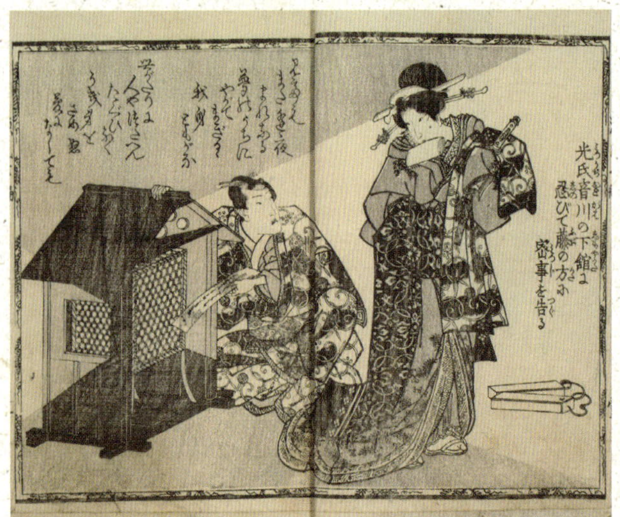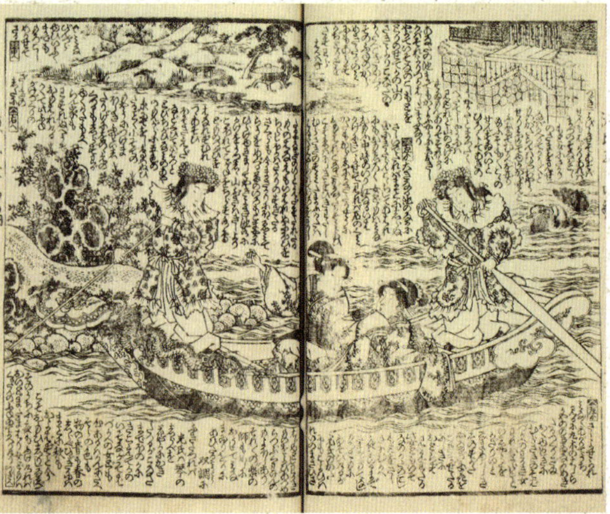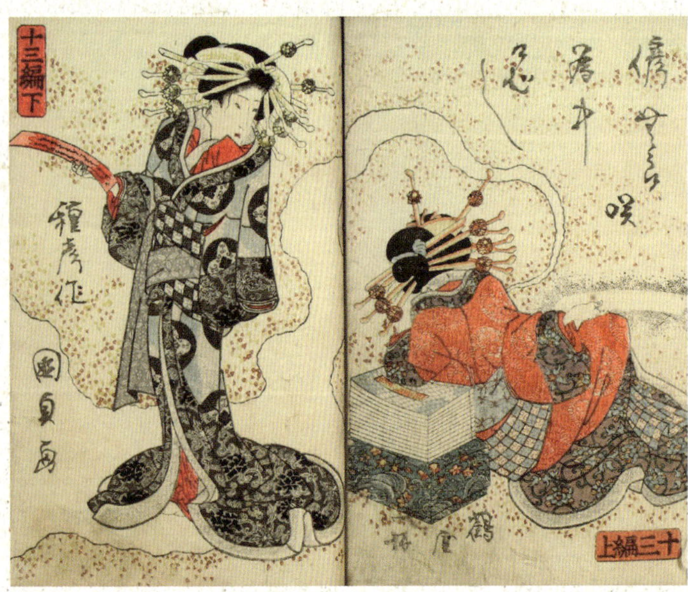

**Top left** Vol. 6, Mitsuuji visits Akogi who holds up an imperial calligraphy.

**Top right** Vol. 9, Murasaki gets into a palanquin.

**Center left** Vol. 7, Mitsuuji hands his outer garments and swords to Karukaya.

**Center right** Vol. 34, two maidservants are rowed by two young girls in Chinese costumes.

**Left** Covers of vol. 13.

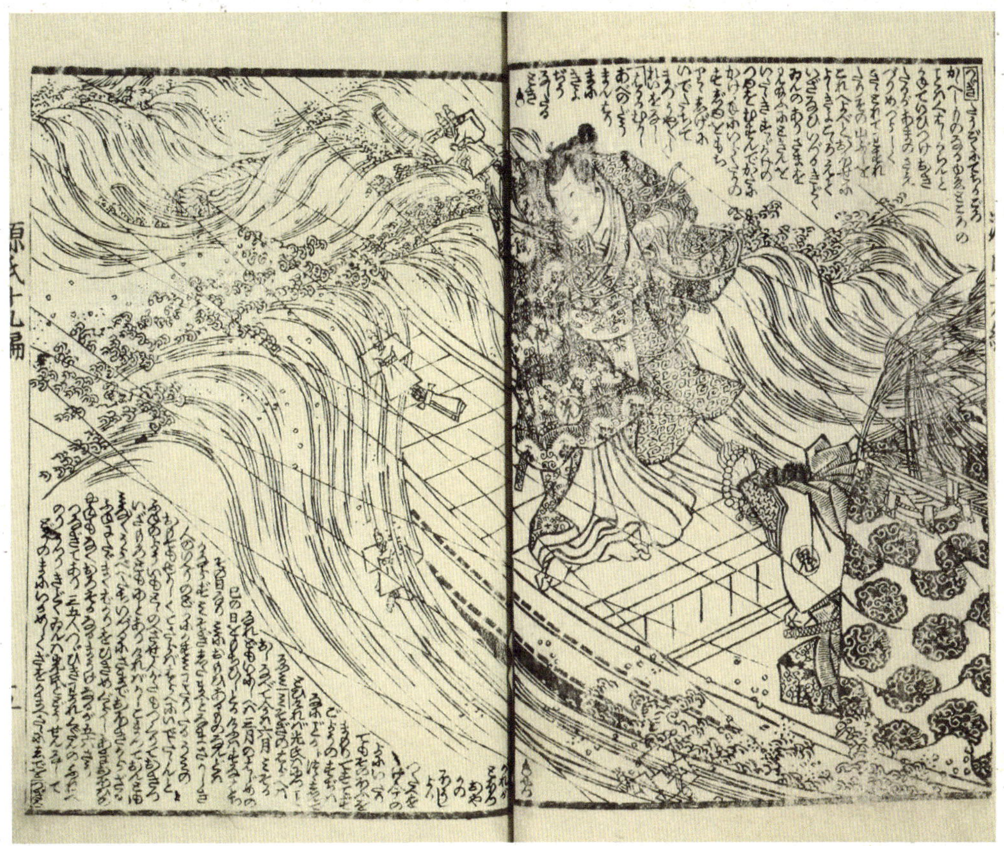

almost 1,300 single prints were published.

All pages of *A Rustic Genji* were printed in black ink, but the covers were produced in full color. Each volume was issued in two booklets. Kunisada designed the two covers for every volume so that they formed a diptych when placed side by side. Each cover depicts one or more characters in the novel against a white background embellished with flecks that look like gold and silver flakes.

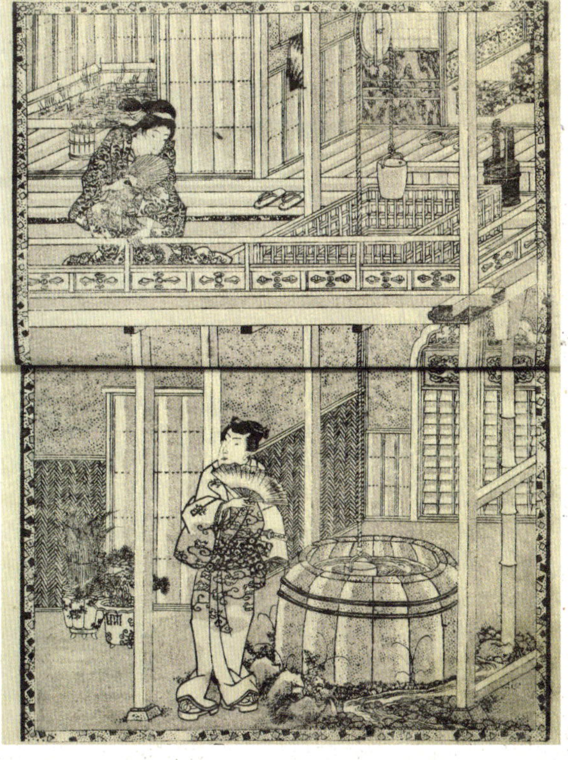

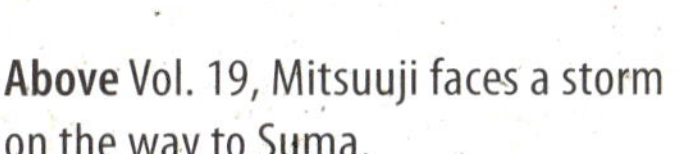

**Above** Vol. 19, Mitsuuji faces a storm on the way to Suma.

**Right** Vol. 21, at a bathhouse, Mitsuuji looks up at Asagiri.

# The Water Margin Digest or The Water Margin in Kana Characters

*Yomihon suiko den / Kanagaki suiko den*

稗史水滸伝／国字水滸伝

1829 (vols. 1–6), 1830 (vols. 7–8), 1831 (vol. 9), 1832 (vol. 10), 1833 (vols. 11–12), 1835 (vol. 13), 1837 (vol. 14), 1838 (vol. 15), 1839 (vol. 16), 1841 (vol. 17), 1847 (vol. 18), 1848 (vol. 19), 1851 (vol. 20)

Authors: vols. 1–6: Santō Kyōzan (1769–1858); vols. 7–9, 13: Ryūtei Tanehiko (1783–1842); vols. 10–12, 14–17: Ryūtei Senka (1806–68); vols. 18–20: Shōtei Kinsui (1795–1862)

Artist: Utagawa Kuniyoshi (1798–1861)

Publisher: Tsuruya Kiemon, et al.

Woodblock printed book (*chūbon*); ink on paper

Waseda University Library

In 1829, a group of six publishers came together to combine their resources to publish an adaptation of the popular fourteenth-century Chinese novel *Shuihu zhuan* (Jp.: *Suiko den*; commonly known in English as *The Water Margin*), written by the popular author Santō Kyōzan. The story revolves around the adventures of a rogue group of heroes, each with particular supernatural powers and specific nicknames, who first fight injustice and later

**Below** Vol. 7, Zhu Gui at the marshes around Mount Liang.

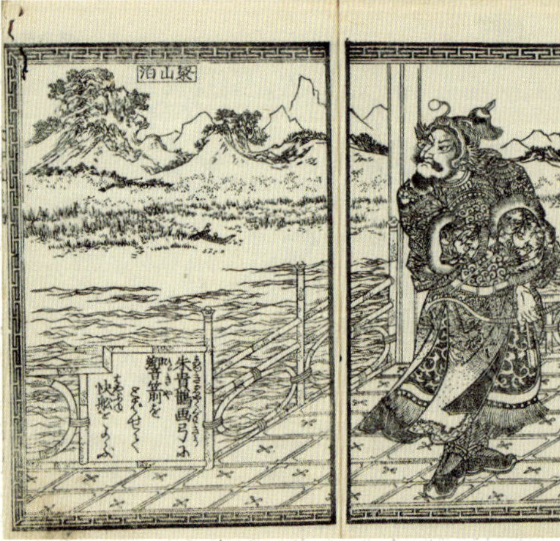

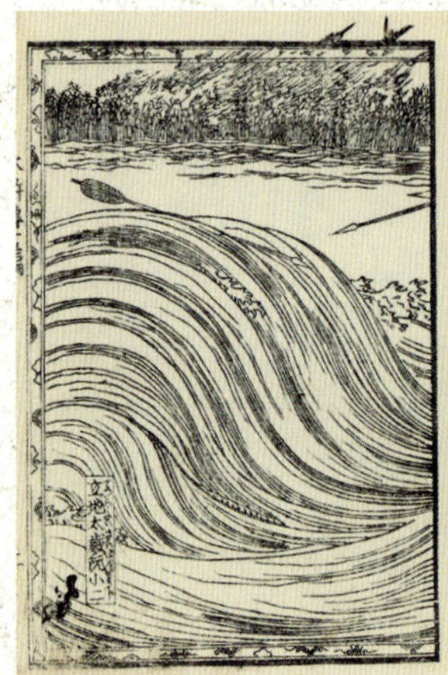
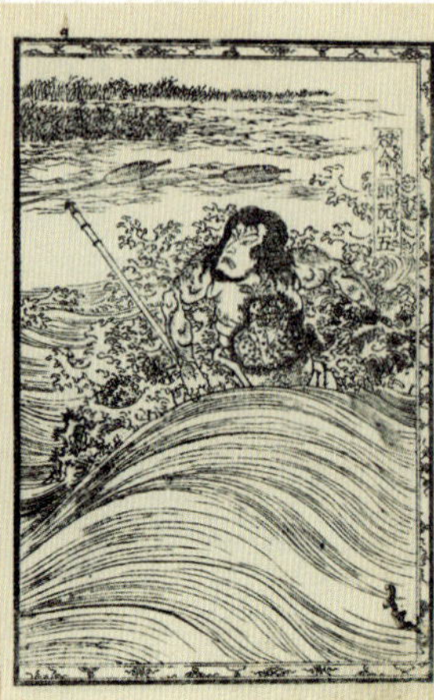

**Above** Vol. 13, Ruan Xiaoer diving after Ruan Xiaowu

serve the emperor. In about 1827, the first prints by Utagawa Kuniyoshi were issued. They portrayed the fictional heroes in a way previously unseen. The print series *One of the 108 Great Men of the Popular Shuihu Zhuan* (*Tsūzoku suiko den gōketsu hyakuhachinin no hitori*), was an immense success and others tried to jump on this bandwagon. To guarantee success for Kyōzan's new novel, *Shuihu Zhuan Digest* (*Yomihon suiko den*), the publishers secured Kuniyoshi himself as the artist for the illustrations. However, Kyōzan's text was not sufficiently captivating and after six volumes of limited success with the buying public the project fell through.

The publishers then turned to Ryūtei Tanehiko and hired him to continue with the story. In 1830, the project was relaunched with the release of volume 7, and to make the break apparent the book's title was revised to *Shuihu Zhuan Written in Kana Characters* (*Kanagaki suiko den*). By volume 10, Tanehiko had asked his student, Ryūtei Senka, to assist and take over, at least for a while. Eventually, Senka continued the story until volume 17, which was published in 1841. Six years later it was revived, and this time the publishers hired Shōtei Kinsui, presumably because Senka was not available as he was tied up in his home province where his father's pawnbroking business went bankrupt. Kinsui continued until the project ended with volume 19, released in 1851.

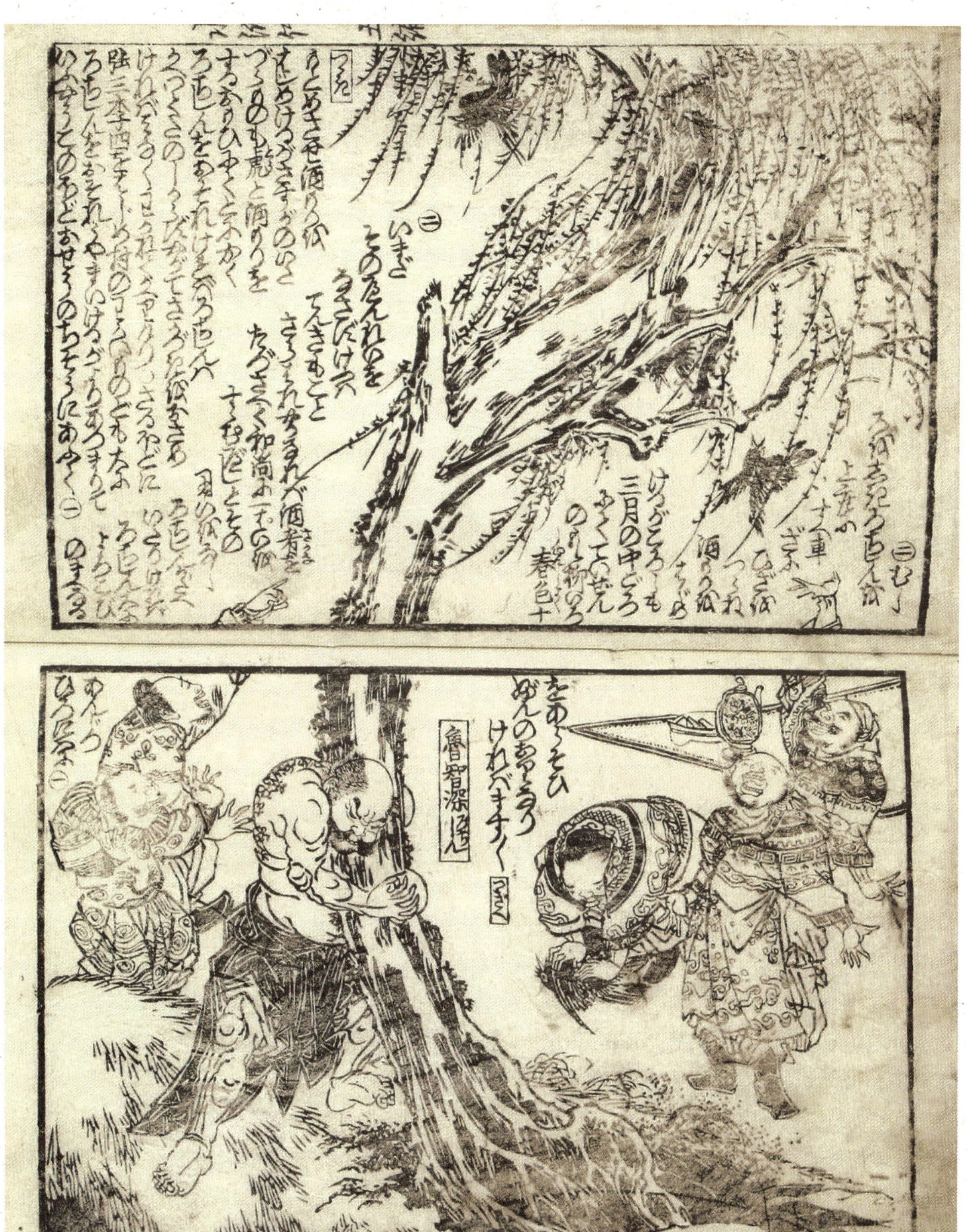

**Above** Vol. 5, Lu Zhishen uprooting a willow tree.

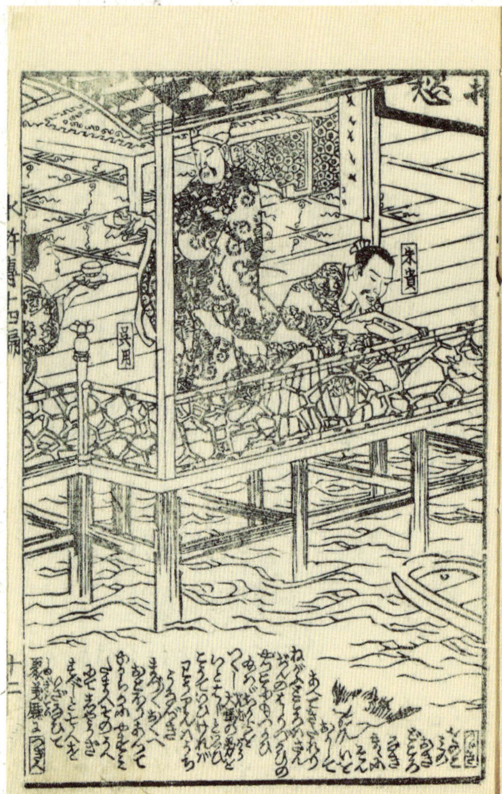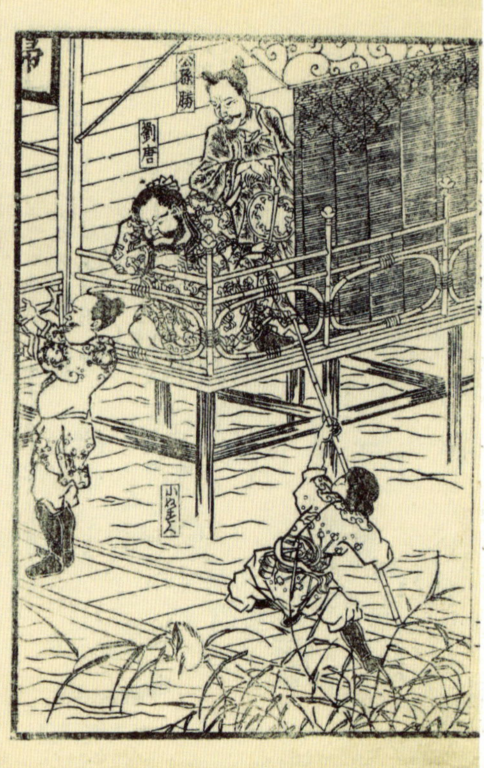

**Above** Vol. 14, Zhu Gui and a messenger.

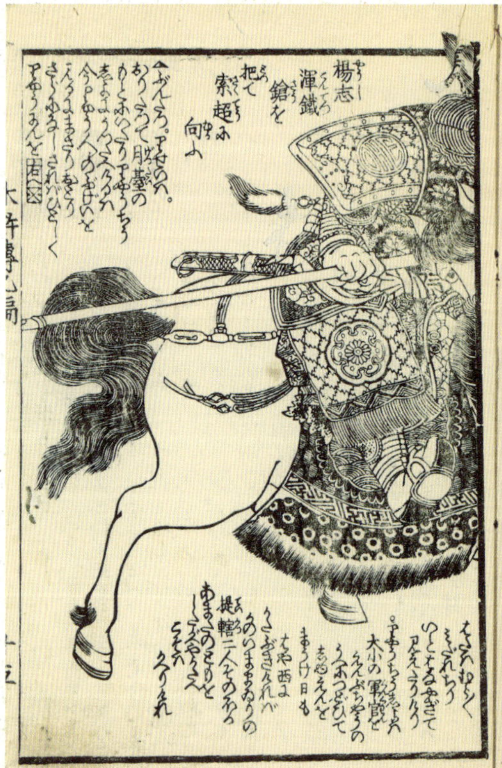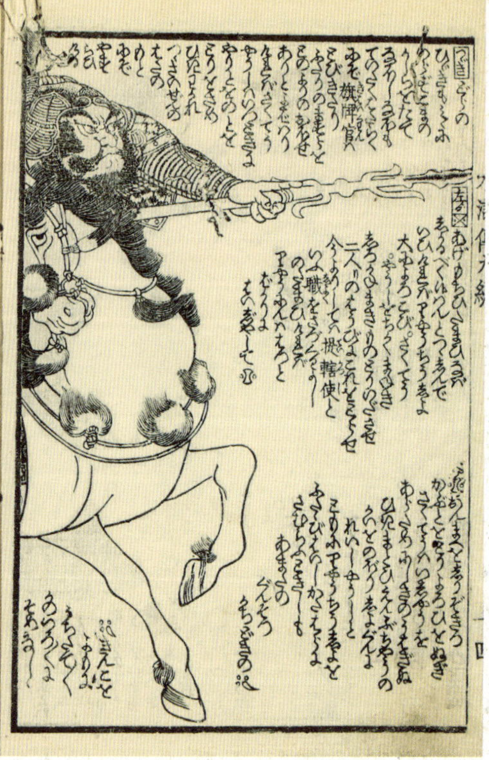

**Right** Vol. 9, Yang Zhi and Suo Chao fight on horseback.

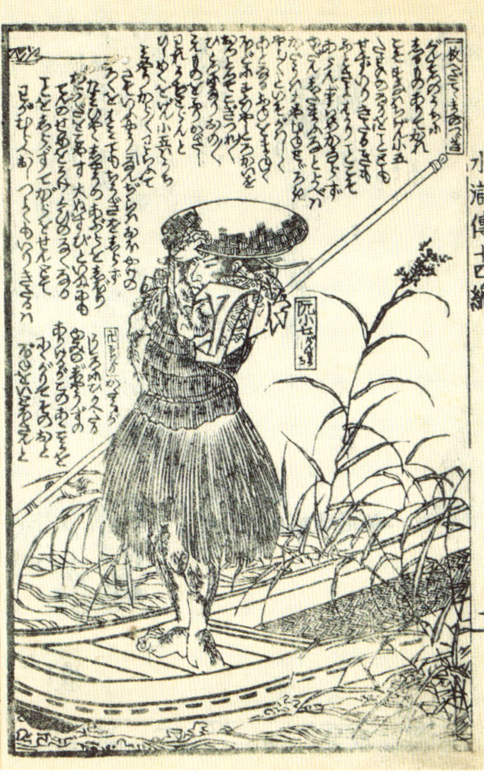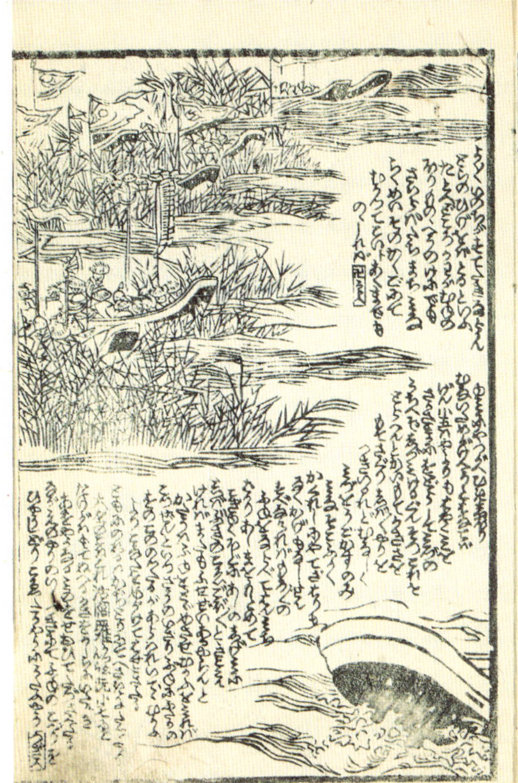

**Above** Vol. 14, Ruan Xiaoqi standing in a boat.

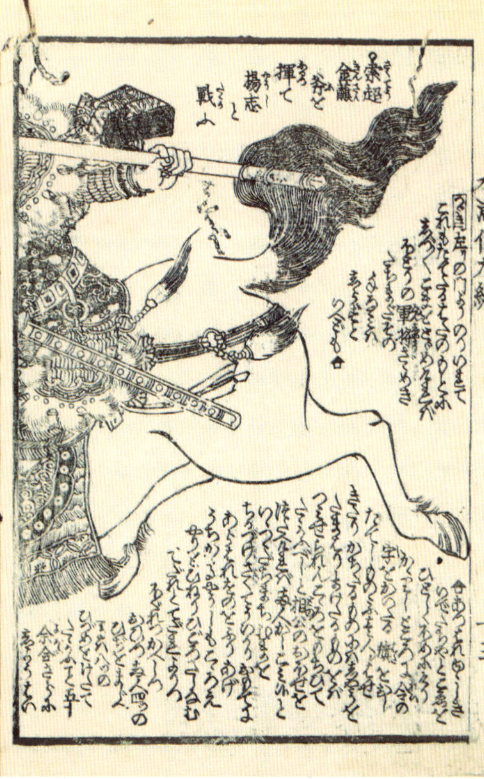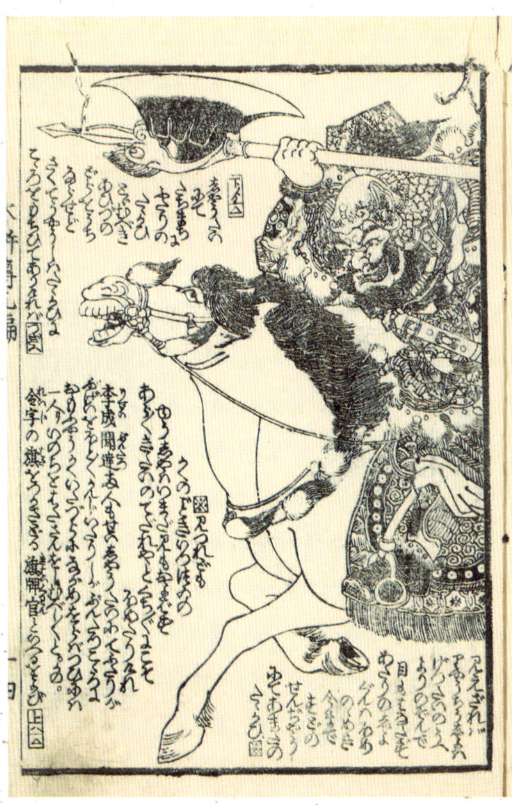

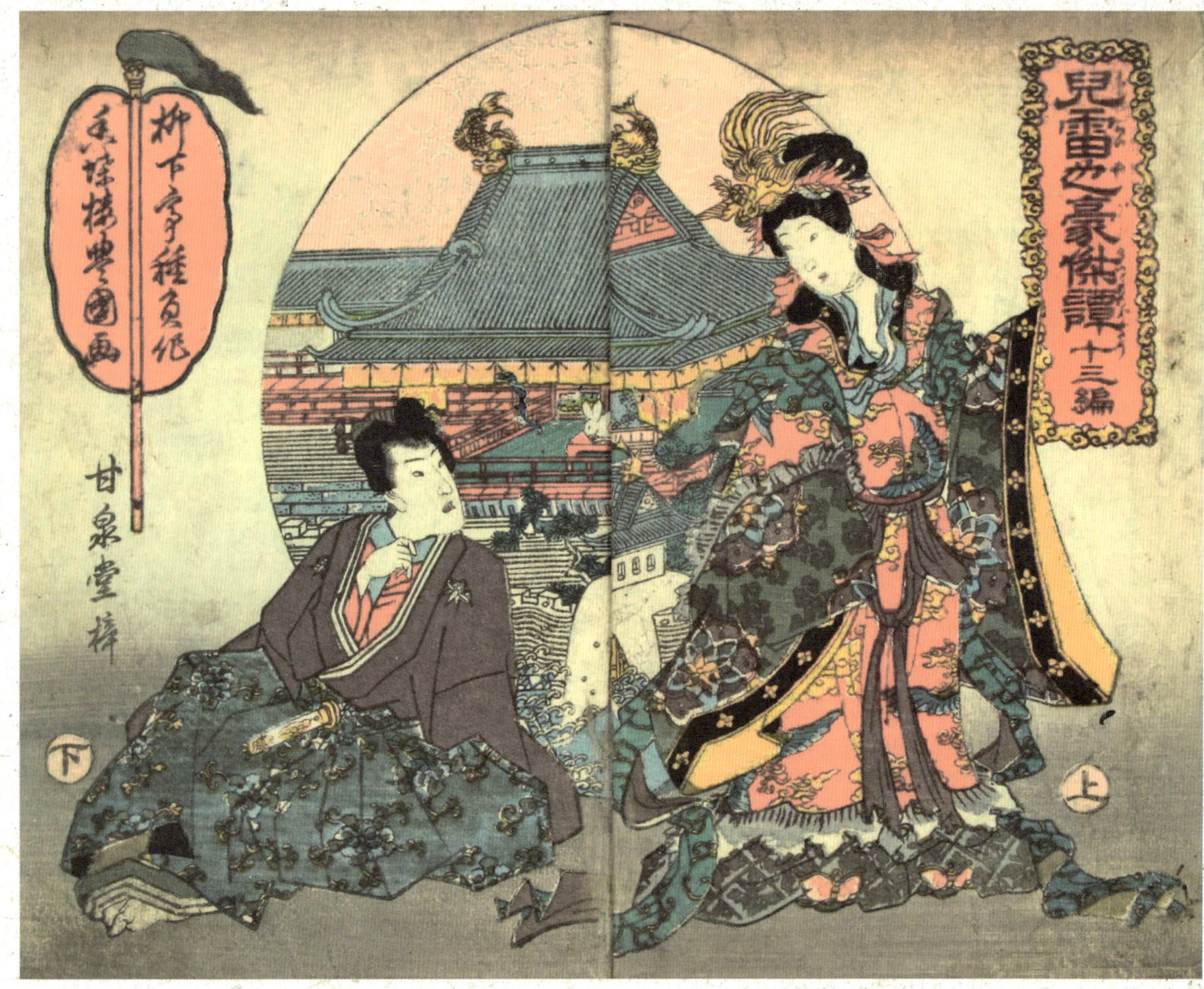

# The Tale of Gallant Jiraiya

### *Jiraiya gōketsu monogatari*

児雷也豪傑譚

1839 (vol. 1), 1841 (vols. 2–3), 1842 (vol. 4), 1846 (vols. 5–6), 1847 (vol. 7), 1848 (vols. 8–9), 1849 (vols. 10–11), 1850 (vols. 12–14), 1851 (vols. 15–17), 1852 (vols. 18–20), 1853 (vols. 21–23), 1854 (vols. 24–25), 1855 (vols. 26–28), 1856 (vol. 29), 1857 (vols. 30–31), 1858 (vols. 32–33), 1859 (vols. 34–36), 1860 (vol. 37), 1861 (vol. 38), 1862 (vol. 39), 1863 (vol. 40), 1864 (vol. 41), 1865 (vol. 42), 1868 (vol. 43)

Authors: vols. 1–11: Mizugaki Egao (1789–1846); vols. 12–36: Ryūkatei Tanekazu (1807–58); vols. 37–43: Ryūsuitei Tanekiyo (1823–1907)

Artists: vols. 1–15, covers vol. 16–36: Utagawa Kunisada (1786–1865); vols. 16–28: Utagawa Kuniteru (1808–76); vols. 29–31: Utagawa Kunimori (active ca. 1840–65); vols. 32–35: Utagawa Kunisada II (1823–80); vols. 36–38: Utagawa Kuniyoshi (1798–1861); vol. 39–41: Utagawa Yoshiiku (1833–1904)

Publisher: Izumiya Ichibei

Woodblock printed book (*chūbon*); ink on paper
Ritsumeikan University Library

The fictional figure Jiraiya made his debut in the novel *The Tale of Jiraiya* (*Jiraiya monogatari*) during 1806–07, penned by Kanwatei Onitake (1760–1818) and illustrated by Katsushika Hokuba (1771–1844). Known as Ogata Shuma Hiroyuki, Jiraiya embodied both virtue and vice. On the one hand he wielded a lethal hand, on the other he donned the mantle of a Robin Hood-type thief. What set him apart was his journey into sorcery under the tutelage of an immortal recluse dwelling on Mount Miyōkō. This immortal could gradually change into a colossal toad, thus imbuing Jiraiya with the arcane art of

**Above** Covers of vol. 13.

**Opposite** Vol. 4, Jiraiya in the mouth of a monster.

toad magic. As a result, depictions of Jiraiya often feature him alongside a toad or engaged in combat against towering serpents armed with firearms.

In 1839, Mizugaki Egao (1789–1846) revived the saga with *The Tale of Gallant Jiraiya* (*Jiraiya gōketsu monogatari*), which surpassed its predecessor in acclaim. Serialized across forty-three volumes between 1839 and 1868, the narrative unfolded under the penmanship of Egao for the initial eleven installments. Subsequently, Ryūkatei Tanekazu (1807–58) took over, guiding the tale to its conclusion, except for volumes 40, 42, and 43, which were written by Tanekazu's disciple, Ryūsuitei Tanekiyo (1823–1907). Richly adorned with illustrations, initially by Utagawa Kunisada (1786–1865), the story pits Jiraiya against his formidable adversary, the youthful swordsman Orochimaru (literally, "Son of a Giant Snake"), harboring the spirit of an ancient serpent entrenched in mountainous depths for a millennium.

Kunisada's fame and popularity as a print designer certainly helped *The Tale of Gallant Jiraiya* bè so successful and run for such a long time. Even when he withdrew as the chief illustrator after volume 15 in favor of his own students (Kuniteru, Kunimori, and Kunisada II), the publisher Izumiya Ichibei retained Kunisada to design the covers of the booklets, which he did until volume 36.

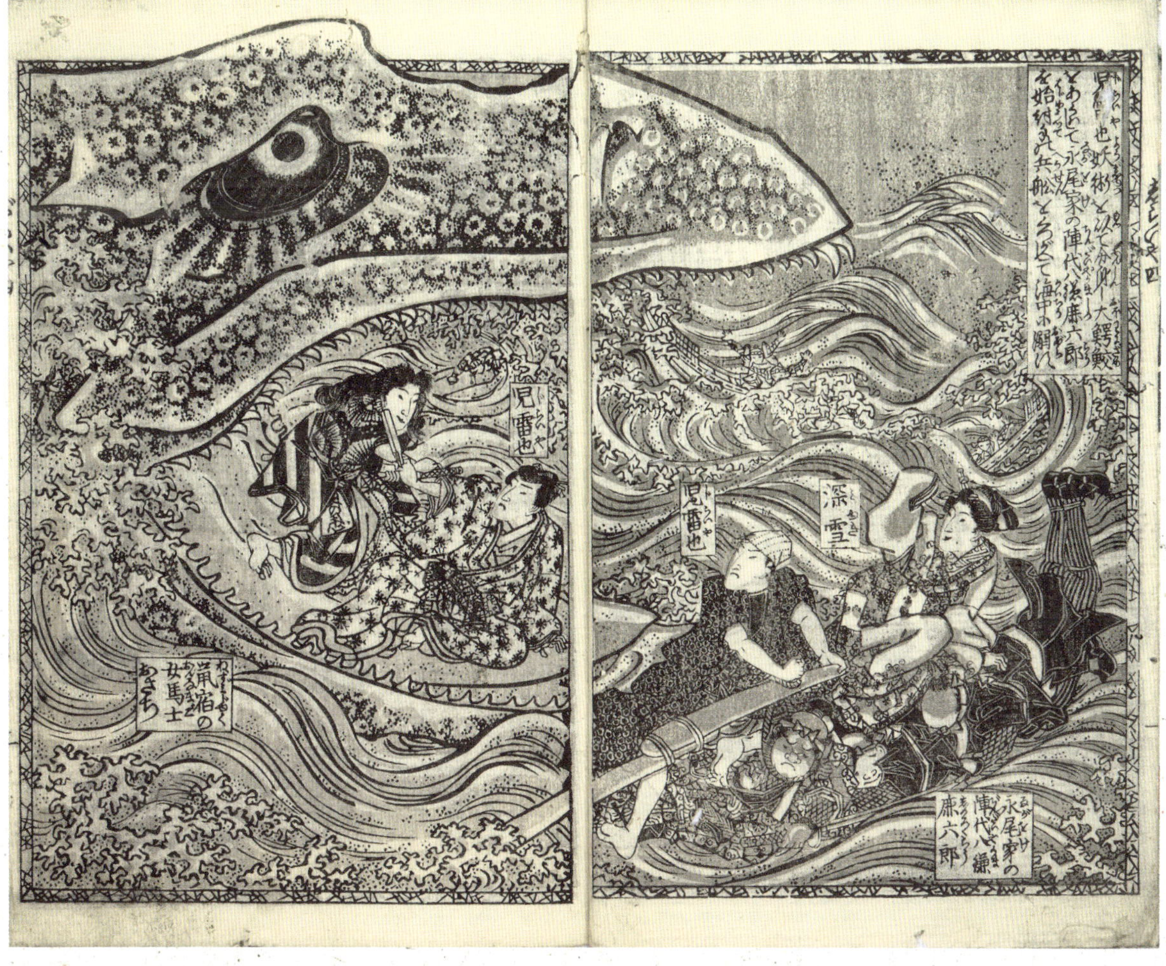

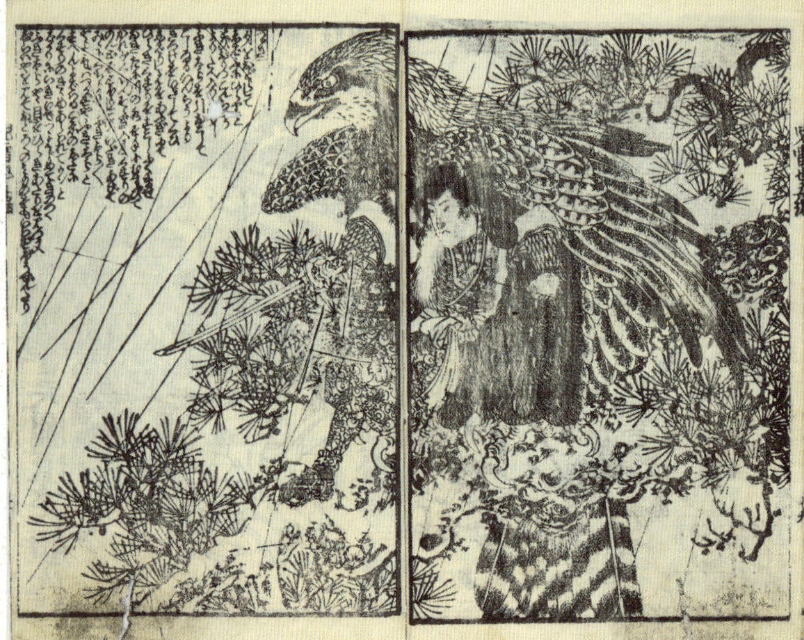

**Left** Vol. 5, Jiraiya in a pine tree.

**Below** Vol. 10, ghosts attack at a graveyard.

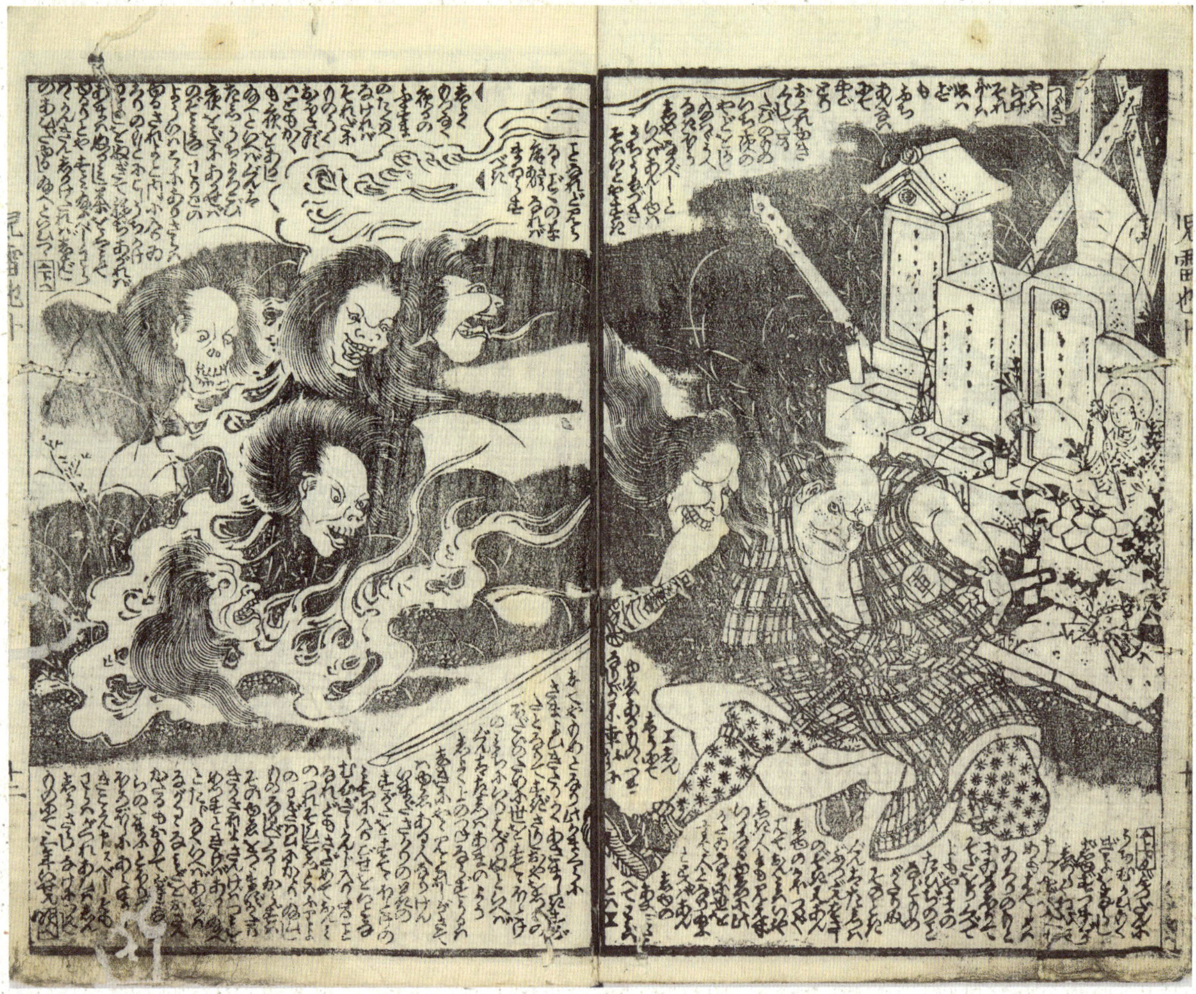

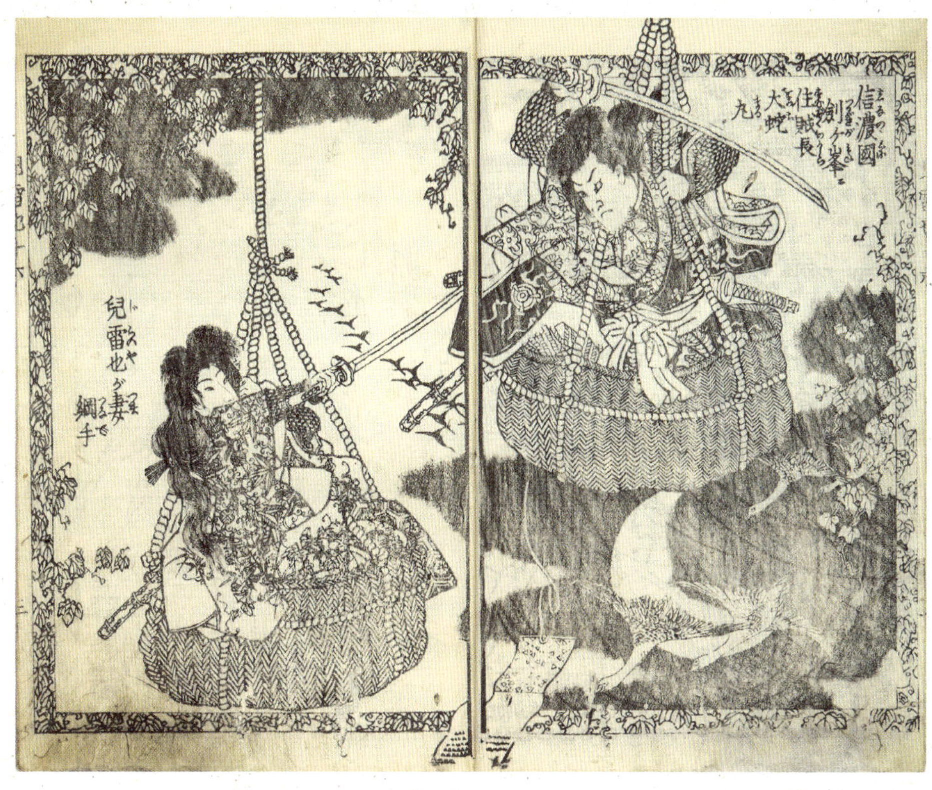

**Above** Vol. 16, Tsunade and Orochimaru.

**Below** Vol. 20, Jiraiya battling a giant snake.

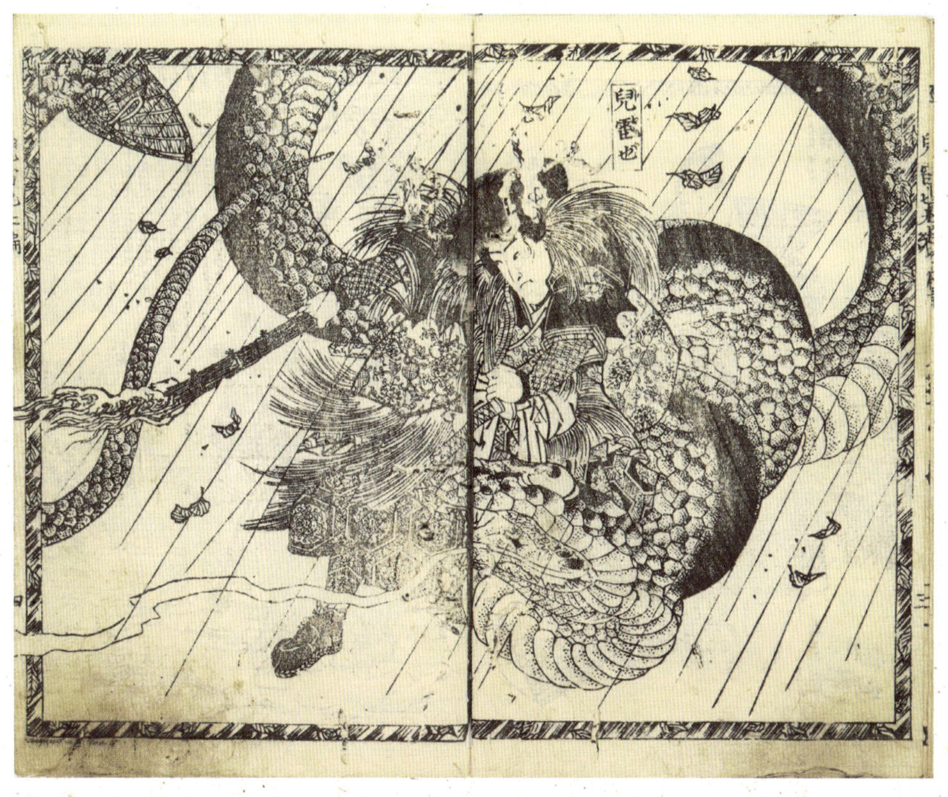

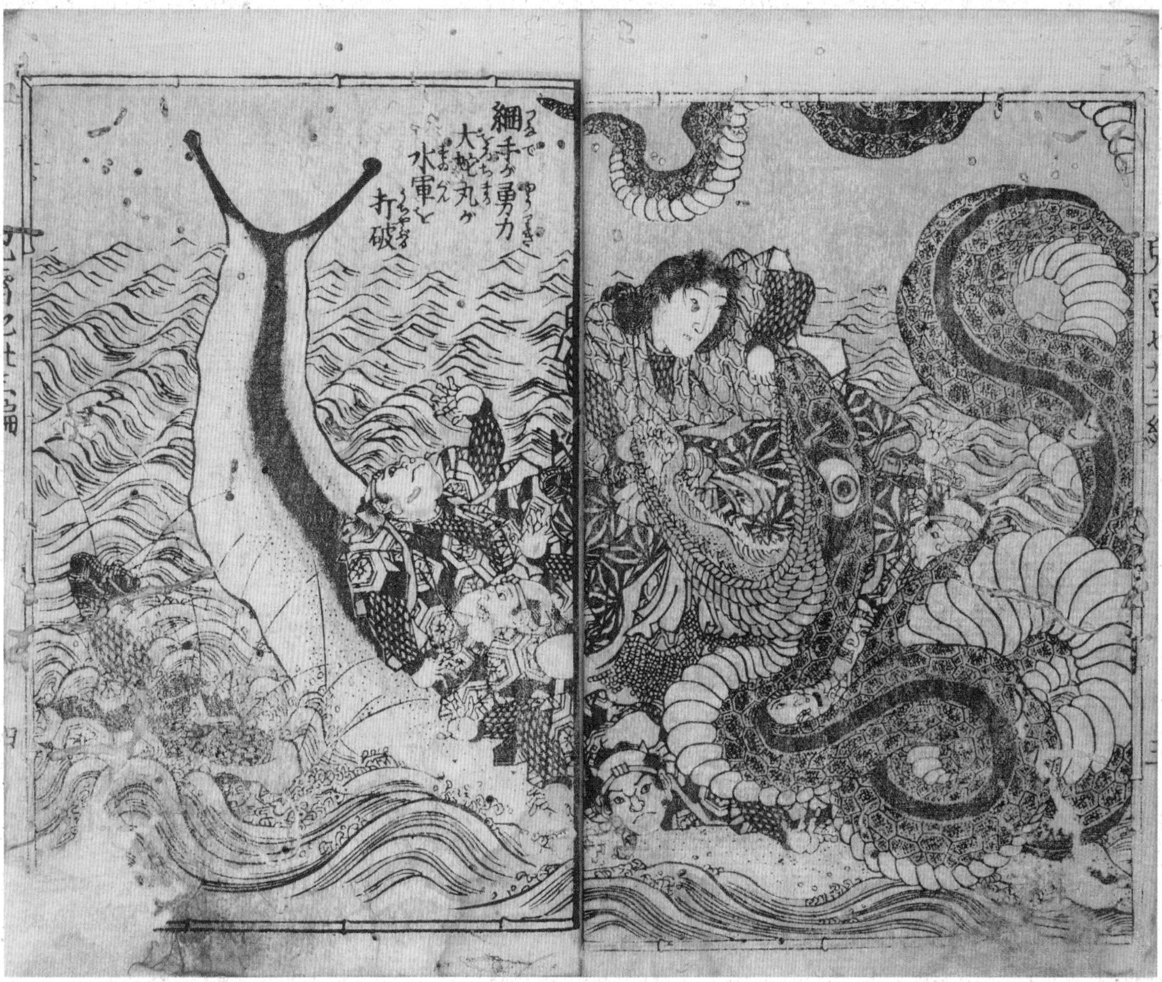

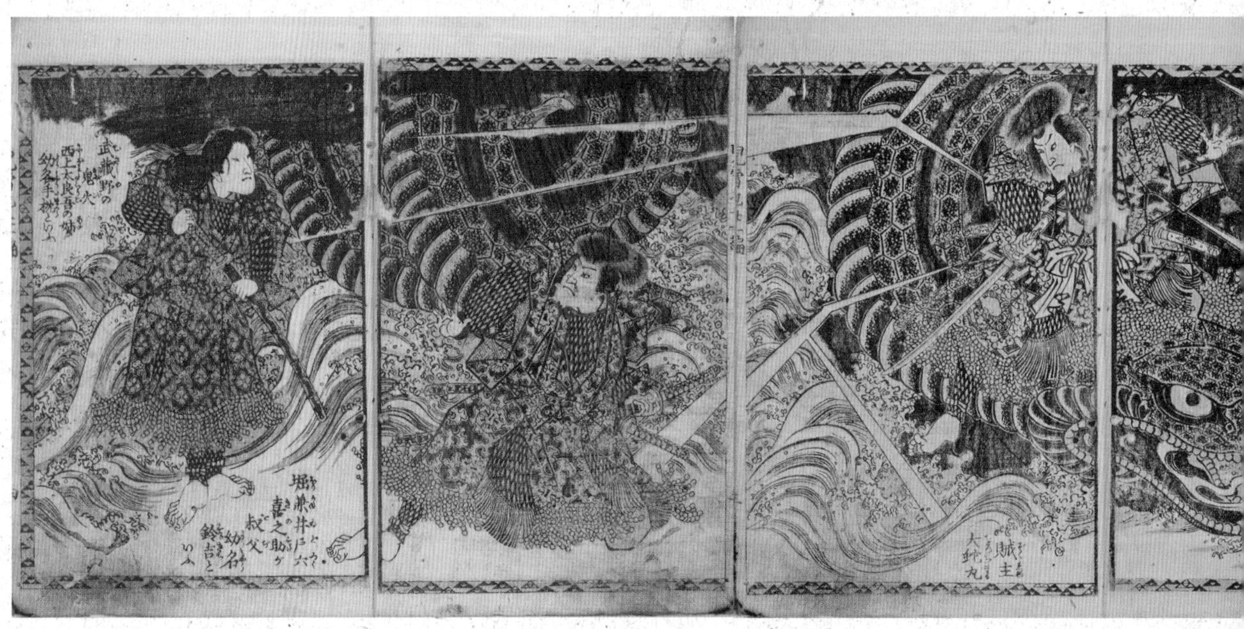

**Above** Vol. 33, Tsunade, riding a giant snail, is attacked by a snake.

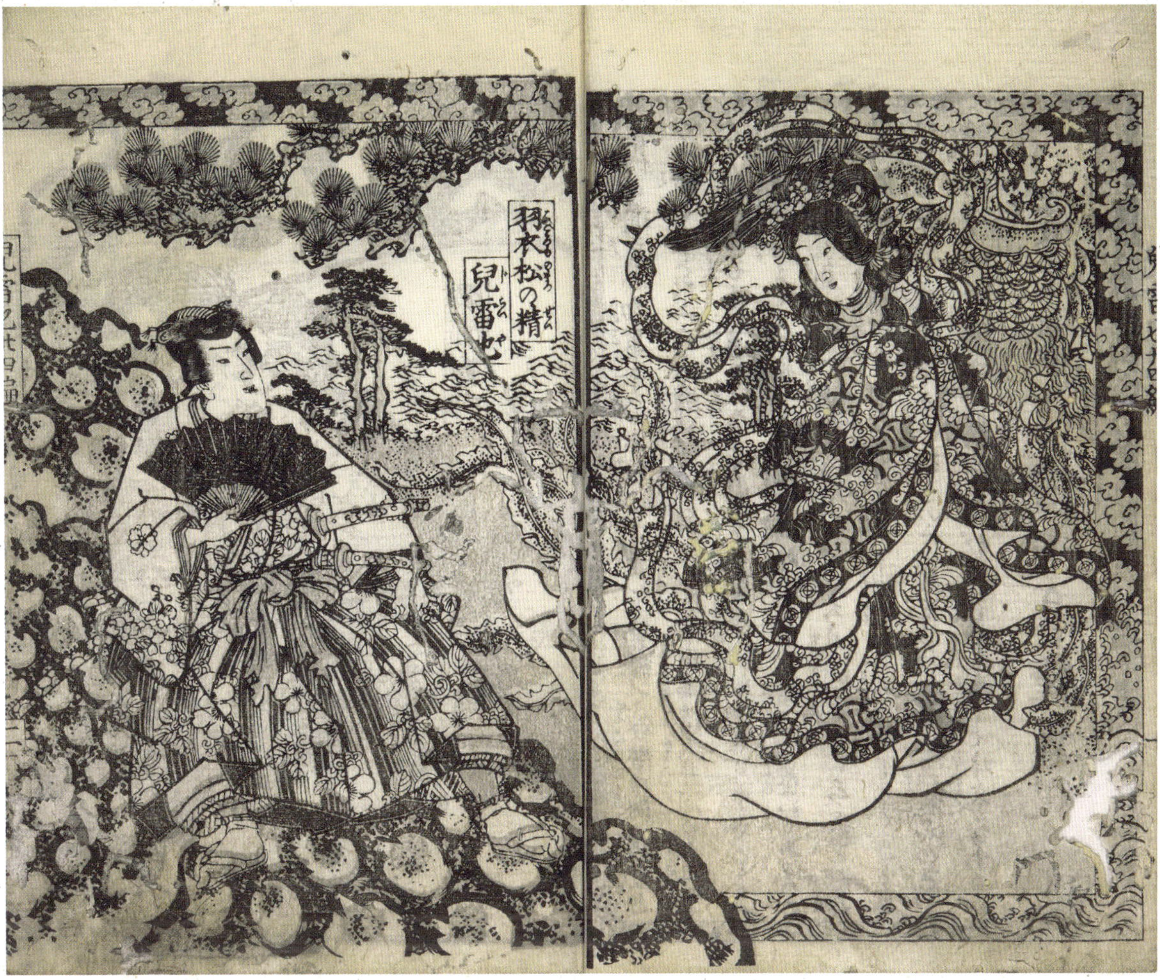

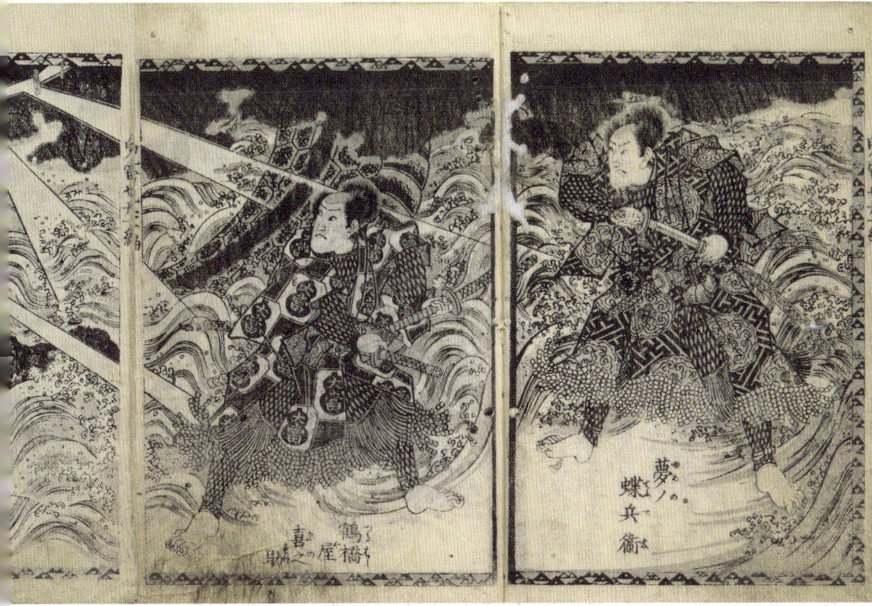

**Above** Vol. 34, Jiraiya and the
Spirit of the Feathered Robe
Pine (*Hagoromo no matsu*).

**Left** Vol. 31, Musashi no
Onibi; Horikane Idoroku;
Orochimaru riding a giant
snake; Tsuruhashiya Kinosuke;
and Yume no Chōbei.

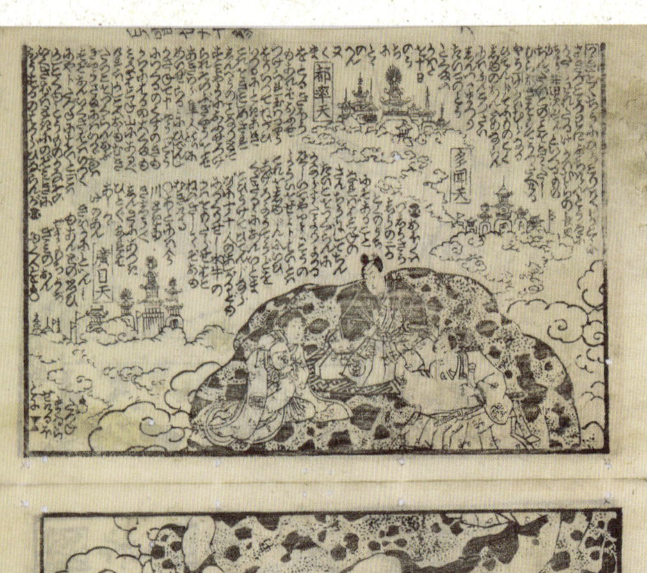

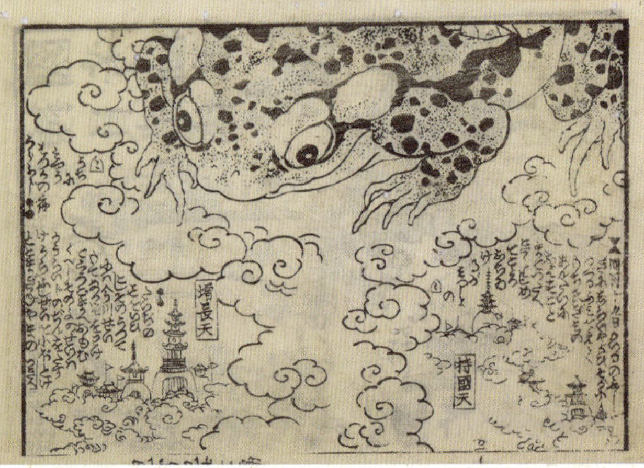

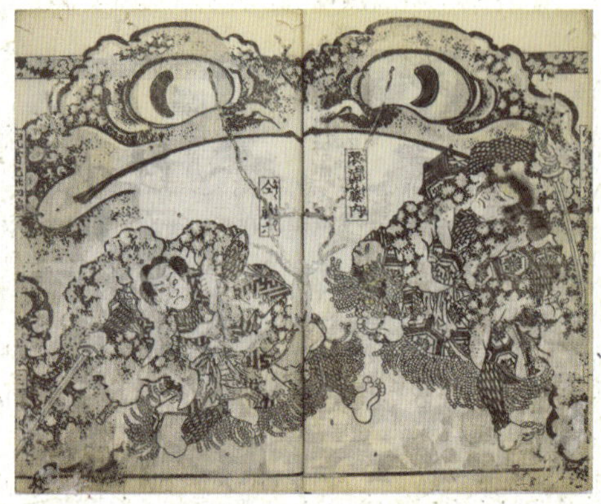

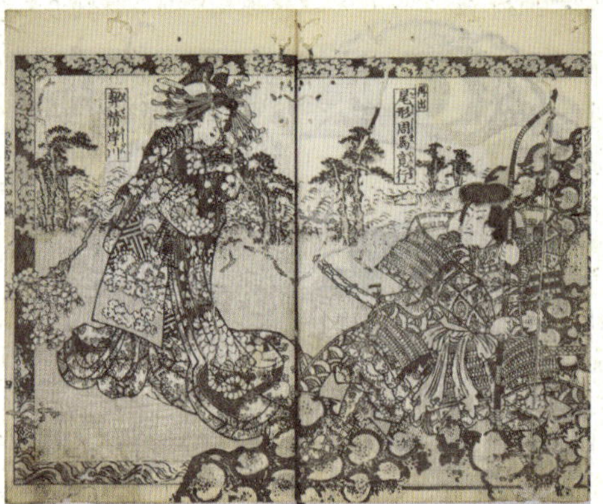

**Above** Vol. 37, Jiraiya and Tsunade sitting on a giant toad.

**Top right** Vol. 34, Tōroku and Tōnai.

**Center right** Vol. 34, the Courtesan Kisegawa and Ogata Shūma Hiroyuki.

**Right** Vol. 37, a giant snake appears.

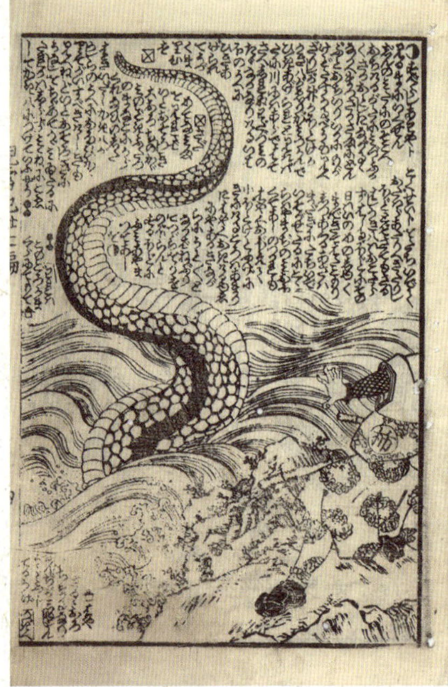

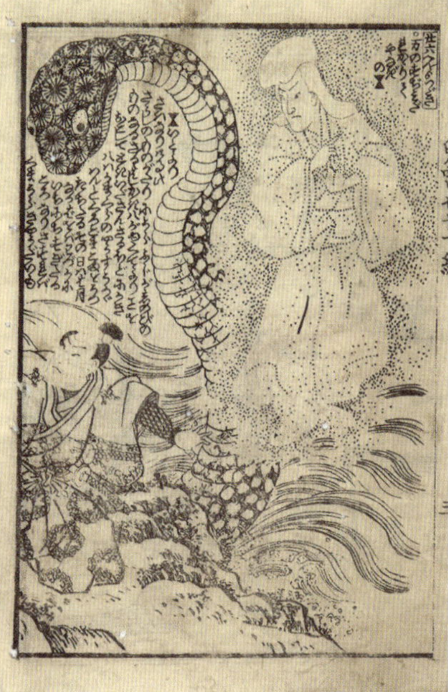

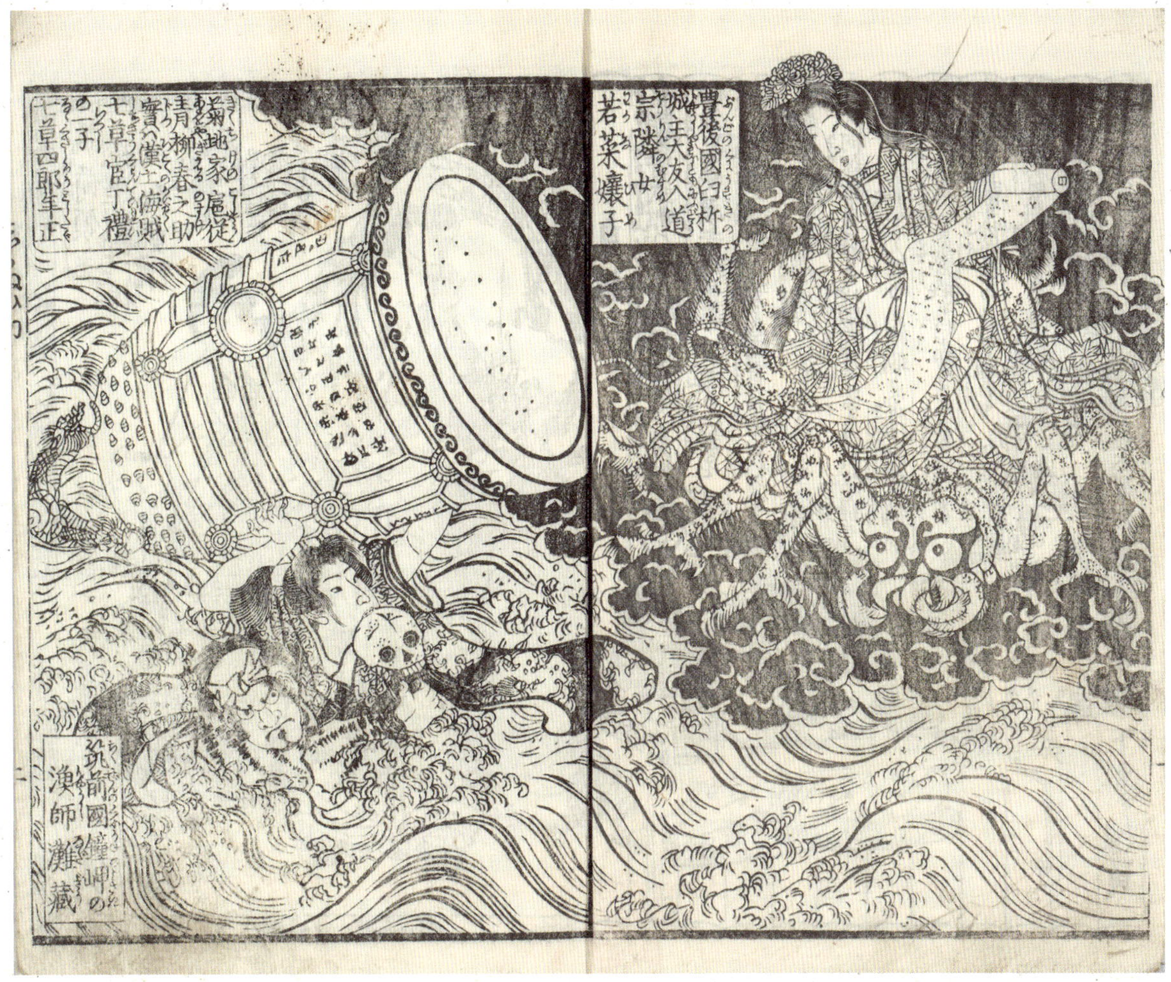

# The Tale of Shiranui

## *Shiranui monogatari*

白縫譚

1849 (vol. 1), 1850 (vols. 2–3), 1851 (vols. 4–6), 1852 (vols. 7–10), 1853 (vols. 11–14), 1854 (vols. 15–18), 1855 (vols. 19–20), 1856 (vols. 21–22), 1857 (vols. 23–24), 1858 (vols. 25–26), 1859 (vols. 27–28), 1860 (vols. 29–31), 1861 (vols. 32–34), 1862 (vols. 35–36), 1863 (vols. 37–40), 1864 (vols. 41–44), 1865 (vols. 45–47), 1866 (vols. 48–51), 1867 (vols. 52–55), 1868 (vols. 56–57), 1869 (vols. 58–59), 1870 (vol. 60), 1871 (vol. 61), 1875 (vol. 62), 1878 (vols. 63–64), 1879 (vols. 65–67), 1880 (vols. 68–70), 1885 (vol. 71), 1909 (vols. 72–90)

Authors: vols. 1–32: Ryūkatei Tanekazu (1807–58); vols. 33–65: Ryūtei Tanehiko II (1806–68); vols. 66–90: Ryūsuitei Tanekiyo (1823–1907)

Artists: vols. 1–8.1, covers of vols. 8.2–36: Utagawa Kunisada (1786–1865); vols. 8.2–36: Utagawa Kunisada II (1823–80); vols. 37–63: Utagawa Yoshiiku (1833–1904); cover vols. 62–63: Toyohara Kunichika (1835–1900); vols. 64–71: Morikawa Chikashige (active ca. 1869–82); vols. 69–71: Toyohara Chikanobu (1838–1912)

Publishers: Fujiokaya Keijirō (vols. 1–20); Ryūkadō (vols. 21–26); Hirookaya Kōsuke (vols. 27–61); Maruya Tetsujirō (vols. 62–71); Hakubunkan (vols. 72–90)

Woodblock printed book (*chūbon*); ink on paper (vols. 1–71)

National Institute of Japanese Literature

**Above** Vol. 1, Nadazō, Nanakusa Shirō Toshisada, and Princess Wakana.

*The Tale of Shiranui* (*Shiranui monogatari*) emerged as a serialized novel in 1849, authored by Ryūkatei Tanekazu with captivating illustrations by Utagawa Kunisada. Its publication journey initially culminated with the release of its 71st volume in 1885. In 1900, the first volume of a reprint without illustrations was issued. The second book followed in 1909 with the continuation of the storyline by Ryūsuitei Tanekiyo until volume 90.

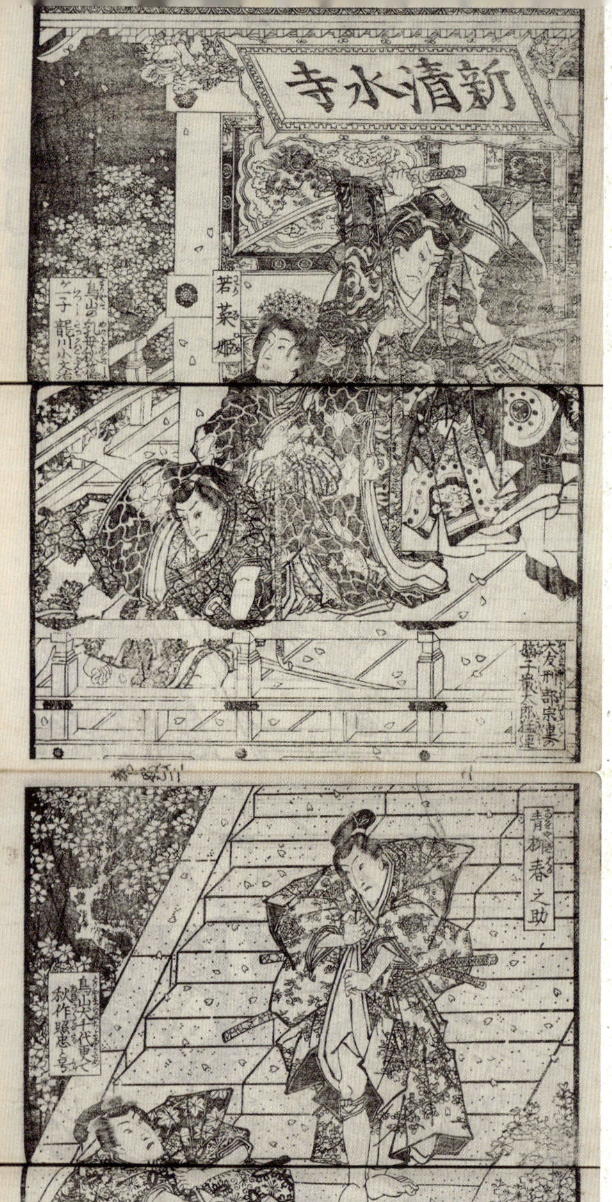
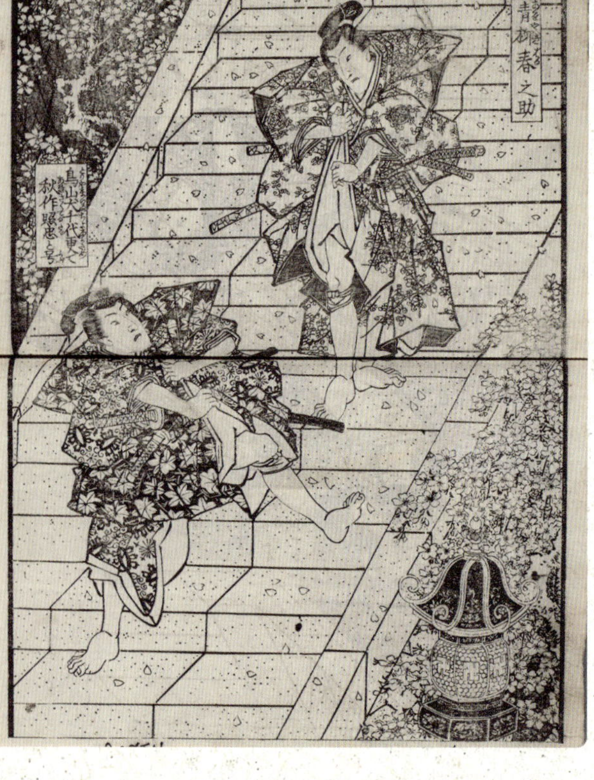



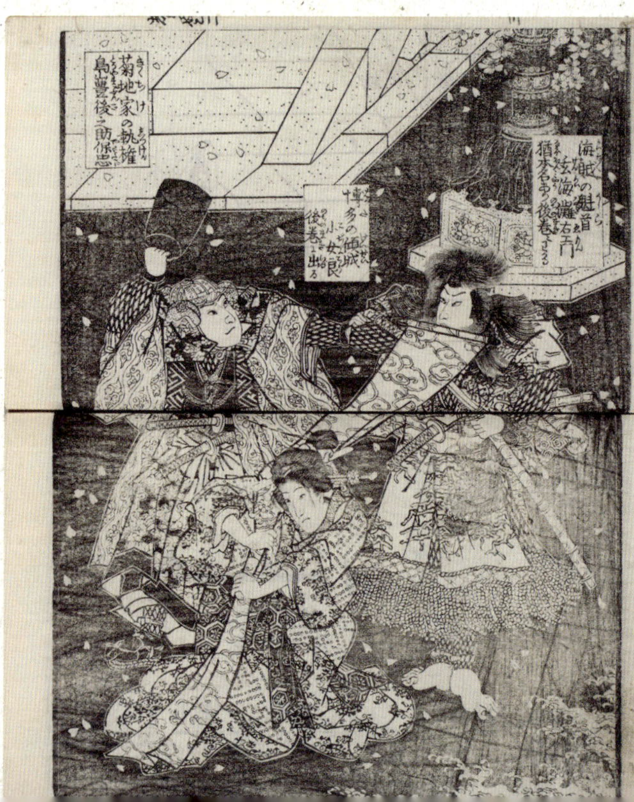

Set in Kyushu, Japan's southern-most large island, renowned for its ethereal *shiranui* ghost lights, the narrative centers on Princess Wakana, the legendary daughter of Ōtomo Sōrin (1530–87), the feudal lord of Bungo Province in eastern Kyushu. Notably, Sōrin, a rare convert to Catholicism amongst feudal lords, found him-self embroiled in a clash with the Shimazu clan over territorial con-trol, a conflict resolved only in 1587 through the intervention of Toyotomi Hideyoshi (1537–98), Japan's revered "Great Unifier," who seized the entire island with Sōrin's assistance. Within the novel's rich tapestry, Sōrin falls under suspicion of rebellion and meets his demise at the hands of henchmen from the rival Kikuchi clan. Wakana, fleeing Bungo in her youth, finds solace and up-bringing under the care of the colossal spider dwelling in Nishi-kigatake, ignorant of her royal lineage. Endowed with a mystical scroll, she unlocks the secrets of spider magic, empowering her quest for retribution against those responsible for her father's un-timely death.

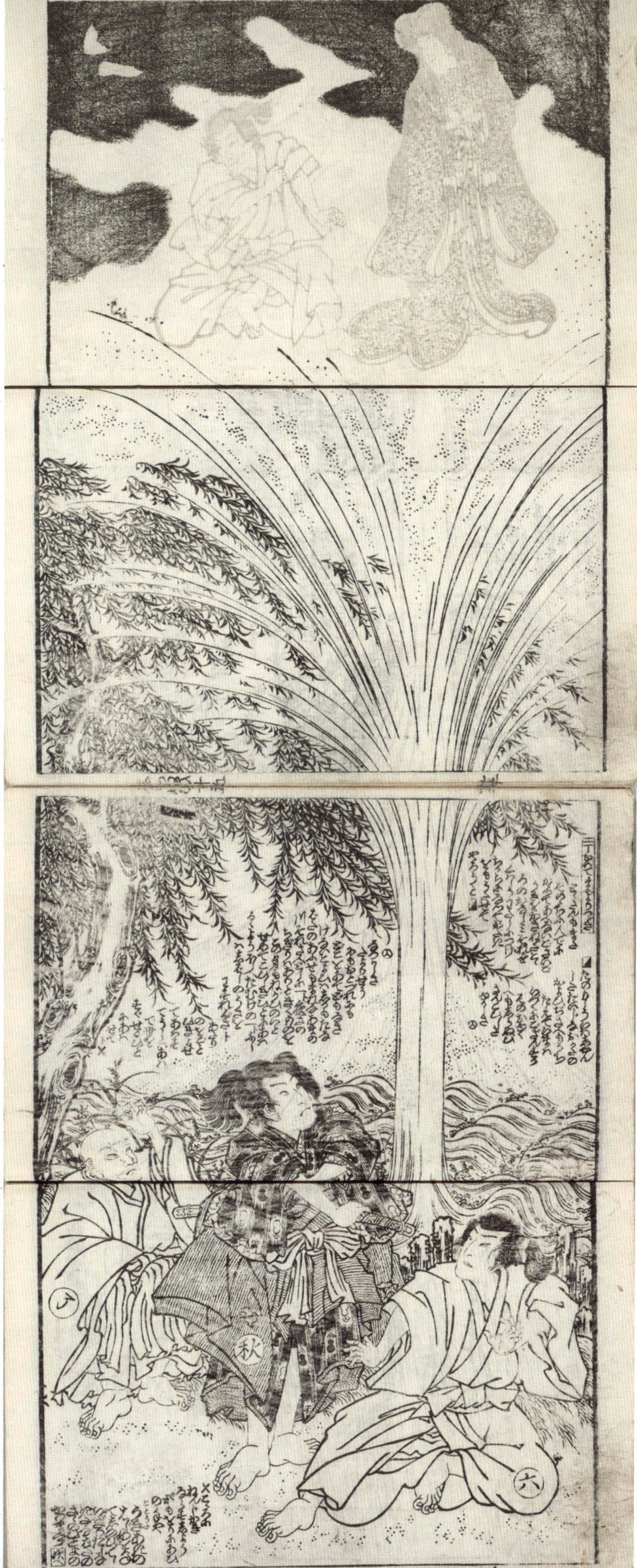

**Right** Vol. 15, Washizu Shichirō and Princess Wakana on top of a fountain.

Until 1852, Kunisada led the project as principal illustrator but then passed it on to his son-in-law, Utagawa Kunisada II. In order to secure high sales through his family name, Kunisada continued to design the covers of the booklets for another ten years, until volume 36. Sometimes Kunisada also designed the first, more luxuriously printed openings, for example, the first booklet of volume 34 where Princess Wakana is watched from the sky by two warriors in a balloon.

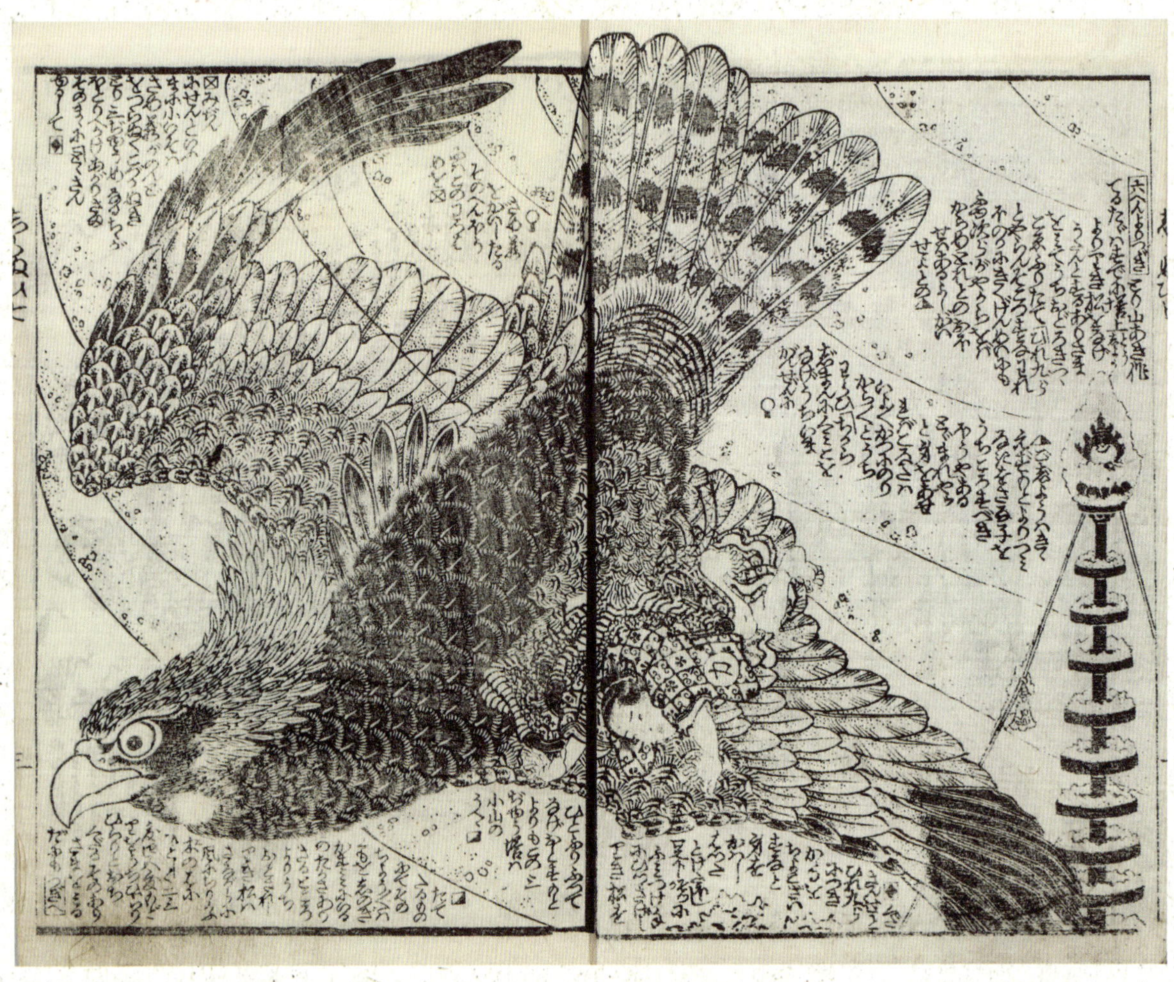

**Below** Vol. 7, a giant eagle.

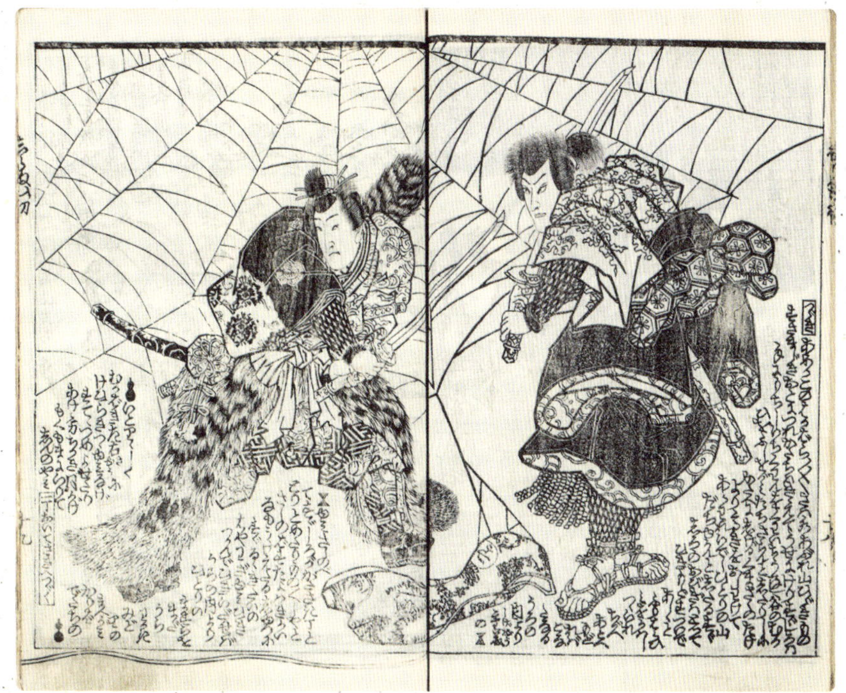

**Right** Vol. 1, Washizu Rokurō and Genkai Nadaemon.

**Below** Vol. 4, a spider with the head of Kojorō.

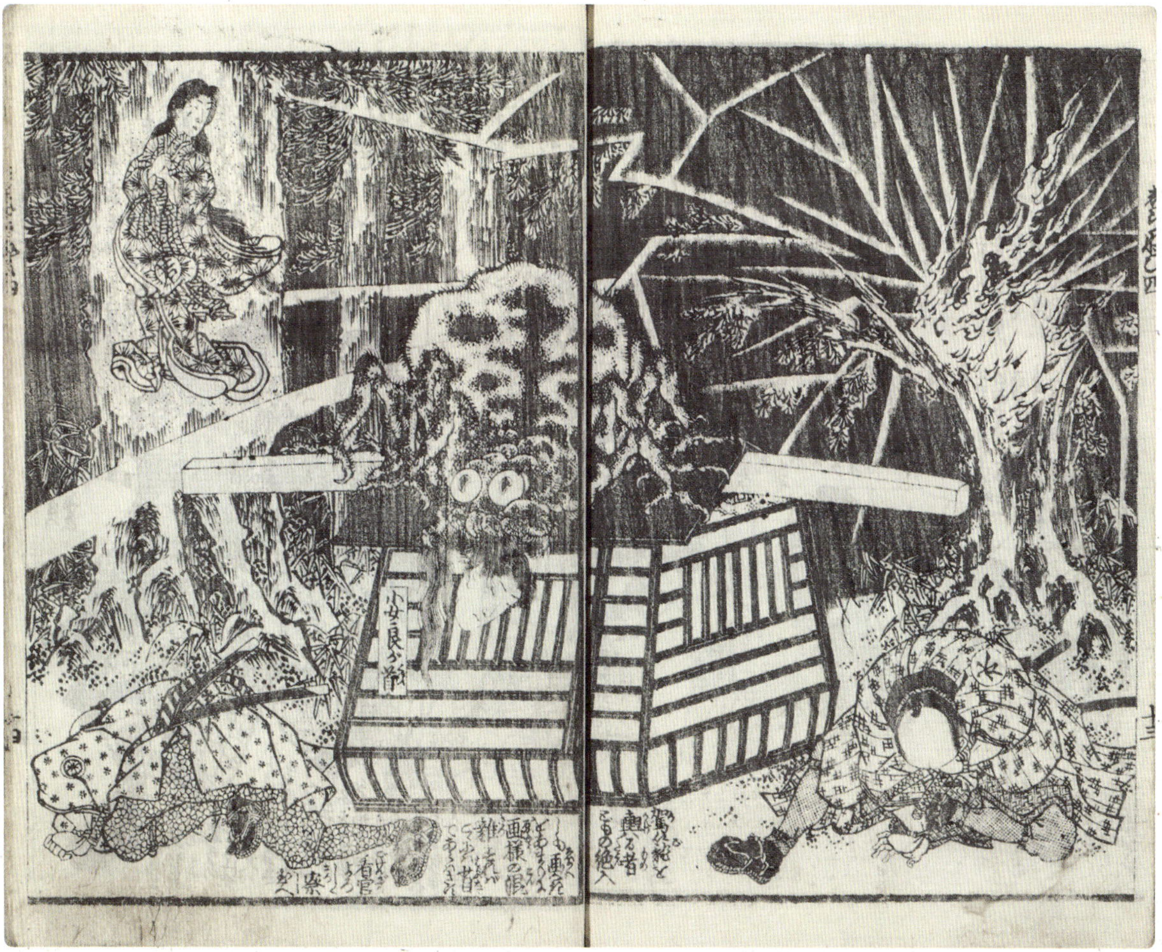

Below Vol. 16, Princess Wakana
and the giant spider.



Bottom Vol. 5, Takigawa Kobunji; Ōtomo
Gyōbu; Washizu Shichirō; Kojorō; Koiso;
Muraoka Shinpe; Washizu Rokurō;
Haramura no Inshi; and Dazai Tsunefusa.

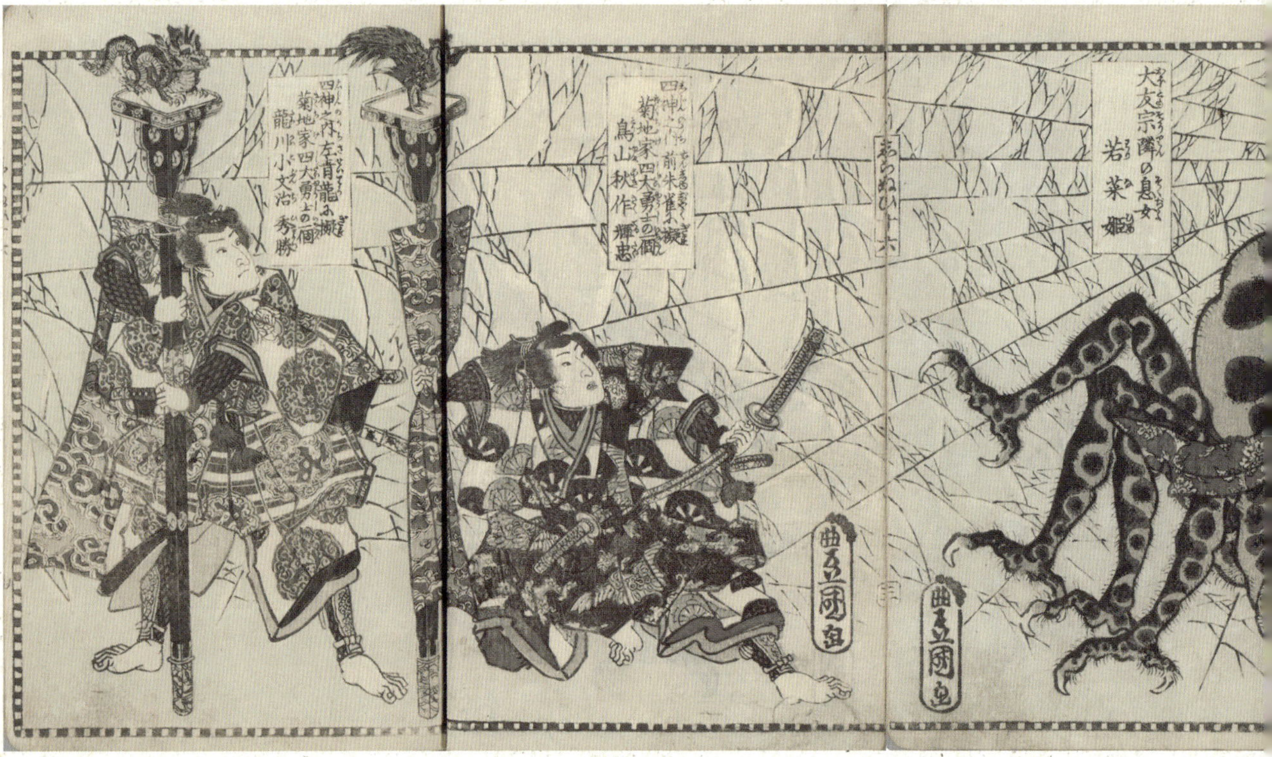

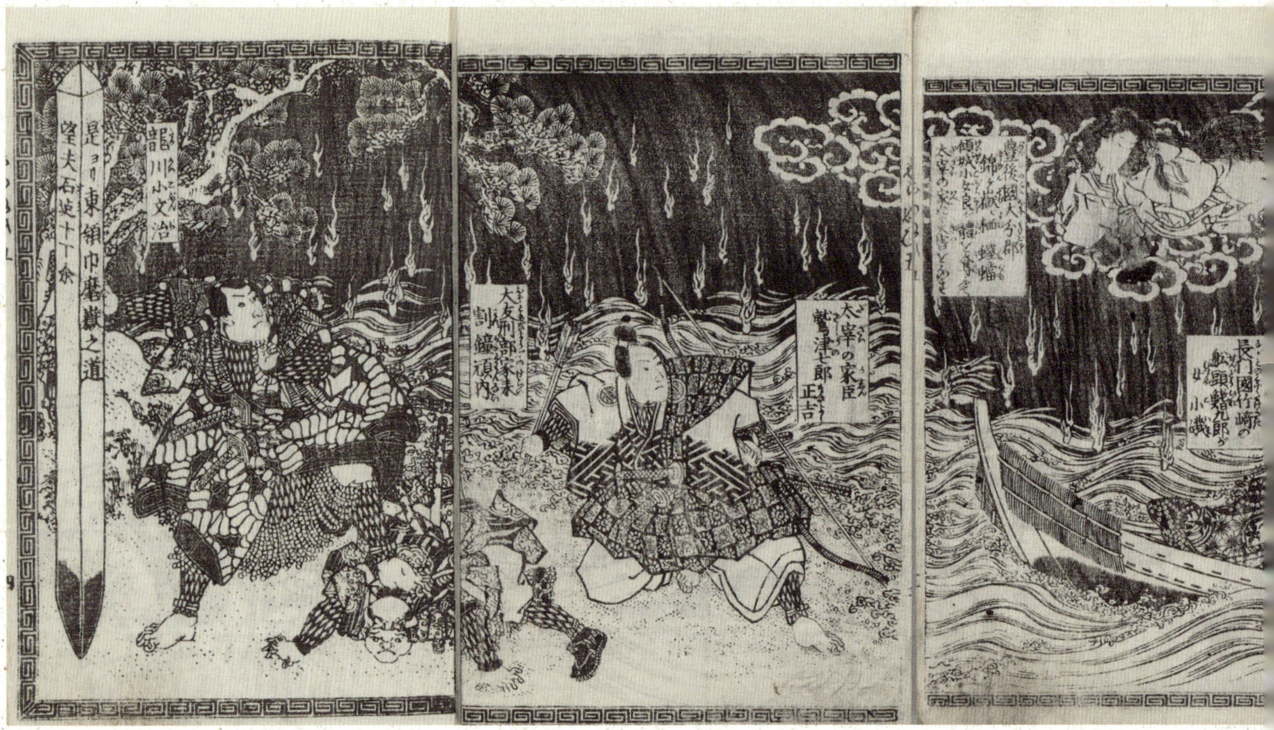

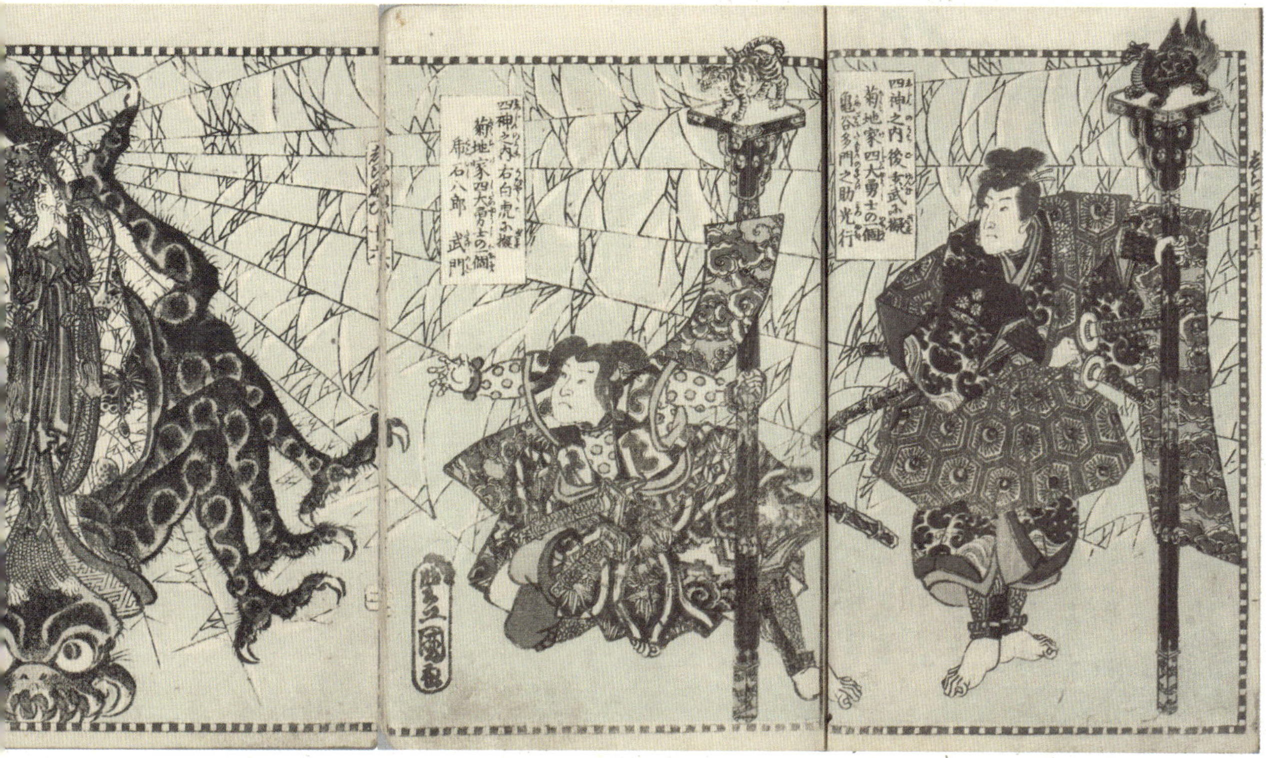

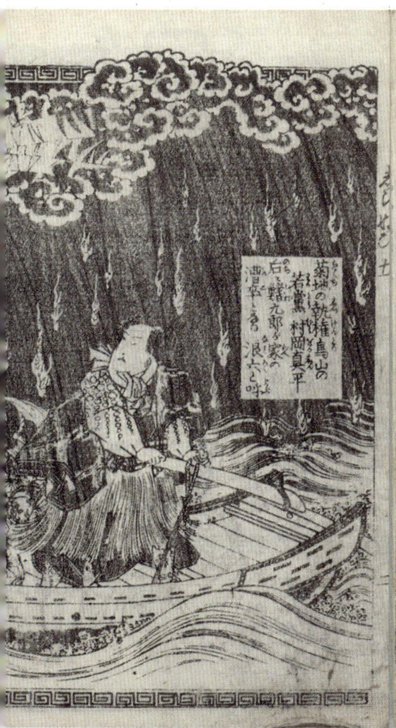
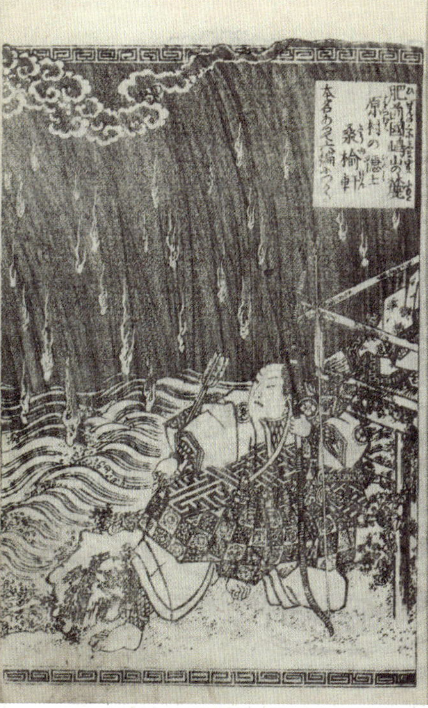
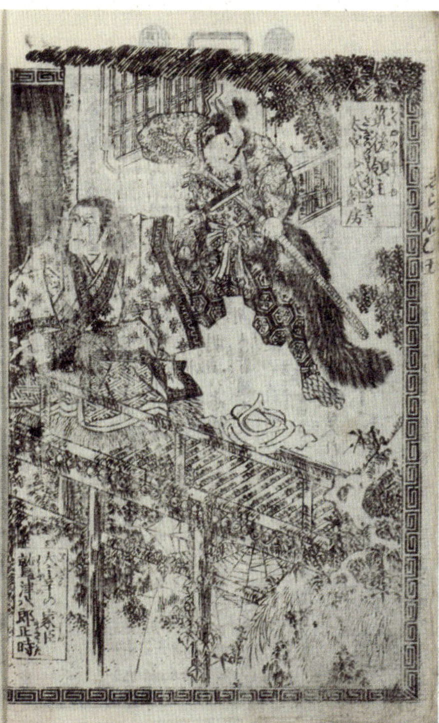

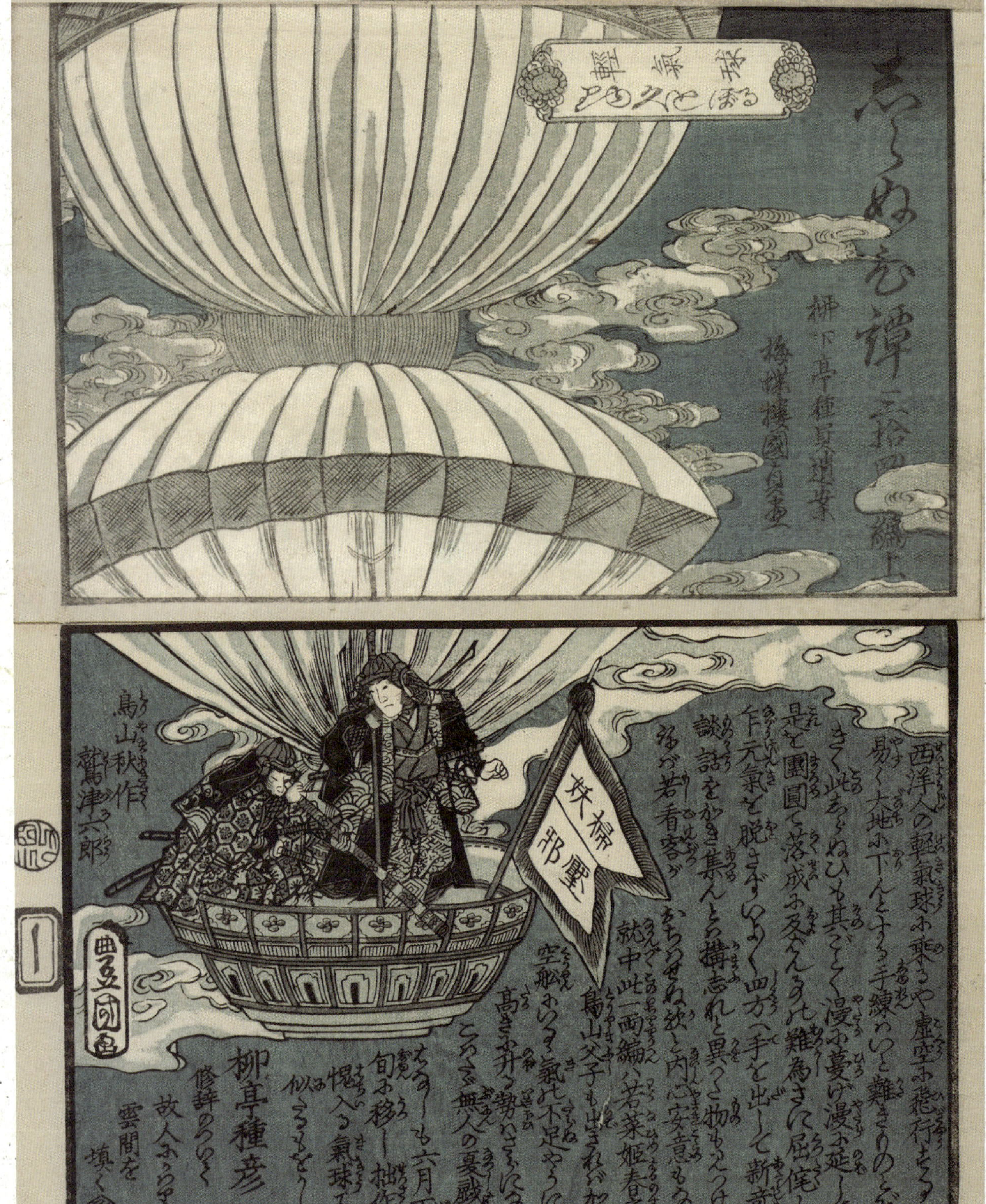

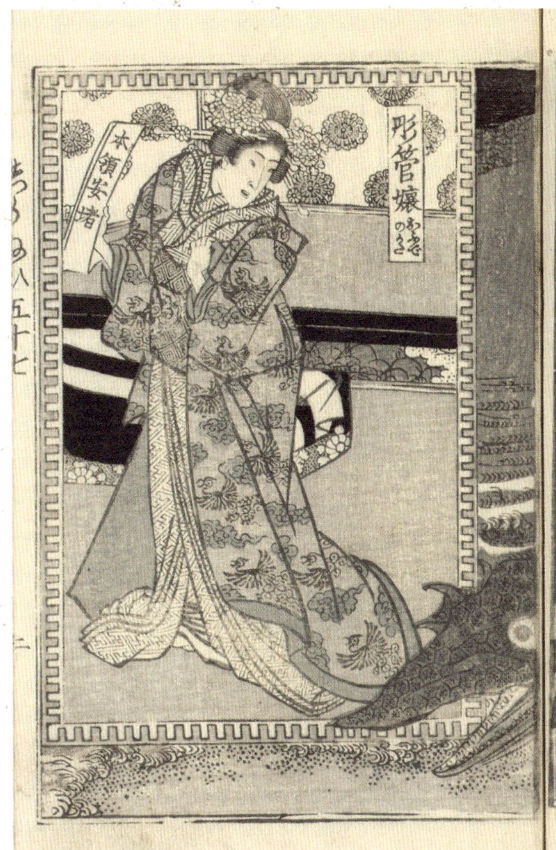

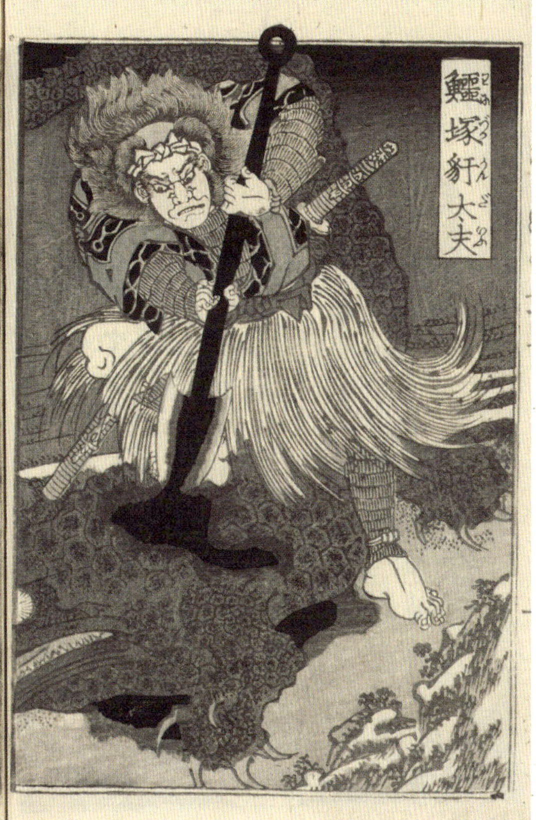

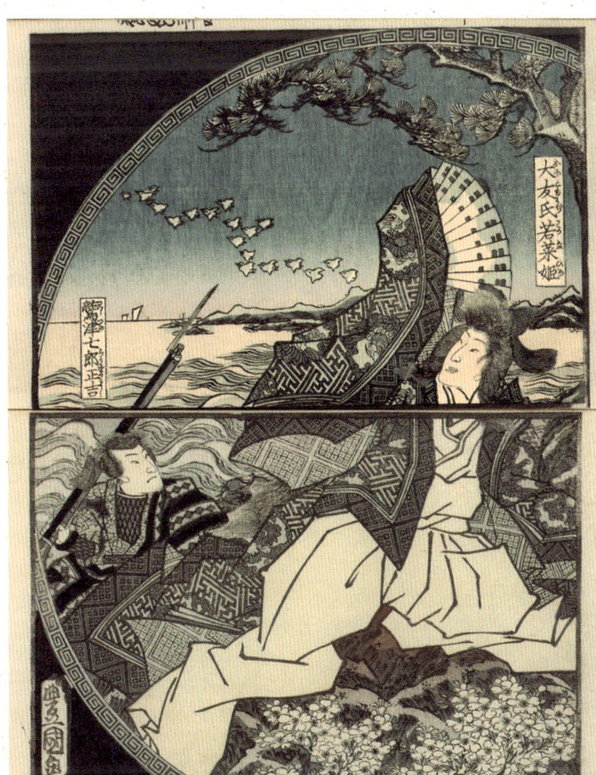

**Opposite** Vol. 34, dirigible balloon (*keikikyū*).

**Above** Vol. 57, Princess Tōkan and Utsuzuka Kandaifu.

**Left** Vol. 34, Princess Wakana spotted through the telescope.

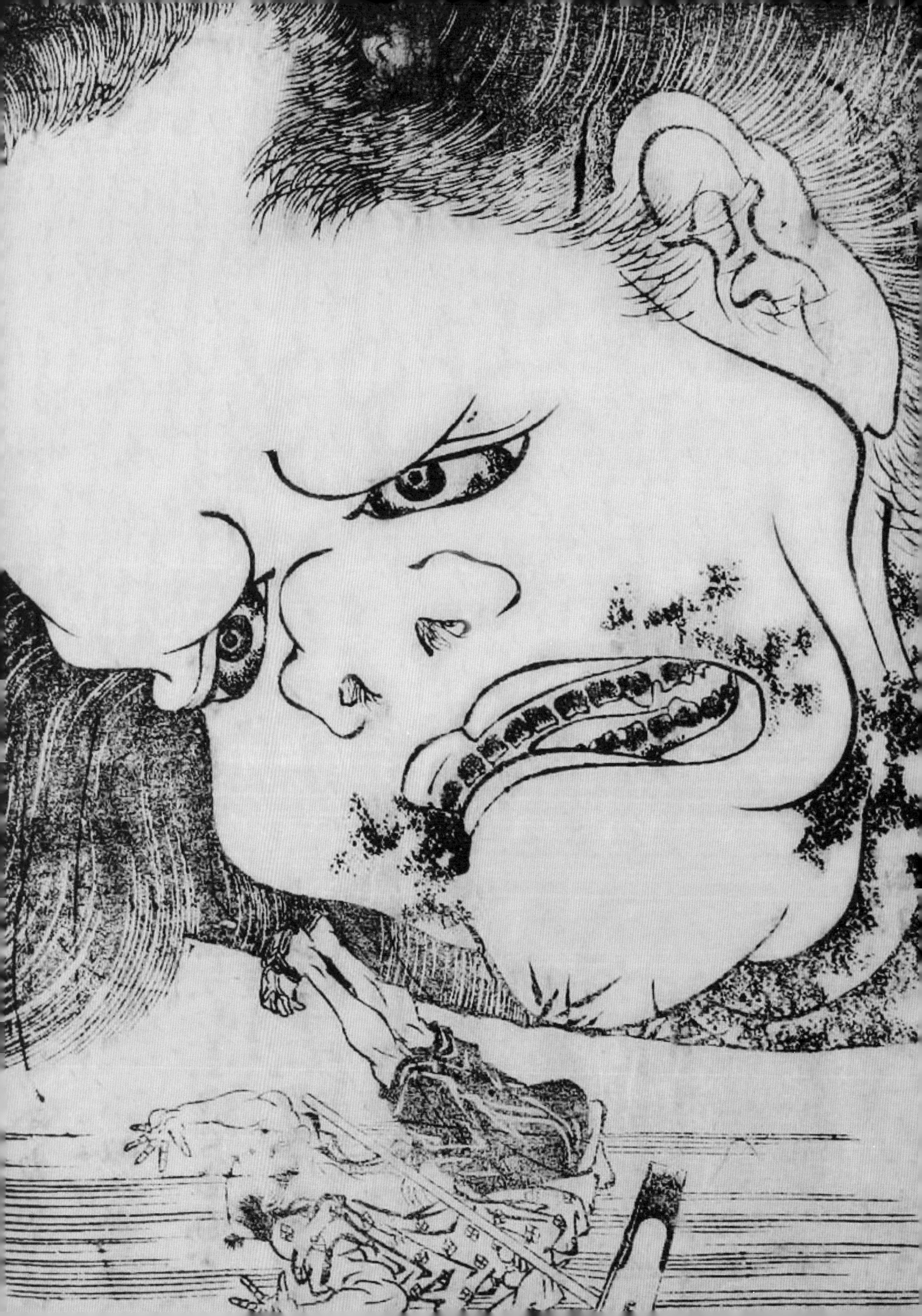

# CHAPTER SIX

# HOKUSAI'S FANTASTICAL SERIAL NOVELS

Katsushika Hokusai (1760–1849), whose worldwide fame today is based on his woodblock print *Under the Wave Off Kanagawa* (*Kanagawa-oki nami-ura*), commonly known as "The Great Wave," was an extremely versatile artist. In addition to designing woodblock prints, Hokusai was a very imaginative painter who also illustrated a large number of books, ranging from painting manuals and poetry to supernatural stories. Most of the supernatural stories are extremely long and complex, with protagonists appearing and disappearing, and some events taking place in distant lands like China where neither Hokusai nor his readers had ever been. From 1803 until 1845, Hokusai worked on thirty-three different series of supernatural novels comprising two hundred volumes and containing almost 1,500 illustrations, all exemplifying his extraordinary talent and sense of imagination.

Hokusai's involvement with adventure and supernatural serial novels began in 1803 when he started to illustrate a new type of book in which the text pages were separated from the illustration pages. The stories were spread over many booklets and their publication could continue for many years. Until 1815, he was the main illustrator of this type of serial novel, and his work on them also generated the lion's share of his income during this period.

Hokusai's first big success was *The New Illustrated Water Margin* (*Shinpen suiko gaden*), an adaptation by the writer Kyokutei Bakin (1767–1848) of the fourteenth-century Chinese novel *Shuihu Zhuan* (Jp.: *Suiko den*; commonly known in English as *The Water Margin*). Publication began in 1805 and new volumes were released until 1838, resulting in almost 200 illustrations. The collaboration between Hokusai and Bakin continued through fifteen more projects until 1815. Noteworthy amongst them is the series *Strange Tales of the Crescent Moon* (*Chinsetsu yumiharizuki*), which began publication in 1807 and ended in 1811. This complex story was told in twenty-nine volumes filled with almost 170 captivating illustrations, many showing the interaction between the hero Tametomo and malevolent demons.

Almost all the supernatural serial stories that Hokusai illustrated were published when he was in his forties. It must have been a tremendous surprise when, in 1843, the first volume of his *Illustrated Book of the Wars of Han and Chu* (*Ehon kanso gundan*) appeared when he was eighty-three. The seventy-three illustrations in this series as well as the twenty-nine in his final adventure story from 1845, *The Life of Shakyamuni Illustrated* (*Shaka goichidaiki zue*), were most likely completed with the assistance of his students.

**Opposite** Detail from *Stars on a Frosty Night*.

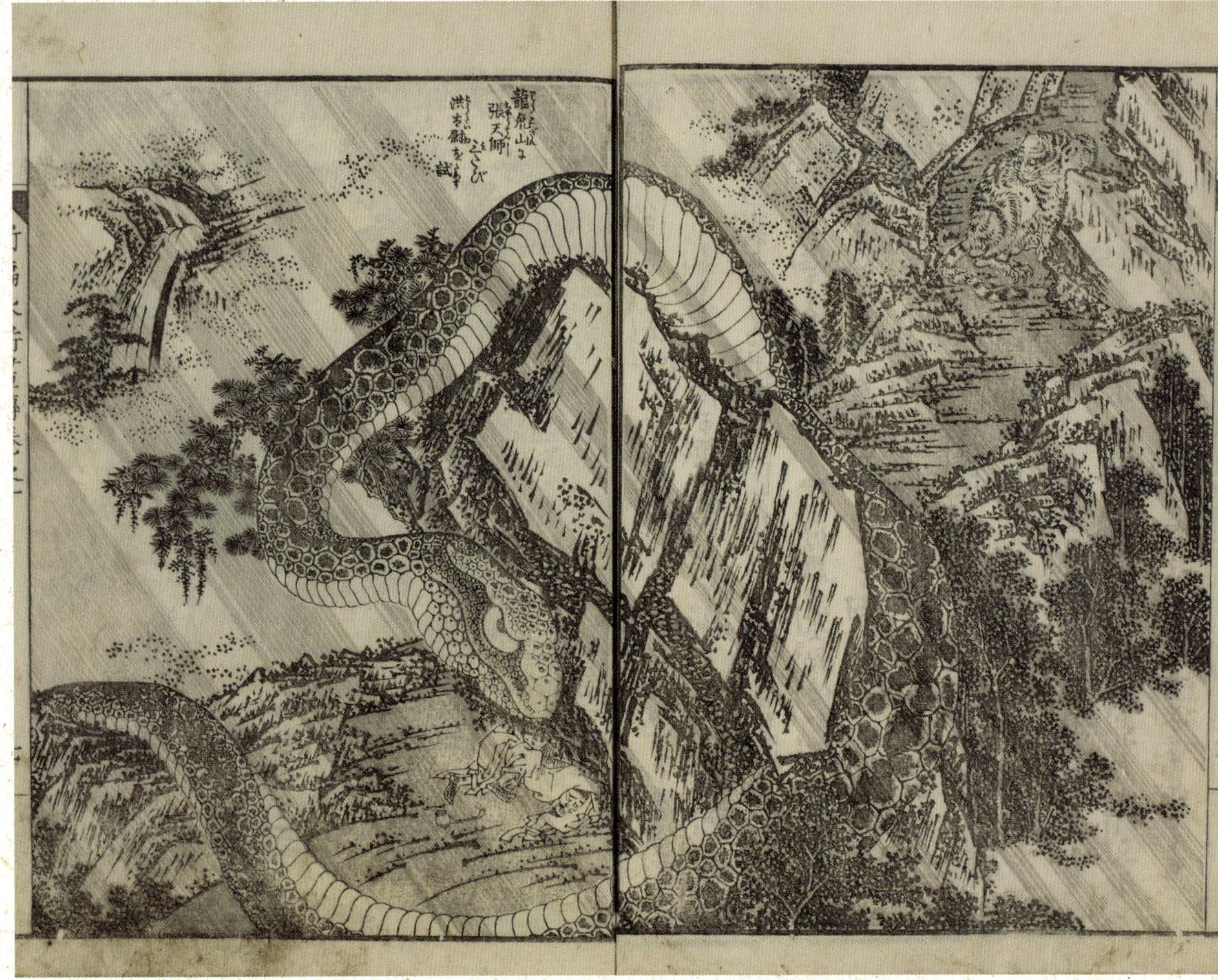

# The New Illustrated Water Margin

## *Shinpen suiko gaden*

新編水滸畫傳

1805 (vol. 1, parts 1–5), 1807 (vol. 1, parts 6–10), 1829 (vol. 2), 1833 (vol. 3), 1835 (vol. 4), 1838 (vols. 5–6)

Authors: vol. 1: Kyokutei Bakin (1767–1848); vols. 2–6: Takai Ranzan (1762–1839)

Artist: Katsushika Hokusai (1760–1849)

Publishers: Kadomaruya Jinsuke and Maekawa Yahei (vols. 1–2); Hanabusaya Heikichi and Chōjiya Heibei (vols. 3–6)

Woodblock printed book (*ōhon*); ink on paper

National Institute of Japanese Literature

From the second half of the eighteenth century, Japanese publishers reprinted the fourteenth-century Chinese novel *Shuihu Zhuan* (Jp.: *Suiko den*; commonly translated as *The Water Margin*). The storyline centers around a band of fictional heroes with superpowers who embark on all kinds of adventures. Each hero is known by a specific nickname, such as "Tattooed Priest" Lu Zhishen, "Flea on a Drum" Shi Qian, and "Panther Head" Lin Chong. Located in the Liangshan Marsh in eastern China, the rogue group eventually has 108 members, who initially fight injustice but later serve the emperor. *Shuihu Zhuan* enjoyed great popularity in Japan, even more so after the first parts of Kyokutei Bakin's adaptation *The New Illustrated Water Margin* (*Shinpen suiko gaden*) were issued in 1805. Between 1805 and 1807, ten volumes with seventy-six monochrome illustrations by Katsushika Hokusai were released, offering a completely new way of visualizing fantastical characters.

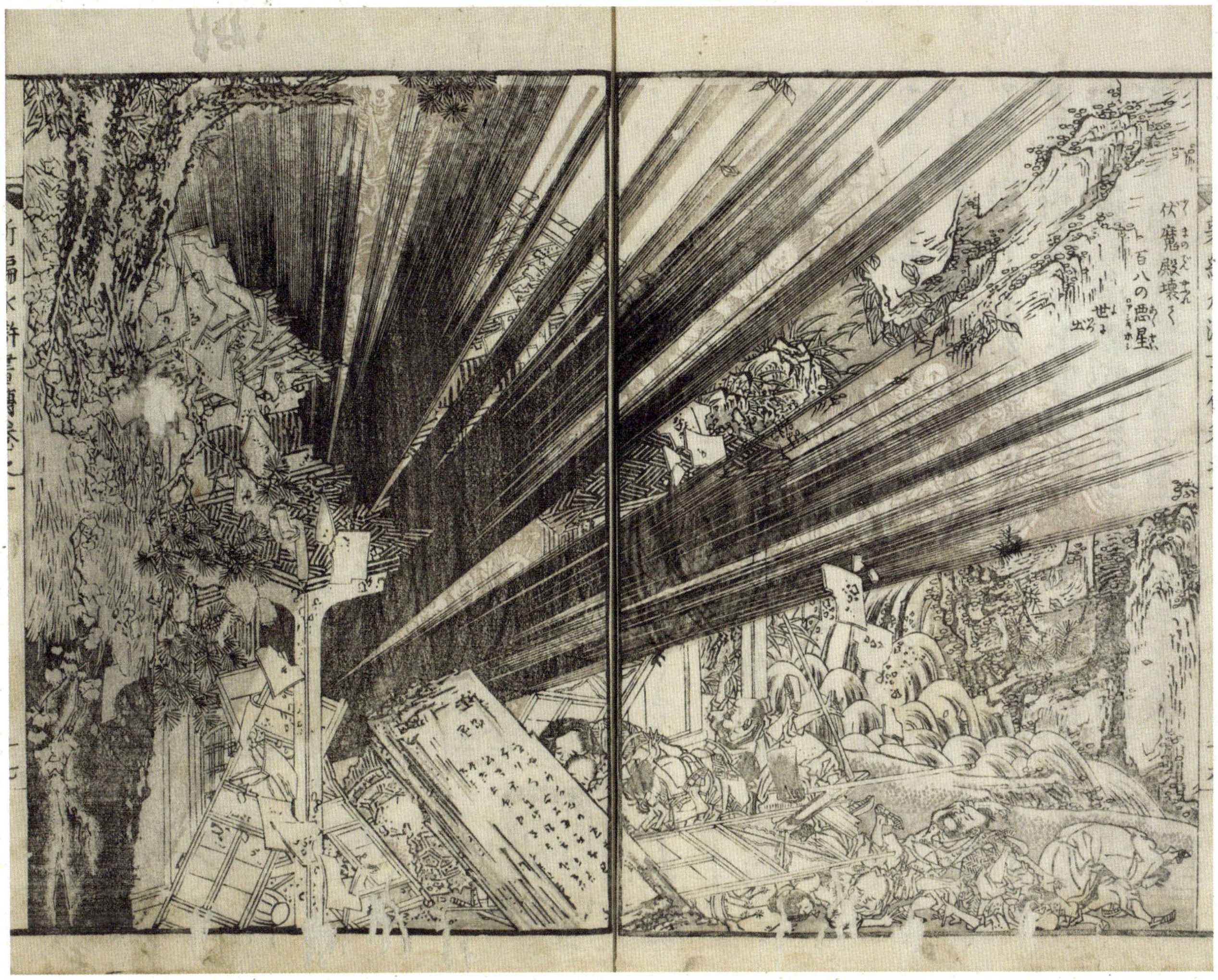

**Opposite** Vol. 1.1, Zhang Tianshi tests Hong Taiwei for the third time on Mount Longhu.

**Above** Vol. 1.1, 108 evil stars that destroy the lair of demons are released into the world.

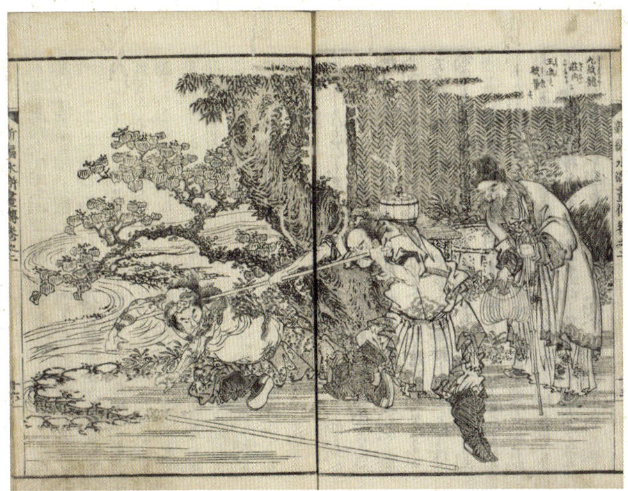

**Above** Vol. 1.2, Wang Jin observes "Nine-dragon Tattooed" Shi Jin.

**Right** Vol. 1.3, "Nine-dragon Tattooed" Shi Jin bravely captures "Stream Leaping Tiger" Chen Da.

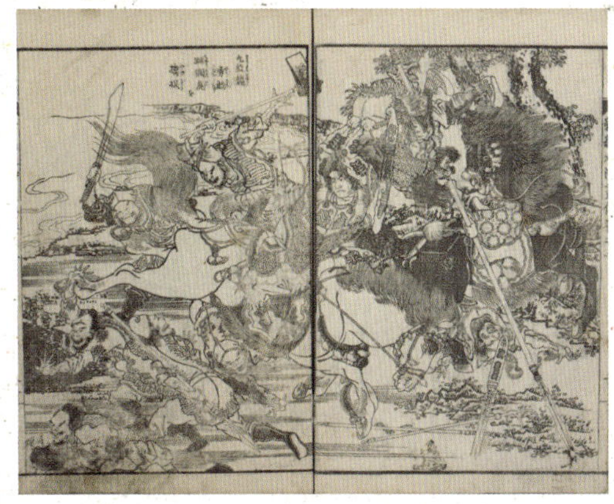

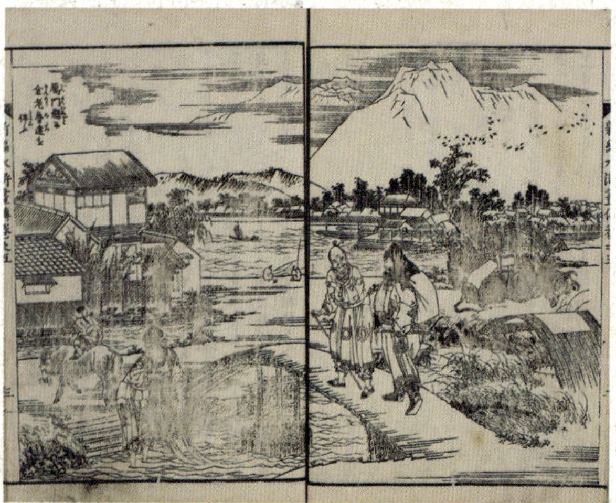

**Above** Vol. 1.5, Lu Zhishen meets Jin Cuilian's father in Yanmen County.

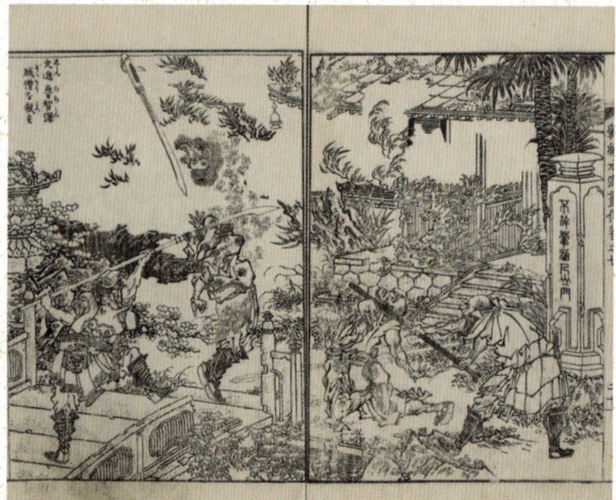

**Above** Vol. 1.7, Shi Jin and Lu Zhishen kill a thief and a monk.

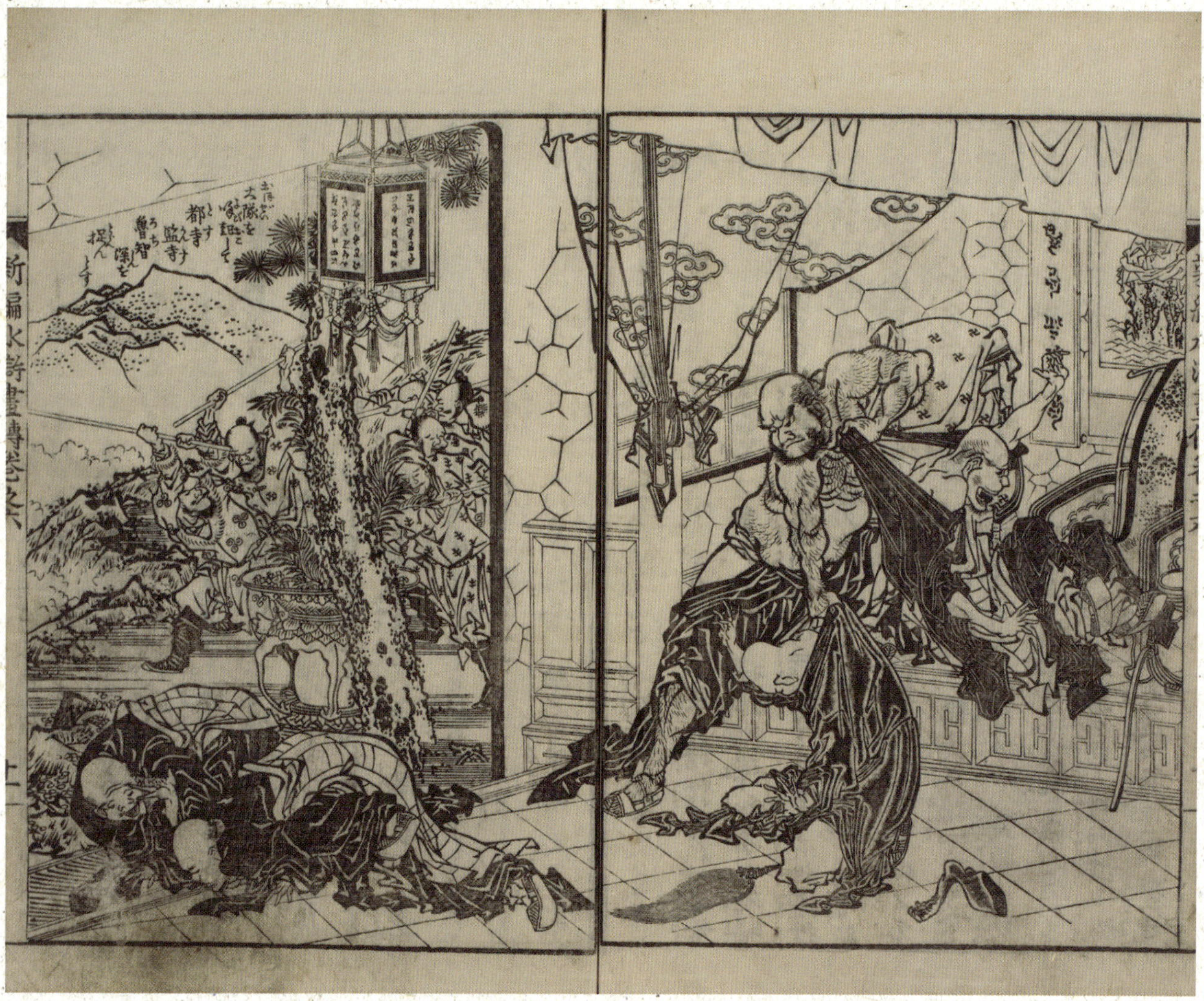

**Above** Vol. 1.6, the administrators of a temple summoned a battalion to capture Lu Zhishen.

Disputes with the publishers led Bakin to withdraw from this project after volume 1 was completed. Twenty years later, the print artist Utagawa Kuniyoshi (1798–1861) designed the first full-color single-sheet portraits in the large *ōban* format. Such warrior prints were previously unknown, and by 1830 seventy-four were released. The original publishers of *The New Illustrated Water Margin* saw an opportunity to relaunch the novel, and they went back to Hokusai but hired Takai Ranzan as author. In 1829, volume 2 was released and more followed until volume 6 was completed in 1838.

In his illustrations, Hokusai tried to do justice to the setting of the stories—China, not Japan—and he therefore portrayed the protagonists in Chinese-style robes and shoes. The weapons they carry are clearly not Japanese and neither is the architecture. What exactly Hokusai used as his source of inspiration is not known but it is certain that he never set foot in China himself.

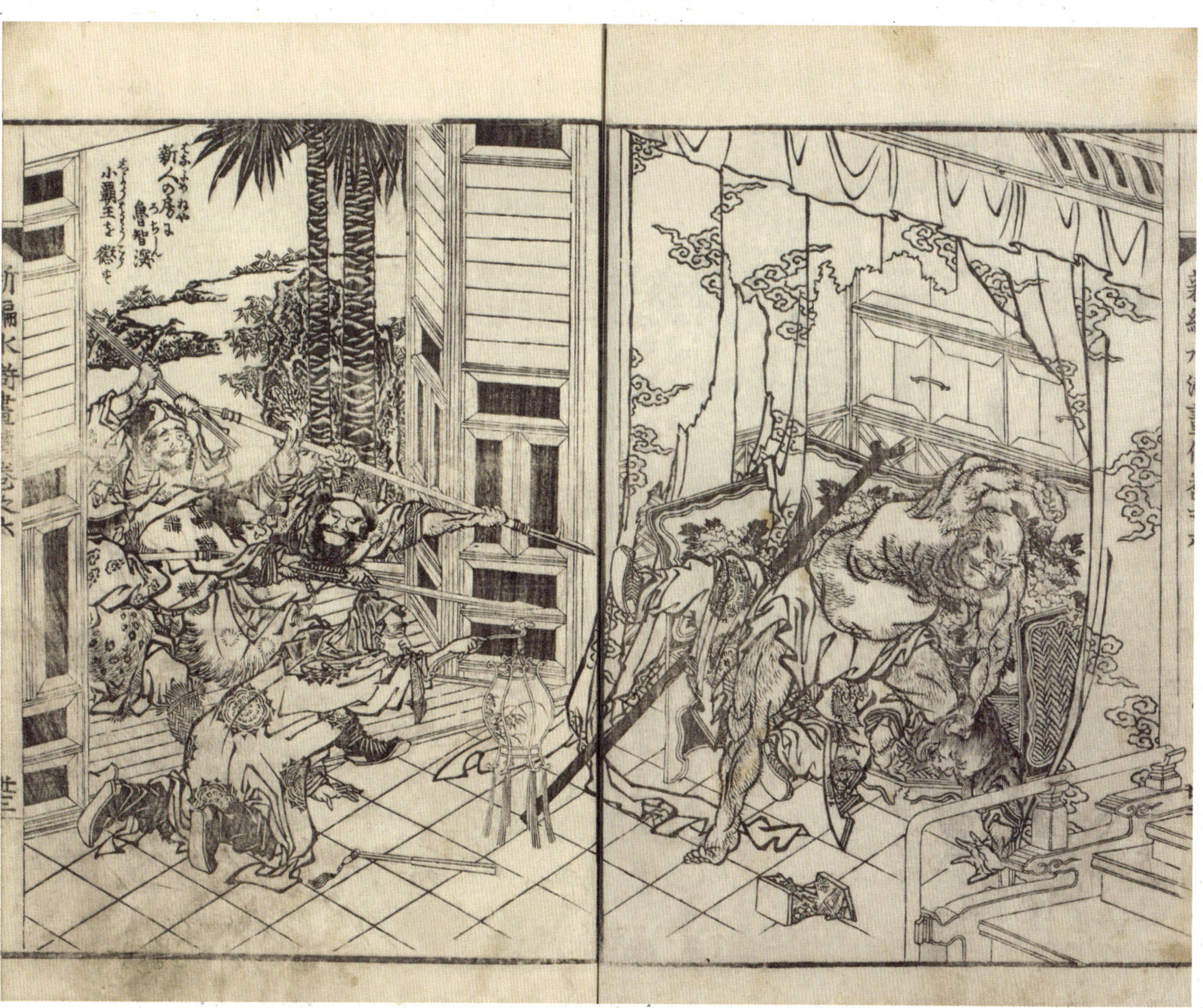

**Above** Vol. 1.6, Lu Zhishen disciplines "The Little Autocrat" Zhou Tong in his new bed.

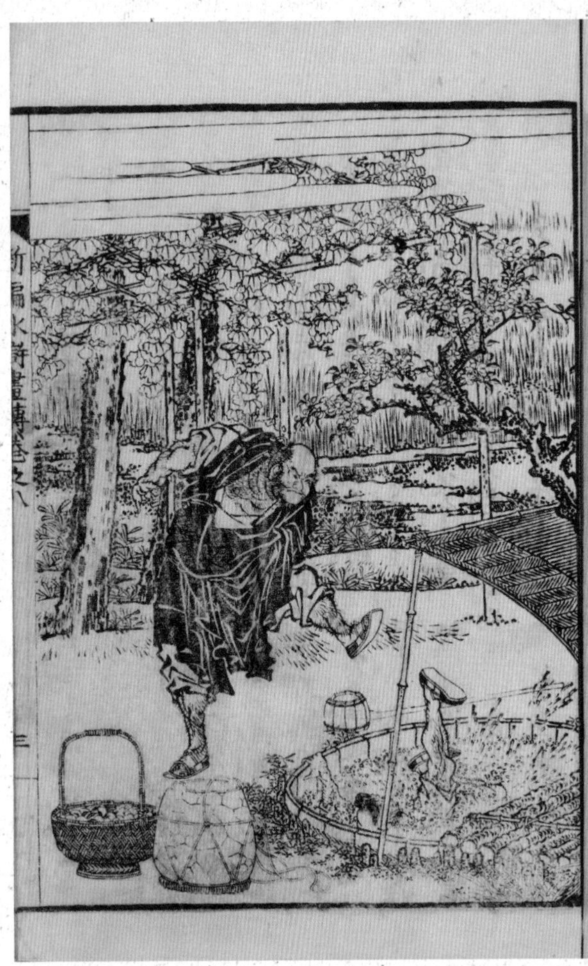

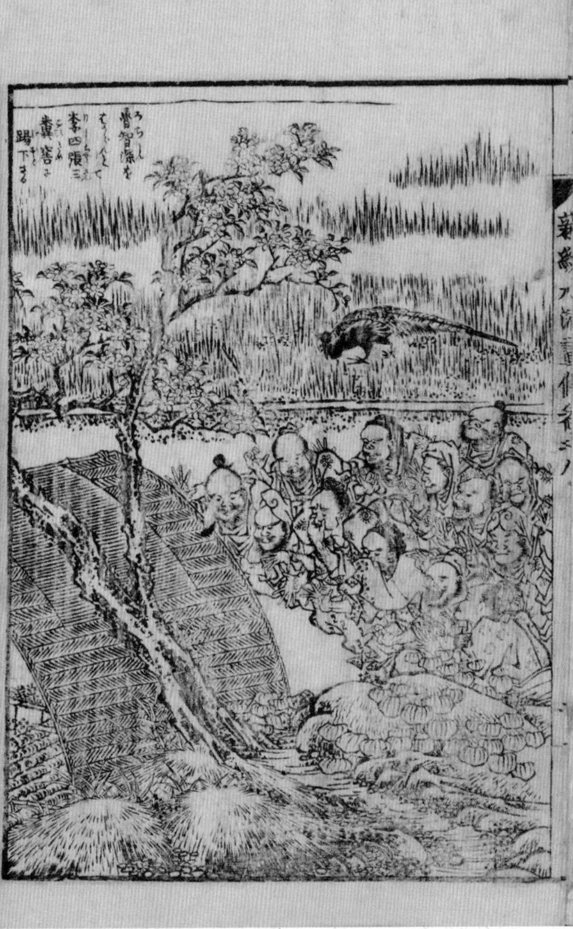

**Above** Vol. 1.8, Lu Zhishen throws Zhang San and Li Si into a pit.

**Left** Vol. 1.10, Lin Chong arrives at his exile in Caoliao.

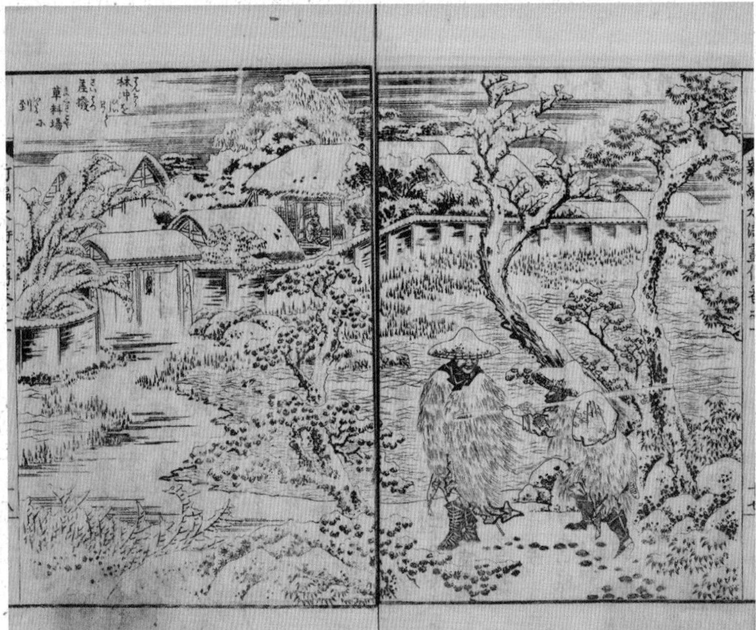

**Opposite above** Vol. 1.8, Lu Zhishen pulls out a tree in the garden.

**Opposite below** Vol. 1.10, Lu Qian and Fu'an clear snow in front of a temple gate.

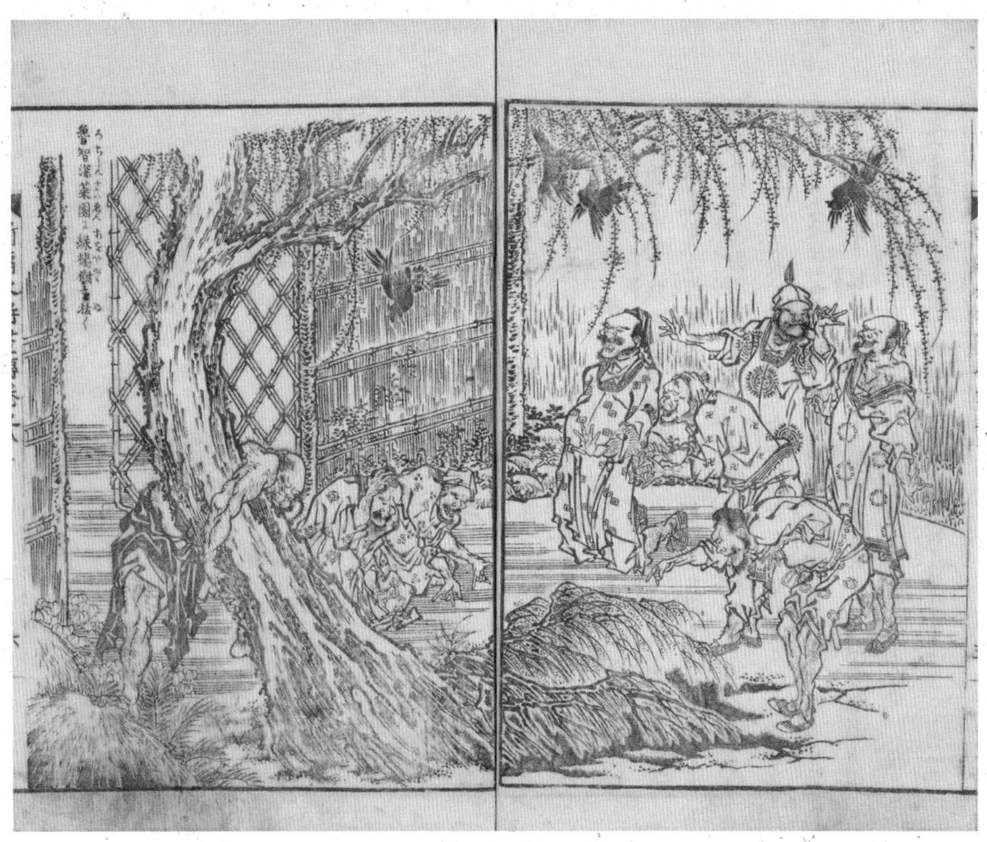

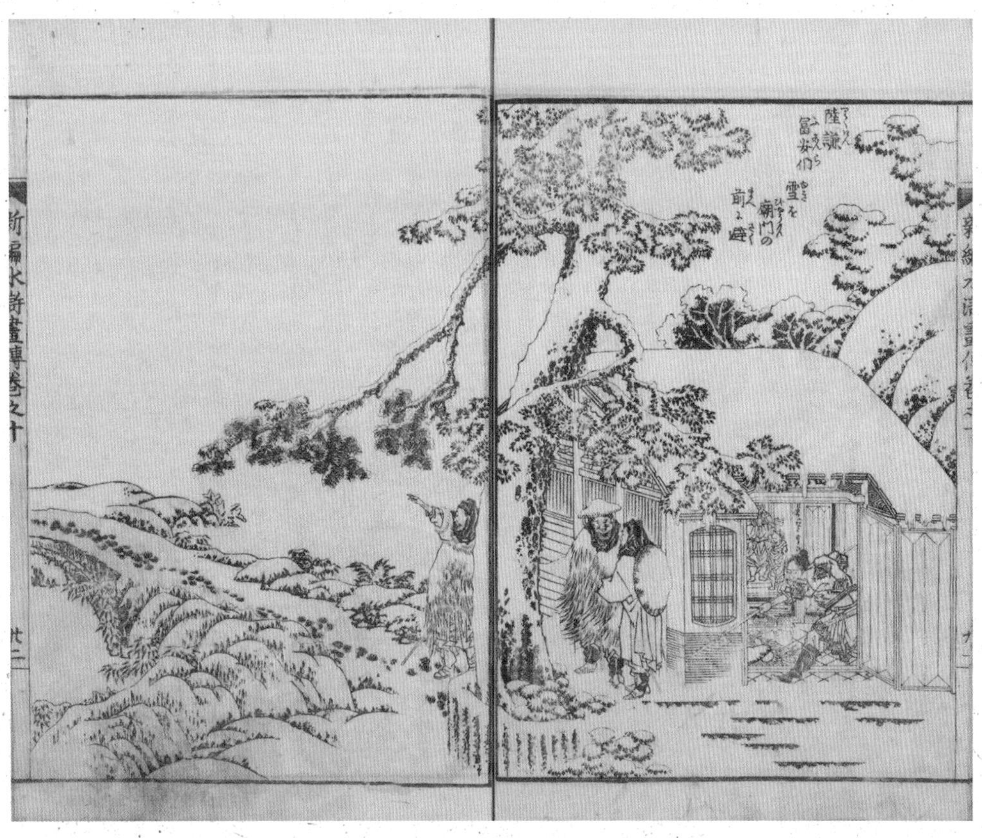

# The New Story of Kasane's Salvation

## *Shin Kasane gedatsu monogatari*
新累解脱物語

1807 (5 vols.)
Author: Kyokutei Bakin (1767–1848)
Artist: Katsushika Hokusai (1760–1849)
Publishers: Tsuruya Kiemon, Kawachiya Tasuke, et al.
Woodblock printed book (*hanshibon*); ink on paper
Waseda University Library

Kyokutei Bakin's novels were all inspired by historical events or legends, which he always adapted in different ways. A very popular writer, Bakin excelled in describing the places where his novels took place.

For *The New Story of Kasane's Salvation* (*Shin Kasane gedatsu monogatari*) a group of four publishers came together—one in Edo (Tsuruya Kiemon), one in Osaka, and two in Kyoto—and hired another favorite to provide the illustrations, Katsushika Hokusai. The novel is based on a folktale about Kasane, a woman with a deformed face who is killed with a sickle by her husband Yoemon. Kasane later returns as a wrathful ghost to haunt him and kill every new woman in his life. This story was first dramatized in the *kabuki* theater in 1731.

In *The New Story of Kasane's Salvation*, Bakin enlarged and restructured the folktale for which Hokusai created thirty-five double-page illustrations that capture the gruesomeness of the story. The publisher in Osaka overseeing the distribution there,

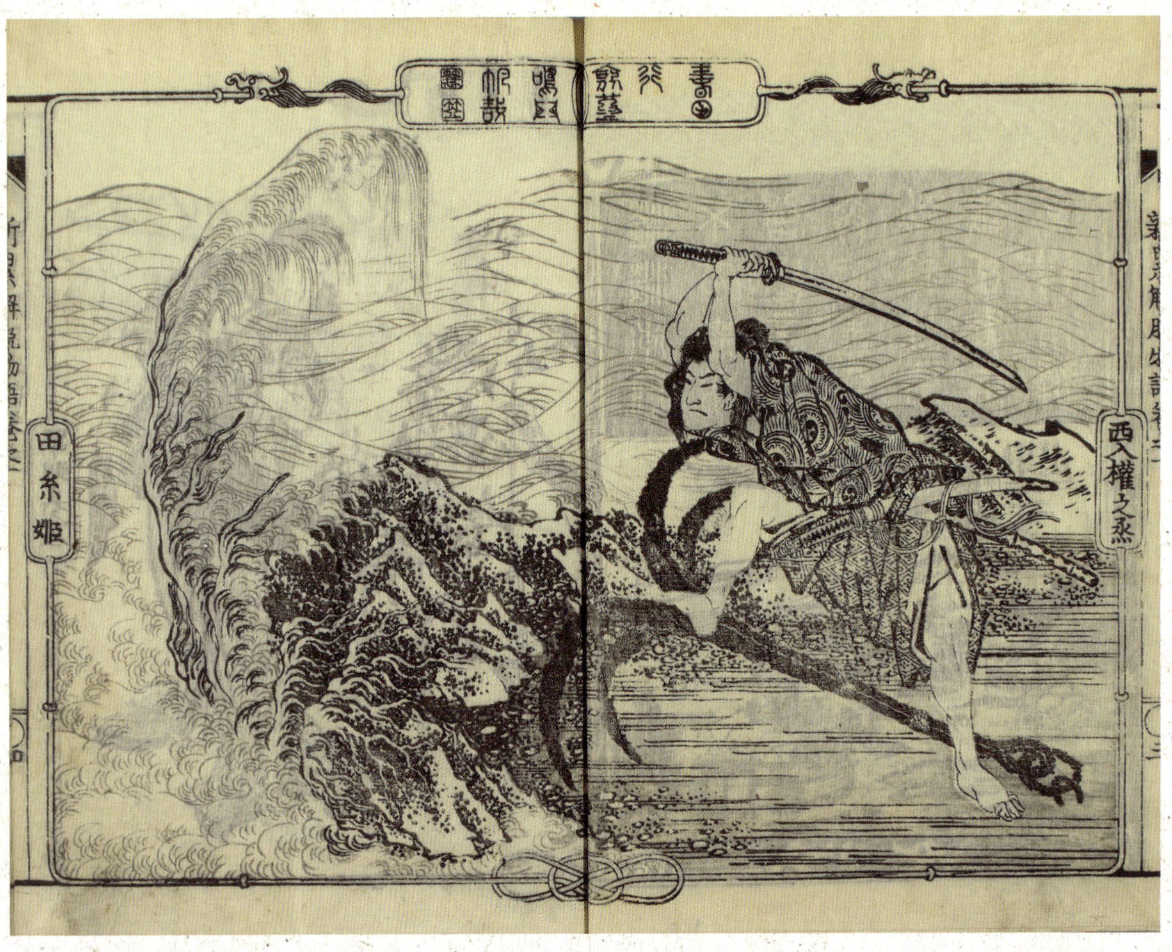

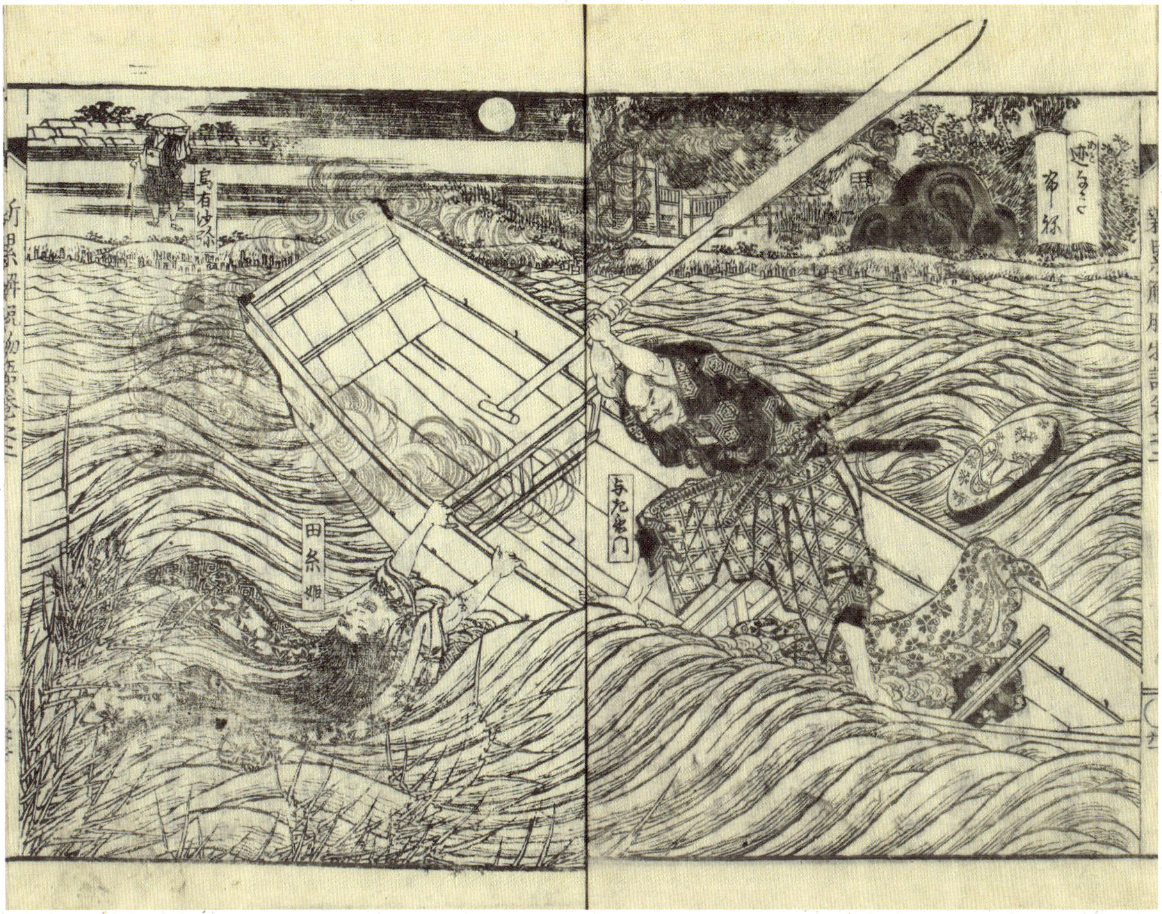

Kawachiya Tasuke, was not entirely happy with the outcome and sent a letter to Bakin complaining that the story was poorly written and not suitable for the eyes and ears of women and children.

Amongst Hokusai's first illustrations is Yoemon on a boat killing Princess Ta'ito, who has fallen overboard, by beatng her with an oar while she clings to the boat with both hands. Some time later, in another boat scene, the ghost of Ta'ito and Suke, both women who refused Yoemon's advances, appear to Yoemon and Kasane. The famous brutal murder of Kasane in the Kinu River is captured in volume 4 where Yoemon stands over her with his sickle while she desperately tries to prevent him from cutting her throat. Volume 5 contains an unusual opening of a priest providing Yoemon with a vision of the Buddhist hell, rendered in a gray fog.

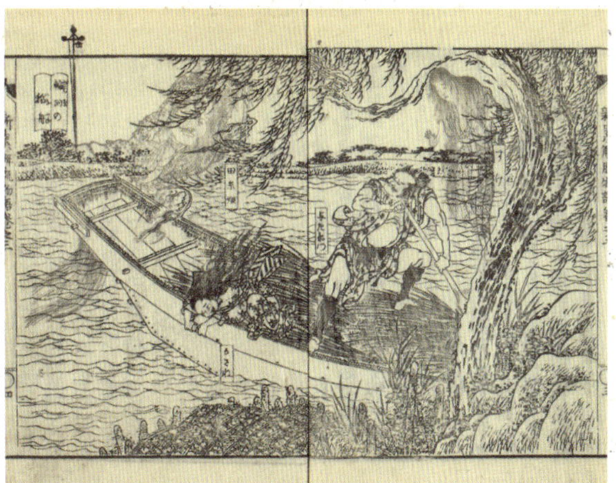

**Opposite** Vol. 1, Princess Ta'ito and Nishiiri Gonnojō.

**Top** Vol. 2, Yoemon kills Princess Ta'ito.

**Above** Vol. 3, the ghosts of Ta'ito and Suke appear to Yoemon and Kasane.

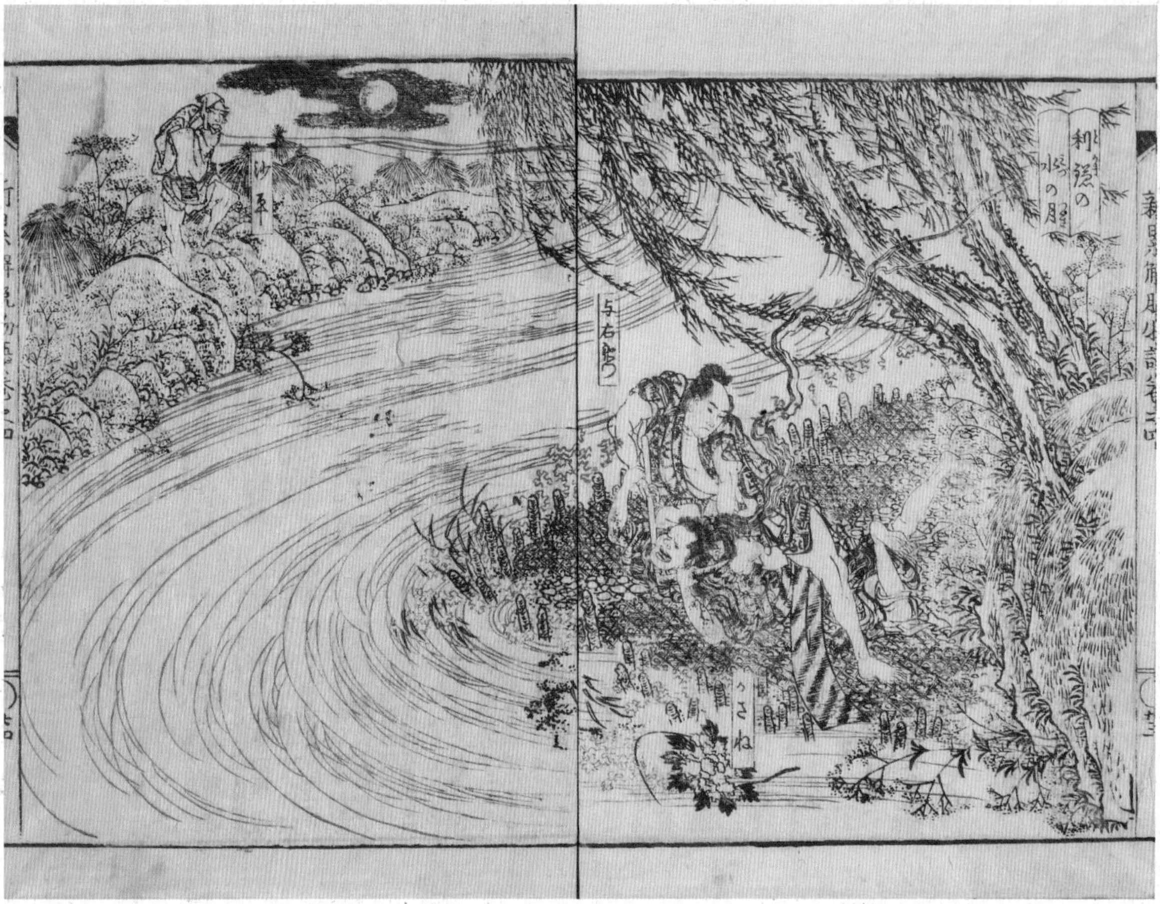

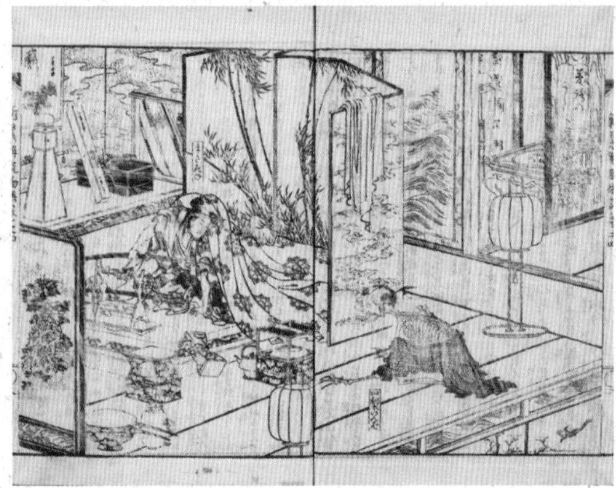

**Above** Vol. 4, Yoemon kills Kasane with a sickle.

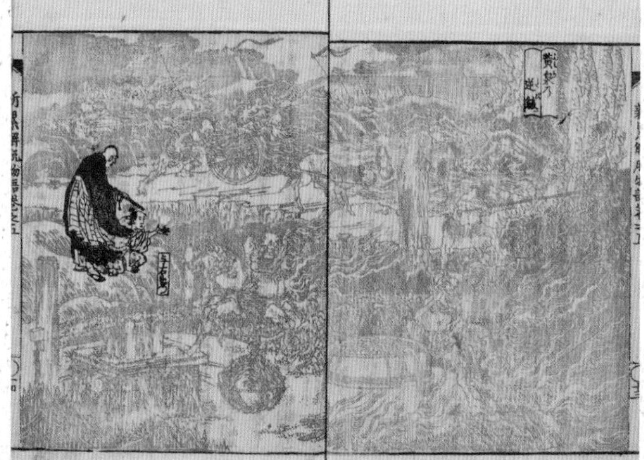

**Above** Vol. 4, Masatane and the ghost of Yamanashi Inba.

**Right** Vol. 5, a priest's vision of the Buddhist hell.

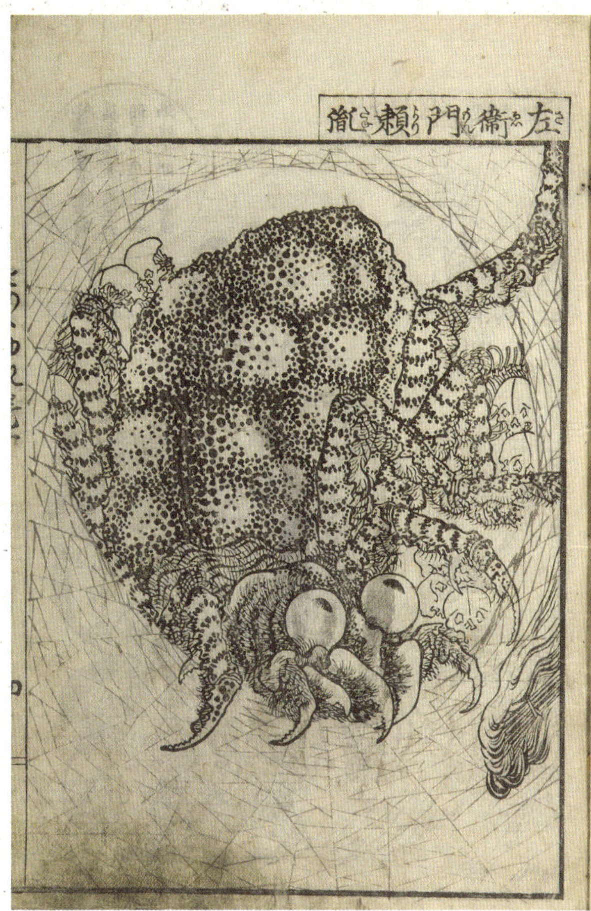
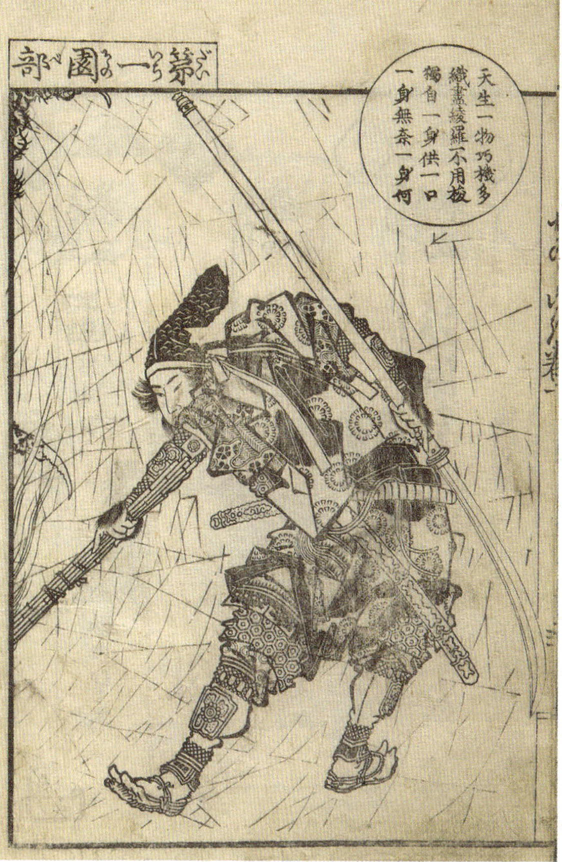



**Above** Vol. 1, no. 1, Sonobe Saemon Yoritsune faces a spider.

# Snow in the Garden

## *Sono no yuki*

園の雪

1807 (5 vols.)
Author: Kyokutei Bakin (1767–1848)
Artist: Katsushika Hokusai (1760–1849)
Publisher: Kadomaruya Jinsuke
Woodblock printed book (*hanshibon*); ink on paper
Wereldmuseum Leiden

As with the novel *The New Story of Kasane's Salvation* (*Shin Kasane gedatsu monogatari*), *Snow in the Garden* (*Sono no yuki*) is also a collaboration between the popular writer Kyokutei Bakin and the esteemed artist Katsushika Hokusai. Both novels were released in 1807 and consist of independent text pages and double-page illustrations. Some scholars consider Hokusai's thirty-three illustrations in *Snow in the Garden* superior to other novels published that year. The first volume includes six frontispieces, mostly of heroes engaged with fantastic and real animals of gigantic size and strength that have supernatural powers. At the beginning is the warrior Sonobe Saemon Yoritsune facing a giant spider, followed by Princess Usuyuki with a carp the size of a whale. Kodono Araheida wrestles with a bear while the strong woman (*gijo*) Magaki aces a huge eagle that holds an unrolled handscroll in its beak.

The storyline is complex, and centers on one side about the princess Usuyuki and her brother Sanewaka, on the other about Kurimon Sajirō and his wife Nagiwai who escape to Fushimi to avoid a conspiracy in Harima. The couple pay for shelter in the house of Suwahiro, but one day a starving monk appears, sets fire to the house, and plucks out the tongues of Suwahiro and his wife. Amongst the most remarkable

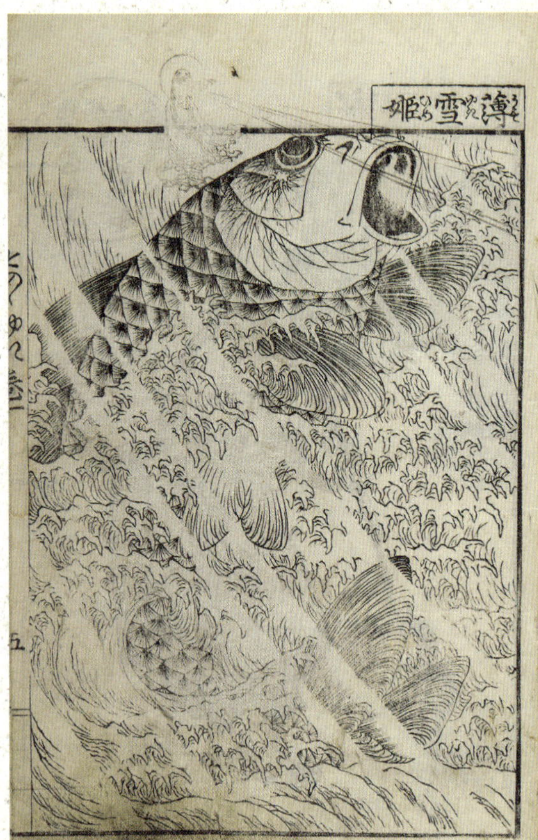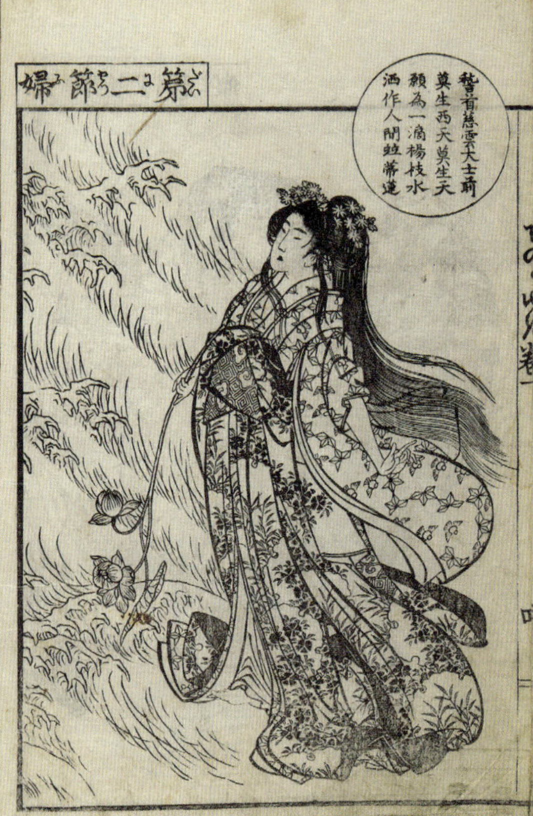

illustrations by Hokusai are how Usuyuki and another woman fight a strong gust of wind that blows their hair and robes behind them and forces them almost to the ground. Shockingly, the final illustration shows the execution of a man, bound to a stick in the ground, being quartered by bulls to which his legs have been tied. The novel ends at this point and Bakin is said to have refused to continue writing because he was displeased with the publisher.

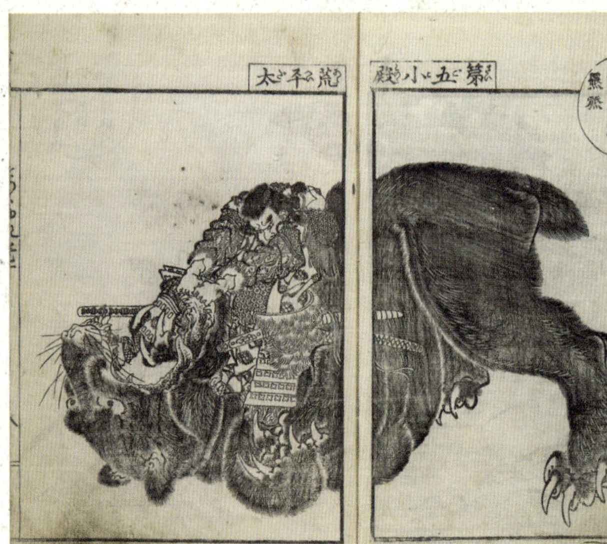

**Top** Vol. 1, no. 2, Princess Usuyuki.

**Above** Vol. 1, no. 5, Kodono Araheida wrestles with a bear.

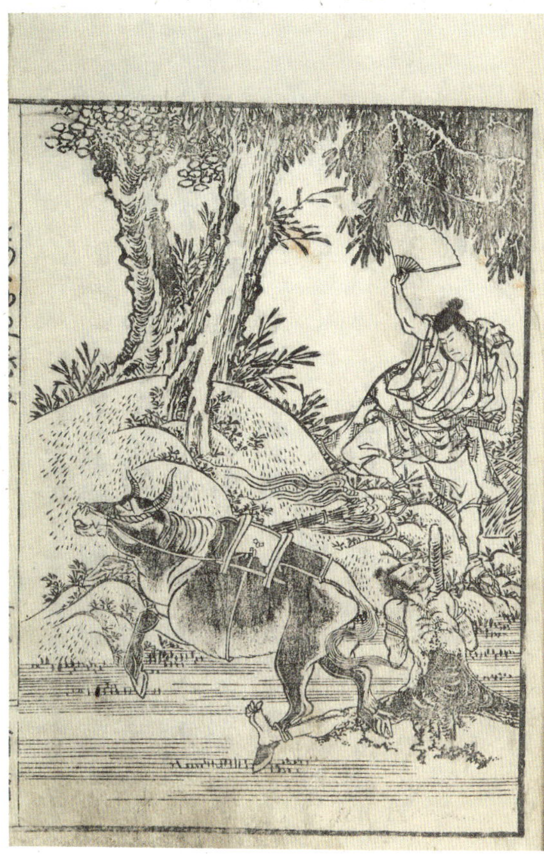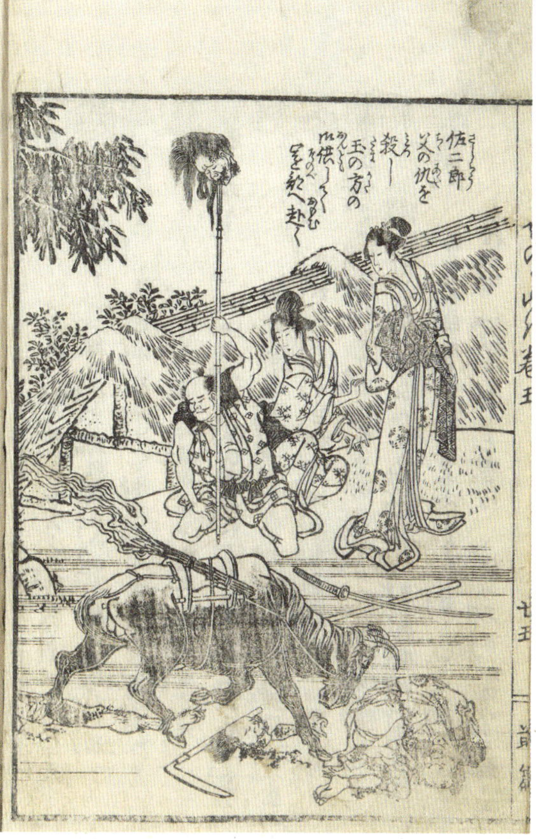

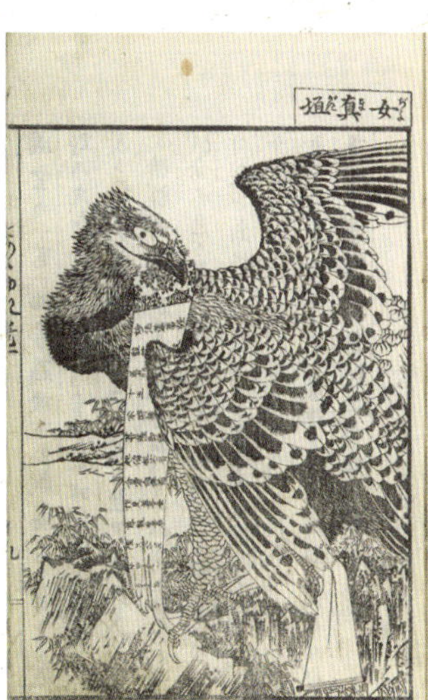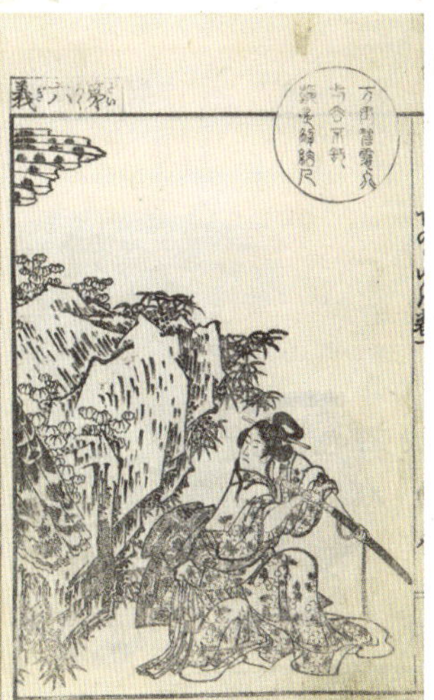

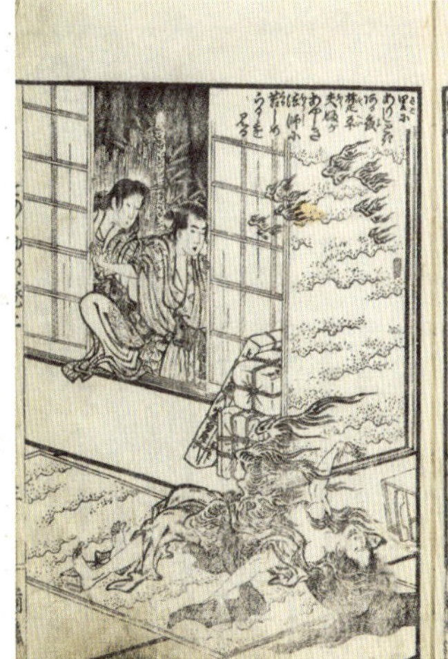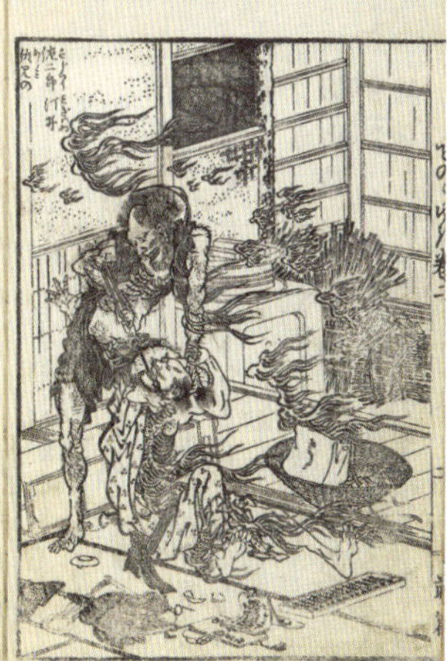

**Top** Vol. 5, execution of a man quartered by bulls.

**Above** Vol. 1, no. 6, the strong woman Magaki faces an eagle.

**Above** Vol. 2, a starving monk plucks out the tongues of Suwahiro and his wife.

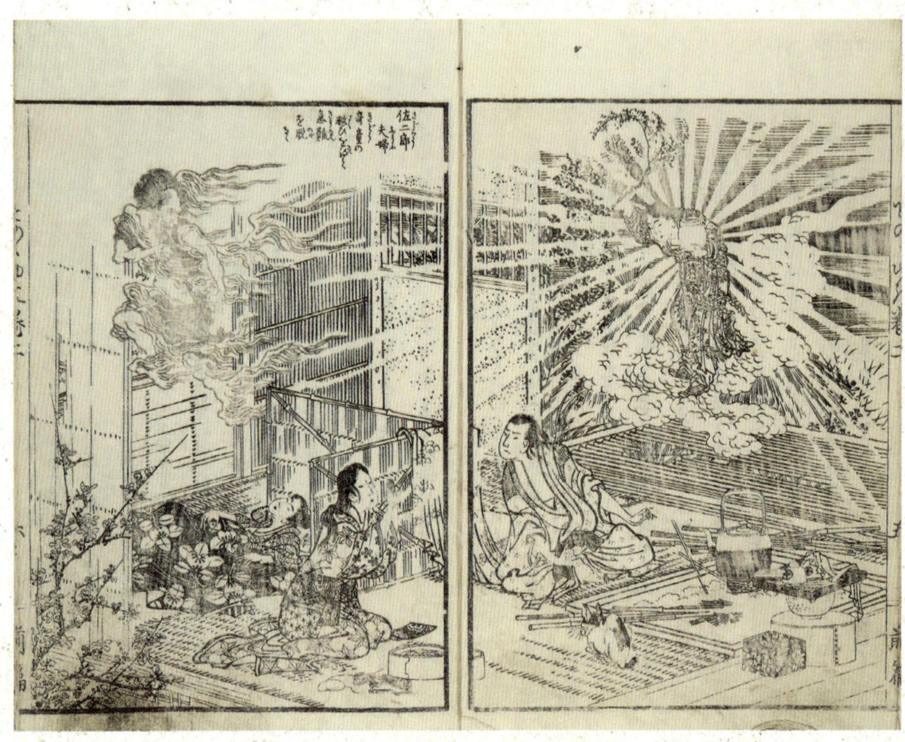

**Right** Vol. 2, Sajirō and his wife are saved.

**Below** Vol. 2, Usuyuki and another woman fight a gust of wind.

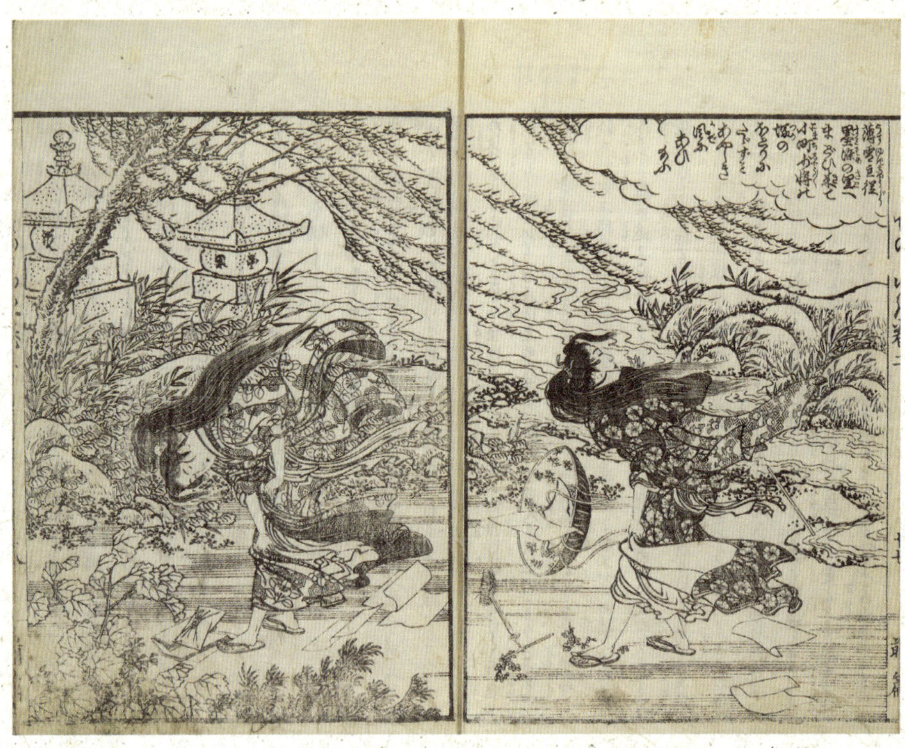

# The Love-dreams Boat

## *Yume no ukihashi*

恋夢艋

1809 (vol. 1), 1814 (vol. 2)

Authors: vol. 1: Rakurakuan Tōei (dates unknown); vol. 2: Ritsujōtei Kiran (1744–1823)

Artists: vol. 1: Katsushika Hokusai (1760–1849); vol. 2: Ōoka Baen (dates unknown)

Publisher: Nishimuraya Genroku, et al.

Woodblock printed book (*hanshibon*); ink on paper

Kansai University Library

"The Floating Bridge of Dreams," or *Yume no ukihashi*, is the title of the 54th and last chapter of *The Tale of Genji* (*Genji monogatari*), the most important novel in Japan's history, dating from the eleventh century. In 1809, the first volume of a new novel written by Rakurakuan Tōei was released. Its title was identical to the last chapter of *Genji monogatari* but was written using different characters that could be translated as *The Love-dreams Boat*. The three publishers who joined forces to finance this project hired the popular Katsushika

**Below** Vol. 1, a gang of bandits from Onizuka.

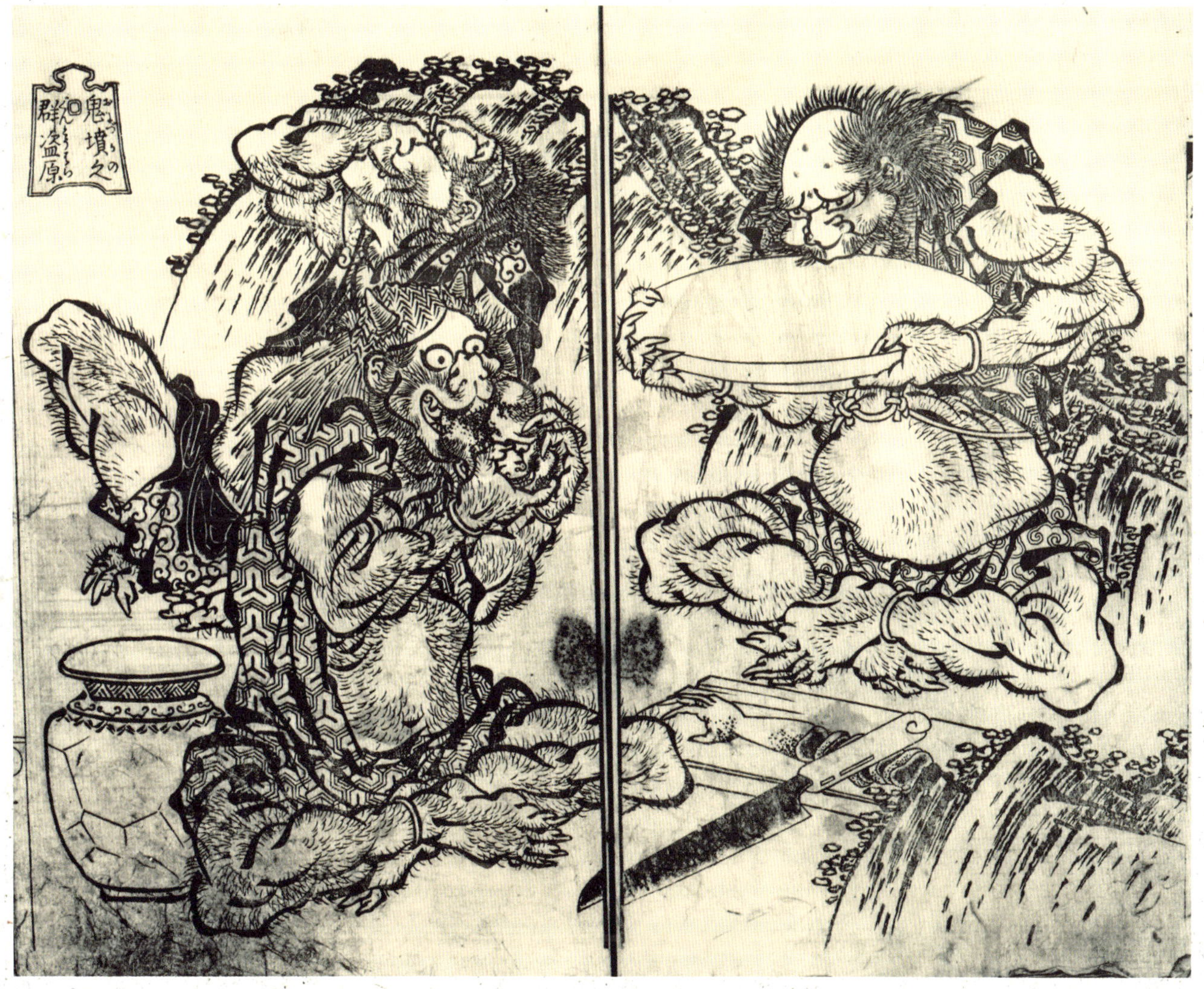

Below Vol. 2, men pulling a giant boar out of a cage.

Bottom Vol. 1, Komichi and the mother of Awaichi.

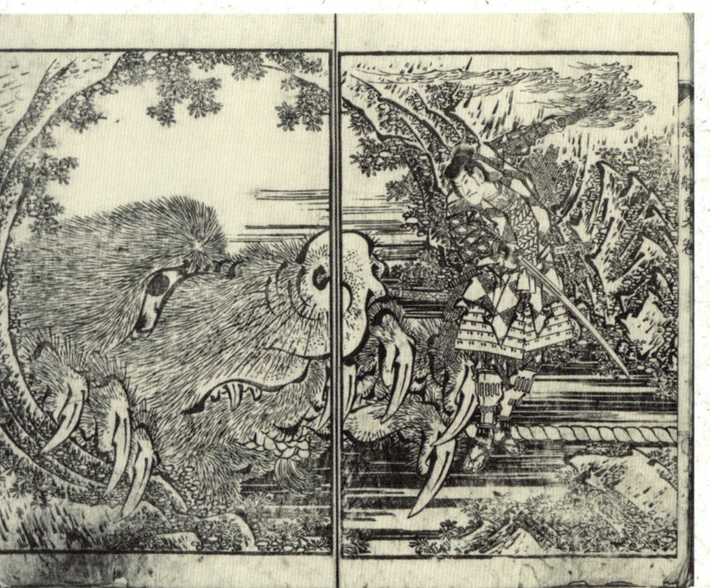

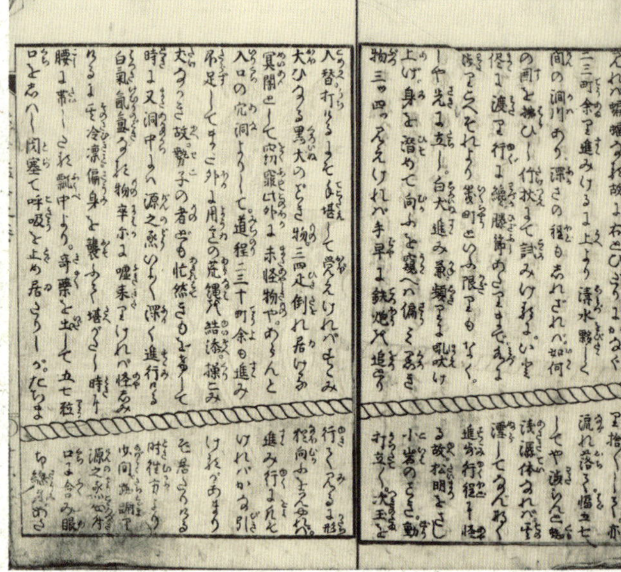

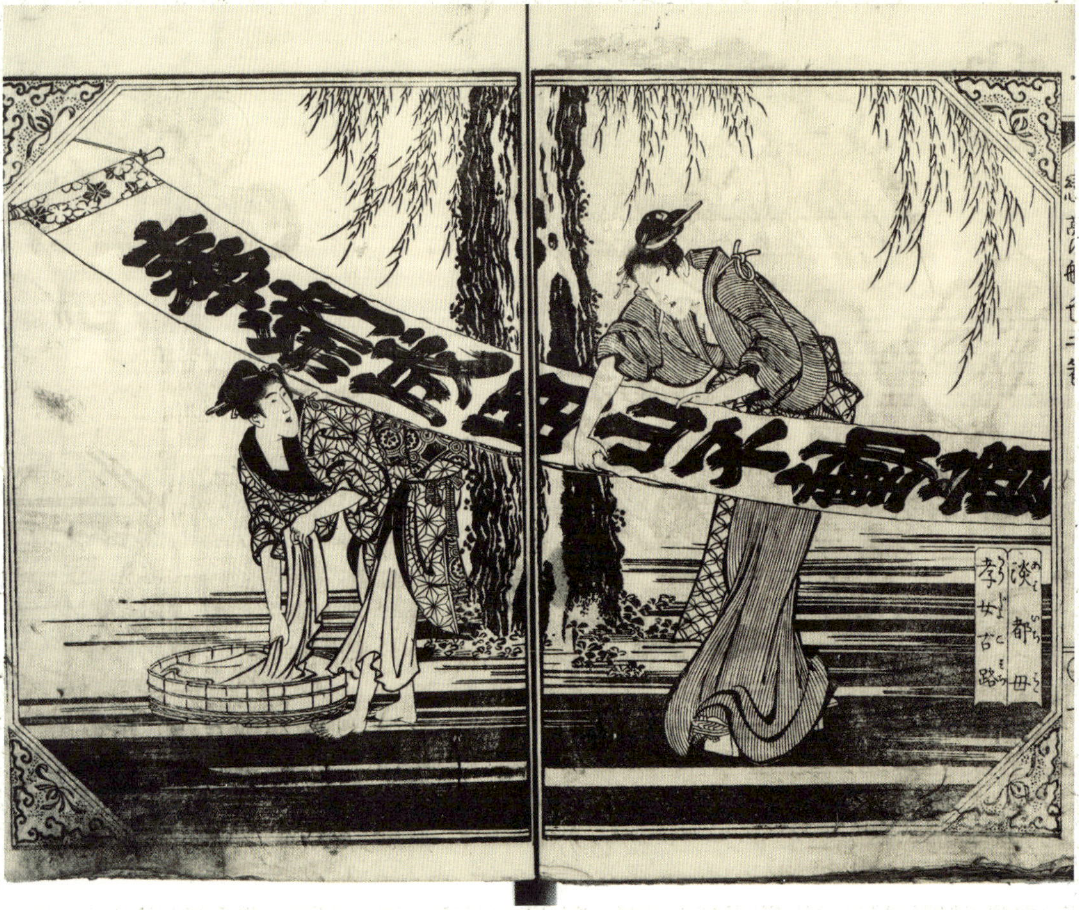

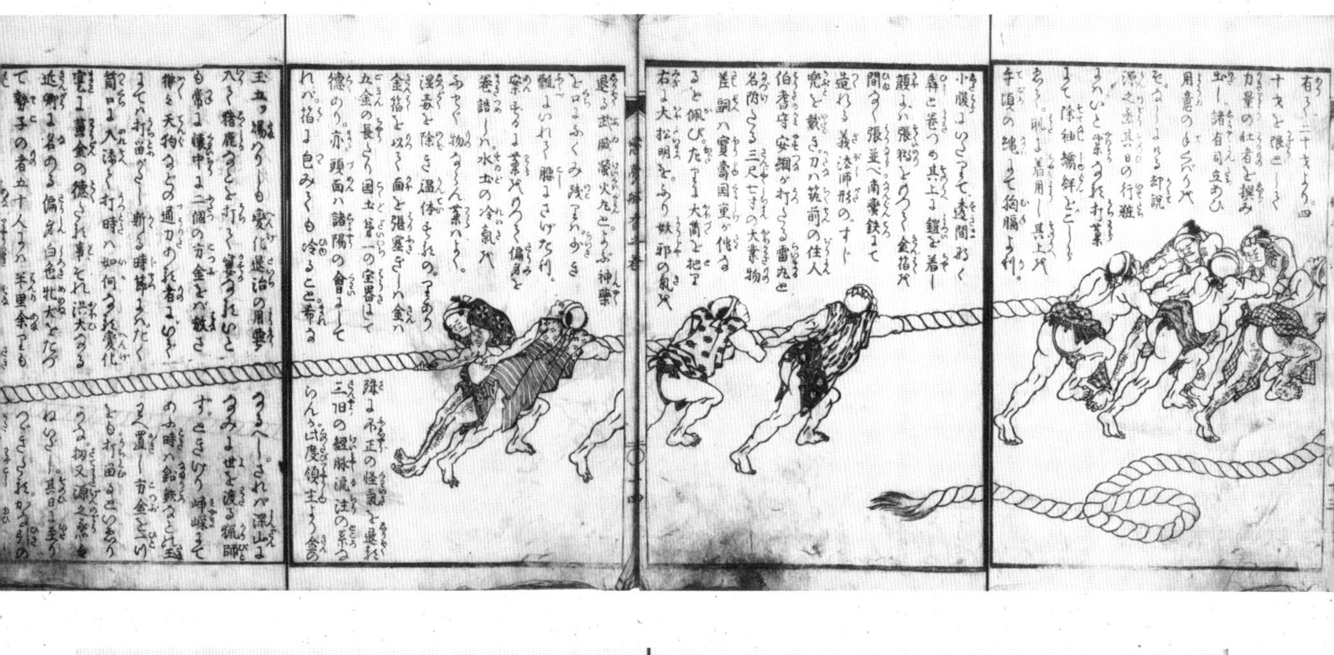

**Bottom** Vol. 1, En'no Gyōja and Tomo no Gennojō Yoshinobu.

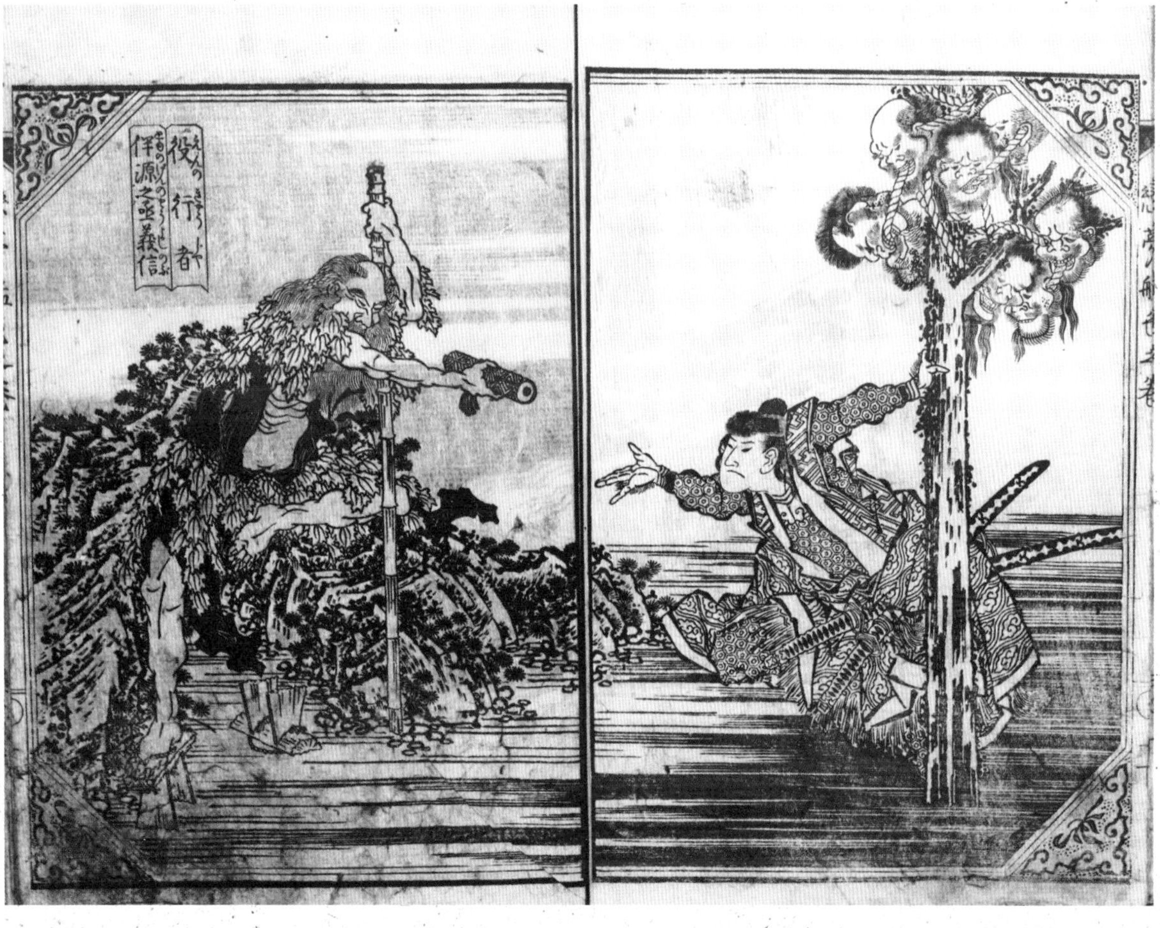

Hokusai as illustrator since this would increase the novel's commercial success. However, instead of creating a long-running serial novel, the project came to an abrupt stop and was only resurrected five years later for a brief time by a different author-artist team: the text by Ritsujōtei Kiran and the illustrations by Hokusai's student Ōoka Baen.

The story follows the warrior Tomo no Gennojō Yoshinobu. Hokusai's illustrations are sometimes gruesome, for example, when he captures Yoshinobu holding onto a pole to which eight decapitated heads have been fixed. Remarkable though is the elongated scene that Hokusai wittily extends over eight pages. At first the reader sees seven half-clad men pulling on a thick rope. Then, flipping over to the next pages there are two more men pulling the same rope. The extraordinary length of this rope is revealed on the third spread when Hokusai captures the tightened rope. Finally, on the fourth spread Yoshinobu sheds light with his torch and reveals that the men have been working hard to pull a gigantic boar with sharp claws out of a cage.

**Below** Vol. 2, judgement of the King of Hell.

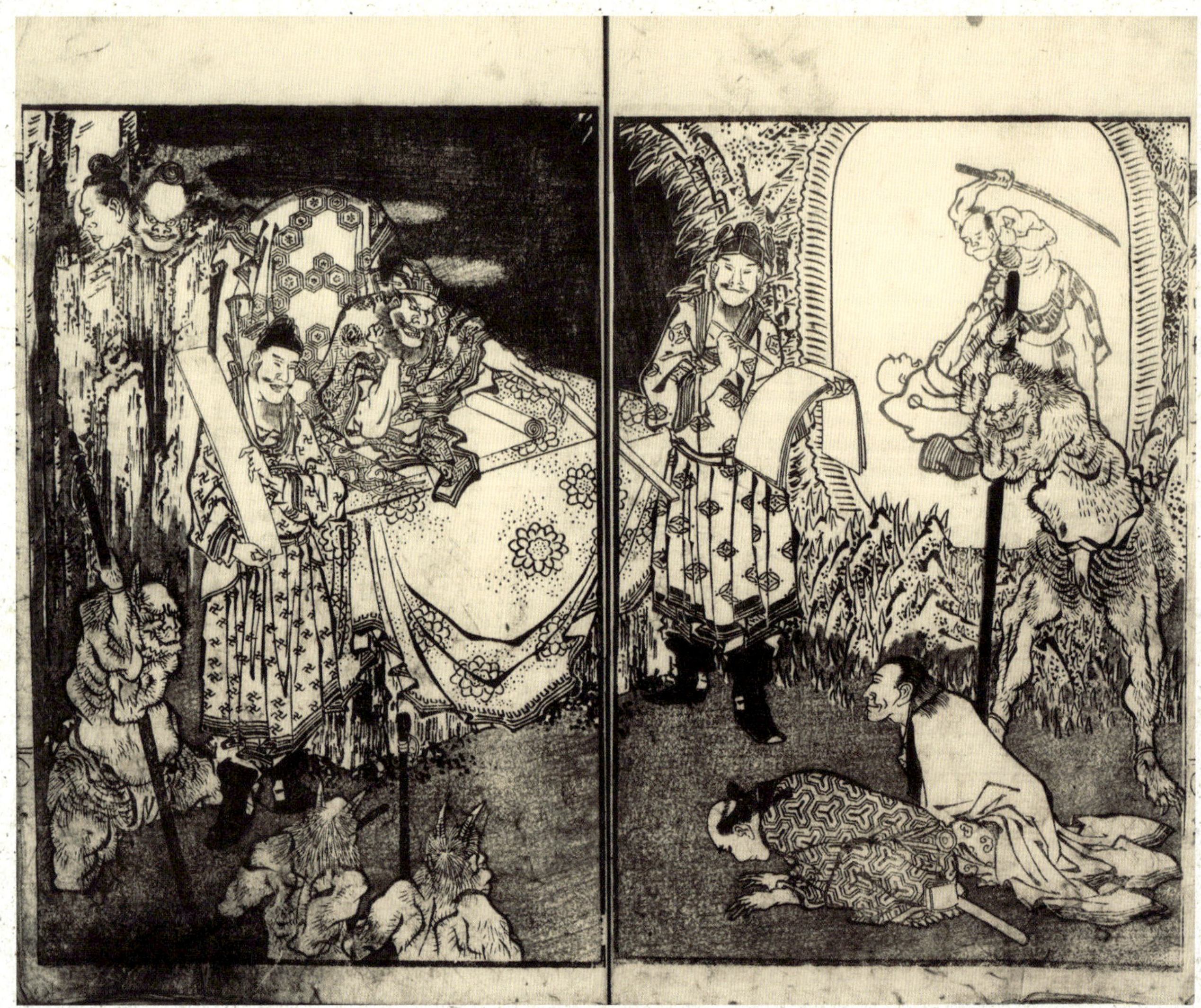

# Stars on a Frosty Night

## *Shimoyo no hoshi*
## 霜夜星

1808 (5 vols.)
Author: Ryūtei Tanehiko (1783–1842)
Artist: Katsushika Hokusai (1760–1849)
Publisher: Yamazakiya Heihachi
Woodblock printed book (*hanshibon*); ink on paper
Waseda University Library

**Below** Vol. 1, Ihyōe is eaten alive by rats.

Ryūtei Tanehiko was of samurai origins and began his literary career as a writer of *kyōka*, or satirical poems. He published his first works of popular fiction in 1807. Two of his three novels, *The Maelstrom of Awa* (*Awa no naruto*) and *Stars on a Frosty Night* (*Shimoyo no hoshi*), were illustrated by Katsushika Hokusai. Although famous today for his single-sheet prints, Hokusai was very popular at that time for his book illustrations, and to engage him as the artist for a newcomer's novel was a brilliant move by the publishers.

*Stars on a Frosty Night* retells the story of the beautiful but unfortunate Ohana who is rescued by Takanishi Ihyōe, a masterless samurai, or *rōnin*. They fall in love, but she is abducted and taken to a brothel where she threatens to bite off her tongue if approached obscenely. For financial reasons, Ihyōe marries the unattractive Osawa, but then discovers Ohana's whereabouts and falls in love with her again. He violates Osawa brutally out of frustration whereupon Osawa drowns herself only to return

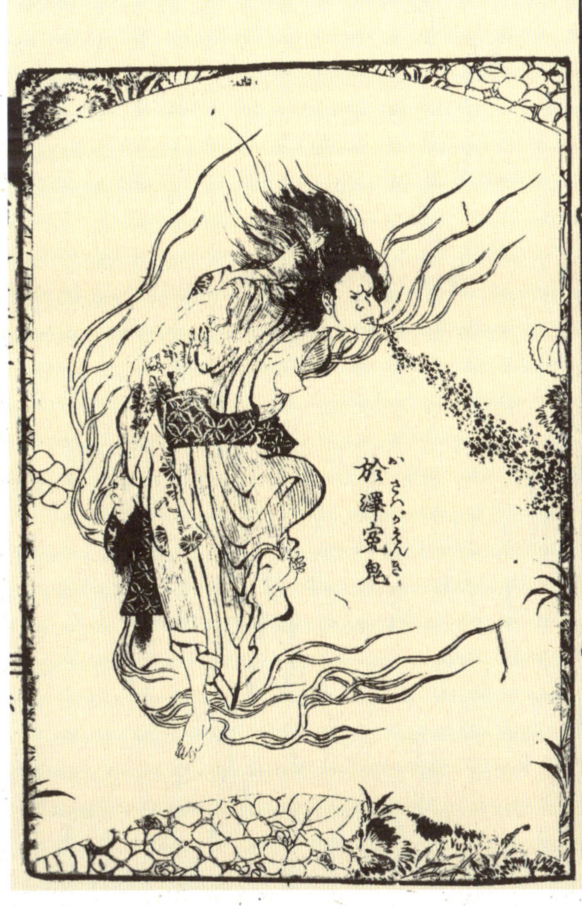
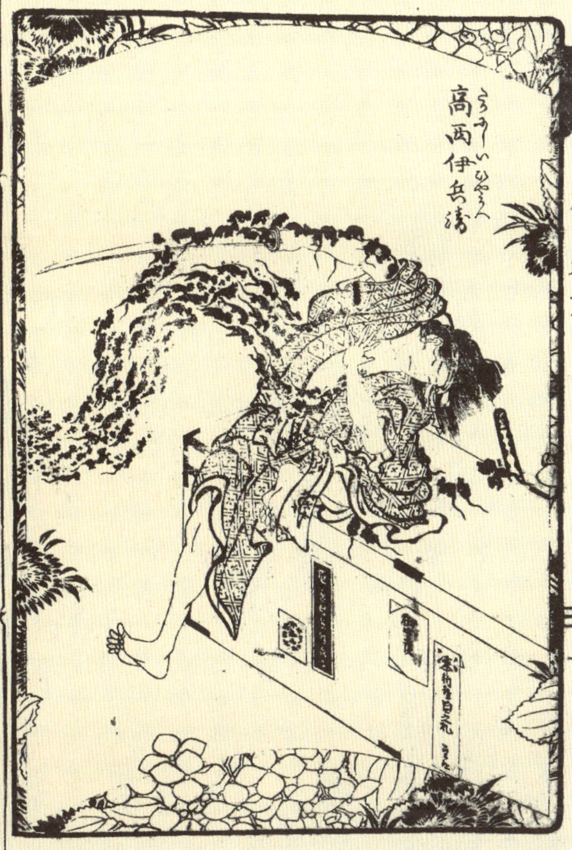

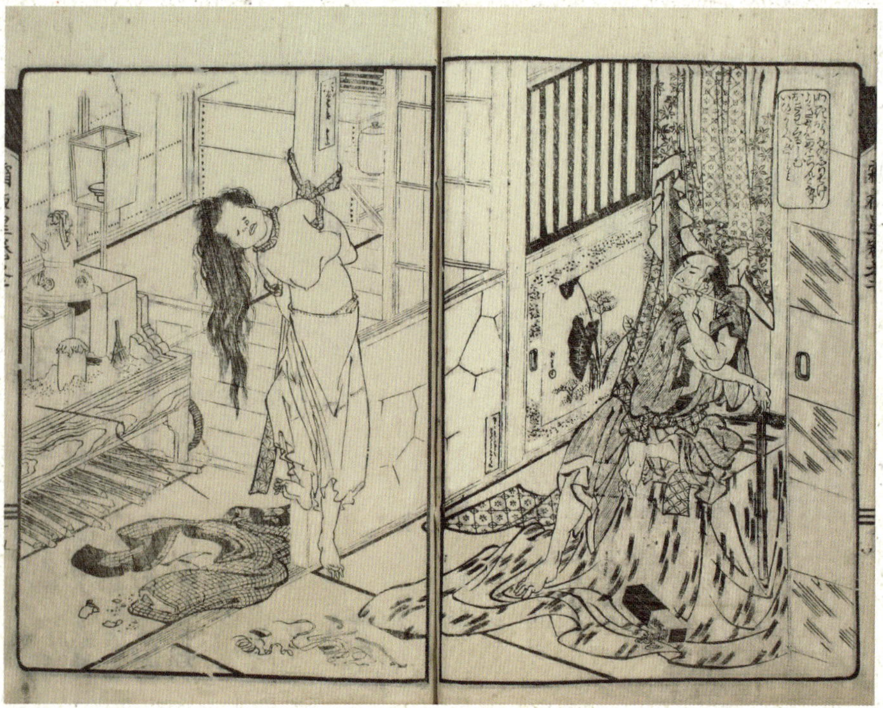



as a serpentine demon with supernatural malice for her tormentors. The demon reserves the most gruesome death for Ihyōe, who is eaten alive by rats. Ohana, untouched by the demon Osawa, then becomes a nun and exorcises Osawa.

In the thirty-seven images in the book, Hokusai masterfully enriches Tanehiko's story of the suffering heroine by visualizing the gruesome behavior of Ihyōe and the eerie demon that Osawa turns into. On one occasion he expands the usual double-page image to four pages depicting Ohana in the house watching Ihyōe kneeling on the veranda and shooting his rifle. The trajectory of the bullet continues to the next spread where the reader sees that Ihyōe, unsuccessfully, was aiming at the demon Osawa, hovering in the sky amidst black clouds and fire.

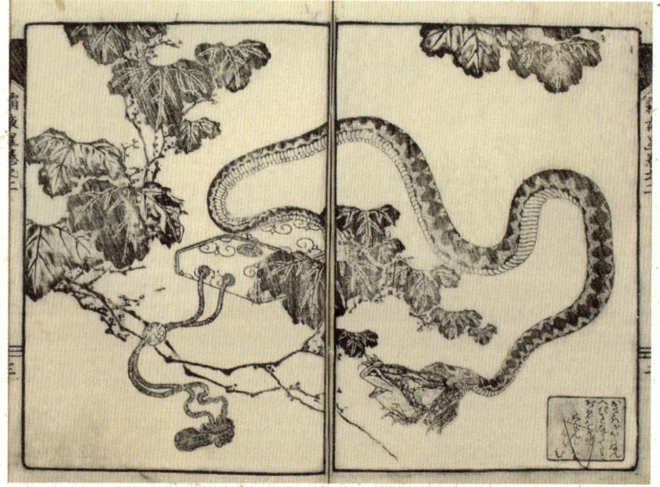

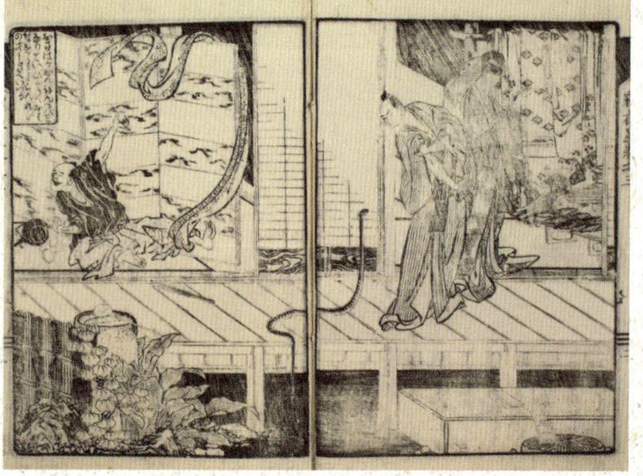

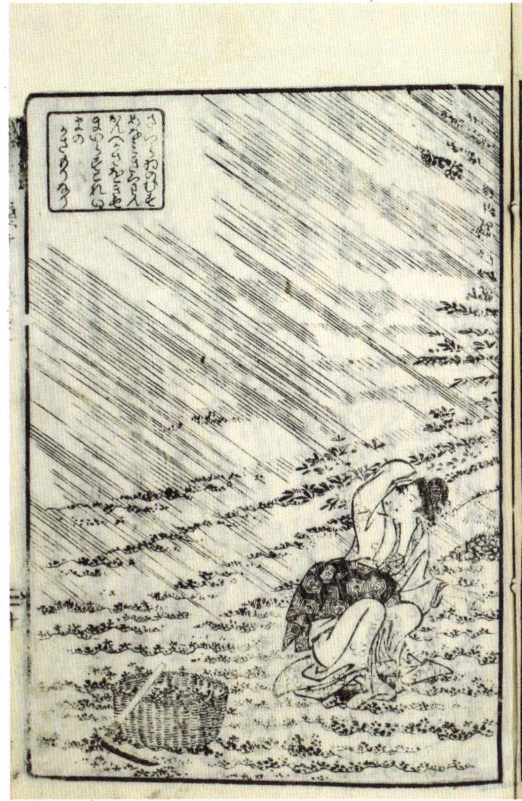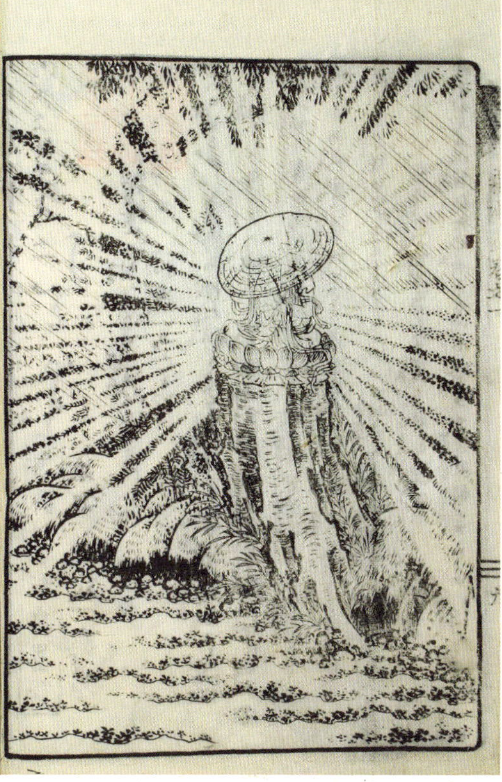

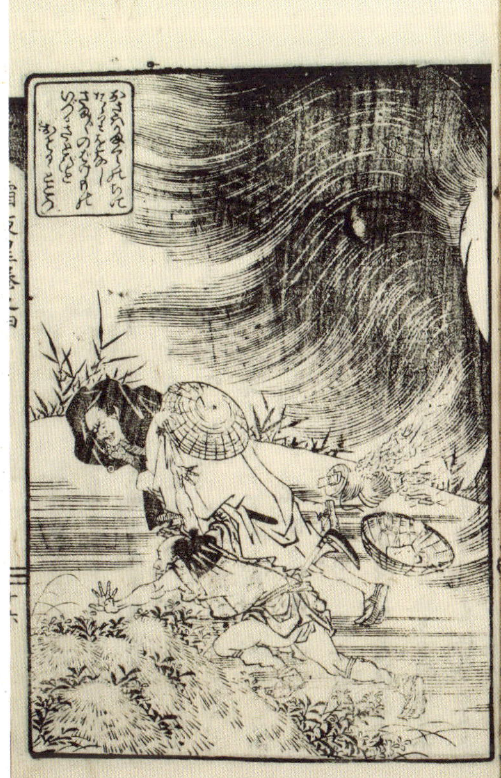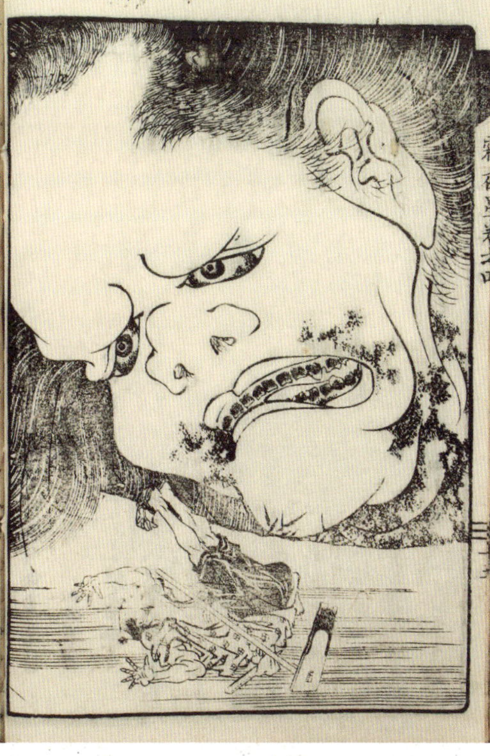

**Left** Vol. 4, giant-head demon.

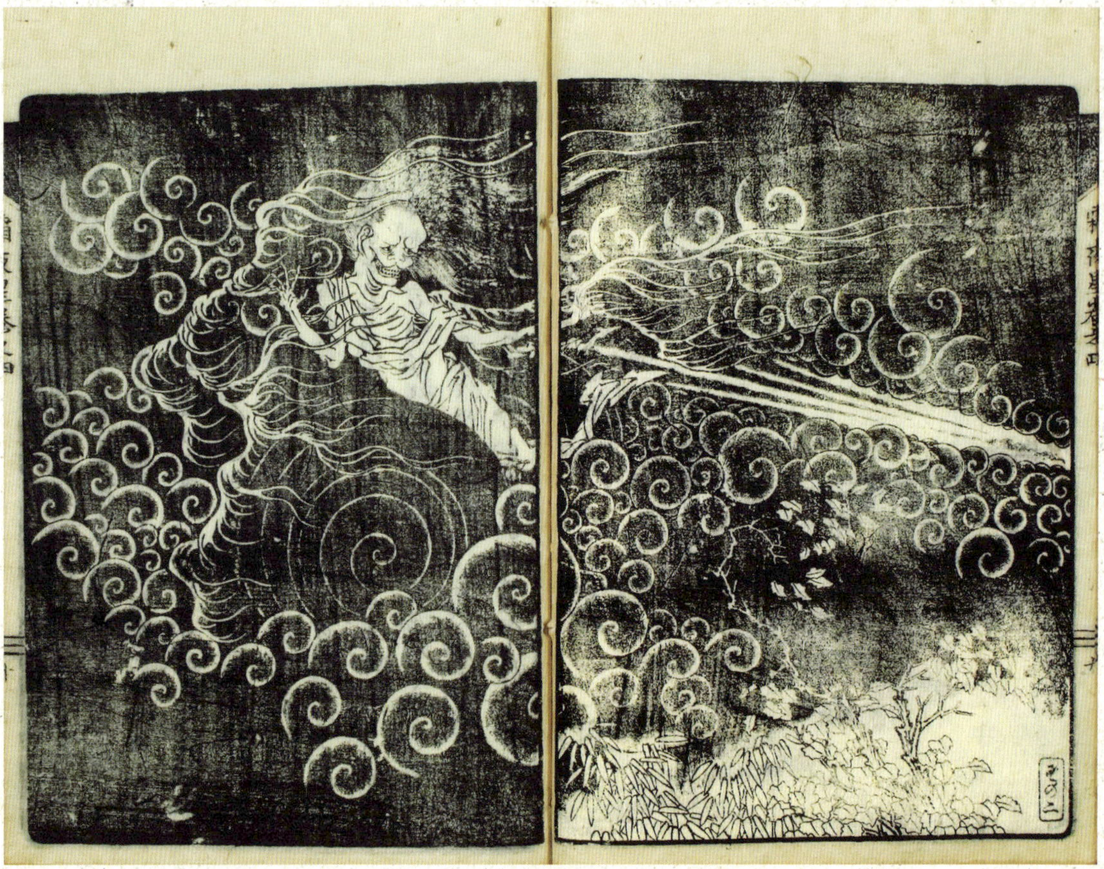

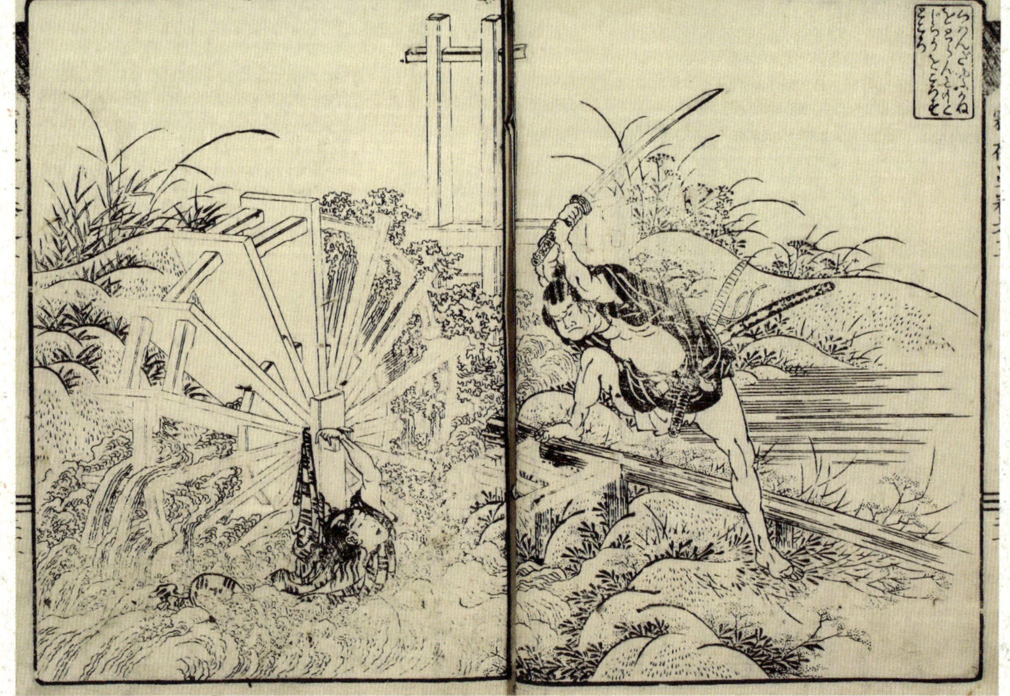



**Above** Vol. 1,
Osawa's ghost.

**Opposite above**
Vol. 3, Ihyōe shoots
at Osawa's ghost:

**Opposite below**
Vol. 5, Enjun beats
a priestess with a
bucket.

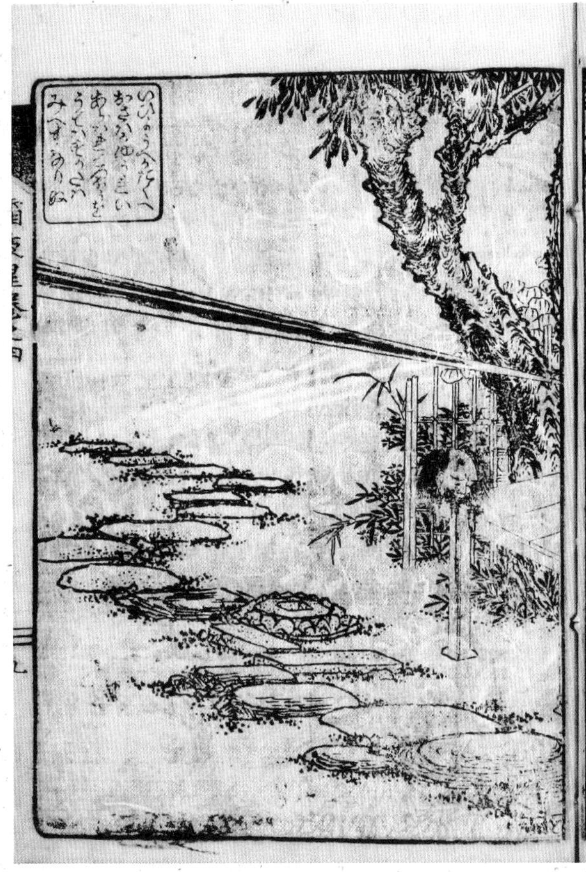
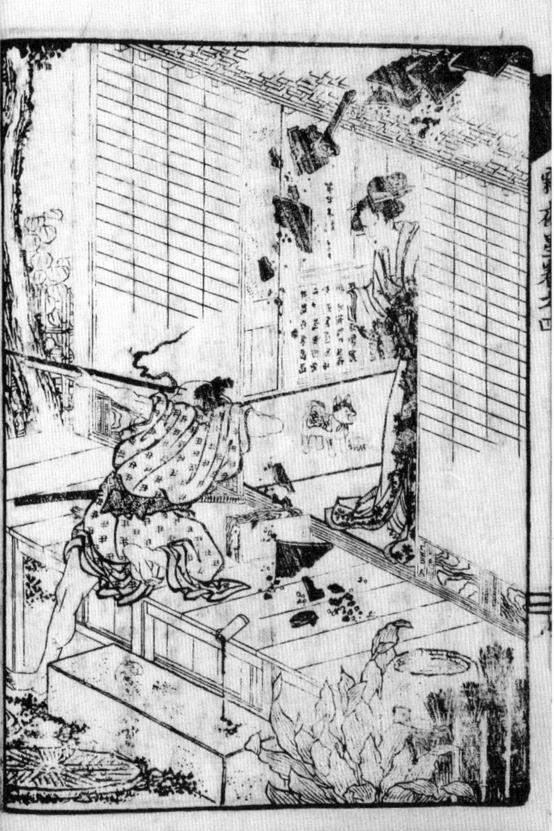
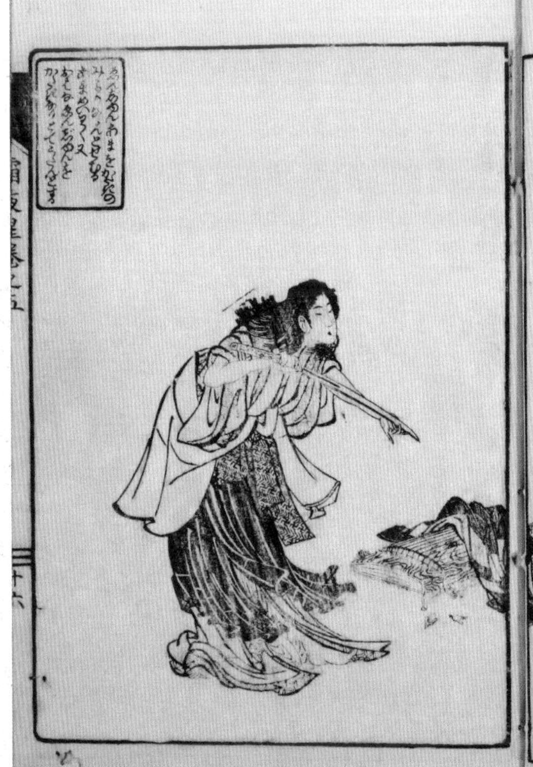
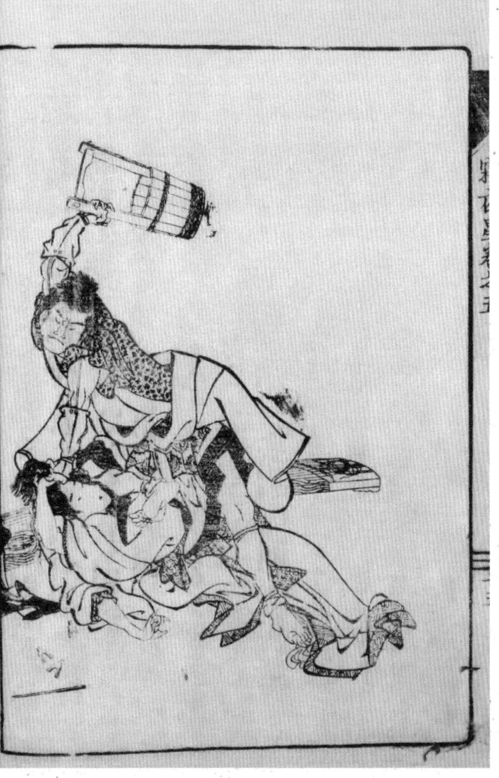

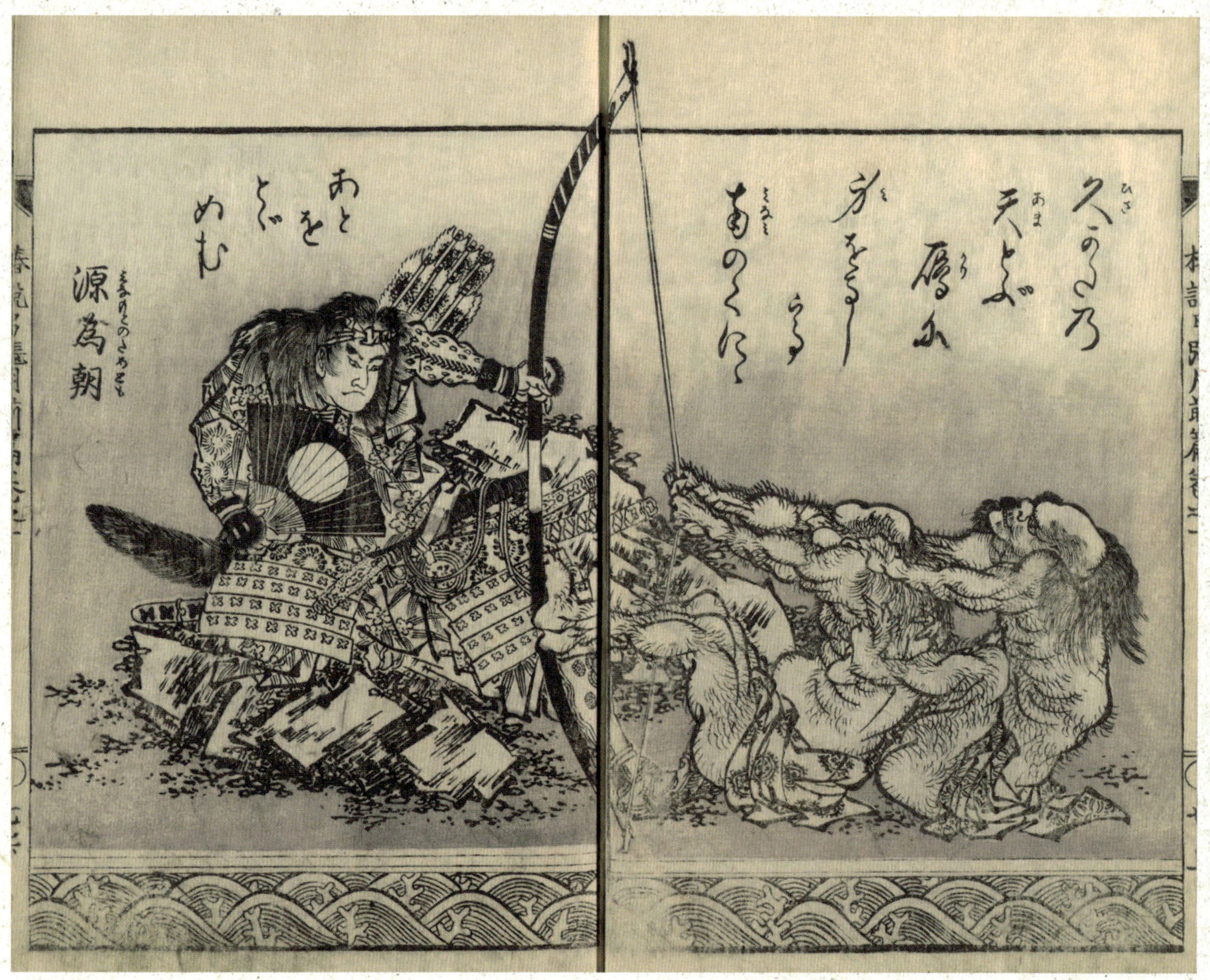


# Strange Tales of the Crescent Moon

## *Chinsetsu yumiharizuki*

椿説弓張月

1807 (vol. 1), 1808 (vols. 2–3), 1810 (vol. 4), 1811 (vol. 5)
Author: Kyokutei Bakin (1767–1848)
Artist: Katsushika Hokusai (1760–1849)
Publishers: Nishimuraya Genroku (vol. 1); Hirabayashiya Shōgorō (vols. 2–5)
Woodblock printed book (*hanshibon*); ink on paper
National Diet Library

*Strange Tales of the Crescent Moon* (*Chinsetsu yumiharizuki*) is Kyokutei Bakin's second-most important novel after his *Lives of the Eight Dog Warriors of the Satomi Clan* (*Nansō Satomi hakkenden*) (see p. 120), which he began writing three years later. Published in twenty-nine volumes over a period of four years, this historical novel is a tale of good and evil. It begins with the story of the twelfth-century hero Minamoto Tametomo, a master archer, who moves to the capital of Kyoto.

In 1156, a dispute erupts about the imperial succession, known as the Hōgen rebellion. Tametomo, who was on the side of the losing faction, was exiled to Ōshima, a large island in the Amami archipelago, far to the south between Kyushu and Okinawa. Bakin describes how, when Tametomo arrives there, instead of letting the story end as the legend does, Bakin expands it, with Tametomo escaping from Ōshima and raising an army. However, instead of sailing back to the mainland, Tametomo is caught in a storm at sea and driven further south to the Ryukyu Islands. Tametomo pacifies rivaling factions there, rescues and marries a princess, and establishes a dynasty. Bakin then makes Tametomo the founder of the Ryukyu kingdom.

A substantial part of the success of *Crescent Moon* must be credited to Katsushika Hokusai and the more than 160 captivating illustrations he provided for the five volumes. Initially, Hokusai masterfully captures the courageous Tametomo in dramatic fights with different monsters and other evil characters. Later, he portrays the faraway Ryukyu Islands which were unreachable for almost anyone at the time, and thus the life there, strongly influenced by nearby China, was perceived as highly exotic for the common townspeople.

**Opposite** Vol. 1, Minamoto Tametomo.

**Below** Vol. 1, Kiheiji chases a ship across the ocean.

**Bottom** Vol. 1, Ikazuchi shoots at Shigesue on Mt. Yufu.

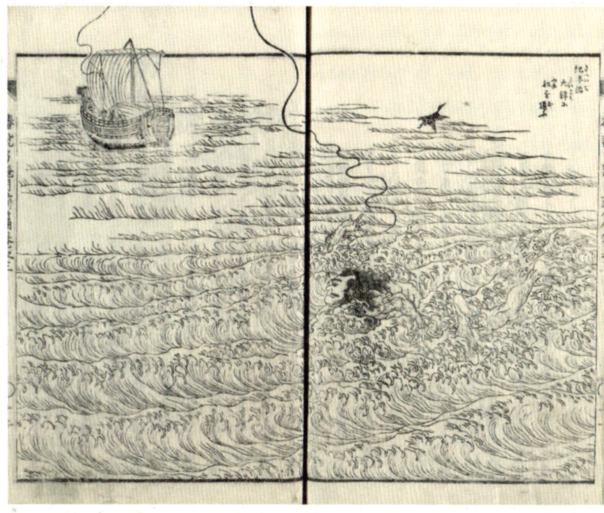

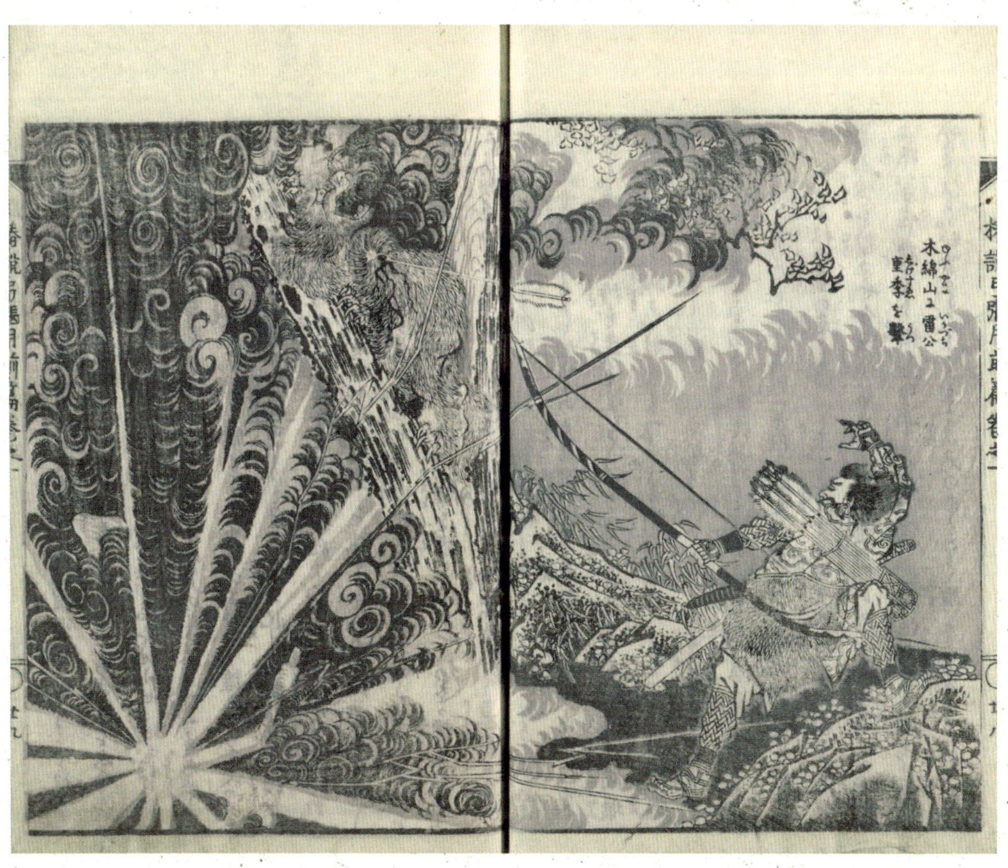

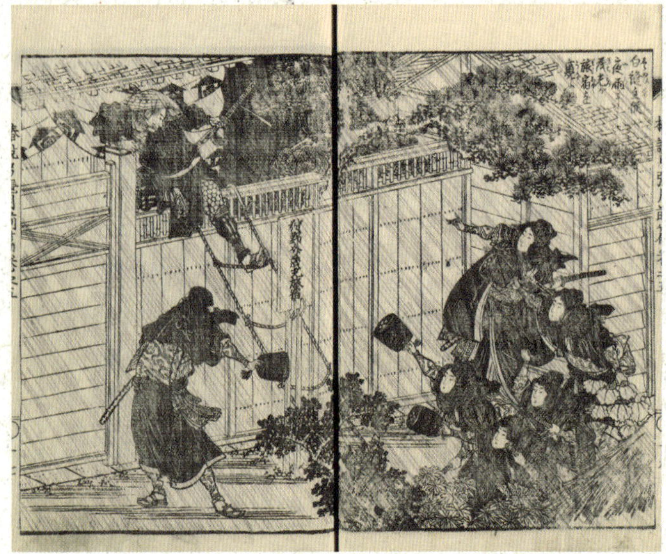

**Left** Vol. 1, Shiranui and followers observing an inn in the night rain.

**Below** Vol. 1, Shin'in (Emperor Sutoku) dies of anger and enters into the demon world.

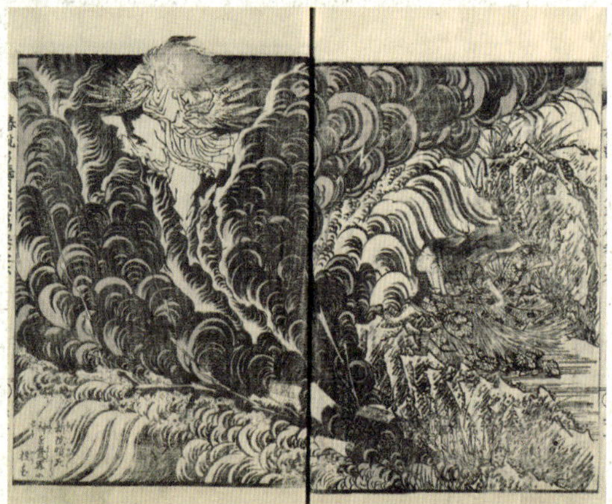

**Below** Vol. 2, Tametomo on Demon Island shoots to the shore.

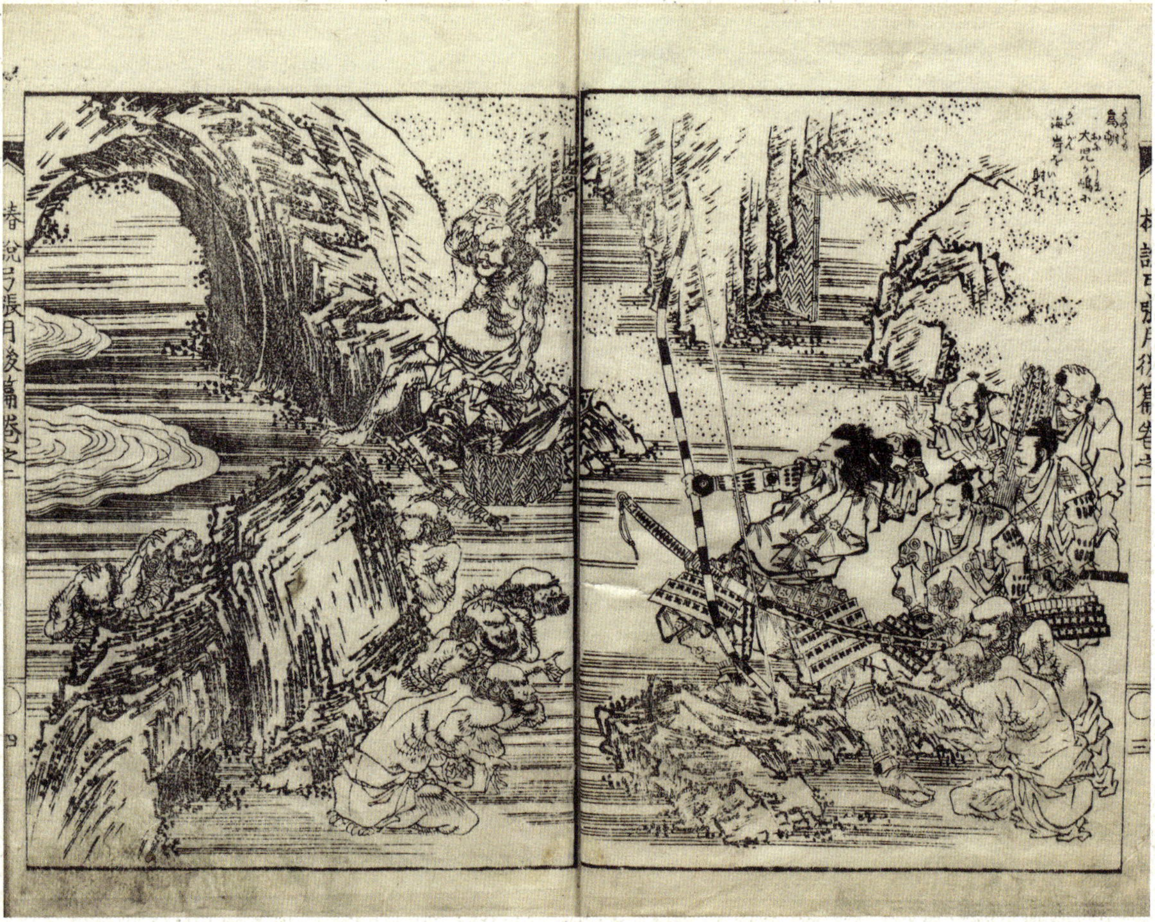

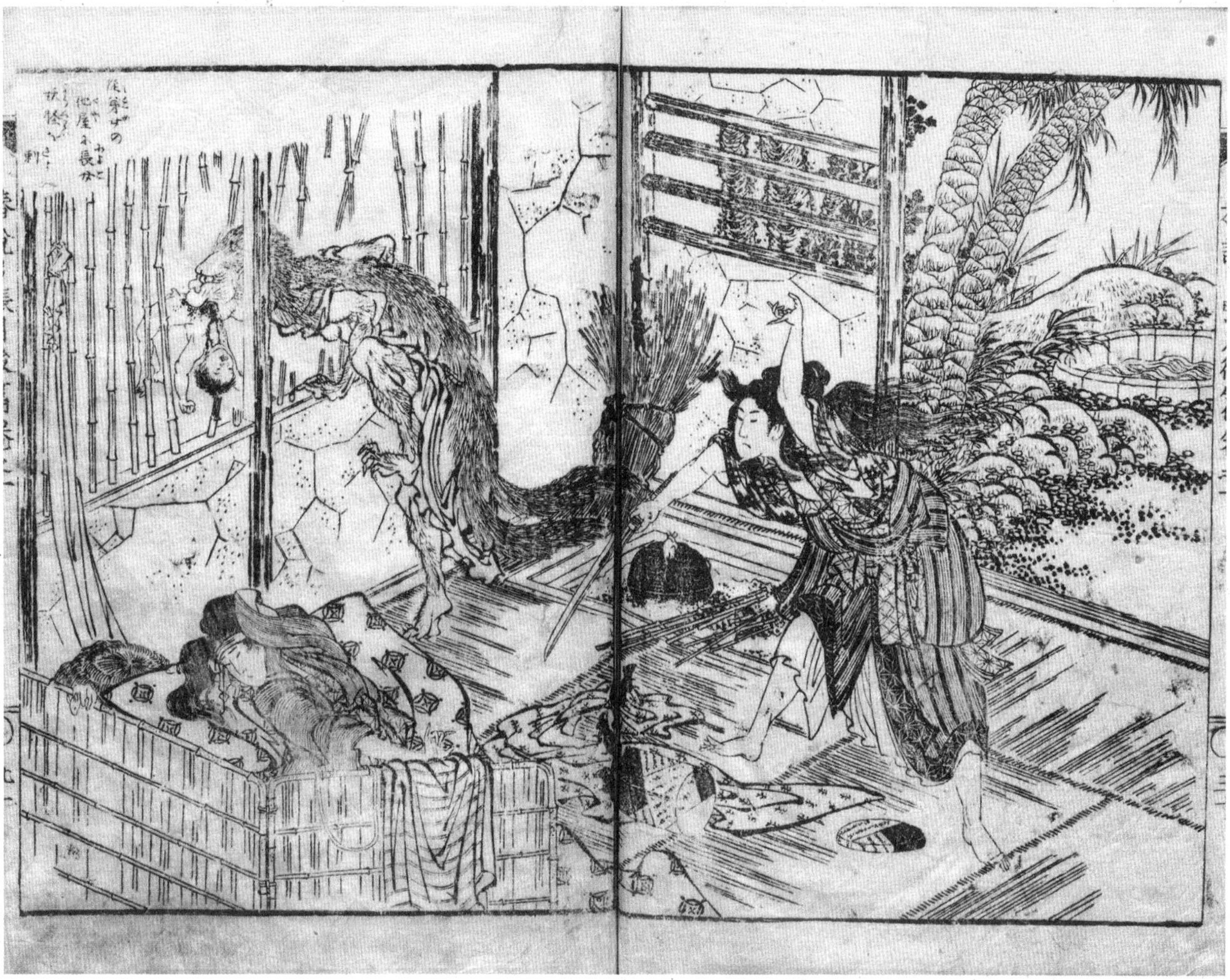

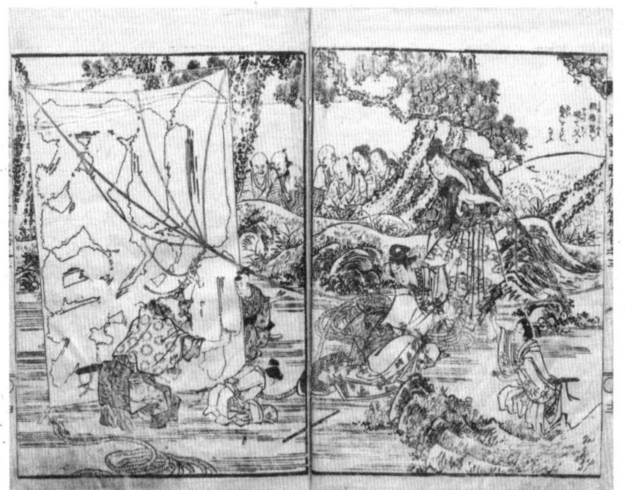

**Above** Vol. 2, a monster kills and carries away a child.

**Above** Vol. 2, Tomowaka is punished for breaking the flute that was a family treasure.

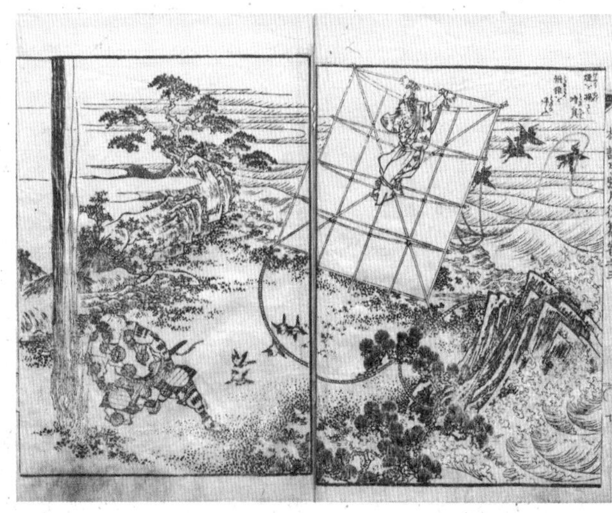

**Above** Vol. 2, Tokikazu makes smoke signals while Tomowaka is tied to a kite.

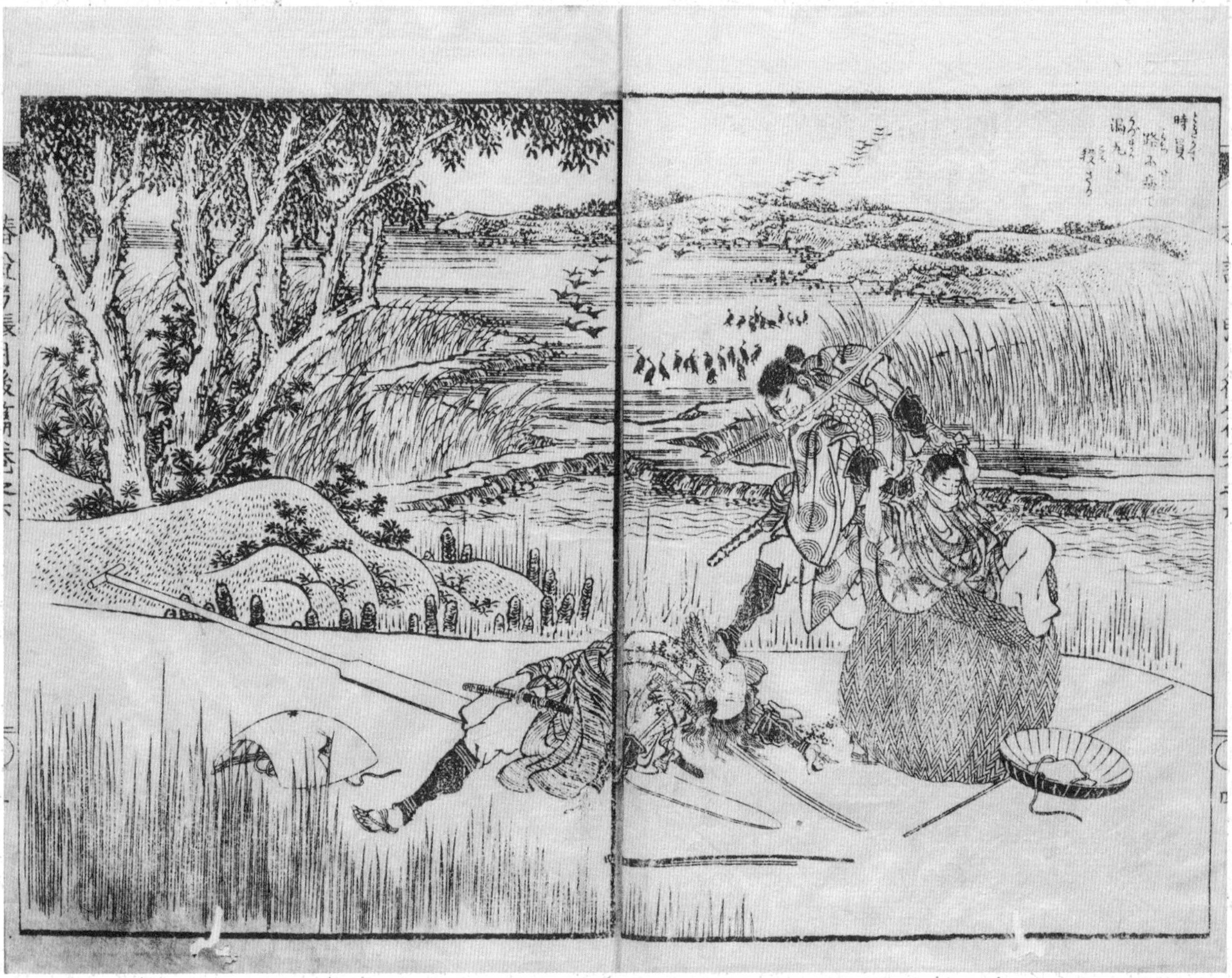

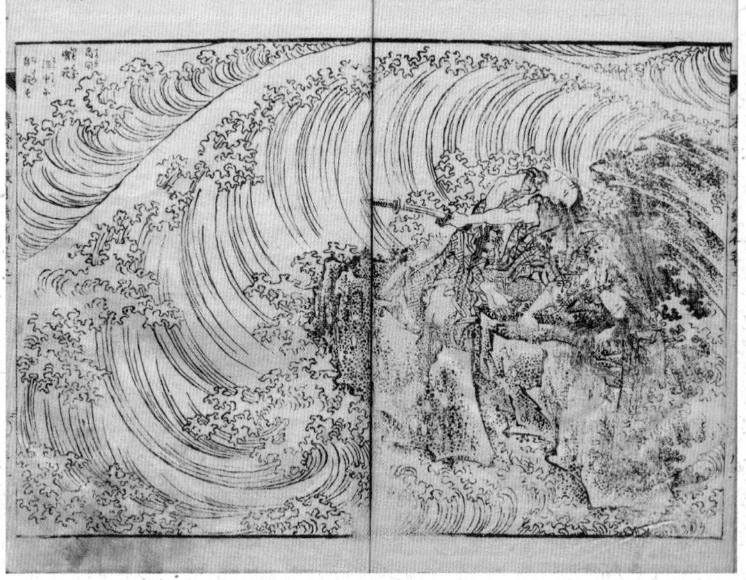

**Above** Vol. 2, Tokikazu becomes sick on the road and is killed by Uzumaru.

**Right** Vol. 3, Takama and Isohagi commit suicide at the ocean.

**Below** Vol. 4, people used as archery targets.

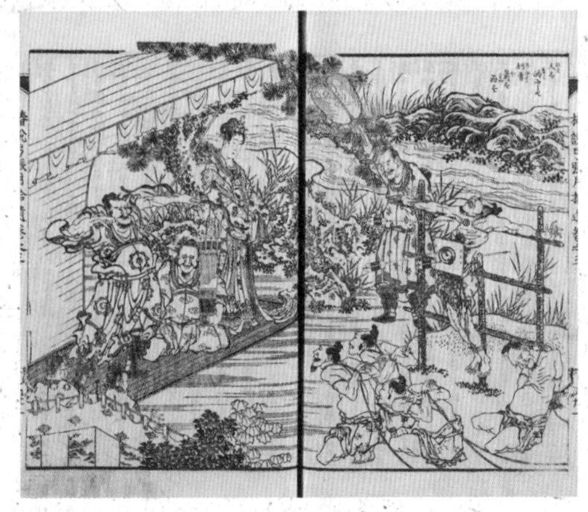

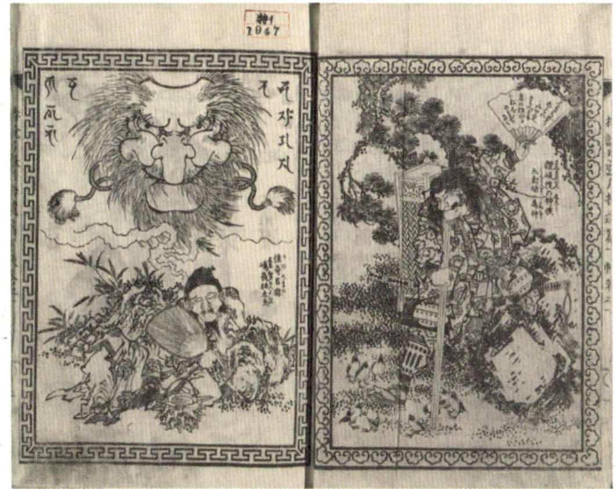

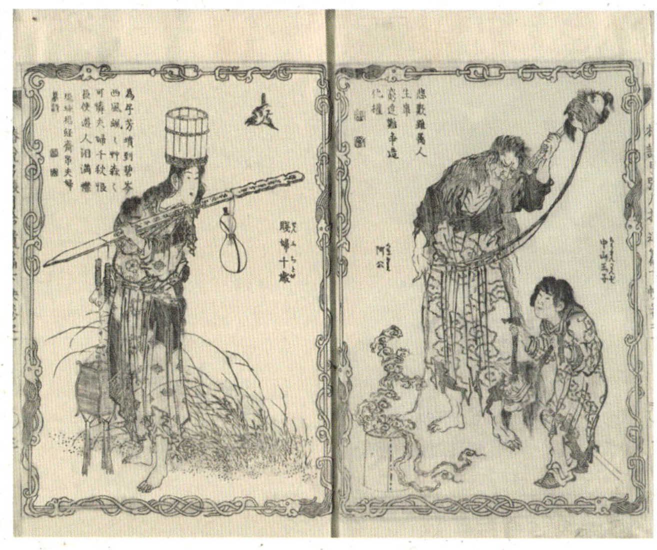

**Above** Vol. 5, the humble woman Chitose, Kumagimi, and Chūsan Wauji.

**Below** Vol. 3, shattering the stone coffin, Mōun appears.

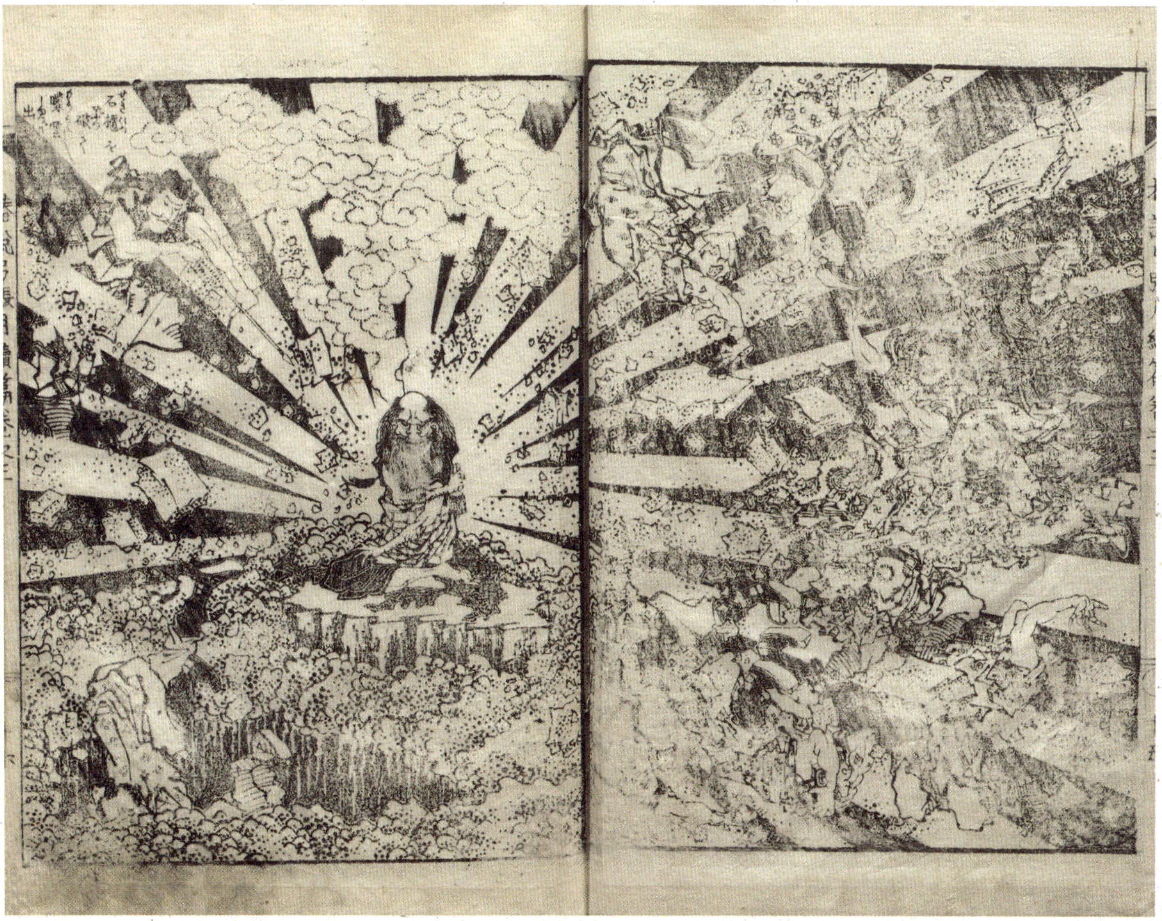

# The Tale of the Craftsman from Hida

*Hida no takumi monogatari*
飛弾匠物語

1809 (6 vols.)
Author: Ishikawa Masamochi (1754–1830)
Artist: Katsushika Hokusai (1760–1849)
Publisher: Kadomaruya Jinsuke
Woodblock printed book (*hanshibon*);
ink on paper
Waseda University Library

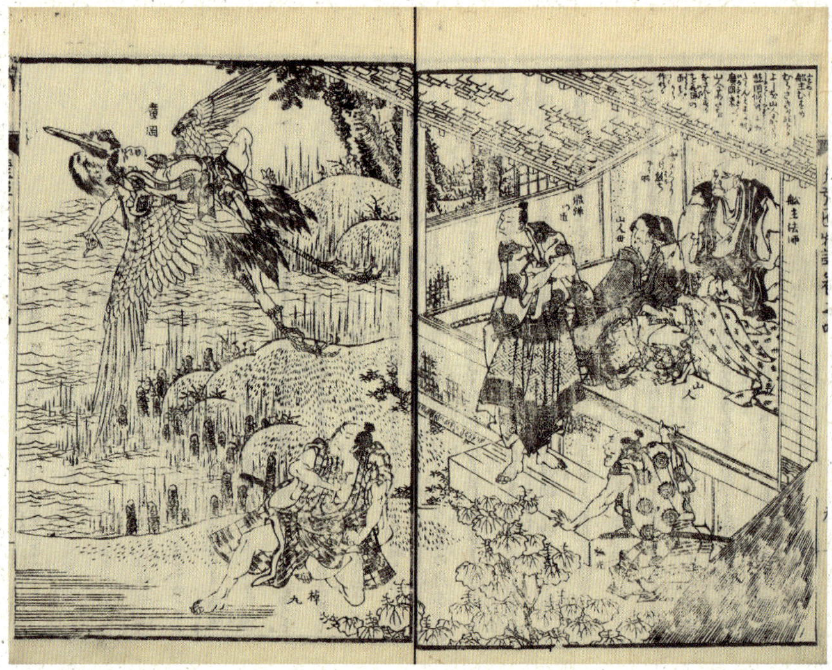

**Above** Vol. 4, Hirooka is carried away by an artificial crane.

**Opposite top** Vol. 3, Yamabito tries to haul the boat with Murasaki.

Ishikawa Masamochi was both a scholar and a famous poet. Since his father was the print artist Ishikawa Toyonobu (1711–85), he was close to the art scene in Edo (today's Tokyo) from childhood. In 1809, Masamochi's novel, *The Tale of the Craftsman from Hida* (*Hida no takumi monogatari*), was published in six volumes with thirty-six illustrations by Katsushika Hokusai, who was arguably the most respected book illustrator of the day.

The story centers around the skilled craftsman Inabe Suminawa from Hida Province in central Japan (present-day Gifu Prefecture). Suminawa is no ordinary carpenter but a wizard with wood, able to create lifelike carvings that surpass reality and are controlled by advanced mechanisms. Early on, Hokusai illustrated some of Suminawa's unrivaled devices, such as a carved rooster that a live rooster cannot stop challenging, a portable bridge, an automated boat, and a moveable house.

Suminawa embarks on a pilgrimage to Mount Hōrai, the paradisical peak in East Asia believed to house immortal Daoist sages. There, he is tutored by mystical beings in the esoteric arts of creation, enhancing his already formidable skills. Upon departing Mount Hōrai, Suminawa encounters Yamabito, a young man entangled in the plight of unrequited love but unable to bridge the social chasm between himself, a commoner, and Murasaki, a princess of lofty lineage. In a whimsical scene, Hokusai captures Yamabito on the shore trying to haul an automated boat carrying Murasaki towards him with the aid of her sash. The villain Hirooka, who is terrorizing Yamabito's parents, is tied by Suminawa to his artificial crane, which is used to carry the villain away.

Employing his ingenuity and clever devices, Suminawa orchestrates a union of true love between the pair. Ultimately, the trio ascend to become immortal sages on Mount Hōrai, bound together by their shared journey and profound connection.

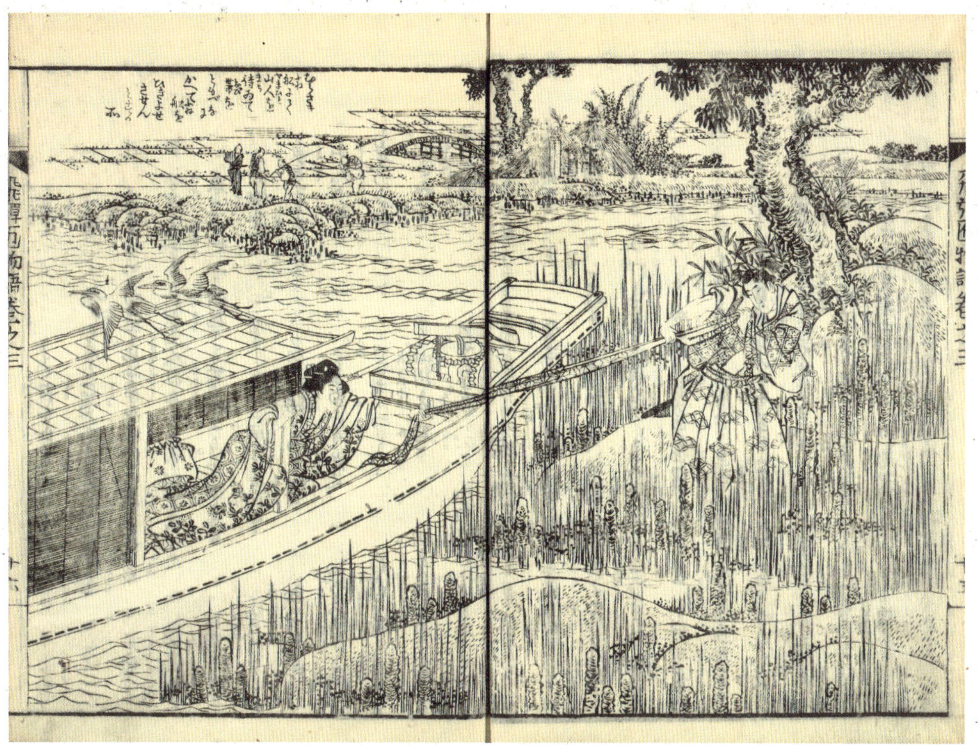

**Below** Vol. 2, a youth drives away Hirooka who had insulted Yamabito and his mother.

**Below** Vol. 1, the mechanical achievements of the craftsman from Hida.

**Bottom** Vol. 1, a carved rooster being challenged by a live rooster.

**Bottom** Vol. 4, Kusakai and his sister try to escape from the corpse of the man they killed.

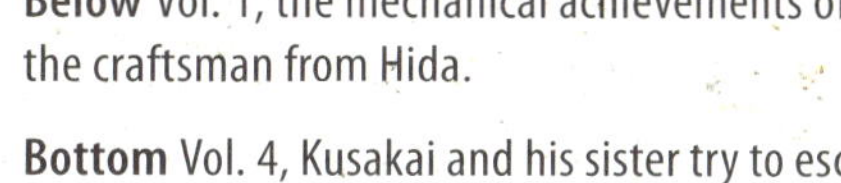

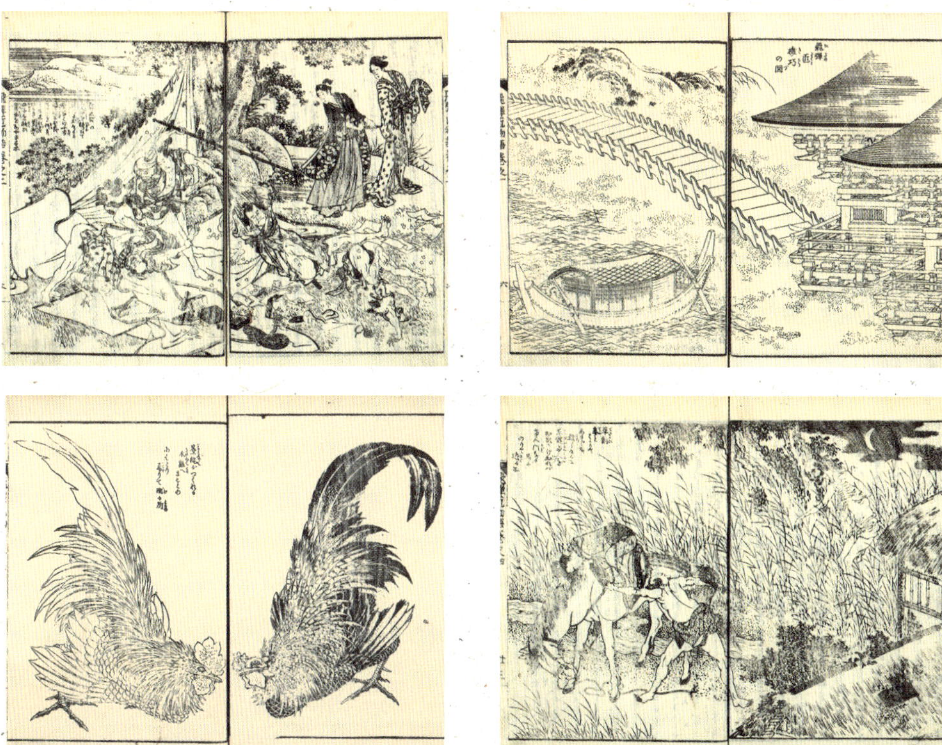

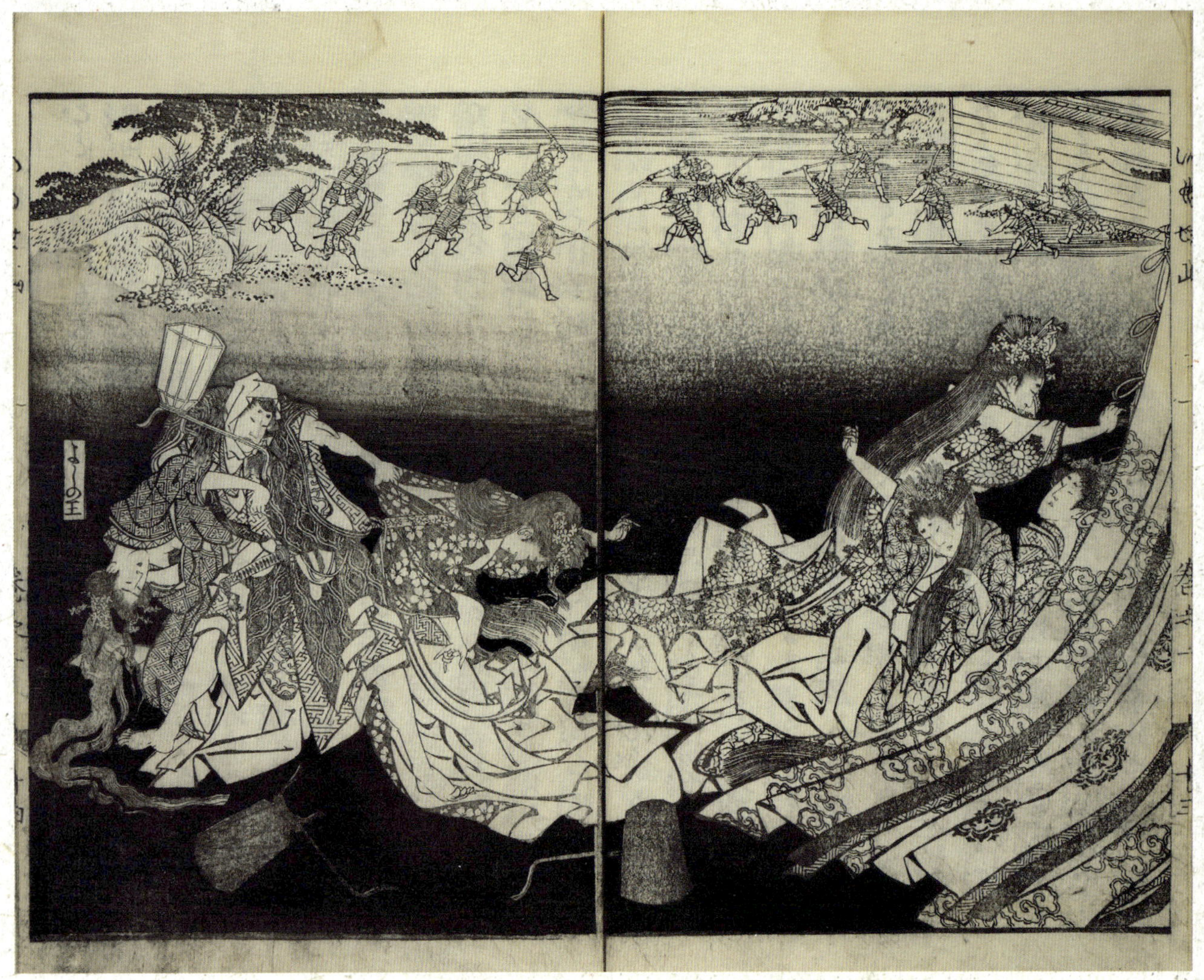

# The Husband and Wife Mountains

*On'yō Imoseyama*

陜陜妹背山

1810 (6 vols.).
Author: Shinrotei (died 1815)
Artist: Katsushika Hokusai (1760–1849)
Publisher: Ishiwatari Risuke
Woodblock printed book (*hanshibon*); ink on paper
The Metropolitan Museum of Art, Purchase, Mary and James G. Wallach Foundation Gift, 2013 (2013.718a–f)

In his youth, the writer Shinrotei is believed to have been a pupil of the artist Torii Kiyonaga before turning to writing *kabuki* plays in 1789. He was very popular in that role and rarely wrote in other genres. However, he did write the novel *The Husband and Wife Mountains* (*On'yō Imoseyama*), published in six volumes in 1810 with thirty-five extraordinary images by Katsushika Hokusai.

The story revolves around two families who dwell on adjacent peaks and are torn apart by their political differences. Amidst this division, Koganosuke, the son of one family, finds himself captivated by the daughter (Hinadori) of the other. Against all odds, their love flourishes, tinged with even greater intrigue. Intertwined with their passion is the shadowy tale of a conspiracy against the reigning emperor, adding a layer of suspense to their star-crossed romance.

Hokusai's illustrations provide a captivating glimpse into his spectral musings. One unveils the evil Fukashichi in a house infamous for its rumored ghostly inhabitants. Fukashichi deliberately selected this eerie locale to evade unwanted interruptions to his covert gatherings. Illuminated by a macabre lamp fashioned from human femurs, a disembodied head emits a flickering flame, casting an ominous aura over the scene. A tree branch resembling bat wings looms over the veranda. Leaning on a massive axe, Fukashichi sits on a wooden board held up by two strong and hairy demons that dwell beneath. Behind him a monster is approaching through spider webs.

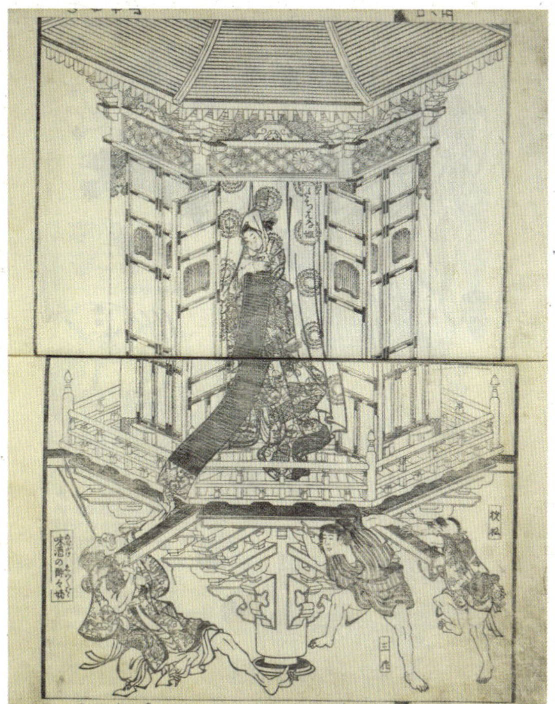

**Above** Vol. 1, revolving sutra repository.

**Opposite and below** Vol. 1, the King of Yoshino.

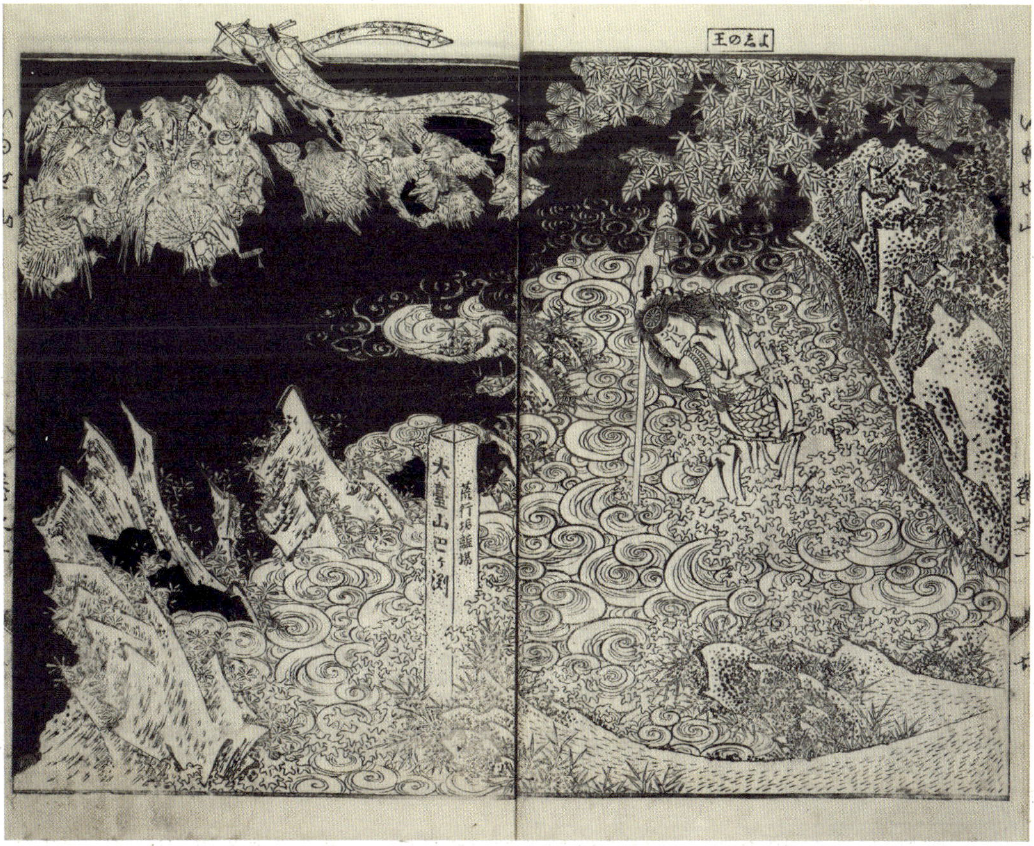

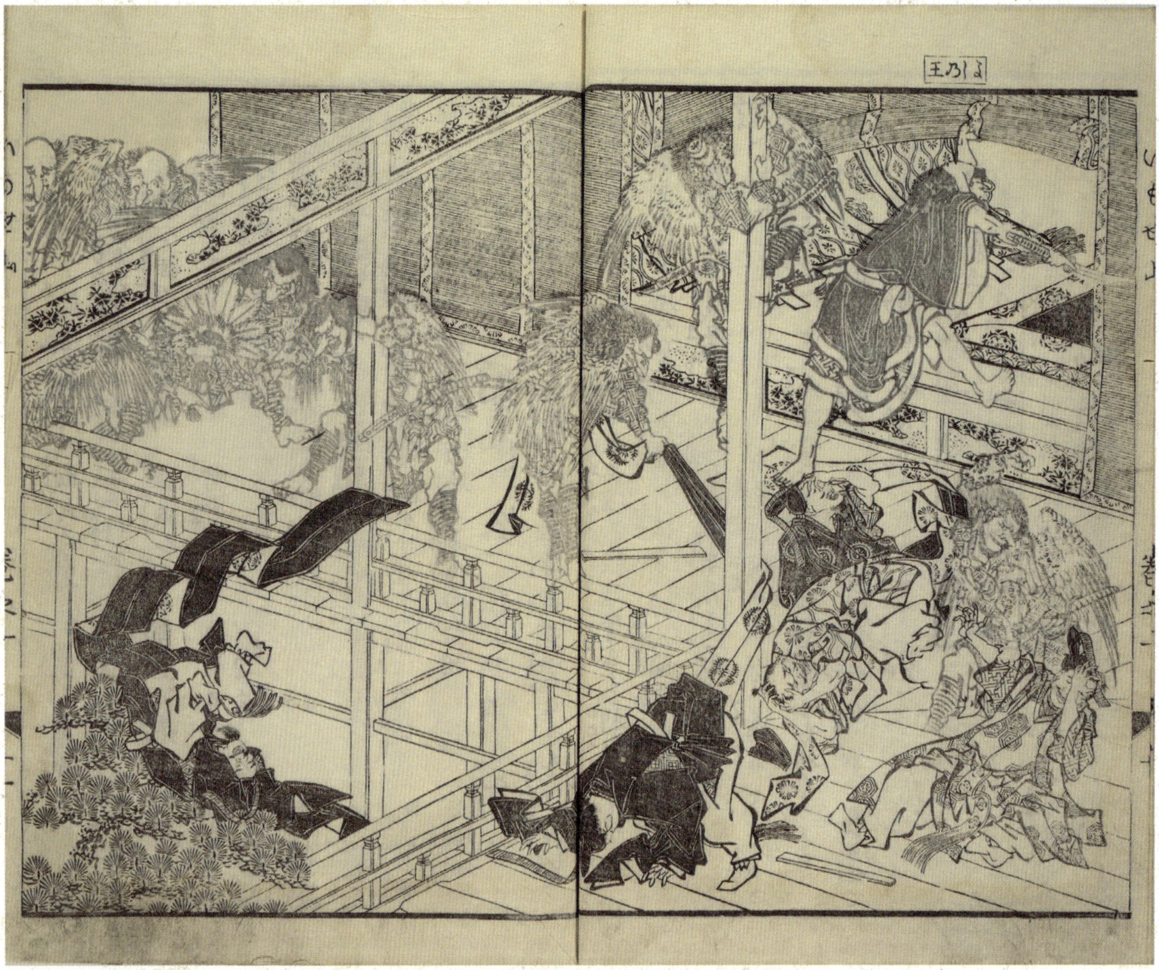

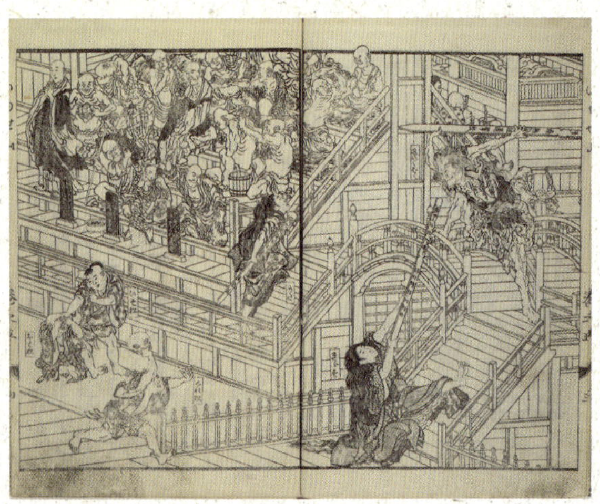

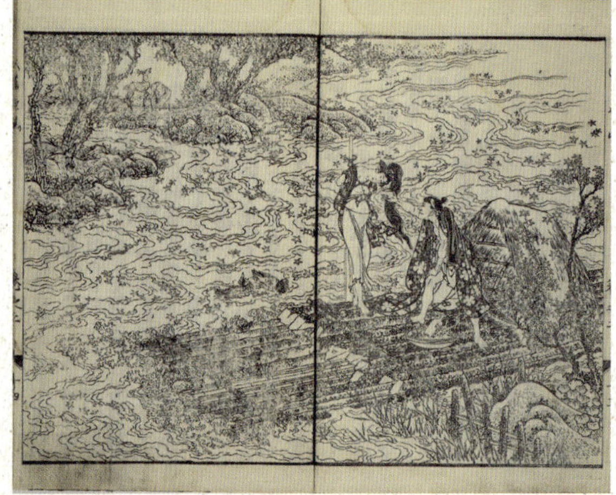

**Below** Vol. 4, Fukashichi in a house of monsters.

**Bottom left** Vol. 6, the King of Yoshino firing against attackers.

**Bottom right** Vol. 6, the King of Yoshino watches Fukashichi pounding children.

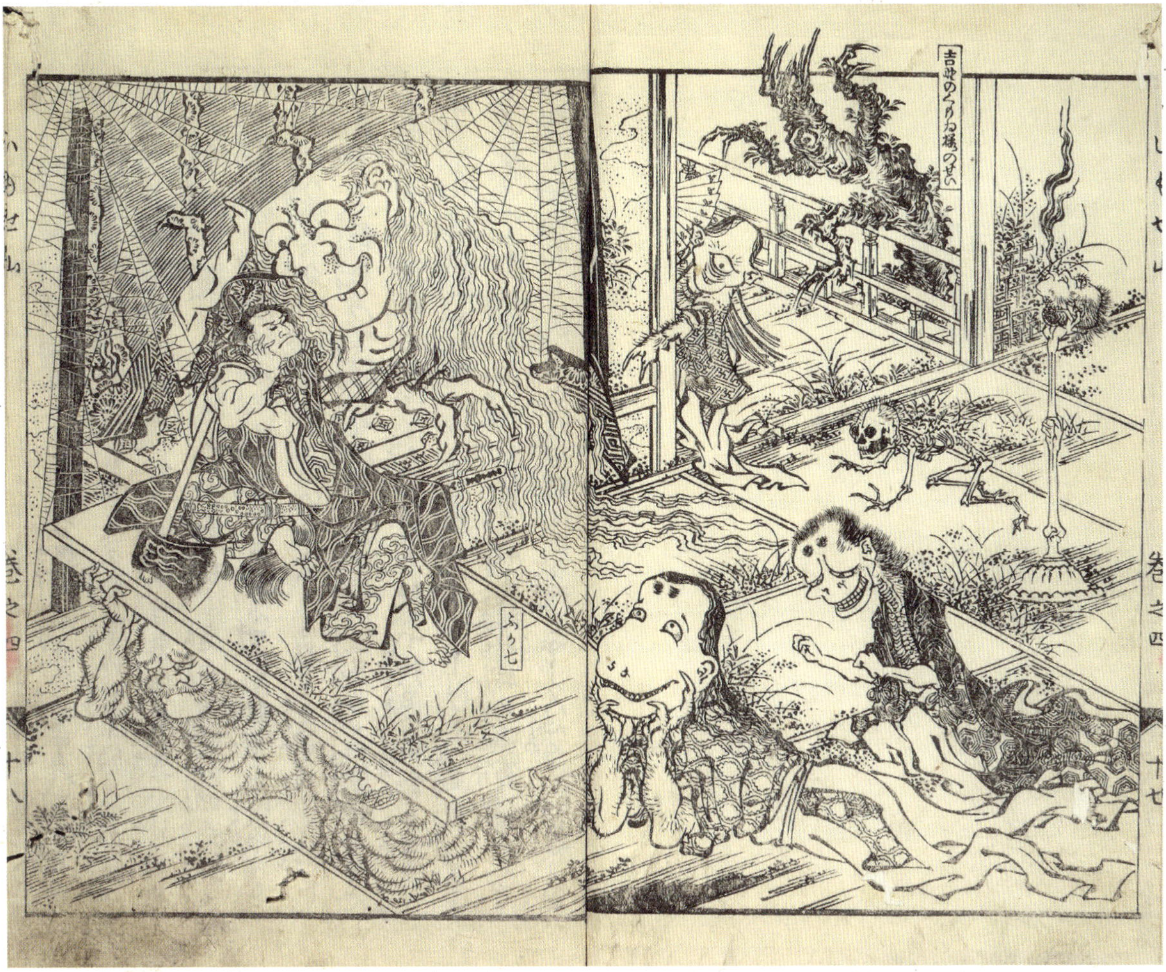

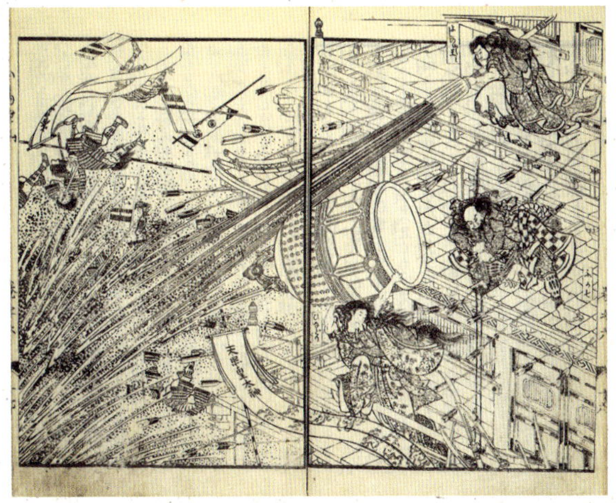

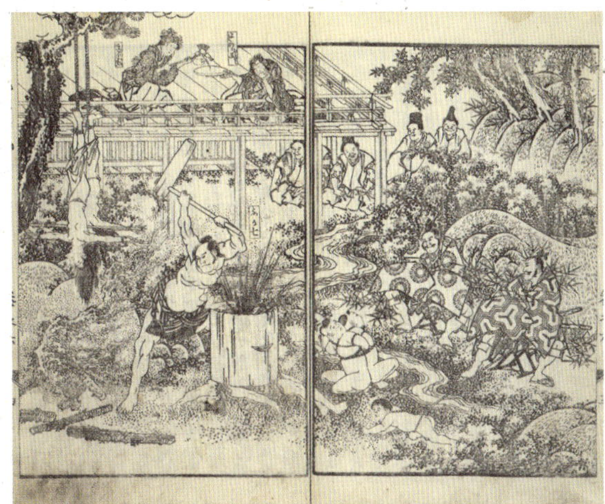

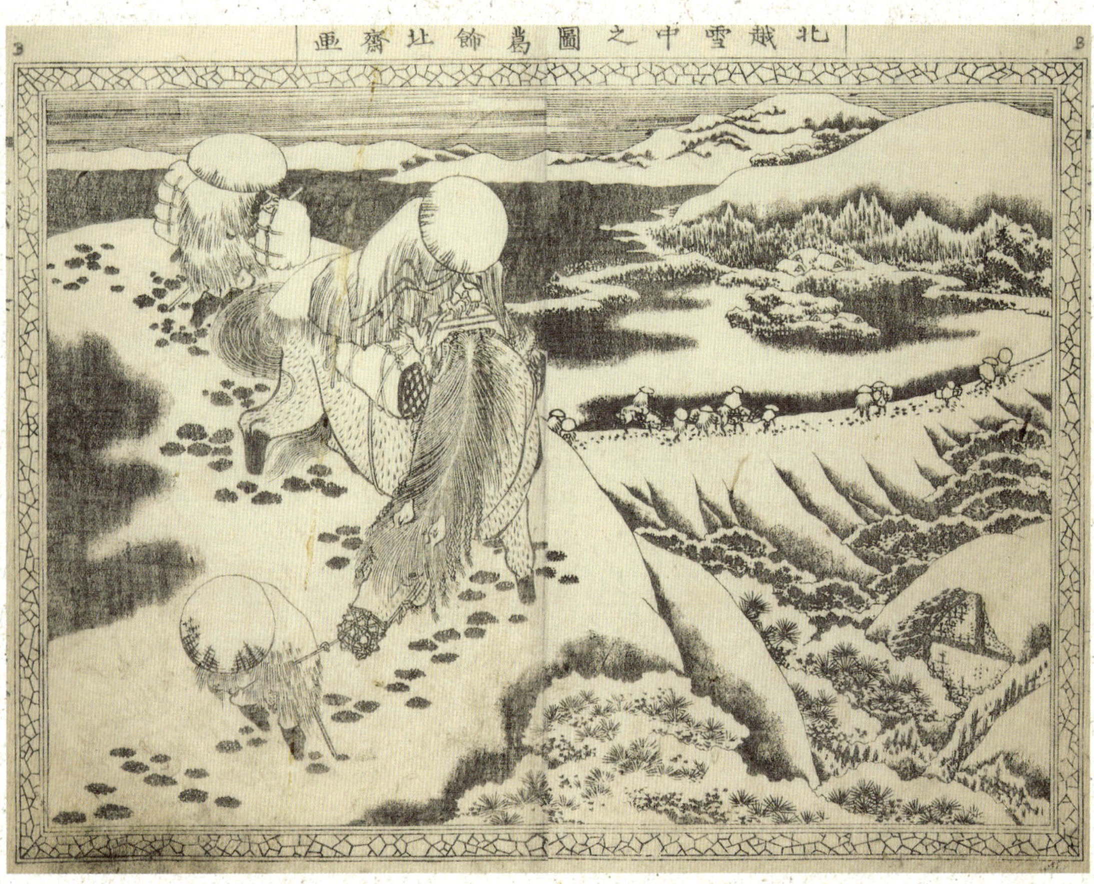



# Strange Stories from the Northern Province of Echigo

## *Hokuetsu kidan*

北越奇談

1813 (6 vols.)
Author: Tachibana Konron (1760–1819)
Preface: Ryūtei Tanehiko (1783–1842)
Artist: Katsushika Hokusai (1760–1849)
Publisher: Nishimuraya Yohachi
Woodblock printed book (*hanshibon*); ink on paper
Private collection

In pre-modern Japan, the north-central province of Echigo, today's Niigata Prefecture, was considered distant and strange. Bordering the Sea of Japan, it has much colder temperatures than the rest of Japan and thus receives a lot of snow. The unfamiliar and harsh climate has been the impetus for strange happenings and supernatural encounters, often retold in folktales. The otherness of Echigo was addressed by the writer Tachibana Konron in his book *Strange Stories from the Northern Province of Echigo* (*Hokuetsu kidan*). Konron himself was from Echigo, but somewhat surprisingly did not incorporate much snow in his book, focusing instead on the supernatural aspects.

The publisher Nishimuraya Yohachi hired the popular artist Katsushika Hokusai to deliver thirty illustrations to support Konron's text. As Konron portrayed Echigo as an uncharted, wild place, it was well suited to Hokusai's fantasy images.

The six volumes in the series contain a collection of stories. One is about the homecoming of the Zen monk Ryōkan (1758–1831) who had lived the life of a

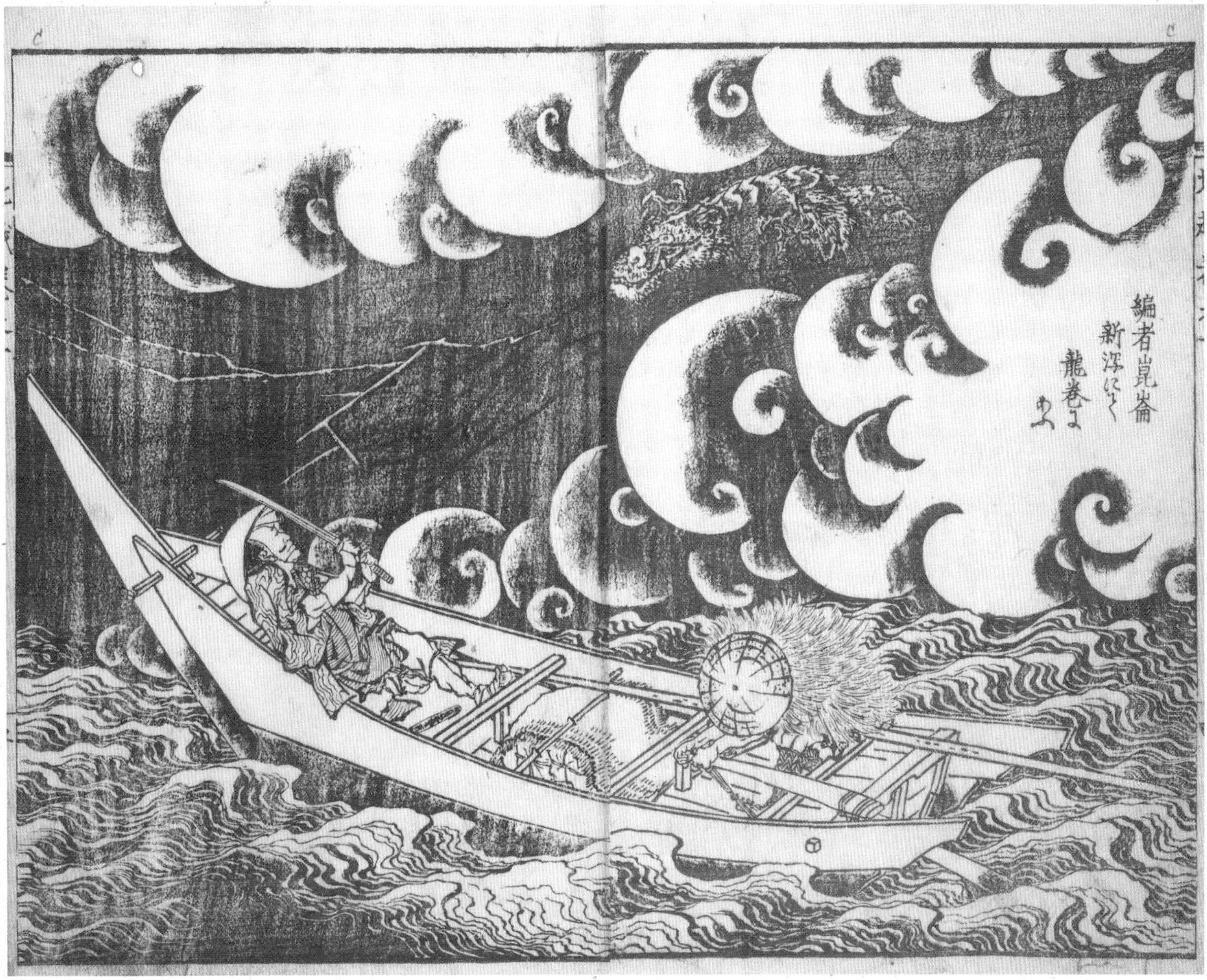

**Opposite** Vol. 1, snow in Hokuetsu.

**Above** Vol. 1, the author Konron is caught by a tornado in Niigata.

**Right** Vol. 4, strange things happen near the monster girl.

hermit in a lonely cottage by the sea. One of Hokusai's earliest illustrations in the book depicts a landscape in the far north, deeply covered in snow. On the left is a man on horseback flanked by one walking in front of him and another behind, all sunk deep into the snow so that their feet are invisible. The poor horse needs to be pulled to make it walk.

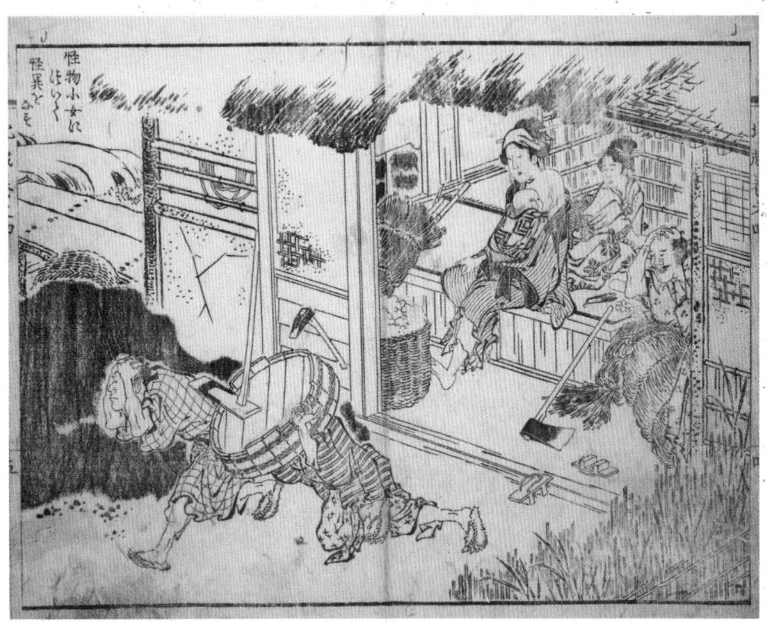

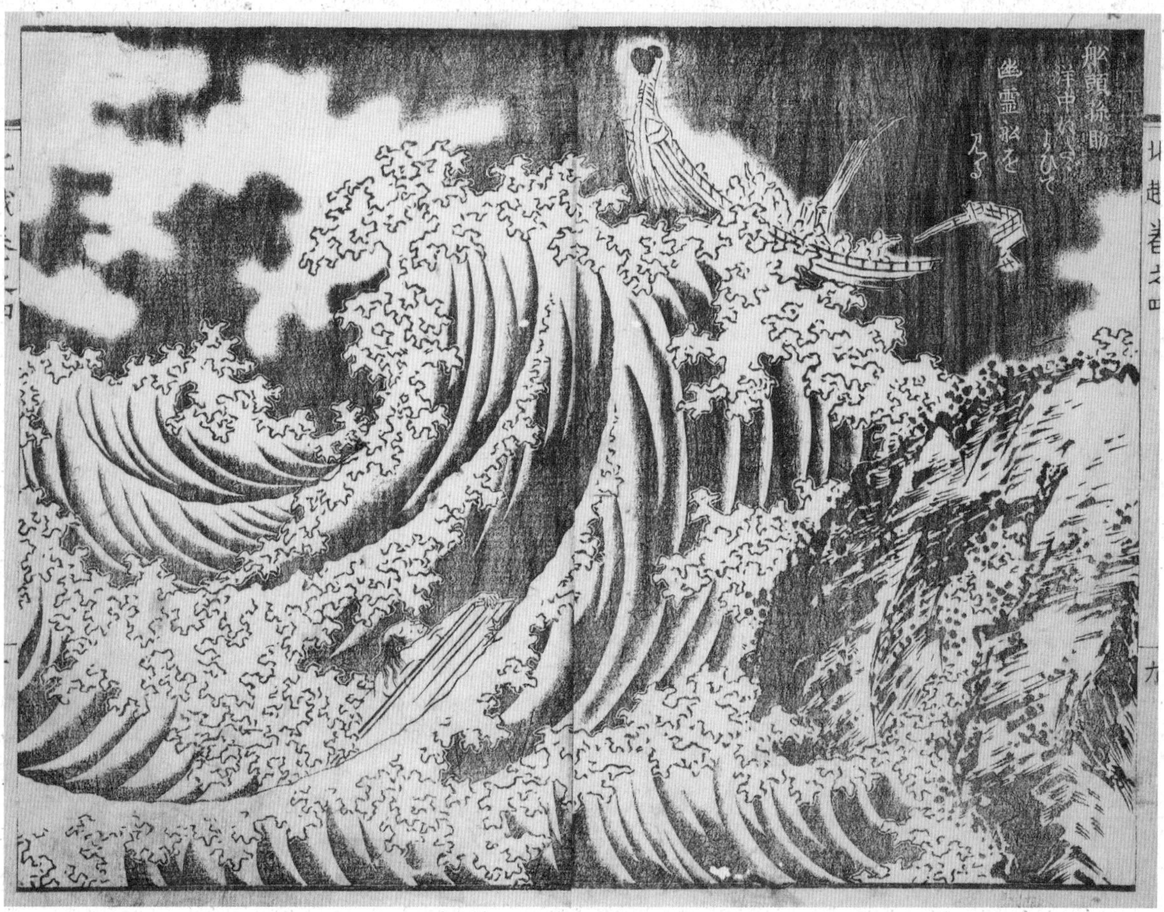

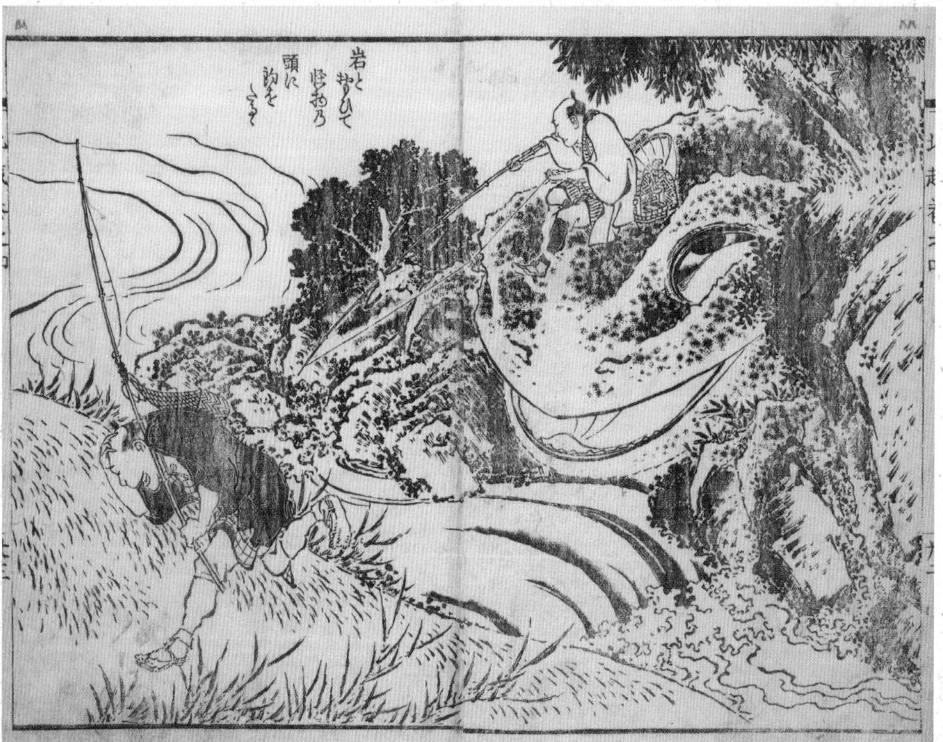


**Above** Vol. 4, the boatman Magosuke encounters the ghost ship.

**Left** Vol. 4, thinking it was a rock, he casts a line from the monster's head.

**Opposite above** Vol. 5, after Kameroku witnessed the mysterious mud turtles, he becomes a monk.

**Opposite below** Vol. 5, in her dreams, the little girl turns into a scary snake.

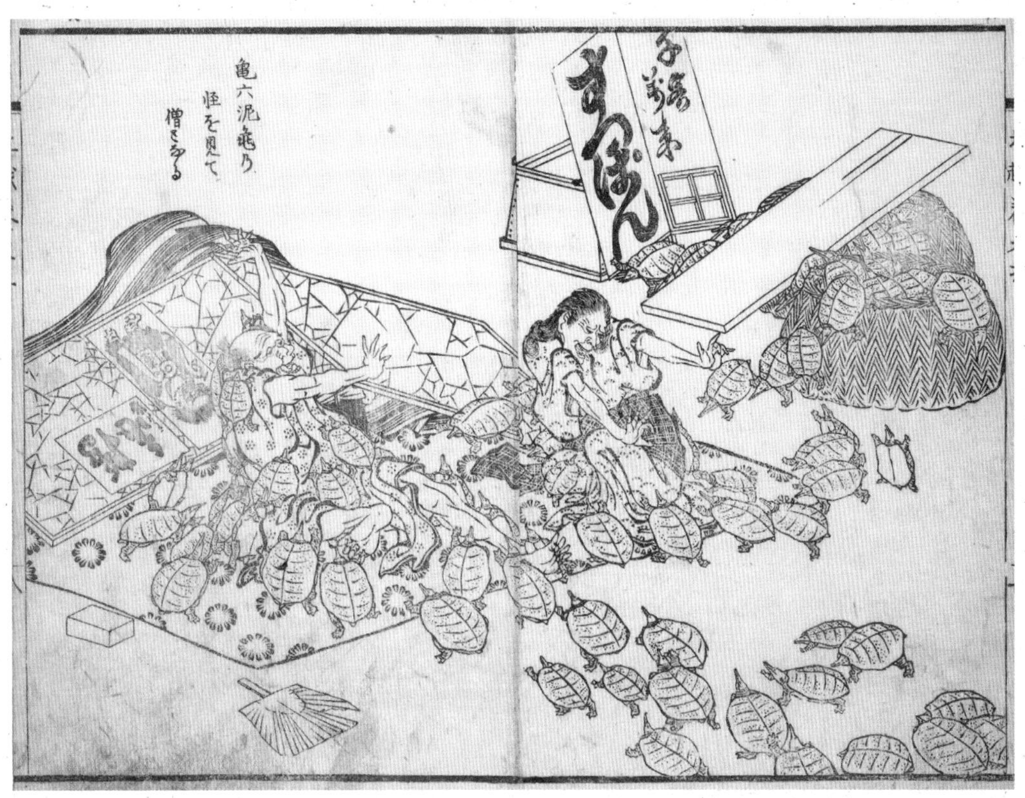
亀六泥亀り
怪を見て
憎さふる
すつぽん

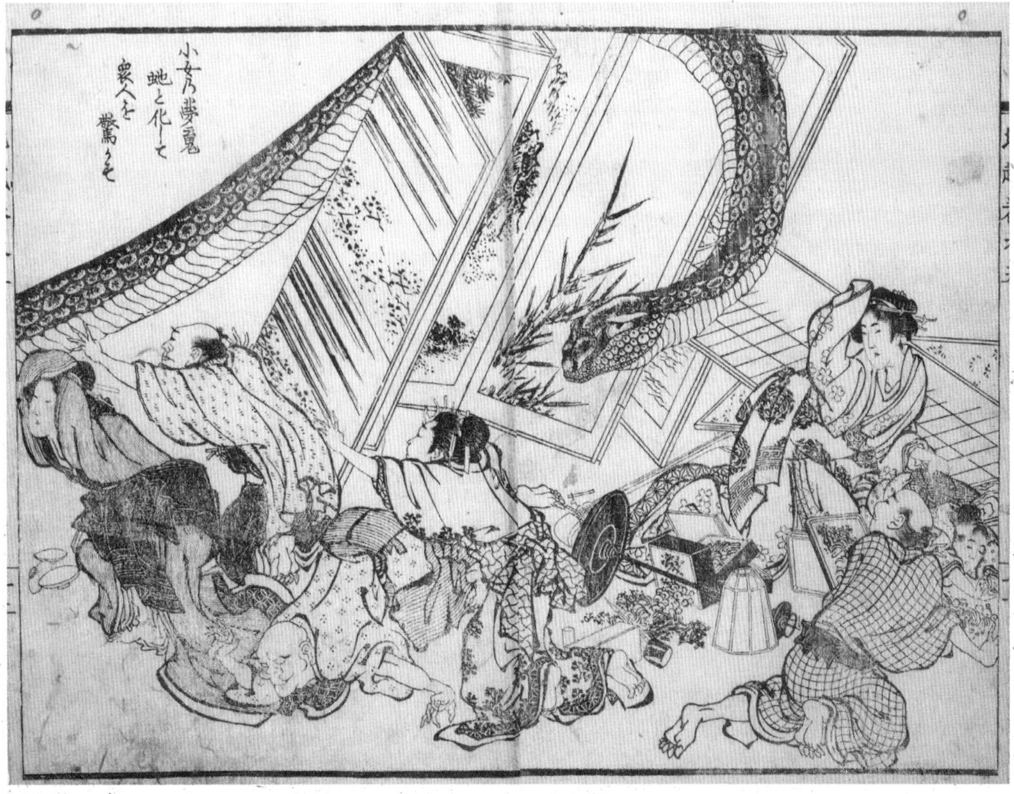
小女乃夢蛇
蛇と化して
喪人を驚るそ

# A Rustic Tale of Two Heirs

## *Beibei kyōdan*
## 皿皿郷談

1815 (8 vols.)
Author: Kyokutei Bakin (1767–1848)
Artist: Katsushika Hokusai (1760–1849)
Publisher: Kawachiya Mohei, et al.
Woodblock printed book (*hanshibon*); ink on paper
Edo-Tokyo Museum

After working together on fifteen projects, *A Rustic Tale of Two Heirs* (*Beibei kyōdan*) was the last collaboration between the writer Kyokutei Bakin and illustrator Katsushika Hokusai. The story focuses on two young girls who are named for plates: Benizara ("crimson plate") and Kakezara ("chipped plate"). The son of a Chinese ambassador and his Japanese wife is left without means after both parents die. He is adopted by a feudal lord, marries, and has two daughters, one named Benizara. In the ensuing civil war, the lord is defeated and his followers are killed, but the adopted son survives. On attempting to find his wife and daughters, he rescues a girl, only to find that she is not his daughter but that of a prince. He becomes a vassal of the prince, remarries, and has another daughter whom he names Kakezara.

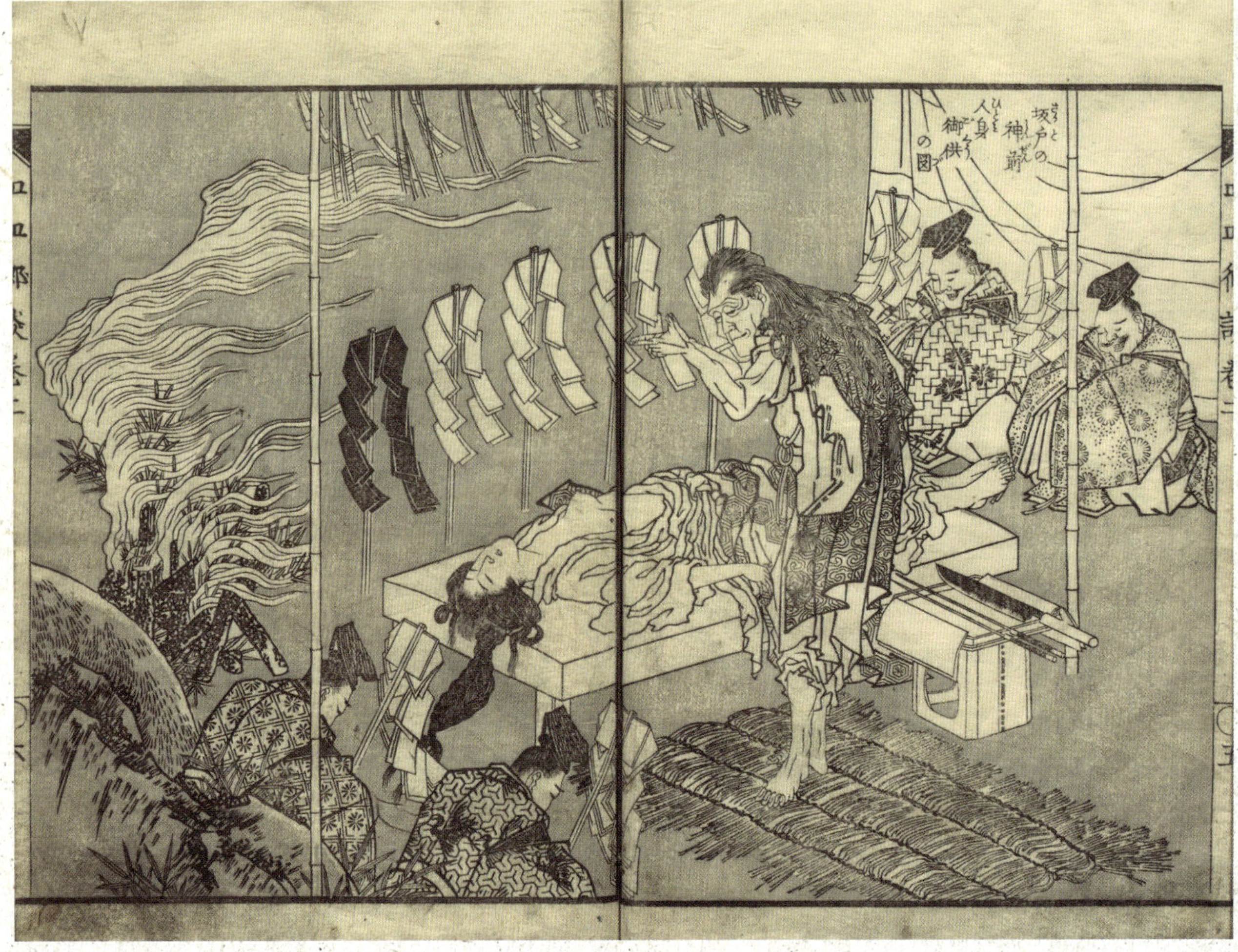

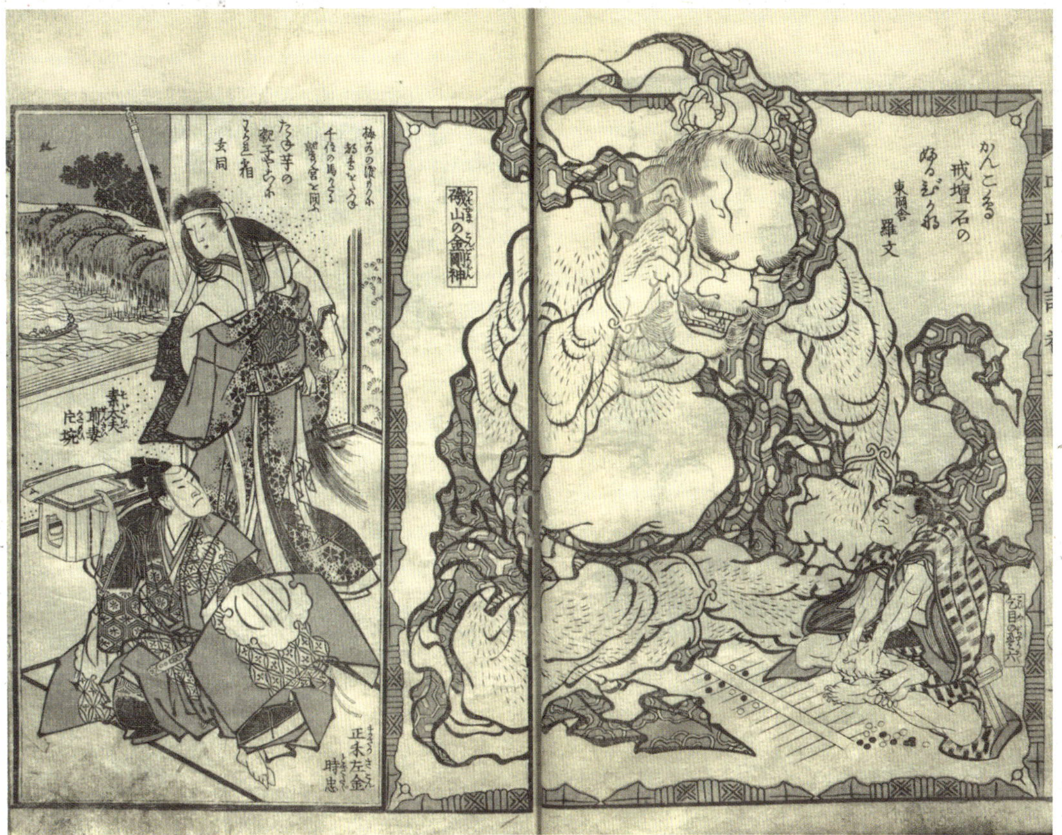

Meanwhile, a bandit plays a game with Niō, the giant guardian statue placed at temple entrances, and wins Niō's strength for three years. The bandit is unsuccessfully hunted by the prince's men. The storyline then becomes very complex with many new characters, twists and turns, some involving already deceased people. The bandit eventually loses his strength and is killed by the adopted son's second wife, who then kills herself. The first wife reappears, but in order for her daughter Benizara to be the heir, she hires an evil priest to kill Kakezara.

Hokusai's twenty-three images greatly enliven the story. One masterpiece is the game between the bandit and the enormous Niō statue who is upset about losing. The Niō later returns in a tumultuous fight scene, barely fitting on the printed page as he is so huge.

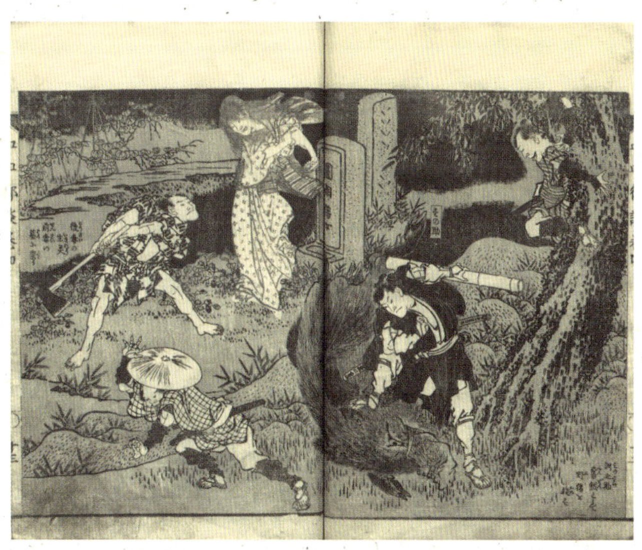

**Opposite** Vol. 2, human sacrifice before the shrine of Sakado.

**Top** Vol. 1, the guardian spirit of Mount Iso.

**Above** Vol. 4, Shinosuke kills a wild boar.

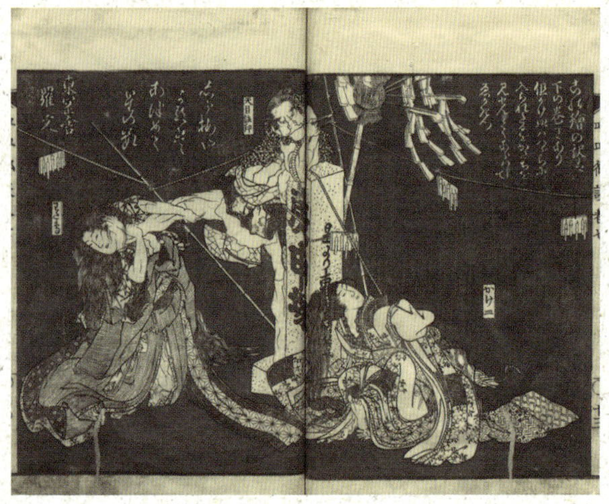

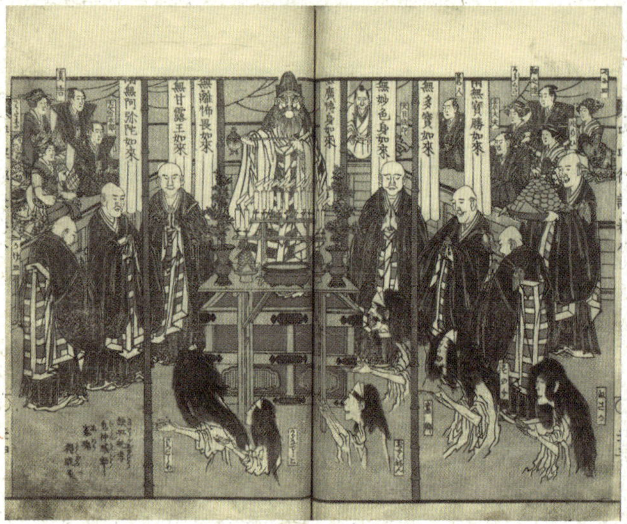

**Above** Vol. 7, the ascetic Hōin capturing Kakezara.

**Right** Vol. 8, the dead souls are liberated.

**Below** Vol. 4, the guardian spirit kills Shinosuke.

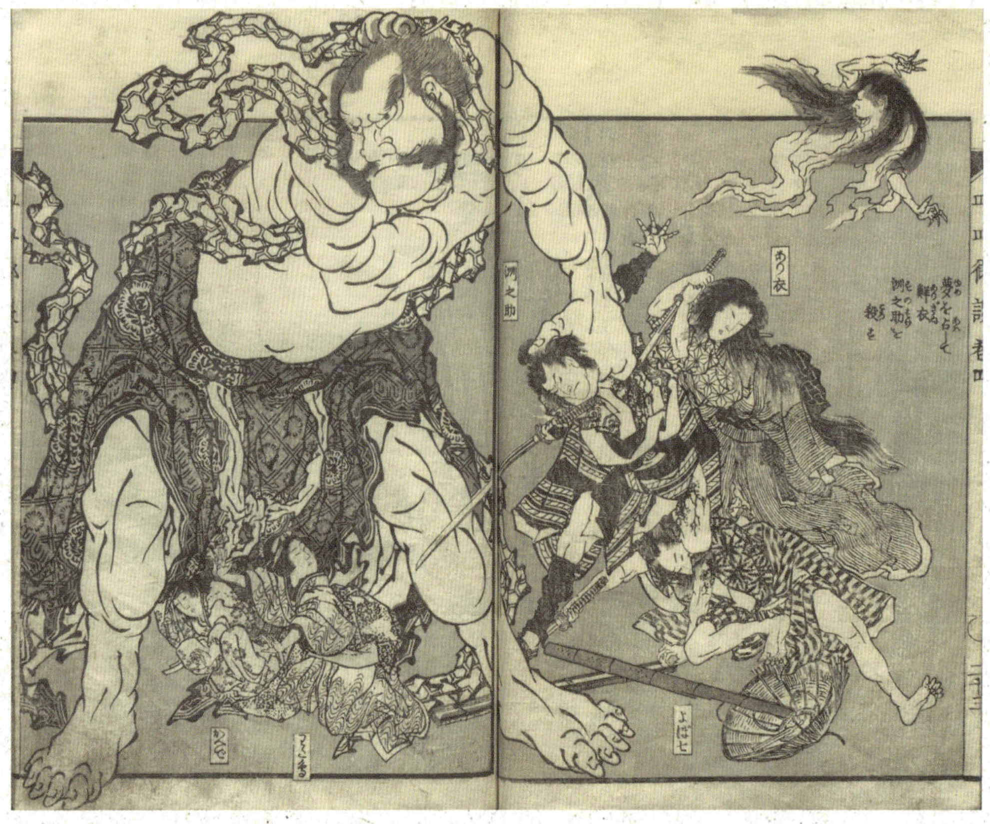

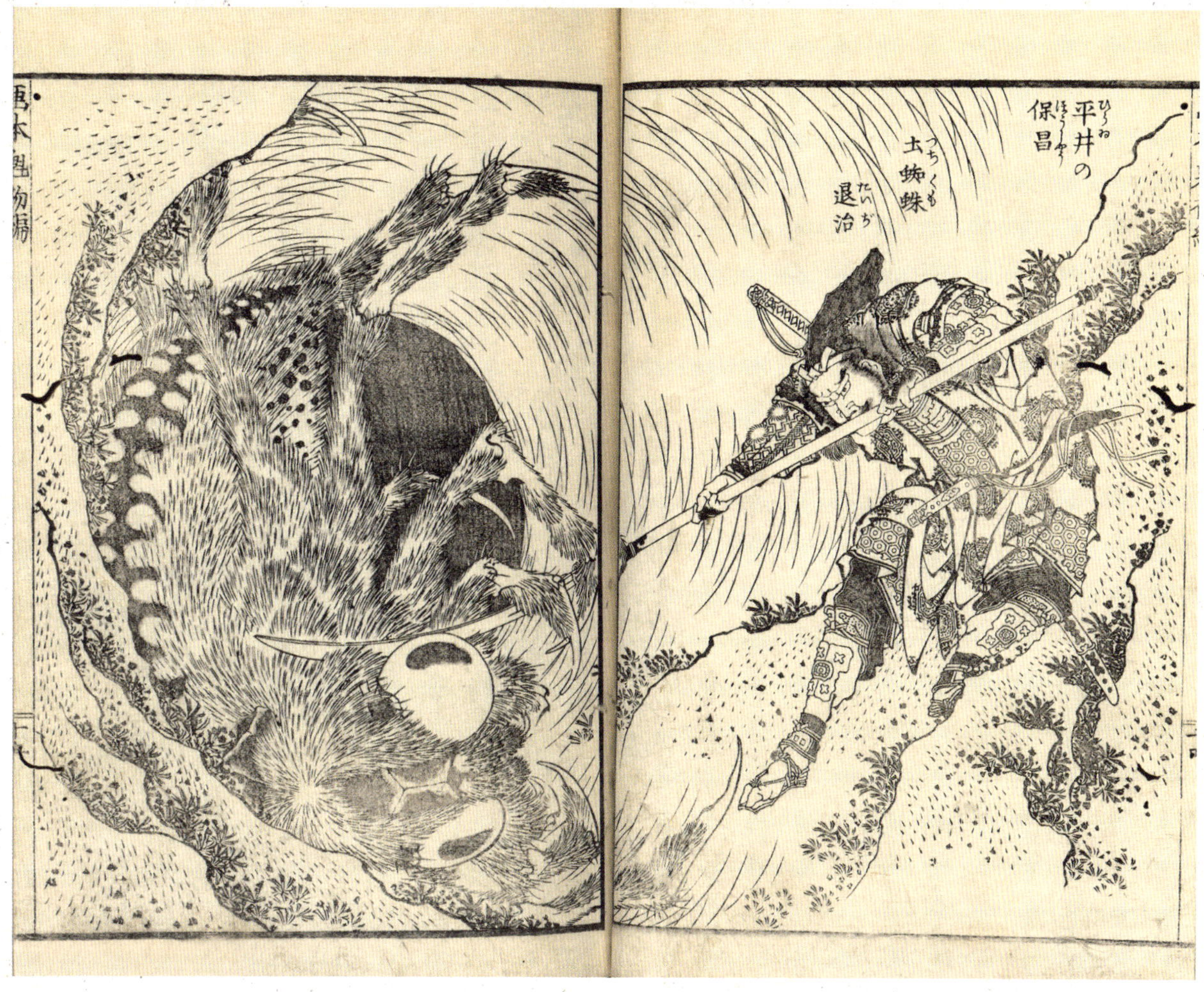


Above Vol. 1, Hirai Yasumasa killing the Earth Spider.

# The Illustrated Book of Military Valor

## Ehon sakigake

絵本魁

1836 (3 vols.)
Artist: Katsushika Hokusai (1760–1849)
Publisher: Akitaya Taemon, et al.
Woodblock printed book (*hanshibon*); ink on paper
Smithsonian Libraries

Warrior tales have a long tradition in Japan, with the earliest dating to the twelfth century. Eventually, Chinese warrior tales also became popular in Japan because of the general belief that Chinese history and culture should be venerated and cherished as part of Japan's cultural heritage. *The Illustrated Book of Military Valor* (*Ehon sakigake*) is purely a picture book; the only texts are brief inscriptions of each portrait. The thirty-two images by Katsushika Hokusai are powerful renderings of popular figures. Some of the illustrations require the book to be turned 90 degrees, for example, when the demon slayer Shōki (Zhong Kui in Chinese) lifts a demon by his throat, or when Benkei is trying to pull the heavy bell of Miidera Temple up the mountain. A dynamic scene shows the famous Chinese commander Zhuge Liang (181–234) fighting a lion during the military campaign he led against the Nanman (lit. "southern barbarians"), indigenous people in South and Southwest China. Yet another scene depicts the warrior Hirai Yasumasa (958–1036) killing the Earth Spider (*tsuchigumo*) monster with a *naginata*, a halberd-like pole weapon.

*The Illustrated Book of Military Valor* (*Ehon sakigake*) was simultaneously released in Osaka, Nagoya, and Edo (today's Tokyo). A letter from Hokusai to the group of six publishers has survived in which he urges them to hire the woodblock carver Egawa Tomekichi (dates unknown) for this project, which they did. He states that his suggestion is not because he would earn a commission from Egawa but because Egawa's work will elevate the books and result in better sales. Hokusai considered his *Manga* (see p. 25) to be well-carved but far from perfect, whereas he was greatly impressed by Egawa's work for his exceptionally illustrated three-volume work, *One Hundred Views of Mount Fuji* (*Fuji hyakkei*).

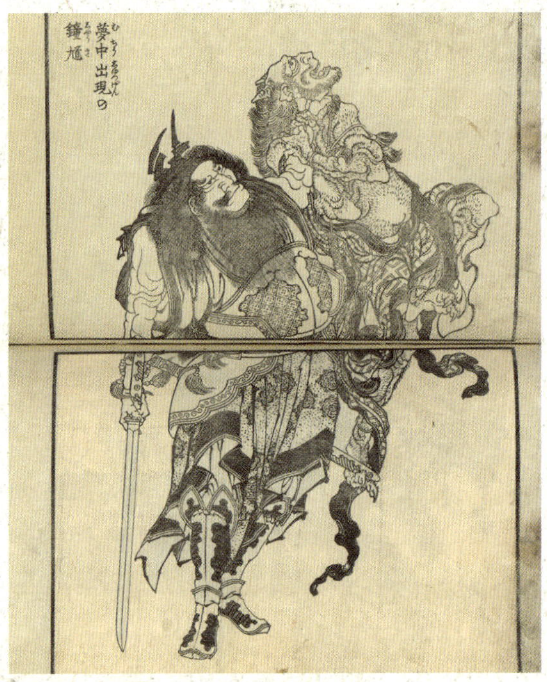

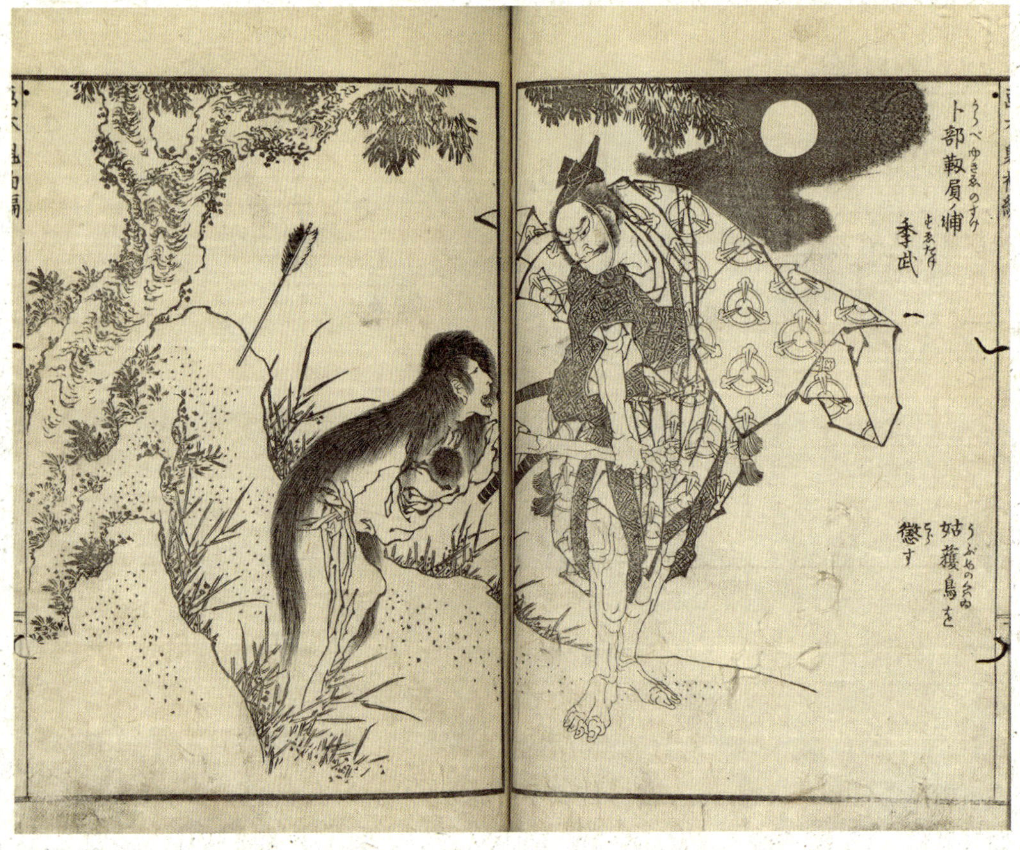

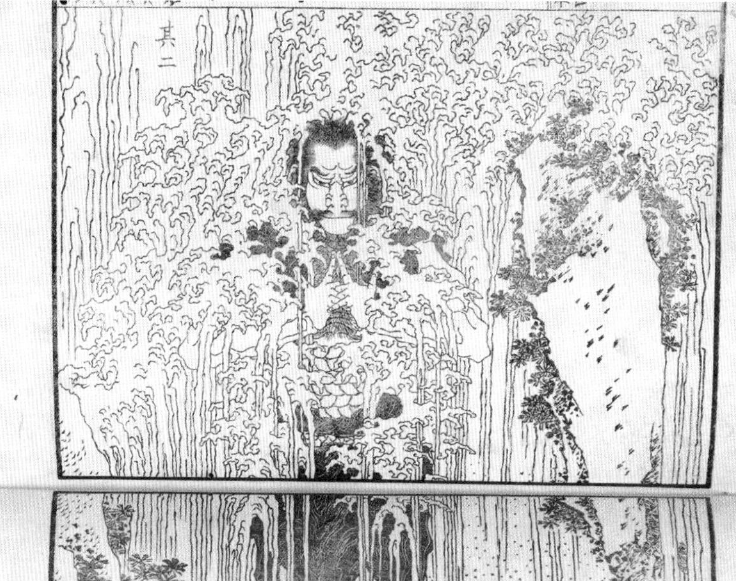

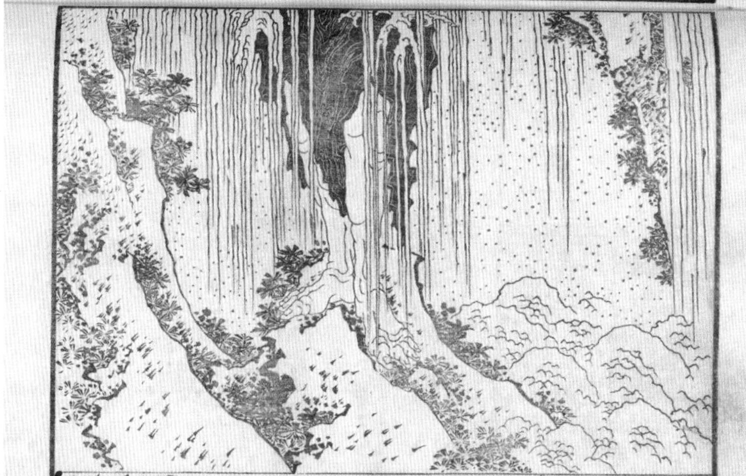

**Left** Vol. 1, Mongaku does penance beneath Nachi Waterfall.

**Below** Vol. 1, Benkei pulling the bell of Miidera Temple.

**Bottom** Vol. 1, Zhuge Liang fighting with a lion.

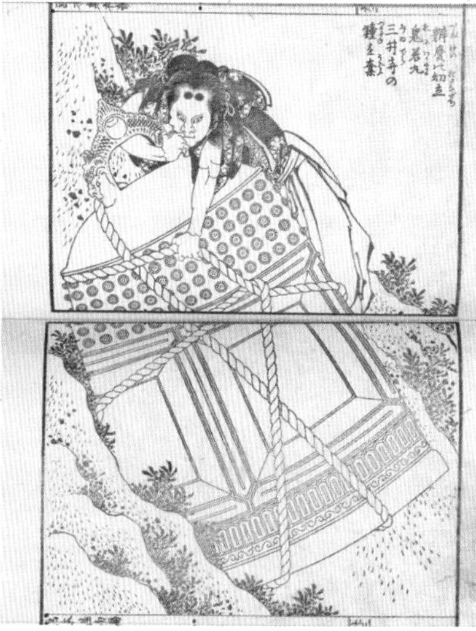

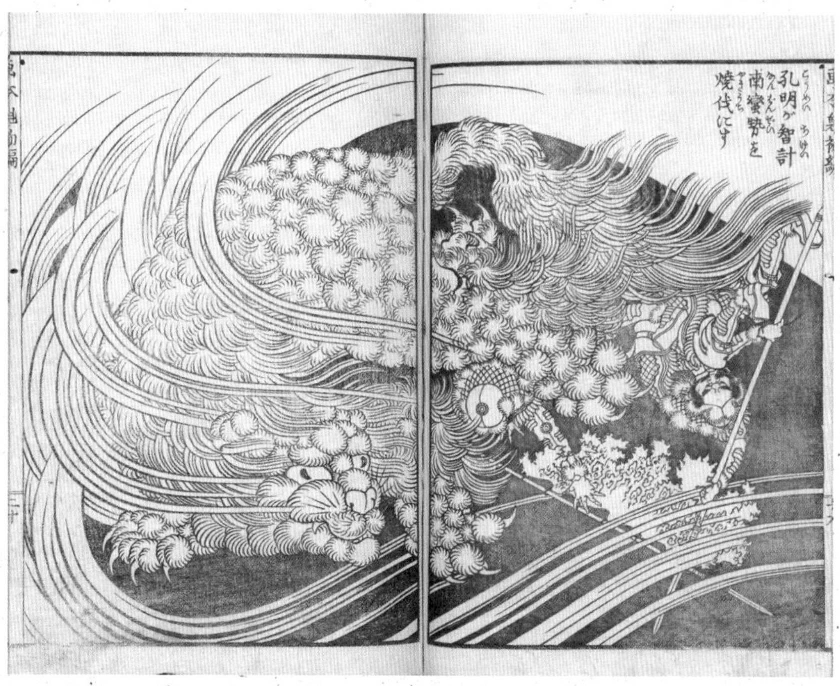

# The Illustrated Book of Wars between the Han and Chu

## *Ehon kanso gundan*
絵本漢楚軍談

1843 (vol. 1), 1845 (vol. 2)
Translator: Tamenaga Shunsui (Sasaki Sadataka; 1790–1844)
Artist: Katsushika Hokusai (1760–1849)
Publisher: Chōjiya Heibei
Woodblock printed book (*hanshibon*); ink on paper
Waseda University Library

In the early decades of his seventy-year career, Katsushika Hokusai was primarily involved in illustrating novels, with this work providing a considerable share of his income. In his later years, when he was in his sixties and seventies, he barely illustrated any novels. Thus, it must have come as a surprise to everyone when, in 1843, the first volume of the novel, *The Illustrated Book of Wars between the Han and Chu* (*Ehon kanso gundan*), was released with illustrations by the then eighty-three-year-old artist.

The first volume was published in ten separate installments (fascicles) that together comprise thirty-five images. The second volume was released two years later, also in ten fascicles and this time with thirty-eight images. It seems likely that Hokusai was not the only person who worked on these, but that he was chosen for his brand name and that his students contributed substantially to the work.

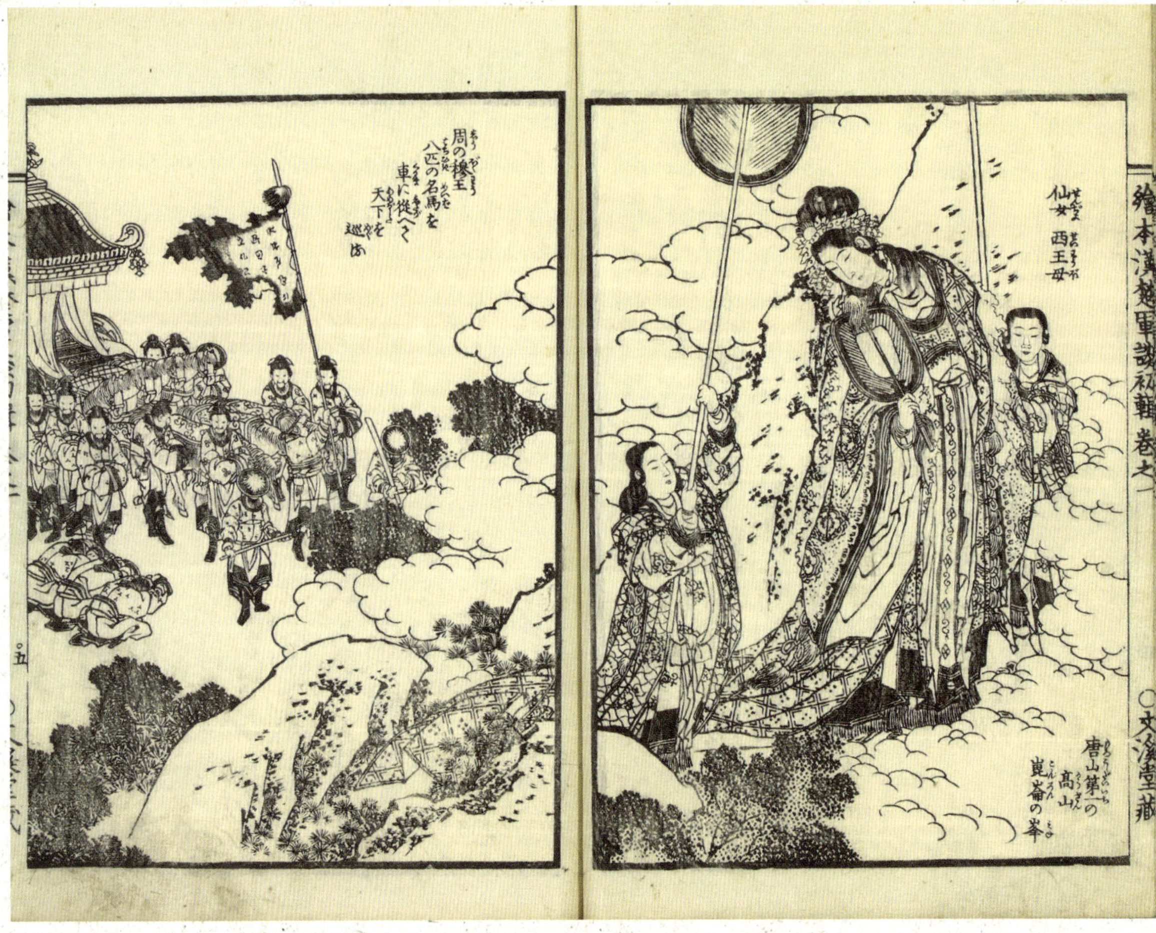

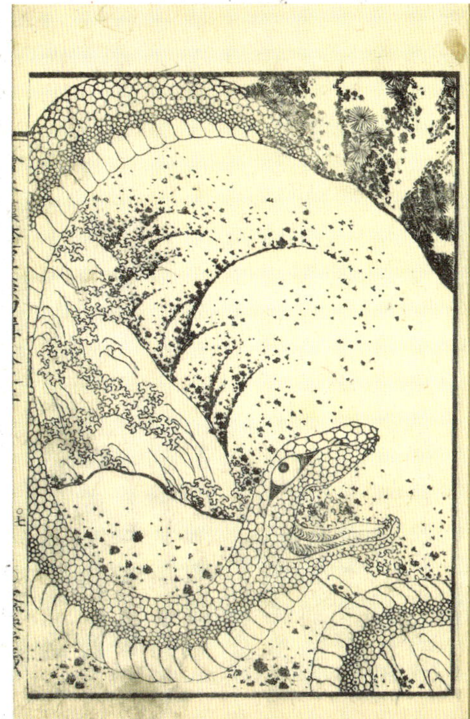

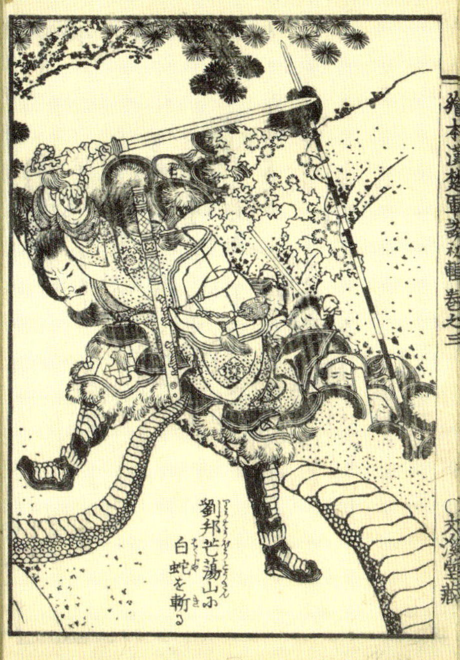




Sasaki Sadataka, better known by his pen name Tamenaga Shunsui, compiled the text based on a Chinese novel. As with the Japanese version of the Chinese novel *Shuihu Zhuan* forty years earlier, the illustrations this time also provide an appealing vision of a foreign country unknown to readers. The robes, architecture, and landscapes are all imaginary, yet believable. The story tells about the fall of Qin Shi Huang (259–210 BC), the first emperor of China who built the Great Wall, and the rise of the Han Dynasty under its first emperor Gaozu (256–195 BC). The conflict between Gaozu und his rival Xiang Yu (232–202 BC) from the state of Chu is the main focus of the novel. One horrifying spread shows how Xiang Yu's men follow his order to kill 5,000 peasants who are loyal to the previous emperor. At top left in the illustration, two men are beheaded, and on the right people gather up the immeasurable number of slain heads. Others march off carrying heavy baskets filled with heads.

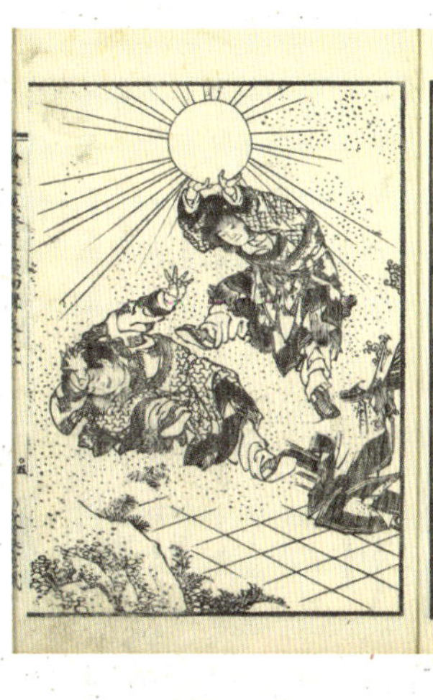

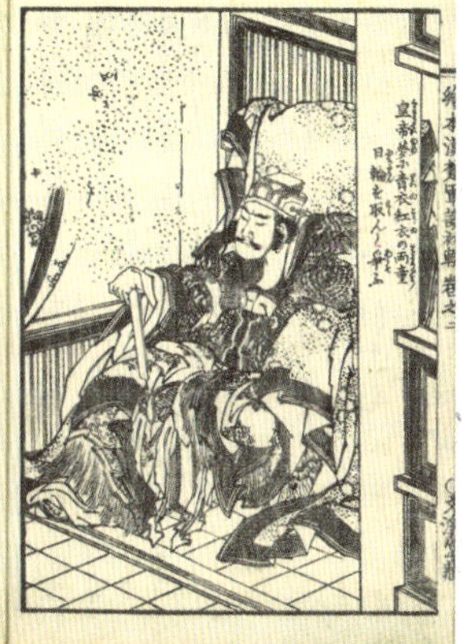

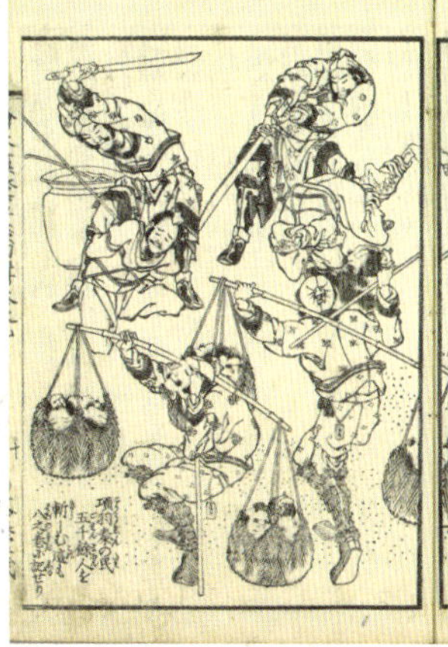

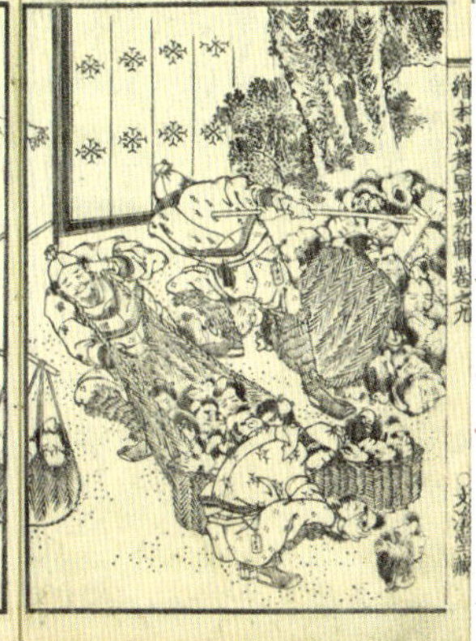

Opposite Vol. 1, Queen Mother of the West (Xiwangmu).

Right Vol. 1, Xiang Yu's men kill 5,000 peasants.

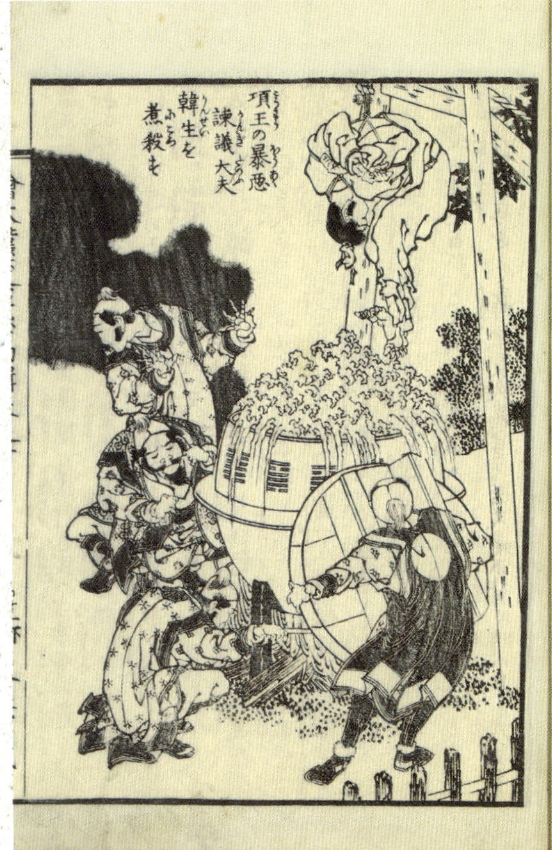

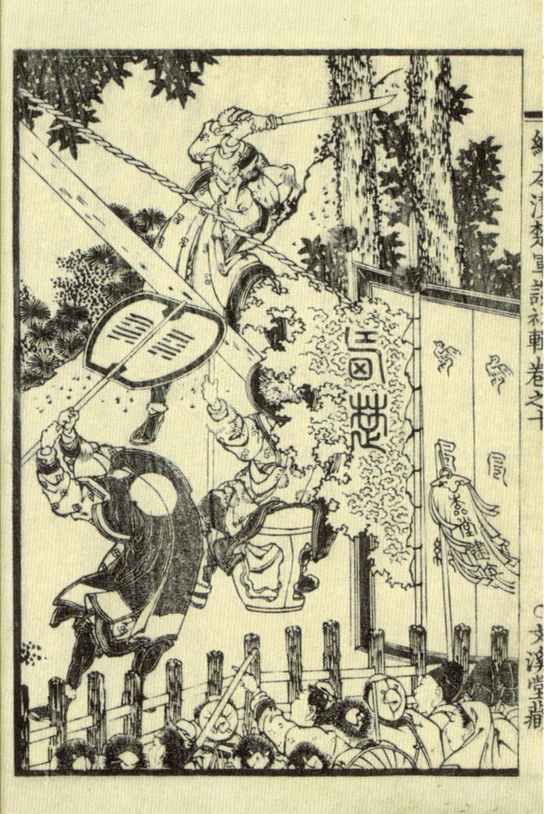

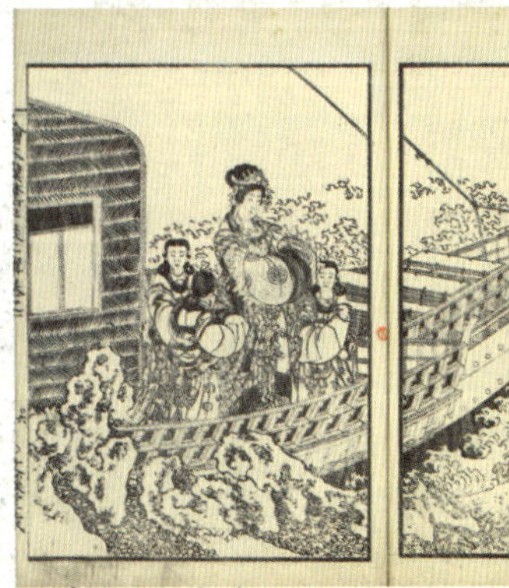

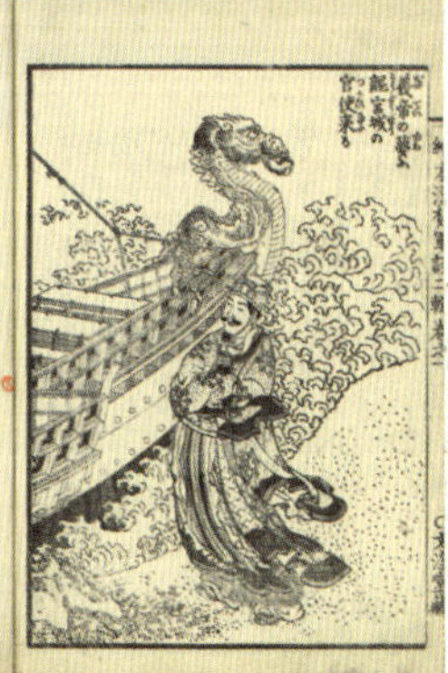

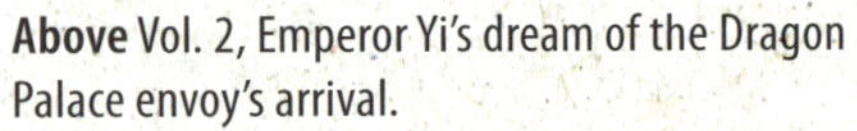

**Above** Vol. 2, Emperor Yi's dream of the Dragon Palace envoy's arrival.

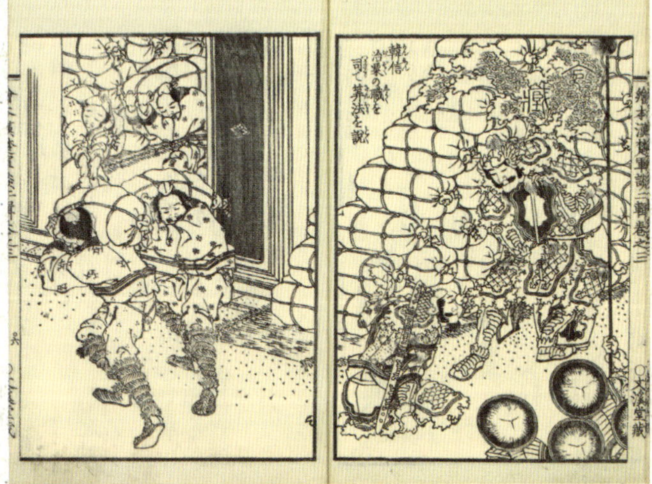

**Right** Vol. 2, Han Xin in charge of government affairs.

# The Life of Shakyamuni Illustrated

## *Shaka goichidaiki zue*
釋迦御一代記圖會

1845 (6 vols.)
Author: Yamada Kakashi (1788–1847)
Artist: Katsushika Hokusai (1760–1849)
Publisher: Kawachiya Mohei, et al.
Woodblock printed book (*hanshibon*); ink on paper
Waseda University Library

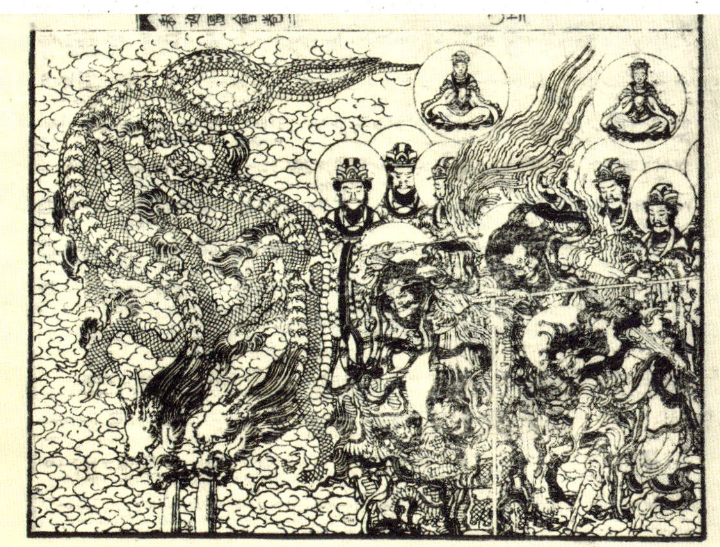

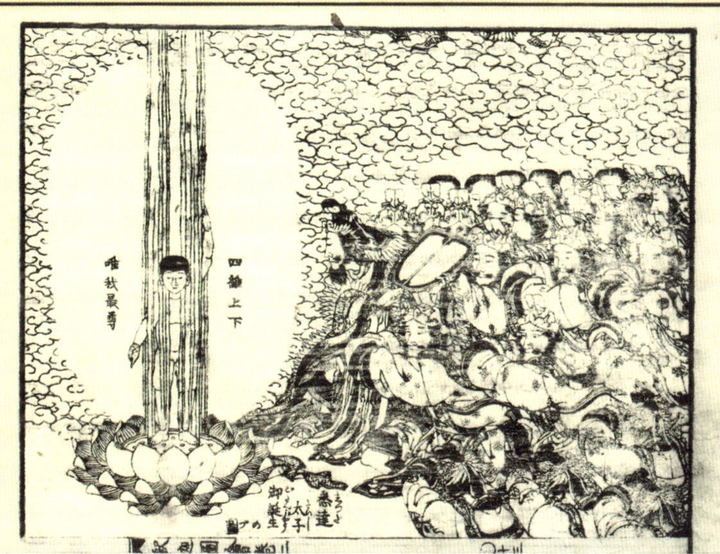

**Above** Vol. 2, the Birth of Shaka.

Few novels center on the life of Shakyamuni, the historic Buddha, which makes Yamada Kakashi's *The Life of Shakyamuni Illustrated* (*Shaka goichidaiki zue*) a rarity. The publishers who jointly financed this project decided to hire the venerated artist Katsushika Hokusai although he was already in his eighties. It is possible that at this age Hokusai was not personally involved in the new project but rather that some of the students in his studio contributed to the twenty-nine illustrations. However, a letter by Hokusai survives in which he expresses a profound interest in illustrating the book himself. Hokusai continued to demand that the publishers hire the carver Egawa Tomekichi (dates unknown), with whom he had worked a few years earlier on his most famous work, *One Hundred Views of Mount Fuji* (*Fuji hyakkei*).

Since the story is set in India, Hokusai was worried that no one other than Egawa would have the skill necessary to carve the curly hair of some of the figures. Whether the publishers obliged him is unknown since the six volumes do not provide the name of the carver.

Hokusai masterfully captures what would have been exotic locations and people to Japanese eyes. He designed several illustrations vertically, forcing the reader to turn the book 90 degrees to view them. This allowed him to enhance the effect of specific scenes and to render tall figures much larger.

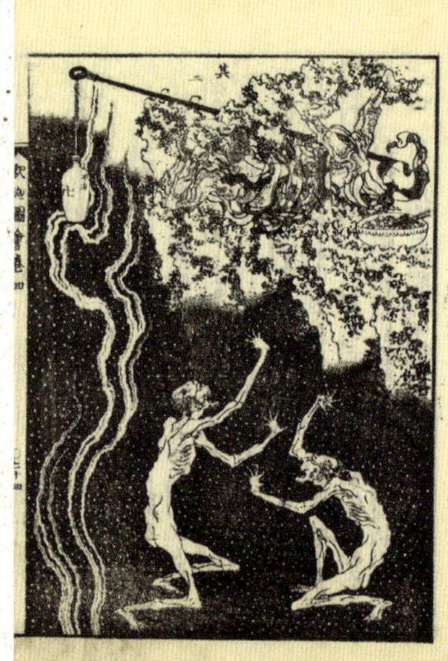

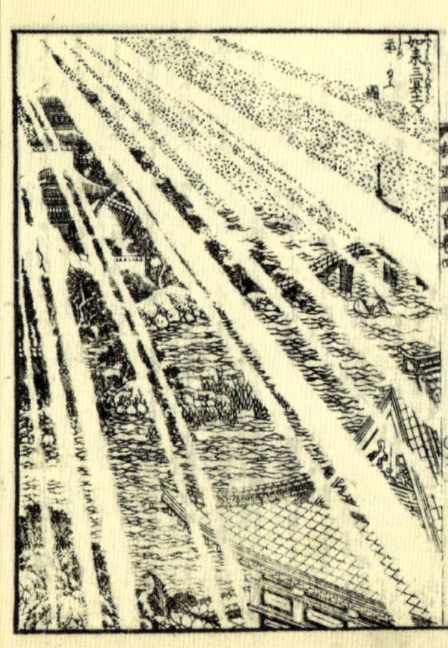

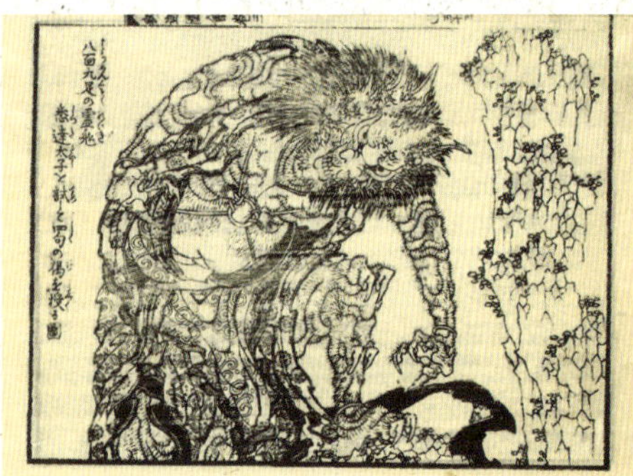

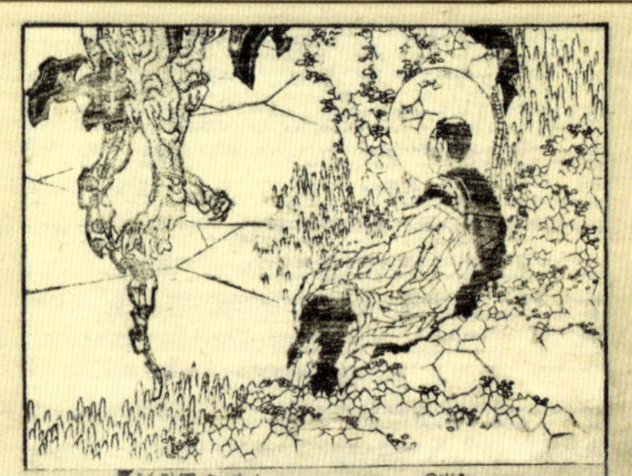

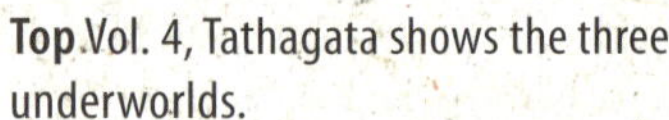

**Top** Vol. 4, Tathagata shows the three underworlds.

**Above** Vol. 3, the Demon with Eight Faces and Nine Legs.

**Right** Vol. 5, Devadatta.

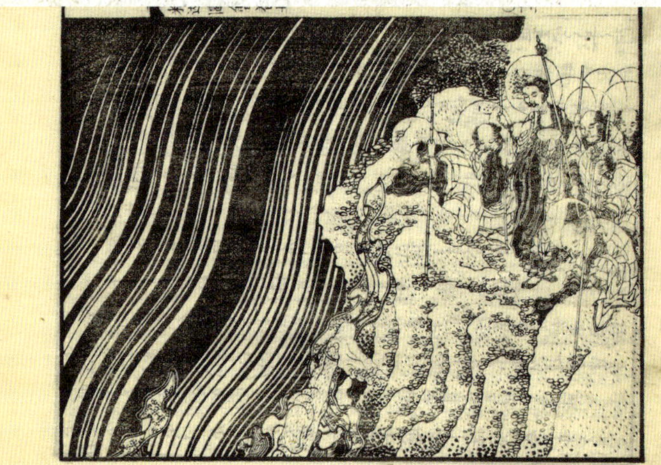

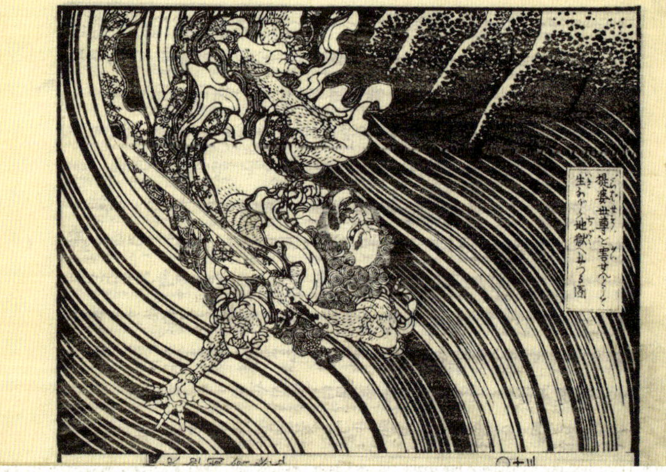

 Vol. 5, Anathapindika.

**Bottom** Vol. 6, the Thunder King burns down the emperor's palace.

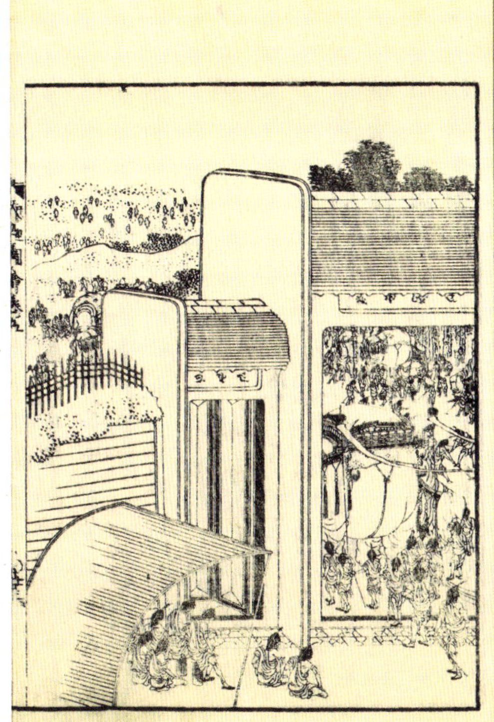
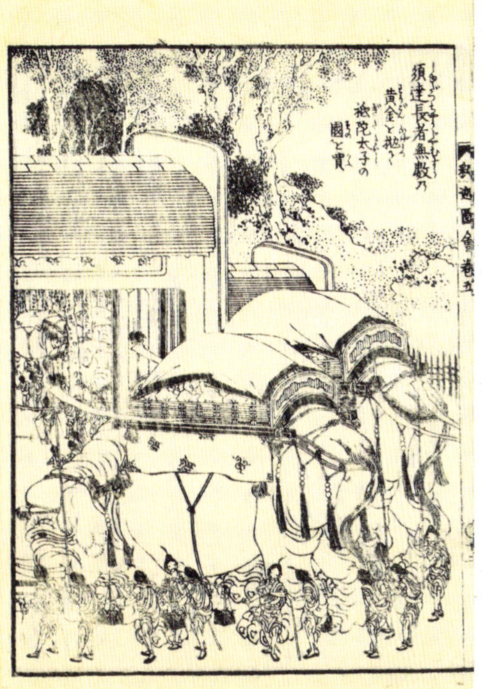

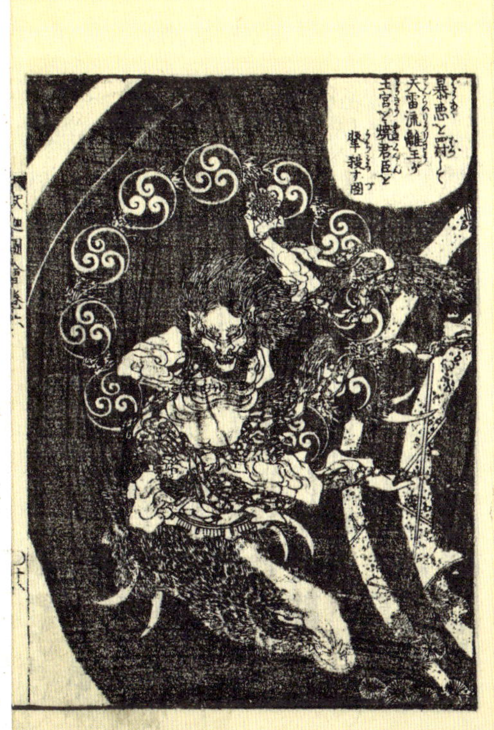
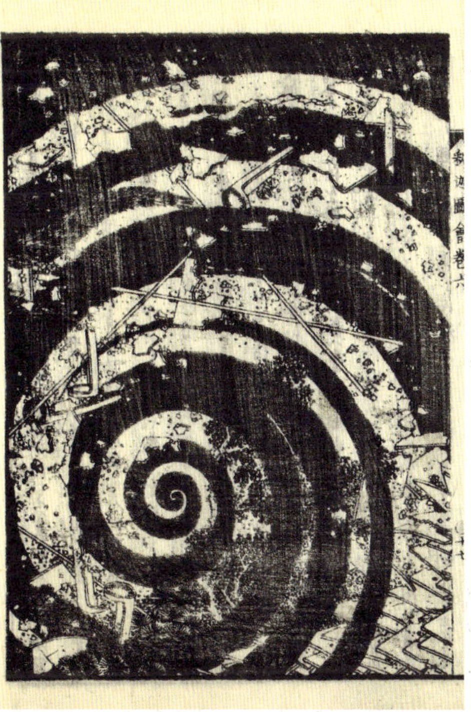

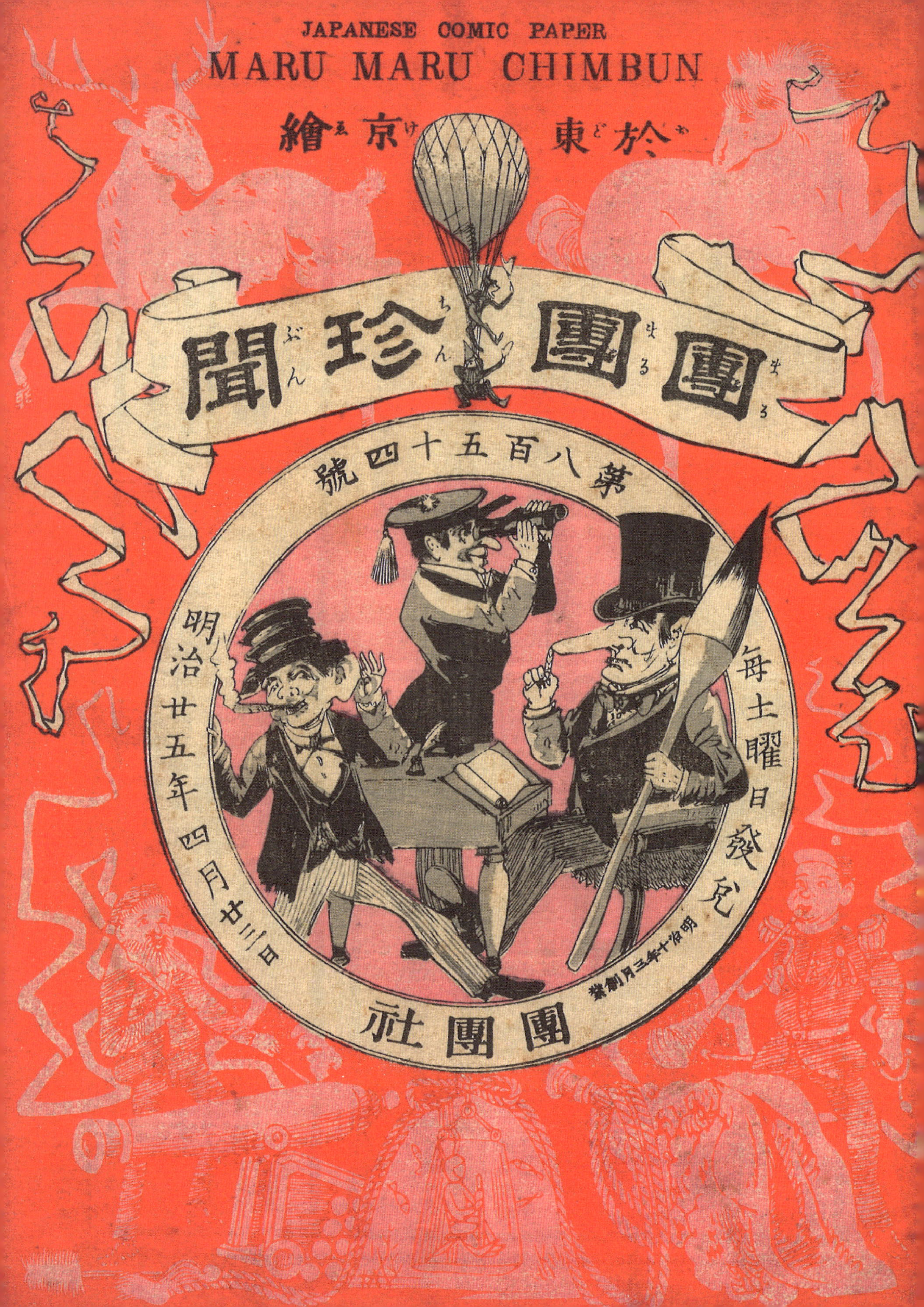
JAPANESE COMIC PAPER
MARU MARU CHIMBUN
於東京繪
團團珍聞
第八百五十四號
明治廿五年四月廿三日
毎土曜日發兌
團團社

# CHAPTER SEVEN

# THE INFLUX OF WESTERN IDEAS

After the forced end to the isolationist policy of the Tokugawa government in the mid-nineteenth century, many Western ideas and concepts gradually found their way into Japanese society. A key moment in the cultural exchange between Japan and the West was the publication of the *The Japan Punch* magazine in 1862 by the British artist Charles Wirgman (1832–81). Wirgman had arrived in Japan the year before as correspondent for the *Illustrated London News*. The inspiration for *The Japan Punch* was the British *Punch*, a weekly magazine of humor and satire founded in London in 1841. It was in this publication that the word "cartoon" was used for the first time to describe comic drawings. Initially, *The Japan Punch* was issued irregularly, but from 1862 until March 1887, Wirgman published over two hundred monochrome issues, each about ten pages long. The illustrations were annotated in English since the target audience was the foreign community in Yokohama where Wirgman lived.

Before *The Japan Punch*, humor and satire existed in the Japanese visual arts, especially in the woodblock prints known today as *ukiyo-e*, but contemporary subjects, especially political ones, were taboo and strictly prohibited by the government. Wirgman showed the Japanese what was possible, and with the reformation process that the Emperor Meiji (1852–1912) introduced in 1868, law after law of the Tokugawa shoguns were repealed. On March 20, 1869, the Meiji government allowed the publication of newspapers and along with them the depiction of current affairs. The prototype satirical comic magazine for a Japanese audience was the *Illustrated Japan News* (*Eshinbun Nipponchi*). Written by Kanagaki Robun (1829–94) and illustrated by Kawanabe Kyōsai (1831–89), the first issue was released in 1874. However, the very simple drawing style was not favored by Japanese readers, and because sales did not do well, the magazine was discontinued after only three issues.

Amongst the earliest Western-inspired satirical magazines that were a commercial success was *Maru Maru Chimbun*, which debuted in 1877. With Japan playing a bigger role internationally, politics became more complex, and some magazines were established that expressed conservative ideas or war propaganda, such as *Nipponchi*, founded in 1904. Several others were produced with varying success, for example, *Tokyo Puck* and *Jōtō Ponchi*. Kitazawa Rakuten, arguably the most important cartoonist during this early period in Japan, was given the opportunity to draw a weekly comic strip in a newspaper from 1902 that he called *Jiji Manga*, the first time the word "manga" was used in the way we use it today. Notably, the cover of *Maru Maru Chimbun* shown left carries the English heading "Japanese Comic Paper."

**Opposite** Detail from *Maru Maru Chimbun*.

# The Japan Punch

Artist: Charles Wirgman (1832–91)

Woodblock printed magazine; ink on paper; cover: 36.5 × 25.4 cm (14⅜ × 10 in); spread 36.5 × 50.8 cm (14⅜ × 20 in)

Philadelphia Museum of Art, Bequest of Vivian Sharples Byrd, 1966 (1966-82-7; 1966-82-6)

**Right** Cover, 1865.

**Below** "Results of our intercourse with Japan."

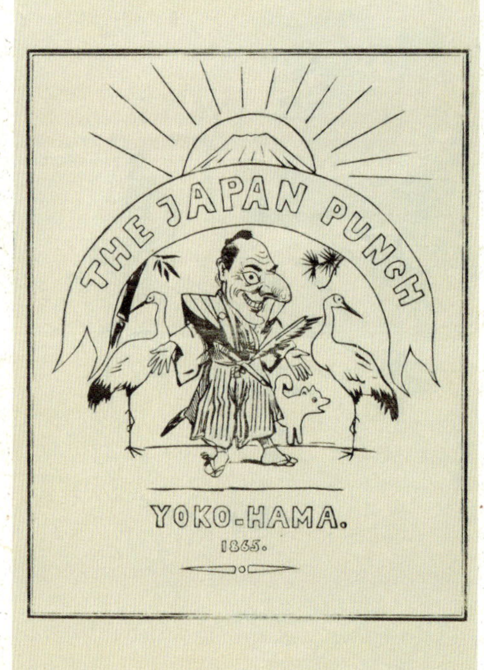

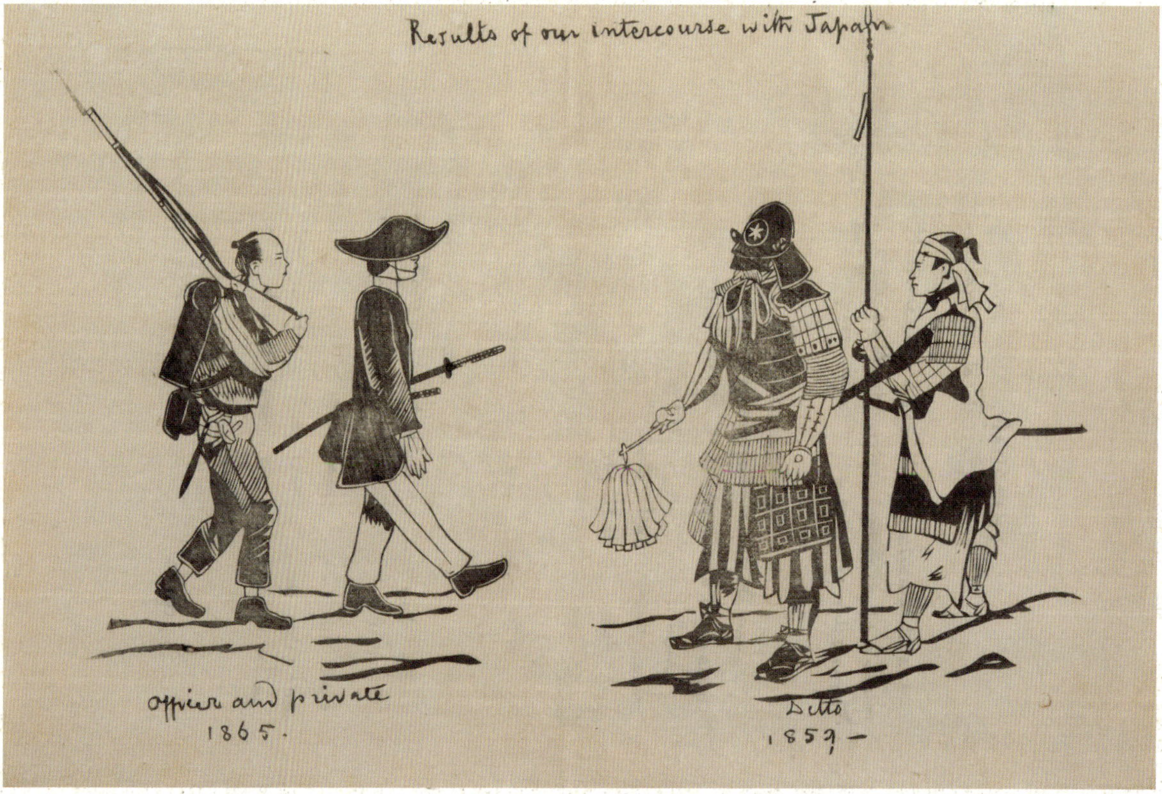

# Brocade Pictures for Moral Education

## *Nishiki-e shūshindan*

## 錦絵修身談

March 1882 (vols. 1–3), July 1882 (vols. 4–6)
Author: Yamana Tomesaburō (dates unknown)
Artist: Tsukioka Yoshitoshi (1839–92)
Publisher: Fukyūsha
Woodblock printed book (*hanshibon*); ink and color on paper
Ritsumeikan University Library

In early 1882, Tsuji Moriyuki (1851–91), an educator and businessman who founded the publishing company Fukyūsha, started publishing the didactic book series *Brocade Pictures for Moral Education* (*Nishiki-e shūshindan*). He hired Masukawa Kan'yū (dates unknown) as editor, Yamana Tomesaburō as writer, and artist Tsukioka Yoshitoshi as illustrator. Each one of the six volumes began with one to three double-page illustrations in color that were followed by text pages with sporadic, mostly half-page illustrations in monochrome ink. The books were intended to provide moral instruction for young children in line with the Ministry of Education's concepts. The underlying fear was that the influx of Western ideas to Japanese society since the opening of the country under Emperor Meiji (1852–1912) was causing moral decay. Publications like this were

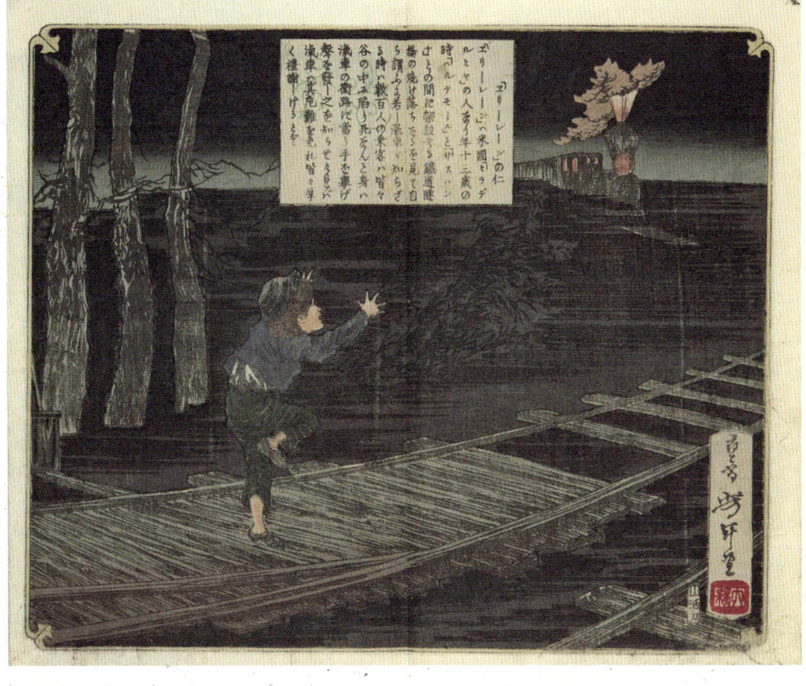

**Above** The benevolence of Harry Lane.

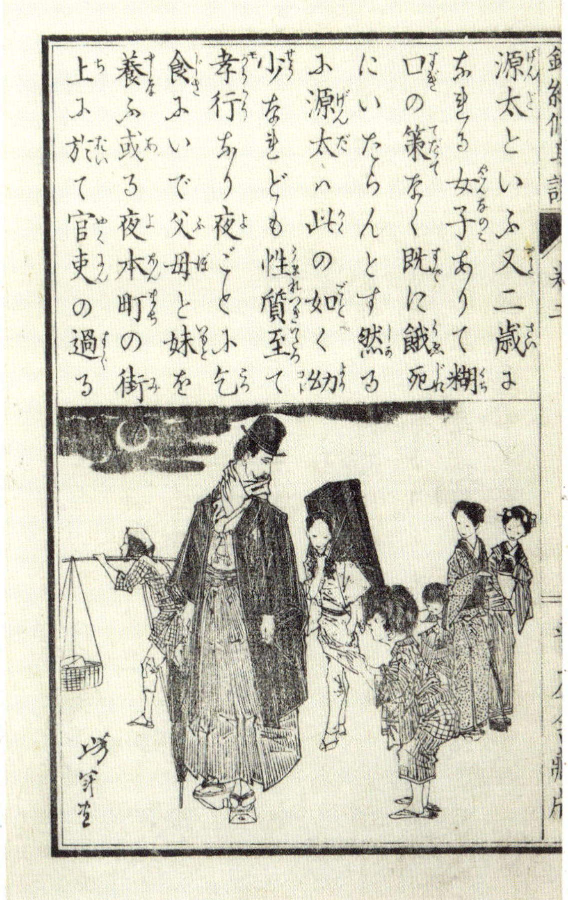

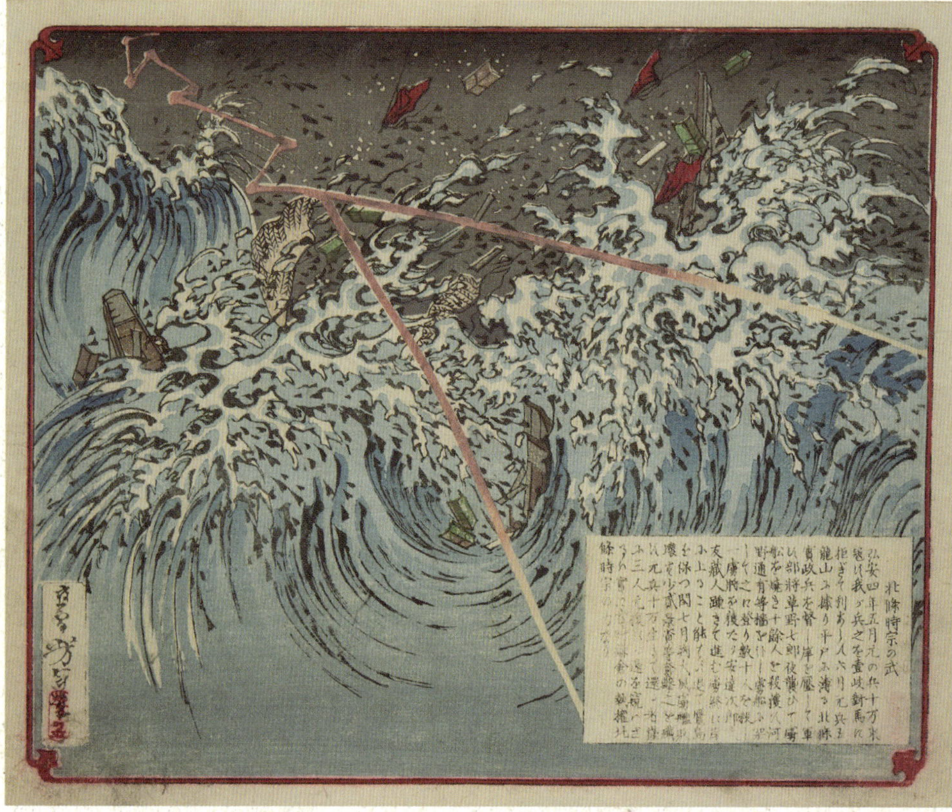



**Left** Hōjō Tokimune's warriors.

**Below** Vol. 2, a son begs for food; artists: Inano Toshitsune and Tominaga Toshichika.

intended to assist schoolteachers by providing support and encouragement to promote strict discipline, while also highlighting the enduring tradition of Confucianist moral concepts in Japan.

The books were so successful that Fukyūsha soon hired a few of Yoshitoshi's students to transpose some of the monochrome illustrations to the vertical *ōban* format which he then printed in full color. The supplemental print series received the same title as the books. Over ninety were produced, designed by Tominaga Toshichika (born 1847), Mizuno Toshikata (1866–1908), Tsutsui Toshimine (1863–1934), Kobayashi Toshimitsu (active ca. 1874–1904), and Inano Toshitsune (1859–1907). One

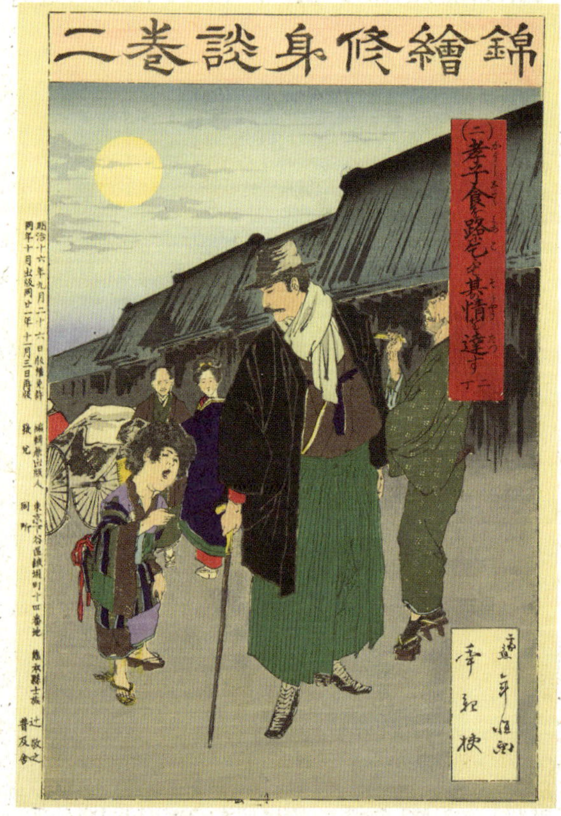

book illustration, for example, that was released as an enlarged color print is titled "Business becomes Commitment" (*Gyō wa tsutomuru ni naru*) and depicts the workshop of a maker of articulated dolls who is proud of his creations.

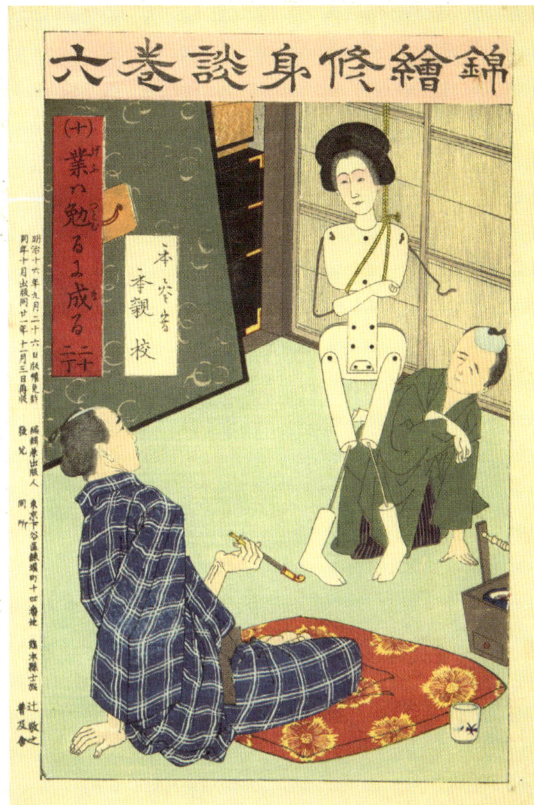

**Left and below** Vol. 6, "Business becomes Commitment;" artists: Kobayashi Toshimitsu and Tominaga Toshichika.

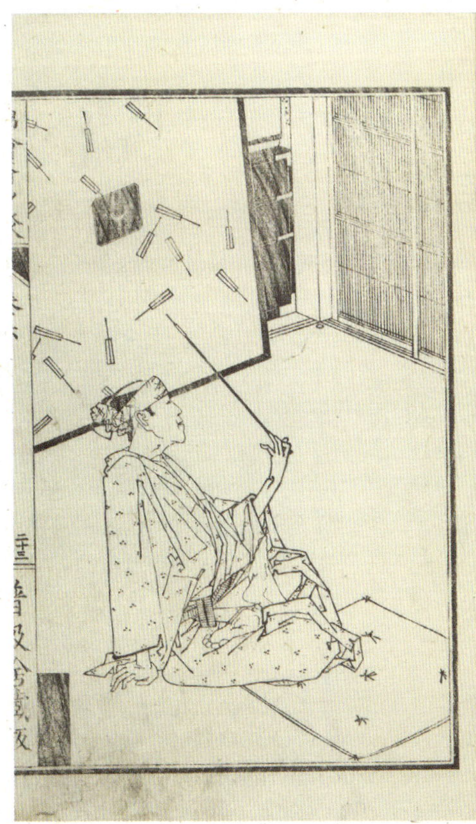

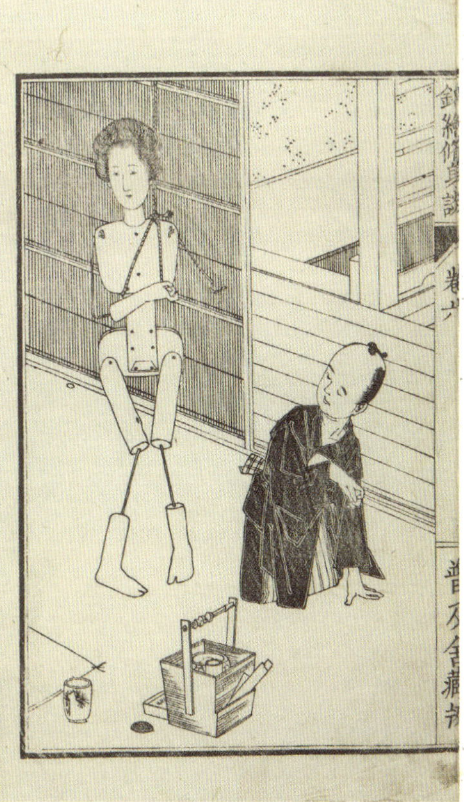

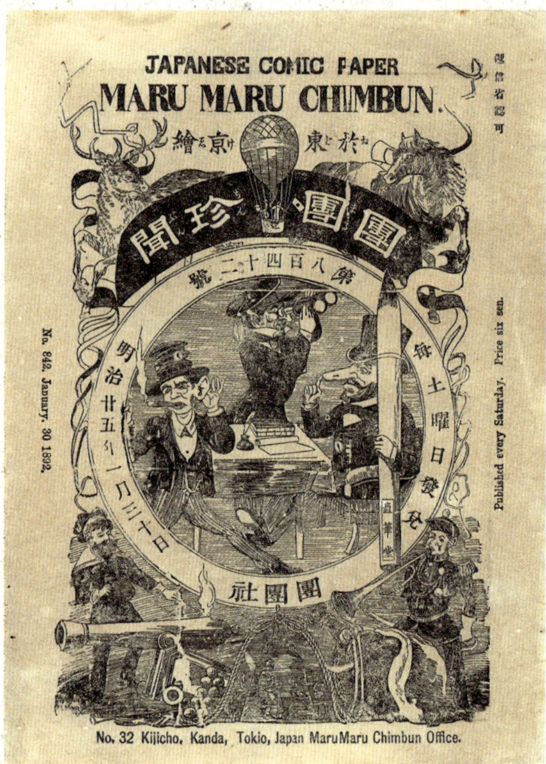


**Above** Cover of no. 842, January 30, 1892.

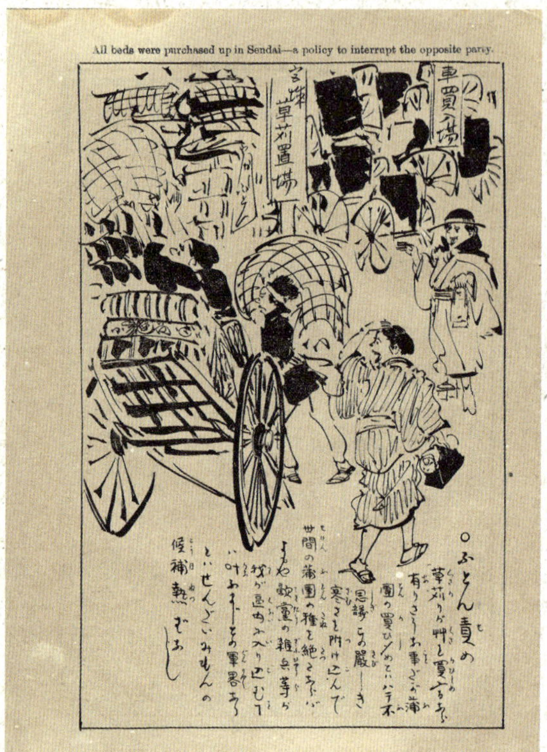


**Above** "All beds were purchased up in Sendai—
a policy to interrupt the opposite party."

# Maru Maru Chimbun

團團珍聞

1877–1907

Artists: Honda Kinkichirō (1851–1921), Kobayashi Kiyochika (1847–1915), Taguchi Beisaku (1864–1903), et al.

Editors: Nomura Fumio (1836–91), Tsuda Jinzaburō (dates unknown), Matsumura Tokuyoshi (dates unknown), et al.

Publishers: Marumarusha, Chinbunkan

Lithograph on paper; 24.6 × 17.6 cm

Collection of the author

Nomura Fumio, a former government official turned journalist, established the magazine *Maru Maru Chimbun* in March 1877 in the style of *Punch*, the British weekly magazine of satire and humor. *Maru Maru Chimbun*, commonly called *Maruchin*, lampooned the government through editorial articles, comic poems, and caricatures, while also advocating for the Freedom and People's Rights Movement of the 1880s. To focus on current affairs, *Maru Maru Chimbun* was originally published weekly on Saturdays, then for a while twice a week on Wednesdays and Saturdays, until it was again published weekly. For a short period, there was a sister magazine called *Kibi Dango*. At first, *Maru Maru Chimbun* was sold through the company Nipposha, publisher of the daily newspaper *Tokyo Nichi Nichi Shimbun*, which became *Mainichi Shimbun* in 1911 and still exists today.

*Maru Maru Chimbun* ceased on July 27, 1907, with number 1654. The magazine was printed with the English title "(New) Japanese Comic Paper Maru Maru Chimbun." The cover illustrations of the early issues were crafted by Western-style painter Honda Kinkichirō. Notably, caricatures were contributed by such artists as Kobayashi Kiyochika and his disciple Taguchi Beisaku, although the actual artist of each issue remains unidentified because the individual illustrations lacked signatures. Kiyochika and Beisaku were amongst the last designers of traditional Japanese woodblock prints, today known as *ukiyo-e*.

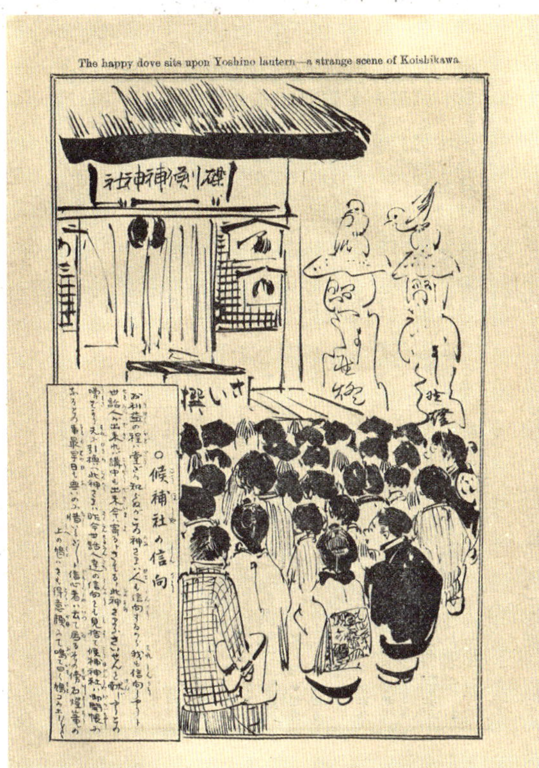

**Above** "The happy dove sits upon Yoshino lantern—a strange scene of Koishikawa."

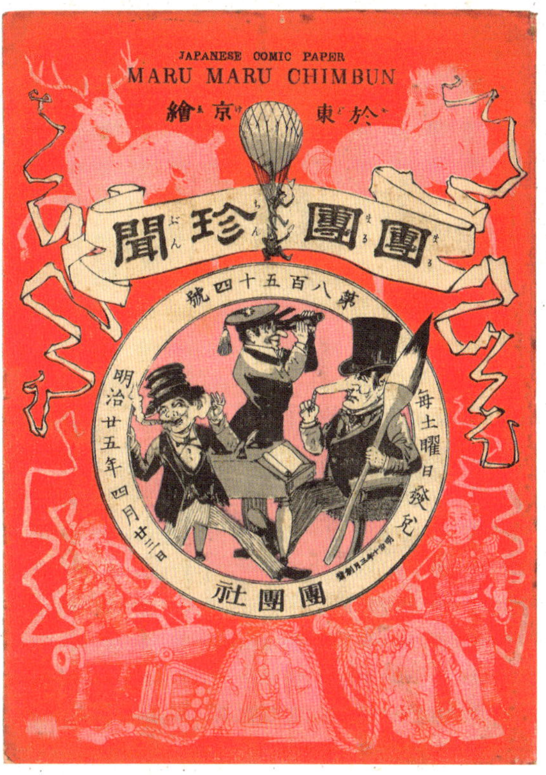


**Above** Cover of no. 854, April 23, 1892.

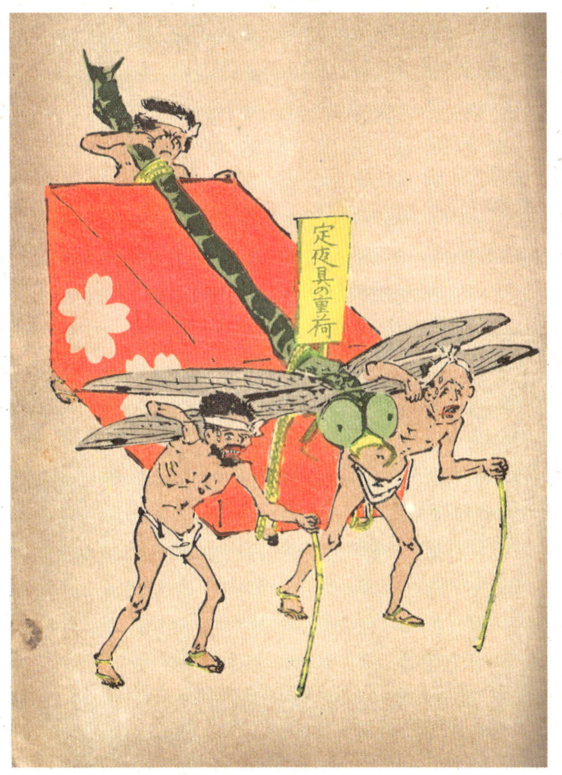

**Above** The heavy burden of the night gear.

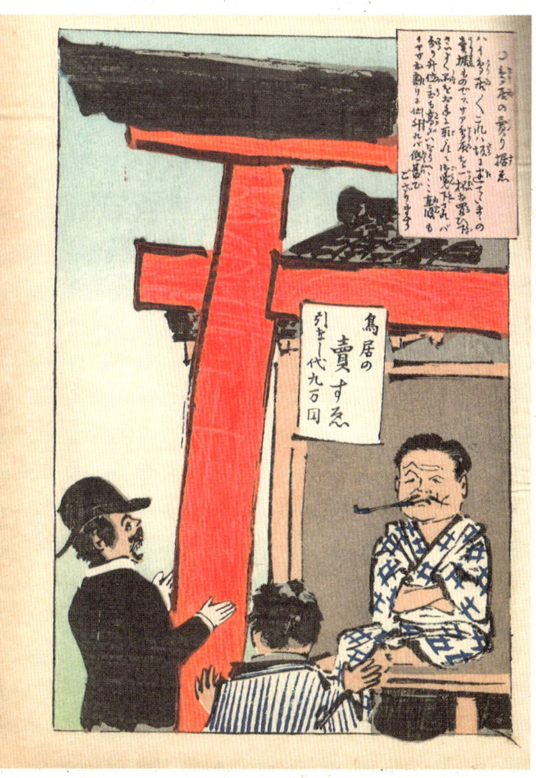

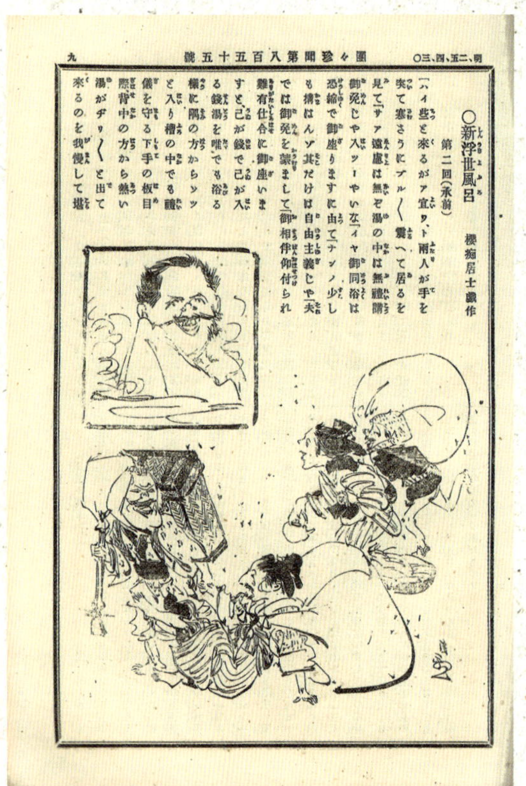

**Below** The umbrella maker's repair.

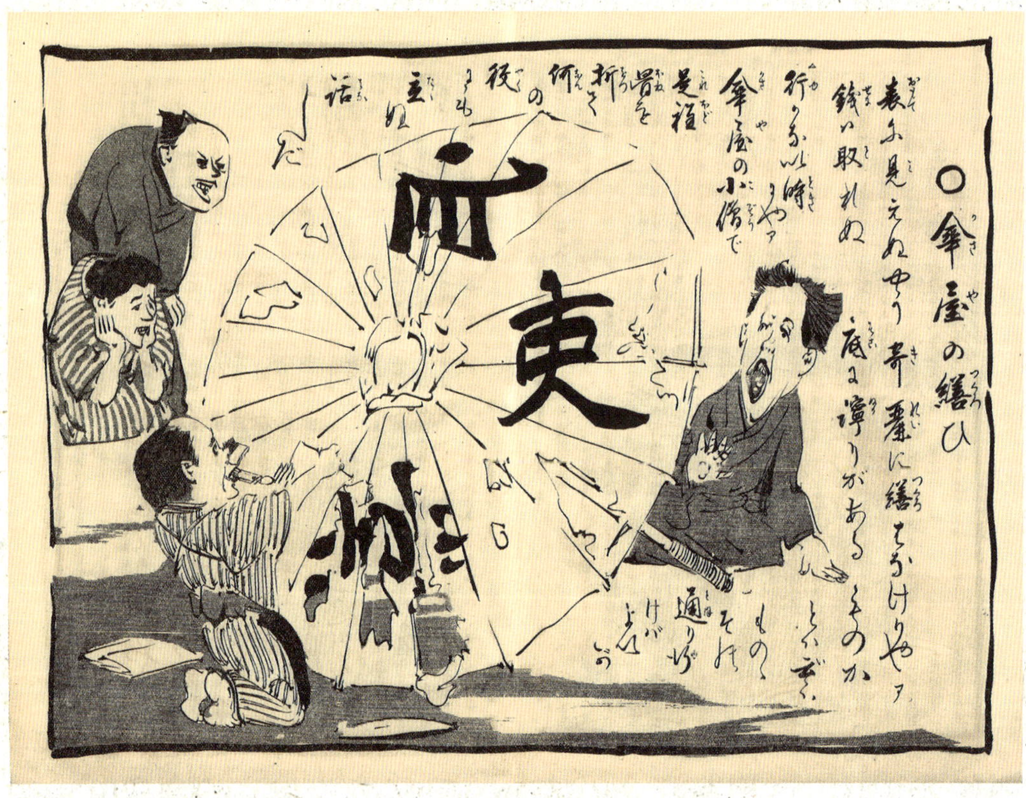

# Nipponchi

日ポン地

1904–06

Artists: Kurosaki Shūsai (born 1877), Nakano Shunkō (dates unknown), Yamamoto Shōkoku (1870–1965), et al.

Editor: Hashimoto Shigeru (dates unknown)

Publisher: Tōyōdō

Lithograph on paper; 25.7 × 18.5 cm

Collection of the author

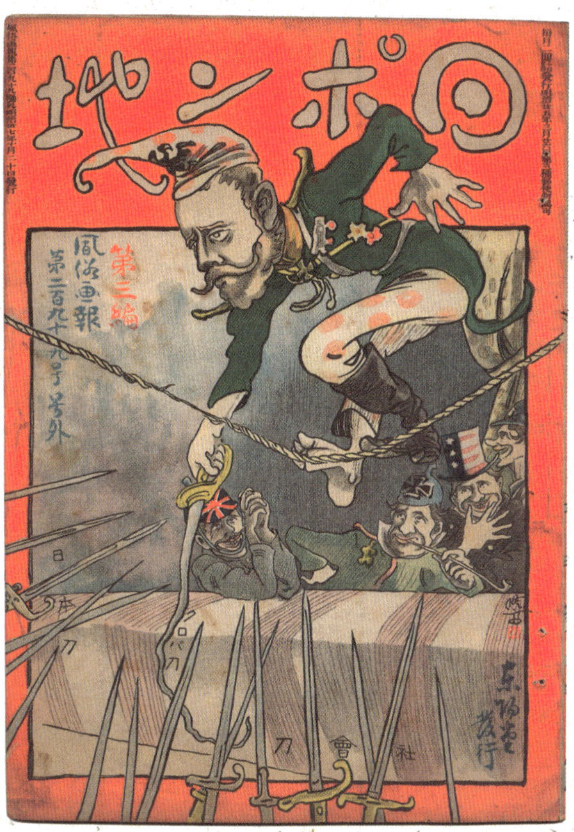

**Above** Cover of no. 3, October 20, 1904.

In 1889, Japan's first graphic magazine, *Fūzoku Gahō*, was published by the firm Tōyōdō, which had been founded in 1876 by Azuma Kenzaburō (1856–1912), a copperplate engraver and lithographer. *Fūzoku Gahō* was produced until 1916, and through the extensive use of illustrations and photographs the magazine addressed such subjects as social customs, literature, history, war, and geography from the Edo period (1603–1868) to the present day.

On September 7, 1904, Azuma published the first issue of *Nipponchi* (which has two meanings, literally "The Land of Japan" and "Japanese Punch") as a supplement to *Fūzoku Gahō*. *Nipponchi* was a satirical propaganda journal which focused especially on the Russo-Japanese War that commenced in February of 1904. Pro-Japanese and anti-Russian propaganda were popular at that time, which also caused the market for woodblock prints to be revived through the creation of many panoramic views of battles. By name, *Nipponchi* refers to the *Illustrated Japan News* (*Eshinbun Nipponchi*)

of which only a few issues were published in 1874 with texts by Kanagaki Robun (1829–94) and illustrations by Kawanabe Kyōsai (1831–89). The new *Nipponchi* was a product of the pro-war atmosphere, but when the war ended in September 1905 its main subject matter disappeared. The magazine was issued twice a month and ended with number 35 in May 1906.

Ōtei Kinshō (1868–1954), who had worked as a journalist for *Maru Maru Chimbun*, also wrote for *Nipponchi*. Kurosaki Shūsai, a student of the print designer Ogata Gekkō (1895–1920), designed the cover illustrations for *Fūzoku Gahō* as well as *Nipponchi*. Amongst the illustrators were Nakano Shunkō, a student of the painter Yamamoto Shunkyo (1872–1933), and Yamamoto Shōkoku (Shōun). Shōkoku, a painter and print artist like Kyōsai, was hired by *Fūzoku Gahō* in 1894 to join their illustrator staff.

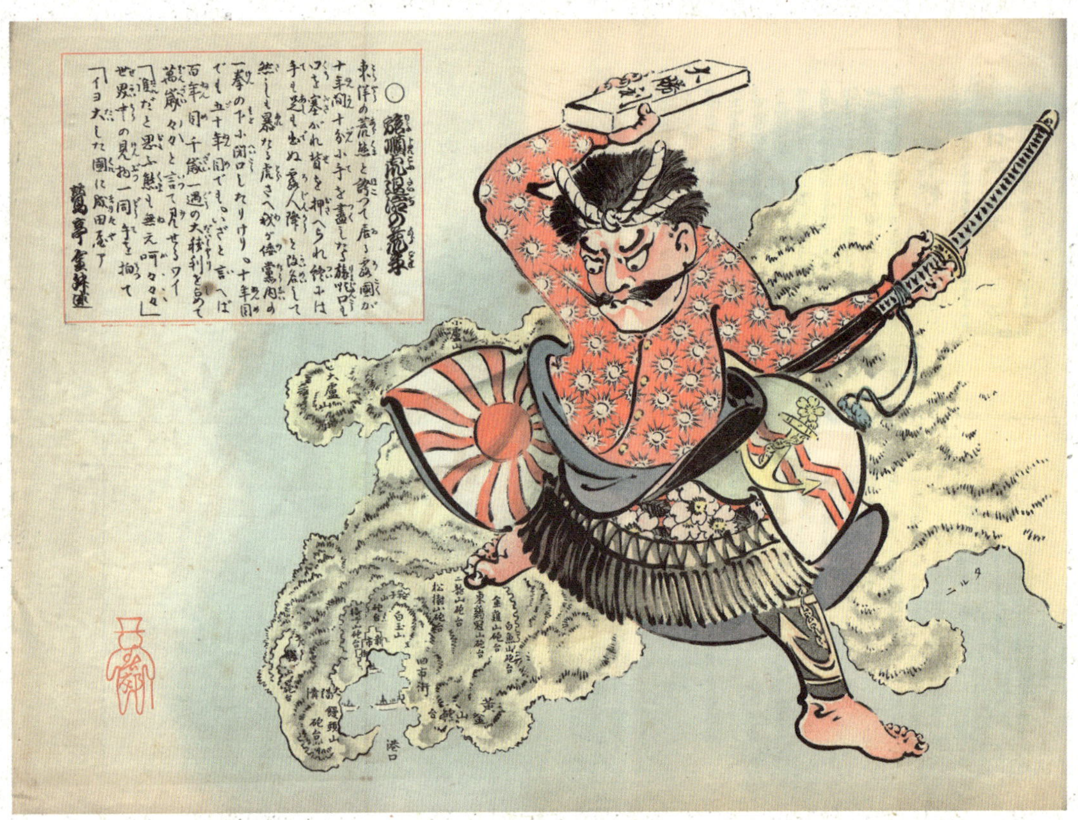

**Above** Exaggerated performance of defeating the Port Arthur tiger; artist: Nakano Shunkō.

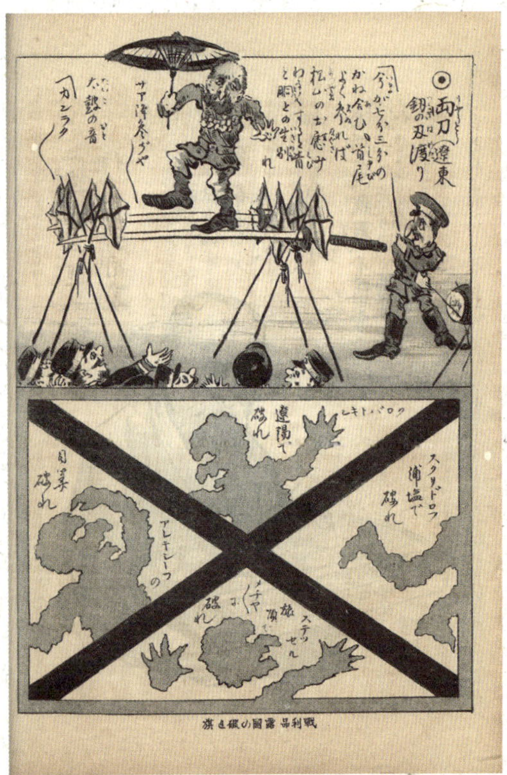

**Below** A collection of faces.

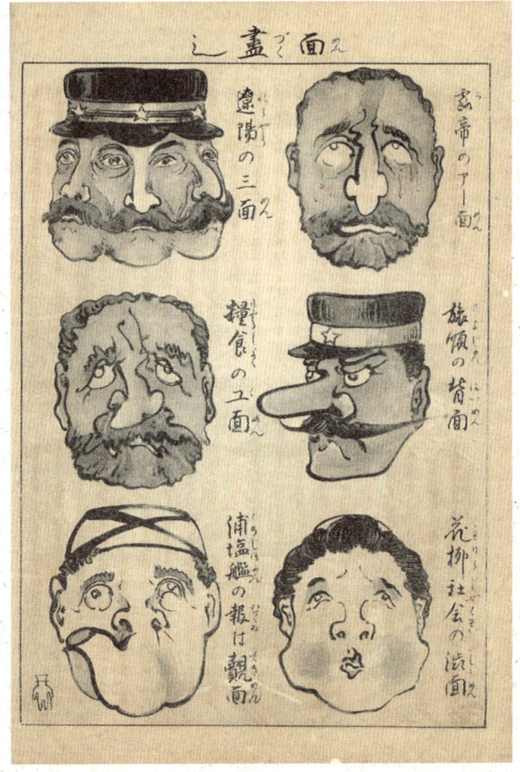

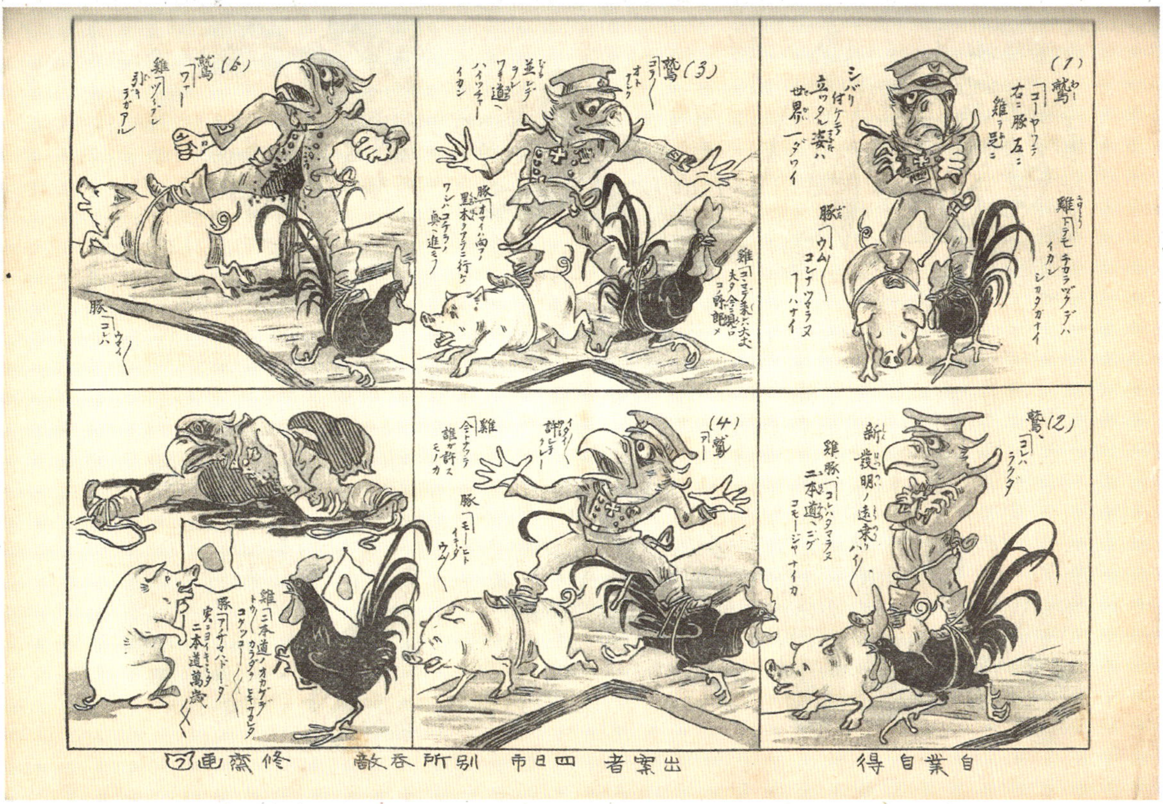

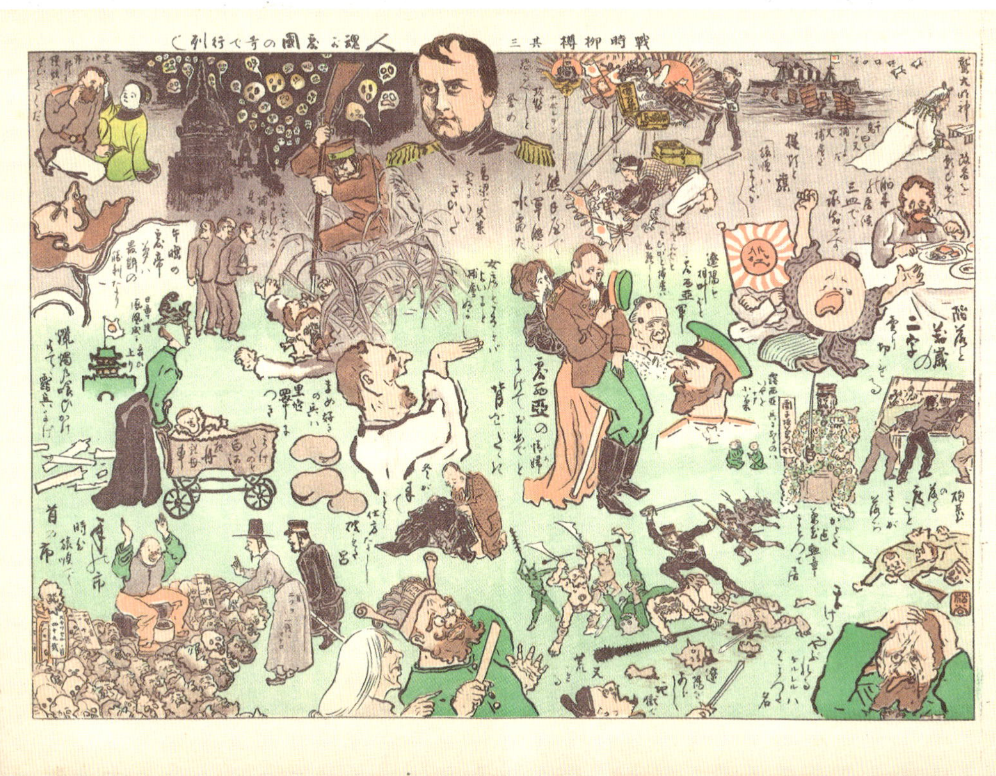

**Below** Wartime Yanagi Barrel no. 3.

# Tokyo Puck

*Tōkyō pakku*

東京パック

1905–15, 1919–23, 1928–41, 1948

Artist/Editor: Kitazawa Rakuten
(1876–1955)

Publishers: Tōkyō pakkusha,
Yūrakusha, et al.

Lithograph on paper; 38.3 × 26.7 cm

Collection of the author

The first issue of the satirical magazine *Tokyo Puck* (*Tōkyō pakku*) was issued on April 15, 1905. The magazine was founded by the popular cartoonist Kitazawa Rakuten who was inspired by his mentor, the Australian Frank Arthur Nankivell (1869–1959), who worked in Japan as a cartoonist until 1894. After arriving in New York, he started working for *Puck*, the first successful humor magazine with multicolor cartoons. Initially, *Tokyo Puck* was critical of the government, but later it expressed more conservative opinions. Contrary to most other satirical magazines, *Tokyo Puck* included English captions, emphasizing that it was also marketed to foreigners living in Japan.

In 1912, Kitazawa left *Tokyo Puck* to start his own magazine, *Rakuten Puck*,

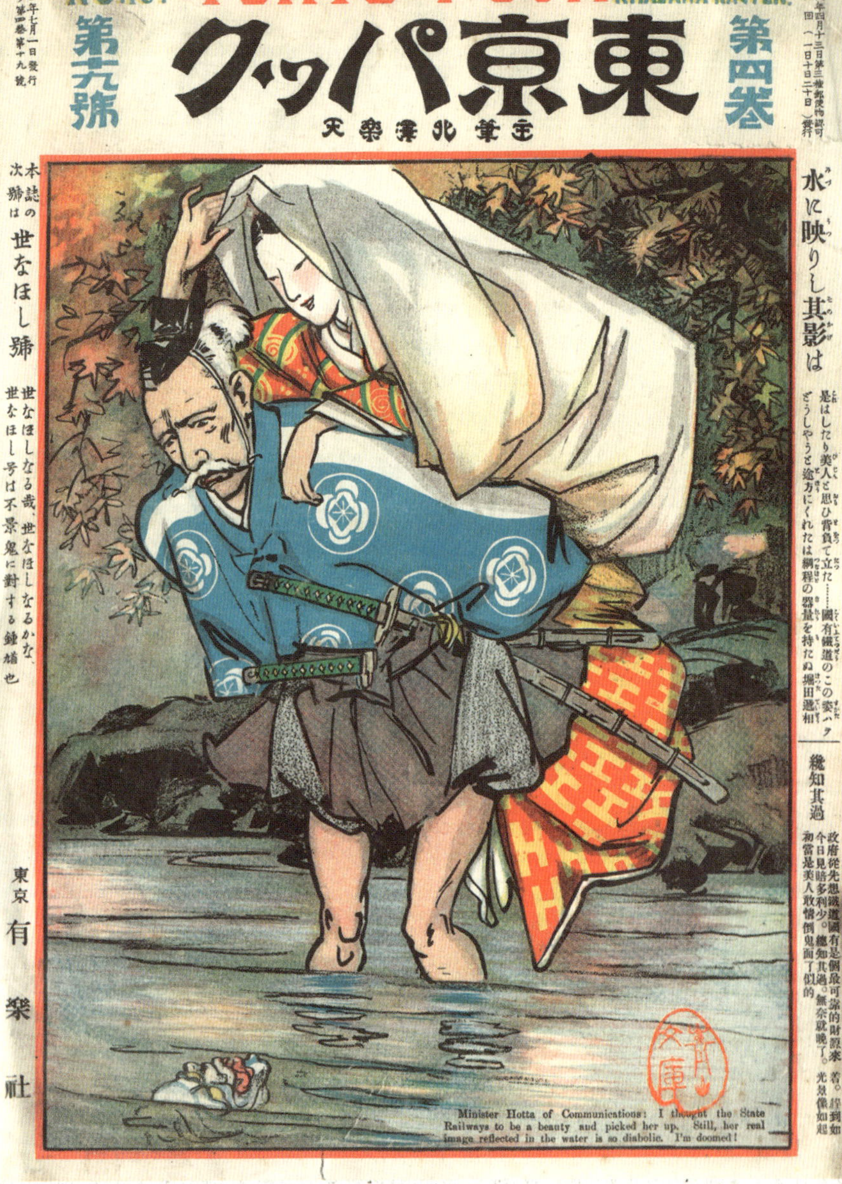


**Above** Cover of vol. 4, no. 19, July 1, 1908, "Minister Hotta of Communications: I thought the State Railways to be a beauty and picked her up. Still, her real image reflected in the water is so diabolic. I'm doomed!"

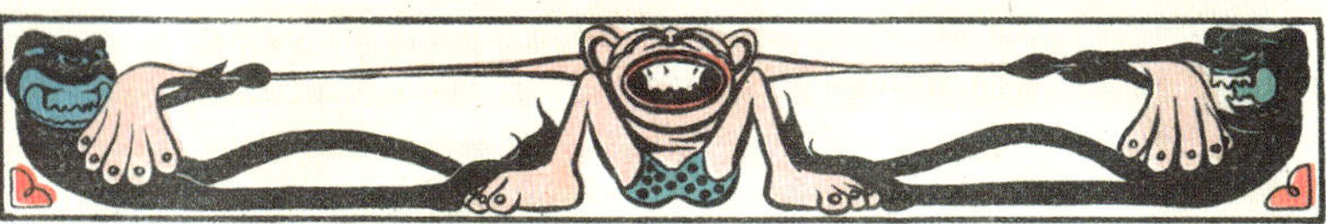

TOKYO PUCK.
Tokyo, July 1.

The United States intends to spend a million and half dollars for participating in the Grand Exhibition of Japan. The authorities here apparently astonished by the huge appropriation made by America is about to propose an increase of the exhibition estimates standing at 10 million yen. This is comparable to a man who hastily dresses himself above his rank, having been surprised by his guest's good dress.

In America, a man's income is 440 and he pays the tax to the amount of 14.28. In Japan an average income is 60 and tax per head 12.62. The comparison is rather remarkable.

In Russia, where a dress exhibition was opened a few years ago, is about to hold an exhibition of ornamental objects. Russia is good in holding technical exhibition. If Japan were called upon to hold one, we would propose an exhibition of shinju (double suicide of lovers).

Shinju is mostly accompanied by other crimes as adultery, etc. Now-a-days, the fair sex seems to be more sinful than the man. This tendency is more conspicuous among educated men.

General Nogi expelled from the Peeresses' School a girl who had been elected the most beautiful woman in Japan. He was severely criticized on that account. Now, he has introduced this same girl as a bride to Marshal Marquis Nodzu's family. This is a retribution worthy of the hero of Port Arthur.

Dr. Koch says that the Japanese shinto prayer "please cleanse, please sweep!" should be applied to sanitary affairs. This is indeed a naive interpretation of our religion. He defeats even Dr. Puck in point of ingenuity.

Dr. Koch saw "Shizuka" of Baiko and said that no actress was wanted in Japan, in view of the actors playing the feminine part so well. That the blatant Kawakami does not say so is because he is afraid to hurt the susceptibilities of his wife, Mme. Sada Yacco.

Two wonderful children are reported to have appeared in the art of Japanese handwriting. We wish wonders should appear in other branches of art. Too many wonders may cause a fall in the value of wonders if not to the extent of the fall of value of doctors by their overproduction.

China promises to open a Diet within three years. The president of the Lower House will be Kang Yuwee or Sun Yatsen, and that of the Upper House Yuan Shihkai or Chang Chihtung. It will be a very interesting sight.

An American is making a round-the-world trip with the remains of his deceased wife. We propose the man should be given a hearty welcome. He may have many sympathizers here.

The Tō-sai-nan-boku will be issued thrice (instead of twice) from this month. The circulation will be trebled and quadrupled. We wish her a brilliant success and prosperity.

有樂閑語

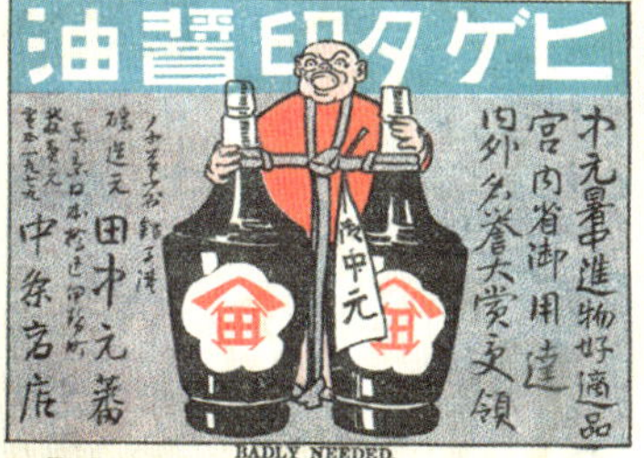


BADLY NEEDED.

The professor had been quizzing his psychology class, and was evidently somewhat disappointed with the result.

"Gentlemen," said he, as the bell rang for dismissal, "it has been said that fish is good for brain food. If that statement is true, I advise some of the men in this class to try a whale."—*The Herald and Presbyter.*



BETTER THAN THAT.

Tramp—"Help me, lady, please. For three years I worked for the grand cause of temperance, ma'am."

Lady—"Were you a temperance orator?"

Tramp—"No, ma'am; I was the horrible example."—*Illustrated Bits.*

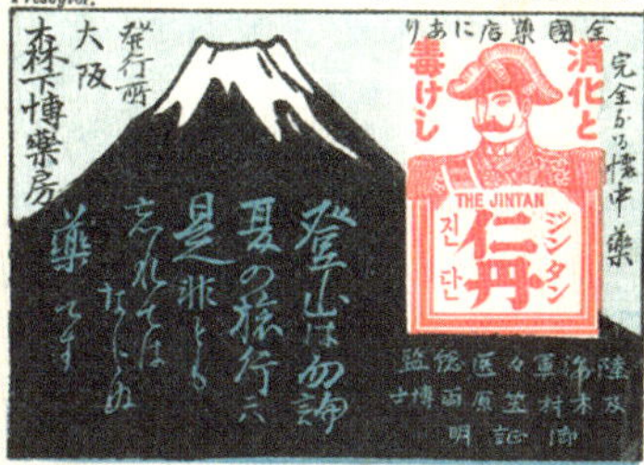


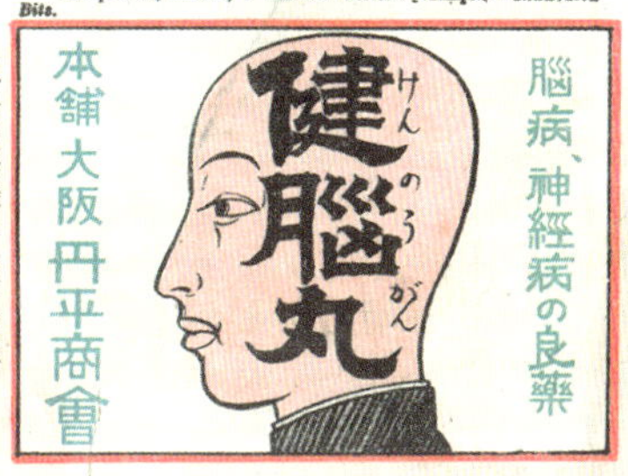


which was not very successful and ceased publication soon after. *Tokyo Puck* continued until 1915 and was revived in 1919. In 1923, the operation ceased again. Publication started once more in 1928 and ended in 1941 until it was briefly relaunched in 1948.

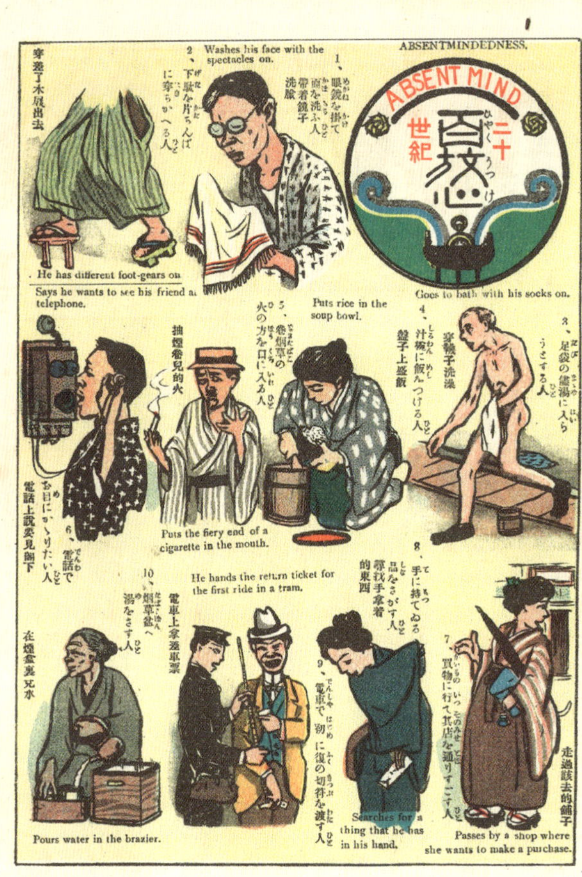


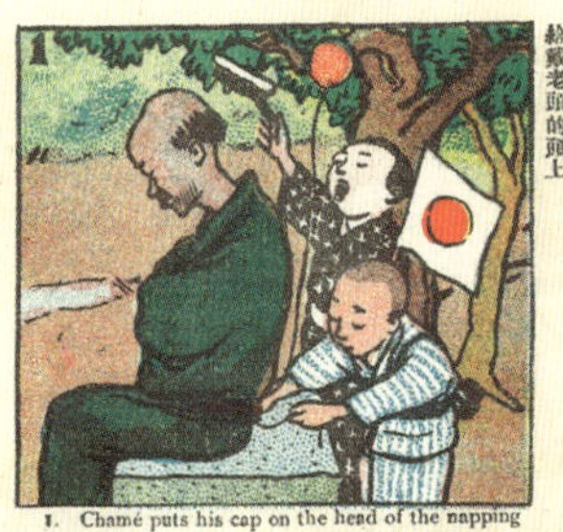
1. Chamé puts his cap on the head of the napping man.

2. Déko has the man decorated with a flag and balloon.

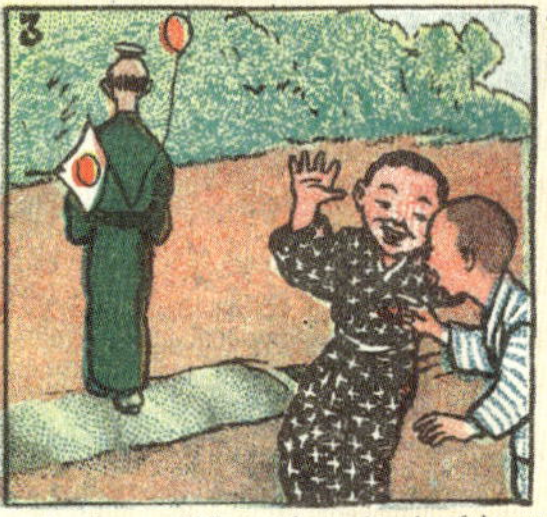
3. Two boys are jubilant at the comic attire of the man.

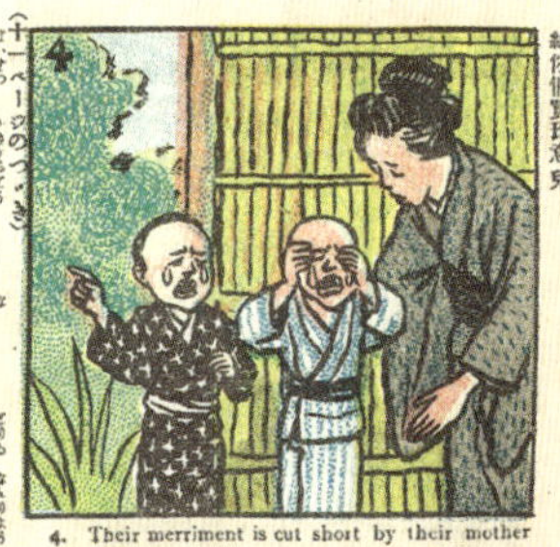
4. Their merriment is cut short by their mother who says they shall have no more cap and toys.

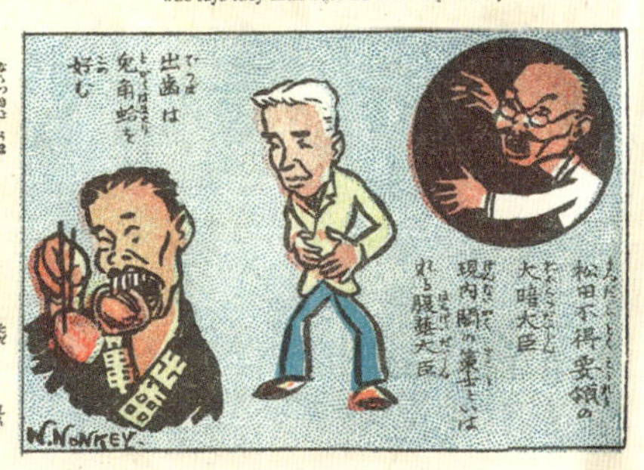

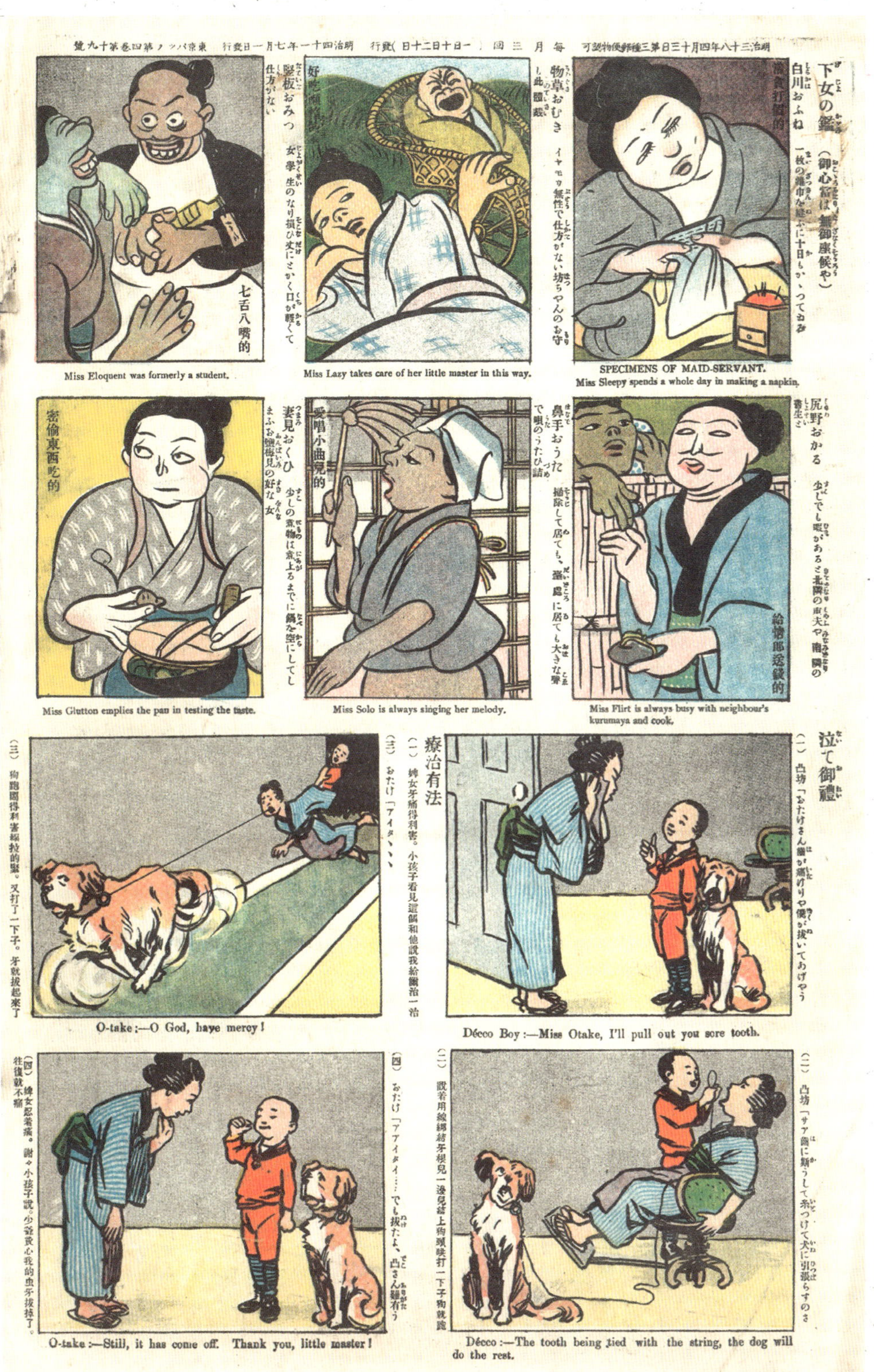
Miss Eloquent was formerly a student.
Miss Lazy takes care of her little master in this way.
SPECIMENS OF MAID-SERVANT.
Miss Sleepy spends a whole day in making a napkin.
Miss Glutton emplies the pan in testing the taste.
Miss Solo is always singing her melody.
Miss Flirt is always busy with neighbour's kurumaya and cook.
O-take:—O God, have mercy!
Décco Boy:—Miss Otake, I'll pull out you sore tooth.
O-take:—Still, it has come off.  Thank you, little master!
Décco:—The tooth being tied with the string, the dog will do the rest.

# Jōtō Ponchi

上等ポンチ

1907–08

Artists: Mitsutani Kunishirō (1874–1936), Kosugi Hōan (1881–1964), et al.

Editor: Kunkida Doppo (1871–1908)

Publisher: Dopposha

Lithograph on paper; 30.8 × 22.7 cm

Collection of the author

*Jōtō Ponchi* (lit. "High-class Punch") was a short-lived satirical magazine that was issued twice a month from August 1907 until January 1908. The novelist Kunkida Doppo, who became a war correspondent in 1894 during the First Sino-Japanese War, was the driving force behind the magazine.

The writer and politician Yano Ryūkei (1851–1931), who worked for the company Keigyōsha, motivated Kunkida to join him in 1902. In March of the following year, Keigyōsha asked Yano to launch the magazine *Tōyō Gahō*, but it was a failure. In September Yano was joined by Kunikida and they renamed the magazine *Kinji Gahō*, which turned out to be much more successful. In 1905, Kunkida founded *Fujin Gahō* (lit. "Illustrated Women's Gazette"), a monthly women's magazine that is still published today. In August of 1907, Kunkida launched *Jōtō Ponchi*, but in the same year he also contracted tuberculosis. When he moved into a sanatorium in early 1908, he was no longer able to continue with *Jōtō Ponchi*. He died on June 23, aged thirty-six.

*Jōtō Ponchi* was distributed through the sales offices of *Kinji Gahō*. Amongst the illustrators of *Jōtō Ponchi* were the Western-style painters Mitsutani Kunishirō and Kosugi Hōan, who had been accepted into the Japan Fine Arts Exhibition (Bunten), a juried event under the supervision of the Ministry of Education, Science, Sports, and Culture, first held in 1907.

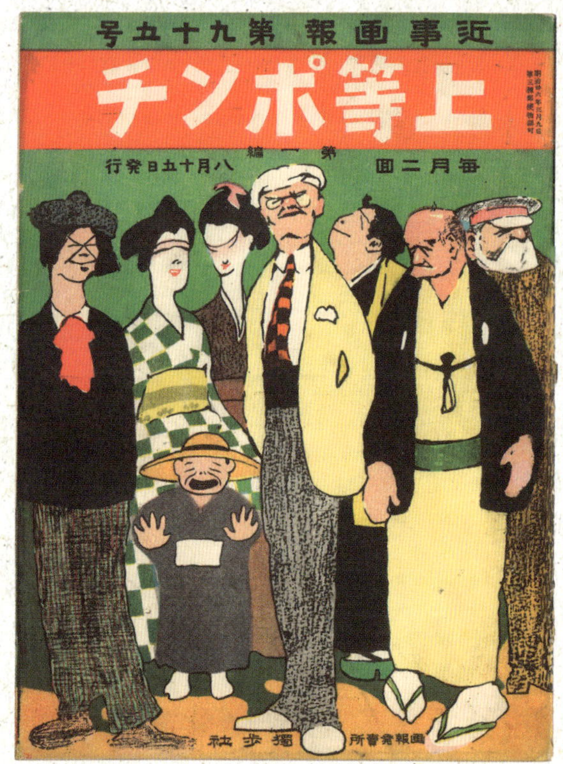

**Above** Cover of no. 1, August 15, 1907.

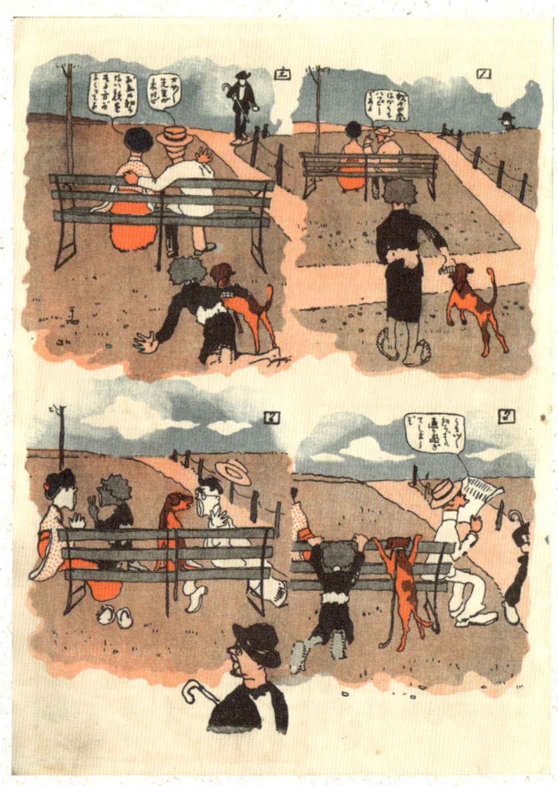

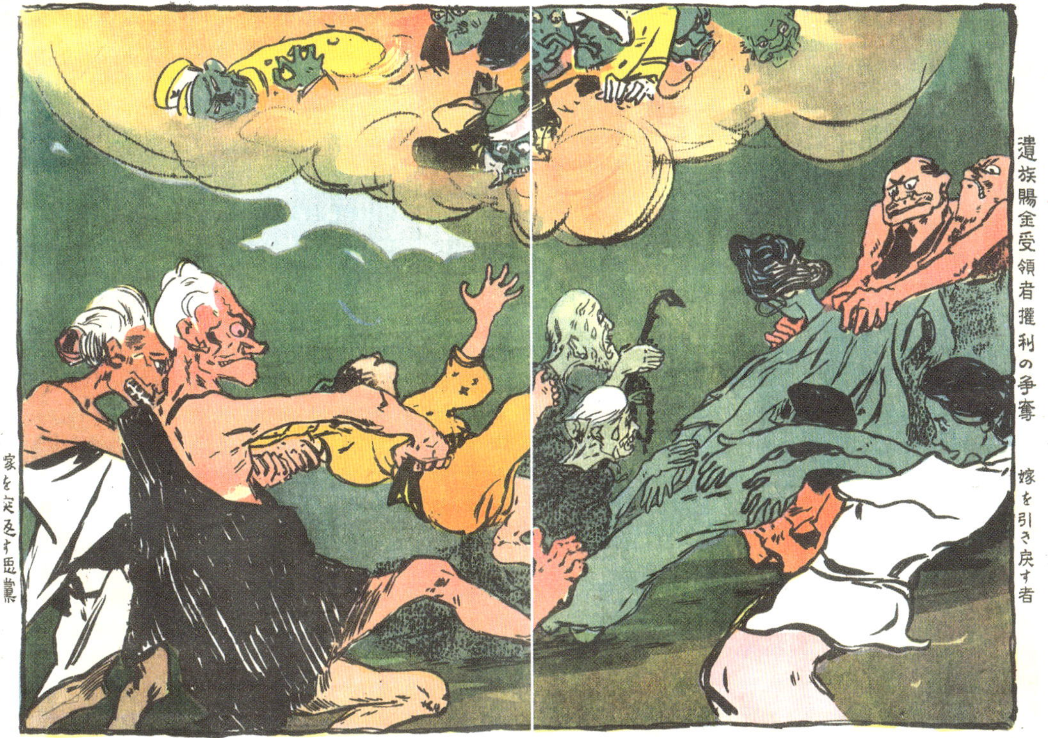

**Above** The struggle for the profits of bereaved family grant recipients.

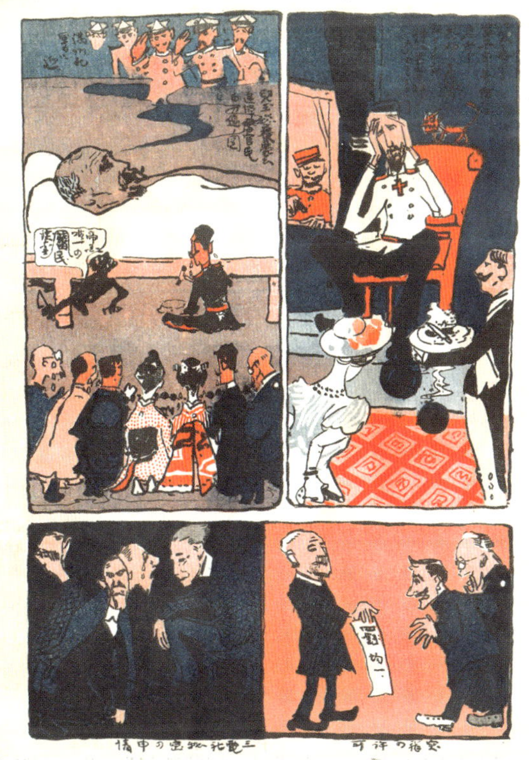

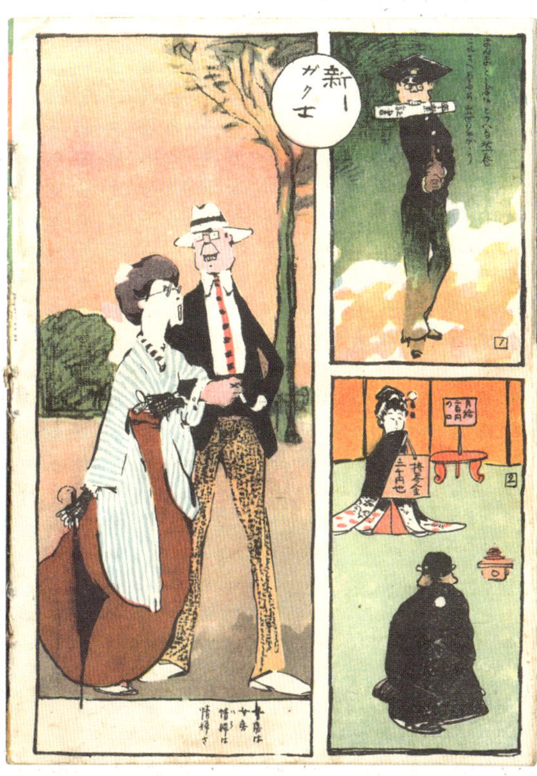

# Jiji Manga

時事漫画

1902–06; 1914–32
Artist/Editor: Kitazawa Rakuten (1876–1955)
Publisher: Jiji Shinpōsha
Lithograph on paper; 40.8 × 26.9 cm
Collection of the author

*Jiji Manga* (lit. "Current Affairs Manga") was the first periodical with the word "manga" in the title. In 1882, the entrepreneur and educator Fukuzawa Yukichi (1835–1901) founded the newspaper *Jiji Shinpō* (lit. "Current Affairs"), which garnered extensive readership, advocating for the people to embrace enlightenment and a moderate political stance amidst the evolving social and political landscape of Japan. In 1899, Kitazawa Rakuten was hired by *Jiji Shinpō* to draw cartoons, which

**Below** Cover of no. 269, June 20, 1926.

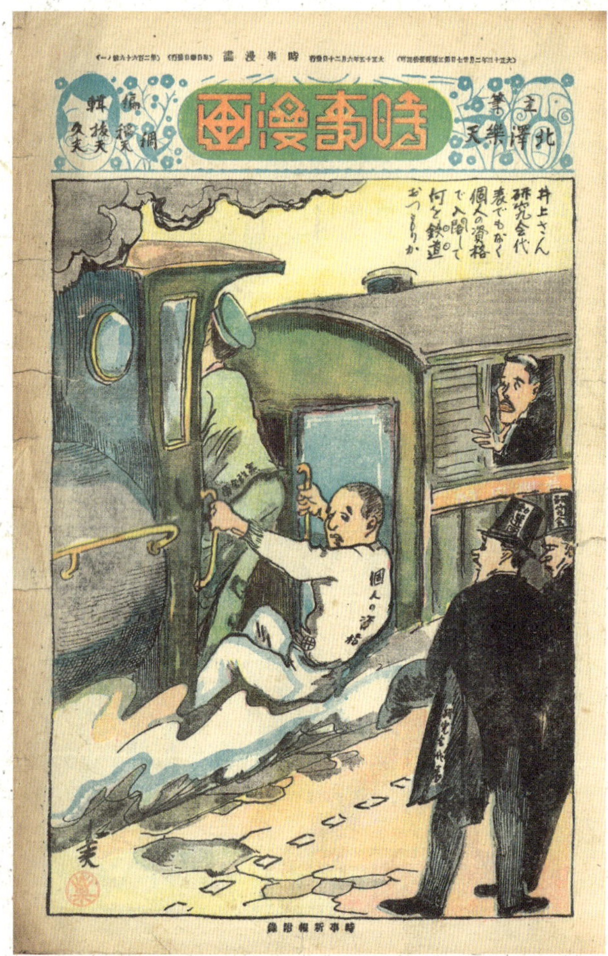

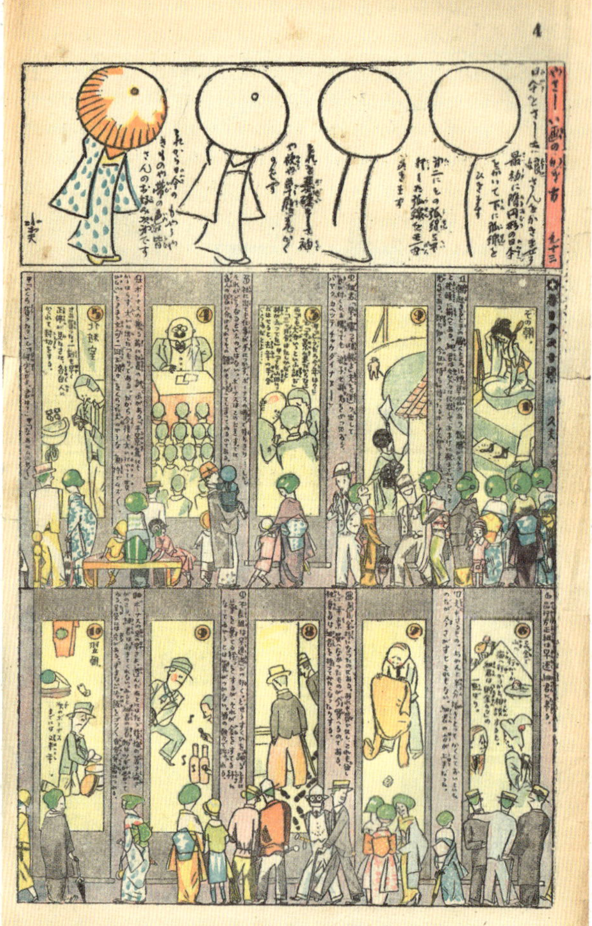

was a ground-breaking step for a Japanese newspaper at that time. The cartoons comprised political satire as well as comics for women and children. Some of Kitazawa's narratives were rooted in Japan's history but the style and design of his cartoons were detached from traditional Japanese visual arts because he was inspired by US comic strips such as *The Katzenjammer Kids* (since 1897) and *The Yellow Kid* (1895–98).

Kitazawa's cartoons became so popular that in 1902 the newspaper established a special section in the Sunday edition, which was called *Jiji Manga*. On February 11, 1921, *Jiji Manga* was launched as an independent supplement to the Sunday edition. The inaugural edition consisted of four pages: a two-page color comic and two pages of mono-chrome photographs and other reading materials. With number 504, *Jiji Manga* was discontinued on June 28, 1932. Its parent newspaper, *Jiji Shinpō*, followed four years later.

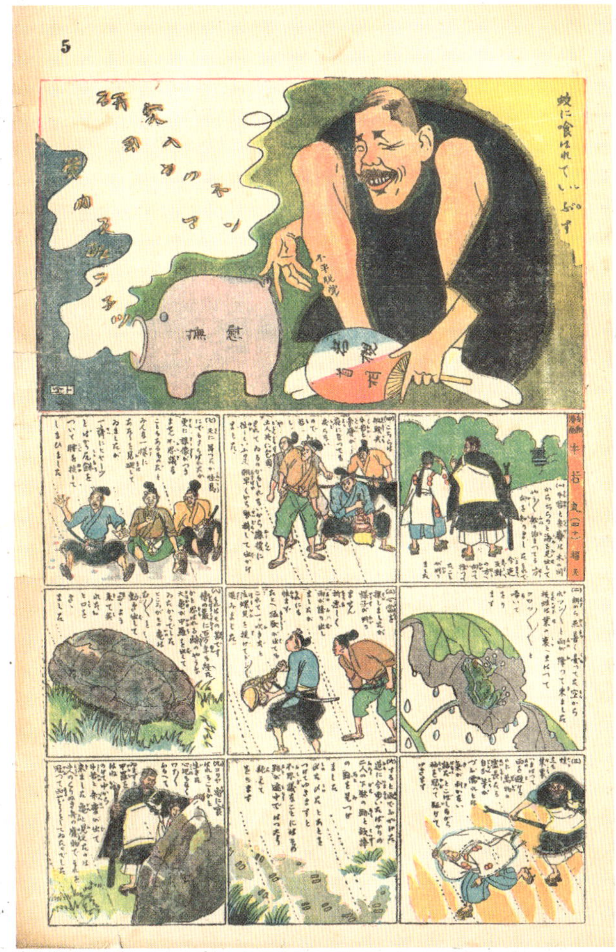

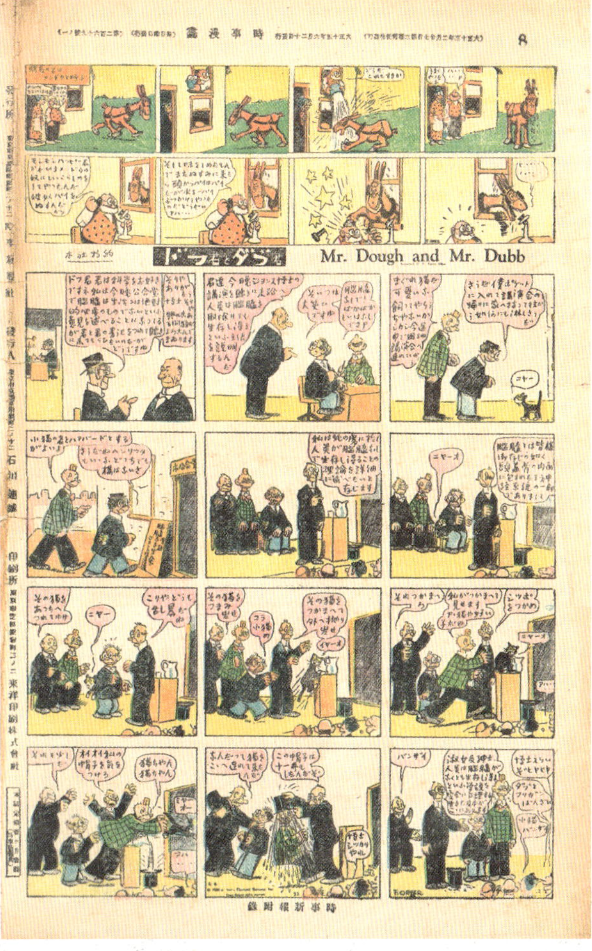

# Bibliography


Achenbach, Nora von, Simon Klingler, and Sabine Schulze, eds. 2016. *Hokusai X Manga: Japanese Pop Culture Since 1680*. Hamburg: Hirmer.

Chibbett, D. G. 1977. *The History of Japanese Printing and Book Illustration*. Tokyo, New York: Kodansha International.

Clark, Timothy. 2021. *Hokusai: The Great Picture Book of Everything*. London: British Museum Press.

Davis, Julie N., ed. 2022. *Arthur Tress and the Japanese Illustrated Book*. Philadelphia: University of Pennsylvania Libraries.

Deutsches Filminstitut, and Museum für Angewandte Kunst, Frankfurt, eds. 2008. *Ga-Netchû! The Manga Anime Syndrome*. Leipzig: Deutsches Filminstitut; Museum für Angewandte Kunst, Frankfurt.

Donath-Wiegand, Margarete. 1963. *Zur literarhistorischen Stellung des Ukiyoburo von Shikitei Samba*. Wiesbaden: Harrassowitz.

Hillier, Jack R. 1987. *The Art of the Japanese Book*. 2 vols. London: Sotheby's.

Keene, Donald. 1955. *Anthology of Japanese Literature, from the Earliest Era to the Mid-Nineteenth Century*. New York: Grove Press.

Keene, Donald. 1999. *World Within Walls: Japanese Literature of the Pre-Modern Era, 1600–1867*. New York: Columbia University Press.

Kerlen, H. 1996. *Catalogue of Pre-Meiji Japanese Books and Maps in Public Collections in the Netherlands*. Japonica neerlandica 6. Amsterdam: Gieben.

Kern, Adam L. 2006. *Manga from the Floating World: Comicbook Culture and the Kibyōshi of Edo Japan*. Harvard East Asian monographs 279. Cambridge, MA: Harvard University Asia Center.

Keyes, Roger S. 2006. *Ehon: The Artist and the Book in Japan*. New York: New York Public Library.

Köhn, Stephan. 2001. "Die Prototypen des Modernen Manga? Das Nise Murasaki Inaka Genji (1829–42) als Paradebeispiel integraler Text/Bild-Literatur der Edo-Zeit." In *11. Deutschsprachiger Japanologentag in Trier 1999: Sprache, Literatur, Kunst, Populärkultur/Medien, Informationstechnik*, edited by Hilaria Gössmann and Andreas Mrugalla, 341–552. Trier: LIT Verlag.

Köhn, Stephan. 2005. *Traditionen visuellen Erzählens in Japan: Eine paradigmatische Untersuchung der Entwicklungslinien vom Faltschirmbild zum narrativen Manga*. Kulturwissenschaftliche Japanstudien 2. Wiesbaden: Harrassowitz.

Köhn, Stephan, and Martina Schönbein. 2000. "Dem Story-Manga auf der Spur: Potentielle Prototypen des modernen Japanischen Comics in der Text/Bild-Tradition der Edo-Zeit." *Japonica Humboldtiana* 4: 21–58.

Kornicki, Peter F. 1998. *The Book in Japan: A Cultural History from the Beginnings to the Nineteenth Century*. Leiden: Brill.

Leutner, Robert W. 1985. *Shikitei Sanba and the Comic Tradition in Edo Fiction*. Cambridge, MA: Harvard University Press.

Marks, Andreas. 2012a. *Genji's World in Japanese Woodblock Prints: From the Paulette and Jack Lantz Collection*. With contributions by B. A. Coats, M. Emmerich, S. Formanek, S. Linhart and R. Paget. Leiden: Hotei.

Marks, Andreas. 2012b. *Kamisaka Sekka: Rinpa Traditionalist, Modern Designer*. San Francisco: Pomegranate.

Marks, Andreas. 2019. *Japanese Woodblock Prints*. Cologne: Taschen.

Marks, Andreas. 2024. *The (Almost) Complete Hokusai*. Cologne: Taschen.

Rousmaniere, Nicole C., and Matsuba Ryoko, eds. 2019. *The Citi Exhibition Manga*. London: Thames & Hudson.

Screech, Timothy Benjamin Mark. 2002. *The Lens Within the Heart: The Western Scientific Gaze and Popular Imagery in Later Edo Japan*. Honolulu: University of Hawai'i Press.

Shimizu, Isao. 1984. *Kindai manga o tsukuriageta Kiyochika: Rakuten to 10-nin no fūshi gaka ten*, edited by Ômiya Shiritsu Manga Kaikan. Tokyo: Ukiyoe Ōta Kinen Bijutsukan.

Shirane, Haruo. 2002. *Early Modern Japanese Literature: An Anthology, 1600–1900*. New York: Columbia University Press.

SteelRiver Studio. 2006. *Mangaka America: Manga by America's Hottest Artists*. New York: Collins Design.

Thompson, Sarah E. 2016. *Hokusai's Lost Manga*. Boston: MFA Publications.

Watanabe, Masako. 2012. *Storytelling in Japanese Art*. New York, New Haven and London: Metropolitan Museum of Art; distributed by Yale University Press.

# Notes

Family names come before given names. Dates followed the lunar calendar until the Gregorian calendar was adopted by Japan on January 1, 1873. Book titles are given in English translation followed by romanized Japanese transliteration and the actual Japanese title. Approximate sizes for closed books are *ōhon*: 25 × 18 cm; *hanshibon*: 23 × 15 cm; *chūbon*: 18 × 13 cm; *kobon*: 15 × 13 cm.

# Acknowledgments

This publication would not have been possible without the generosity of the following institutions to whom I am greatly indebted: Chester Beatty; Edo-Tokyo Museum; Kansai University Library; The Metropolitan Museum of Art; Minneapolis Institute of Art; National Diet Library; National Institute of Japanese Literature; New York Public Library; Ritsumeikan University Library; Smithsonian Libraries; Staatsbibliothek zu Berlin— Preußischer Kulturbesitz; Tokyo Metropolitan Library; Waseda University Library; Wereldmuseum Leiden.

# Index of Authors, Artists, and Publishers

## Publishers

Published by Tuttle Publishing, an imprint of Periplus Editions (HK) Ltd

www.tuttlepublishing.com



ISBN: 978-4-8053-1901-7

Distributed by

**North America, Latin America & Europe**
Tuttle Publishing
364 Innovation Drive, North Clarendon
VT 05759-9436 U.S.A.
Tel: 1 (802) 773-8930
Fax: 1 (802) 773-6993
info@tuttlepublishing.com
www.tuttlepublishing.com

**Japan**
Tuttle Publishing
Yaekari Building 3rd Floor, 5-4-12 Osaki
Shinagawa-ku, Tokyo 141-0032
Tel: (81) 3 5437-0171
Fax: (81) 3 5437-0755
sales@tuttle.co.jp
www.tuttle.co.jp

**Asia Pacific**
Berkeley Books Pte. Ltd.
3 Kallang Sector #04-01
Singapore 349278
Tel: (65) 6741-2178
Fax: (65) 6741-2179
inquiries@periplus.com.sg
www.tuttlepublishing.com

**GPSR representative**
Matt Parsons
matt.parsons@upi2mbooks.hr
UPI-2M PLUS d.o.o., Medulićeva 20, 10000 Zagreb, Croatia

28 27 26 25      5 4 3 2 1

Printed in China   2506EP



## "Books to Span the East and West"

**Tuttle Publishing** was founded in 1832 in the small New England town of Rutland, Vermont [USA]. Our core values remain as strong today as they were then—to publish best-in-class books which bring people together one page at a time. In 1948, we established a publishing outpost in Japan—and Tuttle is now a leader in publishing English-language books about the arts, languages and cultures of Asia. The world has become a much smaller place today and Asia's economic and cultural influence has grown. Yet the need for meaningful dialogue and information about this diverse region has never been greater. Over the past seven decades, Tuttle has published thousands of books on subjects ranging from martial arts and paper crafts to language learning and literature—and our talented authors, illustrators, designers and photographers have won many prestigious awards. We welcome you to explore the wealth of information available on Asia at **www.tuttlepublishing.com.**

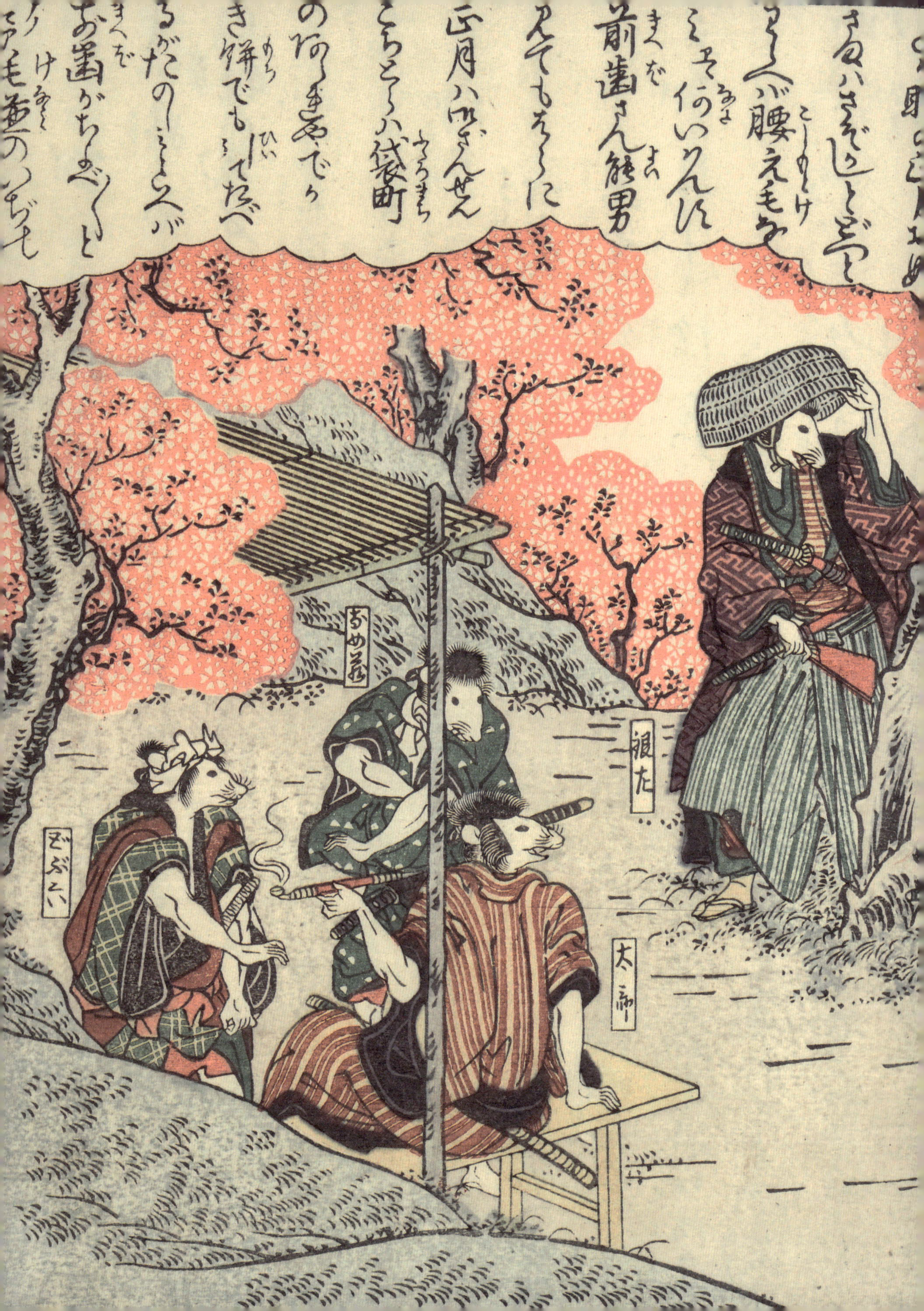
あめ屋
どぶい
娘た
大